The Art and Science of Analyzing Software Data

The Art and Science of Analyzing Software Data

Christian Bird

Microsoft Research, Redmond, WA, USA

Tim Menzies

North Carolina State University, Raleigh, NC, USA

Thomas Zimmermann

Microsoft Research, Redmond, WA, USA

AMSTERDAM • BOSTON • HEIDELBERG • LONDON
NEW YORK • OXFORD • PARIS • SAN DIEGO
SAN FRANCISCO • SINGAPORE • SYDNEY • TOKYO

Morgan Kaufmann is an imprint of Elsevier

Acquiring Editor: Todd Green
Editorial Project Manager: Lindsay Lawrence
Project Manager: Punithavathy Govindaradjane
Designer: Mark Rogers

Morgan Kaufmann is an imprint of Elsevier
225 Wyman Street, Waltham, MA 02451, USA

ISBN: 978-0-12-411519-4

British Library Cataloguing in Publication Data
A catalogue record for this book is available from the British Library

Library of Congress Cataloging-in-Publication Data
A catalog record for this book is available from the Library of Congress

For information on all MK publications
visit our website at www.mkp.com

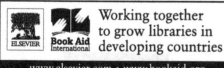

Working together
to grow libraries in
developing countries

www.elsevier.com • www.bookaid.org

Contents

List of Contributors

Alberto Bacchelli
Department of Software and Computer Technology, Delft University of Technology, Delft, The Netherlands

Olga Baysal
School of Computer Science, Carleton University, Ottawa, ON, Canada

Ayse Bener
Mechanical and Industrial Engineering, Ryerson University, Toronto, ON, Canada

Christian Bird
Microsoft Research, Redmond, WA, USA

Aditya Budi
School of Information Systems, BINUS University, Jakarta, Indonesia

Bora Caglayan
Mechanical and Industrial Engineering, Ryerson University, Toronto, ON, Canada

Gul Calikli
Department of Computing, Open University, Milton Keynes, UK

Joshua Charles Campbell
Department of Computing Science, University of Alberta, Edmonton, AB, Canada

Jacek Czerwonka
Microsoft Corporation, Redmond, WA, USA

Kostadin Damevski
Mathematics and Computer Science Department, Virginia State University, Peterburg, VA, USA

Madeline Diep
Fraunhofer Center for Experimental Software Engineering, College Park, MD, USA

Robert Dyer
Department of Computer Science, Bowling Green State University, Bowling Green, OH, USA

Linda Esker
Fraunhofer Center for Experimental Software Engineering, College Park, MD, USA

Davide Falessi
Fraunhofer Center for Experimental Software Engineering, College Park, MD, USA

Xavier Franch
Department of Service and Information System Engineering, Universitat Politècnica de Catalunya, Barcelona, Spain

Thomas Fritz
Department of Informatics, University of Zurich, Zurich, Switzerland

Nikolas Galanis
Department of Service and Information System Engineering, Universitat Politècnica de Catalunya, Barcelona, Spain

Marco Aurélio Gerosa
Software Engineering & Collaborative Systems Research Group (LAPESSC), University of São Paulo (USP), São Paulo, Brazil

Ruediger Glott
University of Maastricht, Maastricht, The Netherlands

Michael W. Godfrey
David R. Cheriton School of Computer Science, University of Waterloo, Waterloo, ON, Canada

Alessandra Gorla
IMDEA Software Institute, Pozuelo de Alarcon, Madrid, Spain

Georgios Gousios
Institute for Computing and Information Sciences, Radboud University Nijmegen, Nijmegen, The Netherlands

Florian Groß
Software Engineering Chair, Saarland University, Saarbrücken, Germany

Randy Hackbarth
Software Technology Research, Avaya Labs, Santa Clara, CA, USA

Abram Hindle
Department of Computing Science, University of Alberta, Edmonton, AB, Canada

Reid Holmes
Department of Computer Science, University of British Columbia, Vancouver, BC, Canada

Lingxiao Jiang
School of Information Systems, Singapore Management University, Singapore

Ron S. Kenett
KPA Ltd., Raanana, Israel; Department of Mathematics, "G. Peano", University of Turin, Turin, Italy

Ekrem Kocaguneli
Microsoft, Seattle, WA, USA

Oleksii Kononenko
David R. Cheriton School of Computer Science, University of Waterloo, Waterloo, ON, Canada

Kostas Kontogiannis
Department of Electrical and Computer Engineering, National Technical University of Athens, Athens, Greece

Konstantin Kuznetsov
Software Engineering Chair, Saarland University, Saarbrücken, Germany

Lucas Layman
Fraunhofer Center for Experimental Software Engineering, College Park, MD, USA

Christian Lindig
Testfabrik AG, Saarbrücken, Germany

David Lo
School of Information Systems, Singapore Management University, Singapore

Fabio Mancinelli
XWiki SAS, Paris, France

Serge Mankovskii
CA Labs, San Francisco, CA, USA

Shahar Maoz
School of Computer Science, Tel Aviv University, Tel Aviv, Israel

Daniel Méndez Fernández
Software & Systems Engineering, Institut für Informatik, Technische Universität München, Garching, Germany

Andrew Meneely
Department of Software Engineering, Rochester Institute of Technology, Rochester, NY, USA

Tim Menzies
Computer Science, North Carolina State University, Raleigh, NC, USA

Audris Mockus
Software Technology Research, Avaya Labs, Santa Clara, CA, USA; The Department of Electrical Engineering and Computer Science, University of Tennessee, Knoxville, TN, USA

Murtuza Mukadam
Department of Computer Science and Software Engineering, Concordia University, Montreal, QC, Canada

Brendan Murphy
Microsoft Research Cambridge, Cambridge, UK

Emerson Murphy-Hill
Computer Science, North Carolina State University, Raleigh, NC, USA

John Mylopoulos
Department of Information Engineering and Computer Science, University of Trento, Trento, Italy

Anil R. Nair
ABB Corporate Research, Bangalore, KN, India

Maleknaz Nayebi
Software Engineering Decision Support Laboratory, University of Calgary, Calgary, AB, Canada

Hoan Nguyen
Department of Electrical and Computer Engineering, Iowa State University, Ames, IA, USA

Tien Nguyen
Department of Electrical and Computer Engineering, Iowa State University, Ames, IA, USA

Gustavo Ansaldi Oliva
Software Engineering & Collaborative Systems Research Group (LAPESSC),
University of São Paulo (USP), São Paulo, Brazil

John Palframan
Software Technology Research, Avaya Labs, Santa Clara, CA, USA

Hridesh Rajan
Department of Computer Science, Iowa State University, Ames, IA, USA

Peter C. Rigby
Department of Computer Science and Software Engineering, Concordia University, Montreal, QC,
Canada

Guenther Ruhe
Software Engineering Decision Support Laboratory, University of Calgary, Calgary,
AB, Canada

Michele Shaw
Fraunhofer Center for Experimental Software Engineering, College Park, MD, USA

David Shepherd
ABB Corporate Research, Raleigh, NC, USA

Forrest Shull
Software Solutions Division, Software Engineering Institute, Arlington, VA, USA

Will Snipes
ABB Corporate Research, Raleigh, NC, USA

Diomidis Spinellis
Department Management Science and Technology, Athens University of Economics
and Business, Athens, Greece

Eleni Stroulia
Department of Computing Science, University of Alberta, Edmonton, AB, Canada

Angelo Susi
Fondazione Bruno Kessler, Trento, Italy

Lin Tan
Department of Electrical and Computer Engineering, University of Waterloo, Waterloo, ON, Canada

Ilaria Tavecchia
SWIFT, La Hulpe, Bruxelles, Belgium

Ayse Tosun Misirli
Faculty of Computer and Informatics, Istanbul Technical University, Istanbul, Turkey

Mohsen Vakilian
University of Illinois at Urbana-Champaign, Champaign, IL, USA

Stefan Wagner
Software Engineering Group, Institute of Software Technology, University of Stuttgart, Stuttgart,
Germany

Shaowei Wang
School of Information Systems, Singapore Management University, Singapore

David Weiss
Computer Science Department, Iowa State University, Ames, IA, USA

Laurie Williams
Department of Computer Science, North Carolina State University, Raleigh, NC, USA

Hamzeh Zawawy
Department of Electrical & Computer Engineering, University of Waterloo, Waterloo, ON, Canada

Andreas Zeller
Software Engineering Chair, Saarland University, Saarbrücken, Germany

Thomas Zimmermann
Microsoft Research, Redmond, WA, USA

PAST, PRESENT, AND FUTURE OF ANALYZING SOFTWARE DATA

Christian Bird*, Tim Menzies†, Thomas Zimmermann*

Microsoft Research, Redmond, WA, USA* Computer Science, North Carolina State University, Raleigh, NC, USA†

CHAPTER OUTLINE

> So much data, so little time.

Once upon a time, reasoning about software projects was inhibited by a lack of data. Now thanks to the Internet and open source, there's so much data about software projects that it's impossible to manually browse through it all. For example, at the time of writing (December 2014), our Web searches shows that Mozilla Firefox has over 1.1 million bug reports, and platforms such as GitHub host over 14 million projects. Furthermore, the PROMISE repository of software engineering data (openscience.us/repo) contains data sets, ready for mining, on hundreds of software projects. PROMISE is just one of more than a dozen open source repositories that are readily available to industrial practitioners and researchers; see the following table.

Repositories of Software Engineering Data	
Repository	URL
Bug Prediction Dataset	http://bug.int.usi.ch
Eclipse Bug Data	http://www.st.cs.uni-saarland.de/softevo/bug-data/eclipse
FLOSSMetrics	http:/flossmetrics.org
FLOSSMole	http://flossmole.org
International Software Benchmarking Standards Group (IBSBSG)	http://www.isbsg.org
Ohloh	http://www.ohloh.net
PROMISE	http://promisedata.googlecode.com
Qualitas Corpus	http://qualitascorpus.com
Software Artifact Repository	http://sir.unl.edu
SourceForge Research Data	http://zeriot.cse.nd.edu
Sourcerer Project	http://sourcerer.ics.uci.edu
Tukutuku	http://www.metriq.biz/tukutuku
Ultimate Debian Database	http://udd.debian.org

It is now routine for any project to generate gigabytes of artifacts (software code, developer emails, bug reports, etc.). How can we reason about it all? The answer is data science. This is a rapidly growing field with immense potential to change the day-to-day practices of any number of fields. Software companies (e.g., Google, Facebook, and Microsoft) are increasingly making decisions in a data-driven way and are in search of data scientists to help them.

1.1 DEFINITIONS

It is challenging to define software analytics for software engineering (SE) since, at different times, SE analytics has meant different things to different people. Table 1.1 lists some of the more recent definitions found in various papers since 2010. Later in this introduction, we offer a short history of work dating back many decades, any of which might be called "SE data analytics."

One reason for this wide range of definitions is the diversity of services and the diversity of audiences for those services. SE data science covers a very wide range of individuals and teams including, but not limited to, the following:

1. Users deciding what funds to allocate to that software;
2. Developers engaged in software development or maintenance;
3. Managers deciding what functionality should be assigned to which developers engaged in that development of maintenance;

Table 1.1 Five Definitions of "Software Analytics"	
Hassan A, Xie T. Software intelligence: the future of mining software engineering data. FoSER 2010: 161-166.	[Software Intelligence] offers software practitioners (not just developers) up-to-date and pertinent information to support their daily decision-making processes.
Buse RPL, Zimmermann T. Analytics for software development. FoSER 2010:77-90.	The idea of analytics is to leverage potentially large amounts of data into real and actionable insights.
Zhang D, Dang Y, Lou J-G, Han S, Zhang H, Xie T. Software analytics as a learning case in practice: approaches and experiences. MALETS 2011.	Software analytics is to enable software practitioners to perform data exploration and analysis in order to obtain insightful and actionable information for data driven tasks around software and services (and software practitioners typically include software developers, tests, usability engineers, and managers, etc.).
Buse RPL, Zimmermann T. Information needs for software development analytics. ICSE 2012:987-996.	Software development analytics . . . empower(s) software development teams to independently gain and share insight from their data without relying on a separate entity.
Menzies T, Zimmermann T. Software analytics: so what? IEEE Softw 2013;30(4):31-7.	Software analytics is analytics on software data for managers and software engineers with the aim of empowering software development individuals and teams to gain and share insight from their data to make better decisions.
Zhang D, Han S, Dang Y, Lou J-G, Zhang H, Xie T. Software analytics in practice. IEEE Softw 2013;30(5):30-7.	With software analytics, software practitioners explore and analyze data to obtain insightful, actionable information for tasks regarding software development, systems, and users.

4. Analysts trying to reduce code runtimes;

5. Test engineers developing work arounds to known problems;

6. And many more besides these five.

It would be very brave, and very inaccurate, to say that one definition of "analytics" holds across this diverse range. For example, Table 1.2 shows nine different information needs seen in interviews with 100+ software managers and developers [1].

Other work has also shown the broad range of information needs for different audiences. For example, the paper "Analyze This! 145 Questions for Data Scientists in Software Engineering" lists over 12 dozen different kinds of questions that have been seen in the information needs of software developers [2]. Note that each of these may require a different kind of analysis before an SE data scientist can answer the particular questions of specific users (as shown in the last column of Table 1.3).

We use the term "data scientist" to denote a person who can handle all these techniques (and more) as well as and adapt them to different information needs. As the following historical notes show, organizations have had "data scientists" for many years—albeit not as high demand or highly paid as in the current environment. Organizations hire these data scientists to explore the local data to find models that most answer the questions of most interest to the local business users [3]. These scientists know

Table 1.2 Space of Information Needs that can be Addressed by Data Science in SE			
	Past	**Present**	**Future**
Exploration Find important conditions.	**Trends** Quantifies how an artifact is changing. Useful for understanding the direction of a project. • Regression analysis.	**Alerts** Reports unusual changes in artifacts when they happen. Helps users respond quickly to events. • Anomaly detection.	**Forecasting** Predicts events based on current trends. Helps users make pro-active decisions. • Extrapolation.
Analysis Explain conditions.	**Summarization** Succinctly characterizes key aspects of artifacts or groups of artifacts. Quickly maps artifacts to development activities or other project dimensions. • Topic analysis.	**Overlays** Compares artifacts or development histories interactively. Helps establish guidelines. • Correlation.	**Goals** Discovers how artifacts are changing with respect to goals. Provides assistance for planning. • Root-cause analysis.
Experimentation Compare alternative conditions.	**Modeling** Characterizes normal development behavior. Facilitates learning from previous work. • Machine learning.	**Benchmarking** Compares artifacts to established best practices. Helps with evaluation. • Significance testing.	**Simulation** Tests decisions before making them. Helps when choosing between decision alternatives. • What-if? analysis.

Table 1.3 Mapping Information Needs (Left) to Automatic Technique (Right)

Information Need	Description	Insight	Relevant Techniques
Summarization	Search for important or unusual factors to associated with a time range.	Characterize events, understand why they happened.	Topic analysis, NLP
Alerts (& Correlations)	Continuous search for unusual changes or relationships in variables	Notice important events.	Statistics, Repeated measures
Forecasting	Search for and predict unusual events in the future based on current trends.	Anticipate events.	Extrapolation, Statistics
Trends	How is an artifact changing?	Understand the direction of the project.	Regression analysis
Overlays	What artifacts account for current activity?	Understand the relationships between artifacts.	Cluster analysis, repository mining
Goals	How are features/artifacts changing in the context of completion or some other goal?	Assistance for planning	Root-cause analysis
Modeling	Compares the abstract history of similar artifacts. Identify important factors in history.	Learn from previous projects.	Machine learning
Benchmarking	Identify vectors of similarity/difference across artifacts.	Assistance for resource allocation and many other decisions	Statistics
Simulation	Simulate changes based on other artifact models.	Assistance for general decisions	What-if? analysis

that before they apply technique XYZ, they first spend much time with their business users learning their particular problems and the specific information needs of their domain.

1.2 THE PAST: ORIGINS

Moving on from definitions, we now offer a historical perspective on SE data analytics. Looking back in time, we can see that this is the fourth generation of data science in SE. This section describes those four generations.

However, before doing that, we add that any historical retrospective cannot reference all work conducted by all researchers (and this is particularly true for a field as large and active as data science in software engineering). Hence, we apologize in advance to any of our colleagues not mentioned in the following.

1.2.1 GENERATION 1: PRELIMINARY WORK

As soon as people started programming, it became apparent that programming was an inherently buggy process. As recalled by Wilkes [4], speaking of his programming experiences from the early 1950s:

> "It was on one of my journeys between the EDSAC room and the punching equipment that 'hesitating at the angles of stairs' the realization came over me with full force that a good part of the remainder of my life was going to be spent in finding errors in my own programs."

It took several decades to gather the experience required to quantify the size/defect relationship. In 1971, Akiyama [5] described the first known "size" law, stating that the number of defects D was a function of the number of LOC; specifically:

$$D = 4.86 + 0.018^*i.$$

In 1976, Thomas McCabe argued that the number of LOC was less important than the complexity of that code [6]. He argued that code is more likely to be defective when its "cyclomatic complexity" measure was over 10.

Not only is programming an inherently buggy process, it's also inherently difficult. Based on data from 63 projects, in 1981 Boehm [7] proposed an estimator for development effort that was exponential on program size:

$$\text{effort} = a^* \text{ KLOC } b^* \text{ EffortMultipliers} \quad (\text{where } 2.4 \leq a \leq 3 \text{ and } 1.05 \leq b \leq 1.2).$$

At the same time, other researchers were finding repeated meta-level patterns in software development. For example, in the late 1970s, Lehman proposed a set of *laws of software evolution* to describe a balance between (1) forces driving new developments and (2) forces that slow down progress [8]. For example, the *law of continuing change* states that an "e-program" (whose behavior is strongly connected to the environment where it runs) must always be continually adapted or it will become progressively less satisfactory.

1.2.2 GENERATION 2: ACADEMIC EXPERIMENTS

From the late 1980s, some data scientists starting analyzing software data using algorithms taken from artificial intelligence research. For example, Selby and Porter found that decision-tree learners could identify which components might be error-prone (or having a high development cost) [9]. After that, very many researchers tried very many other AI methods for predicting aspects of software projects. For example, some researchers applied decision trees and neural networks to software effort estimation [10] or reliability-growth modeling [11]. Yet other work explored instance-based reasoning by analogy [12] or rough sets [13] (again, for effort estimation).

1.2.3 GENERATION 3: INDUSTRIAL EXPERIMENTS

From around the turn of the century, it became more common for workers at industrial or government organizations to find that data science can be successfully applied to their software projects.

For example, Norman Schneidewind explored quality prediction via Boolean discriminant functions for NASA systems [14]. Also at NASA, Menzies and Feather et al. used AI tools to explore trade-offs in early lifecycle models [15] or to guide software inspection teams [16].

Further over at AT&T, Ostrand and Weyuker and Bell used binomial regression functions to recognize 20% of the code that contained most (over 80%) of the bugs [17]. Other prominent work in this time frame included:

- Zimmermann et al. [18] who used association rule learning to find patterns of defects in a large set of open source projects.
- Nagappan, Ball, Williams, Vouk et al. who worked with Nortel Networks and Microsoft to show that data from those organizations can predict for software quality [19, 20].

1.2.4 GENERATION 4: DATA SCIENCE EVERYWHERE

After the above, it became harder to track the massive growth in data science for SE. Many organizations such as Google, Facebook, and Microsoft (and others) routinely apply data science methods to their data. Since 2005, at many conferences, it has became routine to find papers from industrial practitioners and/or academics applying data science methods to software projects. Additionally, since 2010, we have seen a dramatic increase in the starting salaries of our graduate students who take industrial data science positions.

Further, various conferences have emerged that devote themselves to SE data science. At the time of writing, it is now routine for many SE conference papers to use data miners. However, during the last decade, two conferences lead the way: the Mining Software Repositories conference and the PROMISE conference on repeatable experiments in SE. Both communities explore data collection and its subsequent analysis with statistics or data mining methods, but each community has a particular focus: the MSR community is mostly concerned with the initial data collection while PROMISE community is more concerned with improving the efficacy and repeatability of that data's analysis. This book focuses more on the MSR community, while another book (*Sharing Data and Models in Software Engineering*, Morgan Kaufmann, 2014) offers the PROMISE perspective on data analysis.

1.3 PRESENT DAY

Data science has became so popular that at the time of writing (May, 2014), there is something of an unsustainable "bubble" in this area. Over the past few years, the volume and types of data related to SE has grown at an unprecedented rate and shows no sign of slowing. This turn of events has led to a veritable gold rush, as many "big data" enthusiasts mine raw data and extract nuggets of insight. A very real danger is that the landscape may become a Wild West where inexperienced software "cowboys" sell hastily generated models to unsophisticated business users, without any concern for best or safe practices (e.g., such as the best practices documented in this book).

To some extent, the current "bubble" in data is not surprising. New technologies such as data science typically follow the "hype curve" of Figure 1.1. Just like the dot-coms in the late 1990s, the current boom in "big data" and data science is characterized by unrealistic expectations. However, as shown in Figure 1.1, if a technology has something to offer, it won't stay in the trough of disillusionment.

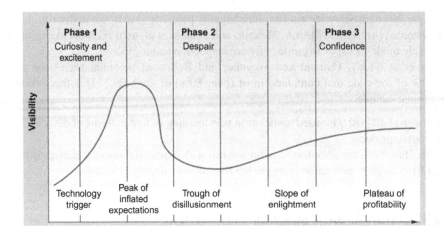

FIGURE 1.1

Standard hype cycle for new technology.

Internet-based computing survived the "dot-gone" meltdown of 1999–2001 and has now risen to a new sustainable (and growing) level of activity. We are confident that data science will also endure and thrive as a important technology for the decades to come.

One goal of this book is to go "behind the hype" and demonstrate proven principles for a sustainable data science industry. One standout result from this book is that *data science needs data scientists.* As shown by the examples in this book, data science for SE can be an intricate task involving extensive and elaborate combinations of tools. Further, it is not enough to merely use those tools—it is also necessary to understand them well enough to adapt and integrate them into some human-level process. Hence, to use data science properly, organizations need skilled practitioners, extensive knowledge of humans and of organizations, a broad skill set, and a *big toolkit* of methods.

For example, consider the technology used in the chapter "Analytical Product Release Planning" by Maleknaz Nayebi and Guenther Ruhe. As shown below, this list of technology is not short. Further, it is representative of the kind of data science solutions being deployed today in many organizations.

The automatic methods discussed in that chapter include:

- Analogical reasoning;
- DBScan (which is a kind of density-based clustering algorithm);
- Attribute weighting; Preprocessing of data (e.g., to filter out erroneous values or to fill in missing values); and
- Methodological tools for assessing a learned model (e.g., leave-n-out experiments; different performance measures).

However, that chapter does not stop at mere automatic methods. Recalling part our definition (shown above), we said that the goal of data science is *"to gain and share insight from data to make better decisions."* Note how this "insight" is a human-reaction to data analysis. Therefore, it is vital that automatic tools be augmented with human-in-the-loop interaction. As examples of that kind of human-level analysis, Nayebi and Ruhe use:

- Qualitative business modeling;
- Amazon's Mechanical Turk;
- Combining algorithmic vs. expert judgement;
- Aggregation of expert judgments.

The bad news is that this kind of analysis is impossible without trained and skilled data scientists. The good news is that the community of trained and skilled data scientists, while not large, is growing. Maryalene LaPonsie calls "data scientists" the "the hottest job you haven't heard of" [21]. She writes that "The University of California San Diego Extension lists data mining and analytics as the second hottest career for college graduates in 2011. Even the Cheezburger Network, home of the web's infamous LOLCats, recently brought a data scientist on board."

In any field with such rapid growth, there are two problems:

1. How do we train the newcomers?
2. How do we manage them?

As to the issue of *training*, most people in SE data science currently get their knowledge about analysis from general data analysis texts such as data mining texts [22], statistical texts [23], etc. While these are useful, they are aimed at a broader audience and do not include common issues in SE (as a simple example, unlike many fields, most SE metrics are not normally distributed). This aim of this book is to focus on how analysis is applied to real-world SE. This book will discuss a range of methods (from manual to automatic and combinations in the middle). Our goal in this book is to give readers an understanding of the breadth of analysis methods possible for a wide range of data taken from SE projects. A companion book *Sharing Data and Models in Software Engineering* takes a different in-depth approach (where the same data is analyzed in-depth by many different ways using many different methods) [24].

As for the issue of *management*, it can be difficult for senior managers to effectively lead teams where the teams are working on technologies that are so novel and disruptive as data science. For such senior managers, we offer the following advice:

- **It ain't all hardware:** In the era of Google-style inference and cloud computing, it's a common belief that a company can analyze large amounts of data merely by building (or renting) a CPU farm, then running some distributed algorithms, perhaps using Hadoop (http://hadoop.apache.org) or some other distributed inference mechanism. This isn't the case. In our experience, while having many CPUs is (sometimes) useful, the factors that determine successful software analytics rarely include the hardware. More important than the hardware is how that hardware is used by skilled data scientists.
- **It ain't all tools:** Another misconception we often see relates to the role of software. Some managers think that if they acquire the right software tools—Weka, Matlab, and so on—then all their analytical problems will be instantly solved. Nothing could be further from the truth. All the standard data analysis toolkits come with built-in assumptions that might be suitable for particular domains. Hence, a premature commitment to particular automatic analysis tools can be counterproductive.

In our view, one vital role for a data scientist is to uncover the right hardware and the right tools for a particular application. At the start of a data science project, when it isn't clear what the important

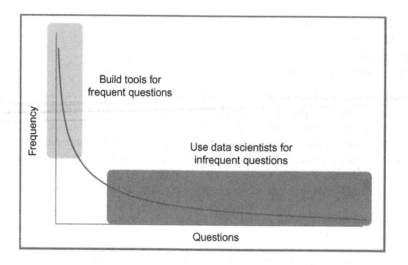

FIGURE 1.2

Data science projects may mature from many ad hoc queries to the repeated use of a limited number of queries.

factors in a domain are, a good data scientist will make many ad hoc queries to clarify the issues in that domain. Subsequently, once the analysis method stabilizes, it will then be possible to define what hardware and software tools would best automate any of the routine and repeated analysis tasks.

We can illustrate this process in Figure 1.2. As shown most data science projects mature by moving up along a curve. Initially, we might start in the darker region (where the queries are many, but the repeated queries are few) and then move into the lighter region (where we repeatedly make a small number of queries). This diagram leads to one of our favorite mantras for managing data science projects:

> For new problems, deploy the data scientists before deploying tools or hardware.

As for other principles for data science, in our Inductive Engineering Manifesto [25], we made some notes on what characterizes best practices in industrial data mining. Combining them with the above, we arrive at six points from this chapter and five further points:

1. *It ain't all hardware.*
2. *It ain't all software.*
3. *Data science needs data scientists*–especially during that initial analysis stage where the goal is to find (a) the most informative queries (that should be automated) and (b) the right hardware and the right tools to automate that query.
4. *Users before algorithms.* Data mining algorithms are only useful in industry if users fund their use in real-world applications. The user perspective is vital to inductive engineering. The space of models that can be generated from any dataset is very large. If we understand and apply user goals, then we can quickly focus an inductive engineering project on the small set of most crucial issues.

5. *Broad skill set, big toolkit.* Successful inductive engineers routinely try multiple inductive technologies. To handle the wide range of possible goals an inductive engineer should be ready to deploy a wide range of tools. Note that the set of useful inductive technologies is large and constantly changing. Therefore, use tools supported by a large ecosystem of developers who are constantly building new learners and fixing old ones.

6. *Deploy the data scientists before deploying tools or hardware*—especially for new problems.

7. *Plan for scale:* In any industrial application, data mining is repeated many times to (a) answer additional questions raised by the users; or (b) make some enhancement and/or bug fix to the method, or (c) to deploy it to a different set of users. That is, for serious studies, to ensure repeatability, the entire analysis should be automated using some high-level scripting language.

8. *Early feedback.* Continuous and early feedback from users allows needed changes to be made as soon as possible and without wasting heavy up-front investment. Prior to conducting very elaborate studies, try applying very simple tools to gain rapid early feedback.

9. *Be open-minded.* It's unwise to enter into an inductive study with fixed hypotheses or approaches, particularly for data that hasn't been mined before. Don't resist exploring additional avenues when a particular idea doesn't work out. We advise this because data likes to surprise: initial results often change the goals of a study when business plans are based on issues irrelevant to local data.

10. *Do smart learning.* Important outcomes are riding on your conclusions. Make sure you check and validate them. There are many such validation methods such as repeat the analysis N times on, say, 90% of the available data—then check how well your conclusions hold across all those samples.

11. *Live with the data you have.* You go mining with the data you have, not the data you might want or wish to have at a later time. Because we may not have control over how data is collected, it's wise to clean the data prior to learning. For example, before learning from a dataset, conduct instance or feature selection studies to see what spurious data can be removed.

1.4 CONCLUSION

This is an exciting time for those of us involved in data science and the analysis of software data. Looking into the very near future, we can only predict more use of data science in SE. By 2020, we predict

- more and different data,
- more algorithms,
- faster decision making with the availability of more data and faster release cycles,
- more people involved in data science as it becomes more routine to mine data,
- more education as more people analyze and work with data,
- more roles for data scientists and developers as this field matures with specialized subareas,
- more real-time data science to address the challenges of quickly finding patterns in big data,
- more data science for software systems such as mobile apps and games, and
- more impact of social tools in data science.

As an example of this last point, check out *Human Boosting* by Harsh Pareek and Pradeep Ravikumar, which discusses how to boost human learning with the help of data miners [26]. In the very near future, this kind of human(s)-in-the-loop analytics will become much more prevalent.

ACKNOWLEDGMENTS

The work of this kind of book falls mostly on the authors and reviewers, and we're very appreciative of all those who took the time to write and comment on these chapters. The work of the reviewers was particularly challenging because their feedback was required in a very condensed timetable. Accordingly, we offer them our heartfelt thanks.

We're also grateful to the Morgan Kaufmann production team for their hard work in assembling this material.

REFERENCES

[1] Buse RPL, Zimmermann T. Information needs for software development analytics. In: ICSE 2012; 2012. p. 987–96.

[2] Begel A, Zimmermann T. Analyze this! 145 questions for data scientists in software engineering. In: ICSE'14; 2014.

[3] Menzies T, Butcher A, Cok D, Marcus A, Layman L, Shull F, et al. Local vs. global lessons for defect prediction and effort estimation. IEEE Trans Softw Eng 2013;29(6).

[4] Wilkes M. Memoirs of a computer pioneer. Cambridge, MA: MIT Press; 1985.

[5] Akiyama F. An example of software system debugging. Inform Process 1971;71:353–9.

[6] Mccabe T. A complexity measure. IEEE Trans Softw Eng 1976;2(4):308–20.

[7] Boehm B. Software engineering economics. Englewood Cliffs: Prentice-Hall; 1981.

[8] Lehman MM. On understanding laws, evolution, and conservation in the large-program life cycle. J Syst Softw 1980; 1:213–21.

[9] Porter AA, Selby RW. Empirically guided software development using metric-based classification trees. IEEE Softw 1990;7(2):46–54.

[10] Srinivasan K, Fisher D. Machine learning approaches to estimating software development effort. IEEE Trans Softw Eng 1995;21(2):126–37.

[11] Tian J. Integrating time domain and input domain analyses of software reliability using tree-based models. IEEE Trans Softw Eng 1995;21(12):945–58.

[12] Shepperd M, Schofield C. Estimating software project effort using analogies. IEEE Trans Softw Eng 1997;23(11):736–43.

[13] Ruhe G. Rough set based data analysis in goal oriented software measurement. In: Proceedings of the 3rd international symposium on software metrics: from measurement to empirical results (METRICS '96); 1996.

[14] Schneidewind NF. Validating metrics for ensuring space shuttle flight software quality. Computer 1994;27(8):50,57.

[15] Feather M, Menzies T. Converging on the optimal attainment of requirements. In: IEEE RE'02; 2002.

[16] Menzies T, Stefano JSD, Chapman M. Learning early lifecycle IV and V quality indicators. In: IEEE symposium on software metrics symposium; 2003.

[17] Ostrand TJ, Weyuker EJ, Bell RM. Where the bugs are. SIGSOFT Softw Eng Notes 2004; 29(4):86–96.

[18] Zimmermann T, Weißgerber P, Diehl S, Zeller A. Mining version histories to guide software changes. In: Proceedings of the 26th international conference on software engineering (ICSE 2004), Edinburgh, United Kingdom; 2004. p. 563–72.

[19] Nagappan N, Ball T. Use of relative code churn measures to predict system defect density. In: ICSE 2005; 2005.

[20] Zheng J, Williams L, Nagappan N, Snipes W, Hudepohl JP, Vouk MA. On the value of static analysis for fault detection in software. IEEE Trans Softw Eng 2006; 32(4):240–53.

[21] LaPonsie M. The hottest job you haven't heard of; 2011. July 5, 2011, URL: http://www.onlinedegrees.com/, http://goo.gl/OjYqXQ.

[22] Witten IH, Frank E, Hall MA. Data mining: practical machine learning tools and techniques. 3rd ed. San Francisco, CA, USA: Morgan Kaufmann Publishers Inc.; 2011.

[23] Duda RO, Hart PE, Stork DG. Pattern classification. 2nd ed. Oxford: Wiley-Interscience; 2000.

[24] Menzies T, Kocaguneli E, Minku L, Peters F, Turhan B. Sharing data and models in software engineering. Waltham, MA: Morgan Kaufmann Publishers; 2014.

[25] Menzies T, Bird C, Kocaganeli E. The inductive software engineering manifesto: principles for industrial data mining; 2011. URL: http://menzies.us/pdf11manifesto.pdf.

[26] Pareek H, Ravikumar P. Human boosting. In: Proceedings of the international conference on machine learning; 2013. URL: http://jmlr.csail.mit.edu/proceedings/papers/v28/pareek13.pdf.

TUTORIAL-TECHNIQUES 1

MINING PATTERNS AND VIOLATIONS USING CONCEPT ANALYSIS

2

Christian Lindig*

Testfabrik AG, Saarbrücken, Germany

CHAPTER OUTLINE

2.1 INTRODUCTION

While classifying something as a software defect requires a specification, we can *find potential defects without a specification*. This is based on the observation that large software systems exhibit *patterns* in their implementation or behavior and that deviations from these patterns correlate with defects [1]. An automatic analysis of such deviations is practical for large systems and is especially suited to find latent bugs.

17

Patterns in code and behavior are a consequence of small and orthogonal interfaces. They force clients to combine functions to implement a certain functionality. For example, implementing in C a function with a varying number of arguments (like `printf`) requires the concerted use of the macros `va_start`, `va_arg`, and `va_end`. Hence, we see many functions that call both `va_start` and `va_end`. For example, the source code for the Ruby 1.8.4 interpreter includes 17 such functions. But it also includes one function (`vafuncall`) that calls `va_start` but not `va_end`. This deviation is indeed a bug that was corrected in a later release.

Mining software for structural patterns and their violations was pioneered by Li and Zhou [2] with PR-Miner,[1] a tool that mines programming rules from source code and flags violations. Patterns are not limited to a known set of patterns or names, but are *purely structural*. Li and Zhou demonstrated the effectiveness and efficiency of this approach by reporting 27 previously unknown bugs in the Linux kernel, PostgreSQL, and Apache HTTP Server. PR-Miner uses frequent itemset mining to detect patterns and their violations. Frequent itemset mining discovers implications such as *every customer who bought bread and butter also bought milk* from itemsets such as shopping carts. Li and Zhou note, however, that *"frequent itemset mining algorithms were not designed exactly for this purpose"* and developed some ad hoc mechanisms such as applying frequent-item mining twice.

The goal of this chapter is *not* to improve on the excellent results of PR-Miner, but is to *improve the foundation for detecting structural patterns and their violations*. Our hope is that this will lead to new applications of the idea that stands behind PR-Miner. In particular, we propose a unified representation for patterns and their instances that uncovers their hierarchical nature and provides an intuitive geometric interpretation.

Our formalism is based on the following insight: any binary relation (such as a call relation) can be represented as a cross table as in Figure 2.1, which shows the call relation of Ruby 1.8.4. A caller f and a callee g are related (marked with a dot) if f calls g. In such a table, rows (callers) and columns (callees)

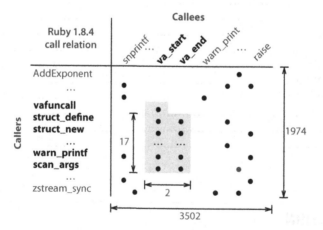

FIGURE 2.1

Call relation for Ruby 1.8.4. The *pattern* {`va_start`, `va_end`} becomes visible as a *block*. It is violated by the function **vafuncall**. This *violation* becomes visible as an *imperfect block*.

---

[1] Programming rule miner.

may be permuted without changing the underlying relation. By picking a suitable permutation, we can *make a pattern visible as a block*. Figure 2.1 shows the block for the *pattern* {va_start, va_end} as well as the 17 functions that are *instances* of this pattern. In addition, the *violation* of this pattern by the function vafuncall becomes visible as an *imperfect block*: vafuncall calls va_start but not va_end, which leaves a *gap* in the block.

Mining patterns from a relation can be understood as finding the blocks of the relation. Analogously, detecting violations of patterns can be understood as finding imperfect blocks. *Patterns and violations can be mined from any binary relation*, not just a call relation. However, for illustration, we shall stick with the call relation as an example for most of this chapter and present another application in Section 2.9.

2.1.1 CONTRIBUTIONS

This chapter makes the following contributions:

- *Blocks unify patterns and their instances*, which were previously treated separately and ad hoc. Furthermore, blocks provide a *geometric interpretation* of patterns and violations.
- A *block hierarchy* captures the recursive relation of blocks and violations: patterns correspond to blocks, and violations correspond to neighboring blocks.
- Case studies show the *efficiency and practicality* of the proposed formalism. Call patterns and their violations can be identified statically for the Python interpreter within 20 seconds, and for the Linux kernel within 1 minute.
- We draw a connection between patterns, their instances and violations, and formal concept analysis [3], which provides a theory to study them.

The remainder of this chapter is organized as follows: Section 2.2 introduces the relation between patterns and blocks, and Section 2.3 shows how to compute them from an input relation. Section 2.4 illustrates the use of COLIBRI/ML to compute patterns and introduces violations of patterns. Section 2.5 introduces violations of patterns formally, and Section 2.6 shows how to identify them efficiently. Section 2.7 explores the recursive relation of patterns and violations. Section 2.8 reports performance numbers gathered from the analysis of open-source projects. Sections 2.9 and 2.10 demonstrate the versatility of the binary relation in program analysis. The chapter closes with a discussion of related work in Section 2.11 and our conclusions in Section 2.12.

2.2 PATTERNS AND BLOCKS

A relation associates *objects* and their *features*, such as callers and callees in the example above. A *pattern* is a set of features shared by objects. These objects are called the *instances* of the pattern. For defect detection, the goal is to find patterns that have many instances because these patterns are likely to capture a universal principle. As we shall see, patterns and instances are unified by blocks.

For example, the Ruby interpreter contains the following pattern: the functions raise and int2inum are called together from 107 different functions. These functions are the *instances* of the *pattern* {raise, int2inum}. The number of instances (107) is called the *support* for the pattern.

Table 2.1 Patterns Found in Open-Source Projects		
Project	**Support**	**Pattern**
Ruby 1.8.4	17	`va_start, va_end`
Apache HTTP 2.2.2	20	`va_start, va_end`
	29	`apr_thread_mutex_lock`
		`apr_thread_mutex_unlock`
Linux 2.6.10	28	`add_wait_queue,`
		`remove_wait_queue`
	53	`acpi_ut_acquire_mutex,`
		`acpi_ut_release_mutex`
	27	`journal_begin,`
		`journal_end`
Linux 2.6.17	31	`kmalloc, copy_from_user,`
		`kfree`
Phyton 2006-06-20	59	`PyEval_SaveThread,`
		`PyEval_RestoreThread`

The column headed "Support" indicates how many instances of that pattern were found in a project.

Table 2.1 illustrates more patterns and their support that we mined from the call relation of systems implemented in C. Most of them show the familiar pattern of allocation and deallocation of a resource. The interesting fact is not that they exist, but that we were able to find them without knowing the names of these functions in advance.

Formally, the relation $R \subseteq \mathcal{O} \times \mathcal{F}$ is a set of pairs. Each pair (o,f) relates an *object* $o \in \mathcal{O}$ and a feature $f \in \mathcal{F}$. A pattern is a set of features $F \subseteq \mathcal{F}$, and its instances are a set of objects $O \subseteq \mathcal{O}$. Given a set of objects O, we can ask what features these objects share; likewise, given a set of features F, we can ask for its instances. Both answers are expressed with the prime operator $'$ (which one can think of as the derivative of a set).

Definition 1 (features, instances). Given the relation $R \subseteq \mathcal{O} \times \mathcal{F}$ and a set of objects $O \subseteq \mathcal{O}$, objects *share* the set $O' \subseteq \mathcal{F}$ of features. Likewise, a set of features $F \subseteq \mathcal{F}$ has *instances* $F' \subseteq \mathcal{O}$, defined as follows:

$$O' = \{f \in \mathcal{F} \mid (o,f) \in R \text{ for all } o \in O\},$$
$$F' = \{o \in \mathcal{O} \mid (o,f) \in R \text{ for all } f \in F\}.$$

A pattern (a set of features) corresponds to a block in a cross table—see Figure 2.2. A block is characterized by two sets: a pattern and its instances, which form the sides of the block. The formal definition interlocks a pattern and its instances:

Definition 2 (block). For the relation $R \subseteq \mathcal{O} \times \mathcal{F}$, a *block* is defined as a pair (O, F) of objects and their features such that $O' = F$ and $F' = O$ holds. The cardinalities $|O|$ and $|F|$ are called the *support* and *pattern width*, respectively.

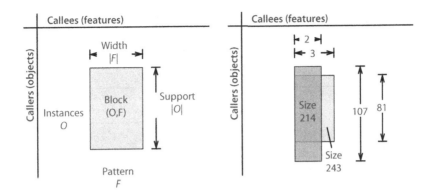

FIGURE 2.2

A block is a pair (O, F) of a pattern F and its instances O. Overlapping patterns lead to overlapping blocks, where large patterns have fewer instances, and vice versa. The size of a block can be used to identify interesting patterns.

A block as defined above is maximal in the sense that it cannot be extended with an additional object (or feature) without our having to remove a feature (or object).

Note that a block is defined as a pair of two *sets*, and therefore objects and features are unordered. However, to visualize a block (O, F) in a cross table, we have to put the elements of O and F next to each other. For this reason, typically not all blocks can be made visible in a table at the same time.

Because patterns are sets, a subset relation may hold between them. For example, the Ruby interpreter exhibits the pattern {raise, int2inum}, which has 107 instances. Of these 107 instances, a subset of 81 instances also call the function funcall2. These 81 instances thus form a *wider* pattern {raise, int2inum, funcall2} with *fewer* instances.

Patterns in a subset relation correspond to overlapping blocks (see Figure 2.2). The pattern {raise, int2inum} is represented by a tall but slim block, whereas the larger pattern {raise, int2inum, funcall2} is represented by a wider but shorter block. The *size* $|O| \times |F|$ of a block (O, F) can be used as a criterion to find interesting patterns—large blocks are good candidates.

Blocks unify patterns and their instances.

2.3 COMPUTING ALL BLOCKS

Finding patterns requires us to identify the blocks of a relation. The crucial question is how to do this efficiently, at least for the blocks that we are most interested in.

The problem of computing all blocks of a relation is solved by *formal concept analysis* [3]. The definition of a block corresponds to a so-called *formal concept*. Concepts (and hence blocks) form a hierarchy which is defined by $(O_1, F_1) \leq (O_2, F_2) \Leftrightarrow O_1 \subseteq O_2$. Indeed, the hierarchy is a lattice (see Figure 2.4). This means, among other things, that any two blocks have a unique common subblock. and any intersection of two blocks in a table is a block in the hierarchy as well. (The intersection may be empty though.)

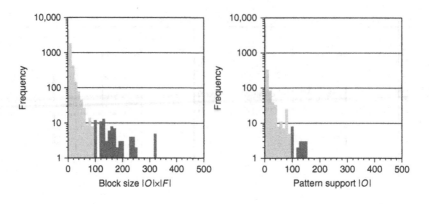

FIGURE 2.3

Distribution of block size $|O| \times |F|$ and pattern support $|O|$ in Ruby 1.8.4. From 7280 blocks, 88 blocks are of size 100 or bigger, and 24 patterns have support 100 or higher—these have dark gray bars.

The call relation for the Ruby interpreter has 7280 blocks. Most blocks are small, as can be seen from the frequency distribution for block size ($|O| \times |F|$) in Figure 2.3. A bar in the diagram for size s represents the number of blocks whose size is in an interval of width 10 that is centered at s. There are 6430 blocks of size 20 or less and 88 blocks of size 100 or more. Likewise, 7043 patterns have a support of 20 or less, and 24 patterns have support of 100 or more. We are most interested in large blocks that exceed a minimum support because they are likely to represent a regularity in the Ruby implementation.

The relation $R \subseteq O \times F$ may have up to 2^n blocks, where $n = \min(|O|, |F|)$. The actual number of blocks strongly depends on the *density* $|R|/(|O| \times |F|)$ of the relation (or table). The exponential case holds only for extremely dense tables. The density of the call relation for Ruby (and other systems—see Table 2.2) is below 1%, which is why the number of blocks is typically dominated by $O(|R|^3)$.

Since we are most interested in the fraction of patterns (or blocks) with high support and large size, it would be wasteful to compute all blocks of a relation. The key observation for an efficient algorithm

Table 2.2 Statistics for the Call Relation of Open-Source Projects

Project	$|O|$	$|F|$	Density	Blocks
		Call Relation		
Ruby 1.8.4	3502	1974	0.002	7280
Linux 2.6.0	11,131	7176	<0.001	11,308
Python 2.4.3	2624	1627	0.002	4870
Lua 5.1	766	664	0.005	1523
Apache 2.2.2	2256	1576	0.002	3301

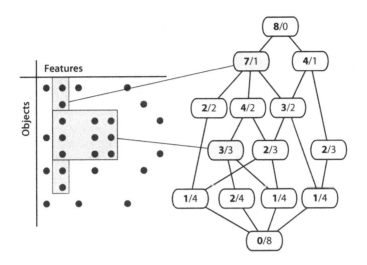

FIGURE 2.4

The blocks of a relation form a lattice. Each block corresponds to a formal concept—two such correspondences are shown. The numbers inside each concept denote $|O|/|F|$: support and width of a rule.

is that the blocks highest in the hierarchy exhibit the highest support (see Figure 2.4). In other words, as we move down in the hierarchy, support $|O|$ decreases monotonically, while $|F|$ increases. The size $|O| \times |F|$ of blocks maximizes toward the middle of the hierarchy. These are interesting characteristics because they combine wide patterns that still have relatively high support.

2.3.1 ALGORITHM IN A NUTSHELL

The best-known algorithm for concept analysis is by Ganter and Wille [3]; it computes efficiently the *set* of all concepts. However, it does not compute the lattice of concepts explicitly, nor does it work breadth-first. Taken together, these facts make it less suitable for the exploration of only the topmost concepts in a lattice. We sketch a better suited, yet simple and efficient, algorithm below. More details can be found in [4].

The top concept (or block) for the relation $R \subseteq \mathcal{O} \times \mathcal{F}$ is $(\{\}', \{\}'')$ and serves as a starting point. Given any concept (O, F), we can compute a subconcept (O_f, F_f) for each feature $f \in \mathcal{F} \setminus F$ that is not already part of (O, F): $(O_f, F_f) = ((F \cup \{f\})', (F \cup \{f\})'')$. The set of subconcepts contains all lower neighbors of (O, F), but may also contain additional concepts. The following criterion holds only for lower neighbors and is used to identify them: (O_f, F_f) is a lower neighbor if and only if for all $x \in F_f \setminus F$ the following holds: $(F \cup \{x\})'' = (F \cup \{f\})''$.

Figure 2.5 shows a small relation R as an example with the corresponding set of concepts shown in Figure 2.6. We look at the concept $(O, F) = \{1, 3, 4, 5\}, \{a\})$ as a starting point to explore its lower neighbors. We compute one concept for each attribute that is not already part of F. Hence, we compute concepts (or at least their attribute sets) F_b through F_e. Each of these belongs to a subconcept of (O, F) but is not necessarily also a lower neighbor of (O, F). Applying the test from above we find that F_b does not belong to a lower neighbor, whereas all other attribute sets F_c, F_d, and F_e do. Intuitively, F_b is

	a	b	c	d	e
1	×		×	×	×
2		×			
3	×				×
4	×			×	
5	×		×		

FIGURE 2.5

Example relation R.

Objects	Attributes
1 2 3 4 5	$\emptyset$
2	b
1 3 4 5	a
1 3	ae
1 4	ad
1 5	ac
1	$acde$
$\emptyset$	$abcde$

FIGURE 2.6

Concepts of relation R.

$(O, F) = (\{1, 3, 4, 5\}, \{a\})$				
$f \in \mathcal{F} \setminus F$	b	c	d	e
$F_f = (F \cup \{f\})''$	$abcde$	ac	ad	ae
$F_f \setminus F$	$bcde$	c	d	e

FIGURE 2.7

Example for computing concepts breadth-first starting from a given concept. We are looking at the subconcepts of $(O, F) = (\{1, 3, 4, 5\}, \{a\})$ and wish to identify those that are its immediate lower neighbors in the lattice. We compute the attribute sets $F_b, F_c, F_d,$ and F_e of the candidates and test which of these belong to lower neighbors. $F_b = \{a, b, c, d, e\}$ is not an attribute set of a lower neighbor of (O, F) because we can find $e \in F_b \setminus F$ with $(F \cup \{e\})'' = \{a, e\} \neq F_b'' = \{a, b, c, d, e\}$.

too large. It contains attributes such as e that, when added to F, result in an attribute set different from F_b (Figure 2.7).

The above algorithm is implemented in COLIBRI/ML, a command-line tool for concept analysis [5]. It takes a textual representation of a relation and computes all blocks and block violations. As sketched above, COLIBRI/ML avoids computing all blocks by starting from the top block and then moving to lower blocks breadth-first as long as blocks still exceed a given minimum support.

COLIBRI/ML worked well for our cases studies (see Section 2.8 for its performance). For very large systems ($|\mathcal{O}| > 20\,000$) the more advanced algorithm by Stumme et al. [6] could provide an alternative, as it is explicitly designed for extreme scalability.

Formal concept analysis computes all blocks from a relation.

2.4 MINING SHOPPING CARTS WITH COLIBRI

To demonstrate the mining of rules and exceptions in practice, we analyze some shopping carts—one of the original applications for frequent itemset mining. The data are the first 1000 shopping carts from the data set of Brijs [7]. It contains lines with numbers, where each line represents a shopping cart and each number represents an item the customer bought. The 1000 shopping carts together contain 3182 distinct products. A little massaging brings the original data in a form suitable for COLIBRI/ML, as shown in Figure 2.8.

As a first task we try to find items that are frequently bought together. Such a set of items is called a rule, and we can control two parameters: the minimum number of items in such a set and the minimum number of customers who need to have bought them together before we report them. Figure 2.9 shows the invocation of COLIBRI/ML and the result.

COLIBRI/ML reports 14 itemsets of size 3 and larger and, under *support*, how often these were bought together. The most popular items bought together are $\{a_{48}, a_{41}, a_{39}\}$, which were bought by 106 of 1000 customers. By default, COLIBRI/ML does not report any itemset that was bought by fewer than 20 customers.

Given this result, the store owner could advertise these items together. He or she might also ask himself or herself whether there are customers who bought some of the items in such a set but not all of them and could advertise the missing item to these customers, assuming that they are likely to be interested. COLIBRI/ML can also detect such incomplete or "flawed" purchases—see Figure 2.10. In a software engineering context, these could represent software defects.

```
o1: a0 a1 a2 a3 a4 a5 a6 a7 a8 a9 a10 a11 a12 a13 a14 a15
    a16 a17 a18 a19 a20 a21 a22 a23 a24 a25 a26 a27 a28 a29 ;
o2: a30 a31 a32 ;
o3: a33 a34 a35 ;
o4: a36 a37 a38 a39 a40 a41 a42 a43 a44 a45 a46 ;
o5: a38 a39 a47 a48 ;
o6: a38 a39 a48 a49 a50 a51 a52 a53 a54 a55 a56 a57 a58 ;
o7: a32 a41 a59 a60 a61 a62 ;
o8: a3 a39 a48 ;
o9: a63 a64 a65 a66 a67 a68 ;
o10: a32 a69 ;
# 990 more lines omitted
```

FIGURE 2.8

Retail data in a format suitable for analysis with COLIBRI/ML. It consists of 1000 shopping carts *o* and 3182 different items *a*.

```
$ colibri rules -rhs 3 retail-1000.dat
rule (support  82): a48 a39 a38
rule (support 106): a48 a41 a39
rule (support  48): a48 a41 a38
rule (support  67): a41 a39 a38
rule (support  41): a48 a41 a39 a38
rule (support  36): a48 a39 a32
rule (support  20): a39 a38 a32
rule (support  27): a39 a38 a36
rule (support  25): a41 a39 a32
rule (support  21): a48 a38 a110
rule (support  24): a39 a38 a110
rule (support  32): a39 a38 a170
rule (support  21): a48 a38 a170
rule (support  24): a48 a39 a1327
```

FIGURE 2.9

Invocation of COLIBRI/ML for rule mining on data from 1000 shopping carts. The tool finds frequent itemsets with a (default) support of at least 20 items and three (as specified by **-rhs 3**) or more items.

```
$ colibri flaws retail-1000.dat
violation (confidence 0.93 support  41 gap   1 flaws   3)
  flaws ( 3)       : o804 o649 o605
  rule (support  41): a38 a36
  rule (support  44): a36
violation (confidence 0.90 support  27 gap   1 flaws   3)
  flaws ( 3)       : o804 o649 o605
  rule (support  27): a39 a38 a36
  rule (support  30): a39 a36
violation (confidence 0.98 support  40 gap   1 flaws   1)
  flaws ( 1)       : o90
  rule (support  40): a38 a110
  rule (support  41): a110
violation (confidence 0.98 support  53 gap   1 flaws   1)
  flaws ( 1)       : o700
  rule (support  53): a38 a170
  rule (support  54): a170
violation (confidence 0.97 support  32 gap   1 flaws   1)
  flaws ( 1)       : o700
  rule (support  32): a39 a38 a170
  rule (support  33): a39 a170
```

FIGURE 2.10

Invocation of COLIBRI/ML for mining "incomplete" purchases. A gap of size 1 means one item was missing in the incomplete purchase. The number of flaws indicates how many carts with this incompleteness were detected.

Forty-one customers bought $\{a_{38}, a_{36}\}$ together, and three customers bought only a_{36} but not a_{38}. It thus might pay off to advertise item a_{38} to them. Likewise, customer o_{90} might be interested in buying a_{38}, which was bought otherwise always together with a_{110}.

2.5 **VIOLATIONS**

When a pattern is represented as a block, a violation of such a pattern is represented by an imperfect block. The initial example in Figure 2.1 shows such an imperfect block formed by the pattern {va_start, va_end}, its instances, and one function that calls only va_start. Adding the missing call to va_end would remove the violation and make the block perfect.

A similar situation is shown more schematically on the left in Figure 2.11. Closer inspection reveals that an imperfect block is really a composition of two blocks. Block A represents a pattern; this pattern is violated by a (small) number of violators belonging to a subset of block B, where the patterns of blocks A and B overlap. This is equivalent to block B being a superblock of block A in the block hierarchy (shown on the right in Figure 2.11). Together they leave a *gap* in a block as wide as block A and as tall as block B. The width of the gap is the number of corrections necessary in any violator to remove the violation.

Just as not every block constitutes an interesting pattern that captures a universal quality, not every gap constitutes an interesting violation of a pattern. We are interested only in gaps within blocks that we have already found interesting. This typically means that we demand a minimum support for block A before we would consider a gap. In addition, we believe that fewer violations of a pattern make these violations more credible. This is expressed in the *confidence* for a violation.

Definition 3 (violation, confidence). Given a pattern represented by block $A = (O_1, F_1)$ and a second block $B = (O_2, F_2)$ with $A < B$, the objects $O_2 \setminus O_1$ violate pattern F_1. The *confidence* that these violations are genuine is $|O_1|/|O_2|$.

Confidence is the probability that any object that exhibits features F_1 also exhibits features F_2. A rule with a support of 100 instances and two violations yields a confidence of $100/102 = 0.98$. In the initial example from Ruby 1.8.4, the rule {va_start, va_end} has support 17 and one violation. This results in a confidence of $17/18 = 0.94$. Table 2.3 shows some additional violated patterns from open-source projects.

A violation is a composition of two blocks.

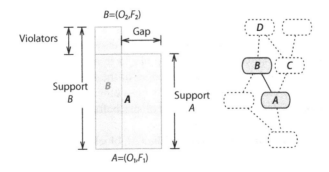

FIGURE 2.11

A pattern and its violation are represented by two blocks that are neighbors in the lattice: block *A* represents a pattern which is violated by block *B*. Our confidence that such a violation is genuine depends on the support of both blocks.

Table 2.3 Some Pattern Violations; The Underlined Call was Missing

Project	Support	Confidence	Violated Pattern
Linux 2.6.17	141	0.97	`mutex_lock,` `mutex_unlock`
Linux 2.6.16	48	0.98	`down_failed, up_wakeup`
Linux 2.6.0	44	0.96	`kmalloc, vmalloc`
Linux 2.6.0	68	0.99	`printk, dump_stack`
Python[a]	59	0.98	`PyEval_RestoreThread,` `PyEval_SaveThread`
Ruby[b]	24	0.96	`id_each, rb_block_call`

[a] *SVN 2006-06-20.*
[b] *CVS 2006-06-20.*

2.6 FINDING VIOLATIONS

An imperfect block such as that on the left in Figure 2.11 can be constructed from block A and any superblock. In the partial block hierarchy on the right in Figure 2.11, these are blocks B, C, and D, as well as all their superblocks.

The violations of block A with the highest confidence are those represented by the upper neighbors of block A in the block hierarchy: blocks B and C in Figure 2.11. The reason is that as we move up in the hierarchy, blocks become slimmer and taller. Since confidence essentially expresses the height ratio of two blocks and we are looking for blocks of almost equal height, *immediate neighbors represent pattern violations with the highest confidence.*

Figure 2.12 shows the block hierarchy from the example in Figure 2.1; the number inside each block indicates the support for the pattern represented by that block. Links between blocks represent violations—some are labeled with the confidence of the violation. As we observed above, support decreases monotonically as we move down in the hierarchy. On the other hand, *confidence is nonmonotonic.* There is no obvious algorithm to identify only the violations with the highest confidence.

A pragmatic approach to identify violations is to consider only those that violate patterns exceeding a minimum support. These are represented by the top blocks in a hierarchy; in Figure 2.12 all blocks with support of at least 3 are shaded. Traversing all edges of the lattice breadth-first, starting from the top element, will find all interesting violations. This is most efficient with an algorithm that computes blocks and their neighbors on demand, rather than all blocks beforehand.

Violations correspond to neighboring blocks in the lattice.

2.7 TWO PATTERNS OR ONE VIOLATION?

The recursive nature of a block hierarchy causes a dilemma: whether a block is a pattern or contributes to the violation of another pattern is a matter of interpretation.

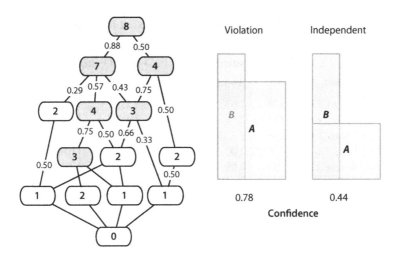

FIGURE 2.12

Block hierarchy for the example from Figure 2.1. Each block is marked with its support; shaded blocks have support of 3 or greater, and edge labels indicate confidence for pattern violations.

When two blocks A and B with $A < B$ have almost the same support, the confidence for a violation of block B is close to 1. This is the situation presented in Figure 2.11 and in the middle in Figure 2.12. In that case we regard block B as a block that contributes to a violation of block A.

An alternative situation is shown in Figure 2.12 on the right: two blocks A and B with $A < B$, where block B has about twice the support of block A. Considering block B as violating block A would result in a low confidence. It is thus more sensible to assume that blocks A and B are overlapping but otherwise independent patterns. This would mean that block A and block B both represent a correct usage, even though one pattern (B) is a subset of the other (A).

We analyzed the call relations of the projects in Table 2.2 for independent but overlapping patterns. We considered all patterns with support of at least 20 and a violation confidence below 60%. We found no such patterns in the Linux 2.6.0 kernel, none in Lua 5.1, one in Apache HTTP, but 59 such patterns in Python 2.4.3, and 49 in Ruby 1.8.4. For example, a typical pair of patterns in Python is {PyType_IsSubtype, PyErr_SetString, PyErr_Format} with support 42 and {PyType_IsSubtype, PyErr_SetString} with support 202. We have no immediate explanation why some systems show many overlapping patterns, while others show none at all. Both systems that show them are interpreters, and we suspect that these include a considerable number of functions which call many functions such that overlapping patterns can emerge.

In addition to confidence, we may use a second criterion to classify two blocks as either independent or violating: the width of the gap (see Figure 2.11), which is the number of corrections needed to make an object an instance of the violated pattern. If a pattern has width 5, it is likely that a true error misses one call, rather than two or three calls. We could thus demand that a violation should have a small gap. As a consequence, we would consider only one block violating another if both blocks have about the same height *and* about the same width.

Table 2.4 Patterns and Violations in the Call Relation of C Programs

Project	Patterns[a]		Violated Patterns[b]		
	No.	Average Width	No.	Violators	Gap
Ruby 1.8.4	143	2.67	39	1.49	2.26
Linux 2.6.0	112	2.52	19	1.21	1.05
Python 2.4.3	163	2.32	8	1.00	1.62
Lua 5.1	5	2.00	0	0.00	0.00
Apache 2.2.2	25	2.08	1	1.00	1.00

[a] With support of 20 or greater.
[b] With confidence of 0.95 or greater.

Using the gap width to identify violations requires patterns of a considerable width. Otherwise the gap width is too bound to be useful as a criterion. This is the case for patterns that we found in C programs, where most patterns have width 2.

Table 2.4 presents some statistics for open-source projects to support this: the columns under the header "Patterns" indicate the number of patterns with support of at least 20 and their average width. The columns under the header "Violated Patterns" indicate how often these were violated, by how many functions (column with header "Violators"), and the average number of missing calls (column with header "Gap"). Because the average gap width is between 1 and 2, it cannot be used as a criterion to classify blocks as violations or patterns.

Patterns and violations are recursive.

2.8 PERFORMANCE

Thinking about patterns and their violations as a hierarchy of blocks is not just a theoretical model, but is also well suited for an implementation. We outlined in Sections 2.3 and 2.5 efficient algorithms to compute all blocks and to find violations of patterns above a minimal support. Here we report some performance numbers gathered with COLIBRI/ML [5], a command-line tool for concept analysis implemented in OCaml.[2]

Our test subjects were the open-source applications written in C that we have used throughout the chapter. These range from the small Lua interpreter (12 kLOC of C code[3]), over-medium-sized systems like the Apache HTTP Server (207 kLOC), the Python and Ruby interpreters (300 kLOC, 209 kLOC), to the Linux 2.6 kernel (3.6 MLOC). For the Linux kernel the actual size of the system depends strongly on the configuration because drivers can be included into the kernel, compiled into modules, or not used at all. We configured a kernel for a small server where all relevant modules are integrated into the kernel.

---

[2] Also available as COLIBRI/JAVA [8].
[3] As reported by David A. Wheeler's SLOCCount.

Table 2.5 Time in Seconds to Analyze Call Relations for Pattern Violations Exceeding a Given Support and Confidence with COLIBRI/ML on a 2 GHz AMD-64 Processor				
Confidence	**0.80**	**0.85**	**0.90**	**0.95**
Support ≥ 20				
Ruby 1.8.4	10.8	10.7	9.9	10.7
Linux 2.6.0	68.9	73.4	68.7	73.4
Python 2.4.3	19.3	17.8	19.3	19.4
Lua 5.1	0.3	0.3	0.3	0.3
Apache 2.2.2	3.1	3.1	2.8	2.9
Support ≥ 30				
Ruby 1.8.4	9.2	8.3	9.1	8.4
Linux 2.6.0	50.7	55.1	55.1	50.7
Python 2.4.3	15.7	14.3	15.7	14.3
Lua 5.1	0.3	0.3	0.2	0.3
Apache 2.2.2	2.8	2.5	2.8	2.5
Support ≥ 40				
Ruby 1.8.4	8.3	7.6	8.3	7.6
Linux 2.6.0	43.4	47.6	43.4	46.8
Python 2.4.3	14.2	12.9	14.3	12.9
Lua 5.1	0.2	0.2	0.2	0.2
Apache 2.2.2	2.7	2.4	2.7	2.7

From each application we extracted the call relation and analyzed it for violations of patterns. We extracted the call relation by building a binary of each application, disassembling it, and analyzing labels and jumps with a small script. This static analysis is fast but misses computed jumps and calls from function pointers. While these are rare in C applications, this simple technique would not work for C++ or Java because method invocation in C++ and Java depends on dynamic dispatch at runtime. For these languages a simple experiment would instrument the code and record method invocations observed at runtime for later analysis.

Table 2.5 reports wall clock times in seconds for the analysis of pattern violations. The analysis was run on a 2 GHz AMD-64 processor on Linux for several levels of minimum support and confidence. For example, analyzing Python for all violations with support of at least 20 instances and confidence of 0.85 or greater took 17.8 s. The analysis of the Linux kernel took about 1 min, while smaller systems could be analyzed within less than 20 s. The analysis is faster for higher confidence and support levels because it must consider fewer blocks; however, the overall impact of these parameters is not prohibitive in any way. The memory requirement was about 100 MB for the Linux analysis and 20 MB for the other systems.

Finding pattern violations is efficient.

2.9 ENCODING ORDER

Our analysis of the call relation is control-flow insensitive: all calls from a function are considered, ignoring their order and whether they are actually possible. This is a good fit for our framework because it is based on sets. However, we wish to demonstrate briefly that a flow-sensitive analysis can be encoded as well by discussing the approach of Wasylkowski [9]. Using our framework, he discovered the previously unknown bug #165631 in the AspectJ compiler.

Wasylkowski observed statically for objects of a Java class C sequences of incoming method calls. The order of these calls is encoded as $C.a \prec C.b$, denoting "call $C.a$ *may* precede call $C.b$." Each observation is local to a method that uses an instance of C as a parameter or local variable. The result is a relation R over methods (that use class C) and pairs $(C.a \prec C.b)$ of methods from class C. An analysis of this relation reveals methods that use class C in an unusual way: for instance, the bug found in AspectJ was detected because the buggy method never called `C.hasNext()` after calling `C.next()`, which was a common observation in other methods. Overall, he analyzed within minutes over 35 000 methods that used almost 3000 classes.

The example shows that sequences and graphs, which do not lend themselves to characterization by feature sets, may be analyzed for patterns using an appropriate encoding. This particular encoding, however, may grow exponentially, and is thus best suited for small graphs or sequences. An alternative is an encoding $\prec_n$ that considers only nodes or events whose distance is bound by n.

Sequences may be encoded as relations to facilitate their analysis.

2.10 INLINING

When a function f calls `lock` but not `unlock`, this is not necessarily an error: f may call g, which in turn calls `unlock`. Hence, f calls `unlock` *indirectly*, as shown in Figure 2.13. Both f and g violate the pattern {`open`, `close`} but we can avoid this false positive by applying *inlining*. Inlining works for any relation $R \subseteq \mathcal{O} \times \mathcal{F}$ where $\mathcal{O} = \mathcal{F}$ holds, as in a call relation. Li and Zhou [2] explain inlining in terms of data flow analysis; we provide here an alternative explanation that works solely on the input relation.

Inlining derives from an existing relation $R^0 \subseteq X \times X$ a new relation $R^1 \supseteq R^0$ according to the following rules:

$$(f, g) \in R^0 \Rightarrow (f, g) \in R^1,$$
$$(f, g) \in R^0 \wedge (g, h) \in R^0 \Rightarrow (f, h) \in R^1.$$

In the derived relation R^1 a function f is related to the function it calls directly (g), as well as to those that it calls indirectly (h) through *one* intermediate function. Inlining may be repeated to capture indirect calls through two intermediate functions, and so on, to account for even more indirect calls.

So far we have fixed f by attributing `close` to it, but have not fixed g yet by attributing `open` to it. This can be easily expressed using the prime operator:

$$(f, g) \in R^0 \Rightarrow (g, x) \in R^1 \quad \text{for } x \in \{g\}''.$$

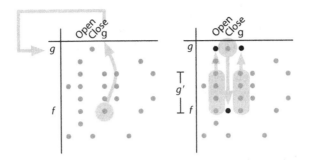

FIGURE 2.13

Inlining: function f calls `open` directly, but calls `close` indirectly through g. Inlining attributes the indirect calls of `close` to f. Likewise, all functions that are called by *all* callers of g are attributed to g as well.

Object set g' is the set of all functions calling g, and g'' is the set of all functions called by all callers of g. These are attributed to g in R^1.

Inlining can be expressed solely on the input relation.

2.11 RELATED WORK

There are many ways to find software defects. The best way is by checking a program against an *independent* specification or test. A failing test then can be used to locate the defect automatically [10]. We focus on a scenario without such external references. Instead, we aim to identify intrinsic *patterns* in a software system's implementation or behavior and *deviations* from these patterns. Such deviations are then suggested as potential defects.

2.11.1 MINING PATTERNS

Mining patterns from programs for program understanding, specification, or documentation has inspired many researchers, especially in the domain of temporal behavior. The following approaches *do not* develop a notion of deviation and therefore are interesting only insofar as they could provide relations that could be mined for deviations.

Finite automata

Cook and Wolf [11] wrote the seminal work on learning *finite-state machines* from event sequences. ADABU by Dallmeier et al. [12] dynamically mines automata from Java classes that characterize the state of objects as seen through observer methods provided by their interface. A similar approach is that of Xie and Notkin [13], where the object state is observed through the return values of methods. This leads to more detailed but also less general automata. In contrast to these dynamic approaches, Henzinger et al. [14] learn *permissive interfaces* by repeatedly generating candidate automata that capture legal method sequences and checking them against an abstract program interpretation. While elegant, it works only for a subset of Java.

Dynamic invariants

Dynamic invariants, as conceived by Ernst et al. [15] and mined with DAIKON, represent logical relations between data that held during test executions. Observed relations such as $a < b$ are suggested as program invariants. DAIKON works by checking a list of fixed relations between pairs of variables and a field and thus cannot infer new invariants. However, by checking a long list of relations between many pairs, a considerable variety of patterns can be mined. A simpler variation of DAIKON was proposed by Hangal and Lam [16].

2.11.2 MINING VIOLATIONS

The most formal and most well established systems for the notion of consistency in software are type systems, and type inference in particular [17]. Undoubtedly, they prevent the introduction of bugs on a routine basis. However, advances in type theory benefit only future programming languages, and type systems of existing languages are often too weak to express consistency. Hence, there is strong interest in mining patterns and violations in *existing software* with the goal to identify defects.

Sets of sequences

Hofmeyr et al. [18] observed sequences of system calls for intrusion detection. Normal behavior is characterized by a set of short overlapping sequences. Abnormal behavior is detected when unknown sequences occur. This approach was refined by Dallmeier et al. [19] for defect localization in Java programs: the AMPLE tool compares sequences of method calls issued by objects across passing and failing test cases. The class that shows the largest deviation in behavior between passing and failing test cases is suggested as a culprit. Hence, this violation does not imply a detailed fix, unlike the method proposed here.

Cluster analysis

Dickinson et al. [20] employed cluster analysis to separate normal program traces from traces triggering bugs. While this can capture a very wide range of behavioral patterns, cluster analysis has very little explanatory power, unlike the patterns and violations we propose here.

Mining correlations

Liblit et al. [21] mined violations in an abstract sense. They observed a statistical correlation of program failure with return values of functions (which are then used in control-flow statements) and predicates. This correlation has high explanatory power, but depends on a high number of varying program executions to develop a statistical notion of normal behavior.

Pairs of functions

Weimer and Necula [22] learn pairs of function calls (such as open/close) from program traces. They looked specifically for violations of these patterns in error-handling code that misses the call to the second function. They detected a considerable number of defects. Their paper is also remarkable for its comparison with other defect localization approaches. Conceptually, this approach learns purely structural patterns and does not depend on prior knowledge—like us. Unlike us, patterns are ordered pairs, whereas we consider unordered sets of any size.

Checking known patterns

Engler et al. [1] coined the slogan of bugs as deviant behavior and introduced a tool that searches for bug patterns. Each instance of such a pattern expresses an inconsistent view of the state of a program and hence a likely bug. The difference from our formalism is that the formalism of Engler et al. can detect only known patterns of inconsistency and cannot find new ones. On the other hand, searching for known patterns results in high precision.

Mining version history

Livshits and Zimmermann [23] mined patterns from the development history which they represented as a sequence of transactions that add new function calls. For each transaction, they mined (using frequent itemset mining) usage patterns of method calls being added together. These patterns are presented to the user for confirmation as being correct; on the basis of them, dynamic tests search for violations of these patterns. The static mining step for patterns is similar to our approach (and could have used it), whereas violation detection is done dynamically using program instrumentation and test cases. The detection of test cases is limited to pairs of functions, whereas we can detect violations of any pattern.

2.11.3 PR-MINER

PR-Miner by Li and Zhou [2] inspired us to propose concept analysis as a better foundation for their analysis that identifies purely structural sets of features and their violations. PR-Miner is based on frequent itemset mining, and mines *closed* feature sets. A violation (called a "rule") is represented as an implication $A \Rightarrow B$, where A and B are closed feature sets.

A closed itemset corresponds to a pattern in our formalism and also to a block, which has the additional benefit that it includes the instances of the pattern. A rule corresponds to neighboring blocks in our formalism, again with the benefit of also representing all instances, and thus making theory and implementation more uniform. The notion of confidence in both formalisms is equivalent.

The short characterization of PR-Miner above might suggest that blocks and formal concepts provide no added benefit. However, we argue that a precise understanding of what PR-Miner does is greatly enhanced by the theory of formal concept analysis. This seems evident both from our simpler and shorter explanation of mining, algorithms and from the discussion of the block hierarchy and its size. Combining patterns and instances into blocks gives access to a rich algebra and intuitive geometric interpretation which simply does not exist for closed itemsets in isolation.

Li and Zhou reported impressive performance numbers using an off-the-shelf implementation for frequent itemset mining. They clearly benefited from years of development of these tools in the data-mining community. However, we believe that the performance of COLIBRI/ML provides a viable alternative for practical problems.

PR-Miner implements some data flow analysis to minimize false positives. It is based on the insight that a pattern $\{a, b\}$ might be implemented not just by calling a and b directly, but also by calling a and c, which in turn calls b. This analysis is independent of the mining, and can be implemented for either system. Indeed, what is expressed as a data flow analysis by Li and Zhou [2] can also be expressed as an operation on the input relation R as in Section 2.10.

PR-Miner analyzes variable declarations in addition to function calls. Again, this is not inherent to the mining, and can be implemented for any system by making these part of the input relation.

2.12 CONCLUSIONS

Formal concept analysis provides a practical and theoretical framework to identify structural patterns and violations in binary relations. The analysis assumes no a priori knowledge such as names or predefined patterns—unlike many previous approaches. Pattern violations have been shown to correlate with bugs in software systems. The main benefit over classical frequent itemset mining [24] is that blocks (or concepts) unify a pattern and its instances. Together they form a rich and well-studied algebra; furthermore, they offer a geometric interpretation which provides intuition: violations correspond to imperfect blocks in a cross table.

A relation (such as a call relation) induces a block hierarchy. Each block corresponds to a pattern, and neighboring blocks correspond either to independent patterns or a violation—depending on the associated confidence. This is the main conceptual result of this chapter.

Formal concept analysis gives us complexity results for pattern mining: the number of blocks (or patterns) induced by a relation may grow exponentially. This happens only for dense relations; call relations, at least, tend to be sparse. In addition, only a small fraction of blocks exceeding a minimum support are of interest and can be computed efficiently using an implementation that we provide [5].

Algorithms for formal concept analysis are practical although they lack the performance tuning that went into algorithms and implementations for frequent itemset mining [25]. We provide an open-source implementation, COLIBRI/ML, that was able to analyze the call relation of the Linux kernel within 1 min, and smaller systems such as the Python interpreter in under 20 s.

Earlier work on detecting anomalies often had a special focus on pairs of function calls [22, 26], rather than the more general patterns we studied. However, we found that most call patterns in open-source projects implemented in C have width between 2 and 3 (see Table 2.4). This is a posteriori a justification for the special interest in such pairs.

The starting point of our analysis is a binary relation. This implies that we analyze *sets* of features related to objects. This seeming limitation may be overcome using clever encodings, as demonstrated by Wasylkowski [9]. We are also encouraged by the success of code query languages such as CodeQuest [27], which represent software at their core using relations. By extending them with our analysis, we would be able to mine many more source code relations for patterns and violations.

Future work

Patterns and violations as we mine them do not capture intrinsically the notion of program execution. We wish to take advantage of this to provide better support of nonexecutable code. By this we mean configuration files for services such as e-mail, HTTP, or firewalls. They control security-critical applications, but almost no support for them exists beyond syntax checkers and syntax highlighting. Patterns can capture best practices that can be learned from existing configuration files. For example, a pattern may represent a combination of flags in a firewall rule. A system administrator could be warned before deploying an unusual flag combination in a firewall rule. We believe that this kind of support could be provided by editors on a routine basis as is done today for syntax highlighting.

All in all, we have shown that formal concept analysis provides an appealing theoretical and practical framework to identify structural patterns and their violations.

ACKNOWLEDGMENTS

Discussions with Silvia Breu, David Schuler, and Valentin Dallmeier helped to improve this chapter.

REFERENCES

[1] Engler D, Chen DY, Chou A. Bugs as inconsistent behavior: a general approach to inferring errors in systems code. In: Proceedings of the 18th ACM symposium on operating systems principles (SOSP-01). New York: ACM Press; 2001 p 57–72.

[2] Li Z, Zhou Y. PR-Miner: automatically extracting implicit programming rules and detecting violations in large software code. In: Proceedings of the 10th European software engineering conf. ESEC/SIGSOFT FSE. New York: ACM; 2005. p. 306–15.

[3] Ganter B, Wille R. Formal concept analysis: mathematical foundations. Berlin/Heidelberg/New York: Springer; 1999.

[4] Lindig C. Fast concept analysis. In: Stumme G, editor. Working with conceptual structures—contributions to ICCS 2000. Aachen, Germany: Shaker Verlag; 2000. p. 152–61.

[5] Lindig C. Colibri/ML. https://github.com/lindig/colibri-ml; 2007. Open-source tool for concept analysis, implements algorithm from [4]. This was previously published on Google Code.

[6] Stumme G, Taouil R, Bastide Y, Pasquier N, Lakhal L. Computing iceberg concept lattices with Titanic. Data and Knowledge Engineering 2002;42(2):189–222.

[7] Brijs T. Retail data from the Frequent Itemset Mining Dataset Repository. http://fimi.ua.ac.be/data/retail.dat; 2014. The dataset was donated by Tom Brijs and contains the (anonymized) retail market basket data from an anonymous Belgian retail store.

[8] Götzmann D. Formal concept analysis in Java. Bachelor thesis, Saarland University, Computer Science Department; 2007. https://code.google.com/p/colibri-java/.

[9] Wasylkowski A. Mining object usage models (doctoral symposium). In: Proceedings of the 29th international conference on software engineering (ICSE 2007), Minneapolis, MN, USA; 2007. For the tool, see https://www.st.cs.uni-saarland.de/models/jadet/.

[10] Cleve H, Zeller A. Locating causes of program failures. In: Proceedings of the 27th international conference on software engineering (ICSE 2005), St. Louis, USA; 2005.

[11] Cook J, Wolf A. Discovering models of software processes from event-based data. ACM Transactions on Software Engineering and Methodology 1998;7(3):215–49.

[12] Dallmeier V, Lindig C, Wasylkowski A, Zeller A. Mining object behavior with Adabu. In: Proceedings of the 2006 international workshop on dynamic system analysis (WODA). New York: ACM Press; 2006. p. 17–24.

[13] Xie T, Notkin D. Automatic extraction of object-oriented observer abstractions from unit-test executions. In: Proceedings of the 6th international conference on formal engineering methods (ICFEM 2004); 2004. p. 290–305.

[14] Henzinger TA, Jhala R, Majumdar R. Permissive interfaces. In: Proceedings of the 10th European software engineering conference, ESEC/SIGSOFT FSE. New York: ACM; 2005. p. 31–40.

[15] Ernst MD, Cockrell J, Griswold WG, Notkin D. Dynamically discovering likely program invariants to support program evolution. IEEE Transactions on Software Engineering 2001;27(2):1–25.

[16] Hangal S, Lam MS. Tracking down software bugs using automatic anomaly detection. In: Proceedings of the 24th international conference on software engineering (ICSE-02). New York: ACM Press; 2002. p. 291–301.

[17] Pierce BC. Types and programming languages. Cambridge, MA: The MIT Press; 2002.

[18] Hofmeyr SA, Forrest S, Somayaji S. Intrusion detection using sequences of system calls. Journal of Computer Security 1998;6(3):151–80.

[19] Dallmeier V, Lindig C, Zeller A. Lightweight defect localization for Java. In: Black A, editor. European conference on object-oriented programming (ECOOP); 2005. p. 528–50.

[20] Dickinson W, Leon D, Podgurski A. Finding failures by cluster analysis of execution profiles In: Proceedings of the 23rd international conference on software engineering, ICSE 2001. Washington, DC, USA: IEEE Computer Society; 2001. p. 339–48.

[21] Liblit B, Naik M, Zheng AX, Aiken A, Jordan MI. Scalable statistical bug isolation. In: Proceedings of the ACM SIGPLAN conference on programming language design and implementation (PLDI); 2005. p. 15–26.

[22] Weimer W, Necula GC. Mining temporal specifications for error detection. In: Tools and algorithms for the construction and analysis of systems (TACAS). Lecture notes in computer science, vol. 3440. Berlin: Springer; 2005. p. 461–76.

[23] Livshits VB, Zimmermann T. Dynamine: finding common error patterns by mining software revision histories. In: Proceedings of the 10th European software engineering conference, ESEC/SIGSOFT FSE. New York: ACM; 2005. p. 296–305.

[24] Agrawal R, Srikant R. Fast algorithms for mining association rules in large databases. In: 20th international conference on very large data bases (VLDB). San Francisco, CA, USA: Morgan Kaufmann Publishers; 1994. p. 487–99.

[25] Hipp J, Güntzer U, Nakhaeizadeh G. Algorithms for association rule mining—a general survey and comparison. SIGKDD Explorations 2000;2(1):58–64.

[26] Yang J, Evans D. Automatically inferring temporal properties for program evolution. In: International symposium on software reliability engineering. Washington, DC, USA: IEEE Computer Society; 2004. p. 340–51.

[27] Hajiyev E, Verbaere M, de Moor O. CodeQuest: scalable source code queries with datalog. In: European conference on object-oriented programming (ECOOP). Lecture notes in computer science, vol. 4067. New York: Springer; 2006. p. 2–27.

ANALYZING TEXT IN SOFTWARE PROJECTS

3

Stefan Wagner*, Daniel Méndez Fernández[†]

Software Engineering Group, Institute of Software Technology, University of Stuttgart, Stuttgart, Germany*
Software & Systems Engineering, Institut für Informatik, Technische Universität München, Garching, Germany[†]

CHAPTER OUTLINE

3.1 INTRODUCTION

Most of the data we produce in software projects is of a textual nature. This ranges from requirement specifications to designs and documentation and customer surveys. Textual data, however, is notoriously difficult to analyze. We have a multitude of techniques and tools which are well known to software developers to process and analyze quantitative data. We handle numerous bugs or lines of code very often. Yet, what should we do with all the textual data? So far, the potential of analyzing this data has not been realized.

Software analytics for practitioners already involves (and will increasingly involve) how to make use of all this textual data. Fortunately, we have seen an interesting development in the research area of analyzing texts. This is often promoted under the umbrella *text mining* or *text analytics*. Both mean roughly the same thing: systematically retrieve and analyze textual data to gain additional insights, in our case additional insights into the software development project.

In this chapter, we first discuss and categorize what kind of textual data we usually encounter in software projects and where we encounter it. On the basis of this categorization, we will discuss the sources of this textual data and how to retrieve them. Next, we will introduce manual coding and analysis as a very flexible but elaborate means to structure and understand different texts. As a means to handle large amounts of text and reduce the manual effort, we will discuss a sample of the currently available automatic analyses of texts such as *n*-grams or clone detection.

Finally, we will employ a running example of textual data which we will analyze with each analysis approach presented. We use the publicly available specifications of the Hypertext Transfer Protocol (HTTP) and the Internet Message Access Protocol (IMAP) as typical representatives for textual requirements specifications. In the case of automatic analyses, we will provide references to the tools used so that the examples can be easily reproduced.

3.2 TEXTUAL SOFTWARE PROJECT DATA AND RETRIEVAL

Textual data appears at many points in a software development project. The main result of a software project—the code—is also textual although we are more concerned with natural language text in this chapter. Yet, source code usually contains also a considerable share of natural language text: the code comments. Apart from that, we have requirements specifications, architecture documentation, or change requests with textual data. There is no generally agreed on classification of the artifacts generated in a software development project, and hence there is also no agreement about textual data contained in these artifacts. As a foundation for the remainder of this chapter, we will therefore first discuss different sources of textual data and then classify them to describe how to retrieve the data for further analysis.

3.2.1 TEXTUAL DATA

Sources of textual data

Although we often consider software developers to be people dealing mostly with formal languages—that is, programming languages—there are many sources of textual data in a software project. Most of this data comes from the developers themselves. A substantial part of any high-quality source code consists of informal or semiformal text code comments. These already contain shorter inline comments as well as longer descriptions of interfaces or classes (as, e.g., with JavaDoc for Java). Apart from that, depending on the development process followed, many other documents are written by the developers or other people in related roles, such as testers, software architects, and requirements engineers. These include requirements specifications, design and architecture documents, test cases, test results, and review results. Yet, we need to think also beyond the "classical" artifacts in software development. Team members nowadays communicate via e-mails and chats, change requests, and commit messages, which all are available electronically as text sources. Finally, in a software project, especially in the context of product development, customer surveys and product reviews are a common means to better understand the requirements for and satisfaction with a software product. These artifacts can also contain open questions which result in textual data to be analyzed.

A classification of textual software project data

We found the general structure of the German standard software process model *V-Modell XT*[1] to be useful to classify artifacts related to software engineering as it is rather general and applies to many application domains. It contains several detailed artifacts that we do not consider in our classification of textual software project data, but we follow the general structure. The classification is shown in Figure 3.1.

The *V-Modell XT* structures the textual artifacts mainly along different process areas or disciplines in the development process. This starts with documents for *contracting* such as requests for proposals or offers. One could, for example, be interested in analyzing public requests for proposals to investigate technological trends. Next, there are several textual documents in project *planning and control*. An example that could be interesting for text analytics is risk lists from projects where we could extract typical risk topics to define mitigation points. We classified the above-mentioned e-mails under *reporting*, which could give relevant insights into the communication between developers or between developers and customers. A now commonly analyzed area in software engineering research is *configuration and change management*. Problem reports, change requests, and commit messages all contain valuable textual information about a project's progress. By *evaluation*, we mean artifacts related to evaluating other artifacts in the project—for example, test case specifications. We could analyze, for instance, the terminology used in the test cases and compare it with the terminology used in the code. The next three categories correspond to the constructive phases of the project: *requirements and analysis*, *software design*, and *software elements*. All contain valuable information about the product. In the latter, we see also the code and with it the code comments, in which we can check the language used by text analytics. Finally, the *logistic elements* contain any further documentation which could also be analyzed for the topics discussed and for relationships between documents.

Running example

As a running example for the remainder of this chapter, we chose the specifications of Internet protocols. They are openly available examples of software requirements specifications. The Internet Engineering Task Force publishes all open protocols as so-called *Requests for Comments* (RFCs) and, hence, these documents are called RFC XXXX, where "XXXX" is the number of the specification. We selected standards concerning two well-known Internet protocols: HTTP and IMAP. We hope that by choosing these, we avoid lengthy introductions and potential misunderstandings about the domain. HTTP is the application-level Internet protocol for most network applications today. IMAP allows access to mailboxes on mail servers. For methods that require a larger text corpus, we add additional RFCs to the corpus that are related to HTTP or IMAP.

The following is a part of RFC 2616 of the specification of HTTP 1.1. It describes valid comments in the HTTP header. It shows that our examples contain text that is similar to text in other requirements specifications:

---

[1] http://www.v-model-xt.de/.

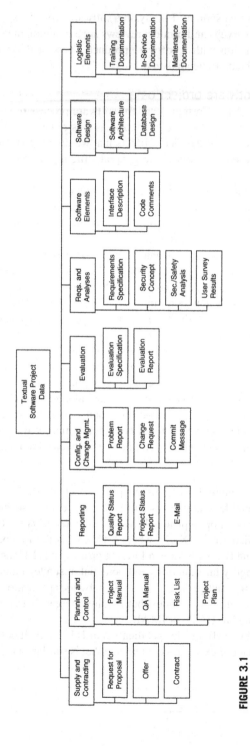

FIGURE 3.1

A classification of textual software project data (based on http://www.v-model-xt.de/).

Comments can be included in some HTTP header fields by surrounding the comment text with parentheses. Comments are only allowed in fields containing "comment" as part of their field value definition. In all other fields, parentheses are considered part of the field value.

Yet, also other kinds of text need to be analyzed. In our industrial studies in Section 3.5, we see that free-text answers in surveys are usually not well-formed, complete sentences. Also code comments are often not complete sentences. Although we will not discuss this in detail in the following, most techniques are able to cope with this.

3.2.2 TEXT RETRIEVAL

With the various sources and classes of different texts in software engineering projects, the first step is to collect or retrieve these texts from their sources. A complete text corpus, consisting of different texts, will often come from different sources, and we want to keep connections between the texts as stored in the sources. For example, we often have pointers from the commit messages in the version control system to specific change requests in the change management system. These links are useful for further

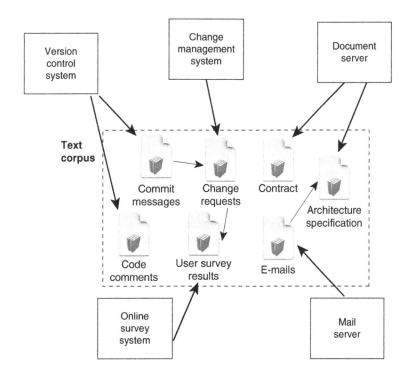

FIGURE 3.2

Text collection from different sources.

analysis and should be retrieved. Figure 3.2 gives an overview of such retained links between texts in the text corpus. In the following, we will go through the categories of textual project data from Section 3.2 and discuss the sources and possible links between texts.

The texts in the supply and contracting category are often not stored with most of the other project documentation. They are usually held either in the form of a formatted document on a file server or as part of a larger enterprise resource planning (ERP) system. Hence, we need either to access the file server and extract the plain text from the formatted document or to access the ERP system, which usually has some kind of application programming interface (API) to retrieve data. We should aim to keep links to the actual project in terms of project IDs or something similar.

Similarly, planning and control texts are also often kept as formatted documents on file servers or in ERP systems. Then, they need to be treated in the same way as supply and contracting texts. They have a better chance, however, of being also kept in a version control system. For example, the above-mentioned risk lists can be maintained also as plain text and, therefore, can be easily handled in Subversion[2] or Git.[3] Then, we can use the APIs of the corresponding version control system for retrieval. This also allows us to retrieve different versions and, hence, the history of documents, which can be necessary for temporal analyses.

Reporting can be done in formatted documents, ERP systems, and version control systems. Quality status reports can also be automatically generated by quality control systems integrated with the continuous integration system. For example, SonarQube[4] or ConQAT[5] can be used to automatically generate quality reports on the basis of data from various sources. These reports can be used directly if they can be retrieved. Usually they provide the possibility to put the report as a file on a server, into a version control system, or into a database. They often provide links to the artifacts analyzed, which should be retained if possible. E-mail can be most easily retrieved if a central mail server is used for the project. While most textual data we retrieve is sensitive, with e-mail we need to take the utmost care not to violate privacy rules established in the organizational context. It is advisable to anonymize the data at this stage and only keep, for example, links to specifications or code explicitly referenced in the e-mails.

Texts from configuration and change management are programatically easy to obtain as they are stored in databases in most companies. We have the above-mentioned version control systems, ticketing systems (e.g., *OSTicket*[6]), and change or issue management systems such as *Bugzilla*[7] and *Atlassian Jira*.[8] They all provide APIs to retrieve the text contained. Depending on the system and possible naming conventions, we can retrieve, besides the texts, links between commit messages and change requests or links between problem reports and change requests.

The further categories are supposed to be held mostly in version control systems. Evaluation (i.e., test or review) reports that sometimes are stored separately on file servers can be exceptions. Also user survey results can be retrieved most easily by going directly to the online survey servers used. They

---

[2] http://subversion.apache.org/.
[3] http://www.git-scm.com/.
[4] http://www.sonarqube.org.
[5] http://www.conqat.org/.
[6] http://www.osticket.com/.
[7] http://www.bugzilla.org/.
[8] https://www.atlassian.com/software/jira.

often provide some kind of API or export functionalities. Otherwise, we need to write a Web crawler or retrieve the results manually. To be able to retrieve code comments, we also need to write an extraction tool that is able to distinguish between code and comments. It can also be useful to distinguish different types of comments as far as this is possible in the retrieval directly. This could also be a further step in the analysis.

3.3 MANUAL CODING

Once we have collected textual data for analysis and interpretation, it needs to be structured and classified. This classification is often referred to as *coding*, where we identify patterns in texts, having an explanatory or a exploratory purpose [1] and serving as a basis for further analysis, interpretation, and validation. Coding can be done in two ways: manually or automated. In this section, we introduce coding as a manual process. A detailed example for applying the manual coding process is provided in Section 3.5.1.

Although manual coding is often associated with interview research, the data we code is not limited to transcripts as we can structure any kind of textual data given in documents, Wikis, or source code (see also Section 3.2.2). This kind of structuring is used in social science research and is also gaining attention in software engineering research. An approach commonly used in these research areas is grounded theory. We briefly describe grounded theory in Sidebar 1, but its theoretical background is not necessary for many practical text analysis contexts.

SIDEBAR 1: GROUNDED THEORY IN A NUTSHELL

Manual coding, as discussed in this chapter, has its origins in grounded theory. Because grounded theory is the most cited approach for qualitative data analysis [1], which comes at the same time with a plethora of different interpretations, we briefly clarify its meaning in a nutshell. Grounded theory describes a qualitative research approach to inductively build a "theory"—that is, it aims to generate testable knowledge from data rather than to test existing knowledge [1]. To this end, we thus make use of various empirical methods to generate data, and we structure and classify the information to infer a theory. A theory, in its essence, "provides explanations and understanding in terms of basic concepts and underlying mechanisms" [2, 3]. In empirical software engineering, we mostly rely on the notion of a *social theory* [4], and refer to a set of falsifiable and testable statements/hypotheses. As most qualitative research methods, grounded theory has its origins in the social sciences, and it was first introduced in 1967 by Glaser and Strauss [5]. A detailed introduction to the background of grounded theory and the delineation with similar concepts arising along the evolution of grounded theory is given by Birks and Miller [1]. For the remainder of the chapter where we introduce a manual coding process, we rely on the terms and concepts as introduced in the context of grounded theory.

3.3.1 CODING PROCESS

Manual coding is a creative process that depends on the experiences, views, and interpretations of those who analyze the data to build a hierarchy of codes. During this coding process, we conceptualize textual data via pattern building. We abstract from textual data—for example, interview transcripts or commit comments stated in natural language—and we build a model that abstracts from the assertions in the form of concepts and relations. During this coding process, we interpret the data manually. Hence, this is a creative process which assigns a meaning to statements and events. One could also say that we try to create a big picture out of single dots.

There are various articles and textbooks proposing coding processes and the particularities of related data retrieval methods such as why and how to build trust between interviewers and interviewees (see, e.g., Birks and Mills [1]). The least common denominator of the approaches lies in the three basic steps of the coding process itself followed by a validation step:

1. *Open coding* aims at analyzing the data by adding codes (representing key characteristics) to small coherent units in the textual data, and categorizing the concepts developed in a hierarchy of categories as an abstraction of a set of codes—all repeatedly performed until a "state of saturation" is reached.
2. *Axial coding* aims at defining relationships between the concepts—for example, "causal conditions" or "consequences."
3. *Selective coding* aims at inferring a central core category.
4. *Validation* aims at confirming the model developed with the authors of the original textual data.

Open coding brings the initial structure into unstructured text by abstracting from potentially large amounts of textual data and assigning codes to single text units. The result of open coding can range from sets of codes to hierarchies of codes. An example is to code the answers given by quality engineers in interviews at one company to build a taxonomy of defects they encounter in requirements specifications. During open coding, we then classify single text units as codes. This can result, for example, in a taxonomy of defect types, such as natural language defects which can be further refined, for example, to sentences in passive voice. During axial coding, we can then assign dependencies between the codes in the taxonomies. For example, the quality engineers could have experienced that sentences in the passive voice have frequently led to misunderstandings and later on to change requests. The axial coding process then would lead to a cause-effect chain that shows potential implications of initially defined defects. The final selective coding then brings the results of open and axial coding together to build one holistic model of requirements defects and their potential impacts.

We subsequently form a process that we applied in our studies and which worked well for us. Figure 3.3 depicts the basic coding process and further steps usually (or ideally) performed in conjunction with the coding process.

The idea of (manual) coding—as it is postulated in grounded theory—is to build a model based on textual data—that is, "grounded" on textual data. As the primary goal is to gather information from text, we need to follow a flexible process during the actual text retrieval and the coding process as well. For example, in the case of conducting interviews, we perform an initial coding of the first transcripts. If we find interesting phenomena for which we would like to have a better understanding of the causes, we might want to change the questions for subsequent interviews; an example is that an interviewee states that a low quality of requirements specifications is also connected with low motivation in a team, leading to new questions on what the root causes for low motivation are. We thereby follow a concurrent data generation and collection along with an emerging model which is also steered according to research or business objectives.

Figure 3.4 shows the coding steps for our running example. During the open coding step (lower part of the figure), we continuously decompose data until we find small units to which we can assign codes ("concept assignment"). This open coding step alone shows that the overall process cannot be performed sequentially. During the open coding step, we found it useful

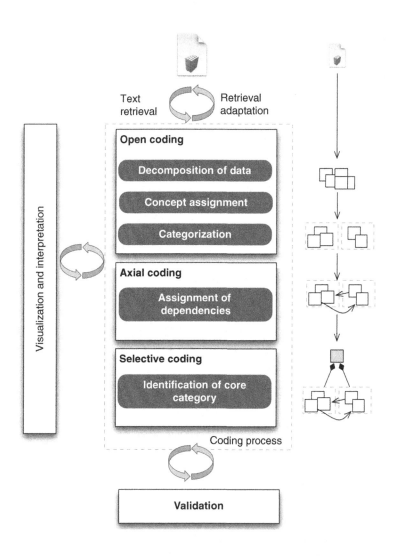

FIGURE 3.3

Coding process.

- to initially browse the textual data (or samples) before coding them to get an initial idea of the content, meaning, and finally, of potential codes we could apply,
- to continuously compare the codes during coding with each other and especially with potentially incoming new textual data, and
- to note down the rationale for each code to keep the coding process reproducible (of special importance if one is relying on independent recoding by another analyst).

Having a set of codes, we allocate them to a category as a means of abstraction. In our running example, we allocate the single codes to the categories "entities" and "dependencies." During axial

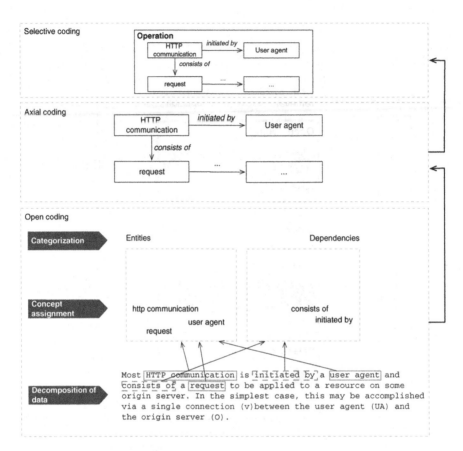

FIGURE 3.4

Manual coding of our running example.

coding, we then assign directed associations between the codes. Finally, the last step in the coding process is supposed to be the identification of the core category, which often can also be predefined by the overall objective; in our case, it is "Operation."

The overall coding process is performed until we reach a theoretical saturation—that is, the point where no new codes (or categories) are identified and the results are convincing to all participating analysts [1].

3.3.2 CHALLENGES

The coding process introduced is subject to various challenges, of which we identify the following three to be the most frequent ones.

1. *Coding as a creative process.* Coding is always a creative process. When analyzing textual data, we decompose it into small coherent units for which we assign codes. In this step, we find appropriate codes that reflect the intended meaning of the data while finding the appropriate level of detail we follow for the codes. This alone shows the subjectivity inherent to coding that demands a validation of the results. Yet, we apply coding with an exploratory or explanatory purpose rather than with a confirmatory one. This means that the validation of the resulting model is usually left to subsequent investigations. This, however, does not justify a creationist view of the model we define. A means to increase the robustness of the model is to apply analyst triangulation, where coding is performed by a group of individuals or where the coding results (or a sample) of one coder are independently reproduced by other coders as a means of internal validation. This increases the probability that the codes reflect the actual meaning of textual units. We still need, if possible, to validate the resulting model with the authors of the textual data or the interviewees represented by the transcripts.

2. *Coding alone or coding in teams.* This challenge considers the validity of the codes themselves. As stated, coding (and the interpretation of codes) is a subjective process that depends on the experiences, expectations, and beliefs of the coder who interprets the textual data. To a certain extent, the results of the coding process can be validated (see also the next point). Given that this is not always the case, however, we recommend applying, again, analyst triangulation as a means to minimize the degree of subjectivism.

3. *Validating the results.* We can distinguish between an internal validation, where we form, for example, teams of coders to minimize the threat to the internal validity (the above-mentioned analyst triangulation), and external validation. The latter aims at validating the resulting theory with further interview participants or people otherwise responsible for the textual data we interpret. This, however, is often not possible; for example, in the case of coding survey results from an anonymous survey. In such cases, the only mitigation we can opt for is to give much attention to the internal validation where we try to increase the reliability of the theory during its construction—for example, by applying analyst triangulation.

3.4 AUTOMATED ANALYSIS

As any manual coding and analysis of textual data is difficult, largely subjective, and very elaborate, automation can have a huge positive effect. Especially in recent years, automated natural language processing has made progress we can exploit for analyzing software data. We cannot replace reading a complete introductory book on natural language processing with this chapter. Yet, we will concentrate on a selected set of promising techniques and corresponding tools that can give us insight into software engineering data complementing manual coding.

3.4.1 TOPIC MODELING

We often want to quickly get an overview of what different texts are about—for example, to decide what to read in-depth or to simply classify the texts. Topic modeling is an automatic approach that attempts to extract the most important topics per text document. The basic assumption of topic modeling [6] is that documents are created using a set of topics the authors want to describe and discuss in the

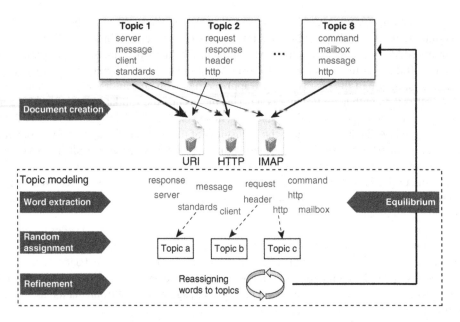

FIGURE 3.5

Overview of document creation based on topics and topic modeling.

documents. The topics might, however, not be explicitly specified in the documents, and might remain only implicitly in the heads of the authors. Nevertheless, for each topic, the authors still use certain words in the documents. Therefore, for this analysis, we say that a topic is formed by a set of related words. Hence, there are probabilities with which certain words appear in the context of several topics. Topic modeling makes use of this by aiming to extract these probabilities and thereby recreating the topics. Figure 3.5 shows the whole process from document creation based on topics and the subsequent topic modeling to rediscover the topics. Hence, the user of topic modeling does not have to specify any topics to look for in the documents, but they are extracted from the text.

Mathematically, we need an algorithm which is able to group the words extracted from documents into probable topics. The most common one used is *latent Dirichlet allocation* [7], but there are others to choose from. The concrete algorithm is mostly uninteresting for the user of the topic modeling method, because all algorithms are not exact. An exact algorithm is impossible to define as the goal (the topics) are not clearly defined. The algorithms typically start by assigning topics to words randomly and then use Bayesian probability to incrementally refine the assignment. Finally, when an equilibrium is reached and the assignments cannot be improved, we have the most probable topics for the corpus of documents.

The uses of topic modeling of software engineering data are vast. For example, if we have a large body of existing specifications to which our software has to conform, we can generate a network of documents based on the topics they share. Fortunately, there is open and usable tool support for building topic maps. *Mallet*[9] is written in Java, and allows users either to run it using the command line or to include it into their own analysis software using an API. Hence, topic modeling is a useful tool for getting an overview of a large corpus of documents.

By applying topic modeling to our running example of RFC specifications using Mallet, we can reconstruct several useful topics related to HTTP and IMAP. Figure 3.5 also illustrates some of the rediscovered topics. The top topic for the uniform resource identifier specification contains *server*, *message*, *client*, and *standards*. For the HTTP specification, we get the terms *request*, *response*, *header*, and *http*, and for the IMAP specification, we get *command*, *mailbox*, *message*, and *http*. Not every word in each topic is helpful. Some can even be confusing, such as *http* in IMAP, but most of the topics give a good idea of what the specification is about. Furthermore, each document can have more than one topic. Figure 3.5 shows this by the thickness of the arrows.

A simple alternative for small documents, which are not suitable for topic modeling, is word clouds (see also Section 3.4.5) or word counts. These cannot show semantic relationships between words, but infer the importance of words by their frequencies. Available Web tools, such as Voyant,[10] can also show the context in which chosen words appear in the text, and thereby, provide an initial semantic flavor.

Topic modeling can give only a rough idea of what the main topics consisting of important words are. The further analysis and interpretation needs manual effort. Yet, especially for larger text corpora, topic modeling can be an interesting preanalysis before manual coding. The topics found can form initial ideas for coding, and we can mark context in which they were found to be checked in detail by the coder.

3.4.2 PART-OF-SPEECH TAGGING AND RELATIONSHIP EXTRACTION

A way to further dig into the meaning of a large text corpus is to analyze its syntax in more detail. A common first step for this is to annotate each word with its grammatical task. This is also referred to as *part-of-speech* (POS) tagging. In its simplest form, this means extracting which word is a noun, verb, or adjective. Contemporary POS taggers [8] are able to annotate more—for example, the tense of a verb. The taggers use machine learning techniques to build models of languages to be able to do the annotations.

We see an example sentence from the HTTP 1.0 specification in Table 3.1. We POS-tagged this sentence using the *Stanford Log-linear Part-Of-Speech Tagger* [9]. The tags are attached to each word with an underscore as a separator. They use a common abbreviation system for the POS. For example, "DT" is a determiner and "NN" is a singular noun. The full list of abbreviations can be found in [10].

This allows us to extract the main nouns which probably form a part of the domain concepts of the specified system. In the example, if we combine consecutive nouns, we will find "Hypertext Transfer Protocol," "HTTP," "protocol," "lightness," "speed," and "hypermedia information systems." These nouns already capture a lot of the main concepts of the specification. We can further qualify them with adjectives. For example, the specification is not only about hypermedia information systems but is

---

[9]http://mallet.cs.umass.edu/.
[10]http://voyant-tools.org.

Table 3.1 A POS-Tagged Sentence from RFC 1945

Original sentence from RFC 1945

The Hypertext Transfer Protocol (HTTP) is an application-level protocol with the lightness and speed necessary for distributed, collaborative, hypermedia information systems.

POS-tagged sentence

The_DT Hypertext_NNP Transfer_NN Protocol_NNP -LRB-_-LRB- HTTP_NNP -RRB-_-RRB- is_VBZ an_DT application-level_JJ protocol_NN with_IN the_DT lightness_NN and_CC speed_NN necessary_JJ for_IN distributed_VBN ,_, collaborative_JJ ,_, hypermedia_NN information_NN systems_NNS ._.

---

also about "collaborative" hypermedia information systems. Yet, we also see a problem in this kind of analysis in this example. The word "distributed" is tagged as a verb ("VBN") instead of as an adjective, which would probably distort an automated analysis.

The possibilities of further analysis having the POS tags in a text are very broad. A concrete example of exploiting this in the context of software engineering is to extract domain information from a specification to generate design models or code skeletons. For example, Chen [11] investigated the structure of English prose specifications to create entity-relationship (ER) diagrams. Put very simply, he mapped nouns to entities and verbs to relationships. For example, the sentence

> Most HTTP communication is initiated by a user agent and consists of a request to be applied to a resource on some origin server.

from RFC 1945 can be transformed into the five entities *HTTP communication*, *user agent*, *request*, *resource*, and *origin server*. They are connected by the relationships *is initiated by*, *consists of*, *to be applied to*, and *on*. The resulting ER diagram is shown in Figure 3.6.

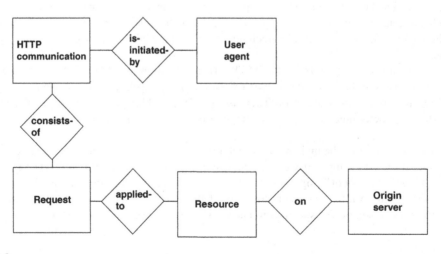

FIGURE 3.6

An ER diagram derived from a sentence from RFC 1945.

Similar approaches were proposed by Abbott [12] to create a first skeleton of Ada code based on a textual specification and by Kof [13], who has built an ontology from a textual specification to infer initial component diagrams and message sequence charts. All these approaches can help to bridge the gap from textual specifications to further, more formal artifacts. Yet, a multitude of other applications of POS tagging are also possible on other kinds of textual software engineering artifacts. For example, we can assess the quality of requirements specifications by detecting requirements smells such as the passive voice [14]. Furthermore, POS tagging can help as a preprocessing step in manual coding by highlighting nouns, adjectives, and verbs with different colors to quickly grasp the main concepts.

3.4.3 *n*-GRAMS

Computational linguists are looking for ways to predict what a next word in a sentence could be. One way to achieve this is by looking at the immediately preceding words. "On the basis of having looked at a lot of text, we know which words tend to follow other words" [15]. Hence, we need a way of grouping these preceding words. A popular way is to construct a model grouping words having the same preceding $n - 1$ words. This model is then called an *n*-gram model. An *n*-gram is a contiguous sequence of n words in a piece of text. The *n*-gram-based analysis of texts does not aim at abstracting the content of the texts but aims at categorizing or predicting attributes of them.

n-gram models have received a lot of interest in recent years. Part of the interest comes from the availability of *Google Ngram Viewer*[11] for the books digitized by Google. It can show the percentage of an *n*-gram in relation to all *n*-grams of all books per year. For example, for the bigram "software engineering," we can see a spike in the early 1990s and a mostly flat line since the 2000s. So, one application of *n*-grams is to compare how frequently words occur together in different texts or over time.

Another interesting application of *n*-grams is for categorizing texts into their languages. On the basis of already learned models for different languages, *n*-grams can indicate in which language a given text is. Imagine your company policy is to write all documents in English, including specifications and code comments. Then, an analyzer using the *n*-gram models could look for non-English text in code and other documents. Another example is to automatically classify specification chapters into technical content and domain content. A useful tool in that context is the *Java Text Categorizing Library*.[12] It comes with *n*-gram models for a set of languages, and is also capable of being trained for other categories. When we sent the RFC specification documents we use as running example into the Java Text Categorizing Library, it correctly classified them as being written in English.

There are further uses of *n*-gram models in software engineering. Hindle et al. [16] investigated the naturalness of source code. They built *n*-gram models for source code and then predicted how to complete code snippets similar to autocompletion in modern integrated development environments. Allamanis and Sutton [17] built on the work by Hindle et al. and created *n*-gram language models of the whole Java corpus available in GitHub. Using these models, they derived a new kind of complexity metric based on how difficult it is to predict the sequence of the given code. The intuition behind this complexity metric is that complex source code is also hard to predict. Hence, the worse the prediction

---

[11] http://books.google.com/ngrams.
[12] http://textcat.sourceforge.net.

matches the actual source code piece, the more complex it is. These applications are not ripe for widespread industrial use, but show the potential of the analysis technique.

3.4.4 CLONE DETECTION

Clone detection is a static analysis technique born in code analysis but usable on all kinds of texts. It is a powerful technique to get an impression of the syntactic redundancy of a piece of software, and it is highly automated at the same time.

What is a clone?

A clone is a part of a software development artifact that appears more than once. Most of the clone detection today concentrates on code clones, but cloning can happen in any artifact. In code, it is usually the result of a normal practice during programming: Developers realize that they have implemented something similar somewhere else. They copy that part of the code and adapt it so that it fits their new requirements. So far, this is not problematic, because we expect that the developer will perform a refactoring afterward to remove the redundancy introduced. Often, however, this does not happen, either because of time pressure or because the developer is not even aware that this can be a problem.

A developer most often does not create an exact copy of the code piece, but changes some identifiers or even adds or removes some lines of code. The notion of a clone incorporates that too. To identify something as a clone, we allow normalization to some degree, such as different identifiers and reformatting. If complete statements (or lines of text) have been changed, added, or deleted, we speak of *gapped clones*. In clone detection, we then have to calibrate how large this gap should be allowed to be. If it is set too large, at some point everything will be a clone. Yet, it can be very interesting to see clones with a difference of three to five lines.

As mentioned above, clone detection is not restricted to source code. If the particular detection approach permits it, we can find clones in any kind of text. For example, we have applied a clone detection tool on textual requirements specifications and found plenty of requirements clones. We will discuss this study in detail in Section 3.5.2. This works because clone detection in the tool ConQAT[13] is implemented on the basis of tokens which we can find in any text. Only normalization cannot be done because we cannot differentiate identifiers.

Impact of cloning

It is still questioned today in research if cloning is really a problem [18], while Martin [19] states that "duplication may be the root of all evil in software." Many factors influence the effects of cloning. In our studies, however, we found two clearly negative impacts of cloning.

First, it is undeniable that the software becomes larger than it needs to be. Every copy of text adds to this increase in size, which could often be avoided by simple refactorings. There are border cases where a rearrangement would add so much additional complexity that the positive effect of avoiding the clone would be compensated. In the vast majority of cases, however, a refactoring would support the readability of the text. The size of a software codebase is correlated to the effort needed to read,

---

[13]http://www.conqat.org/.

change, review, and test it. The review effort increases massively, and the reviewers become frustrated because they have to read a lot of similar text.

Second, we found that cloning can also lead to unnecessary faults. We conducted an empirical study [20] with several industrial system as well as an open-source system in which we particularly investigated the gapped clones in the code of those systems. We reviewed all gapped clones found and checked whether the differences were intentional and whether they constitute a fault. We found that almost every other unintentional inconsistency (gap) between clones was a fault. This way, we identified 107 faults in five systems that have been in operation for several years. Hence, cloning is also a serious threat to program correctness.

Clone detection techniques

There are various techniques and tools to detect clones in different artifacts [21]. They range from token-based comparison [22] to the analysis of abstract syntax trees [23] to more semantics-close analyses such as memory states [24]. In the following example, we work with the tool ConQAT mentioned above. It is applied in many practical environments to regularly check for cloning in code and other artifacts. The measure we use to analyze cloning is predominantly *clone coverage*, which describes the probability that a randomly chosen line of text exists more than once (as a clone) in the system. In our studies, we often found code clone coverage values for source code between 20% and 30%, but also 70% to 80% is not rare. The best code usually has single-digit values for clone coverage. For other artifacts, it is more difficult to give average values, but we have also found clone coverage up to 50% in requirements specifications [25].

In general, false positives tend to be a big problem in static analysis. For clone detection, however, we have been able to get rid of this problem almost completely. It requires a small degree of calibration of the clone detection approach for a context, but then the remaining false positive rates are negligible. ConQAT, for example, provides black listing of single clones and can take regular expressions describing text to be ignored, such as copyright headers or generated code. Finally, we use several of the visualizations the dashboard tool ConQAT provides to control cloning: A trend chart shows if cloning is increasing or a tree map shows us which parts of our systems are affected more or less strongly by cloning.

Running example

We now run the standard text clone detection of ConQAT on the HTTP and IMAP RFCs. By inspecting the found clones, we find several false positives—for example, the copyright header, which is similar in all documents. While these are copies, we do not care because we do not have to read them in detail or compare them for differences. We ignore the headers by giving ConQAT a corresponding regular expression. Figure 3.7 shows an example of a remaining clone in RFC 2616. It describes two variations of HTTP types which are mostly the same. A manual check of what is the same and what is different between the two clone instances would be boring and error-prone. Hence, clone analysis could be used to point to text parts that should be removed and, thereby, make understanding of the specifications easier.

Overall, we have a clone coverage of 27.7% over all 11 analyzed documents from the HTTP and IMAP specifications. The clone coverage is rather evenly distributed, as shown in the tree map in Figure 3.8. The tree map displays each file as a rectangle. The size of the rectangle is relative to the

```
Media Type name:          message
Media subtype name:       http
Required parameters:      none
Optional parameters:      version, msgtype
  version: The HTTP-Version number of the enclosed message
           (e.g., "1.1"). If not present, the version can be
           determined from the first line of the body.
  msgtype: The message type — "request" or "response". If not
           present, the type can be determined from the first
           line of the body.
Encoding considerations:
```

```
Media Type name:          application
Media subtype name:       http
Required parameters:      none
Optional parameters:      version, msgtype
  version: The HTTP-Version number of the enclosed messages
           (e.g., "1.1"). If not present, the version can be
           determined from the first line of the body.
  msgtype: The message type — "request" or "response". If not
           present, the type can be determined from the first
           line of the body.
Encoding considerations:
```

FIGURE 3.7

A text clone of RFC 2616.

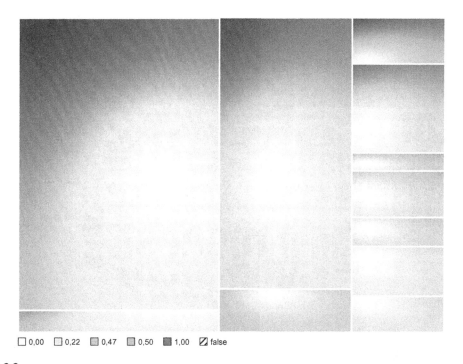

☐ 0,00   ☐ 0,22   ☐ 0,47   ☐ 0,50   ■ 1,00   ▨ false

FIGURE 3.8

A tree map of the cloning in the analyzed RFCs.

size of the file and the color indicates the clone coverage. The darker a rectangle is, the higher the clone coverage for this file. This can quickly give us an overview of even a large number of documents.

Manual coding as well as automatic techniques, such as POS tagging or topic modeling, aim at providing a concise abstraction of the text. We can use it to describe, summarize, and better understand the text. Clone detection, however, has the goal to describe the redundancy created by copy and paste in the text. Hence, a possibility is to use clone detection as a first analysis step to exclude clones from the further analysis. Simply copied texts will otherwise distort the other analyses.

3.4.5 VISUALIZATION

"A picture is worth a thousand words" is a cliché, but a graphical visualization can help strongly in understanding the results of text analyses. In the previous sections, we have already seen a tree map in Figure 3.8 to quickly get an overview of cloning in different text files. It could be used to visualize the distribution of all kinds of metrics over files. A further visualization is the ER diagram in Figure 3.6, which shows the domain concepts in a text in an abstract form well known to computer scientists.

The support for analysts by visualization is a very active research area, often denoted by the term *visual analytics*. Also for visualizing unstructured textual data, several new methods and tools have

FIGURE 3.9

A word cloud of HTTP and IMAP.

appeared in recent years. Alencar et al. [26] give a good overview of this area. We will base our discussion on their work and will highlight three exemplary visualizations.

Word cloud

A well-known, simple, but effective visualization of text is called a *word cloud*, *tag crowd*,[14] or *wordle*.[15] Different implementations give different concrete visualizations, but the idea is always to extract the most frequent words and show them together with the size of each word in relation to its frequency. Our example of the HTTP and IMAP RFCs gives us the word cloud in Figure 3.9. A useful tool for that is Voyant,[16] which we have already mentioned in the context of topic modeling (Section 3.4.1). It can create a word cloud out of a text corpus and allows us interactively to change its appearance, include stop word lists (to avoid having "the" as the largest word) and to click on any word to see its frequency and context. The word cloud in Figure 3.9 was created using Voyant. A word cloud can be a good first step for finding the most important terms in a set of texts. For example, it could be an input into a manual coding process for identifying a set of prior codes likely to appear often in the texts.

---

[14]http://tagcrowd.com/.
[15]http://www.wordle.net/.
[16]http://voyant-tools.org.

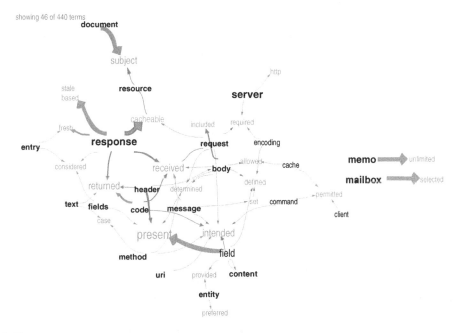

showing 46 of 440 terms

FIGURE 3.10

A phrase net of HTTP and IMAP with the relationship "is" created with IBM's Many Eyes.

Phrase net

A comparable visualization that adds a bit more semantics is a *Phrase net* [27]. It not only presents very frequent words, but also presents their relationship to other frequent words. The kind of relationship can be configured: for example, the connection of both words by another word such as "the" or "is" can be a relationship. Figure 3.10 shows a phrase net for the RFC corpus with the selected relationship "is." It shows frequent words, the larger the more frequent, as well as arrows between words that are connected by an "is." The arrow becomes thicker the more frequently the relationship occurs in the text. For example, the RFCs often contain the word "response"—as we already saw in the word cloud—but we additionally see that "response" is frequently connected by "is" to "state-based" and "cacheable." If the data are publicly accessible, the IBM Many Eyes[17] system is an easy tool to create phrase nets. It is a more complicated visualization than word clouds, but gives more information. It could be used as an alternative to create domain models as with POS tagging (Section 3.4.2) or to check and extend those domain models. Furthermore, it could provide a more comprehensive input to manual coding as it contains not only single words but also important relationships between words.

---

[17]http://www-958.ibm.com/software/analytics/labs/manyeyes/.

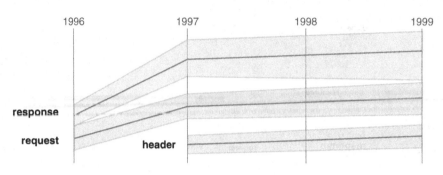

FIGURE 3.11

A TextFlow sketch of the different HTTP RFCs over time.

Temporal change

A next step in visualizing textual data was to introduce a further dimension in the visualization such as the change over time in texts. This can be interesting for the analysis of several versions of a document or survey results collected regularly. We can see changes in the interest in different topics, for example. Havre et al. [28] proposed *ThemeRiver* to visualize topics as streams horizontally over time, with the thickness of the stream related to the strength of the topic at that point in time. Chi et al. [29] extended this with their approach *TextFlow*, which adds specific events extracted from the texts such as the birth or death of a topic to the streams. At present, there is no tool available to perform this kind of analysis.

A text flow of the different versions of the RFC on HTTP is sketched in Figure 3.11 to show the concept. We see that in 1996, the stream for "request" is bigger than that for "response" and, hence, was more often used. This changes in the later versions. The word "header" comes in as a very frequent word only in 1997, and continues to increase in importance in 1999.

3.5 TWO INDUSTRIAL STUDIES

We further illustrate the application of text analytics in software engineering by two industrial studies: first, a survey on requirements engineering (RE) we manually coded and analyzed, and, second, clone detection on RE which we combined with manual coding of the requirements clones found.

3.5.1 NAMING THE PAIN IN REQUIREMENTS ENGINEERING: A REQUIREMENTS ENGINEERING SURVEY

We conducted this survey study in 2013 as a collaboration between Technische Universität München and the University of Stuttgart. We have been working with industrial partners on RE for several years and had a subjective understanding of typical problems in this area. Yet, we often stumbled on the fact that there is no more general and systematic investigation of the state of the practice and contemporary problems of performing RE in practice. Therefore, we developed a study design and questionnaire to tackle this challenge called *Naming the Pain in Requirements Engineering* (NaPiRE). While you are not likely to perform the same study, the way we analyzed the free-text answers to our open questions is applicable to any kind of survey. You can find more information on the complete survey in [30, 31] and on the website http://www.re-survey.org/.

Goals and design

Our long-term research objective is to establish an open and generalizable set of empirical findings about practical problems and needs in RE that allows us to steer future research in a problem-driven manner. To this end, we wanted to conduct a continuously and independently replicated, globally distributed survey on RE that investigates the state of the practice and trends, including industrial expectations, status quo, problems experienced, and what effects those problems have. The survey presented in the following describes the first run of our survey in Germany.

On the basis of these goals, we developed a set of research questions and derived a study design and questionnaire. For most of the aspects we were interested in, we designed closed questions that can be analyzed with common quantitative analyses from descriptive statistics. Often we used the Likert scale from "I fully agree" to "I do not agree at all" to let the survey respondents rate their experiences. We often complemented closed questions with an open question to let the respondents voice additional opinions. At the end of the questionnaire, we asked open questions about the personal experiences with RE in their projects. Our design included a manual analysis using manual coding (Section 3.3) of all the textual data we would get from the open questions. We wanted to derive an improved and extended understanding of potential problems which we would then include in the closed questions of the next survey run.

Example questions and answers

Let us look at two examples of open questions we asked in the questionnaire and some answers we got. The first question we discuss is as follows:

> If you use an internal improvement standard and not an external one, what were the reasons?

The context was that we first asked about normative standards, defined by external parties, that they use for improving their RE practices. An example of such a standard would be the Capability Maturity Model Integration (CMMI) of the US Software Engineering Institute and adaptations of that standard for RE. We were interested in how satisfied the respondents are with such standards and, in turn, why they did not use them. Answers included "We want to live our own agility," "We do not use any standard," and "I am not convinced of the external standards."

The second question we look at provoked longer answers from most respondents. It is also the one from which we could get the most with our manual coding later. It was as follows:

> Considering your personally experienced most critical problems (selected in the previous question), how do these problems manifest themselves in the process, e.g., in requests for changes?

We had presented a set of problems we encountered in practice before in the previous question. Now, we wanted to better understand what problems the respondents consider most critical. From this, we wanted to learn about the context of the problems, potential causes, and candidates for new problems. The answers we got included "Requirements emerge and change priority once the system is deployed. Again, this is no problem but the environment. It becomes a problem if you're not prepared to deal with it" and "Hard negotiations regarding the CR/Bug question, mostly leading to bad relationship with the customer on project lead level."

Coding process and challenges

To analyze the free-text answers, we followed the manual coding procedure as introduced in Section 3.3. However, we already have a predefined set of codes (given RE problems) for which we want to know how the participants see their implications. For this reason, we had to adjust our procedure from the standard procedure and rely on a mix of bottom-up and top-down approaches. We start with selective coding and build the core category with two subcategories—namely, *RE problems* with a set of codes each representing one RE problem and *Implications*, which then groups the codes defined for the answers given by the participants. For the second category, we conducted open coding and axial coding for the answers until we reached a saturation for a hierarchy of (sub-)categories, codes, and relationships.

During the coding process, we had to tackle several challenges. One was the lack of appropriate tool support for manual coding, especially when working in distributed environments. Another one was the missing possibility to validate the results by getting feedback from the respondents. Figure 3.12 shows the procedure we followed during manual coding.

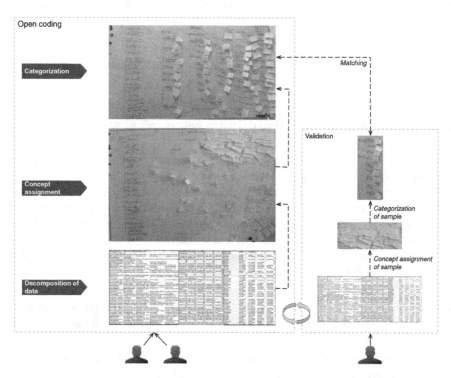

FIGURE 3.12

Open coding and validation procedure.

For this reason, we relied on analyst triangulation during the open coding step as this was essentially the step which most depended on subjectivity (during interpretation of the answers to the open questions). During this open coding step, we decomposed the data using spreadsheets and worked with paper cards, where we also denoted the rationale for selected codes. In a third step, we arranged the cards according to categories using a whiteboard. A third analyst then repeated, as a validation step, independently the open coding process on a sample.

Coding results

Because of the resulting complexity in the answers given and the resulting coding scheme, we describe the results stepwise. To this end, we first introduce the full results from the open coding, followed by the full results of the axial coding. In a last step, we present a condensed overall view of the results as a graph with a minimal saturation. We show only those results having a minimal occurrence in the answers to include only those in our theory.

Figure 3.13 summarizes the full results from the open coding. We distinguish a hierarchy of categories as an abstraction of those codes defined for the answers given in the questionnaire. For each code, we furthermore denote the number of occurrences. Not included in the coding are statements that cannot be unambiguously allocated to a code—for example, the statement "never ending story" as an implication of the problem "incomplete/hidden requirements."

Given that we asked what implications the problems have, we would expect two top-level categories. The participants also stated, however, reasons for the problems, and occasionally also how they would expect to mitigate the problem. As shown in Figure 3.13, we thus categorize the results into the predefined category *RE Problems*, *Implications*, and the additional category *Reasoning*.

Regarding the implications, we distinguish three subcategories: consequences of problems in the RE phase itself, consequences to be seen in further phases of the software life cycle other than RE, and more abstract consequences for the overall project quality. The highest occurrence of statements is given for the code *Change Request*, being stated 22 times. Other codes resulted from only one statement, but they were unique, specific formulations that could not be merged with other statements. For instance, the code *Weak Relationship Customer & Project Lead* in the category *Overall SW Project Quality* resulted from a statement which we could not allocate to another code without interpretation and potentially misinterpreting the statement (given that no validation with the respondents is possible).

Regarding the reasoning for the given RE problems, we distinguish the category *Rationale* as a justification of why particular problems occurred, and *Improvement/Mitigation* for statements that suggested how to mitigate particular problems. The first category can be further divided into *Factors in RE* and *General Factors*.

Also here, we encountered very mixed statements, including detailed ones we had to allocate to codes having in the end only one occurrence and vague statements we could accumulate with (consequently vague) codes. The subsequent original statements should give an impression of the answers given:

Code   *Missing Abstraction from Solution Level:* "Stakeholders like to discuss on solution level, not on requirements level. Developers think in solutions. The problem is: even Product Managers and Consultants do it."

Code   *No RE explicitly planned (in tendering):* "A common situation is to take part in a tender process—where requirements are specified very abstract—most of these tender processes do

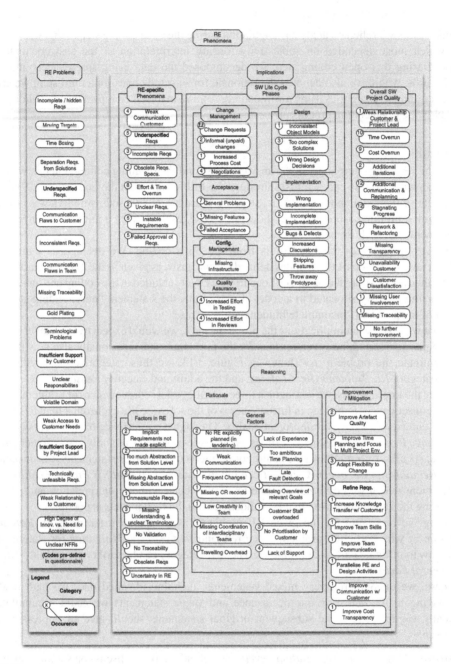

FIGURE 3.13

Categories and codes resulting from open coding.

not include a refinement stage, as a supplier we are bound to fulfill vague requests from the initial documents."

Code   *Weak Communication:* "The communication to customer is done not by technicians, but by lawyers."

Code   *Too Ambitious Time Planning:* "Delivery date is known before requirements are clear."

Code   *Implicit Requirements not made explicit:* "Referencing common sense as a requirement basis."

Code   *Failed Acceptance:* "After acceptance testing failed, the hidden requirements came up and had to be fixed on an emergency level."

Code   *Missing Coordination of Interdisciplinary Teams:* "Missing coordination between different disciplines (electrical engineering, mechanical engineering, software etc.)."

The axial coding defines the relationships between the codes. As a consequence of the categories introduced in the previous section, we distinguish two types of relationships:

1. The consequences of given RE problems for the category *Implications*.
2. The consequences of the codes in the category *Reasoning* for the RE problems, including rationales and improvement suggestions.

We cannot show the full results of the axial coding here. We further refrain from interpreting any transitive relationships from reasonings to implications because of the multiple input/output relationships between the codes of the different categories; for instance, while "Too ambitious time planning" was stated as an exclusive reason for "time boxing" as an RE problem, the problem "incomplete/hidden requirements" has multiple reasons as well as multiple consequences.

We are especially interested in a condensed result set that omits the codes and the dependencies with limited occurrences in corresponding statements. The reason is that we need a result set with a minimal saturation to propose its integration into the questionnaire for the next run of the survey. After testing the results with different values for the minimal occurrences, we defined a graph including only codes with a minimal occurrence level of 7. This resulting graph is shown in Figure 3.14. Nodes represent a selection of codes, and edges represent a selection of relationships between nodes.

With the chosen minimal occurrence level, the final graph does not include statements coded in the category *Reasoning*, leaving us with a selection of RE problems interconnected with their implications. The three nodes with the highest occurrence in their underlying statements are "Additional communication and replaning," "Stagnating progress," and "Change requests." Change requests (in the center of the figure) are stated as the most frequent consequence of various RE problems such as time boxing or incomplete/hidden requirements. Additional communication and replanning (upper part of the figure) was another frequently stated consequence of interconnected RE problems, similarly to a stagnating process (left side of the figure).

3.5.2 CLONE DETECTION IN REQUIREMENTS SPECIFICATIONS

We performed this case study in 2009 in a collaboration between Technische Universität München and itestra GmbH as an exploratory study on the extent of cloning in commercial requirements specifications. We had a subjective feeling that there is a lot of textual redundancy in those specifications from experiences with project partners but we had not this investigated systematically before. All details of the study can be found in [25]. It is an example for clone detection on natural language texts (Section 3.4.4) as well as for manual coding (Section 3.3).

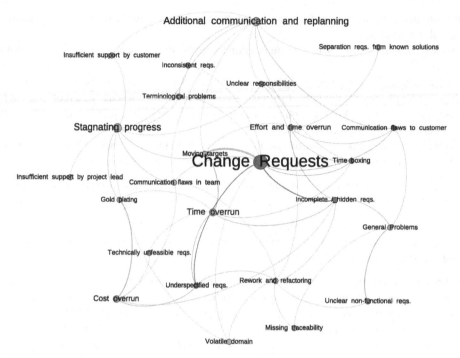

FIGURE 3.14

Condensed view of axial coding with minimal weighting of 7 in the nodes.

What is the problem with clones in specifications?

Requirements specifications are a central artifact in most software development processes. They capture the goals of the software to be developed and constitute the connection between the customer/user and the developers. Many call the specifications the determining part for project success or failure. Yet, as with any other development artifact, requirements specifications contain redundancy. Semantic redundancies are the source of many potential problems in a development project, but are also extremely hard to detect. Yet, there are also syntactic redundancies: Specifications are written by people who tend to copy (and adapt) text if they need similar things in different parts of the document or in different documents. These syntactic redundancies can be found by clone detection (see Section 3.4.4).

In our collaborations with various industry partners on their RE processes, we often found syntactic redundancies in their specifications. They lead to various problems. The most direct is the sheer increased size of the specifications, which, in turn, leads to greater efforts for reading, reviewing, and changing them. In addition, similarly to code cloning [20], redundancy can introduce inconsistencies. The copies of the text drift apart over time as some copies are adapted, for example, to changes in the requirements of the customer, while others are forgotten. We now have conflicting requirements, and the developers can introduce faults into the software. Finally, an undesired effect of clones in requirements specifications is also that the developers introduce redundancy by cloning the implementation or, even worse, develop the same functionality more than once.

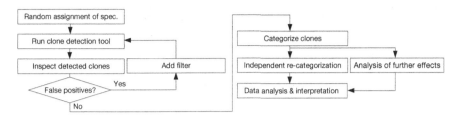

FIGURE 3.15

Our approach to analyze cloning in requirements specifications.

Analysis approach

To better understand the actual extent of cloning in industrial requirements specifications, we designed a study in which we used automated clone detection on a set of industrial specifications and then classified the clones found with manual coding. The former gives us a quantification of the phenomenon and the latter gives us qualitative insight into what information is cloned. We worked in several research pairs and followed the process shown in Figure 3.15.

We assembled a set of 28 requirements specifications of various lengths and for a wide variety of systems and domains. We first assigned the specifications randomly among pairs of analysts. Each pair ran a clone detection without any filters using the tool ConQAT. We then inspected the clones found for false positives (pieces of text reported as clones but not actual redundancies). As expected, we found a few false positives such as copyright headers and footers. We added corresponding filters in the form of regular expressions so that the false positives will be ignored. Afterward, we ran the clone detection again and inspected the results. This continued until we could not find any false positives in a random sample of the clones. This gave us the quantitative results of the study.

Afterward, we manually coded a random sample of the clones to form categories of the type of information that was cloned. We had no predefined codes, but developed them while inspecting the clones. As we did not need any larger theory, we skipped axial coding (Section 3.3). The coding gave us a complete set of categories. To validate the more subjectively developed categories, we performed an independent recoding of a sample of the categorized clones and found a substantial agreement between the raters. Besides, we also noted additional effects such as the impact on the implementation. This gave us the qualitative results of the study.

Results of automatic analysis

All the quantitative results of our study are shown in Table 3.2. The outcome is clear: there are many industrial requirements specifications that contain cloning, several with high clone coverage values between 30% and 70%. The third column gives the number of clone groups per specification. A clone group is a set of clones, the individual copies. There are several specifications with more than 100 clone groups. Hence, there has been a lot of copy and paste in these documents. There are also several specifications, however, with no or almost no cloning. Therefore, it seems to be possible to create specifications without copy and paste.

Table 3.2 Automatic Analysis Results of Cloning in Requirements Specifications

Specification	Clone Coverage (%)	Clone Groups	Clones
H	71.6	71	360
F	51.1	50	162
A	35.0	259	914
G	22.1	60	262
Y	21.9	181	553
L	20.5	303	794
Z	19.6	50	117
C	18.5	37	88
K	18.1	19	55
U	15.5	85	237
X	12.4	21	45
AB	12.1	635	1818
V	11.2	201	485
B	8.9	265	639
N	8.2	159	373
D	8.1	105	479
P	5.8	5	10
I	5.5	7	15
AC	5.4	65	148
W	2.0	14	31
O	1.9	8	16
S	1.6	11	27
M	1.2	11	23
J	1.0	1	2
E	0.9	6	12
R	0.7	2	4
Q	0.0	0	0
T	0.0	0	0
Average	13.6		
Sum		2631	7669

Results of manual classification

The manual coding of a sample of clones resulted in 12 categories of cloned information being encountered. The categories we identified are described in Table 3.3 [25]. Overall, we coded a sample of over 400 clone groups almost 500 times because we sometimes assigned a clone group to more than one category, especially if the clones were longer and, hence, contained different aspects. To better understand these different categories and how they occur in practice, we quantified the results by counting the number of clone groups per category in our sample (Figure 3.16). The highest number of assigned codes belongs to the category "Detailed use case steps," with 100 assignments.

Table 3.3 Descriptions of the Categories of Cloned Information in Requirements Specifications

Detailed use case steps	Description of one or more steps in a use case that specifies in detail how a user interacts with the system, such as the steps required to create a new customer account in a system.
Reference	Fragment in a requirements specification that refers to another document or another part of the same document. Examples are references in a use case to other use cases or to the corresponding business process.
UI	Information that refers to the (graphical) user interface. The specification of which buttons are visible on which screen is an example for this category.
Domain knowledge	Information about the application domain of the software. An example is details about what is part of an insurance contract for software that manages insurance contracts.
Interface description	Data and message definitions that describe the interface of a component, function, or system. An example is the definition of messages on a bus system that a component reads and writes.
Precondition	A condition that has to hold before something else can happen. A common example is preconditions for the execution of a specific use case.
Side condition	Condition that describes the status that has to hold during the execution of something. An example is that a user has to remain logged in during the execution of a certain functionality.
Configuration	Explicit settings for configuring the described component or system. An example is timing parameters for configuring a transmission protocol.
Feature	Description of a piece of functionality of the system on a high level of abstraction.
Technical domain knowledge	Information about the technology used for the solution and the technical environment of the system—for example, bus systems used in an embedded system.
Postcondition	Condition that describes what has to hold after something has finished. Analogous to the preconditions, postconditions are usually part of use cases to describe the system state after the use case execution.
Rationale	Justification of a requirement. An example is the explicit demand by a certain user group.

"Reference" (64) and "UI" (63) follow. The least number of assignments belongs to the category "Rationale" (8).

Overall, this study was a beneficial combination of manual and automatic text analyses to better understand the extent and type of cloning in requirements specifications. The automatic analysis has the advantage that we could integrate it into a regular quality analysis—for example, contained in the nightly build of the corresponding system. This way, introduced clones could be detected and removed early and easily. Nevertheless, it is interesting to regularly also inspect the clones and categorize them to understand if new types of clones appear.

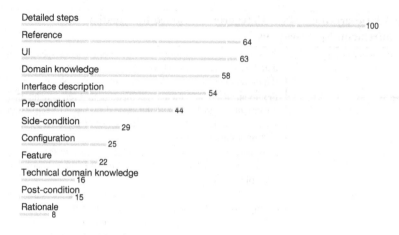

FIGURE 3.16

Cloning: found categories of requirements clones.

3.6 SUMMARY

Textual data constitutes most of the data that is generated in a software project. Yet, we often do not make use of the information and insights contained in this textual data. The problem is that many analysis methods are focused on quantitative data. There are various possibilities of manual as well as automatic analyses now available that help us in employing textual data in better understanding our software projects.

In this chapter, we discussed first manual coding to analyze any kind of textual data. We assigned different types of codes to the text to abstract and interpret it. This is a highly subjective task which needs appropriate means such as triangulation of analysts to make it more objective. Yet, it can be flexibly applied and allows the analysts to bring their own expertise to the data analysis. The biggest problem, however, is the large amount of effort necessary for the analysis.

Therefore, we discussed a sample of automatic analyses available, mostly with easily accessible tool support. For example, clone detection is an easy and viable means to detect any syntactic redundancy in textual software artifacts. Topic modeling is another example that can help us to investigate dependencies between documents or quickly get an overview of topics contained in the documents. Visualizations can greatly support all of these automatic analyses to make them easier to comprehend, especially for large text corpora.

Research on text analytics is still very active, and we expect to see many more innovations that we will be able to exploit also for analyzing textual project data from software projects. The possibilities are huge.

REFERENCES

[1] Birks M, Mills J. Grounded theory—a practical guide. Thousand Oaks: Sage Publications, Inc.; 2011.

[2] Hannay J, Dag S, Tore D. A systematic review of theory use in software engineering experiments. IEEE Trans Softw Eng 2007:87–107.

[3] Wohlin C, Runeson P, Höst M, Ohlsson M, Regnell B, Wesslen A. Experimentation in software engineering. Berlin: Springer; 2012.

[4] Popper K. The logic of scientific discovery. New York: Routledge; 2002.

[5] Glaser B, Strauss A. The discovery of grounded theory: strategies for qualitative research. Chicago: Aldine Transaction; 1967.

[6] Steyvers M, Griffiths T. Probabilistic topic models. In: Landauer T, McNamara D, Dennis S, Kintsch W, editors. Latent semantic analysis a road to meaning. Mahwah, NJ: Laurence Erlbaum; 2007.

[7] Blei DM, Ng AY, Jordan MI. Latent Diriclet allocation. J Mach Learn Res 2003;3:993–1022.

[8] Brill E. Part-of-speech tagging. In: Dale R, Moisl H, Somers H, editors. Handbook of natural language processing. Boca Raton, FL: CRC Press; 2000.

[9] Toutanova K, Manning CD. Enriching the knowledge sources used in a maximum entropy part-of-speech tagger. In: Proceedings of the joint SIGDAT conference on empirical methods in natural language processing and very large corpora (EMNLP/VLC-2000); 2000. p. 63–70.

[10] Marcus M, Santorini B, Marcinkiewicz M. Building a large annotated corpus of English: the Penn Treebank. Comput Linguist 1993;19(2):313–30.

[11] Chen PSP. English sentence structure and entity-relationship diagrams. Inform Sci 1983;29:127–49.

[12] Abbott RJ. Program design by informal English descriptions. Commun ACM 1983;26(11): 882–94.

[13] Kof L. Text analysis for requirements engineering. Ph.D. thesis, Technische Universität München; 2005.

[14] Femmer H, Kucera J, Vetro' A. On the impact of passive voice requirements on domain modelling. In: Proceedings of the ACM/IEEE international symposium on empirical software engineering and measurement; 2014.

[15] Manning CD, Schütze H. Foundations of statistical natural language processing. Cambridge, MA: MIT Press; 1999.

[16] Hindle A, Barr ET, Su Z, Gabel M, Devanbu P. On the naturalness of software. In: 34th international conference on software engineering (ICSE, 2012); 2012. p. 837–47.

[17] Allamanis M, Sutton C. Mining source code repositories at massive scale using language modeling. In: 10th IEEE working conference on mining software repositories (MSR). Piscataway, NJ: IEEE Press; 2013. p. 207–16.

[18] Kapser C, Godfrey MW. Cloning considered harmful" considered harmful: patterns of cloning in software. Empir Softw Eng 2008;13(6):645–92.

[19] Martin RC. Clean code: a handbook of agile software craftmanship. Upper Saddle River, NJ: Prentice Hall; 2008.

[20] Juergens E, Deissenboeck F, Hummel B, Wagner S. Do code clones matter? In: ICSE'09; 2009.

[21] Koschke R. Survey of research on software clones. Internationales Begegnungs-und Forschungszentrum für Informatik; 2007.

[22] Juergens E, Deissenboeck F, Hummel B. CloneDetective—a workbench for clone detection research. In: Proceedings of the 31st international conference on software engineering (ICSE'09). Washington, DC, USA: IEEE Computer Society; 2009. p. 603–6. ISBN 978-1-4244-3453-4. doi:10.1109/ICSE.2009.5070566.

[23] Jiang L, Misherghi G, Su Z, Glondu S. DECKARD: scalable and accurate tree-based detection of code clones. In: Proceedings of the international conference on software engineering (ICSE'07); 2007.

[24] Kim H, Jung Y, Kim S, Yi K. MeCC: memory comparison-based clone detector. In: Proceedings of the 33rd international conference on software engineering (ICSE '11). New York: ACM; 2011.

[25] Juergens E, Deissenboeck F, Feilkas M, Hummel B, Schaetz B, Wagner S, et al. Can clone detection support quality assessments of requirements specifications? In: ICSE '10: proceedings of the 32nd ACM/IEEE international conference on software engineering. New York: ACM; 2010.

[26] Alencar AB, de Oliveira MCF, Paulovich FV. Seeing beyond reading: a survey on visual text analytics. Wiley Interdiscip Rev Data Min Knowl Discov 2012;2(6):476–92.

[27] van Ham F, Wattenberg M, Viegas FB. Mapping text with Phrase Nets. IEEE Trans Vis Comput Graph 2009;15:1169–76.

[28] Havre S, Hetzler E, Whitney P, Nowell L. ThemeRiver: visualizing thematic changes in large document collections. IEEE Trans Vis Comput Graph 2002;8:9–20.

[29] Cui W, Liu S, Tan L, Shi C, Song Y, Gao Z, et al. TextFlow: towards better understanding of evolving topics in text. IEEE Trans Vis Comput Graph 2011;17:2412–21.

[30] Méndez Fernández D, Wagner S. Naming the pain in requirements engineering: design of a global family of surveys and first results from Germany. In: Proceedings of the 17th international conference on evaluation and assessment in software engineering (EASE'13). New York: ACM Press; 2013. p. 183–94.

[31] Méndez Fernández D, Wagner S. Naming the pain in requirements engineering—NaPiRE report 2013. Technical report, TUM-I1326, Technische Universität München; 2013.

SYNTHESIZING KNOWLEDGE FROM SOFTWARE DEVELOPMENT ARTIFACTS

4

Olga Baysal*, Oleksii Kononenko[†], Reid Holmes[‡], Michael W. Godfrey[†]

School of Computer Science, Carleton University, Ottawa, ON, Canada* David R. Cheriton School of Computer Science, University of Waterloo, Waterloo, ON, Canada[†] Department of Computer Science, University of British Columbia, Vancouver, BC, Canada[‡]

CHAPTER OUTLINE

4.1 PROBLEM STATEMENT

The data is out there. The problem is making practical use of it.

It can be challenging, if not impossible, to process the myriad development artifacts that accrue in repositories, such as issue tracking and version control systems. The sheer size of the data, arriving in unrelenting streams, makes it impractical to perform manual processing for comprehension of the current state of the project, let alone seek historical trends. Help is needed to corral the information, organize it in a helpful and intuitive way, and provide an overview of development progress. With this in mind, we introduce a data pattern called the *lifecycle model*, which is a graph-based representation of specific properties within a development artifact and how they change over time.

Lifecycle models can be applied to any data that changes its state, or is annotated with new data, over time. For example, "issues" in issue-tracking systems often start their lives as *OPEN*, but are eventually *RESOLVED* or marked as *WONTFIX*. A lifecycle model for issues aggregates data to provide a graphical representation of how bugs flow through these three states. For example, the lifecycle model would capture the proportion of bugs that are reopened from a *WONTFIX* state that might be interesting for a manager considering adjustments to their issue triage process. Such lifecycle models often exist in process models (if defined). Therefore, extracting one from the history enables comparing the defined lifecycle with the actual one.

In this chapter, we apply lifecycle models to capture how the patch review process works within the Mozilla, WebKit, and Blink projects. We demonstrate how these models can expose interesting trends within individual projects, while at the same are succinct enough to permit an analyst to easily compare traits between projects.

4.2 ARTIFACT LIFECYCLE MODELS

Using metadata history, lifecycle models can be extracted for any data elements that change over time, such as the change status of issues, patches under review, or evolving lines of code. By examining how each artifact evolves, we can build a summary that captures common dynamic evolutionary patterns. Each node in a lifecycle model represents a state that can be derived by examining the evolution of an artifact.

4.2.1 EXAMPLE: PATCH LIFECYCLE

To model the patch lifecycle, e.g., for the Mozilla project, we first examine Mozilla's code review policy and processes. Mozilla employs a two-tier code review process for validating submitted patches — *review* and *super-review* [1]. The first type of a review is performed by a module owner or peers of the module; a reviewer is someone who has domain expertise in a problem area. The second type of review is called a super-review; these reviews are required if the patch involves integration or modifies core codebase infrastructure. We then extract the states a patch can go through and define the final states it can be assigned to.

Figure 4.1 illustrates a lifecycle model of a patch as a simple graph: the nodes show the various states a patch can go through during the review process, while the edges capture the transitions between lifecycle states. A transition represents an event that is labeled as a flag and its status reported during the review process. For simplicity, we show only the key code review patches that have "review" (r) and "super-review" (sr) flags attached to them.[1]

The code review process begins when a patch is submitted and a review is requested; the initial transition is labeled "r? OR sr?," i.e., a review or super-review has been requested. A patch can be assigned to one of three states: *Submitted*, *Accepted*, or *Rejected*. Once the review is requested (a flag contains a question mark "?" at the end), the patch enters the *Submitted* state. If a reviewer assigns "+"

---

[1]Other flags on a patch such as "feedback," "ui-review," "checkin," "approval aurora," or "approval beta," as well as patches with no flags were excluded from the analysis.

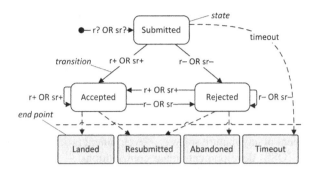

FIGURE 4.1

Lifecycle of a patch.

to a flag (e.g., "*r +*" or "*sr +*"), the patch is marked as *Accepted*; if a flag is reported with a status "–" (e.g., "*r–*" or "*sr–*"), the patch is *Rejected*.

Note that both the *Accepted* and *Rejected* states permit self-transitions. These self-transitions, when taken together with the transitions between the *Accepted* and *Rejected* states, illustrate the double-review process. The double-review process takes place when a reviewer believes the patch can benefit from additional reviews, or when code modifications affect several modules and thus needs to be reviewed by a reviewer from each affected module.

There are four possible terminal states for a patch:

- *Landed*—a patch meets the code review criteria and is incorporated into the codebase.
- *Resubmitted*—a patch is superseded by additional refinements after being accepted or rejected.
- *Abandoned*—a patch is not improved after being rejected.
- *Timeout*—a patch with review requests that are never answered.

By definition, the cumulative number of the patches in *Landed*, *Resubmitted*, *Abandoned*, and *Timeout* is equal to the number of the *Submitted* patches.

Each edge may be presented with quantitative data, such as the time required for a patch to pass from one state to another or the percentage of the total patches that appear in a certain state (e.g., how many patches are positively evaluated by reviewers).

4.2.2 MODEL EXTRACTION

We now demonstrate the process of extracting patch lifecycle models. Lifecycle models can be generated as follows:

1. Determine the key states of the system or process (e.g., a number of events that could occur) and their attributes.
2. Define the necessary transitions between the states and specify an attribute for each transition.
3. Define the terminal outcomes (optional).
4. Define and gather qualitative or quantitative measurements for each state transition and, if present, for the final outcomes. In addition to these measurements, the time spent in the state or the transition to another state can also be considered and analyzed.

The pattern provides means to model, organize, and reason about the data or underlying processes otherwise hidden in individual artifacts. While lifecycle models can be modified or extended depending on the needs, they work best when the state space is well defined. Applying this pattern to complex data may require some abstraction.

4.3 CODE REVIEW

Code review is a key element of any mature software development process. It is particularly important for open source software (OSS) development, since contributions — in the form of bug fixes, new features, documentation, etc. — may come not only from core developers but also from members of the greater user community [2–5]. Indeed, community contributions are often the life blood of a successful open source project; however, the core developers must also be able to assess the quality of the incoming contributions, lest they negatively impact the overall quality of the system.

The code review process evaluates the quality of source code modifications (submitted as patches) before they are committed to a project's version control repository. A strict review process is important to ensuring the quality of the system, and some contributions will be championed and succeed while others will not. Consequently, the carefulness, fairness, and transparency of the process will be keenly felt by the contributors.

Here, we want to explore whether code review in a project is "democratic," i.e., are contributions reviewed "equally," regardless of the developers' previous involvement on a project. For example, do patches from core developers have a higher chance of being accepted? Do patches from casual contributors take longer to get feedback?

4.3.1 MOZILLA PROJECT

As we said earlier, Mozilla employs a two-tiered code review process for evaluating code modifications: reviews and super-reviews [1]. A *review* is typically performed by the owner of the module or a "peer"; the reviewer has domain expertise in the problem area. A *super-review* is required if the patch involves integration or modifies core Mozilla infrastructure. Currently, there are 29 super-reviewers [6] spread across all Mozilla modules, with 18 reviewers (peers) on the Firefox module alone [7]. However, any person with level 3 commit access — i.e., core product access to the Mercurial version control system — can become a reviewer.

Bugzilla users flag patches with metadata to capture code review requests and evaluations. A typical patch review process consists of the following steps:

1. Once a patch is ready, its owner requests a review from a module owner or a peer. The review flag is set to "*r?*". If the patch owner decides to request a super-review, he may also do so and the flag is set to "*sr?*".
2. When the patch passes a review or a super-review, the flag is set to "*r+*," or "*sr+*," respectively. If it fails, the reviewer sets the flag to "*r−*" or "*sr−*" and provides explanation on a review by adding comments to a bug in Bugzilla.
3. If the patch is rejected, the patch owner may resubmit a new version of the patch that will undergo a review process from the beginning. If the patch is approved, it will be checked into the project's official codebase.

4.3.2 **WebKit PROJECT**

WebKit is an HTML layout engine that renders web pages and executes embedded JavaScript code. The WebKit project was started in 2001 as a fork of the KHTML project. Prior to April 2013, developers from more than 30 companies actively contributed to WebKit, including Google, Apple, Adobe, BlackBerry, Digia, Igalia, Intel, Motorolla, Nokia, and Samsung. Google and Apple are the two primary contributors, submitting 50% and 20% of patches, respectively.

The WebKit project employs an explicit code review process for evaluating submitted patches; in particular, a WebKit reviewer must approve a patch before it can land in the project's version control repository. The list of official WebKit reviewers is maintained through a system of voting to ensure that only highly-experienced candidates are eligible to review patches. A reviewer will either accept a patch by marking it "*review+*" or ask for further revisions from the patch owner by annotating the patch with "*review−*". The review process for a particular submission may include multiple iterations between the reviewer and the patch writer before the patch is accepted (lands) in the version control repository.

4.3.3 **BLINK PROJECT**

Google forked WebKit to create the Blink project in April 2013 because they wanted to make larger-scale changes to WebKit to fit their own needs that did not align well with the WebKit project itself. Several of the organizations that contributed to WebKit migrated to Blink after the fork.

Every Blink patch is submitted to the project's issue repository. The reviewers on the Blink project approve patches by annotating it "LGTM" ("Looks Good To Me," case-insensitive) on the patch and reject patches by annotating "not LGTM." In this work, we consider WebKit's "*review+*"/"*review−*" flags and Blink's "*lgtm*"/"*not lgtm*" annotations as equivalent. Since Blink does not have an explicit review request process (e.g., "*review?*"), we infer requests by adding a "*review?*" flag to a patch as soon as it is submitted to the repository. Since patches are typically committed to the version control system by an automated process, we define landed patches as those followed by the automated message from the "commit bot." The last patch on the issue is likely to be the patch that eventually lands to the Blink's source code repository. Committers can optionally perform a manual merge of the patches to the version control system, although we do not consider these due to their infrequence.

4.4 **LIFECYCLE ANALYSIS**

We now apply lifecycle models to the code review processes to highlight how code reviews happen in practice. Here, the goal of creating the model is to identify the ways in which patches typically flow through the code review process, and also to identify exceptional review paths. We have extracted the code review lifecycle model for Mozilla Firefox (Section 4.4.1), WebKit (Section 4.4.2), and Blink (Section 4.4.3).

4.4.1 **MOZILLA FIREFOX**

We modeled the patch lifecycle by examining Mozilla's code review policy and processes and compared them to how developers worked with patches in practice. To generate lifecycle models all events have been extracted from Mozilla's public Bugzilla instance. We extracted the states a patch can go through and defined the final states it can be assigned to.

All code committed to Mozilla Firefox undergoes code review. Developers submit a patch containing their change to Bugzilla and request a review. Reviewers annotate the patch either positively or negatively to reflect their opinion of the code under review. For highly-impactful patches super-reviews may be requested and performed. Once the reviewers approve a patch it can be applied to the Mozilla source code repository.

We generated the model by applying the four steps given in Section 4.2.2:

1. *State identification*: Patches exist in one of three key states: Submitted, Accepted, and Rejected.
2. *Transition extraction*: Code reviews transition patches between the three primary states. A review request is annotated with "*r?*". Positive reviews are denoted with a "*r+*". Negative reviews are annotated "*r−*". Super-reviews are prepended with an *s* (e.g., "*sr+*"/"*sr−*").
3. *Terminal state determination*: Patches can also exist in four terminal states, which are defined considering entire patch history to resolve an issue. Landed patches are those that pass the code review process and are included in the version control system. Resubmitted patches are patches a developer decides to further refine based on reviewer feedback. Abandoned patches capture those patches the developer decided to abandon based on the feedback they received. Finally, the Timeout state represents patches for which no review was given even though it was requested.
4. *Measurement*: For this study we measured both the number of times each transition happened along with the median time taken to transition between states.

Figure 4.2 illustrates the lifecycle model of the patch review process for core Mozilla contributors. *Core contributors* are those developers who submitted 100 patches or more during the studied period, while *casual contributors* are defined as those ones who wrote 20 patches or fewer [8]. Contributors who submitted more than 20 and fewer than 100 patches (12% of all contributors) were not included in this analysis.

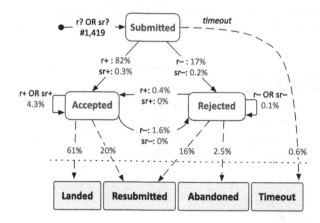

FIGURE 4.2

Mozilla Firefox's patch lifecycle for core developers.

Table 4.1 Median Time of a Transition (in Minutes) for Mozilla Firefox		
Transition	**Core Contributors**	**Casual Contributors**
r? → r+	534	494
r? → r−	710	1024
r+ → r−	390	402
r− → r+	1218	15
sr? → sr+	617	n/a
sr? → sr−	9148	n/a

The lifecycle demonstrates some interesting transitions that might not otherwise be obvious. For instance, a large proportion of accepted patches are still resubmitted by authors for revision. We can also see that rejected patches are usually resubmitted, easing concerns that rejecting a borderline patch could cause it to be abandoned. We also see that very few patches timeout in practice. From the timing data for core contributors (refer to Table 4.1) we see that it takes an average of 8.9 hours to get an initial "r+" review, while getting a negative "r−" review takes 11.8 hours.

We also measured the time it takes for a patch to go from one state to another. Table 4.1 reports the median time (in minutes) each transition of the model takes. The transition "r? → r+" is a lot faster than "r? → r−" showing that reviewers provide faster responses if a patch is of good quality. To our surprise, the fastest "r? → r+" is detected for casual developers. Our findings show that contributions from casual developers are less likely to get a positive review; however, if they do, the median response rate is about 8 hours (in contrast to 9 hours for core developers). Super-reviews, in general, are approved very quickly, within 8−10 hours. This finding conforms to the Mozilla's code review policy: super-reviewers are supposed to respond within 24 hours of a super-review request. However, it takes much longer — 4 to 6 days — for a super-reviewer to reject a patch that requires an integration, as these patches often require extensive discussions with others. "r− → r+" is a lot slower for core developers, mainly because there is only one occurrence of this transition for the "casual" group.

Comparing the lifecycles for core (Figure 4.2) and casual contributors (Figure 4.3), we note that, in general, casual contributors have 7% fewer patches that get accepted or checked into the codebase and have 6% more patches that get rejected. The amount of the patches from casual contributors that received no response or are being abandoned is increased by the factor of 3.5x and 3.12x respectively. Review requests with timeouts are likely those that are directed to the wrong reviewers or to the "General" component that does not have an explicit owner. If a review was requested from a default reviewer, a component owner, the patch is likely to get no response due to heavy loads and long review queues the default reviewer has. Since contributors decide what reviewer to request an approval from, they might send their patch to the "graveyard" by asking the wrong person to review their patch. The process, by design, lacks transparency on the review queues of the reviewers.

Moreover, casual contributors are more likely to give up on a patch that fails a review process — 16% fewer patches are resubmitted after rejection. Unlike patches from core developers, once rejected patches from the "casual" group do not get a chance to get in (0% on the "Rejected" to "Accepted" transition) and are three times more likely to receive a second negative response.

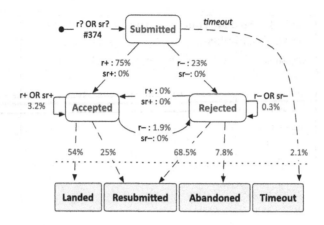

FIGURE 4.3

Mozilla Firefox's patch lifecycle for casual developers.

The results show that patches submitted by casual developers do not require super-reviews, as we found no super-review requests on these patches. This was unsurprising since community members who participate occasionally in a project often submit small and trivial patches [9].

Our findings suggest that patches from casual contributors are more likely to be abandoned by both reviewers and contributors themselves. Thus, it is likely that these patches should receive extra care to both ensure quality and encourage future contributions from the community members who prefer to participate in the collaborative development on a less regular basis.

The results of our analysis of the code review process of Firefox — and comparing the lifecycle models for patch review between core and casual contributors — generated discussion and raised some concerns among the developers on the Mozilla Development Planning team [10]:

> "... rapid release has made life harder and more discouraging for the next generation of would-be Mozilla hackers. That's not good. . . So the quality of patches from casual contributors is only slightly lower (it's not that all their patches are rubbish), but the amount of patches that end up abandoned is still more than 3x higher. :-("
>
> **[Gerv Markham]**
>
> "I do agree that it's worth looking into the "abandoned" data set more carefully to see what happened to those patches, of course."
>
> **[Boris Zbarsky]**

4.4.2 WebKit

The lifecycle model can be easily modified according to the dataset at hand. For example, we have applied the pattern to study the code review process of the WebKit project [11]. The model of the patch lifecycle is shown in Figure 4.4.

Since WebKit is an industrial project, we were particularly interested to compare its code review process to that of Mozilla, which was run in more traditional open source development style. To do so,

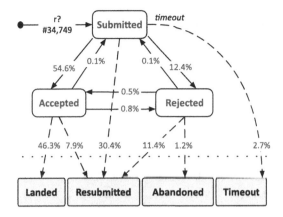

FIGURE 4.4

WebKit's patch lifecycle.

we extracted WebKit's patch lifecycle (Figure 4.4) and compared it with the previously studied patch lifecycle of Mozilla Firefox [8] (Figure 4.2).

The patch lifecycle captures the various states patches undergo during the review process, and characterizes how the patches transition between these states. The patch lifecycles enable large data sets to be aggregated in a way that is convenient for analysis. For example, we were surprised to discover that a large proportion of patches that have been marked as accepted are subsequently resubmitted by authors for further revision. We can also see that rejected patches are usually resubmitted, which might ease concerns that rejecting a borderline patch could cause it to be abandoned.

While the set of states in our patch lifecycle models of both WebKit and Firefox are the same, WebKit has fewer state transitions; this is because the WebKit project does not employ a "super-review" policy. Furthermore, unlike in Mozilla, there are no self-edges on the "Accepted" and "Rejected" states in WebKit; this is because Mozilla patches are often reviewed by two people, while WebKit patches receive only individual reviews. Finally, the WebKit model introduces a new edge between "Submitted" and "Resubmitted"; WebKit developers frequently "obsolete" their own patches and submit updates before they receive any reviews at all. One reason for this behavior is that submitted patches can be automatically validated by the external test system and developers can thus submit patches before they are to be reviewed to see if they fail any tests. All together, however, comparing the two patch lifecycles suggests that the WebKit and Firefox code review processes are fairly similar in practice.

4.4.3 BLINK

Blink's patch lifecycle is depicted in Figure 4.5, which shows that 40% of the submitted patches receive positive reviews, while only 0.3% of the submitted patches are rejected. Furthermore, a large portion of patches (40.4%) are resubmitted. This is because Blink developers often update their patches prior receiving any reviews; as with WebKit, this practice enables the patches to be automatically validated. At first glance, outright rejection does not seem to be part of the Blink code review practice; the *Rejected*

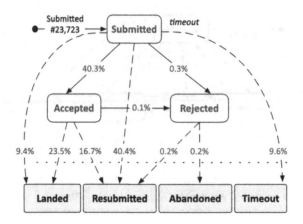

FIGURE 4.5

Blink's patch lifecycle.

state seems to under-represent the number of patches that have been actually rejected. In fact, reviewers often leave comments about patch improvements, before the patch is accepted.

The model also illustrates the iterative nature of the patch lifecycle, as patches are frequently "Resubmitted". The edge from "Submitted" to "Landed" represents patches that have been merged into Blink's source code repository, often after one or more rounds of updates. Developers often fix "nits" (minor changes) after their patch has been approved, and land the updated version of the patch without receiving additional explicit approval. The lifecycle also shows that nearly 10% of patches are being neglected by the reviewers (i.e., "Timeout" transition); "Timeout" patches in Blink can be considered as "informal" rejects.

Comparing the patch lifecycle models of WebKit and Blink, we noticed that Blink has fewer state transitions. In particular, the edges from the "Accepted" and "Rejected" back to "Submitted" are absent in Blink. Since Blink does not provide any indication of the review request on patches, we had to reverse engineer this information for all patches by considering the timestamps on each item (patch) in the series. We automated this process by putting the "Submitted" label to the patch at the time the patch was filed to the issue repository.

Blink also accepts a smaller portion of patches (about 40% of all contributions compared to the WebKit's 55% of submitted patches), but officially rejects less than 1%. "Timeouts" are more frequent for Blink patches than WebKit ones. Blink appears to exhibit a larger portion of patches being resubmitted (a 10% increase compared to the WebKit patches), including resubmissions after patches are successfully accepted (16.7%).

Finally, a new edge is introduced between "Submitted" and "Landed", accounting for those contributions that were committed to the code base without official approval from the reviewers; these cases typically represent patch updates. Both WebKit and Blink developers frequently "obsolete" their own patches and submit updates before they receive any reviews at all.

Comparing the two patch lifecycle models suggests that the WebKit and Blink code review processes are similar in practice; at the same time, it appears that Google's review policy may not be as strict as the one employed by Apple on the WebKit project.

4.5 OTHER APPLICATIONS

Software projects put considerable effort into defining and documenting organizational rules and processes. However, the prescribed processes are not always followed in practice. Lifecycle models provide practitioners with fact-based views about their projects (e.g., code review as described in this chapter). Supporting practitioners with better insights into their processes and systems, these models help them make better data-driven development decisions.

The lifecycle model is a flexible approach that can be used in a variety of software investigation tasks. For example:

- Issues: As developers work on issues their state changes. Common states here would include *NEW*, *ASSIGNED*, *WONTFIX*, *CLOSED*, although these may vary from project to project.
- Component/Priority assignments: Issues are often assigned to specific code components (and are given priority assignments). As an issue is triaged and worked upon these assignments can change.
- Source code: The evolutionary history of any line or block of source code can be considered capturing *Addition*, *Deletion*, and *Modification*. This data can be aggregated at the line, block, method, or class level.
- Discussions: Online discussions, e.g., those on StackOverflow, can have status of *CLOSED*, *UNANSWERED*, *REOPENED*, *DUPLICATE*, and *PROTECTED*.

4.6 CONCLUSION

In this chapter we introduced the lifecycle model data pattern. This pattern can be used to capture both common and exceptional cases in the evolution of software artifacts. We have applied it successfully to code review in Mozilla, WebKit, and Blink and have received positive feedback from Mozilla developers as they investigated their own code review processes. Lifecycle models can be easy to generate and interpret, making them practical for use in a wide variety of data modeling applications.

Software developers and managers make decisions based on the understanding they have of their software systems. This understanding is both built up experientially and through investigating various software development artifacts. While artifacts can be investigated individually, being able to summarize characteristics about a set of development artifacts can be useful. In this chapter we proposed artifact lifecycle models as an effective way to gain an understanding of certain development artifacts. Lifecycle models capture the dynamic nature of how various development artifacts change over time in a graphical form that can be easily understood and communicated. Lifecycle models enables reasoning of the underlying processes and dynamics of the artifacts being analyzed. We described how lifecycle models can be generated and demonstrated how they can be applied to the code review processes of three industrial projects.

REFERENCES

[1] Mozilla. Code review FAQ. June 2012. URL: https://developer.mozilla.org/en/Code_Review_FAQ.
[2] Asundi J, Jayant R. Patch review processes in open source software development communities: a comparative case study. In: Proceedings of the 40th annual Hawaii international conference on system sciences, HICSS '07; 2007. p. 166c.

[3] Nurolahzade M, Nasehi SM, Khandkar SH, Rawal S. The role of patch review in software evolution: an analysis of the Mozilla Firefox. In: Proceedings of the joint international and annual ERCIM workshops on principles of software evolution (IWPSE) and software evolution (Evol) workshops; 2009. p. 9–18.

[4] Rigby P, German D. A preliminary examination of code review processes in open source projects. Canada: University of Victoria, January 2006. Technical Report DCS-305-IR.

[5] Rigby PC, German DM, Storey MA. Open source software peer review practices: a case study of the apache server. In: Proceedings of the 30th international conference on software engineering; 2008. p. 541–50.

[6] Mozilla. Code review policy; June 2012. The-super-reviewers, URL: http://www.mozilla.org/hacking/reviewers.html#.

[7] MozillaWiki. Modules firefox; June 2012. URL: https://wiki.mozilla.org/Modules/Firefox.

[8] Baysal O, Kononenko O, Holmes R, Godfrey MW. The secret life of patches: a firefox case study. In: Proceedings of the 19th working conference on reverse engineering, WCRE '12; 2012. p. 447–55.

[9] Weissgerber P, Neu D, Diehl S. Small patches get in! In: Proceedings of the 2008 international working conference on mining software repositories; 2008. p. 67–76.

[10] Mozilla. The Mozilla development planning forum.

[11] Baysal O, Kononenko O, Holmes R, Godfrey MW. The influence of non-technical factors on code review. In: Proceedings of the 20th working conference on reverse engineering, WCRE '13; 2013.

A PRACTICAL GUIDE TO ANALYZING IDE USAGE DATA

5

Will Snipes*, Emerson Murphy-Hill†, Thomas Fritz‡, Mohsen Vakilian§, Kostadin Damevski¶,
Anil R. Nair‖, David Shepherd*

ABB Corporate Research, Raleigh, NC, USA* Computer Science, North Carolina State University, Raleigh, NC, USA†
Department of Informatics, University of Zurich, Zurich, Switzerland‡ University of Illinois at Urbana-Champaign,
Champaign, IL, USA§ Mathematics and Computer Science Department, Virginia State University, Peterburg, VA, USA¶
ABB Corporate Research, Bangalore, KN, India‖

CHAPTER OUTLINE

5.1 **INTRODUCTION**

As software development evolved, many developers began using integrated development environments (IDEs) to help manage the complexity of software programs. Modern IDEs such as Eclipse and Visual Studio include tools and capabilities to improve developer productivity by assisting with tasks such as navigating among classes and methods, continuous compilation, code refactoring, automated testing, and integrated debugging. The breadth of development activities supported by the IDE makes collecting editor, command, and tool usage data valuable for analyzing developers' work patterns.

Instrumenting the IDE involves extending the IDE within a provided application programming interface (API) framework. Eclipse and Visual Studio support a rich API framework allowing logging of many commands and actions as they occur. We discuss tools that leverage this API to observe all the commands developers use, developer actions within the editor such as browsing or inserting new code, and other add-in tools developers use. In Section 5.3, we provide a how-to guide for implementing tools that collect usage data from Eclipse or Visual Studio.

Collecting IDE usage data provides an additional view of how developers produce software to help advance the practice of software engineering. The most obvious application of usage data is to analyze how developers spend their time in the IDE by classifying the events in the usage log and tracking the time between each event. Through usage data analysis, we gain a better understanding of the developer's time allocation and can identify opportunities to save time such as reducing build time or improving source code search and navigation tools. Beyond time analysis, researchers have applied usage data to quantify developers' use of practices such as the study of types of refactoring by Murphy-Hill et al. [1], who found developers mostly perform minor refactoring while making other changes. In another example, Carter and Dewan [2] leveraged usage data to discover areas of the code where developers have difficulty with comprehension and should ask for assistance from more experienced developers. One study determined whether developers are doing test-driven development properly by writing the tests first then writing code that passes the tests, or are doing it improperly by writing tests against previously written code [3]. Maalej et al. [4] describe how to collect and process data for recommendation systems including tools and analysis methods, and they discuss important findings from developer usage data analysis. These works provide good examples of how usage data provides necessary information to answer interesting research questions in software engineering.

There are limits, however, to what IDE usage data can tell us. The missing elements include the developer's mental model of the code, and how developers intend to alter the code to suit new requirements. We must also separately obtain data on the developers' experience, design ideas, and constraints they keep in mind during an implementation activity.

Looking forward, we see usage data from development environments provides a platform for greater understanding of low-level developer practices. We expect to uncover more nuggets of how developers work to comprehend source code, how they perform mini trial-and-error experiments, and what might result in further productivity improvements for all developers.

5.2 USAGE DATA RESEARCH CONCEPTS

In this section we discuss the background on usage data research and provide motivation for analyzing usage data by describing what we can learn from it. With a review of goal-question-metric, we discuss how to focus usage data collection with specific research goals. To round out the concepts, we discuss additional considerations such as privacy and additional data sources that may be useful.

5.2.1 WHAT IS USAGE DATA AND WHY SHOULD WE ANALYZE IT?

We refer to the data about the interactions of software developers with an IDE as the *IDE usage data*, or simply *usage data*. The interactions include commands invoked, files viewed, mouse clicks, and add-on tools used.

Several stakeholders benefit from capturing and analyzing usage data. First, IDE vendors leverage the data to gain insight into ways to improve their product on the basis of how developers use the IDE in practice. Second, researchers both develop usage data collectors and conduct rigorous experiments to (1) make broader contributions to our understanding of developers' coding practices and (2) improve the state-of-the-art programming tools (e.g., debuggers and refactoring tools). Finally, developers benefit from the analysis conducted on the usage data because these analyses lead to more effective IDEs that make developers more productive.

At a high level, an IDE can be modeled as a complex state machine. In this model, a developer performs an action at each step that moves the IDE from one state to another. To capture usage data, researchers and IDE vendors have developed various usage data collectors (Section 5.3). Depending on the goals of the experiments, the usage data collector captures data about a subset of the IDE's state machine. While a combination of video recordings of the IDE with the keyboard strokes and mouse clicks of a developer would provide a fairly complete set of usage data, it is difficult to automatically analyze video data and therefore this is mostly limited to small laboratory studies and is not part of the usage data collectors developed.

An example of a usage data collection and analysis project with wide adoption in practice is the Mylyn project (previously known as Mylar). Mylyn started as a research project that later became part of Eclipse and it exhibits both of the advantages of understanding programmers' practices and improving tool support.

Mylyn created by Kersten and Murphy [5] was one of the first usage data collectors in IDEs. It was implemented as a plug-in for the Eclipse IDE and captured developers' navigation histories and their command invocations. For example, it records changes in selections, views, and perspectives as well as invocations of commands such as delete, copy, and automated refactoring. The Mylyn project now ships with the official distribution of Eclipse.

The Mylyn project has been used to collect and then analyze usage data to gather empirical evidence on the usage frequency of various features of Eclipse (see, e.g., [6]). In addition to collecting usage data, Mylyn introduces new features to the Eclipse IDE that leverage the usage data to provide a task-focused user interface and increase a developer's productivity [7]. In particular, Mylyn introduces the concept of a *task context*. A task context comprises a developer's interactions in the IDE that are related to the task, such as selections and edits of code entities (e.g., files, classes, and packages). Mylyn analyzes the interactions for a task and uses the information to surface relevant information with less clutter in various features, such as outline, navigation, and autocompletion. More information on collecting data from Mylyn is given in Section 5.3.2.

Later, Eclipse incorporated a system similar to Mylyn, called the Eclipse Usage Data Collector (UDC),[1] as part of the Eclipse standard distribution package for several years. UDC collected data from hundreds of thousands of Eclipse users every month. To the best of our knowledge, the UDC data set[2] is the largest set of IDE usage data that is publicly available. As described in [8, 9], several authors, including Vakilian and Johnson [10], Vakilian et al. [9], and Murphy-Hill et al. [1], mined this large data set to gain insight into programmers' practices and develop new tools that better fit programmers' practices. For more information on UDC, see Section 5.3.1 on using UDC to collect usage data from Eclipse.

Studies of automated refactoring are another example of interesting research results from analyzing usage data. Vakilian et al. [9] and Murphy-Hill et al. [1] analyzed the Eclipse UDC data, developed custom usage data collectors [11], and conducted survey and field studies [1, 10, 12] to gain more insight into programmers' use of the existing automated refactorings. Murphy-Hill et al. [1] and Negara et al. [12] found that programmers do not use the automated refactorings as much as refactoring experts expect. This finding motivated researchers to study the factors that lead to low adoption of automated refactorings [1, 11] and propose novel techniques for improving the usability of automated refactorings [1, 8, 13–17].

With this background on usage data collection and research based on usage data, we look next at how to define usage data collection requirements on the basis of your research goals.

5.2.2 SELECTING RELEVANT DATA ON THE BASIS OF A GOAL

Tailoring usage data collection to specific needs helps optimize the volume of data and privacy concerns when collecting information from software development applications. While the general solutions described in the next sections collect all events from the IDE, limiting the data collection to specific areas can make data collection faster and more efficient and reduce noise in the data collected. A process for defining the desired data can follow structures such as goal-question-metric defined by Basili and Rombach [18] that refines a high-level goal into specific metrics to be generated from data. For example, in the experiences gamifying software development study [19], we focused on the navigation practices of developers. The study tried to encourage developers to use structured navigation practices

---

[1]http://www.eclipse.org/epp/usagedata/.
[2]http://archive.eclipse.org/projects/usagedata/.

(navigating source code by using commands and tools that follow dependency links and code structure models). In that study, we defined a subset of the available data on the basis of a goal-question-metric structure as follows:

- Goal: Assess and compare the use of structured navigation by developers in our study.
- Possible question(s)
  What is the frequency of navigation commands developers use when modifying source code?
  What portion of navigation commands developers use are structured navigation rather than unstructured navigation?
- Metric: The navigation ratio is the ratio of the number of structured navigation commands to the number of unstructured navigation commands used by a developer in a given time period (e.g., a day).

The specific way to measure the navigation ratio from usage data needs further refinement to determine how the usage monitor can identify these actions from available events in the IDE. Assessing commands within a time duration (e.g., a day) requires, for instance, that we collect a timestamp for each command. Simply using the timestamp to stratify the data according to time is then a straightforward conversion from the timestamp to the data and grouping the events by the day. Similarly the timestamp can be converted to the hour to look at events grouped by the hour of any given day. Calculating the duration or elapsed time for a command or set of commands adds new requirements to monitoring—specifically, the need to collect events such as window visibility events from the operating system that relate to when the application or IDE is being used and when it is in the background or closed.

5.2.3 PRIVACY CONCERNS

Usage data can be useful; however, there are some privacy concerns your developers might and often have regarding the data collection and who the data is shared with. These privacy concerns arise mainly since the data collected may expose individual developers or it may expose parts of the source code companies are working on. How you handle information privacy in data collection affects what you can learn from the data during analysis (see Section 5.4).

To minimize privacy concerns about the data collected, steps such as encrypting sensitive pieces of information, for instance, by using a one-way hash-function can be taken. Hashing sensitive names, such as developer names, window titles, filenames or source code identifiers, provides a way to obfuscate the data and reduce the risk of information allowing identification of the developers or the projects and code they are working on. While this obfuscation makes it more difficult to analyze the exact practices, using a one-way hash-function will still allow differentiation between distinct developers, even if the remain anonymous.

Maintaining developer privacy is important, but there may be questions for which you need the ground truth that confirms what you observe in the usage data. Thus, you may need to know who is contributing data so you can ask that person questions that establish the ground truth. A privacy policy statement helps participants and developers be more confident in sharing information with you when they know they can be identified by the information. The policy statement should specifically state who will have access to the data and what they will do with it. Limiting statements such as not reporting data at the individual level helps to reduce a developer's privacy concerns.

5.2.4 STUDY SCOPE

Small studies that examine a variety of data can generate metrics that you can apply to data collected in bigger studies where the additional information might not be available. For instance, Robillard et al. [20] defined a metric on structured navigation in their observational study on how developers discover relevant code elements during maintenance. This metric can now be used in a larger industrial study setting in which structured navigation command usage is collected as usage data, even without the additional information Robillard et al. gathered for their study.

Finally, and most importantly, usage data may not be enough to definitively solve a problem or inquiry. While usage data tells us what a developer is doing in the IDE, it usually leaves gaps in the story (see Section 5.5). Augmenting usage data with additional data sources such as developer feedback, task descriptions, and change histories (see Section 5.4.7) can fill in the details necessary to understand user behavior.

Now that we have discussed aspects to consider, we are ready to dig deeper into the specifics on how to collect data from developer IDEs. The next section covers several options for tooling that collects usage data from IDEs.

5.3 HOW TO COLLECT DATA

There are many options for collecting usage data from IDEs. Existing tools can provide solutions for commonly used IDEs, and some support collecting data from additional sources. Another way to start is to study data collected in previous projects such as data available in the Eclipse archive for UDC data. This archive contains a wealth of data collected by UDC when UDC was integrated with each Eclipse version in 2009 and 2010. The data is currently available at http://archive.eclipse.org/projects/usagedata/.

You may have more specific questions than those that can be answered with the UDC data or you may need to collect usage data for a specific experiment. In this section we discuss details on how to use existing data collection tools for Eclipse, including UDC, Mylyn Monitor, and CodingSpectator (Section 5.3.3). Then we will walk through creating a usage data collection extension to Microsoft Visual Studio. Before we go into the details, we provide an overview of some existing frameworks.

Eclipse: UDC, discussed in Section 5.3.1, collects commands executed in the environment and editors and views that are invoked.

Eclipse: Mylyn Monitor, described in Section 5.3.2, collects task-oriented events and information about what code elements the programmers work with.

Eclipse: CodingSpectator , discussed in Section 5.3.3, focuses on refactoring actions and the context in which they are taken.

Visual Studio: Section 5.3.4 describes in detail how to build your own Visual Studio extension that collects all command events from the IDE.

Visual Studio: CodeAlike[3] is a Visual Studio extension for personal analytics and research of usage data related to coding efficiency.

---

[3]https://codealike.com.

Table 5.1 A Summary of the Four Tools Discussed in Depth in This Section			
Tool Name	**Advantages**	**Disadvantages**	**Examples**
Eclipse Usage Data Collector	Well tested, widely deployed	Collects data only on tools; sometimes missing data	[26–28]
Mylyn Monitor	Collects data both about tools and the program elements the tools are used on	No details about code beyond element names collected	[7, 29, 30]
CodingSpectator	Very detailed information collected	Information collected largely customized to observe usage of refactoring tools	[11, 21, 31]
Build-Your-Own for Visual Studio	A high degree of customizability. One of the few Visual Studio monitoring tools	Extra work required to collect a wider variety of events	[19]

Eclipse: CodingTracker, created by Negara et al. [21], is a usage data collector for the Eclipse IDE that records every character insertion and deletion. CodingTracker records the code edits so accurately that it can later replay them to show the changes in action. CodingTracker has been used to conduct empirical studies and accurately infer high-level changes such as refactorings [12].
Eclipse: Fluorite, created by Yoon and Myers [22], is an Eclipse-based tool that captures usage data such as invoked commands, typed characters, cursor movements, and text selections. Fluorite has been used to study programmers' backtracking strategies in [23] and visualizing code histories in [24].
Eclipse and Visual Studio: Hackystat, created by Johnson et al. [25], provides a framework to collect usage data from many sources.

The remainder of this section discusses in detail how to implement the top four tools from the list above. Where the section describes code, listings are provided that are based on the open source code available on GitHub (https://github.com/wbsnipes/AnalyzingUsageDataExamples). In Table 5.1, we summarize the advantages and disadvantages of each of the four tools we discuss in this chapter, as well as example papers that reported use of these tools.

5.3.1 ECLIPSE USAGE DATA COLLECTOR

This section outlines how to collect IDE usage data using Eclipse's UDC. The UDC framework was originally build by the Eclipse Foundation as a way to measure how the community was using the Eclipse IDE. While UDC was included in official Eclipse releases and data was collected from hundreds of thousands of Eclipse users between 2008 and 2011, the project was eventually shut down, and UDC was removed from official Eclipse releases. However, the source code for UDC remains available for collecting data.

5.3.1.1 Collected data

The Eclipse UDC records the following types of Eclipse information:

- The run-time environment, such as the operating system and Java virtual machine
- Environment data, such as which bundles are loaded and when Eclipse starts up and shuts down
- Actions and commands that are executed, via menus, buttons, toolbars, and hotkeys
- Views, editors, and perspectives that are invoked

Let us look at an example of an event that UDC produces on a developer's machine:

what	kind	bundleId	bundleVersion	description	time
executed	command	org.eclipse.ui	3.7.0.v20110928-1505	org.eclipse.ui.edit.paste	1389111843130

The first column tells us what kind of thing happened—in this case, something was executed. The second column tells us what was executed—in this case, a command. The third column tells us the name of the bundle (a set of resources and code installed in Eclipse) this event belonged to—in this case, Eclipse's user interface bundle. The fourth column gives us the version of the bundle. The fifth column tells us the name of the command that was executed—in this case, paste. The final column, a Unix timestamp that tells us when the command was executed, in Greenwich Mean Time—in this case, January 7, 2014 at 16:24:03 Greenwich Mean Time.

5.3.1.2 Limitations

Apart from the general limitations in collecting usage data (Section 5.5), one significant limitation of UDC that we have found is that sometimes it has unexpectedly incomplete data. For example, in planning a study involving when people ran their JUnit tests, we found that UDC recorded an event when the "Run > Run As > Run as JUnit Test" menu item was selected, but not when the "Run As" button was pressed on the toolbar. We suspect that the reason has to do with how different user interface accordances invoke the same functionality. In general, when you are planning to perform a study with UDC, be sure to know what types of events you are looking for, and test them to make sure UDC captures those events.

5.3.1.3 How to use it

Collecting usage data is fairly straightforward with Eclipse UDC, and we describe how to do so here. We also provide an accompanying screencast that shows the basics.[4]

Gathering data using the UDC client

Let us talk about how data is collected on a developer's machine. Since UDC was last included in the Eclipse Indigo SR2 release,[5] if you have the option of which Eclipse version to use, we recommend you use that version. By default, UDC starts collecting data when Eclipse is started. You can verify this by going to "Windows > Preferences," then select the "Usage Data Collector" item (Figure 5.1). The *Enable capture* option should be checked.

Before looking at the data, execute a few commands and open a few views in Eclipse. Then, on your file system, open the following path as a subdirectory of your current workspace (Figure 5.2):

.metadata /. plugins /org. eclipse .epp.usagedata. recording

---

[4]http://youtu.be/du4JTc9UB-g.
[5]http://www.eclipse.org/downloads/packages/release/indigo/sr2.

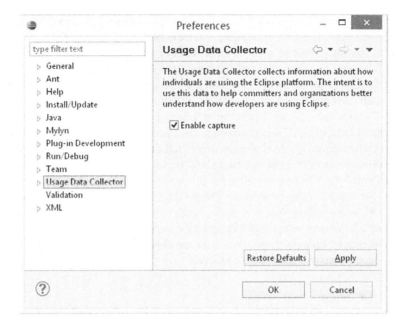

FIGURE 5.1

Eclipse UDC preference page.

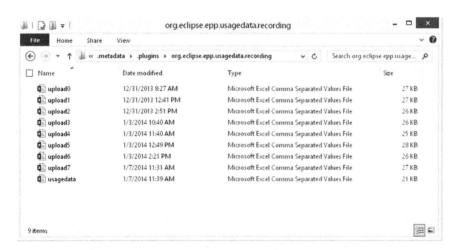

FIGURE 5.2

UDC data files.

In that folder, depending on how many UDC events have been gathered, a number of comma-separated value (CSV) files will appear, where upload0.csv is the oldest and usagedata.csv is the newest. Open usagedata.csv—you should notice a large number and a large variety of events. Be sure to look specifically for events that you executed and views that you opened earlier.

Before doing a study, be aware that Eclipse will ask you and periodically attempt to upload data to the Eclipse Foundation server. You should *not* allow it to do this, because each time data is uploaded, the underlying CSV files are deleted. Furthermore, because the UDC project is no longer officially supported, the official Eclipse UDC server no longer accepts the data, so your usage data is, in effect, lost permanently. Unfortunately, there is no easy way to tell the UDC client to permanently store usage data. An easy work-around is to increase the upload period to allow enough time to complete the experiment(see Figure 5.3). The long-term fix for this issue is to either use some other tool, such as CodingSpectator (Section 5.3.3), to periodically submit the UDC data to your servers, or to modify the source code of UDC, as we will explain how to do shortly, to never upload data.

If you are doing a laboratory experiment, collecting data should be simply a matter of copying and deleting the CSV files after each participant has done the experiment. You can concatenate each file to the previous file, or put them in a database for analysis.

Modifying the UDC client
You may wish to modify the UDC client yourself, perhaps to add a custom filter for events or to disable data uploading. Whatever the reason, making modifications to the client is fairly easy.

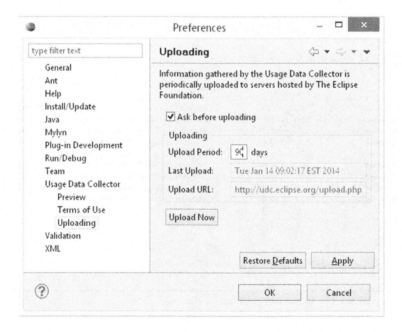

FIGURE 5.3

Changing the UDC upload frequency.

The first step is to check out the UDC source code into your Eclipse workspace using git.[6] Here we will again use Eclipse Indigo SR2, but we will specifically be using the "Eclipse for RCP and RAP Developers" download package because we will modify Eclipse plug-ins. Before you import the necessary plug-ins, we recommend your switching to the Indigo SR2 tag, to ensure compatibility with Eclipse. To do so, clone the git repository[7] locally, open up "Tags," right click on "Indigo SR 2," and then choose "Checkout."

To import the projects into Eclipse, right click on the repository, then click on "Import Projects," then click on "Import Existing Projects." The three core projects to import are as follows:

```
1  org. eclipse .epp. usagedata. internal . gathering
2  org. eclipse .epp. usagedata. internal . recording
3  org. eclipse .epp. usagedata. internal . ui
```

Next, we recommend a quick smoke test to determine whether you can actually make changes to the UDC client. Open `UsageDataRecordingSettings.java`, then modify the value of `UPLOAD_URL_DEFAULT` to `"my_changed_server"`. Then, create a new debug configuration that is an Eclipse Application, and press "Debug" (Figure 5.4). Finally, you can verify that your change

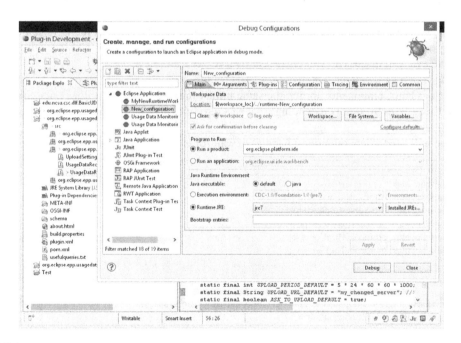

FIGURE 5.4

Debugging the UDC client.

---

[6]http://git-scm.com/.

[7]http://git.eclipse.org/c/epp/org.eclipse.epp.usagedata.git/.

worked by going to UDC's Uploading preference page, noticing that the Upload URL is now "my_changed_server."

From here, you can make any changes to the UDC client that you wish. One thing you may want to do is upgrade UDC to work with more recent versions of Eclipse. The code is likely currently out of date because it has not been maintained since the UDC project was shut down. Another thing you may wish to do is to make available your new version of UDC via an Eclipse update site to the developers you want to study. There are many resources on the Web for plug-in deployment instructions, such as Lars Vogel's tutorial on creating plug-ins.[8]

Transmitting data over the Internet

If you do not plan on doing a laboratory study where you can manually collect UDC usage files, you will want to have the UDC client send the data to you directly. As already mentioned, the best way to do this is probably by changing the default server URL in the client source code. An easy way to change the server when debugging is by adding the following Java virtual machine arguments:

```
1  -Dorg.eclipse.epp.usagedata.recording.upload-url=http://localhost:8080
```

However, simply changing the client to point at a new URL is insufficient, because there actually has to be a working server at that URL ready to receive UDC data. While the source code of the official Eclipse server was not officially made available, Wayne Beaton from the Eclipse Foundation unofficially released some of the PHP code from the Eclipse Foundation's server.[9] Since our PHP skills are rusty, next we will discuss how to create our own server using Java.

Creating your own server that receives UDC data is fairly straightforward. Let us create a simple one using Apache's HttpComponents library, the same library that UDC uses to upload data. Specifically, we can create a server by simply extending Apache's tutorial Web server.[10] You can find this server in our GitHub repository.[11]

First, we will need a generic request handler to wait for HTTP connections:

```
1  import java.io.IOException;
2  import org.apache.http.ConnectionClosedException;
3  import org.apache.http.HttpException;
4  import org.apache.http.HttpServerConnection;
5  import org.apache.http.protocol.BasicHttpContext;
6  import org.apache.http.protocol.HttpContext;
7  import org.apache.http.protocol.HttpService;
8
9  /**
10  * Based on
11  * http://hc.apache.org/httpcomponents-core-ga/httpcore/examples/org/apache
12  * /http/examples/ElementalHttpServer.java
13  */
14  class WorkerThread extends Thread {
```

---

[8]http://www.vogella.com/tutorials/EclipsePlugIn/article.html#deployplugin_tutorial.

[9]https://bugs.eclipse.org/bugs/show_bug.cgi?id=221104.

[10]http://hc.apache.org/httpcomponents-core-ga/httpcore/examples/org/apache/http/examples/ElementalHttpServer.java.

[11]https://github.com/wbsnipes/AnalyzingUsageDataExamples.

```
15
16          private  final  HttpService  httpservice ;
17          private  final  HttpServerConnection conn;
18
19          public  WorkerThread( final  HttpService  httpservice ,  final  HttpServerConnection conn) {
20                  super () ;
21                  this . httpservice  =  httpservice ;
22                  this .conn = conn;
23          }
24
25          @Override
26          public  void  run () {
27                  System.out. println (”New connection thread”);
28                  HttpContext  context  = new BasicHttpContext( null );
29                  try {
30                          while  (! Thread. interrupted () && this.conn.isOpen()) {
31                                  this . httpservice .handleRequest( this .conn,  context );
32                          }
33                  } catch  (ConnectionClosedException ex) {
34                          System.err . println (”Client closed  connection”);
35                  } catch  (IOException ex) {
36                          System.err . println (”I/O error :  ” + ex.getMessage());
37                  } catch  (HttpException ex) {
38                          System.err . println (”Unrecoverable HTTP protocol violation :  ” + ex.getMessage());
39                  } finally  {
40                          try {
41                                  this .conn.shutdown();
42                          } catch  (IOException ignore ) {
43                          }
44                  }
45          }
46 }
```

We will also need a generic request listener:

```
1 import java . io .IOException;
2 import java . io . InterruptedIOException ;
3 import java . net . ServerSocket ;
4 import java . net . Socket ;
5
6 import org.apache. http . HttpConnectionFactory ;
7 import org.apache. http . HttpServerConnection ;
8 import org.apache. http . impl . DefaultBHttpServerConnection ;
9 import org.apache. http . impl . DefaultBHttpServerConnectionFactory ;
10 import org.apache. http . protocol . HttpService ;
11
12 /**
13  * Based on
14  * http :// hc.apache.org/httpcomponents−core−ga/httpcore/examples/org/apache
15  * / http /examples/ElementalHttpServer .java
16  */
17 class  RequestListenerThread  extends  Thread {
```

```
18
19          private  final  HttpConnectionFactory<DefaultBHttpServerConnection> connFactory;
20          private  final  ServerSocket  serversocket ;
21          private  final  HttpService  httpService ;
22
23          public  RequestListenerThread ( final  int  port ,  final  HttpService  httpService )
24                          throws  IOException {
25                  this .connFactory  =  DefaultBHttpServerConnectionFactory .INSTANCE;
26                  this . serversocket  = new ServerSocket( port );
27                  this . httpService  =  httpService ;
28          }
29
30          @Override
31          public  void  run () {
32                  System.out. println ("Listening  on  port  " + this . serversocket . getLocalPort ());
33                  while  (!Thread. interrupted ()) {
34                          try {
35                                  // Set  up  HTTP  connection
36                                  Socket  socket  =  this . serversocket . accept ();
37                                  System.out. println ("Incoming connection from" + socket.getInetAddress ());
38                                  HttpServerConnection  conn  =  this .connFactory. createConnection ( socket );
39
40                                  // Start  worker  thread
41                                  Thread  t  = new WorkerThread(this. httpService ,  conn);
42                                  t .setDaemon(true);
43                                  t . start ();
44                          } catch  ( InterruptedIOException  ex) {
45                                  break ;
46                          } catch  (IOException e) {
47                                  System.err . println ("I/O error   initialising   connection  thread :  " +
                                              e.getMessage());
48                                  break ;
49                          }
50                  }
51          }
52  }
```

And finally, we will need the guts of our server:

```
1  import java . io .IOException;
2  import org.apache. http . HttpEntityEnclosingRequest ;
3  import org.apache. http .HttpException ;
4  import org.apache. http .HttpRequest;
5  import org.apache. http .HttpResponse;
6  import org.apache. http . protocol .HttpContext ;
7  import org.apache. http . protocol . HttpProcessor ;
8  import org.apache. http . protocol . HttpProcessorBuilder ;
9  import org.apache. http . protocol .HttpRequestHandler;
10 import org.apache. http . protocol . HttpService ;
11 import org.apache. http . protocol .ResponseConnControl;
12 import org.apache. http . protocol .ResponseContent;
13 import org.apache. http . protocol .ResponseDate;
```

```
14  import org.apache.http . protocol .ResponseServer;
15  import org.apache.http . protocol .UriHttpRequestHandlerMapper;
16  import org.apache.http . util . EntityUtils ;
17
18  /**
19   * Based on
20   * http :// hc.apache.org/httpcomponents−core−ga/httpcore/examples/org/apache
21   * / http /examples/ElementalHttpServer . java
22   */
23  public class BasicUDCServer {
24
25          public  static  void main(String [] args ) throws IOException {
26
27          int  port  = 8080;
28
29          HttpProcessor  httpproc  = HttpProcessorBuilder . create ()
30                      .add(new ResponseDate()).add(new ResponseServer())
31                      .add(new ResponseContent().add(new ResponseConnControl()).build () ;
32
33          UriHttpRequestHandlerMapper reqistry  = new UriHttpRequestHandlerMapper();
34          reqistry . register ("*", new HttpRequestHandler() {
35
36                  public  void handle(HttpRequest request , HttpResponse response,
37                              HttpContext  context ) throws HttpException , IOException {
38
39                          HttpEntityEnclosingRequest  entityRequest =
40                              ( HttpEntityEnclosingRequest ) request ;
41
42                          String  userID = request .getHeaders("USERID")[0].getValue();
43                          String  workspaceID = request .getHeaders("WORKSPACEID")[0].getValue();
44                          long  time = Long.parseLong(request .getHeaders("TIME")[0].getValue());
45
46                          System.out. println (userID + "," + workspaceID + "," + time);
47                              System.out. println ( EntityUtils . toString ( entityRequest . getEntity ( ) ));
48                  }
49          });
50
51          HttpService  httpService  = new HttpService( httpproc ,  reqistry );
52
53          Thread t  = new RequestListenerThread(port ,  httpService );
54          t .setDaemon(false );
55          t . start () ;
56      }
57  }
```

When this server is running and it receives a UDC upload, it will print a UserId, WorkspaceId, and the time of the upload. UserIds are randomly generated on the client side and are stored in a file in the developer's home directory. As long as that file remains intact, future uploads from that developer will contain that UserId. WorkspaceIds are identifiers contained in each workspace, and can be used to uniquely (but anonymously) identify which workspace a set of data is uploaded from. Thus, there is normally only one UserId per computer, but there can be multiple WorkspaceIds per computer.

While there is some coding involved, setting up the UDC for Eclipse can provide thorough usage data collection for a project using Eclipse. For laboratory studies, not much setup is required. For larger or distributed studies, some infrastructure (a Web server) and code (the UDC data server) are required. Next we look at Mylyn and the Eclipse Mylyn Monitor component, which collects tool data like UDC, but also includes information about what program elements the programmer is working with.

5.3.2 MYLYN AND THE ECLIPSE MYLYN MONITOR

Kersten and Murphy [7] created Mylyn, a task-focused user interface, a top-level project of the Eclipse IDE that is part of many of the Eclipse IDE configurations. To better support developers in managing and working on multiple tasks, Mylyn makes tasks a first class entity, monitors a developer's interaction with the IDE for each task, and logs it in a so-called *task context*.

The first versions of Mylyn, originally called Mylar, were developed as part of the PhD research of Mik Kersten, and contained an explicit Mylyn Monitor component to collect and upload a developer's activity within the Eclipse IDE. While the source code of the Mylyn Monitor can still be found online, it is not an active part of the Mylyn project anymore.

5.3.2.1 Data collected

Mylyn captures three types of developer interactions with the Eclipse development environment:

1. The *selection* of elements.
2. The *editing* of elements.
3. *Commands* in the IDE, such as saving or refactoring commands.

These interaction events are monitored and then stored in XML format in a log file. An interaction event log example of a developer selecting a Java class `TaskEditorBloatMonitor.java` in the package explorer of the Eclipse IDE is as follows:

```
1   <InteractionEvent
2       StructureKind="java"
3       StructureHandle="=org.eclipse.mylyn.tasks.ui/src&lt;org.eclipse.mylyn.
4           internal.tasks.ui{TaskEditorBloatMonitor.java"
5       StartDate="2012-04-10 02:05:53.451 CEST"
6       OriginId="org.eclipse.jdt.ui.PackageExplorer"
7       Navigation="null"
8       Kind="selection"
9       Interest="1.0"
10      EndDate="2012-04-10 02:05:53.451 CEST"
11      Delta="null"
12  />
```

The log entry contains among other information the kind of interaction event, in this case a selection, the full identifier of the element the developer interacted with, a Java type called TaskEditorBloatMonitor, the time when the interaction event occurred, in this case October 4, 2012, at

02:05:52 Central European Summer Time (CEST), and the place where the interaction event occurred, in this case the package explorer view of Eclipse.

You may notice that the log also contains an interest value, in this case 1.0. This value is used by Mylyn to calculate the interest a developer shows in a code element, the so-called degree of interest. The degree of interest of a code element, such as a class, method, or field, is based on the recency and frequency of interactions while working on a task. The more frequent and recent a developer selected and/or edited a code element, the higher the degree of interest. This degree-of-interest value is then used to highlight and/or filter elements in views of the IDE (see [7, 32]).

5.3.2.2 Logging interactions with the Mylyn Monitor

While the code for the Mylyn Monitor is not part of the active Mylyn project anymore, the code for the monitor and example code for using it can be found in the Incubator project online.[12, 13] In the following, we will present relevant parts of the code from these examples to log the interactions.

To be able to use the Mylyn Monitor code and log the events of interest, there are two important classes you have to implement. First, you will need a plug-in class that extends the following plug-in:

```
1  org.eclipse.ui.plugin.AbstractUIPlugin
```

Then, add a listener for the events that you are interested in to

```
1  org.eclipse.mylyn.internal.monitor.ui.MonitorUiPlugin
```

Second, you will need to write the listener that creates the interaction event objects when an interaction event occurs. Let us assume you want to write a listener for selections of Java elements in the IDE. In this case you can extend the class `org.eclipse.mylyn.monitor.ui.AbstractUserInteractionMonitor` and simply override the `selectionChanged` method. By extending the `AbstractUserInteractionMonitor`, you will automatically add your listener as a postselection listener to all windows in the current workbench so that all selection events in the windows are forwarded to your listener. The relevant code for the `selectionChanged` method is as follows:

```
1  /**
2   * Based on
3   * http://git.eclipse.org/c/mylyn/org.eclipse.mylyn.incubator.git/tree/
4   * org.eclipse.mylyn.examples.monitor.study/src/org/eclipse/mylyn/examples/
5   * monitor/study/SelectionMonitor.java
6   */
7  import org.eclipse.jface.viewers.ISelection;
8  import org.eclipse.jface.viewers.StructuredSelection;
9  import org.eclipse.mylyn.monitor.core.InteractionEvent;
10 import org.eclipse.jdt.core.IJavaElement;
11
12 ...
13
14     @Override
```

---

[12]http://git.eclipse.org/c/mylyn/org.eclipse.mylyn.incubator.git/tree/.
[13]http://wiki.eclipse.org/Mylyn_Integrator_Reference#Monitor_API.

```
15    public void selectionChanged(IWorkbenchPart part, ISelection selection) {
16            InteractionEvent.Kind interactionKind = InteractionEvent.Kind.SELECTION;
17            if (selection instanceof StructuredSelection) {
18                    StructuredSelection structuredSelection = (StructuredSelection) selection;
19                    Object selectedObject = structuredSelection.getFirstElement();
20                    if (selectedObject == null) {
21                            return;
22                    }
23
24                    if (selectedObject instanceof IJavaElement) {
25                            IJavaElement javaElement = (IJavaElement) selectedObject;
26                            structureKind = STRUCTURE_KIND_JAVA;
27                            elementHandle = javaElement.getHandleIdentifier();
28                    }
29            }
30
31            ...
32
33            InteractionEvent event = new InteractionEvent(interactionKind, structureKind,
34                            elementHandle, ...);
35            MonitorUiPlugin.getDefault().notifyInteractionObserved(event);
36    }
37
38  ...
```

The code first checks what type the selection has. If the selection is structured, and the first part of it is a Java Element, it collects the relevant information, and then creates an `InteractionEvent` with the information gathered, such as the interaction kind, the structure kind, and the element handle. At the end of the method, the `MonitorUiPlugin` is notified about the observed interaction event. The `MonitorUiPlugin` will then go through all registered interaction event listeners and forward the event to them. Since there is an `InteractionEventLogger` registered as part of the Mylyn code, the interaction event object will be forwarded to the logger and then written out into a file.

5.3.3 CODINGSPECTATOR

CodingSpectator[14] is an extensible framework for collecting Eclipse usage data. Although researchers at the University of Illinois at Urbana-Champaign developed CodingSpectator primarily for collecting detailed data about the use of the Eclipse refactoring tool, it also provides a reusable infrastructure for *submitting usage data* from developers to a central repository. CodingTracker,[15] described by Negara et al. [12, 21], is another data collector developed at the University of Illinois at Urbana-Champaign, and collects finer-grained IDE actions while reusing the data submission infrastructure provided by CodingSpectator.

---

[14]http://codingspectator.cs.illinois.edu/.
[15]http://codingtracker.web.engr.illinois.edu/.

5.3.3.1 Data collected

CodingSpectator was designed for capturing detailed data about the use of automated refactorings. It collects three kinds of refactoring events: `canceled`, `performed`, and `unavailable`. If a programmer starts an automated refactoring but quits it before it finishes, CodingSpectator records a `canceled` refactoring event. If a programmer applies an automated refactoring, CodingSpectator records a `performed` refactoring event. Finally, if a programmer invokes an automated refactoring but the IDE refuses to start the automated refactoring, indicating that the refactoring is not applicable to the selected program element, CodingSpectator records an `unavailable` refactoring event.

Eclipse creates a *refactoring descriptor* object for each `performed` refactoring event and serializes it in an XML file. CodingSpectator saves more data in Eclipse refactoring descriptors of `performed` refactorings. In addition, it creates and serializes refactoring descriptors for canceled and `unavailable` refactoring events. CodingSpectator supports 23 of the 33 automated refactorings that Eclipse supports.

We show a concrete example of the data that CodingSpectator collects for an invocation of the automated Extract Method refactoring in Eclipse, which extracts a piece of code into a new method. This refactoring moves a selected piece of code into a new method and replaces the selected code by an invocation to the new method. To use the automated Extract Method refactoring, a programmer has to go through multiple steps. First, the programmer selects a piece of code (Figure 5.5). Second, the programmer invokes the automated Extract Method and configures it (Figure 5.6). In this case, the programmer sets the name of the new method. The configuration page provides a number of other options, including method accessibility, the ordering and names of method parameters, and the generation of method comments. Third, after configuring the refactoring, the programmer hits the "Preview" button, and the automated refactoring reports the problems that the refactoring may introduce (Figure 5.7). In this example, the automated refactoring complains that the selected name

```
package org.elasticsearch.action.support.single.custom;

import org.elasticsearch.action.ActionRequestBuilder;
/**
 */
public abstract class SingleCustomOperationRequestBuilder<Request extends SingleCustomOperationRequest<Request>, Response extends ActionResponse
        extends ActionRequestBuilder<Request, Response, RequestBuilder> {

    protected SingleCustomOperationRequestBuilder(InternalGenericClient client, Request request) {
        super(client, request);
    }

    /**
     * Controls if the operation will be executed on a separate thread when executed locally.
     */
    @SuppressWarnings("unchecked")
    public final RequestBuilder setOperationThreaded(boolean threadedOperation) {
        request.operationThreaded(threadedOperation);
        return (RequestBuilder) this;
    }

    /**
     * if this operation hits a node with a local relevant shard, should it be preferred
     * to be executed on, or just do plain round robin. Defaults to <tt>true</tt>
     */
    @SuppressWarnings("unchecked")
    public final RequestBuilder setPreferLocal(boolean preferLocal) {
        request.preferLocal(preferLocal);
        return (RequestBuilder) this;
    }
}
```

FIGURE 5.5

A programmer selects a piece of code to extract into a new method. The selected code is part of the class SingleCustomOperationRequestBuilder from commit bdb1992 of the open-source Elasticsearch project (https://github.com/elasticsearch/elasticsearch).

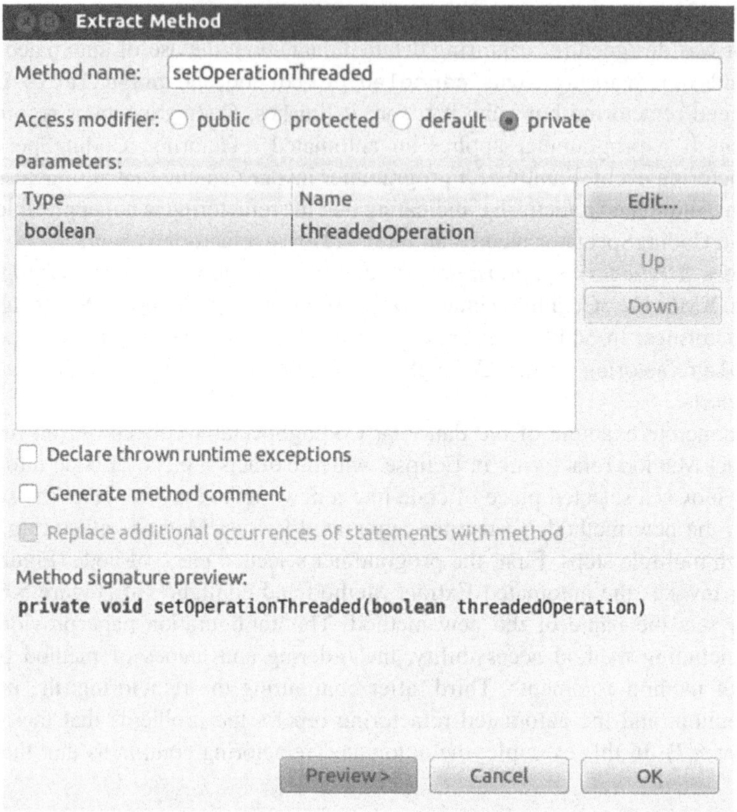

FIGURE 5.6

A programmer configures an automated Extract Method refactoring by entering the desired name of the new method.

of the new method conflicts with the name of an existing method. Finally, the programmer decides to cancel the refactoring, and CodingSpectator records a refactoring descriptor for this `canceled` refactoring, as shown in Figure 5.8. The type of refactoring event (i.e., `unavailable`, `canceled`, or `performed`) can be inferred from the directory in which the XML file containing the refactoring descriptor resides. CodingSpectator captures the following attributes for the canceled automated Extract Method refactoring in the above example:

1. `captured-by-codingspectator`: indicates that CodingSpectator created the refactoring descriptor.
2. `stamp`: a timestamp recording when the refactoring event occurred.
3. `code-snippet`, `selection`, `selection-in-code-snippet`, `selection-text`: the location and contents of the selection that the programmer made before invoking the automated refactoring.
4. `id`: the automated refactoring's identifier.

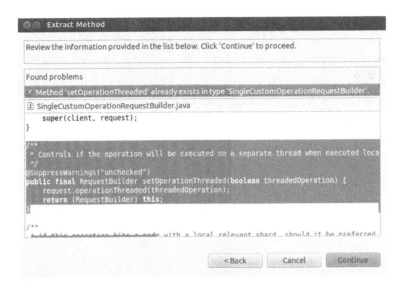

FIGURE 5.7

The Extract Method refactoring reports a name conflict problem to the programmer. The programmer can ignore the problem and continue the refactoring, go back to the configuration page to provide a different name, or cancel the refactoring.

5. `comment, description, comments, destination, exceptions, flags, input, name, visibility`: configuration options—for example, input elements, project, and settings that programmers can set to control the effect of the refactoring.
6. `status`: any problems reported by the automated refactoring to the programmer.
7. `navigation-history`: when the programmer pressed a button to navigate from one page of the refactoring wizard to another.
8. `invoked-through-structured-selection, invoked-by-quick-assist`: selection method (e.g., structured or textual selection and whether the automated refactoring was invoked using Quick Assist.

5.3.3.2 Deploying CodingSpectator

Deploying CodingSpectator consists of two main steps: (1) setting up a Subversion repository and (2) setting up an Eclipse update site.

1. **Setting up a Subversion repository.** CodingSpectator regularly submits developers' data to a central Subversion repository. To collect CodingSpectator's data automatically, you need to set up a Subversion repository and create accounts for your developers. To allow the developers to submit their data to the Subversion repository, you should grant them appropriate write accesses to the repository.

Node	Content
?-? xml	version="1.0" encoding="UTF-8"
▼ ⓔ session	
ⓐ version	1.0
▼ ⓔ refactoring	
ⓐ captured-by-codingspectator	true

ⓐ code-snippet	`/**`
	`*/`
	`public abstract class SingleCustomOperationRequestBuilder<Request extends SingleCustomOperationReque`
	  `extends ActionRequestBuilder<Request, Response, RequestBuilder> {`
	
	  `protected SingleCustomOperationRequestBuilder(InternalGenericClient client, Request request) {`
	    `super(client, request);`
	  `}`
	
	  `/**`
	  `* Controls if the operation will be executed on a separate thread when executed locally.`
	  `*/`
	  `@SuppressWarnings("unchecked")`
	  `public final RequestBuilder setOperationThreaded(boolean threadedOperation) {`
	    `request.operationThreaded(threadedOperation);`
	    `return (RequestBuilder) this;`
	  `}`
	
	  `/**`
	  `* if this operation hits a node with a local relevant shard, should it be preferred`
	  `* to be executed on, or just do plain round robin. Defaults to <tt>true</tt>`
	  `*/`
	  `@SuppressWarnings("unchecked")`
	  `public final RequestBuilder setPreferLocal(boolean preferLocal) {`
	    `request.preferLocal(preferLocal);`
	    `return (RequestBuilder) this;`
	  `}`
	`}`

ⓐ comment	Extract method 'private void setOperationThreaded(boolean threadedOperation)' from 'org.elasticsearch.ac - Original project: 'elasticsearch' - Method name: 'setOperationThreaded' - Destination type: 'org.elasticsearch.action.support.single.custom.SingleCustomOperationRequestBuilder' - Declared visibility: 'private'
ⓐ comments	false
ⓐ description	Extract method 'setOperationThreaded'
ⓐ destination	0
ⓐ exceptions	false
ⓐ flags	786434
ⓐ id	org.eclipse.jdt.ui.extract.method
ⓐ input	/src\/main\/java<org.elasticsearch.action.support.single.custom{SingleCustomOperationRequestBuilder.java
ⓐ invoked-by-quickassist	false
ⓐ invoked-through-structured-selection	false
ⓐ name	setOperationThreaded
ⓐ navigation-history	{[Extract Method,BEGIN_REFACTORING,1390255987858],[ExtractMethodInputPage,Previe&w >,139025599846
ⓐ parameter1	boolean threadedOperation threadedOperation
ⓐ replace	false
ⓐ selection	1710 45
ⓐ selection-in-code-snippet	697 45
ⓐ selection-text	request.operationThreaded(threadedOperation);
ⓐ stamp	1390256000993

ⓐ status	`<ERROR`
	
	`ERROR: Method 'setOperationThreaded' already exists in type 'SingleCustomOperationRequestBuilder'.`
	`Context: [Working copy] SingleCustomOperationRequestBuilder.java [in org.elasticsearch.action.support.sing`
	`package org.elasticsearch.action.support.single.custom`
	`import org.elasticsearch.action.ActionRequestBuilder`
	`import org.elasticsearch.action.ActionResponse`
	`import org.elasticsearch.client.internal.InternalGenericClient`
	`class SingleCustomOperationRequestBuilder`
	  `SingleCustomOperationRequestBuilder(InternalGenericClient, Request)`
	  `RequestBuilder setOperationThreaded(boolean)`
	  `RequestBuilder setPreferLocal(boolean)`
	`code: none`
	`Data: null`
	`>`

ⓐ version	1.0
ⓐ visibility	2

FIGURE 5.8

An example refactoring descriptor recorded by CodingSpectator.

Using a version control system such as Subversion as the data repository has several advantages:

(a) Subversion makes all revisions of each file easily accessible. This makes troubleshooting easier.

(b) For textual files, Subversion submits only the *changes* made to the files as opposed to the entire new file. This differential data submission leads to faster submissions.

(c) There are libraries such as SVNKit[16] that provide an API for Subversion operations such as add, update, remove, and commit. CodingSpectator uses SVNKit for submitting developers' data to the central repository.

(d) Setting up a Subversion server is a well-documented process. This avoids the burden of setting up a specialized server.

On the other hand, a disadvantage of using Subversion as the data repository is that it requires the developers to maintain a copy of their data on their file systems. The Subversion working copy on the developers' systems takes *space*, and can also cause *merge conflicts*—for example, if a developer restores the contents of the file system to an earlier version. To handle merge conflicts, CodingSpectator has built-in support for automatic conflict detection and resolution. When CodingSpectator detects a merge conflict, it removes the developer's data from the central repository and then submits the new data. Despite removal of the data from the central repository, it is possible to locate the merge conflicts and restore the data that was collected before the conflicts occurred.

CodingSpectator prompts the developers for their Subversion user names and passwords when CodingSpectator is about to submit their data. CodingSpectator gives the developers the option to save their passwords in Eclipse securely. See http://codingspectator.cs.illinois.edu/documentation for more information on the features of CodingSpectator for developers.

2. **Setting up an Eclipse update site.** Users of CodingSpectator install it from an Eclipse update site.[17] An Eclipse update site is an online repository of the JAR and configuration files that Eclipse requires for installing a plug-in.

You will have to customize CodingSpectator at least by specifying the URL of the Subversion repository to which CodingSpectator should submit developers' data. You may also want to customize the message that CodingSpectator shows to the developers when it prompts them for their Subversion credentials. You can customize these aspects of CodingSpectator by changing the configuration files that are packed in the existing JAR files hosted on the Eclipse update site of CodingSpectator. If you need to customize CodingSpectator in more complex ways that involve changes to its source code, you should follow the instructions for building CodingSpectator's update site from source code.

5.3.3.3 *Extending CodingSpectator*

In addition to collecting detailed refactoring data, CodingSpectator provides a reusable infrastructure for collecting Eclipse usage data. Extending CodingSpectator frees you from having to develop many features from scratch—for example, Subversion communications, automatic merge conflict detection and resolution, secure storage of Subversion credentials, and periodic update reminders.

---

[16]http://svnkit.com/.
[17]http://codingspectator.cs.illinois.edu/installation.

CodingSpectator provides an Eclipse extension point (id = `edu.illinois.codingspectator.mo nitor.core.submitter`) and the following interface:

```
1  public interface  SubmitterListener {
2     //  hook before  svn add
3     void preSubmit();
4     //  hook after  svn add and before  svn commit
5     void preCommit();
6     //  hook after  svn commit
7     void postSubmit(boolean succeeded);
8  }
```

The above interface provides three hooks to CodingSpectator's submission process. CodingSpectator checks out the Subversion repository into a folder, which we refer to as the *watched folder*. Then, it executes the Subversion commands (e.g., add and commit) on the watched folder. A plug-in that extends the `submitter` extension point and implements the `SubmitterListener` interface can perform actions before or after two of the Subversion commands that CodingSpectator executes: add and commit. For example, CodingSpectator overrides the method `preSubmit` to copy the recorded refactoring descriptors to the watched folder. As another example, the developers of CodingSpectator made the Eclipse UDC plug-in use the `submitter` extension point and copy the UDC data to the watched folder. As a result, CodingSpectator submits the UDC data to the Subversion repository. Effectively, this is an alternative method to the one presented in Section 5.3.1.3 for collecting UDC data in a central repository.

5.3.4 **BUILD IT YOURSELF FOR VISUAL STUDIO**

This section shows how to implement a usage data collection tool for Visual Studio that generates the navigation ratio metric (see Section 5.2.2) daily, giving the developer insight into his or her own navigation patterns. Readers attempting the tutorial should be familiar with C# as well as have working knowledge of Visual Studio.

Because this extension is illustrative, some simplifications have been made that would need to be addressed in a widely deployed extension. For instance, this example extension does not perform any background processing; thus, the developer may notice a delay during Visual Studio start-up.

5.3.4.1 *Creating a visual studio extension*

1. **Create a new extension solution.** With the Visual Studio software development kit installed, create a new Visual Studio Extension project with a project name of "Collector" and a solution named "VisualStudioMonitor." Set up the extension to provide a menu command named "Stop Monitoring" with a command ID of "StopMonitoring." To separate the Visual Studio Extension setup code from the core functionality of the extension, create a second project within the same solution called "Monitor."

2. **Ensure the extension loads on start-up.** The next step is to instruct the extension package to load when Visual Studio starts, by setting the attribute ProvideAutoLoad on the package class (CollectorPackage.cs). The globally unique ID (GUID) value in the listing below will load the package when Visual Studio starts:

```
1    // This attribute  starts  the package when Visual Studio starts
2    [ProvideAutoLoad("{ADFC4E64−0397−11D1−9F4E−00A0C911004F}")]
3    [Guid(GuidList. guidCollectorPkgString )]
4    public sealed class CollectorPackage : Package
```

3. **Create the Monitor project.** Add a class library type project to the "VisualStudioMonitor" solution. Because the class library must be signed, go to the "Properties" for the Monitor project and select "Signing" from the list at the right. In the "Signing" tab, check the "sign the assembly" checkbox, then under "Choose a strong name key file," select "Browse" and browse over to the Key.snk file in the collector project (the file was created with the solution).

4. **Create the monitoring class.** The next step is to create a static class that will manage the log file, including starting, stopping recording data, and inserting data into the log file. Rename the class created by Visual Studio in the Monitor project as "DataRecorder." Because we do not want more than one recorder running at a time and we want to access this class without instantiating it, make the class static. Create a method to start the recorder that generates a file name for the log file and sets a flag that the recording has started. A Stop method resets that flag and perhaps clears the file name. A method to write a log message to the file completes DataRecorder.

5. **Connecting the extension framework with the recorder.** Finally, insert a call to DataRecorder.Start() at the end of the Initialize() method in the CollectorPackage class. This will start the monitoring each time Visual Studio starts. You will need to add a reference for the Monitor project to the Collector project, make sure you sign the Monitor project, then rebuild the solution. See the listings for CollectorPackage.cs in Listing 5.1 and DataRecorder.cs in Listing 5.2.

5.3.4.2 Create the data model

The next step creates a data model for storing and managing event monitoring for Visual Studio. This includes designing the main event types and implementing a factory to create these events.

1. **Implement the base class.** Create the AbstractMonitoredEvent class in the Monitor project in Visual Studio. Then add properties for EventName and Classification as follows:

```
1    [XmlInclude(typeof( MonitoredCommandEvent))]
2    [XmlRoot(ElementName = "MonitoredEvent", Namespace = "http://Monitor")]
3    public abstract class AbstractMonitoredEvent
4    {
5        // / <summary>
6        // / Default constructor  to use in serialization
7        // / </summary>
8        protected AbstractMonitoredEvent()
9        {
10       }
11
12       public String EventName { get; set ; }
13       public String Classification    { get; set ; }
14   }
```

2. **Enable serialization in the base class.** So that we can store events in a configuration file then manipulate that configuration file later, we provision this abstract class for XML serialization of itself and its derived classes. .NET attributes support the XML serialization in this structure.

The first attribute tells XML serialization that the MonitoredCommandEvent class is a derived class of AbstractMonitoredEvent that we will create next. This provides the ability to serialize and deserialize the public objects of the derived class by referencing the type of AbstractMonitoredEvent when creating a serializer. The second attribute creates an XML namespace that all derived classes will share with the AbstractMonitoredEvent class.

3. **Create the concrete subclass.** The next step is to create a derived class called MonitoredCommandEvent that inherits from AbstractMonitoredEvent. MonitoredCommandEvent implements a constructor that builds a MonitoredCommandEvent object from the Command class of the DTE.

The EnvDTE.Command object contains fields for Guid (a GUID string), ID and integer sub-id, and Name, a readable name for the command. To register an event handler for a EnvDTE.Command, you need to get an object reference for the command using the Guid and ID to identify the command. The Guid is a GUID for command events in Visual Studio; however, some command events share a GUID and distinguish themselves with different EventIDs. Thus, both elements are necessary to link a Command event from the DTE to an event handler in this extension. The Name is useful information to understand what the command is. There are several versions of the DTE object corresponding to versions of Visual Studio. Depending on the commands of interest, each version may need to be queried for its commands.

The constructor that takes a Command as input, simply extracts the necessary and relevant fields from the DTE's Command object and transfers the matching information into the corresponding fields from this class and the AbstractMonitoredEvent class.

4. **Enable serialization in concrete subclass.** Ensure the class also includes a constructor that builds from an XElement and an output method ToXElement translates the object to XML for saving. Add using statements for System.Xml.Serialization, and EnvDTE and their corresponding references in the project References configuration.

```
1   [ XmlRoot(ElementName = "MonitoredEvent", Namespace = "http://Monitor")]
2   public  class  MonitoredCommandEvent : AbstractMonitoredEvent {
3
4       public  int  EventID { get;  set ;  }
5   public  String  Guid { get;  set ;  }
6
7   public  MonitoredCommandEvent()
8   {
9   }
10
11  public  MonitoredCommandEvent(Command DTECommandObj) {
12      if  (DTECommandObj != null) {
13          this . EventName = DTECommandObj.Name;
14          this . Classification    = EventName.Split('. ')[0];    // use the first    part  of event  name
15          this . Guid = DTECommandObj.Guid;
16          this . EventID = DTECommandObj.ID;
17      }
18      else  {
19          throw  new ArgumentNullException("DTECommandObj");
20      }
21  }
```

The attribute for XMLRoot is the same attribute assigned to the AbstractMonitoredEvent class which tells XML Serialization that this type is a type belonging to the abstract class. In this class, create two public fields, EventID as int and Guid as string, that will save important information from the Visual Studio DTE object needed to engage monitoring for each command.

5. **Create the event factory.** To complete the Simple Factory pattern, a static factory class provides static factory methods that create an object of type MonitoredCommandEvent from a DTE Command object and returns it as an AbstractMonitoredEvent. For now the only class to consider is the MonitoredCommandEvent derived class; however, a future step will add more derived classes.

5.3.4.3 Storing visual studio command event information

Our extension is now wired to listen for events; however, events also need to be saved for later analysis. In this step we discuss how the data is collected and its persistence.

1. **Create the collection manager class.** In this step, build the MonitoredEventCollection class shown in Listing 5.6 that manages a List object of AbstractMonitoredEvent type.
2. **Create and populate the configuration.** Configuration data is stored in the List object. The List object is populated from an XML file that stores the configuration data. The MonitoredEventCollection class provides a method to query the DTE for all commands and initialize the list. Another method called after the DTE query stores the List contents in the same XML format file. These two methods should be called in sequence the first time the extension launches. After that, it reads the XML file on start-up to initialize the List. Call the method(s) to query, store, and load the event list from the Start() method of the DataRecorder class in the previous step so that the Monitor will load the commands on start-up.

Fortunately, the DTE object has a query method that lists all the commands it manages. The DTE Commands object returns an IEnumerable collection of EnvDTE.Command objects. The listing below provides a method to try to get an instance of the DTE. It depends on references to EnvDTE, Microsoft.VisualStudio.Shell.12.0, and Microsoft.VisualStudio.OLE.Interop, so be sure to add those to the project's References list.

```
1
2    using EnvDTE;
3    using Microsoft.VisualStudio.Shell; // 12.0
4    private static DTE tryGetDTEObject()
5    {
6        DTE dteobj=null;
7        try
8        {
9            dteobj = ((EnvDTE.DTE)ServiceProvider.GlobalProvider.GetService(typeof(
                 EnvDTE.DTE).GUID)).DTE;
10
11       }
12       // Important to catch the following exception if the DTE object is unavailable
13       catch (System.Runtime.InteropServices.InvalidComObjectException)
14       {}
```

```
15          // Important to catch the following exception if the DTE object is busy
16          catch (System.Runtime.InteropServices . COMException)
17          {}
18          return dteobj ;
19      }
```

Once you have a reference to the DTE object from the tryGetDTEObject method, use the DTE to query the Commands object. Then process each command into the List managed by MonitoredEventCollection. Example code from the QueryVSForAddDTECommands method in MonitoredEventCollection.cs in Listing 5.6 is highlighted below, making use of the MonitoredEventFactory to generate each AbstractMonitoredEvent stored in the List. The try-catch here is necessary because the saved DTE object could be disposed while the loop processes the Commands.

```
1       try
2       {
3           foreach (Command DTE_CommandEventObj in dteobj.Commands)
4           {
5               AbstractMonitoredEvent NewEvent =
                    MonitoredEventFactory.GetMonitoredEvent(DTE_CommandEventObj);
6               if (NewEvent != null)
7               {
8                   EventList . Add(NewEvent);
9               }
10          }
11      }
12      // This exception happens during dispose/finalize when VS exits, just return null
13      catch (System.Runtime.InteropServices . InvalidComObjectException)
14      {
15          return null ;
16      }
```

3. **Enable persistence of the configuration.** A persistent configuration file helps independently manage the events that are monitored for a study, and makes the configuration of all possible events easier to manage. Using the framework's ToXelement methods, build methods in MonitoredEventCollection to save the List of AbstractMonitoredEvents to the configuration file and load them from the configuration file. Below is the core code for the saveEventInterestTable method in MonitoredEventCollection.cs in Listing 5.6 that creates an XML serializer for the List object then writes that to the file stream:

```
1       var serializer = new
                System.Xml.Serialization . XmlSerializer (typeof(List <AbstractMonitoredEvent>));
2       using (Stream file = new FileStream(filepath , FileMode.Create, FileAccess . Write))
3       {
4           serializer . Serialize (file , eventList );
5           file . Flush() ;
6       }
```

5.3.4.4 Register event handlers

Now that the framework is complete and a configuration file for all command events to be monitored is ready, the methods to hook Visual Studio into event handlers that log each command can be created. This step will add methods and member objects to the AbstractMonitoredEvent and MonitoredCommandEvent classes to register event handlers with the DTE and dispose of them appropriately when necessary. The MonitoredEventCollection class gets a new method to perform the registration from the objects in the list and another method to deregister them.

1. **Define the registration interface.** The AbstractMonitoredEvent class should get a virtual RegisterEventForMonitoring method that takes an object parameter we will use to pass a DTE reference in. The method returns a bool based on successful registration. The class also gets a nonvirtual Dispose() method and a virtual Dispose(bool disposing) method, with the former calling the latter and the latter setting the field isDisposed to true. This is the typical dispose structure. Finally, the abstract class holds the nonvirtual method to write the event log information (the abstract class's fields and a timestamp) to the log via the DataRecorder class. This unites logs for all derived classes into a common format.

2. **Implement the registration routine.** The MonitoredCommandEvent class in Listing 5.4 overrides the virtual RegisterEventForMonitoring method to implement registering an event handler for Command events. Registering first must find the event in the DTE and assign it to the field, then attach a new event hander to the event. Looking at the method listing below, we see the Guid and EventID are used as parameters to query the DTE Events object for the specific command event in this instance. The result is assigned to a field, eventTypeObject. With this reference to the event, the next block adds an event handler that runs after the command is executed. After all that, if the eventTypeObject is not null, the method returns true for success.

```
1    public  override  bool RegisterEventForMonitoring ( object  dte )
2    {
3        if  ( ! isDisposed  && eventTypeObject == null && dte != null )
4        {
5            eventTypeObject  = ( dte  as  DTE ).Events.get_CommandEvents(Guid, EventID) as
                 CommandEvents;
6        }
7        if  ( eventTypeObject  != null )
8        {
9            eventTypeObject. AfterExecute  += new
10                   _dispCommandEvents_AfterExecuteEventHandler(OnAfterExecute);
11       }
12       return  ( eventTypeObject  != null );
13   }
```

With the above method in Visual Studio, the missing fields and methods can be automatically generated via the "Generate" context menu command.

The last step with MonitoredCommandEvent is to create the Dispose method that will deregister the event handler. This looks as follows:

```
1    protected  override  void  Dispose(bool  disposing )
2    {
3        if  (eventTypeObject  != null )
4            eventTypeObject. AfterExecute  −= OnAfterExecute;
5        this . isDisposed  = true ;
6    }
```

Use the Visual Studio "Generate" command to generate a method stub for OnAfterExecute and the code will compile. In the OnAfterExecute method, call ToLog so the event data is captured in the log.

3. **Register all commands.** MonitoredEventCollection in Listing 5.6 now needs methods to perform registration and deregistration on all the events in the list. As the following listing shows, RegisterEventInventoryForEventMonitoring() must get the DTE object, then walk through the IDEEventListenerRegistry list calling the abstract method RegisterEventForMonitoring with the DTE. If one of them succeeds, then this method considers it successful.

```
1    public  bool  RegisterEventInventoryForEventMonitoring ()
2    {
3        DTE dteobj = tryGetDTEObject();
4        bool somethingRegistered  = false ;
5        if  (dteobj  != null  && IDEEventListenerRegistry != null  && IDEEventListenerRegistry.Count > 0)
6        {
7            foreach  (AbstractMonitoredEvent  command in IDEEventListenerRegistry)
8            {
9                if  (command.RegisterEventForMonitoring(dteobj))
10               {
11                   somethingRegistered  = true ;
12               }
13           }
14       }
15       return  somethingRegistered ;
16   }
```

4. **Connect to the package life cycle.** Refactor the MonitoredEventCollection object in DataRecorder to a static class field. Then add a call to RegisterEventInventoryForEventMonitoring() in the Start() method of DataRecorder. Add a call to the deregister method of MonitoredEventCollection in the Stop() method of DataRecorder.

5. **Execute the extension.** Run the solution and use a few commands in Visual Studio, then give the Stop Collector command and check the log file. You should see output like the following:

```
Collector Started
2014-02-02 13:46:52Z,Tools.AddinManager,Tools
2014-02-02 13:46:56Z,Tools.ExtensionsandUpdates,Tools
Collector Stopped
```

Below are descriptions of the code listings for the example code we discussed in this section. Code listings can be found in Section 5.7.

- The listing for AbstractMonitoredEvent.cs in Listing 5.3 shows the additions to that class.
- The listing for CommandMonitoredEvent.cs in Listing 5.4 shows methods implemented for registration and disposal.
- The listing for MonitoredEventCollection.cs in Listing 5.6 shows list processing in calls to respective registration and deregistration methods for the List object.
- The DataRecorder class is shown in Listing 5.2.

With this demonstration, you see how to build a usage monitor for Visual Studio that records most commands the developer can issue in the IDE. What is missing? Well, there are other areas of the DTE to explore, such as editor events, unit test events, and build and debug session events that provide greater context to the developer experience. For brevity, capturing those events is left to readers to explore on their own.

Thus far we have been focusing on concrete usage data collection frameworks and the specific data collected by these frameworks. With options to collect data from both Visual Studio and Eclipse, we hopefully have provided a good resource to get you started on collecting and analyzing usage data. Next, let us look at methods and challenges in analyzing usage data.

5.4 HOW TO ANALYZE USAGE DATA

The tools described in this chapter provide the usage data you can use to study developer interactions, but leave the selection of the methods for analyzing the data to the reader. In this section we discuss several data analysis techniques that you may apply to usage data. We will discuss attributes of the data, including format and anonymity of the data, categorizing the records, defining sequences, using state models, and other techniques to extract information from the usage data.

5.4.1 DATA ANONYMITY

Nonanonymous data, where sensitive information, including source code snippets, change sets, and even access to the source code base, is provided, has obvious advantages. We can replay the developers' activity stream, affording them a deep understanding of their actions [11]. There are few limits on how this data can be analyzed, and *nonanonymous data is well suited for exploratory studies*. Unfortunately, there are some key disadvantages. First, it may not be permitted for developers to participate in a study; typical enterprise developers may face termination of their contracts if they were to leak even parts of their source code base. Second, while playback and other deep analyses are possible, these analyses can be costly in terms of time and resources.

Anonymous data, where only records of activities and anonymous facts about artifacts are recorded, may at first seem strictly inferior. Indeed, there are some limitations on what can be learned from anonymous activity streams, yet there are key advantages. First, Snipes et al. [19] report that developers are more receptive to sharing anonymous data, and thus the ability to collect a large amount of information from many developers increases greatly. Second, because the data set is relatively large and is harvested from working developers, conclusions are ultimately more reliable.

In this section we focus on analyzing anonymous data sources. We do so because analyzing anonymous activity streams is similar to analyzing nonanonymous data streams (i.e., they are both activity streams) and because the unlimited variation of analysis permitted by nonanonymous data affords few generalities. As we discuss analyzing usage data, we start with straightforward magnitude analysis, build to a categorization system for activity streams, discuss dividing streams into sessions, and finally discuss state-based analysis.

5.4.2 USAGE DATA FORMAT

Most usage data is collected as an activity stream with varying levels of supporting detail. In Figure 5.9 we present an abstraction of a typical activity stream. It includes a timestamp, followed by the activity, appended with (often anonymous) details concerning that activity. We can apply this model to the examples discussed earlier. For instance, the event recorded by UDC corresponds to a row in our theoretical model. It includes a timestamp (i.e., time), an activity description (i.e., what, kind, and description), and additional information (i.e., bundleId, bundleVersion). Similarly, the CodingSpectator example includes a timestamp (i.e., stamp), an activity description (i.e., id), and a much larger set of additional information (i.e., code-snippet, selection, selection-in-code-snippet, etc.). Because these and other usage data activity streams can easily be described using our abstraction, we will refer to it as we describe data analysis techniques.

5.4.3 MAGNITUDE ANALYSIS

A major advantage of anonymous usage data is the fact that it captures developers in their natural habitat, without any observational bias. Deriving conclusions from hours of developers' fieldwork is naturally more convincing than deriving conclusions from hour-long, in-laboratory developer studies. One type of question that usage data is well suited to answer uses measurement of the magnitude of occurrence of a specific event. For instance, we may want to know how often developers invoke pull-up refactoring or how often a file search is invoked. By performing a count of a specific message in the collected logs, researchers can easily calculate the frequencies of specific actions, which can often be sufficient to answer important questions.

However, there are a few common issues with magnitude analysis. First, in any sufficiently large set of user logs there is a small set of developers who will use the feature/tool under analysis orders

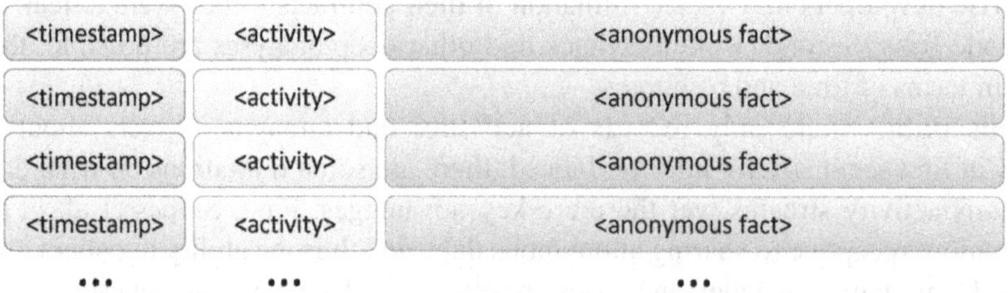

FIGURE 5.9

Abstract model of developer activity streams.

of magnitude more often than the general population, potentially skewing the data. Second, attempts to attribute time to individual activities are fraught with difficulties. For instance, there is a temptation to report the percentage of time spent doing activity X. Yet, because the data is based on a stream of activities, any time calculation requires making unsound assumptions about what happens in between these events.

The work by Murphy et al. [6] on understanding Eclipse IDE usage provides several examples of magnitude analysis being used effectively. By simply counting instances of events in developers' activity streams, they were able to present how often developers accessed certain views, the top 10 commands executed by developers, and the percentage of developers who used each specific refactoring command. In spite of the simplicity of this analysis, it is ideal for identifying heavily used features for improvements and unused features for removal, as well as for getting a sense of how developers are currently working.

5.4.4 CATEGORIZATION ANALYSIS

While magnitude analysis is well suited for answering questions about the use of a single IDE command, many questions are related to a specific feature or tool in the IDE, which usually maps to multiple activities. For instance, the question "How often are refactorings performed?" cannot be answered via magnitude analysis alone, as refactorings can be triggered through a number of different IDE commands. These commands first need to be categorized, after which magnitude analysis can be used.

When focusing on a concrete subtask, such as refactoring, one may find it easy to categorize activities. In this case, all refactoring commands, such as pull-up or extract method, can be classified as refactorings. However, when focusing on more general behavior, such as editing, navigating, and searching, one may find categorization difficult. It is impossible to say, for instance, from a single click in the File Explorer window whether that click represents a search, as the developers browses a few promising files, or a navigation, as he or she implicitly opens a type declaration of a variable he or she was just browsing. Thus, categorization without context can produce noisy data in certain cases. However, categorization is a powerful tool, especially when there is little ambiguity in the IDE commands that are analyzed.

To illustrate both the power and the limitations of category analysis, consider the following IDE data stream, asking the question "Do developers use code search tools?"

For this question, the category of log events related to code search tools should be identified and counted. Modern IDEs commonly offer several code search tools, which operate at the global or local scale, such as the Find-in-Files and Quick Find tools. An example log from Visual Studio with these tools is shown in Figure 5.10. Using categorization analysis, we can identify three log events related to usage of code search tools, and report various statistics aimed at answering the question (e.g., number of code search events per day, number of code search events per developer; see Figure 5.11). However, the IDE usage data can sometimes be affected by noise, which cannot be avoided by categorization analysis. For instance, the second query to Find-in-Files is not followed by a developer click, which is a failed interaction with the Find-in-Files tool and should likely not be included in answering the question.

```
Collector Started
2014-02-02 13:21:22 - User submitted query to Find-in-Files
2014-02-02 13:24:36 - Find-in-Files retrieved 42 results
2014-02-02 13:32:21 - User clicked on result 2
2014-02-02 13:46:56 - User submitted query to Quick Find
2014-02-02 14:07:12 - Open definition command; input=class
2014-02-02 14:46:52 - User submitted query to Find-in-Files
2014-02-02 14:46:56 - Find-in-Files retrieved 0 results
2014-02-02 14:48:02 - Click on File Explorer
```

FIGURE 5.10

Log file search category example.

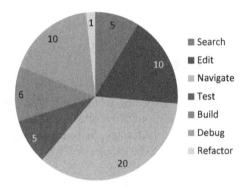

FIGURE 5.11

Categorized log events with search category.

5.4.5 SEQUENCE ANALYSIS

Magnitude analysis and categorization are both appropriate for answering questions that are simply manifested in the IDE usage log. However, a more powerful way of analyzing activity logs is through sequence analysis, which first breaks the IDE data stream into a number of sequences, according to some criteria, and then reports on the characteristics of each sequence. A sequence in the IDE usage data corresponds to a software engineering task or subtask accomplished by the developer (e.g., refactoring or looking for a starting point for a maintenance task), consisting of all of IDE events in a given time span. For instance, answering the question "Are developers successful at finding initial points in the code for a software maintenance task?" requires that the sequence of IDE events corresponding to each maintenance task be identified before we can perform further analysis using either magnitude or categorization analysis. The granularity of a sequence is determined by the guiding question. For certain questions, we may be interested in a smaller sequence (e.g., searching the code base), while for others we may need to consider a longer time span (e.g., implementing a new feature, fixing a bug). According to Zou and Godfrey [33], the larger and more complex the task or subtask to extract, the harder it is for sequence analysis to determine its starting and stopping point in the activity log.

In many cases, extracting activity sequences can be challenging as it impossible to know exactly when a developer begins or ends a particular task or subtask without understanding the developer's underlying thought process. There are several possibilities in how sequence extraction can be performed, based on the specific question. One possibility is to use sentinels, which are specific actions that indicate the beginning and end of a sequence. For instance, in the context of the code search question mentioned above, submitting a query to the code search tool begins a sequence, while performing an edit or structural navigation (e.g., following the call graph) ends the sequence. Another possibility is to use the passage of time to extract sequences, where time without any activity is used as a signal of task start or finish. Yet another possibility is to use locations in the code base to identify a sequence in the activity log. This is the key insight used in the algorithm of Coman and Sillitti [34], which uses periods of activity on the same program elements to represent the core of a task, and the time gap between such events to extract sequences corresponding to developer tasks. Laboratory validation studies of this algorithm have shown very high accuracy (80%) when compared with the ground truth reported by developers. Zou and Godfrey [33] found that this accuracy may not hold up in an industrial setting, where tasks are longer, code bases are more complex, and developer interruptions are common. Also, the algorithm requires that information regarding program elements be kept in the activity log, which may conflict with many developers' privacy and anonymity requirements.

We illustrate sequence analysis with the usage log shown in Figure 5.12 and the question "Are developers successful at finding initial points in the code for a software maintenance task?" To answer the question, sequence analysis can extract two separate sequences in the log from Figure 5.12 by using sentinels indicative of start/end of a code search activity, among other possible sequence identification approaches. Both of the extracted search sequences can be deemed as successful since for each of the queries to the `Find-in-Files` code search tool the developer clicks on a retrieved result, followed by a structured navigation event (open caller/callee) or editing event (developer-edited code). Therefore, it would seem that the developer is successful at finding initial points in the code for his or her software maintenance task. However, on closer inspection of the second sequence, we observe that there is a large time gap between clicking on a result and editing code. The reason for this time gap is open to interpretation, as the developer may have returned to the previous results, continuing the search session, or may have started on a completely new development activity. Certain types of sequence analysis, such

```
Collector Started
2014-02-02 13:46:52 - User submitted query to Find-in-Files
2014-02-02 13:46:56 - Find-in-Files retrieved 121 results
2014-02-02 13:52:21 - User clicked on result 2
2014-02-02 13:58:01 - User clicked on result 8
2014-02-02 13:59:57 - Open caller/callee command
...
2014-02-02 14:46:52 - User submitted query to Find-in-Files
2014-02-02 14:46:56 - Find-in-Files retrieved 19 results
2014-02-02 15:01:08 - User clicked on result 11
2014-02-02 17:30:12 - User edited code
...
```

FIGURE 5.12

Log file sequence example.

as Coman's algorithm, take time into account when identifying sequences, while others, such as the sentinel approach used above, do not. Neither of these approaches, however, helps to resolve the origin of ambiguous events, which is left to the reader to characterize.

5.4.6 STATE MODEL ANALYSIS

Another way to analyze log data is to view the log as a sequence of events occurring in a state machine. Using state models, we can quantify the occurrences of repeating actions and describe a usage pattern in statistical analysis. Nagappan and Robinson [35] used sequence analysis to generate a graphical view of a profile of how users interacted with the components of a system from log data. In state model analysis, the sequential data is converted to nodes and edges of a graph which represents the entire data in states and transitions between them. A Markov state model provides information about the probability of occurrence of each state and the transitional probability of each activity. The statistics provided in a Markov state model include the quantity of time the developer is in each state and the probability of the developer being in each state. From a given state, the model calculates the probability of each transition to different unique states. State models answer specific questions such as the following: What is the probability that once a developer searches the code, that developer edits a code element listed in the find results? Expanding this question, the probability of an entire use case or set of transitions through the usage model is calculable from the state model.

State model graphs make it easy to identify the most active states, and edges provide information about the important activities in the data set. As the number of states increases, the weighted directed graph (WDG) becomes more complex and hence more difficult to understand. When this occurs, summarizing the detailed event data into higher-level categories effectively combines the states to get more meaningful information. For example, classifying events in usage data of similar types into categories results in fewer states with the same number of transitions as the original data.

We generate a state model from a usage log by transforming the serially ordered events in sequence data to a WDG data structure. We can group the information in the log line to any level, such as event level, event category level, tool level, or application level. In the sequence data, each event is important as a stand-alone event; however, in the WDG representation, the importance shifts to adjacent pairs of events. Therefore, each group in the sequence data is represented by a unique node in the WDG. For example, suppose we choose to create a WDG at the level of an event. The analysis that generates the graph creates a node for each unique event name, then determines the transitions that occur in the log before and after that event name.

To understand how to interpret a state model, look at our example graph in Figure 5.14. We see that an edge exists from one node (head) to another (tail) if there is an occurrence of the event representing the tail node immediately after the event representing the head node in the log file. For example if event B follows event A in the log file, then there is a directed edge from node A to node B in the WDG. The edges are labeled with the number of times this transition has occurred. For example if event B occurs 50 times after event A in the log file, then the edge from node A to node B in the WDG is labeled with 50. Typically, we keep track of the actual count as the weight of the edge when building the graph. In the graph we display the percentage as the label. This percentage is proportional to the total number of transitions. The cumulative probability of out-edges of a node is 1. The transitional probabilities of each out-edge is calculated by dividing the number of transactions of that out-edge by the sum of all outward transactions from that node. We could also store the dynamic parameter information in each log line as a list along the edges.

As an example, consider the sample log file shown in Figure 5.13 and the corresponding state model graph in Figure 5.14. Intuitively, you can see how the state model represents the log states and transitions between them in the sequence of events.

Converting a log into a state model requires three steps. We use Java Usage Model Builder (JUMBL) from the Software Quality Research Laboratory (SQRL) of the University of Tennessee. Details on input formats and JUMBL tools are available on SourceForge.[18]

```
2013-03-21 18:18:32Z,A
2013-03-21 18:18:33Z,B
2013-03-21 18:20:49Z,C
2013-03-21 18:20:50Z,A
2013-03-21 18:20:56Z,B
2013-03-21 18:20:57Z,A
2013-03-21 18:21:08Z,C
2013-03-21 18:21:08Z,D
2013-03-21 18:21:08Z,E
2013-03-21 18:21:08Z,A
```

FIGURE 5.13

Sample log file for conversion to the state model.

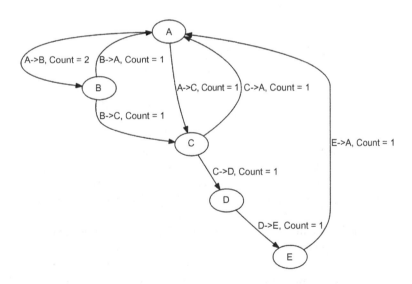

FIGURE 5.14

WDG of the example log.

[18]http://jumbl.sourceforge.net/.

1. First, convert the log file into a representation for each transition called a sequence-based specification. The format for a sequence-based specification in CSV files is described in the JUMBL user guide. This representation contains the following information with one row for each transition:

   - State transition
   - Count of transitions
   - Total time elapsed
   - State in information
   - State out information

2. After the sequence-based specification has been imported, JUMBL can write out the representation of a state model as a TML script or in several other formats, including Graph Modeling Language (GML), that graph tools can import. The TML script has information about the nodes, the out-edges from each node, and the number of transitions from each node to another node. The corresponding graph for the usage log example is depicted in Figure 5.14.

With the use of state models, sequence data with hundreds of thousands of lines can be quickly converted to more meaningful graphical representation using this method. Once the TML file has been generated, we can use JUMBL to find out the state probabilities of each state. Using the state probability and the usage patterns, we can draw conclusions about the occupancy of individual states and the use cases that involve transitions through several states.

5.4.7 THE CRITICAL INCIDENT TECHNIQUE

The critical incident technique (CIT) is a general method for improving a process or system with respect to a set of objectives. The CIT prescribes a systematic study of the *critical incidents*. Critical incidents are *positive* or *negative* events that have a significant effect on the objectives.

The CIT was developed and published in its current form by Flanagan [36] in 1954. Nevertheless, it is believed that the technique was introduced even earlier by Galton (ca 1930). Variations of the CIT have been widely used in the field of human factors [37].

Del Galdo et al. [38] applied the CIT to human-computer interaction as part of evaluating the documentation of a conferencing system. They asked the study participants to perform a task and report any incident that they ran into. The researchers observed the participants during the study, analyzed the reported incidents, and proposed improvements to the documentation accordingly.

In the context of IDEs, Vakilian and Johnson [10] adapted the CIT to automated refactorings. The goal of this study was to identify the usability problems of automated refactorings by analyzing refactoring usage data. The researchers found that certain events such as cancellations, reported messages, and repeated invocations are likely indicators of the usability problems of automated refactorings. By locating these events in the usage data and analyzing their nearby events, the researchers were able to identify 15 usability problems of the Eclipse refactoring tool. For instance, the usage data indicated that six participants invoked the Move Instance Method refactoring a total of 16 times, but none finished the refactoring successfully. In all cases, the participants either canceled the refactoring or could not proceed because of an error that the refactoring tool reported. By inspecting these critical incidents, the researchers were able to infer two usability problems related to the Move Instance Method.

To apply the CIT on a set of usage data, you should follow several steps. First, identify the objectives. Finding usability problems is only one example. Second, identify a set of events that may be critical incidents. These are events they may have significant effects on your objectives. Usually, the negative critical incidents, which may have negative effects on the objectives, are better indicators of problems than the positive ones. Third, identify the critical incidents in your usage data. Fourth, collect sufficient contextual information to interpret the critical incidents. This may include events that have occurred in close time proximity to the critical incidents. You may even have to interview the developers or ask them to report their explanations of the incidents during the study. Although the developer reports may be short or incomplete, they can provide more insight into the nature of the problems. Finally, evaluate the effectiveness of the critical incidents and revisit the steps above. The process that we described for applying the CIT on usage data is iterative in nature—that is, it is natural to go back to a previous step from each step.

5.4.8 INCLUDING DATA FROM OTHER SOURCES

Other data sources, such as developer feedback, task descriptions, and change histories, can provide context for usage data and yield new opportunities for supporting developers. In this section, we briefly outline some related work in this area.

5.4.8.1 Developer feedback

Usage data collection can be augmented by explicit developer feedback to establish a ground truth. For instance, if you want to understand a developer's opinion of a tool or his or her purpose for using an IDE feature, it is best to ask about it. A postanalysis interview can shed light on your observations and confirm your analysis or point out different aspects.

Information on a developer's activities can provide an additional rationale to the usage data and explain the developer's actions. Asking questions about how well the developer knows the code he or she is working on can explain a developer's navigation patterns and usage of code search [19], while questions about the task—for example, implementing a new feature versus fixing a bug—can explain other characteristics, such as the amount of editing versus testing.

5.4.8.2 Tasks

As mentioned earlier, Mylin is a popular extension to the Eclipse IDE that supports task management, reducing the effort for a developer to switch between tasks and maintaining relevant information for each task [7]. In the context of a specific task, Mylin collects usage data in order to compute a degree-of-interest value for each program element, which represents the interest the developer has in the program element for the task at hand. Program elements that a developer interacted with frequently and recently have a higher degree-of-interest value. Using these calculated degree-of-interest values, Mylyn highlights the elements relevant for the current task and filters unnecessary information from common views in the IDE.

5.4.8.3 Change history

The FastDash tool created by Biehl et al. [39] enables real-time awareness of other developers' actions (e.g., focus or edits to a specific file) by utilizing usage data in concert with the source files and directories. FastDash's purpose is to reduce faults caused by lack of communication and lack of awareness of activities that other developers are performing on the same code base. The tool highlights other developer's activity as it is occurring using a sophisticated dashboard on the developer's screen or on a team's dashboard.

Using this overview of analysis techniques should give you a good start in analyzing usage data. The ideas you bring to your usage data analysis process provide the real opportunities for innovating usage-data-based research. Next we discuss limitations we have observed when collecting and analyzing usage data.

5.5 LIMITS OF WHAT YOU CAN LEARN FROM USAGE DATA

Collecting usage data can have many interesting and impactful applications. Nonetheless, there are limits to what you can learn from usage data. In our experience, people have high expectations about what they can learn from usage data, and those expectations often come crashing down after significant effort implementing and deploying a data collection system. So before you begin your usage data collection and analysis, consider the following two limitations of usage data.

1. **Rationale is hard to capture.** Usage data tells you what a software developer did, but not why he or she did it. For example, if your usage data tells you that a developer used a new refactoring tool for the first time, from a trace alone you cannot determine whether (a) the developer learned about the tool for the first time, (b) the developer had used the tool earlier, but before you started collecting data, or (c) the developer's finger slipped and the developer pressed a hotkey by accident. We do not know whether the developer is satisfied with the tool and will use it again in the future. It may be possible to distinguish between these by collecting additional information, such as asking the developer just after he or she had used the tool why he or she used it, but it is impossible to definitively separate these on the basis of the usage data alone.

2. **Usage data does not capture everything.** It is practically impossible to capture "everything," or at least everything that a developer does, so using the goal-question-metric method helps narrow the scope of data required. If you have a system that captures all key presses, you are still lacking information about mouse movements. If you have a system that also captures mouse movements, you are still missing the files that the developer is working with. If your system also captures the files, you are still lacking the histories of those files. And so on. In a theoretical sense, one could probably collect all observable information about a programmer's behavior, yet the magnitude of effort required to do so would be enormous. Furthermore, a significant amount of important information is probably not observable, such as rationale and intent. Ultimately, usage data is all about fitness for purpose—is the data you are analyzing fit for the purpose of your questions?

To avoid these limitations, we recommend thinking systemically about how the data will be used while planning rather than thinking about usage data collection abstractly. Invent an ideal usage data trace, and ask yourself:

- Does the data support my hypothesis?
- Are there alternative hypotheses that the data would support?

- Do I need additional data sources?
- Can the data be feasibly generated?

Answering these questions will help you determine whether you can sidestep the limitations of collecting and analyzing usage data.

5.6 CONCLUSION

Analyzing IDE usage data provides insights into many developer activities which help identify ways we can improve software engineering productivity. For example, one study found developers spend more than half of their time browsing and reading source code (excluding editing and all other activities in the IDE) [19]. This finding supports initiatives to build and promote tools that improve the navigation experience by supporting structural navigation. Other references mentioned in this chapter leveraged usage data to identify opportunities to improve refactoring tools [8, 10]. By identifying task contexts through usage data, Mylyn made improvements to how developers manage their code and task context [7].

If the last two decades can be labeled the era of big data collection, the next two decades will surely be labeled as the era of smarter big data analysis. Many questions still remain: How do we balance data privacy and data richness? What are the long-term effects of developer monitoring? How can we maximize the value of data collection for as many questions as possible, and reduce the strain on developers providing the data? How can we provide the right data to the right person at the right time with the least effort? Answering these questions will help the community advance in usage data collection and analysis.

Usage data, while now widely collected, still remains a resource largely untapped by practitioners and researchers. In this chapter, we have explained how to collect and analyze usage data, which we hope will increase the ease with which you can collect and analyze your own usage data.

5.7 CODE LISTINGS

The following code listings show the code mentioned in Section 5.3.4.

Listing for CollectorPackage.cs

```
1  using  System;
2  using  System.Diagnostics ;
3  using  System.Globalization ;
4  using  System.Runtime.InteropServices ;
5  using  System.ComponentModel.Design;
6  using  Microsoft. Win32;
7  using  Microsoft. VisualStudio ;
8  using  Microsoft. VisualStudio . Shell . Interop ;
9  using  Microsoft. VisualStudio . OLE.Interop;
10 using  Microsoft. VisualStudio . Shell ;
11 using  Monitor;
```

```
12
13  namespace Microsoft. Collector
14  {
15      // / <summary>
16      // / This is the class that implements the package exposed by this assembly.
17      // /
18      // / The minimum requirement for a class to be considered a valid package for Visual Studio
19      // / is to implement the IVsPackage interface and register itself with the shell .
20      // / This package uses the helper classes defined inside the Managed Package Framework (MPF)
21      // / to do it : it derives from the Package class that provides the implementation of the
22      // / IVsPackage interface and uses the registration attributes defined in the framework to
23      // / register itself and its components with the shell .
24      // / </summary>
25      // This attribute tells the PkgDef creation utility (CreatePkgDef.exe) that this class is
26      // a package.
27      [PackageRegistration ( UseManagedResourcesOnly = true)]
28      // This attribute is used to register the information needed to show this package
29      // in the Help/About dialog of Visual Studio.
30      [InstalledProductRegistration ("#110", "#112", "1.0", IconResourceID = 400)]
31      // This attribute is needed to let the shell know that this package exposes some menus.
32      [ProvideMenuResource("Menus.ctmenu", 1)]
33      // This attribute starts the package when Visual Studio starts
34      [ProvideAutoLoad("{ADFC4E64−0397−11D1−9F4E−00A0C911004F}")]
35      [Guid(GuidList. guidCollectorPkgString )]
36      public sealed class CollectorPackage : Package
37      {
38          // / <summary>
39          // / Default constructor of the package.
40          // / Inside this method you can place any initialization code that does not require
41          // / any Visual Studio service because at this point the package object is created but
42          // / not sited yet inside Visual Studio environment. The place to do all the other
43          // / initialization is the Initialize method.
44          // / </summary>
45          public CollectorPackage ()
46          {
47              Debug.WriteLine(string . Format(CultureInfo . CurrentCulture , "Entering constructor for : {0}",
                      this . ToString() ));
48          }
49
50
51
52          // /////////////////////////////////////////////////////////////////////
53          // Overridden Package Implementation
54          #region Package Members
55
56          // / <summary>
57          // / Initialization of the package; this method is called right after the package is sited , so this is
                      the place
58          // / where you can put all the initialization code that rely on services provided by VisualStudio .
59          // / </summary>
60          protected override void Initialize ()
61          {
```

```
62    Debug.WriteLine (string . Format(CultureInfo . CurrentCulture , "Entering Initialize  ()  of: {0}",
           this . ToString( ) ));
63    base. Initialize  () ;
64
65    //  Add our command handlers for menu (commands must exist in  the  . vsct  file  )
66    OleMenuCommandService mcs = GetService(typeof(IMenuCommandService)) as
           OleMenuCommandService;
67    if  (  null  != mcs )
68    {
69       //  Create  the  command for the menu item.
70       CommandID menuCommandID = new CommandID(GuidList.guidCollectorCmdSet,
              (int)PkgCmdIDList.StopMonitoring);
71       MenuCommand menuItem = new MenuCommand(MenuItemCallback, menuCommandID );
72       mcs.AddCommand( menuItem );
73    }
74    DataRecorder.Start () ;
75    }
76    #endregion
77
78    // /  <summary>
79    // /  This function  is  the  callback  used to  execute  a command when the a menu item is  clicked .
80    // /  See the  Initialize   method to see how the menu item is  associated  to this  function  using
81    // /  the  OleMenuCommandService service and the MenuCommand class.
82    // /  </summary>
83    private  void MenuItemCallback(object sender,  EventArgs e)
84    {
85       DataRecorder.Stop() ;
86       //  Show a Message Box to prove we were here
87       IVsUIShell uiShell  = (IVsUIShell)GetService( typeof ( SVsUIShell));
88       Guid clsid  = Guid.Empty;
89       int  result ;
90       Microsoft. VisualStudio . ErrorHandler. ThrowOnFailure(uiShell. ShowMessageBox(
91              0,
92              ref  clsid ,
93              "Collector",
94              string . Format(CultureInfo . CurrentCulture ,  "Collector Stopped"),
95              string . Empty,
96              0,
97              OLEMSGBUTTON.OLEMSGBUTTON_OK,
98              OLEMSGDEFBUTTON.OLEMSGDEFBUTTON_FIRST,
99              OLEMSGICON.OLEMSGICON_INFO,
100             0,        //  false
101             out  result ));
102   }
103
104   }
105 }
```

LISTING 5.1

CollectorPackage.

Listing for DataRecorder.cs

```csharp
1  using System;
2
3  namespace Monitor
4  {
5      public static class DataRecorder
6      {
7          public static void Start ()
8          {
9              logDirectoryPath = System.IO.Path. GetTempPath();
10             logFileName = System.IO.Path. Combine(logDirectoryPath, "collector " + DateTime.Now.ToString("yyyy
                   -MM-dd HH.mm.ss") + ".log");
11             try
12             {
13                 using (System.IO.StreamWriter streamWriter = new System.IO.StreamWriter(
14                     new System.IO.FileStream(logFileName, System.IO.FileMode.OpenOrCreate,
                           System.IO.FileAccess. Write,  System.IO.FileShare . ReadWrite)
15                     ))
16                 {
17                     streamWriter. WriteLine("Collector Started");
18                 }
19             }
20             catch (System.IO.IOException ioexception )
21             {
22                 Console. WriteLine("Error creating log file  " + ioexception );
23             }
24             myEvents = new MonitoredEventCollection();
25             myEvents.RegisterEventInventoryForEventMonitoring () ;
26         }
27
28         public static void Stop()
29         {
30             myEvents.DeRegisterEventMonitoringForInventory();
31             WriteLog("Collector Stopped");
32         }
33
34         public static void WriteLog(string logToWrite)
35         {
36             try
37             {
38                 using (System.IO.StreamWriter streamWriter = new System.IO.StreamWriter(
39                     new System.IO.FileStream(logFileName, System.IO.FileMode.Append,
                           System.IO.FileAccess. Write,  System.IO.FileShare . ReadWrite)
40                     ))
41                 {
42                     streamWriter. WriteLine(logToWrite);
43                 }
44             }
45             catch (System.IO.IOException ioexception )
46             {
47                 Console. WriteLine("Error writing to log file  " + ioexception );
48             }
```

```
49              }
50
51              static   MonitoredEventCollection  myEvents;
52              private  static   string  logFileName;
53              private  static   string  logDirectoryPath ;
54          }
55  }
```

LISTING 5.2

DataRecorder.

Listing for AbstractMonitoredEvent.cs

```
1   using  System;
2   using  System.IO;
3   using  System.Text;
4   using  System.Xml.Linq;
5   using  System.Xml.Serialization ;
6
7   namespace Monitor
8   {
9
10      [XmlInclude(typeof(MonitoredCommandEvent))]
11      [XmlRoot(ElementName = "MonitoredEvent", Namespace = "http://Monitor")]
12      public  abstract  class  AbstractMonitoredEvent
13      {
14          // /  <summary>
15          // /  Default  constructor  to  use  in  serialization
16          // /  </summary>
17          protected  AbstractMonitoredEvent()
18          {
19          }
20
21          //  User friendly  event  name used for  recording  in  logs
22          public  String  EventName { get;  set ;  }
23
24          //  Configured classification    for  the  log
25          public  String  Classification    { get ;  set ;  }
26
27          //  Stores  information  related  to  artifacts   such  as  window titles   active   during  the  event
28          public  String  ArtifactReference    { get ;  set ;  }
29
30          public  void  ToLog()
31          {
32              DataRecorder. WriteLog(String. Join (",", System.DateTime.UtcNow.ToString("u"), this.EventName,
                        this.Classification  ));
33          }
34
35          #region  event  handler  registration    and  disposal
36
37          public  virtual   bool  RegisterEventForMonitoring ( object  dte )
38          {
39              return   false ;
```

```
40          }
41
42
43          public void Dispose()
44          {
45
46              this . Dispose(true );
47
48              // GC.SuppressFinalize(this );
49
50          }
51
52          protected virtual void Dispose(bool disposing )
53          {
54              this . isDisposed = true ;
55          }
56
57          protected bool isDisposed;
58
59          #endregion
60      }
61 }
```

LISTING 5.3

AbstractMonitoredEvent.

Listing for MonitoredCommandEvent.cs

```
1 using System;
2 using System.Xml.Linq;
3 using EnvDTE;
4 using System.Xml.Serialization ;
5
6 namespace Monitor
7 {
8
9      [XmlRoot(ElementName = "MonitoredEvent", Namespace = "http://Monitor")]
10     public class MonitoredCommandEvent : AbstractMonitoredEvent
11     {
12
13         // /  <summary>
14         // /  DTE object EventID integer  distinguishes  events  with a shared  GUID.
15         // /  </summary>
16         public int EventID { get; set; }
17
18         // /  <summary>
19         // /  GUID of the DTE event from Visual  Studio
20         // /  </summary>
21         public String Guid { get; set; }
22
23         // /  <summary>
24         // /  Default constructor  to use in serialization
25         // /  </summary>
```

```
26      public  MonitoredCommandEvent()
27      {
28      }
29
30      // /  <summary>
31      // /  Create  an object  from the  Command class of the  DTE
32      // /  </summary>
33      // /  <param name="DTECommandObj">Command class of the DTE</param>
34      public  MonitoredCommandEvent(Command DTECommandObj)
35      {
36          if  (DTECommandObj != null)
37          {
38              this . EventName = DTECommandObj.Name;
39              this . Classification   = EventName.Split('. ')[0];    // use the  first   part of event  name
40              this . Guid = DTECommandObj.Guid;
41              this . EventID = DTECommandObj.ID;
42          }
43          else
44          {
45              throw new ArgumentNullException("DTECommandObj");
46          }
47      }
48
49      #region Event registration  , disposal ,  and hander
50      // /<summary>
51      // /The event  type object  holds the  event class  type  for this   interceptor   for example CommandEvents
52      // /the RegisterEvent  method registers   the  event
53      // /</ summary>
54      private   CommandEvents eventTypeObject;
55
56      public  override  bool RegisterEventForMonitoring (object  dte )
57      {
58          if  (! isDisposed  && eventTypeObject == null && dte != null )
59          {
60              eventTypeObject = (dte  as  DTE).Events.get_CommandEvents(Guid, EventID) as CommandEvents;
61          }
62          if  (eventTypeObject != null )
63          {
64              eventTypeObject. AfterExecute  += new
                      _dispCommandEvents_AfterExecuteEventHandler(OnAfterExecute);
65          }
66          return  (eventTypeObject != null );
67      }
68
69
70      // /  <summary>
71      // /  Remove the event  from the  handler  list
72      // /  </summary>
73      // /  <param name="disposing"></param>
74      protected  override  void Dispose(bool disposing )
75      {
76          if  (eventTypeObject  != null )
```

```
77              eventTypeObject. AfterExecute  −= OnAfterExecute;
78          this . isDisposed  = true ;
79      }
80
81
82      // /  <summary>
83      // /  Method receives  event  after   the  command completes execution.   Adds  the  end  of
84      // /  the  command event to the  log
85      // /  </summary>
86      // /  <param name="Guid">Guid of the command</param>
87      // /  <param name="ID">numeric id of the command</param>
88      // /  <param name="CustomIn"></param>
89      // /  <param name="CustomOut"></param>
90      private   void OnAfterExecute(string  Guid, int  ID, object  CustomIn, object  CustomOut)
91      {
92          this . ToLog();
93      }
94      #endregion
95  }
96 }
```

LISTING 5.4

MonitoredCommandEvent.

Listing for MonitoredEventFactory.cs

```
 1 using  System;
 2 using  System.IO;
 3 using  System.Text;
 4 using  System.Xml.Linq;
 5 using  System.Xml.Serialization  ;
 6 using  EnvDTE;
 7
 8 namespace Monitor
 9 {
10     public  static   class  MonitoredEventFactory
11     {
12
13         public  static   AbstractMonitoredEvent GetMonitoredEvent(Command DTECommandObj)
14         {
15             object  eventObj  = new MonitoredCommandEvent(DTECommandObj);
16             return  (AbstractMonitoredEvent)eventObj;
17
18         }
19
20     }
21 }
```

LISTING 5.5

MonitoredEventFactory.

Listing for MonitoredEventCollection.cs

```
1   using  System;
2   using  System.Collections . Generic;
3   using  System.IO;
4   using  System.Reflection ;
5   using  System.Xml;
6   using  System.Xml.Linq;
7   using  EnvDTE;
8   using  Microsoft. VisualStudio . Shell ;
9   using  System.Xml.Serialization  ;  // 12.0
10
11  namespace Monitor
12  {
13      public  class  MonitoredEventCollection
14      {
15          // /  <summary>
16          // /  Object  to store  all  the  MonitoredEvents we have on file
17          // /  </summary>
18          private  List <AbstractMonitoredEvent> IDEEventListenerRegistry ;
19
20          // /  <summary>
21          // /  Constructor  that  reads  events  from a file  or queries  Visual  Studio  for  the  command events
22          // /  if  the  file  does not  exist . Then saves  the  events  to  the  file  for  next  time.
23          // /  </summary>
24          public  MonitoredEventCollection ()
25          {
26              String  EventInventoryFilePath  =
                        Path. Combine(Path.GetDirectoryName(Assembly.GetExecutingAssembly().Location), "
                        CommandGUIDs.xml");
27              MonitoredEventCollectionInitialize   (EventInventoryFilePath );
28          }
29
30          private  void  MonitoredEventCollectionInitialize   (String  EventInventoryFilePath ) {
31              if  (File . Exists (EventInventoryFilePath )) {
32                  IDEEventListenerRegistry  = LoadEventsFromFile(EventInventoryFilePath );
33              }
34              else  {
35                  IDEEventListenerRegistry  = QueryVSForAllDTECommands();
36
37              }
38              if  (IDEEventListenerRegistry != null ) {
39                  saveEventInterestTable  (IDEEventListenerRegistry ,  EventInventoryFilePath );
40              }
41          }
42
43          private  List <AbstractMonitoredEvent> LoadEventsFromFile(string  filepath  )
44          {
45              try
46              {
47                  List <AbstractMonitoredEvent> eventList  = new List<AbstractMonitoredEvent>();
48                  var  serializer   = new System.Xml.Serialization . XmlSerializer (typeof (List <
                        AbstractMonitoredEvent>));
```

```
49        using (Stream file  = new FileStream(filepath , FileMode.Open, FileAccess.Read))
50        {
51            eventList  = (List <AbstractMonitoredEvent>)serializer .Deserialize (file );
52        }
53        return eventList ;
54    }
55    catch (System.IO.IOException)
56    {
57        Console.WriteLine("Error opening file  with event inventory" + filepath );
58        return null ;
59    }
60 }
61
62 private void saveEventInterestTable (List <AbstractMonitoredEvent> eventList , string filepath )
63 {
64    try
65    {
66        var serializer  = new System.Xml.Serialization .XmlSerializer (typeof (List <
                AbstractMonitoredEvent>));
67        using (Stream file  = new FileStream(filepath , FileMode.Create, FileAccess .Write))
68        {
69            serializer .Serialize (file , eventList );
70            file .Flush() ;
71        }
72    }
73    catch (System.IO.IOException)
74    {
75        Console.WriteLine("Error creating file  for storing monitored events with file  path:" +
                filepath );
76    }
77
78 }
79 // / <summary>
80 // / Query the DTE Commands object for all events it provides . Could be useful to determine whether
            new commands from
81 // / Add–Ins or Extensions appeared since we built the inventory . Returns a collection of Events with
            Immediate type
82 // / </summary>
83 // / <returns >List of AbstractMonitoredEvents in the DTE object</returns >
84 private List <AbstractMonitoredEvent> QueryVSForAllDTECommands()
85 {
86    List <AbstractMonitoredEvent> EventList = new List <AbstractMonitoredEvent>();
87    DTE dteobj = tryGetDTEObject();
88    if (dteobj != null )
89    {
90
91        try
92        {
93            foreach (Command DTE_CommandEventObj in dteobj.Commands)
94            {
95                AbstractMonitoredEvent NewEvent =
                        MonitoredEventFactory.GetMonitoredEvent(DTE_CommandEventObj);
```

```
 96                          if  (NewEvent != null)
 97                          {
 98                              EventList . Add(NewEvent);
 99                          }
100                      }
101                  }
102              // This exception happens during dispose / finalize   when VS exits, just  return  null
103              catch  ( System.Runtime.InteropServices . InvalidComObjectException)
104              {
105                  return  null ;
106              }
107          }
108          return  EventList ;
109      }
110
111
112      // /  <summary>
113      // /  Gets a DTE object for the  currently  running Visual  Studio  instance .   Requires references
114      // /  to EnvDTE, Microsoft.VisualStudio . Shell .12.0,   and Microsoft. VisualStudio . OLE.Interop.
115      // /  </summary>
116      // /  <returns ></returns >
117              private  static   DTE tryGetDTEObject()
118              {
119                      DTE dteobj=null;
120          try
121          {
122              dteobj  = (( EnvDTE.DTE)ServiceProvider.GlobalProvider.GetService(typeof( EnvDTE.DTE).GUID)).
                        DTE;
123          }
124          catch  (NullReferenceException)
125          { }
126          catch  ( System.Runtime.InteropServices . InvalidComObjectException)
127          { }
128          catch  ( System.Runtime.InteropServices . COMException)
129          { }
130                      return   dteobj ;
131              }
132
133      public  bool  RegisterEventInventoryForEventMonitoring ()
134      {
135
136          DTE dteobj = tryGetDTEObject();
137          bool somethingRegistered  = false ;
138          if (dteobj  != null  && IDEEventListenerRegistry != null  && IDEEventListenerRegistry.Count > 0)
139          {
140
141              foreach  (AbstractMonitoredEvent command in IDEEventListenerRegistry)
142              {
143                  if  (command.RegisterEventForMonitoring(dteobj))
144                  {
145                      somethingRegistered  = true ;
146                  }
```

```
147                   }
148
149
150               }
151
152           return  somethingRegistered ;
153       }
154
155       public  void  DeRegisterEventMonitoringForInventory ()
156       {
157
158           foreach  (AbstractMonitoredEvent  monitoredEvent  in  IDEEventListenerRegistry )
159           {
160               monitoredEvent.Dispose() ;
161           }
162
163       }
164
165   }
166 }
```

LISTING 5.6

MonitoredEventCollection.

ACKNOWLEDGMENTS

The authors thank the software developer community's contribution in sharing their usage data and the support of their respective institutions for the research work behind this chapter. This material is based in part on work supported by the National Science Foundation under grant number 1252995.

REFERENCES

[1] Murphy-Hill E, Parnin C, Black AP. How we refactor, and how we know it. IEEE Trans Softw Eng 2012;38:5–18. doi:10.1109/TSE.2011.41.

[2] Carter J, Dewan P. Are you having difficulty? In: Proceedings of the 2010 ACM conference on computer supported cooperative work, CSCW '10. New York, NY, USA: ACM; 2010. p. 211–4. ISBN 978-1-60558-795-0. doi:10.1145/1718918.1718958.

[3] Kou H, Johnson P, Erdogmus H. Operational definition and automated inference of test-driven development with Zorro. Autom Softw Eng 2010;17(1):57–85. doi:10.1007/s10515-009-0058-8.

[4] Maalej W, Fritz T, Robbes R. Collecting and processing interaction data for recommendation systems, chap. Recommendation systems in software engineering. Berlin: Springer; 2014.

[5] Kersten M, Murphy GC. Mylar: a degree-of-interest model for ides. In: Proceedings of the 4th international conference on aspect-oriented software development, AOSD '05. New York, NY, USA: ACM; 2005. p. 159–68. ISBN 1-59593-042-6. doi:10.1145/1052898.1052912.

[6] Murphy GC, Kersten M, Findlater L. How are Java software developers using the Elipse IDE? IEEE Softw 2006;23(4):76–83. doi:10.1109/MS.2006.105.

[7] Kersten M, Murphy GC. Using task context to improve programmer productivity. In: Proceedings of the 14th ACM SIGSOFT international symposium on foundations of software engineering, SIGSOFT '06/FSE-14. New York, NY, USA: ACM; 2006. p. 1–11. ISBN 1-59593-468-5. doi:10.1145/1181775.1181777.

[8] Murphy-Hill E, Jiresal R, Murphy GC. Improving software developers' fluency by recommending development environment commands. In: Foundations of software engineering; 2012.

[9] Vakilian M, Chen N, Moghaddam RZ, Negara S, Johnson RE. A compositional paradigm of automating refactorings. In: Proceedings of the European conference on object-oriented programming (ECOOP); 2013. p. 527–51.

[10] Vakilian M, Johnson RE. Alternate refactoring paths reveal usability problems. In: Proceedings of the international conference on software engineering (ICSE); 2014. p. 1–11.

[11] Vakilian M, Chen N, Negara S, Rajkumar BA, Bailey BP, Johnson RE. Use, disuse, and misuse of automated refactorings. In: Proceedings of the international conference on software engineering (ICSE); 2012. p. 233–43.

[12] Negara S, Chen N, Vakilian M, Johnson RE, Dig D. A comparative study of manual and automated refactorings. In: Proceedings of the European conference on object-oriented programming (ECOOP); 2013. p. 552–76.

[13] Murphy-Hill E, Black AP. Breaking the barriers to successful refactoring: observations and tools for extract method. In: Proceedings of the 30th international conference on software engineering, ICSE '08. New York, NY, USA: ACM; 2008. p. 421–30. ISBN 978-1-60558-079-1. doi:10.1145/1368088.1368146.

[14] Lee YY, Chen N, Johnson RE. Drag-and-drop refactoring: intuitive and efficient program transformation. In: Proceedings of the 35th international conference on software engineering (ICSE); 2013. p. 23–32. doi:10.1109/ICSE.2013.6606548.

[15] Murphy-Hill ER, Ayazifar M, Black AP. Restructuring software with gestures. In: VL/HCC; 2011. p. 165–72.

[16] Ge X, DuBose Q, Murphy-Hill E. Reconciling manual and automatic refactoring. In: Proceedings of the 34th international conference on software engineering (ICSE); 2012. p. 211–21. doi:10.1109/ICSE.2012.6227192.

[17] Foster S, Griswold WG, Lerner S. Witchdoctor: IDE support for real-time auto-completion of refactorings. In: Proceedings of the 34th international conference on software engineering (ICSE); 2012. p. 222–32. doi:10.1109/ICSE.2012.6227191.

[18] Basili VR, Rombach HD. The TAME project: towards improvement-oriented software environments. IEEE Trans Softw Eng 1988;14(6):758–73. doi:10.1109/32.6156.

[19] Snipes W, Nair A, Murphy-Hill E. Experiences gamifying developer adoption of practices and tools. In: IEEE 36th international conference on software engineering, ICSE 2014; 2014.

[20] Robillard MP, Coelho W, Murphy GC. How effective developers investigate source code: an exploratory study. IEEE Trans Softw Eng 2004;30:889–903. doi:10.1109/TSE.2004.101.

[21] Negara S, Vakilian M, Chen N, Johnson RE, Dig D. Is it dangerous to use version control histories to study source code evolution? In: Proceedings of the European conference on object-oriented programming (ECOOP); 2012. p. 79–103.

[22] Yoon Y, Myers BA. Capturing and analyzing low-level events from the code editor. In: Proceedings of the 3rd ACM SIGPLAN workshop on evaluation and usability of programming languages and tools; 2011. p. 25–30.

[23] Yoon Y, Myers BA. An exploratory study of backtracking strategies used by developers. In: Proceedings of the 5th international workshop on cooperative and human aspects of software engineering (CHASE); 2012. p. 138–44.

[24] Yoon Y, Myers BA, Koo S. Visualization of fine-grained code change history. In: Proceedings of the 2013 IEEE symposium on visual languages and human-centric computing (VL/HCC); 2013. p. 119–26.

[25] Johnson PM, Kou H, Agustin J, Chan C, Moore C, Miglani J, et al. Beyond the personal software process: metrics collection and analysis for the differently disciplined. In: Proceedings of the 25th international conference on software engineering. Washington, DC, USA: IEEE Computer Society; 2003.

[26] Liu H, Gao Y, Niu Z. An initial study on refactoring tactics. In: IEEE 36th annual computer software and applications conference (COMPSAC). Washington, DC, USA: IEEE Computer Society; 2012. p. 213–8.

[27] Parnin C, Rugaber S. Resumption strategies for interrupted programming tasks. Softw Qual J 2011; 19(1):5–34.

[28] Murphy-Hill E, Parnin C, Black AP. How we refactor, and how we know it. IEEE Trans Softw Eng 2012;38(1):5–18.

[29] Ying AT, Robillard MP. The influence of the task on programmer behaviour. In: IEEE 19th international conference on program comprehension (ICPC), 2011. Washington, DC, USA: IEEE Computer Society; 2011. p. 31–40.

[30] Murphy GC, Viriyakattiyaporn P, Shepherd D. Using activity traces to characterize programming behaviour beyond the lab. In: IEEE 17th international conference on program comprehension, ICPC'09. Washington, DC, USA: IEEE Computer Society; 2009. p. 90–4.

[31] Vakilian M, Chen N, Negara S, Rajkumar BA, Zilouchian Moghaddam R, Johnson RE. The need for richer refactoring usage data. In: Proceedings of the workshop on evaluation and usability of programming languages and tools (PLATEAU); 2011. p. 31–8.

[32] Kersten M. Focusing knowledge work with task context. Ph.D. thesis, The University of British Columbia; 2007.

[33] Zou L, Godfrey MW. An industrial case study of Coman's automated task detection algorithm: what worked, what didn't, and why. In: Proceedings of the 2012 IEEE international conference on software maintenance (ICSM), ICSM '12. Washington, DC, USA: IEEE Computer Society; 2012. p. 6–14. ISBN 978-1-4673-2313-0. doi:10.1109/ICSM.2012.6405247.

[34] Coman ID, Sillitti A. Automated identification of tasks in development sessions. In: Proceedings of the 2008 16th IEEE international conference on program comprehension, ICPC '08. Washington, DC, USA: IEEE Computer Society; 2008. p. 212–7. ISBN 978-0-7695-3176-2. doi:10.1109/ICPC.2008.16.

[35] Nagappan M, Robinson B. Creating operational profiles of software systems by transforming their log files to directed cyclic graphs. In: Proceedings of the 6th international workshop on traceability in emerging forms of software engineering, TEFSE '11. ACM; 2011. p. 54–7.

[36] Flanagan JC. The critical incident technique. Psychol Bull 1954:327–58

[37] Shattuck LG, Woods DD. The critical incident technique: 40 years later. In: Proceedings of HFES; 1994. p. 1080–4.

[38] del Galdo EM, Williges RC, Williges BH, Wixon DR. An evaluation of critical incidents for software documentation design. In: Proceedings of HFES; 1986. p. 19–23.

[39] Biehl JT, Czerwinski M, Smith G, Robertson GG. Fastdash: a visual dashboard for fostering awareness in software teams. In: Proceedings of the SIGCHI conference on human factors in computing systems, CHI '07. New York, NY, USA: ACM; 2007. p. 1313–22. ISBN 978-1-59593-593-9. doi:10.1145/1240624.1240823.

LATENT DIRICHLET ALLOCATION: EXTRACTING TOPICS FROM SOFTWARE ENGINEERING DATA

Joshua Charles Campbell*, Abram Hindle*, Eleni Stroulia*

Department of Computing Science, University of Alberta, Edmonton, AB, Canada*

CHAPTER OUTLINE

6.1 INTRODUCTION

Whether they consist of code, bug/issue reports, mailing-list messages, requirements specifications, or documentation, software repositories include text documents. This textual information is an invaluable source of information, and can potentially be used in a variety of software-engineering activities. The textual descriptions of bugs can be compared against each other to recognize duplicate bug reports. The textual documentations of software modules can be used to recommend relevant source code fragments. E-mail messages can be analyzed to better understand the skills and roles of software developers, and to recognize their concerns about the project status and their sentiments about their work and teammates. This is why we have recently witnessed numerous research projects investigating the application of text-analysis methods to software text assets.

The simplest approach to analyzing textual documents is to use a *vector-space model*, which views documents (and queries) as frequency vectors of words. For example "the" occurred once, "my" occurred twice, "bagel" occurred zero times, and so on. Effectively, a vector-space model views terms as dimensions in a high-dimensional space, so that each document is represented by a point in that space on the basis of the frequency of terms it includes. This model suffers from two major shortcomings. First, it makes the consideration of all words impractical: since each word is a dimension, considering all words would imply expensive computations in a very high-dimensional space. Second, it assumes that all words are independent. In response to these two assumptions, methods for extracting *topic models*—that is, thematic topics corresponding to related bags of words, were developed.

A thematic topic is a collection of words which are somehow related. For example, a topic might consist of the words "inning," "home," "batter," "strike," "catcher," "foul," and "pitcher," which are all related to the game of baseball. The most well known topic-model methods are latent semantic indexing (LSI) and *latent Dirichlet allocation* (LDA). LSI employs singular-value decomposition to describe relationships between terms and concepts as a matrix. LDA arranges and rearranges words into buckets, which represent topics, until it estimates that it has found the most likely arrangement. In the end, having identified the topics relevant to a document collection (as sets of related words) LDA associates each document in the subject collection with a weighted list of topics.

LDA has recently emerged as the method of choice for working with large collections of text documents. There is a wealth of publications reporting its applications in a variety of text-analysis tasks in general and software engineering in particular. LDA can be used to summarize, cluster, link, and preprocess large collections of data because it produces a weighted list of topics for every document in a collection dependent on the properties of the whole. These lists can then be compared, counted, clustered, paired, or fed into more advanced algorithms. Furthermore, each topic comprises a weighted list of words which can be used in summaries.

This chapter provides an overview of LDA and its relevance to analyzing textual software-engineering data. First, in Section 6.2, we discuss the mathematical model underlying LDA. In Section 6.3, we present a tutorial on how to use state-of-the-art software tools to generate an LDA model of a software-engineering corpus. In Section 6.4, we discuss some typical pitfalls encountered when using LDA. In Section 6.5, we review the mining-software repositories literature for example applications of LDA. Finally, in Section 6.6, we conclude with a summary of the important points one must be aware of when considering using this method.

6.2 APPLICATIONS OF LDA IN SOFTWARE ANALYSIS

The LDA method was originally formulated by Blei et al. [1], and it soon became quite popular within the software-engineering community. LDA's popularity comes from the variety of its potential applications.

LDA excels at feature reduction, and can employed as a preprocessing step for other models, such as machine learning algorithms. LDA can also be used to augment the inputs to machine learning and clustering algorithms by producing additional features from documents. One example of this type of LDA usage was described by Wang and Wong [2], who employed it in a recommender system. Similarly, labeled LDA can be used to create vectors of independent features from arbitrary feature sets such as tags.

An important use of LDA is for linking software artifacts. There are many instances of such artifact-linking applications, such as measuring coupling between code modules [3] and matching code modules with natural-language requirement specifications [4] for traceability purposes. Asuncion et al. [5] applied LDA on textual documentation and source-code modules and used the topic-document matrix to indicate traceability between the two. Thomas et al. [6] focused on the use of LDA on yet another traceability problem, linking e-mail messages to source-code modules. Gethers et al. [7] investigated the effectiveness of LDA for traceability-link recovery. They combined information retrieval techniques, including the Jenson-Shannon model, the vector space model, and the relational topic model using LDA. They concluded that each technique had its positives and negatives, yet the integration of the methods tended to produce the best results. Typically steeped in the information retrieval domain, Savage et al. [8], Poshyvanyk [9], and McMillan et al. [10] have explored the use of information retrieval techniques such as LSI [11] and LDA to recover software traceability links in source code and other documents. For a general literature survey related to traceability techniques (including LDA), the interested reader should refer to De Lucia et al. [12].

Baldi et al. [13] labeled LDA-extracted topics and compared them with aspects in software development. Baldi et al. claim that some topics do map to aspects such as security, logging, and cross-cutting concerns, which was somewhat corroborated by Hindle et al. [14].

Clustering is frequently used to compare and identify (dis)similar documents and code, or to quantify the overlap between two sets of documents. Clustering algorithms can potentially be applied to topic probability vectors produced by LDA. LDA has been used in a clustering context, for issue report querying, and for deduplication. Lukins et al. [15] applied LDA topic analysis to issue reports, leveraging LDA inference to infer if queries, topics, and issue reports were related to each other. Alipour et al. [16] leveraged LDA topics to add context to deduplicate issue reports, and found that LDA topics added useful contextual information to issue/bug deduplication. Campbell et al. [17] used LDA to examine the coverage of popular project documentation by applying LDA to two collections of documents at once: user questions and project documentation. This was done by clustering and comparing LDA output data.

Often LDA is used to summarize the contents of large datasets. This is done by manually or automatically labeling the most popular topics produced by unlabeled LDA. Labeled LDA can be used to track specific features over time—for example, to measure the fragmentation of a software ecosystem as in Han et al. [18].

Even though LDA topics are assumed to be implicit and not observable, there is substantial work on assessing the interpretability of those summaries by developers. Labeling software artifacts using

LDA was investigated by De Lucia et al. [19]. By using multiple information retrieval approaches such as LDA and LSI, they labeled and summarized source code and compared it against human-generated labels. Hindle et al. [20] investigated if developers could interpret and label LDA topics. They reported limited success, with 50% being successfully labeled by the developers, and that nonexperts tend to do poorly at labeling topics on systems they have not dealt with.

Finally, there has been some research on the appropriate choice of LDA hyperparameters and parameters: α, β, K topics. Grant and Cordy [21] were concerned about K, where K is the number of topics. Panichella et al. [22] proposed LDA-GA, a genetic algorithm approach to searching for appropriate LDA hyperparameters and parameters. LDA-GA needs an evaluation measure, and thus Panichella et al. used software-engineering-specific tasks that allowed their genetic algorithm optimized the number of topics for cost-effectiveness.

6.3 HOW LDA WORKS

The input of LDA is a collection of documents and a few parameters. The output is a probabilistic model describing (a) how much words belong to topics and (b) how associated topics are with documents. A list of topics, often containing some topics repeatedly, is generated at random on the basis of (b). That list is the same length as the number of words in the document. Then, that list of topics is transformed into a list of words by turning each topic into a word on the basis of (a).

LDA is a generative model. This means that it works with the probability of observing a particular dataset given some assumptions about how that dataset was created. At its core is the assumption that a document is generated by a small number of "topics." An LDA "topic" is a probability distribution, assigning to each word in the collection vocabulary a probability.

Topics are considered hypothetical and unobservable, which is to say that they do not actually exist in documents. This means that, first, we know that documents are not actually generated from a set of topics. Instead, we are using the concept of a topic as a simplified model for what must be a more complicated process, the process of writing a document. Second, documents do not come with information about what topics are present, what words those topics contain, and how much of each topic is in each document. Therefore, we must infer the topic characteristics from a collection of collections of words. Each document is usually assumed to be generated by a few of the total number of possible topics. So, every word in every document is assumed to be attributable to one of the document's topics.

Though, of course, words do a have a particular order in a document, LDA does not consider their order. Each word is assigned an individual probability of being generated. That is, the probability of a topic k generating a word v is a value $\phi_{k,v}$ [23]. The sum of these probabilities for a topic k must be 1:

$$\sum_v \phi_{k,v} = 1.$$

Furthermore, the $\phi_{k,v}$ values are assumed to come from a random variable ϕ_k, with a symmetric Dirichlet distribution (which is the origin of the name of the LDA method). The symmetric Dirichlet distribution has one parameter, β, which determines whether a topic is narrow (i.e., focuses on a few words) or broad (i.e., covers a bigger spread of words). If β is 1, the probability of a topic generating a word often is the same as the probability of a topic generating a word rarely. If β is less than 1, most words will be extremely unlikely, while a few will make up the majority of the words generated. In other words, larger values of β lead to broad topics, and smaller values of β lead to narrow topics.

In summary, words are assumed to come from topics, with the probability of a word coming from a specific topic coming from a Dirichlet distribution. Thus, if we know that β is a very small positive integer, we know that a topic which would generate any word with equal probability is itself very unlikely to exist.

The "document" is an important concept involved in understanding how LDA works. A document is also a probability distribution. Every possible topic has a probability of occurring from 0 to 1, and the sum of these probabilities is 1. The probability that a document d will generate a word from a specific topic k is $\theta_{d,k}$. Again, the $\theta_{d,k}$ probabilities are probabilities, but the probabilities of $\theta_{d,k}$ taking on a particular probability value comes from a Dirichlet distribution of parameter α. The topics that a document is observed to generate are a vector, Z_d. This vector is N_d words long, representing every word in the document. If α is near 1, we expect to see documents with few topics and documents with many topics in equal proportion. If α is less than 1, we expect most documents to only use a few topics. If α is greater than 1, we expect most documents to use almost every topic.

To summarize, words come from topics. The probability of a word being generated by a specific topic comes from a symmetric Dirichlet distribution. The probability of a document containing a word from a specific topic is dictated by a different symmetric Dirichlet distribution. The words that a document is observed to generate are a vector, W_d, which is formed by observing the topic indicated by the entries in the Z_d vector.

Figure 6.1 shows the words present in each document coming from topic 1 in nine different LDA models of varying parameters. Additionally, it shows α, β, θ, ϕ, Z, and W. By following the arrows, we can see how each prior generates each observed posterior. Figure 6.1 shows the effects that α has on θ, that θ has on Z, and that Z has on W. As we increase α, we observe that more documents contain words from topic 1. Additionally, it shows the effect that β has on ϕ and that ϕ has on W. As we increase β, we end up with topic 1 including a larger variety of vocabulary words. For example, the plot in column 1 and row 1 in Figure 6.1 shows that each document uses a much smaller subset of the possible vocabulary than the plot in column 1 and row 3 below it. Similarly, the plot in column 3 and row 1 shows that many more documents contain words from topic 1 than the plot in column 1 and row 1.

The LDA process consists in allocating and reallocating weights (or probabilities if normalized) in θ and ϕ until the lower bound of the total probability of observing the input documents is maximized. Conceptually, this is accomplished by dividing up topics among words and by dividing up documents among topics. This iterative process can be implemented in many different ways.

Technically, the generative process LDA assumes is as follows, given a corpus of M documents, each of length N_i [1]:

1. For every topic $k \in \{1, \ldots, K\}$, choose $\vec{\phi_k} \sim \text{Dir}(\beta)$.
2. For every document $d \in \{1, \ldots, M\}$
   (a) choose $\vec{\theta_d} \sim \text{Dir}(\alpha)$.
   (b) for every word $j \in 1, \ldots, N_d$ in document d
      i. choose a topic $z_{d,j} \sim \text{multinomial}\left(\vec{\theta_d}\right)$.
      ii. choose a word $w_{d,j} \sim \text{multinomial}\left(\vec{\phi_{z_{d,j}}}\right)$.

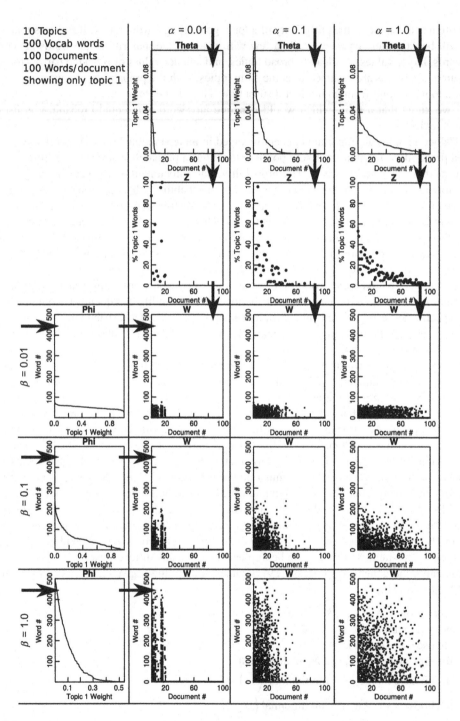

FIGURE 6.1

9 Example LDA models produced by varying **α** and **β**. Arrows show the relationship between prior and posterior.

Thus, the probability of a topic k generating a word v at a position j in a document d is $p\left(w_{d,j} = v \mid \alpha, \beta, K\right)$:

$$\int_{\Theta} \sum_{k=1}^{K} \int_{\Phi} p\left(w_{d,j} = v \mid \vec{\phi}_k\right) p\left(z_{d,j} = k \mid \vec{\theta}_d\right) p\left(\vec{\phi}_k \mid \beta\right) p\left(\vec{\theta}_d \mid \alpha\right) \, d\vec{\phi}_k \, d\vec{\theta}_d,$$

integrating over all possible probability vectors of length K (Θ) and of length V (Φ). The goal of LDA software is to maximize the probability

$$p\left(\theta, Z \mid W, \alpha, \beta, K\right)$$

by choosing θ and Z given a corpus W and parameters α and β. Unfortunately, this problem is intractable [1], so the values of θ and ϕ that maximize the above probability are estimated by LDA software. The exact technique employed to estimate the maximum differs between different pieces of software.

6.4 LDA TUTORIAL

In this tutorial, we illustrate the LDA method in the context of analyzing textual data extracted from the issue-tracking system of a popular project.

1. The first task involves acquiring the issue-tracker data and representing it in a convenient format such as JavaScript Object Notation (JSON).
2. Then we transform the text of the input data—namely, we convert the text to word counts, where words are represented as integer IDs.
3. We apply LDA software on the transformed documents to produce a topic-document matrix and a topic-word matrix.
4. We then summarize the top words from the topic-word matrix to produce topic-word summaries, and store the topic-document matrix.
5. Finally, we analyze the document matrix and the topics. The objective of this analysis step is to (a) examine the latent topics discovered, (b) plot the topic relevance over time, and (c) cluster the issues (i.e., input documents) according to their associated topics.

6.4.1 MATERIALS

This tutorial will use source code that the authors have developed to run LDA on issues collected in issues-tracking systems. For the sake of simplicity, the authors have provided a configured Ubuntu 64bit x86 virtual machine for VirtualBox[1] with all the software and appropriate data already loaded and available. The file is called `LDA-Tutorial.ova`, and can be downloaded from http://archive.org/details/LDAinSETutorial/ and https://archive.org/29/items/LDAinSETutorial/.

---

[1]https://www.virtualbox.org/.

Download the ova file and import it into VirtualBox. Alternatively, use VirtualBox to export it to a raw file to write directly to a USB stick or hard drive. The username and the password of this virtual image are tutorial. On boot-up the virtual image will open to an Lubuntu 14.04 desktop. The source code for this tutorial is located in the /home/tutorial/lda-chapter-tutorial directory, which is also linked to from the desktop.

To access and browse the source code of the tutorial, visit http://bitbucket.org/abram/lda-chapter-tutorial/ and git clone that project, or download a zip file of the tutorial data and source code from http://webdocs.cs.ualberta.ca/~hindle1/2014/lda-chapter-tutorial.zip. The data directory contains the issue-tracker data for the bootstrap project. The important source code file is lda_from_json.py, which depends on lda.py. We use lda_from_json.py to apply the LDA algorithm, implemented by Vowpal Wabbit,[2] on issue-tracker issues. It is highly recommended to use the virtual machine as Vowpal Wabbit and other dependencies are already installed and configured.

6.4.2 ACQUIRING SOFTWARE-ENGINEERING DATA

The data source for this tutorial will be the issues and comments of the Bootstrap[3] issue tracker. Bootstrap is a popular JavaScript-based Website front-end framework that allows preprocessing, templating, and dynamic-content management of webpages. Bootstrap is a very active project, and its developer community is regularly reporting issues regarding Web browser compatibility and developer support. As of March 2014, Bootstrap had 13,182 issues in its issue tracker.

Our first task is to acquire the issue-tracker data for Bootstrap. To achieve this result we have written a Github issue tracker-extractor that relies on the Github application programming interface (API) and the Ruby Octokit library. Our program github_issues_to_json.rb (included in the chapter tutorial repository) uses the Github API to download the issues and comments from the Github issue tracker. One must first sign up to Github as a registered user and provide the GHUSERNAME and GHPASSWORD in the config.json file in the root of the chapter repository. One can also specify GHUSER (target Github user) and GHPROJECT (target Github user's project to mirror) in config.json or as an environment variable. github_issues_to_json.rb downloads issue-tracker data and every page of issues and issue comments. It saves this data to a JSON file, resembling the original format obtained from the Github API. The JSON file created, large.json, contains both issues and comments, stored as a list of JSON objects (issues), each of which contains a list of comments. Mirroring Bootstrap takes a couple of minutes because of the thousands of issues and thousands of comments within Bootstrap's issue tracker.

Once we have downloaded the Bootstrap issues (and comments) into large.json, we need to load and prepare that data for LDA. Most LDA programs will require that documents are preprocessed.

6.4.3 TEXT ANALYSIS AND DATA TRANSFORMATION

In this section we will cover preprocessing the data for LDA. Generally those who use LDA apply the following prepossessing steps:

- Loading text
- Transforming text
- Lexical analysis of text
- Optionally removing stop words
- Optionally stemming
- Optionally removing uncommon or very common words
- Building a vocabulary
- Transforming each text document into a word bag

6.4.3.1 Loading text

Loading the text is usually a matter of parsing a data file or querying a database where the text is stored. In this case, it is a JSON file containing Github issue-tracker API call results.

6.4.3.2 Transforming text

The next step is to transform the text into a final textual representation. This will be the textual representation of the documents. Some text is structured and thus must be processed. Perhaps section headers and other markup need to be removed. If the input text is raw HTML, perhaps one needs to strip HTML from the text before use. For the issue-tracker data we could include author names in the comments and in the issue description. This might allow for author-oriented topics, but might also confuse future analysis when we notice there was no direct mention of any of the authors. In this tutorial we have chosen to concatenate the title and the full description of the issue report, so that topics will have access to both fields.

Many uses of LDA in software analysis include source code in the document texts. Using source code requires lexing, parsing, filtering, and often renaming values. When feeding source code to LDA, some users do not want comments, some do not want identifiers, some do not want keywords, and some want only identifiers. Thus, the task of converting documents to a textual representation is nontrivial, especially if documents are marked up.

6.4.3.3 Lexical analysis

The next step is the lexical analysis of the texts. We need to split the words or tokens out of the text in order to eventually count them.

With source code we apply lexical analysis, where one extracts tokens from source code in a fashion similar to how compilers perform lexical analysis before parsing.

With natural language text, words and punctuation are separated where appropriate. For example, some words, such as initialisms, contain periods, but most of the time a period indicates the end of a sentence and is not a part of the word. With texts about source code, it might be useful to have some tokens start with a period—for instance, if you are analyzing cascading style sheets (CSS) or texts with CSS snippets, where a period prefix indicates a CSS class.

6.4.3.4 Stop word removal

Often words appear in texts which are not useful in topic analysis. Such words are called stop words. It is common in natural language processing and information retrieval systems to filter out stop words before executing a query or building a model. Stop words are words that are not relevant to the desired analysis. Whether a word is considered a stop word or not depends on the analysis, but there are some sets of common stop words available. Some users of natural language processing and LDA tools view terms such as "the," "at," and "a" as unnecessary, whereas other researchers, depending on the context, might view the definitives and prepositions as important. We have included stop_words, a text file that contains various words that we do not wish to include in topics in this tutorial. For each word extracted from the document, we remove those found within our stop word list.

6.4.3.5 Stemming

Since words in languages such as English have multiple forms and tenses, it is common practice to *stem* words. Stemming is the process of reducing words to their original root. Stemming is optional and is often used to reduce vocabulary sizes. For instance, given the words "act," "acting," "acted," and "acts," the stem for all four words will be "act." Thus, if a sentence contains any of the words, on stemming, we will resolve it to the same stem. Unfortunately, sometimes stemming reduces the semantic meaning of a term. For example, "acted" is in the past tense, but this information will be lost if the word is stemmed. Stemming is not always necessary.

Stemming software is readily available. NLTK[4] comes with an implementation of the Porter and Snowball stemmers. One caveat with stemmers is they often produce word roots that are not words or that conflict with other words. Sometimes this leads to unreadable output from LDA unless one keeps the original documents and their original words.

6.4.3.6 Common and uncommon word removal

Since LDA is often used to find topics, it is common practice to filter out exceptionally common words and infrequent words. Words that appear in only one document are often viewed as unimportant, because they will not form a topic with multiple documents. Unfortunately, if very infrequent words are left in, some documents which do not contain the word will be associated with that word via the topics that include that word. The common words are often skipped because they muddle topic summaries and make interpretation more difficult.

Once the documents have been preprocessed and prepared via lexing, filtering, and stemming, we can start indexing them for use as documents within an LDA implementation.

6.4.3.7 Building a vocabulary

In this tutorial, we use the Vowpal Wabbit software of Langford et al. [24]. Vowpal Wabbit accepts a sparse document-word matrix format where each line represents a document and each element of the line is an integer word joined by a colon to its count within that document. We provide lda.py, found within the lda-chapter-tutorial directory, a program to convert text to Vowpal Wabbit's input format, and parse its output format.

One difficulty encountered using LDA libraries and programs is that often you have to maintain your own vocabulary or dictionary. We also have to calculate and provide the size of the vocabulary as $\lceil \log_2(|words|) \rceil$.

---

[4]http://www.nltk.org/howto/stem.html.

6.4.4 **APPLYING LDA**

We choose 20 for the number of topics for the sake reading and interpreting the topics. The number of topics depends on the intent behind the analysis. If one wants to use LDA for dimensionality reduction, perhaps keeping the number of topics low is important. If one wants to cluster documents using LDA a larger number of topics might be warranted. Conceptual coupling might be best served with many topics over fewer topics.

We provide our parameters to Vowpal Wabbit: α set to 0.01, β set to 0.01 (called ρ in Vowpal Wabbit), and K, the number of topics. The value 0.01 is a common default for α and β in many pieces of LDA software. These parameters should be chosen on the basis of the desired breadth of documents and topics, respectively.

- If documents that discuss only a few topics and never mention all others are desired, α should be set small, to around $1/K$. With this setting, almost all documents will almost never mention more than a few topics.
- Inversely, if documents that discus almost every possible topic but focus on some more than others are desired, α should be set closer to 1. With this setting, almost all documents will discuss almost every topic, but not in equal proportions.
- Setting β is similar to setting α except that β controls the breadth of words belonging to each topic.

Vowpal Wabbit reads the input documents and parameters and outputs a document-topic matrix and a topic-word matrix. `predictions-00.txt`, where 00 is the number of topics, is a file containing the document-topic matrix. Each document is on one line, and each row is the document-topic weight. If multiple passes are used, the last M lines of `predictions-00.txt`, where M is the number of documents, are the final predictions for the document-topic matrix. The first token is the word ID, and the remaining K tokens are the allocation for each topic (topics are columns).

6.4.5 **LDA OUTPUT SUMMARIZATION**

Our program `lda.py` produces `summary.json`, a JSON summary of the top topic words for each topic extracted, ranked by weight. Two other JSON files are created, `document_topic_matrix.json` and `document_topic_map.json`. The first file (matrix) contains the documents and weights represented by JSON lists. The second file (map) contains the documents represented by their ID mapped to a list of weights. `document_topic_map.json` contains both the original ID and the document weight, where as the matrix it uses indices as IDs. `lda-topics.json` is also produced, and it lists the weights of words associated with each topic, as lists of lists. `lids.json` is a list of document IDs in the order presented to Vowpal Wabbit and the order used in the `document_topic_matrix.json` file. `dicts.json` maps words to their integer IDs. You can download the JSON and comma separated value (CSV) output of our particular run from
https://archive.org/29/items/LDAinSETutorial/bootstrap-output.zip.

6.4.5.1 Document and topic analysis

Since the topics have been extracted, let us take a look! In Table 6.1 we see a depiction of 20 topics extracted from the Bootstrap project issue tracker. The words shown are the top 10 ranking words from each of the topics, the most heavily allocated words in the topic.

Table 6.1 The Top 10 Ranked Words of the 20 Topics Extracted from Bootstrap's Issue-Tracker Issues

Topic No.	Top 10 Topic Words
1	*grey blazer cmd clipboard packagist webview kizer ytimg vi wrench*
2	*lodash angular betelgeuse ree redirects codeload yamlish prototypejs deselect manufacturer*
3	*color border background webkit image gradient white default rgba variables*
4	*asp contrast andyl runat hyperlink consolidating negatory pygments teuthology ftbastler*
5	*navbar class col css width table nav screen http span*
6	*phantomjs enforcefocus jshintrc linting focusin network chcp phantom humans kevinknelson*
7	*segmented typical dlabel signin blockquotes spotted hyphens tax jekyllrb hiccups*
8	*modal input button form btn data http tooltip popover element*
9	*dropdown issue chrome menu github https http firefox png browser*
10	*zepto swipe floor chevy flipped threshold enhanced completeness identified cpu*
11	*grid width row container columns fluid column min media responsive*
12	*div class li href carousel ul data tab id tabs*
13	*parent accordion heading gruntfile validator ad mapped errorclass validclass collapseone*
14	*bootstrap github https css http js twitter docs pull don*
15	*left rtl support direction location hash dir ltr languages offcanvas*
16	*percentage el mistake smile spelling plnkr portuguese lokesh boew ascii*
17	*font icon sm lg size xs md glyphicons icons glyphicon*
18	*tgz cdn bootstrapcdn composer netdna libs yml host wamp cdnjs*
19	*npm js npmjs lib http install bin error ruby node*
20	*license org mit apache copyright xl cc spec gpl holder*

Each topic is assigned a number by LDA software; however, the order in which it assigns numbers is arbitrary and has no meaning. If you ran LDA again with different seeds or a different timing (depending on the implementation), you would get different topics or similar topics but in different orders. Nonetheless, we can see in Table 6.1 that many of these topics are related to the Bootstrap project. Topic summaries such as these are often your first canary in the coal mine: they give you some idea of the health of your LDA output. If they are full of random tokens and numbers, one might consider stripping out such tokens from the analysis. If we look to topic 20, we see a set of terms: *license org mit apache copyright xl cc spec gpl holder*. MIT, Apache, GPL, and CC are all copyright licenses, and all of these licenses have terms and require attribution. Perhaps documents related to topic 20 are related to licensing. How do we verify if topic 20 is about licensing or not?

Using the document-topic matrix, we can look at the documents that are ranked high for topic 20. Thus, we can load the CSV file, `document_topic_map.csv`, or the JSON file, `document_topic_map.json`, with our favorite spreadsheet program (LibreOffice is included with the virtual machine), R, or Python, and sort then data in descending order on the T20 (topic 20)

Table 6.2 Issue Texts of the Top Documents Related to Topic 20 (Licensing) from `document_topic_map.csv`

https://github.com/twbs/bootstrap/issues/2054	cweagans

Migrate to MIT License

I'm wanting to include Bootstrap in a Drupal distribution that I'm working on. Because I'm using the Drupal.org packaging system, I cannot include Bootstrap because the APLv2 is not compatible with GPLv2 ...

https://github.com/twbs/bootstrap/issues/3942	justinshepard

License for Glyphicons is unclear

The license terms for Glyphicons when used with Bootstrap needs to be clarified. For example, including a link to Glyphicons on every page in a prominent location isn't possible or appropriate for some projects. ...

https://github.com/twbs/bootstrap/issues/3057	englishextra

bootstrap-dropdown.js clearMenus() needs ; at the end

bootstrap-dropdown.js when minified with JSMin::minify produces error in Firefox error console saying clearMenus()needs ; ...

https://github.com/twbs/bootstrap/issues/10811	picomancer

"PhantomJS must be installed locally" error running qunit:files task

I'm attempting to install Bootstrap in an LXC virtual machine, getting "PhantomJS must be installed locally" error. ...

https://github.com/twbs/bootstrap/issues/6342	mdo

WIP: Bootstrap 3

While our last major version bump (2.0) was a complete rewrite of the docs, CSS, and JavaScript, the move to 3.0 is equally ambitious, but for a different reason: Bootstrap 3 will be mobile-first. ...

MIT License is discussed.

https://github.com/twbs/bootstrap/issues/966	andrijas

Icons as font instead of img

Hi
Any reason you opted to include image based icons in bootstrap which are limited to the 16px dimensions? For example http://somerandomdude.com/work/iconic/ is available as open source fonts—means you can include icons in headers, buttons of various size etc since its vector based. ...

License of icons is discussed.

---

column. Right at the top is issue 2054. Browsing `large.json` or by visiting issue 2054 on Github,[5] we can see that the subject of the issue is "Migrate to MIT License." The next issues relate to licensing for image assets (#3942), JavaScript minification (unrelated, but still weighted heavily toward topic 20) (#3057), phantomJS error (#10811), and two licensing issues (#6342 and #966). Table 6.2 provides more details about these six issues. The LDA Python program also produces the file `document_topic_map_norm.csv`, which has normalized the topic weights. Reviewing the top

---

[5]https://github.com/twbs/bootstrap/issues/2054.

Table 6.3 Issue Texts of the Top Normalized Documents Related to Topic 20 (Licensing) from `document_topic_map_norm.csv`

https://github.com/twbs/bootstrap/pull/12366	mdo
Change a word	
...	
	Blank + Documentation change
https://github.com/twbs/bootstrap/pull/9987	cvrebert
Change 'else if' to 'else'	
...	
	Blank + Provided a patch changing else if to else
https://github.com/twbs/bootstrap/pull/10693	mdo
Include a copy of the CC-BY 3.0 License that the docs are under	
This adds a copy of the Creative Commons Attribution 3.0 Unported license to the repo. /cc @mdo	
https://github.com/twbs/bootstrap/issues/855	mistergiri
Can i use bootstrap in my premium theme?	
Can i use bootstrap in my premium cms theme and sell it?	
https://github.com/twbs/bootstrap/issues/216	caniszczyk
Add CC BY license to documentation	
At the moment, there's no license associated with the bootstrap documentation. We should license it under CC BY as it's as liberal as the software license (CC BY). ...	
https://github.com/twbs/bootstrap/issues/11785	tlindig
License in the README.md	
At bottom of README.md is written: Copyright and license Copyright 2013 Twitter, Inc under the Apache 2.0 license. With 3.1 you switched to MIT. It looks like you forgott to update this part too.	

weighted documents from the normalized CSV file reveals different issues, but four of the six top issues are still licensing relevant (#11785, #216, #855, and #10693 are licensing related but #9987 and #12366 are not). Table 6.3 provides more details about these six normalized issues.

6.4.5.2 Visualization

Looking at the numbers and topics is not enough, usually we want to visually explore the data to tease out interesting information. One can use simple tools such as spreadsheets to make basic visualizations.

Common visualization tasks with LDA include the following:

- Plotting document to topic association over time.
- Plotting the document-topic matrix.
- Plotting the document-word matrix.
- Plotting the association between two distinct kinds of documents within the same LDA run.

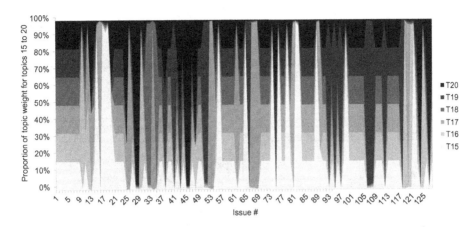

FIGURE 6.2

Example of using simple spreadsheet charting to visualize part of the document-topic matrix of Bootstrap (topics 15-20 of the first 128 issues).

Given the CSV files, one can visualize the prevalence of topics over time. Figure 6.2 depicts the proportional topic weights of the first 128 issues over time against topics 15-20 from Table 6.1.

From the spreadsheet inspection, the reader should notice that the document topic weights are somewhat noisy and hard to immediately interpret. For instance, it is hard to tell when a topic is popular and when it becomes less popular. Alternatively, one might ask if a topic is constantly referenced over time or if it is periodically popular. One method of gaining an overview is to bin or group documents by their date (e.g., weekly, biweekly, monthly) and then plot the mean topic weight of one topic per time bin over time. This allows one to produce a visualization depicting peaks of topic relevance over time. With the tutorial files we have included an R script called `plotter.R` that produces a summary of the 20 topics extracted combined with the dates extracted from the issue tracker. This R script produces Figure 6.3, a plot of the average relevance of documents per 2-week period over time. This plot is very similar to the plots in Hindle et al. [20]. If one looks at the bottom right corner of Figure 6.3, in the plot of topic 20 one can see that topic 20 peaks from time to time, but is not constantly discussed. This matches our perception of the licensing discussions found within the issue tracker: they occur when licenses need to be clarified or change, but they do not change all the time. This kind of overview can be integrated into project dashboards to give managers an overview of issue-tracker discussions over time.

Further directions for readers to explore include using different kinds of documents, such as documentation, commits, issues, and source code, and then relying on LDA's document-topic matrix to link these artifacts. We hope this tutorial has helped illustrate how LDA can be used to gain an overview of unstructured data within a repository and infer relationships between documents.

6.5 PITFALLS AND THREATS TO VALIDITY

This section summarizes the threats to validity that practitioners may face when using LDA. In addition, this section describes potential pitfalls and hazards in using LDA.

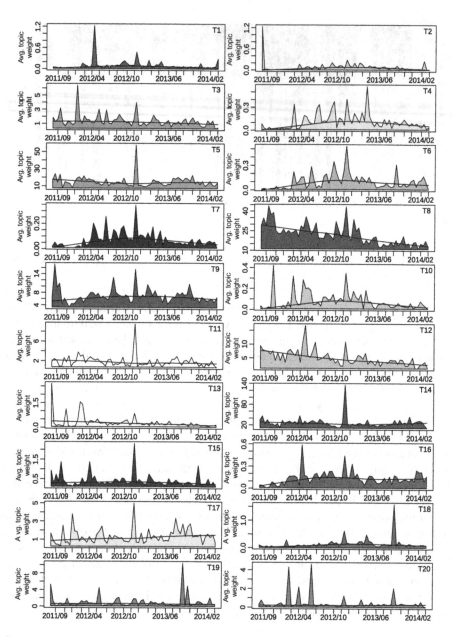

FIGURE 6.3

Average topic weight for Bootstrap issues in 2-week bins. The topics are clearly described in Table 6.1.

One pitfall is that different pieces of LDA software output different types of data. Some LDA software packages report probabilities, while others report word counts or other weights. While one can convert between probabilities and word counts, it is important to consider whether each document receives equal weight, or whether longer documents should receive more weight than shorter documents.

6.5.1 CRITERION VALIDITY

Criterion validity relates to the ability of a method to correspond with other measurements that are collected in order to study the same concept. LDA topics are not necessarily intuitive ideas, concepts, or topics. Therefore, results from LDA may not correspond with results from topic labeling performed by humans.

A typical erroneous assumption frequently made by LDA users is that an LDA topic will represent a more traditional topic that humans write about such as sports, computers, or Africa. It is important to remember that LDA topics may not correspond to an intuitive domain concept. This problem was explored in Hindle et al. [20]. Thus, working with LDA-produced topics has some hazards: for example, even if LDA produces a recognizable sports topic, it may be combined with other topics or there may be other sports topics.

6.5.2 CONSTRUCT VALIDITY

Construct validity relates to the ability of research to measure what it intended to measure. LDA topics are independent topics extracted from word distributions. This independence means that correlated or co-occurring concepts or ideas will not necessarily be given their own topic, and if they are, the documents might be split between topics.

One should be aware of the constraints and properties of LDA when trying to infer if LDA output shows an activity or not. LDA topics are not necessarily intuitive ideas, concepts, or topics. Comparisons between topics in terms of document association can be troublesome owing to the independence assumption of topics.

Finally, it is necessary to remember that LDA assumes that topic-word probabilities and document-topic probabilities are Dirichlet distributions. Furthermore, many pieces of LDA software use symmetric Dirichlet distributions. This implies the assumption that the Dirichlet parameters are the same for every word (β) or topic (α), respectively, and that these parameters are known beforehand. In most software, this means that α and β must be set carefully.

6.5.3 INTERNAL VALIDITY

Internal validity refers to how well conclusions can be made about casual effects and relationships. An important aspect of LDA is that topics are independent; thus, if two ideas are being studied to see if one causes the other, one has to guard against LDA's word allocation strategy.

This means that a word can come only from a single topic. Even if LDA produced a recognizable "sports" topic and a recognizable "news" topic, their combination is assumed never to occur. "Sports news," may then appear as a third topic, independent from the first two. Or, it may be present in other

Table 6.4 Topic-Topic Correlation Matrix (95% Confidence Intervals of the Correlation Amount)

	Topic 1	Topic 2	Topic 3	Topic 4	Topic 5
Topic 1	1	−0.22 to 0.17	−0.21 to 0.18	−0.22 to 0.17	−0.16 to 0.24
Topic 2	−0.22 to 0.17	1	−0.22 to 0.17	−0.23 to 0.16	−0.23 to 0.16
Topic 3	−0.21 to 0.18	−0.22 to 0.17	1	−0.22 to 0.18	−0.22 to 0.18
Topic 4	−0.22 to 0.17	−0.23 to 0.16	−0.22 to 0.18	1	−0.23 to 0.16
Topic 5	−0.16 to 0.24	−0.23 to 0.16	−0.22 to 0.18	−0.23 to 0.16	1
Topic 6	−0.11 to 0.28	−0.22 to 0.17	−0.21 to 0.18	−0.22 to 0.17	−0.21 to 0.19
Topic 7	−0.22 to 0.17	−0.23 to 0.16	−0.21 to 0.18	−0.23 to 0.16	−0.23 to 0.16
Topic 8	−0.22 to 0.17	−0.23 to 0.16	−0.21 to 0.18	−0.23 to 0.17	−0.23 to 0.16
Topic 9	−0.23 to 0.17	−0.24 to 0.15	−0.19 to 0.21	−0.23 to 0.16	−0.24 to 0.16
Topic 10	−0.22 to 0.17	−0.23 to 0.16	−0.21 to 0.18	−0.23 to 0.16	−0.11 to 0.28
	Topic 6	**Topic 7**	**Topic 8**	**Topic 9**	**Topic 10**
Topic 1	−0.11 to 0.28	−0.22 to 0.17	−0.22 to 0.17	−0.23 to 0.17	−0.22 to 0.17
Topic 2	−0.22 to 0.17	−0.23 to 0.16	−0.23 to 0.16	−0.24 to 0.15	−0.23 to 0.16
Topic 3	−0.21 to 0.18	−0.21 to 0.18	−0.21 to 0.18	−0.19 to 0.21	−0.21 to 0.18
Topic 4	−0.22 to 0.17	−0.23 to 0.16	−0.23 to 0.17	−0.23 to 0.16	−0.23 to 0.16
Topic 5	−0.21 to 0.19	−0.23 to 0.16	−0.23 to 0.16	−0.24 to 0.16	−0.11 to 0.28
Topic 6	1	−0.2 to 0.2	−0.22 to 0.18	−0.22 to 0.17	−0.22 to 0.18
Topic 7	−0.2 to 0.2	1	−0.21 to 0.18	−0.21 to 0.18	−0.23 to 0.17
Topic 8	−0.22 to 0.18	−0.21 to 0.18	1	−0.23 to 0.16	−0.22 to 0.17
Topic 9	−0.22 to 0.17	−0.21 to 0.18	−0.23 to0.16	1	−0.05 to 0.33
Topic 10	−0.22 to 0.18	−0.23 to 0.17	−0.22 to 0.17	−0.05 to 0.33	1

From the same LDA model as Figure 6.1.

topics whose focus is neither sports nor news. The independence of topics makes their comparison problematic.

For example, it might be desirable to ask if two topics overlap in some way. Table 6.4 depicts the correlation between every pair of topics as described by the document-topic matrix. Because of their independence they are not allowed to correlate: the output of LDA has topic-to-topic correlation values that are never significantly different from zero, as shown by the confidence intervals in Table 6.4.

To show that an event caused a change in LDA output, one should use a different data source and manual validation. LDA output changes given different α and β parameters, and sometimes given a test one, could tune these parameters to pass or fail this test. One has to provide motivation for the choice of α and β in order for any conclusions drawn from LDA output to be convincing.

6.5.4 EXTERNAL VALIDITY

External validity is about generalization and how broadly findings can be made. LDA topics are relevant to the corpora provided their topics and words associated with the topics might not be generalizable.

Alternatively LDA can be applied to numerous collections of documents, and thus external validity can be addressed in some situations.

6.5.5 RELIABILITY

Reliability is about how well one can repeat the findings of a study. With LDA, the exact topics found will not be found again without sharing of initial parameters or seeds. Thus, all LDA studies should report their parameters. Yet, even if parameters are reported, LDA implementations will return different results, and the same implementation might produce different topics or different topic orderings each time it is run. Others might not be able to replicate the exact topics found or the ordering of the topics found.

Since LDA models are found iteratively, it is important to ensure that they have had adequate time to converge before use. Otherwise, the model does not correspond to the input data. The time required for convergence depends on the number of topics, documents, and vocabulary words. For example, given Vowpal Wabbit with 100 topics and 20,000 documents, each pass takes a matter of seconds on modest hardware, but at least two passes is recommended. To choose the correct number of passes, the output should be examined and the number of passes should be increased until the output stops changing significantly.

6.6 CONCLUSIONS

LDA is a powerful tool for working with collections of structured, unstructured, and semistructured text documents, of which there are plenty in software repositories. Our literature review has documented the abundance of LDA applications in software analysis, from document clustering for issue/bug de-duplication, to linking for traceability between code, documentation, requirements, and communications, to summarizing association of events and documents with software life cycle activities.

We have demonstrated a simple case of using LDA to explore the contents of an issue-tracker repository and showed how the topics link back to documents. We also discussed how to visualize the output.

LDA, however, relies on a complex underlying probabilistic model and a number of assumptions. Therefore, even though off-the-shelf software is available to compute LDA models, the user of this software must be aware of potential pitfalls and caveats. This chapter has outlined the basics of the underlying conceptual model and discussed these pitfalls in order to enable the informed use of this powerful method.

REFERENCES

[1] Blei DM, Ng AY, Jordan MI. Latent Dirichlet allocation. J Mach Learn Res 2003;3:993–1022.
[2] Wang H, Wong K. Recommendation-assisted personal web. In: IEEE ninth world congress on services (SERVICES). Washington, DC, USA: IEEE Computer Society; 2013. p. 136–40.
[3] Poshyvanyk D, Marcus A. The conceptual coupling metrics for object-oriented systems. In: 22nd IEEE international conference on software maintenance, ICSM'06. Washington, DC, USA: IEEE Computer Society; 2006. p. 469–78.

[4] Ramesh B. Factors influencing requirements traceability practice. Commun ACM 1998;41(12):37–44. doi: 10.1145/290133.290147.

[5] Asuncion HU, Asuncion AU, Taylor RN. Software traceability with topic modeling. In: Proceedings of the 32nd ACM/IEEE international conference on software engineering, ICSE '10, vol. 1. New York, NY, USA: ACM; 2010. p. 95–104. ISBN 978-1-60558-719-6. doi:10.1145/1806799.1806817.

[6] Thomas SW, Adams B, Hassan AE, Blostein D. Validating the use of topic models for software evolution. In: Proceedings of the 10th IEEE working conference on source code analysis and manipulation, SCAM '10. Washington, DC, USA: IEEE Computer Society; 2010. p. 55–64. ISBN 978-0-7695-4178-5. doi:10.1109/SCAM.2010.13.

[7] Gethers M, Oliveto R, Poshyvanyk D, Lucia AD. On integrating orthogonal information retrieval methods to improve traceability recovery. In: Proceedings of the 27th IEEE international conference on software maintenance (ICSM). Washington, DC, USA: IEEE Computer Society; 2011. p. 133–42.

[8] Savage T, Dit B, Gethers M, Poshyvanyk D. Topicxp: exploring topics in source code using latent Dirichlet allocation. In: Proceedings of the 2010 IEEE international conference on software maintenance, ICSM '10. Washington, DC, USA: IEEE Computer Society; 2010. p. 1–6. ISBN 978-1-4244-8630-4. doi: 10.1109/ICSM.2010.5609654.

[9] Poshyvanyk D. Using information retrieval to support software maintenance tasks. Ph.D. thesis, Wayne State University, Detroit, MI, USA; 2008.

[10] McMillan C, Poshyvanyk D, Revelle M. Combining textual and structural analysis of software artifacts for traceability link recovery. In: Proceedings of the 2009 ICSE workshop on traceability in emerging forms of software engineering, TEFSE '09. Washington, DC, USA: IEEE Computer Society; 2009. p. 41–8. ISBN 978-1-4244-3741-2. doi:10.1109/TEFSE.2009.5069582.

[11] Marcus A, Sergeyev A, Rajlich V, Maletic JI. An information retrieval approach to concept location in source code. In: Proceedings of the 11th working conference on reverse engineering, WCRE '04. Washington, DC, USA: IEEE Computer Society; 2004. p. 214–23. ISBN 0-7695-2243-2.

[12] De Lucia A, Marcus A, Oliveto R, Poshyvanyk D. Information retrieval methods for automated traceability recovery. In: Software and systems traceability. Berlin: Springer; 2012. p. 71–98.

[13] Baldi PF, Lopes CV, Linstead EJ, Bajracharya SK. A theory of aspects as latent topics. In: Proceedings of the 23rd ACM SIGPLAN conference on object-oriented programming systems languages and applications, OOPSLA '08. New York, NY, USA: ACM; 2008. p. 543–62. ISBN 978-1-60558-215-3. doi:10.1145/1449764.1449807.

[14] Hindle A, Ernst NA, Godfrey MW, Mylopoulos J. Automated topic naming to support cross-project analysis of software maintenance activities. In: Proceedings of the 8th working conference on mining software repositories. New York, NY, USA: ACM; 2011. p. 163–72.

[15] Lukins SK, Kraft NA, Etzkorn LH. Source code retrieval for bug localization using latent Dirichlet allocation. In: Proceedings of the 2008 15th working conference on reverse engineering, WCRE '08. Washington, DC, USA: IEEE Computer Society; 2008. p. 155–64. ISBN 978-0-7695-3429-9. doi:10.1109/WCRE.2008.33.

[16] Alipour A, Hindle A, Stroulia E. A contextual approach towards more accurate duplicate bug report detection. In: Proceedings of the tenth international workshop on mining software repositories. Piscataway, NJ, USA: IEEE Press; 2013. p. 183–92.

[17] Campbell JC, Zhang C, Xu Z, Hindle A, Miller J. Deficient documentation detection: a methodology to locate deficient project documentation using topic analysis. In: MSR; 2013. p. 57–60.

[18] Han D, Zhang C, Fan X, Hindle A, Wong K, Stroulia E. Understanding Android fragmentation with topic analysis of vendor-specific bugs. In: WCRE; 2012. p. 83–92.

[19] De Lucia A, Di Penta M, Oliveto R, Panichella A, Panichella S. Using IR methods for labeling source code artifacts: is it worthwhile? In: IEEE 20th international conference on program comprehension (ICPC). Washington, DC, USA: IEEE Computer Society; 2012. p. 193–202.

[20] Hindle A, Bird C, Zimmermann T, Nagappan N. Relating requirements to implementation via topic analysis: do topics extracted from requirements make sense to managers and developers? In: ICSM; 2012. p. 243–52.

[21] Grant S, Cordy JR. Estimating the optimal number of latent concepts in source code analysis. In: Proceedings of the 10th IEEE working conference on source code analysis and manipulation, SCAM '10. Washington, DC, USA: IEEE Computer Society; 2010. p. 65–74. ISBN 978-0-7695-4178-5.

[22] Panichella A, Dit B, Oliveto R, Di Penta M, Poshyvanyk D, De Lucia A. How to effectively use topic models for software engineering tasks? An approach based on genetic algorithms. In: Proceedings of the 2013 international conference on software engineering. Piscataway, NJ, USA: IEEE Press; 2013. p. 522–31.

[23] Wikipedia. Latent Dirichlet allocation—Wikipedia, the free encyclopedia; 2014. http://en.wikipedia.org/w/index.php?title=Latent_Dirichlet_allocation&oldid=610319663 [Online; accessed 15.07.14].

[24] Langford J, Li L, Strehl A. Vowpal Wabbit; 2007. Technical report, http://hunch.net/~vw/.

TOOLS AND TECHNIQUES FOR ANALYZING PRODUCT AND PROCESS DATA

7

Diomidis Spinellis*

*Department Management Science and Technology, Athens University of Economics and Business, Athens, Greece**

CHAPTER OUTLINE

7.1 INTRODUCTION

The analysis of data from software products and their development process [1] is tempting, but often non-trivial. It is tempting, because the software development process generates ample data that we should be able use in order to optimize it. Unfortunately, it is also difficult, because many tasks cannot be readily accomplished, despite the development of many platforms that collect software data and allow its analysis. Examples of such platforms and related tools include Hackystat [2], Hipikat [3], Kenyon [4], Evolizer [5], Sourcerer [6, 7], Tesseract [8], Moose [9], Churrasco [10], and Alitheia Core [11, 12]. The difficulty in using these platforms occurs for a number of reasons. First, the software artifact or the type of analysis that is required may not be covered by an existing platform. Then, the disparate data sources, which are the norm when organizations build their development process in an organic way, may be difficult to combine using the analysis facilities provided by integrated development environments or platforms. Furthermore, the analysis to be performed may be highly specialized, involving an organization's domain-specific scenario or a novel research question. Finally, due to the ease with which software process records data, the volume of the data to be examined can be enormous, making it difficult to scale some existing tools to handle real-world data.

Line-oriented textual data streams are the lowest useful common denominator for many software analysis tasks. It is often effective to combine Unix tool-chest programs [13] into a pipeline that forms the following pattern: fetching, selecting, processing, and summarizing. We examine this approach in Section 7.2, which builds on a previously published column [14].

In other cases, scripting languages, such as Python, Ruby, and Perl, can also be remarkably effective. For research purposes, also worth looking at are platforms and projects that gather and analyze data from open source software repositories. These include FLOSSmole [15], Flossmetrics [16], Sourcerer, Alitheia Core, and GHTorrent [17], with FLOSSmole having the widest adoption outside the research team that produced it [18].

Many useful source code analysis tasks do not require implementing a full lexical analysis and parser, but can be performed using simple heuristics implemented through regular expressions [19]. In other cases, piggy-backing the analysis onto existing compiler front-ends can be just as effective (Section 7.3). Another useful technique involves processing compiled code. Object file symbols and Java byte code are two particularly rich sources of accurate data (see Section 7.4).

The best viewpoint of the software development process comes through data obtained from its configuration management (version control) system. This provides information regarding developers, progress, productivity, working hours, teamwork, and many other attributes. Three powerful analysis methods involve the processing of snapshots in a time series, revision logs, and the so-called blame listings. We examine these and more in Section 7.5.

Numerous tools can aid exploratory data analysis and visualization. Notable ones include the GraphViz graph drawing tools [20], the GMT toolset for map drawing [21], the *gnuplot* plotting program, the R Project for statistical computing [22], and Python's diverse visualization libraries. Automating the publication of analyzed results can increase the researcher's productivity and aid the reproducibility of the results. We will see some examples of visualization tools in Section 7.6, which is also loosely based on a previously published paper [14].

7.2 A RATIONAL ANALYSIS PIPELINE

Line-oriented textual data streams are the lowest useful common denominator for much of the data that passes through our hands. Such streams can represent program source code, feature requests, version control history, file lists, symbol tables, archive contents, error messages, profiling data, and so on. For many routine, everyday tasks, we might be tempted to process the data using a Swiss army knife scripting language, such as Perl, Python, or Ruby. However, to do that we often need to write a small, self-contained program and save it into a file. By that point we may have lost interest in the task, and end up doing the work manually, if at all. Often, a more effective approach is to combine programs of the Unix toolchest into a short and sweet pipeline we can run from our shell's command prompt. With modern shell command-line editing facilities we can build our command bit by bit, until it molds into exactly the form that suits us. Today, the original Unix tools are available on many different systems, such as GNU/Linux, Mac OS X, and Microsoft Windows (through Cygwin),[1] so there is no reason why we should not add this approach to our arsenal. Documentation for these tools is always available, either through the *man* command, or, often, by invoking a command with the --help option.

Many of the analysis one-liners we will build around the Unix tools follow a pattern whose parts we will examine in the following sections. It goes roughly like this: fetching (Section 7.2.1), selecting (Section 7.2.2), processing (Section 7.2.3), and summarizing (Section 7.2.4). We will also need to apply some plumbing to join these parts into a whole (Section 7.2.5).

7.2.1 GETTING THE DATA

In many cases our data will be text (e.g., source code) we can directly feed to the standard input of a tool. If this is not the case, we need to adapt our data. If we are dealing with object files or executable programs, we will have to use a tool such as *nm* (Unix), *dumpbin* (Windows), or *javap* (Java) to dig into them. We examine these approaches in Sections 7.4.2 and 7.4.4. If we are working with files grouped into an archive, then a command such as *tar*, *jar*, or *ar* will list the archive's contents. In addition, the *ldd* command will print shared library dependencies associated with Unix executables, object files, and libraries. If our data comes from a (potentially large) collection of files stored on locally accessible

---

[1]http://www.cygwin.com/.

storage *find* can locate those that interest us. Here is how we would use the *find* command to list the (header) files residing in the directory /usr/include.[2]

```
find /usr/include -type f
/usr/include/pty.h
/usr/include/time.h
/usr/include/printf.h
/usr/include/arpa/nameser_compat.h
/usr/include/arpa/telnet.h
/usr/include/arpa/inet.h
[...]
```

On the other hand, to get our data over the Web, we can use *wget* or *curl* (see Section 7.5.1). We can also use *dd* (and the special file /dev/zero), *yes*, or *jot* to generate artificial data, perhaps for running a quick test or a benchmark. Finally, if we want to process a compiler's list of error messages, we will want to redirect its standard error to its standard output; the incantation 2>&1 will do this trick.

There are many other cases we have not covered here: relational databases, version control systems (see Section 7.5), mailing lists, issue management systems, telemetry data, and so on. A software system's issue management system (bugs) database can provide insights regarding a product's maturity and the adequacy of the resources devoted to it. Issues are often coupled with software changes, allowing even more detailed analyses to be performed. A dynamic view of a system's operation can be obtained by analyzing software telemetry data. This can include precise user interaction metrics, crash dump reports [23], and server logs. Always keep in mind that we are unlikely to be the first ones who need the application's data converted into a textual format; therefore, someone has probably already written a tool for that job. For example, the *Outwit* tool suite [24][3] can convert into a text stream data coming from the Windows clipboard, an ODBC source, the event log, or the Windows registry.

7.2.2 SELECTING

Given the generality of the textual data format, in most cases we will have on our hands more data than what we require. We might want to process only some parts of each row, or only a subset of the rows. To select a specific column from a line consisting of elements separated by white space or another field delimiter, we can use *awk* with a single print $n command. If our fields are of fixed width, we can separate them using *cut*. And, if our lines are not neatly separated into fields, we can often write a regular expression for a *sed* substitute command to isolate the element we want.

The workhorse for obtaining a subset of the rows is *grep*. We can specify a regular expression to get only the rows that match it, and add the --invert-match[4] flag to filter out rows we do not want to process.

Here is how we could use *grep* to list lines in the FreeBSD kernel source code file vfs_subr.c containing the XXX sequence, which is commonly used to flag questionable code. The first part of

---

[2]The text in the sans serif font denotes the commands we would write at the Unix shell command-line prompt (often ending in $), while the text in typewriter font is part of the command's output.

[3]http://www.spinellis.gr/sw/outwit.

[4]In the interest of readability, the examples use the GNU non-standard long form of the command flags.

the fetch-selection pipeline uses *curl* to fetch the corresponding file from the FreeBSD repository. The backslash at the end of the line indicates that the line is continued on the one below, containing the URL where the file resides. The | (pipeline) symbol specifies that the output of *curl* (the `vfs_subr.c` file's contents) will be sent for further processing to the command following it, which is *grep*.

```
curl --silent https://svnweb.freebsd.org/base/head/sys/kern/vfs_subr.c?view=co |
grep XXX
```

```
 * XXX desiredvnodes is historical cruft and should not exist.
   * XXX We could save a lock/unlock if this was only
  * Wait for I/O to complete. XXX needs cleaning up. The vnode can
    if (bp->b_bufobj != bo) { /* XXX: necessary ? */
  * XXX Since there are no node locks for NFS, I
 vp = bp->b_vp;    /* XXX */
 vp = (*bo)->__bo_vnode; /* XXX */
          /* XXX audit: privilege used */
/* XXX - correct order? */
[...]
```

We can use the *grep* flags `--files-with-matches` and `--files-without-match` to obtain only the names of files that contain (or do not contain) a specific pattern. We can run *fgrep* with the `--file` flag if the elements we are looking for are fixed strings stored in a file (perhaps generated in a previous processing step). If our selection criteria are more complex, we can often express them in an *awk* pattern expression. We will often find ourselves combining a number of these approaches to obtain the result that we want. For example, we might use *grep* to get the lines that interest us, `grep -invert-match` to filter-out some noise from our sample, and finally *awk* to select a specific field from each line.

Many examples in this chapter use *awk* for some of their processing steps. In general, *awk* works by applying a recipe we give it as an argument on each line of its input. This recipe consists of patterns and actions; actions without a pattern apply to all input lines, and a pattern without an action will print the corresponding line. A pattern can be a /-delimited regular expression or an arbitrary boolean expression. An action consists of commands enclosed in braces. Lines are automatically split into space-separated fields. (The -F option can be used to specify arbitrary field delimiters.) These fields are then available as variables named $*n*. For example, the following shell command will print the names of header files included by the C files in the current directory.

```
awk '/#include/ {print $2}' *.c
```

7.2.3 PROCESSING

Data processing frequently involves sorting our lines on a specific field. The *sort* command supports tens of options for specifying the sort keys, their type, and the output order. Having our results sorted we then often want to count how many instances of each element we have. The *uniq* command with the `--count` option will do the job here; often we will post-process the result with another instance of *sort*, this time with the `--numeric` flag specifying a numerical order, to find out which elements appear most frequently. In other cases, we might want to the compare results between different runs. We can use *diff* if the two runs generate results that should be similar (perhaps we are comparing two versions of the file), or *comm* if we want to compare two sorted lists. Through *comm* we can perform set intersection and difference operations. To piece together results coming from unrelated processing steps based on a key, we can first sort them and then apply the *join* command on the two lists. We can handle more complex tasks using, again, *awk*.

Here are the steps of how to build a pipeline that generates a list of header files ordered by the number of times they are included. First, use *grep* to obtain a list of include directives.

```
grep --no-filename '^#include' *.c
#include <sys/cdefs.h>
#include <sys/param.h>
#include <sys/exec.h>
#include <sys/imgact.h>
#include <sys/imgact_aout.h>
#include <sys/kernel.h>
#include <sys/lock.h>
[...]
```

Then, use *awk* to get from each line the included file name, which is the second field. While at it, we can replace the original *grep* with an *awk* selection pattern.

```
awk '/^#include/ {print $2}' *.c
<sys/cdefs.h>
<sys/param.h>
<sys/exec.h>
<sys/imgact.h>
<sys/imgact_aout.h>
<sys/kernel.h>
[...]
```

Our next step is to sort the file names, in order to bring the same ones together, so that they can be counted with *uniq*.

```
awk '/^#include/ {print $2}' *.c |
sort
"clock_if.h"
"cpufreq_if.h"
"linker_if.h"
"linker_if.h"
"linker_if.h"
"opt_adaptive_lockmgrs.h"
"opt_adaptive_mutexes.h"
"opt_alq.h"
[...]
```

We then use *uniq* to count same consecutive lines (file names).

```
awk '/^#include/ {print $2}' *.c |
sort |
uniq --count
      1 "clock_if.h"
      1 "cpufreq_if.h"
      3 "linker_if.h"
      1 "opt_adaptive_lockmgrs.h"
      1 "opt_adaptive_mutexes.h"
      1 "opt_alq.h"
      1 "opt_bus.h"
     30 "opt_compat.h"
      1 "opt_config.h"
     34 "opt_ddb.h"
[...]
```

The final step involves sorting the output again, this time in reverse numerical order, in order to obtain a list of header file names in a descending order according to the number of times they occurred in the source code.

```
awk '/^#include/ {print $2}' *.c |
sort |
uniq --count |
sort --reverse --numeric
  162 <sys/cdefs.h>
  161 <sys/param.h>
  157 <sys/systm.h>
  137 <sys/kernel.h>
  116 <sys/proc.h>
  114 <sys/lock.h>
  106 <sys/mutex.h>
   94 <sys/sysctl.h>
[...]
```

7.2.4 SUMMARIZING

In many cases the processed data are too voluminous to be of use. For example, we might not care which symbols are defined with the wrong visibility in a program, but we might want to know how many there are. Surprisingly, many problems involve simply counting the output of the processing step using the humble *wc* (word count) command and its --lines flag. Here again is the preceding example, this time counting the number of lines containing the characters XXX.

```
curl --silent \
https://svnweb.freebsd.org/base/head/sys/kern/vfs_subr.c?view=co |
grep XXX |
wc --lines
    20
```

If we want to know the top or bottom 10 elements of our result list, we can pass our list through *head* or *tail*. To format a long list of words into a more manageable block that we can then paste in a document, we can use *fmt* (perhaps run after a *sed* substitution command tacks on a comma after each element). Also, for debugging purposes we might initially pipe the result of intermediate stages through *more* or *less*, to examine it in detail. As usual, we can use *awk* when these approaches do not suit us; a typical task involves summing up a specific field with a command such as sum += $3. In other cases, we might use *awk*'s associative arrays to sum diverse elements.

7.2.5 PLUMBING

All the wonderful building blocks we have described are useless without some way to glue them together. For this we will use the Bourne shell's facilities. First and foremost comes the pipeline (|), which allows us to send the output of one processing step as input to the next one, as we saw in the preceding examples. We can also redirect output into a file; this is done by ending our command with the >*file-name* construct. In other cases, we might want to execute the same command with many different arguments. For this we will pass the arguments as input to the *xargs* command. A typical pattern involves obtaining a list of files using *find* and processing them using *xargs*. Commands that can only handle a single argument can be run by *xargs* if we specify the --max-args=1 option. If our processing is more complex, we can always pipe the arguments into a while read loop. (Amazingly, the Bourne shell allows us to pipe data into and from all its control structures.) When everything else fails, we can use a couple of intermediate files to juggle our data.

Note that by default the Unix shell will use spaces to separate command-line arguments. This can cause problems when we process file names that contain spaces in them. Avoid this by enclosing variables that represent a file name in double quotes, as in the following (contrived) example that will count the number of lines in the Java files residing in the directories under org/eclipse.

```
find org/eclipse —type f —name \*.java —print |
while read f
do
  cat "$f"   # File name in quotes to protect spaces
done | wc ——lines
```

When using *find* with *xargs*, which is more efficient than the loop in the preceding example, we can avoid the problem of embedded spaces by using the respective arguments -print0 and --null. These direct the two commands to have file names separated with a null character, instead of a space. Thus, the preceding example would be written as

```
find org/eclipse —type f —name \*.java —print0 |
xargs ——null cat |
wc ——lines
```

7.3 SOURCE CODE ANALYSIS

Source code can be analyzed with various levels of accuracy, precision, and detail. The analysis spectrum spans heuristics, lexical analysis, parsing, semantic analysis, and static analysis.

7.3.1 **HEURISTICS**

Heuristics allow us to easily obtain rough-and-ready metrics from the code. The main advantage of heuristics in source code analysis is that they are easy, often trivial, to implement. They can therefore often be used as a quick way to test a hypothesis. In most cases, the use of heuristics entails the use of regular expressions and corresponding tools, such as the family of the Unix *grep* programs, to obtain measures that are useful, but not 100% accurate. For instance, the following command will display the number of top-level classes defined in a set of Java files.

```
grep ——count ^class *.java
```

The heuristic employed here is based on the assumption that the word `class` appears in the beginning of a line if and only if it is used to define a top-level class. Similarly, the number of subclasses defined in a set of files can be found through the following command.

```
fgrep ——count ——word—regexp extends *.java
```

Again, the preceding command assumes that the word `extends` is only used to refer to a subclass's base class. For example, the count can be set off by the word `extends` appearing in strings or comments. Finally, if the files were located in various folders in a directory tree, we could use the *grep*'s --recursive flag, instructing it to traverse the directory tree starting from the current directory (denoted by a dot). An invocation of *awk* can then be used to sum the counts (the second field of the colon-separated line).

```
grep ——recursive ——count ^class . |
awk —F: '{s += $2} END {print s}'
```

The preceding command assumes that the keyword `class` always appears at the beginning of a line, and that no other files that might contain lines beginning with the word `class` are located within the directory hierarchy.

7.3.2 **LEXICAL ANALYSIS**

When more accuracy is required than what a heuristic can provide, or when the analysis cannot be easily expressed through a heuristic, flow-blown lexical analysis has to be performed. This allows us to identify reserved words, identifiers, constants, string literals, and rudimentary properties of the code structure. The options here include expressing the lexical analyzer as a state machine or creating code with a lexical analyzer generator.

7.3.2.1 *State machines*

A hand crafted state machine can be used for recognizing strings and comments, taking into account a language's escaping rules. As an example, the following states can be used for recognizing various elements of C++ source code.

```
enum e_cfile_state {
       s_normal,
       s_saw_slash,        // After a / character
       s_saw_str_backslash, // After a \ character in a string
       s_saw_chr_backslash, // After a \ character in a character
```

```
    s_cpp_comment,      // Inside C++ comment
    s_block_comment,    // Inside C block comment
    s_block_star,       // Found a * in a block comment
    s_string,           // Inside a string
    s_char,             // Inside a character
};
```

Given the preceding definition, a state machine that processes single characters counting the number of characters appearing within character strings can be expressed as follows.

```
static void
process(char c)
{
    static enum e_cfile_state cstate = s_normal;

    switch (cstate) {
    case s_normal:
        if (c == '/')
            cstate = s_saw_slash;
        else if (c == '\'')
            cstate = s_char;
        else if (c == '"') {
            cstate = s_string;
            n_string++;
        }
        break;
    case s_char:
        if (c == '\'')
            cstate = s_normal;
        else if (c == '\\')
            cstate = s_saw_chr_backslash;
        break;
    case s_string:
        if (c == '"')
            cstate = s_normal;
        else if (c == '\\')
            cstate = s_saw_str_backslash;
        break;
    case s_saw_chr_backslash:
        cstate = s_char;
        break;
    case s_saw_str_backslash:
        cstate = s_string;
        break;
    case s_saw_slash:   // After a / character
        if (c == '/')
            cstate = s_cpp_comment;
        else if (c == '*')
            cstate = s_block_comment;
        else
            cstate = s_normal;
        break;
```

```
case s_cpp_comment:    // Inside a C++ comment
    if (c == '\n')
        cstate = s_normal;
    break;
case s_block_comment:   // Inside a C block comment
    if (c == '*')
        cstate = s_block_star;
    break;
case s_block_star:      // Found a * in a block comment
    if (c == '/')
        cstate = s_normal;
    else if (c != '*')
        cstate = s_block_comment;
    break;
    }
}
```

Given that the preceding code has a precise picture of what type of lexical elements it processes, it can be easily extended to count more complex elements, such as the number or nesting level of blocks.

The driver for the `process` function could be a simple filter-style program that will report the number of strings contained in the code provided in its standard input.

```
#include <stdio.h>

static int n_string;
static void process(char c);

int
main(int argc, char *argv[])
{
    int c;

    while ((c = getchar()) != EOF)
        process(c);
    printf("%d\n", n_string);
    return 0;
}
```

Running the driver with its source code as input will report 1 (one string found) on its standard output.

```
count <count.c
```

```
1
```

7.3.2.2 Lexical analyzer generator

For heavy lifting a lexical analyzer generator [25], such as *lex* or its modern open-source incarnation *flex*, can be used to identify efficiently and accurately all of a language's tokens. The following code excerpt can be fed to the *lex* generator to create a self-standing program that will count the number of times each C lexical token has appeared in its standard input.

```
LET [a-zA-Z_]
DIG [0-9]

%{
int n_auto, n_break, n_case, n_char, n_const;
int n_volatile, n_while, n_identifier;
// [...]

%}

%%
"auto"              { n_auto++; }
"break"             { n_break++; }
"case"              { n_case++; }
"char"              { n_char++; }
"const"             { n_const++; }
// [...]
"while"             { n_while; }

{LET}({LET}|{DIG})* { n_identifier++; }

">>="               { n_right_shift_assign++; }
"<<="               { n_left_shift_assign++; }
// [...]
">>"                { n_right_shift++; }
"<<"                { n_left_shift++; }
// [...]
"<="                { n_less_than++; }
">="                { n_greater_than++; }
"=="                { n_compare++; }
// [...]
"="                 { n_assign++; }
.                   { /* ignore other characters */ }

%%

yywrap() { return(1); }

main()
{
     while (yylex())
          ;
     printf("auto %d\n", n_auto);
     printf("break %d\n", n_break);
     // [...]
}
```

The lexical analyzer specification begins with the definition of regular expressions for C letters (LET) and digits (DIG). Then come the C definitions of the counter variables, which are enclosed in the %{ %} block. The analyzer's main body, which starts after the %% line, consists of regular expressions on the left-hand side, followed by C code in braces on the right-hand side. The C code is executed when the program's input matches the corresponding regular expression. The lexical analysis specification can be easily modified to handle other languages and types of input. Note that because the specified regular expressions are matched in the order specified, longer elements and more specific elements must be specified before the corresponding shorter or more general ones. This can be clearly seen in the example illustrating the handling of identifiers and operators.

The C code after the second %% line contains a loop to iterate over all input tokens and statements to print the collected figures. This allows the generated code to be compiled and run as a single program. The program assumes that the code it reads has already been preprocessed to handle preprocessing commands and comments. This can be easily done by passing the source code through the C preprocessor, *cpp*.

7.3.3 PARSING AND SEMANTIC ANALYSIS

Parsing and semantic analysis [26] is required when we want to extract more sophisticated measures from the code, involving, for instance, the scoping of identifiers, the handling of exceptions, and class hierarchies. Most modern languages are large complex beasts and therefore this form of processing is not for the faint-hearted. The effort involved can easily require writing tens of thousands of lines of code. Therefore, if this level of analysis is required it is best to adapt the code of an existing compiler. Compilers for most languages are available as open source software, and can therefore can be modified to perform the requisite analysis.

An interesting case is the LLVM compiler infrastructure [27] and in particular its Clang front-end, which can be used as a library to parse and analyze C-like languages, such as C, C++, and Objective C. For instance, we can build an analyzer that will print a C program's global variable declarations in about 100 lines of C++ code.[5]

7.3.4 THIRD-PARTY TOOLS

A final option to analyze source code is to piggy-back third-party tools that analyze code. Here are some tools and ideas on how to use them.

The *CScout* program is a source code analyzer and refactoring browser for collections of C programs [28]. It can process workspaces of multiple projects (think of a project as a collection of C source files that are linked together) mapping the complexity introduced by the C preprocessor back into the original C source code files. CScout takes advantage of modern hardware (fast processors and large memory capacities) to analyze C source code beyond the level of detail and accuracy provided by current compilers, linkers, and other source code analyzers. The analysis CScout performs takes into account the identifier scopes introduced by the C preprocessor and the C language proper scopes and namespaces. After the source code analysis CScout can process sophisticated queries on identifiers, files, and functions, locate unused or wrongly-scoped identifiers, and compute many metrics related to files, functions, and identifiers. Figure 7.1 illustrates the metrics collected for functions.

CCFinderX[6] is a tool that detects duplicated code fragments in source code written in many modern programming languages. The tool is a redesign of CCFinder [29], which has been used for research published in many papers. The command-line version of the tool will print its results as a text file.

---

[5]https://github.com/loarabia/Clang-tutorial/blob/master/CItutorial6.cpp.
[6]http://www.ccfinder.net/.

Function Metrics

Number of elements: 229

Metric	Total	Min	Max	Avg
Number of characters	92771	13	3686	405.114
Number of comment characters	7114	0	482	31.0655
Number of space characters	20762	2	1062	90.6638
Number of line comments	0	0	0	0
Number of block comments	295	0	14	1.28821
Number of lines	4247	1	185	18.5459
Maximum number of characters in a line	10519	9	107	45.9345
Number of character strings	344	0	32	1.50218
Number of unprocessed lines	0	0	0	0
Number of C preprocessor directives	0	0	0	0
Number of processed C preprocessor conditionals (ifdef, if, elif)	0	0	0	0
Number of defined C preprocessor function-like macros	0	0	0	0
Number of defined C preprocessor object-like macros	0	0	0	0
Number of preprocessed tokens	28102	4	1084	122.716
Number of compiled tokens	33064	0	1930	144.384
Number of statements or declarations	3214	0	153	14.0349
Number of operators	4509	0	176	19.69
Number of unique operators	1153	0	19	5.03493
Number of numeric constants	988	0	64	4.31441
Number of character literals	369	0	67	1.61135
Number of if statements	599	0	32	2.61572
Number of else clauses	179	0	21	0.781659
Number of switch statements	25	0	2	0.10917
Number of case labels	189	0	28	0.825328
Number of default labels	21	0	2	0.0917031
Number of break statements	111	0	16	0.484716
Number of for statements	105	0	9	0.458515
Number of while statements	28	0	4	0.122271
Number of do statements	8	0	2	0.0349345
Number of continue statements	9	0	3	0.0393013
Number of goto statements	9	0	2	0.0393013
Number of return statements	263	0	13	1.14847
Number of project-scope identifiers	1887	0	98	8.24017
Number of file-scope (static) identifiers	476	0	47	2.0786
Number of macro identifiers	1081	0	102	4.72052
Total number of object and object-like identifiers	7321	0	270	31.9694
Number of unique project-scope identifiers	938	0	36	4.09607
Number of unique file-scope (static) identifiers	318	0	27	1.38865
Number of unique macro identifiers	676	0	34	2.95197
Number of unique object and object-like identifiers	2444	0	68	10.6725
Number of global namespace occupants at function's top	166333	0	1070	726.345
Number of parameters	330	0	6	1.44105
Maximum level of statement nesting	283	0	7	1.23581
Number of goto labels	7	0	2	0.0305677
Fan-in (number of calling functions)	719	0	61	3.13974
Fan-out (number of called functions)	881	0	34	3.84716
Cyclomatic complexity (control statements)	994	1	36	4.34061
Extended cyclomatic complexity (includes branching operators)	1196	1	42	5.22271
Maximum cyclomatic complexity (includes branching operators and all switch branches)	1360	1	69	5.93886
Structure complexity (Henry and Kafura)	440199	0	238144	1922.27
Halstead complexity	72126.2	0	3416.45	314.961
Information flow metric (Henry and Selig)	2.51256e+006	0	1.5552e+006	10971.9

FIGURE 7.1

CScout-derived function metrics for the *awk* source code.

The output file format of *CCFinderX* is simple, but not trivial. Its first section lists for each file that has been analyzed its numerical identifier, its path, and the number of tokens it contains. Here is an excerpt corresponding to the Linux kernel.

```
source_files {
...
19 arch/i386/kernel/bootflag.c 314
20 arch/i386/kernel/cpuid.c 841
21 arch/i386/kernel/i8237.c 147
22 arch/i386/kernel/microcode.c 1673
23 arch/i386/kernel/msr.c 1287
24 arch/i386/kernel/quirks.c 154
25 arch/i386/kernel/topology.c 133
26 arch/i386/mm/hugetlbpage.c 1084
27 arch/i386/oprofile/backtrace.c 310
28 arch/i386/oprofile/init.c 67
...
}
```

A list of detected code clones then follows. Each line contains the clone's identifier, followed by a pair of source code clone specifications. Each one has the file identifier, the beginning token, and the end token of the cloned code.

In the following example we see code cloned within the same file (`microcode.c`—clone 7329), as well as code cloned between different files (e.g., `cpuid.c` and `msr.c`—clone 6981).

```
clone_pairs {
...
6981 20.785-840 23.1231-1286
10632 20.625-690 934.1488-1553
7329 22.660-725 22.884-949
...
}
```

The generated file can be further analyzed to derive additional measures. As an example, the following Perl program when given as input the base name of a CCFinderX result file will print the percentage of cloned tokens in it. A high percentage of cloning can often lead to higher maintenance costs, because fixes and enhancements need to be carefully duplicated in multiple places.

```
open(IN, "ccfx.exe P $ARGV[0].ccfxd|") || die;
while (<IN>) {
  chop;
  if (/^source_files/ .. /^\}/) {
    # Initialize file map as non-cloned tokens
    ($id, $name, $tok) = split;
```

```perl
    $file[$id][$tok - 1] = 0 if ($tok > 0);
    $nfile++;
  } elsif (/^clone_pairs/ .. /^\}/) {
    # Assign clone details to corresponding files
    ($id, $c1, $c2) = split;
    mapfile($c1);
    mapfile($c1);
  }
}

# Given a detected clone, mark the corresponding tokens
# in the file map as cloned
sub mapfile {
  my($clone) = @_;
  ($fid, $start, $end) = ($clone =~ m/^(\d+)\.(\d+)\-(\d+)$/);
  for ($i = $start; $i <= $end; $i++) {
    $file[$fid][$i] = 1;
  }
}

# Sum up the number of tokens and clones
for ($fid = 0 ; $fid <= $#file; $fid++) {
  for ($tokid = 0; $tokid <= $#{$file[$fid]}; $tokid++) {
    $ntok++;
    $nclone += $file[$fid][$tokid];
  }
}

print "$ARGV[0] nfiles=$nfile ntok=$ntok nclone=$nclone ",
    $nclone / $ntok * 100, "\n";
```

General-purpose tools can often be just as helpful as the specialized ones we have seen. If we want to perform some processing on comments in C, C++, or Objective-C code, then the GCC version of the C preprocessor can help us. Consider a case where we want to count the number of comment characters in a source code file. Preprocessing the file with the -fpreprocessed flag will remove the comments, but won't perform any other expansion. Thus, subtracting the number of characters in the file with the comments removed from the original number will give us the number of comment characters. The following *sh* code excerpt will print the number of comment characters in file.c.

```sh
expr $(wc --chars <prog.c) - $(cpp -fpreprocessed prog.c | wc --chars)
```

We can also pass the -H flag to the C preprocessor in order to obtain a list of included header files. This output can, for instance, then be used to map code reuse patterns. Here is some representative output. (The dots at the beginning of each line indicate nested include levels, and can be used to study a project's module layering.)

```
. /usr/include/stdlib.h
.. /usr/include/machine/ieeefp.h
.. /usr/include/_ansi.h
```

```
...  /usr/include/newlib.h
...  /usr/include/sys/config.h
....  /usr/include/machine/ieeefp.h
....  /usr/include/sys/features.h
....  /usr/include/cygwin/config.h
..  /usr/lib/gcc/i686-pc-cygwin/4.8.2/include/stddef.h
..  /usr/include/sys/reent.h
...  /usr/include/_ansi.h
...  /usr/lib/gcc/i686-pc-cygwin/4.8.2/include/stddef.h
...  /usr/include/sys/_types.h
....  /usr/include/machine/_types.h
.....  /usr/include/machine/_default_types.h
....  /usr/include/sys/lock.h
....  /usr/lib/gcc/i686-pc-cygwin/4.8.2/include/stddef.h
```

Another useful family of general-purpose tools we can repurpose for source code analysis are documentation generators, such as *Doxygen* and *Javadoc*. These parse source code and documentation comments to create code reference documents. The simplest way to use these tools is to analyze the resulting HTML text. The text's structure is simpler than the corresponding code, and, in addition, it may contain data that would be difficult to get from the original code. The trick in this case is to look at the generated HTML code (right-click—This Frame—View Source in many browsers) to determine the exact pattern to search for. For example, the following shell code will go through the Java development kit HTML documentation to count the number of methods that are declared to implement some interface (7752 methods in total).

```
grep --recursive --count '<strong>Specified by:' . |
awk -F: '{s += $2} END {print s}'
```

If the generated documentation does not contain the information we want, we can extend *Javadoc* through custom so-called *doclets*. These have a method that is called after *Javadoc* has processed the source code. The method gets as an argument a document tree of the code's element, which can then be easily processed to extract and print the results we want. As an example, the *UMLGraph* system uses this approach to create UML diagrams out of Java code [30].

Regarding the analysis of the code's adherence to some style conventions, a useful approach is to apply a source code formatter, such as *indent*, on the source code, and then compare the original source code with the formatter's output. The number of differences found is an indication of how closely the code follows the code style conventions: a large number of differences indicates a poor adherence to the style conventions. A problem of this approach is that for some languages, such as C and C++, there are many acceptable style conventions. In these cases, either the code style tool has to be configured according to the documented code conventions, or the code's conventions have to be deduced from the actual code [31].

The following shell script will deduce the code's conventions by perturbing the (far too many) settings passed to the *indent* program, and keeping the setting that minimizes the number of lines that do not match the specified style each time. After it is executed with FILES set to a (hopefully representative) set of files on which to operate, it will set the variable INDENT_OPT to the *indent* options that match the code's style more closely.

```
# Return number of style violations when running indent on
# $FILES with $INDENT_OPT options
style_violations()
{
        for f in $FILES
        do
                indent -st $INDENT_OPT $1 $f |
                diff $f -
        done |
        grep '^<' |
        wc --lines
}

VIOLATIONS $(style_violations)

# Determine values for numerical options
for TRY_OPT in i ts bli c cbi cd ci cli cp d di ip l lc pi
do
        BEST=$VIOLATIONS
        # Find best value for $TRY_OPT
        for n in 0 1 2 3 4 5 6 7 8
        do
                NEW=$(style_violations -$TRY_OPT$n)
                if [ $NEW -lt $BEST ]
                then
                        BNUM=$n
                        BEST=$NEW
                fi
        done
        if [ $BEST -lt $VIOLATIONS ]
        then
                INDENT_OPT="$INDENT_OPT -$TRY_OPT$BNUM"
                VIOLATIONS=$BEST
        fi
done

# Determine Boolean options
for TRY_OPT in bad bap bbb bbo bc bl bls br brs bs cdb cdw ce cs bfda \
    bfde fc1 fca hnl lp lps nbad nbap nbbo nbc nbfda ncdb ncdw nce \
    ncs nfc1 nfca nhnl nip nlp npcs nprs npsl nsaf nsai nsaw nsc nsob \
    nss nut pcs prs psl saf sai saw sc sob ss ut
do
        NEW=$(style_violations -$TRY_OPT)
        if [ $NEW -lt $VIOLATIONS ]
        then
                INDENT_OPT="$INDENT_OPT -$TRY_OPT"
                VIOLATIONS=$NEW
        fi
done
```

Running *indent* on the Windows Research Kernel without any options results in 389,547 violations found among 583,407 lines. After determining the appropriate *indent* options with the preceding script (-i4 -ts0 -bli0 -c0 -cd0 -di0 -bad -bbb -br -brs -bfda -bfde -nbbo -ncs) the number of lines found to be violating the style conventions shrinks to 118,173. This type of analysis can pinpoint, for example, developers and teams that require additional mentoring or training to help them adhere to an organization's code style standards. An increase of these figures over time can be an indicator of stress in an organization's development processes.

7.4 COMPILED CODE ANALYSIS

Analyzing the artifacts of compilation (assembly language code, object files, and libraries) has the obvious advantage that the compiler performs all the heavy lifting required for the analysis. Thus, the analysis can be efficiently performed and its results will accurately match the actual semantics of the language. In addition, this analysis can be performed on proprietary systems, repositories of binary code, such as those of the Maven ecosystem [32], and also on mixed code bases where an application's source code is shipped together with library binaries. The following sections list tools and corresponding examples.

7.4.1 ASSEMBLY LANGUAGE

Most compilers provide a switch that directs them to produce assembly language source code, rather than binary object code. The corresponding flag for most Unix compilers is -S. Assembly language files can be easily processed using text tools, such as *grep*, *sed*, and *awk*. As an example, we will see a script that counts the code's basic blocks.

A *basic block* is a portion of code with exactly one entry and exit point. It can be valuable to analyze code in terms of basic blocks, since it allows measuring things like code complexity and test coverage requirements.

We can obtain information regarding the basic blocks of GCC-compiled code by passing to the compiler the --coverage flag in conjunction with the -S flag to produce assembly language output. The generated code at the entry or exit of a basic block looks like the following excerpt (without the comments).

```
movl  ___gcov0.stat_files+56, %eax  ; Load low part of 64-bit value
movl  ___gcov0.stat_files+60, %edx  ; Load hight part of 64-bit value
addl  $1, %eax                      ; Increment low part
adcl  $0, %edx                      ; Add carry to high part
movl  %eax, ___gcov0.stat_files+56  ; Store low part
movl  %edx, ___gcov0.stat_files+60  ; Store high part
```

From the above code it is easy to see that the counter associated with each basic block occupies 8 data bytes. The compiler stores the counters in common data blocks allocated on a per-function basis, like the ones in the following example obtained by analyzing a small C program.[7]

---

[7]http://www.spinellis.gr/sw/unix/fileprune/.

```
.lcomm ___gcov0.execute_schedule,400,32
.lcomm ___gcov0.prunefile,48,32
.lcomm ___gcov0.bytime,8,8
.lcomm ___gcov0.print_schedule,24,8
.lcomm ___gcov0.create_schedule,184,32
.lcomm ___gcov0.parse_dates,80,32
.lcomm ___gcov0.stat_files,72,32
.lcomm ___gcov0.xstrdup,16,8
.lcomm ___gcov0.xmalloc,24,8
.lcomm ___gcov0.D,8,8
.lcomm ___gcov0.main,816,32
.lcomm ___gcov0.error_pmsg,40,32
.lcomm ___gcov0.error_msg,24,8
.lcomm ___gcov0.usage,24,8
```

The three arguments to each `lcomm` pseudo-op are the block's name, its size, and alignment. By dividing the size by 8 we can obtain the number of basic block boundaries associated with each function. Thus, we can process a set of assembly language files produced by compiling code with the `--coverage` option and then use the following script to obtain a list of functions ordered by the number of basic blocks boundaries embedded in them.

```
# Compile code with coverage analysis
gcc −S −−coverage −o /dev/stdout file.c |

# Print the blocks where coverage data is stored
sed −−quiet '/^\.lcomm ___gcov0/s/[.,]/ /gp' |

# Print name and size of each block
awk '{print $3, $4 / 8}' |

# Order by ascending block size
sort −−key=2 −−numeric
```

Here is an example of the script's output for the preceding program.

```
D 1
bytime 1
xstrdup 2
error_msg 3
print_schedule 3
usage 3
xmalloc 3
error_pmsg 5
prunefile 6
stat_files 9
parse_dates 10
create_schedule 23
execute_schedule 50
main 102
```

The number of basic blocks in each function can be used to assess code structure, modularity, and (together with other metrics) locate the potential trouble spots.

7.4.2 MACHINE CODE

On Unix systems we can analyze object files containing machine code with the *nm* program.[8] This displays a list of defined and undefined symbols in each object file passed as an argument [33, pp. 363–364]. Defined symbols are preceded by their address, and all symbols are preceded by the type of their linkage. The most interesting symbol types found in user-space programs in a hosted environment are the following.

B   Large uninitialized data; typically arrays
C   Uninitialized "common" data; typically variables of basic types
D   Initialized data
R   Read-only symbols (constants and strings)
T   Code (known as text)
U   Undefined (imported) symbol (function or variable)

Lowercase letter types (e.g., "d" or "t") correspond to symbols that are defined locally in a given file (with a `static` declaration in C/C++ programs).

Here is as an example the output of running *nm* on a C "hello, world" program.

```
00000000 T main
         U printf
```

As a first example of this technique, consider the task of finding all symbols that a (presumably) large C program should have declared as `static`. Appropriate `static` declarations, minimize name space pollution, increase modularity, and can prevent bugs that might be difficult to locate. Therefore, the number of elements in such a list could be a metric of a project's maintainability.

```
# List of all undefined (imported) symbols
nm *.o | awk '$1 == "U" {print $2}' >imports

# List of all defined globally exported symbols
nm *.o | awk 'NF == 3 && $2 ~ /[A-Z]/ {print $3}' | sort >exports

# List of all symbols that were globally exported but not imported
# (-2: don't show only imports, -3: don't show common symbols)
comm -2 -3 exports imports
```

Our second example derives identifier metrics according to their type. The script we will see can analyze systems whose object files reside in a directory hierarchy and therefore uses *find* to locate all object files. After listing the defined symbols with *nm*, it uses *awk* to tally in an associative array (map) the count and total length of the identifiers of each identifier category. This allows it in the end to print the average length and count for each category.

---

[8]A program with similar functionality, called *dumpbin*, is also distributed with Microsoft's Visual Studio.

```
# Find object files
find . —name \*.o |

# List symbols
xargs nm |

awk '
  # Tally data for each symbol type
  NF == 3 {
    len[$2] += length($3)
    count[$2]++
  }
  END {
    # Print average length for each type
    for (t in len)
      printf "%s %4.1f %8d\n", t, len[t] / count[t], count[t]
  }' |

# Order by symbol type
sort --ignore-case
```

Running the preceding script on a compiled kernel of FreeBSD produces the following results.

```
A  6.0        5
b 13.2     2306
B 16.7     1229
C 10.9     2574
D 19.1     1649
d 23.0    11575
R 13.2      240
r 40.9     8244
T 17.5    12567
t 17.9    15475
V 17.0        1
```

From these results we can see that in each category there are more local (static) symbols (identified by a lowercase letter) than global ones (shown with the corresponding uppercase letter), and that global functions (T) are far more common (12567) than global variables (D: 1649) and arrays (B: 1229). This allows us to reason regarding the encapsulation mechanisms used in the specific system.

Binary code analysis can go into significantly more depth than the static analysis techniques we have discussed in other sections. The code sequences can be analyzed in considerably more detail, while dynamic analysis methods can be used to obtain information from running programs. Tool support can help in both regards; a recently published survey of available tools [34] provides a good starting point.

7.4.3 DEALING WITH NAME MANGLING

Some of the techniques covered in this section work well with code written in older languages, such as C and Fortran. However, if we try them on code written in relatively newer ones, such as Ada, C++, and Objective-C, we will get gibberish, as illustrated in the following example.

```
_ZL19visit_include_files6FileidMS_KFRKSt3mapIS_10IncDetails
St4lessIS_ESaISt4pairIKS_S1_EEEvEMS1_KFbvEi 53
_ZL9call_pathP12GraphDisplayP4CallS2_b 91
_ZL11cgraph_pageP12GraphDisplay 96
_ZL12version_infob 140
```

The reason for this is *name mangling*: a method C++ compilers use to reconcile linkers that were designed for simpler languages with the requirement of C++ for type-correct linking across separately compiled files. To achieve this feat the compiler adorns each externally visible identifier with characters that specify its precise type.

We can undo this mangling by passing the resulting text through the *c++filt* tool, which ships with GNU binutils. This will decode each identifier according to the corresponding rules, and provide the full language-dependent type associated with each identifier. For instance, the demangled C++ identifiers of the preceding example are the following.

```
visit_include_files(Fileid, std::map<Fileid, IncDetails,
std::less<Fileid>, std::allocator<std::pair<Fileid const,
IncDetails> > > const& (Fileid::*)() const, bool
(IncDetails::*)() const, int) 53
call_path(GraphDisplay*, Call*, Call*, bool) 91
cgraph_page(GraphDisplay*) 96
version_info(bool) 140
```

7.4.4 BYTE CODE

Programs and libraries associated with the JVM environment are compiled into portable byte code. This can be readily analyzed to avoid the complexity of analyzing source code. The *javap* program, which comes with the Java development kit, gets as an argument the name of a class, and, by default, prints its public, protected, and package-visible members. For instance, this is the *javap* output for a "hello, world" Java program.

```
Compiled from "Test.java"
class Hello {
  Hello();
  public static void main(java.lang.String[]);
}
```

Here is how we can use the output of *javap* to extract some basic code metrics of Java programs (in this case the *ClassGraph* class).

```
# Number of fields and methods in the ClassGraph class
javap org.umlgraph.doclet.ClassGraph |
grep '^ ' |
wc --lines
```

```
# List of public methods of a given class
javap —public org.umlgraph.doclet.ClassGraph |
sed ——quiet '
 # Remove arguments of each method
 s/(.*/(/
 # Remove visibility and return type of each method; print its name
 s/^ .* \([^(]*\)(/\1/p'
```

The *javap* program can also disassemble the Java byte codes contained in each class file. This allows us to perform even more sophisticated processing. The following script prints virtual method invocations, ordered by the number of times each class invokes a method.

```
# Disassemble Java byte code for all class files under the current directory
javap —c **/*.class |

# Print (class method) pairs
awk '
 # Set class name
 /^[^ ].* class / {
  # Isolate from the line the class name
  # It is parenthesized in the RE so we can refer to it as \1
  class = gensub("^.* class ([^ ]*) .*", "\\1", "g")
 }
 # Print class and method name
 /: invokevirtual/ {
  print class, $6
 }' |

# Order same invocations together
sort |

# Count number of same invocations
uniq ——count |

# Order results by number of same invocations
sort ——numeric—sort ——reverse
```

Running the above script on the UMLGraph's compiled method allows us to determinate that the `org.umlgraph.doclet.Options` class calls the method `String.equals` 158 times. Measures like these can be used to build a dependency graph, which can then expose refactoring opportunities.

If the output of *javap* is too low-level for our purpose, another alternative for processing Java byte code is the *FindBugs* program [35]. This allows the development of plug-ins that are invoked when specific code patterns are encountered. For instance, a simple plugin can detect instances of `BigDecimal` types that are created from a `double` value,[9] while a more complex one can locate arbitrary errors in method arguments that can be determined at the time of the analysis [36].

---

[9]http://code.google.com/p/findbugs/wiki/DetectorPluginTutorial.

7.4.5 DYNAMIC LINKING

Modern systems have their executable programs link dynamically at runtime to the libraries they require in order to run. This simplifies software updates, reduces the size on disk of each executable program, and allows the running programs to share each library's code in memory [37, p. 281]. Obtaining a list of the dynamic libraries a program requires allows us to extract information regarding software dependencies and reuse.

On Unix systems the *ldd* program will provide a list of the libraries an executable program (or an other library) requires in order to run. Here is an example of running the *ldd* command on bin/ls on a Linux system.

```
ldd /bin/ls
    linux-gate.so.1 =>  (0xb7799000)
    libselinux.so.1 => /lib/i386-linux-gnu/libselinux.so.1 (0xb776d000)
    librt.so.1 => /lib/i386-linux-gnu/i686/cmov/librt.so.1 (0xb7764000)
    libacl.so.1 => /lib/i386-linux-gnu/libacl.so.1 (0xb7759000)
    libc.so.6 => /lib/i386-linux-gnu/i686/cmov/libc.so.6 (0xb75f5000)
    libdl.so.2 => /lib/i386-linux-gnu/i686/cmov/libdl.so.2 (0xb75f1000)
    /lib/ld-linux.so.2 (0xb779a000)
    libpthread.so.0 => /lib/i386-linux-gnu/i686/cmov/libpthread.so.0 (0xb75d8000)
    libattr.so.1 => /lib/i386-linux-gnu/libattr.so.1 (0xb75d2000)
```

As usual, we can then process this output with additional tools to generate higher-level results. As an example, the following pipeline will list the libraries required by all programs in the /usr/bin directory, ordered by the number of programs that depend on them. The pipeline's output can be used to study the dependencies between modules and software reuse.

```
# List dynamic library dependencies, ignoring errors
ldd /usr/bin/* 2>/dev/null |

# Print library name
awk '/=>/{print $3}' |

# Bring names together
sort |

# Count same names
uniq --count |

# Order by number of occurrences
sort --reverse --numeric-sort
```

These are the first ten lines of the preceding pipeline's output on a FreeBSD system,

```
392 /lib/libc.so.7
 38 /lib/libz.so.5
 38 /lib/libm.so.5
 35 /lib/libncurses.so.8
 30 /lib/libutil.so.8
```

```
30 /lib/libcrypto.so.6
29 /lib/libcrypt.so.5
22 /usr/lib/libstdc++.so.6
22 /usr/lib/libbz2.so.4
22 /lib/libmd.so.5
```

and these on a Linux system.

```
587 /lib/i386-linux-gnu/i686/cmov/libc.so.6
208 /lib/i386-linux-gnu/i686/cmov/libdl.so.2
148 /lib/i386-linux-gnu/i686/cmov/libm.so.6
147 /lib/i386-linux-gnu/libz.so.1
118 /lib/i386-linux-gnu/i686/cmov/libpthread.so.0
 75 /lib/i386-linux-gnu/libtinfo.so.5
 71 /lib/i386-linux-gnu/i686/cmov/librt.so.1
 41 /lib/i386-linux-gnu/libselinux.so.1
 38 /lib/i386-linux-gnu/libgcc_s.so.1
 38 /lib/i386-linux-gnu/i686/cmov/libresolv.so.2
```

7.4.6 LIBRARIES

Library files contain compiled object files packed together so that they can be easily shipped and used as a unit. On Unix systems *nm* can be applied to see the symbols defined and referenced by each library member (see Section 7.4.2), while the *ar* program can be run to list the files contained in the library. As an example, the following pipeline will list the C library's files ordered by their size.

```
# Print a verbose table for file libc.a
ar tvf libc.a |

# Order numerically by size (the third field)
sort --reverse --key=3 --numeric-sort
```

Here are the first few lines of the pipeline's output on a Linux system.

```
rw-r--r-- 2308942397/2397 981944 Dec 18 01:16 2013 regex.o
rw-r--r-- 2308942397/2397 331712 Dec 18 01:16 2013 malloc.o
rw-r--r-- 2308942397/2397 277648 Dec 18 01:16 2013 getaddrinfo.o
rw-r--r-- 2308942397/2397 222592 Dec 18 01:16 2013 strcasestr-nonascii.o
rw-r--r-- 2308942397/2397 204552 Dec 18 01:16 2013 fnmatch.o
rw-r--r-- 2308942397/2397 196848 Dec 18 01:16 2013 vfwprintf.o
```

Such a listing can provide insights on a library's modularity, and modules that could be refactored into units of a more appropriate size.

The corresponding program for Java archives is *jar*. Given the name of a Java `.jar` file it will list the class files contained in it. The results can then be used by other programs for further processing.

Consider the task of calculating the Chidamber and Kemerer metrics [38] for a set of classes. These metrics comprise for a class the following following values:

WMC	: Weighted methods per class
DIT	: Depth of inheritance tree
NOC	: Number of children
CBO	: Coupling between object classes
RFC	: Response for a class
LCOM	: Lack of cohesion in methods

The metrics can be used to assess the design of an object-oriented system and to improve the corresponding process.

The following example will calculate the metrics for the classes contained in the `ant.jar` file and print the results ordered by the weighted methods per class. For the metrics calculation it uses the *ckjm* program [39],[10] which expects as its input pairs of files and class names.

```
# Print table of files contained in ant.jar
jar tf ant.jar |

# Add "ant.jar " to the beginning of lines ending with .class
# and print them, passing the (file name class) list to ckjm
# c metrics
sed --quiet '/\.class$/s/^/ant.jar /p' |

# Run ckjm, calculating the metrics for the file name class
# pairs read from its standard input
java -jar ckjm-1.9.jar 2>/dev/null |

# Order the results numerically by the second field
# (Weighted methods per class)
sort --reverse --key=2 --numeric-sort
```

Here are, as usual, the first few lines of the pipeline's output.

```
org.apache.tools.ant.Project 127 1 0 33 299 7533 368 110
org.apache.tools.ant.taskdefs.Javadoc 109 0 0 35 284 5342 8 83
org.apache.tools.ant.taskdefs.Javac 88 0 1 19 168 3534 14 75
org.apache.tools.ant.taskdefs.Zip 78 0 1 44 269 2471 5 36
org.apache.tools.ant.DirectoryScanner 70 1 2 15 169 2029 43 34
org.apache.tools.ant.util.FileUtils 67 1 0 13 172 2181 151 65
org.apache.tools.ant.types.AbstractFileSet 66 0 3 31 137 1527 9 63
```

The preceding metrics of object-oriented code can be further processed to flag classes with values that merit further analysis and justification [37, pp. 341–342], [40], and to locate opportunities for refactoring. In this case, some of the preceding classes, which comprise more than 50 classes each, may need refactoring, because they violate a rule of a thumb stating that elements consisting of more than 30 subelements are likely to be problematic [41, p. 31].

---

[10]http://www.spinellis.gr/sw/ckjm/.

7.5 ANALYSIS OF CONFIGURATION MANAGEMENT DATA

Analysis of data obtained from a configuration management system [42, 43], such as *Git* [44], *Subversion* [45], or cvs [46], can provide valuable information regarding software evolution [47, 48], the engagement of developers [49], defect prediction [50, 51], distributed development [52, 53], and many other topics [54]. There are two types of data that can be obtained from a configuration management system.

> **Metadata** are the details associated with each commit: the developer, the date and time, the commit message, the software branch, and the commit's scope. In addition, the commit message, apart from free text, often contains other structured elements, such as references to bugs in the corresponding database, developer user names, and other commits.
> **Snapshots** of a project's source code can be obtained from the repository, reflecting the project's state at each point of time a commit was made. The source code associated with each snapshot can be further analyzed using the techniques we saw in Section 7.3.

7.5.1 OBTAINING REPOSITORY DATA

Before a repository's data can be analyzed, it is usually preferable to obtain a local copy of the repository's data [55]. Although some repositories allow remote access to clients, this access is typically provided to serve the needs of software developers, i.e., an initial download of the project's source code, followed by regular, but not high-frequency, synchronization requests and commits. In contrast, a repository's analysis might involve many expensive operations, like thousands of checkouts at successive time points, which can stress the repository server's network bandwidth, cpu resources, and administrators. Operations on a local repository copy will not tax the remote server, and will also speed up significantly the operations run on it.

The techniques used for obtaining repository data depend on the repository type and the number of repositories that are to be mirrored. Repositories of distributed version control systems [56] offer commands that can readily create a copy of a complete repository from a remote server, namely `bzr branch` for *Bazaar* [57], `git clone` for *Git*, and `hg clone` for *Mercurial* [58]. Projects using the *Subversion* or cvs system for version control can sometimes be mirrored using the *rsync* or the *svnsync* (for *Subversion*) command and associated protocol. The following are examples of commands used to mirror a diverse set of repositories.

```
# Create a copy of the GNU cpio Git repository
git clone git://git.savannah.gnu.org/cpio.git

# Create a copy of the GNU Chess Subversion repository using rsync
rsync —avHS rsync://svn.savannah.gnu.org/svn/chess/ chess.repo/

# Create a copy of the Asterisk Bazaar repository
bzr branch lp:asterisk

# Create a copy of the Mercurial C Python repository
hg clone http://hg.python.org/cpython
```

Using *svnsync* is more involved; here is an example of the commands used for mirroring the *Subversion* repository of the JBOSS application server.

```
svnadmin create jboss-as
svnsync init file://$(pwd)/jbossas https://svn.jboss.org/repos/jboss-as
cd jboss-as
echo '#!/bin/sh' > hooks/pre-revprop-change
chmod +x hooks/pre-revprop-change
cd ..
svnsync init file://$(pwd)/jboss-as http://anonsvn.jboss.org/repos/jbossas
svnsync sync file://$(pwd)/jboss-as
```

Alternatively, if a friendly administrator has shell-level access to the site hosting the Subversion repository, the repository can be dumped into a file and restored back from it using the commands svnadmin dump and svnadmin load.

When multiple repositories are hosted on the same server, their mirroring can be automated by generating cloning commands. These can often be easily created by screen-scrapping a web page that lists the available repositories. As an example consider the *Git* repositories hosted on git.gnome.org.

Each project is listed with an HTML line like the following.

```
<tr><td class='sublevel-repo'><a title='archive/gcalctool'
href='/browse/archive/gcalctool/'>archive/gcalctool</a>
</td><td><a href='/browse/archive/gcalctool/'>Desktop calculator</a>
</td><td></td><td><span class='age-months'>11 months</span></td></tr>
```

The name of the corresponding *Git* repository can be readily extracted from the URL. In addition, because the projects are listed in multiple web pages, a loop is required to iterate over them, specifying the project list's offset for each page. The following short script will download all repositories using the techniques we saw.

```
# List the URLs containing the projects
perl -e 'for ($i = 0; $i < 1500; $i += 650) {
  print "https://git.gnome.org/browse/?ofs=$i\n"}' |

# For each URL
while read url
do
  # Read the web page
  curl "$url" |

  # Extract the Git repository URL
  sed --quiet '/sublevel-repo/s|.*href='\''/browse/\([^'\'']*\)'\''.*|\
  git://git.gnome.org/\1|p' |

  # Run git clone for the specific repository
  xargs --max-args=1 git clone
done
```

In recent years GitHub has evolved to be an amazingly large repository of open source projects. Although GitHub offers an API to access the corresponding project data (see Figure 7.2), it does not offer a comprehensive catalog of the data stored in it [59]. Thankfully, large swathes of the data can be obtained as database dump files in the form of a torrent [17].

7.5.2 ANALYZING METADATA

Metadata analysis can easily be performed by running the version control system command that outputs the revision log. This can then be analyzed using the process outlined in Section 7.2.

As examples of metadata, consider the following *Git* log entry from the Linux kernel

```
commit fa389e220254c69ffae0d403eac4146171062d08
Author: Linus Torvalds <torvalds@linux-foundation.org>
Date:   Sun Mar 9 19:41:57 2014 -0700

    Linux 3.14-rc6
```

and an older CVS log entry from FreeBSD's *sed* program.

```
revision 1.28
date: 2005/08/04 10:05:11;  author: dds;  state: Exp;  lines: +8 -2
Bug fix: a numeric flag specification in the substitute command would
cause the next substitute flag to be ignored.
While working at it, detect and report overflows.

Reported by:    Jingsong Liu
MFC after:      1 week
```

The following example illustrates how we can obtain the time of the first commit from various types of repositories.

```
# Git
git rev-list --date-order --reverse --pretty=format:'%ci' master |
sed --quiet 2p

# Bazaar
bzr log | grep timestamp: | tail -1

# Mercurial
hg log | grep 'date:' | tail -1

# CVS
cvs log -SN |
sed --quiet 's/^date: \(..........\).*/\1/p' |
sort --unique |
head -1
```

Some version control systems, such as *Git*, allow us to specify the format of the resulting log output. This makes it easy to isolate and process specific items. The following sequence will print the author

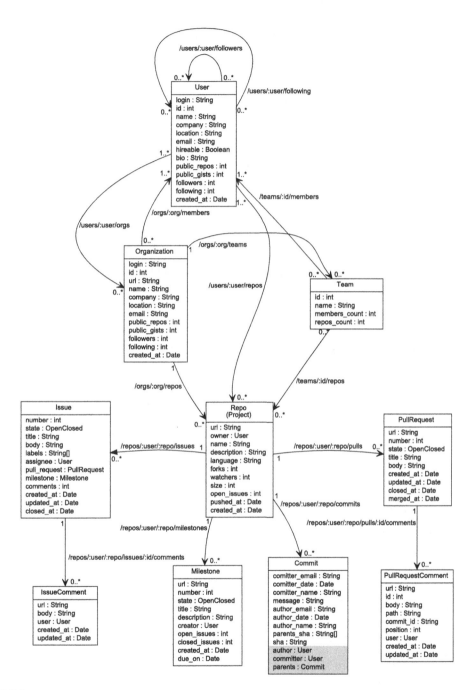

FIGURE 7.2

Schema of the data available through GitHub.

names of the 10 most prolific contributors associated with a *Git* repository, ordered by the number of commits they made.

```
# Print author names
git log ——format='%an' |

# Order them by author
sort |

# Count number of commits for each author
uniq ——count |

# Order them by number of commits
sort ——numeric—sort ——reverse |

# Print top 10
head —10
```

The result of running the preceding script on the last 10 years of the Linux kernel is the following.

```
20131 Linus Torvalds
 8445 David S. Miller
 7692 Andrew Morton
 5156 Greg Kroah-Hartman
 5116 Mark Brown
 4723 Russell King
 4584 Takashi Iwai
 4385 Al Viro
 4220 Ingo Molnar
 3276 Tejun Heo
```

Such lists can be used to gain insights into the division of labor within teams and developer productivity.

Aggregate results can be readily calculated using *awk*'s associative arrays. The following example shows the lines contributed by each developer in a cvs repository.

```
# Print the log
cvs log —SN |

# Isolate the author and line count
sed —n '/^date:/s/[+;]//gp' |

# Tally lines per author
awk '{devlines[$5] += $9}
     END {for (i in devlines) print i, devlines[i]}' |

# Order entries by descending number of lines
sort ——key=2 ——numeric—sort ——reverse
```

The first 10 lines from the output of the preceding command run on the FreeBSD kernel are the following.

```
gallatin 956758
mjacob 853190
sam 749313
jchandra 311499
jmallett 289413
peter 257575
rwatson 239382
jhb 236634
jimharris 227669
vkashyap 220986
```

7.5.3 **ANALYZING TIME SERIES SNAPSHOTS**

Creating a series of source code snapshots from a repository requires us

- to perform accurate data calculations,
- to represent the dates in a format that can be unambiguously parsed by the repository's version control system, and
- to check out the corresponding version of the software.

Accurate date calculations on time intervals can be performed by expressing dates in seconds from the start of an epoch (1970-01-01 on Unix systems). The Unix *date* command allows the conversion of an arbitrary start date into seconds since Epoch. Unfortunately, the way this is done differs between various Unix-like systems. The following Unix shell function expects as its first argument a date expressed in ISO-8601 basic date format (YYYYMMDD). It will print the date as an integer representing seconds since Epoch.

```
iso_b_to_epoch()
{
  case $(uname) in
  FreeBSD)
    date -j "$1"0000.00 '+%s' ;;
  Darwin)
    # Convert date to "mmdd0000yyyy.00" (time is 00:00:00)
    MDHMY=$(echo $1 | sed 's/\(....\)\(..\)\(..\)/\2\30000\1.00/')
    date -j "$MDHMY" '+%s'
    ;;
  CYGWIN*)
    date -d "$1" '+%s' ;;
  Linux)
    date -d "$1" '+%s' ;;
  *)
    echo "Unknown operating system type" 1>&2
    exit 1
  esac
}
```

The reverse conversion, from Epoch seconds to the ISO-8601 extended format (YYYY-MM-DD), which most version control systems can parse unambiguously, again depends on the operating system flavor.

The following Unix shell function expects as its first argument a date expressed as seconds since Epoch. It will print the corresponding date in ISO format.

```
epoch_to_iso_e()
{
  case $(uname) in
  Darwin)
    date -r $1 '+%Y-%m-%d' ;;
  FreeBSD)
    date -r $1 '+%Y-%m-%d' ;;
  CYGWIN*)
    date -d @$1 '+%Y-%m-%d' ;;
  Linux)
    date -d @$1 '+%Y-%m-%d' ;;
  *)
    echo "Unknown operating system type" 1>&2
    exit 1
  esac
}
```

As we would expect, the code used to check out a snapshot of the code for a given date depends on the version control system in use. The following Unix shell function expects as its first argument an ISO-8601 extended format date. In addition, it expects that the variable $REPO is set to one of the known repository types, and that it is executed within a directory where code from that repository has already been checked out. It will update the directory's contents with a snapshot of the project stored in the repository for the specified date. In the case of a *Bazaar* repository, the resulting snapshot will be stored in **/tmp/bzr-checkout**.

```
date_checkout()
{
  case "$REPO" in
  bzr)
    rm -rf /tmp/bzr-checkout
    bzr export -r date:"$1" /tmp/bzr-checkout
    ;;
  cvs)
    cvs update -D "$1"
    ;;
  git)
    BRANCH=$(git config --get-regexp branch.*remote |
      sed -n 's/^branch.//;s/\.remote origin//p')
    HASH=$(git rev-list -n 1 --before="$1" $BRANCH)
    git checkout $HASH
    ;;
  hg)
    hg update -d "$1"
    ;;
  rcs)
    # Remove files under version control
    ls RCS | sed 's/,v$//' | xargs rm -f
    # Checkout files at specified date
```

```
    co −f −d"$1" RCS/*
    ;;
  svn)
    svn update −r "{$1}"
    if [ −d trunk ]
    then
      DIR=trunk
    else
      DIR=.
    fi
    ;;
  *)
    echo "Unknown repository type: $REPO" 1>&2
    exit 1
    ;;
  esac
}
```

Given the building blocks we saw, a loop to perform some processing on repository snapshots over successive 10 day periods starting from, say, 2005-01-01, can be written as follows.

```
# Start date (2005-01-1) in seconds since Epoch
START=$(iso_b_to_epoch 20050101)

# End date in seconds since Epoch
END=$(date '+%s')

# Time increment (10 days) in seconds
INCR=$(expr 10 \* 24 \* 60 \* 60)

DATE=$START
while [ $DATE −lt $END ]
do
      date_checkout $DATE
      # Process the snapshot
      DATE=$(expr $DATE + $INCR)
done
```

7.5.4 ANALYZING A CHECKED OUT REPOSITORY

Given a directory containing a project checked out from a version control repository, we can analyze it using the techniques listed in Section 7.3. Care must be taken to avoid processing the data files associated with the version control system. A regular expression that can match these files, in order to exclude them, can be set as follows, according to the repository type.

```
case "$REPO" in
bzr)
  # Files are checked out in a new directory; nothing to exclude
  EXCLUDE=///
  ;;
cvs) EXCLUDE='/CVS/' ;;
git) EXCLUDE=.git ;;
```

```
hg) EXCLUDE='/.hg/' ;;
rcs) EXCLUDE='/RCS/' ;;
svn) EXCLUDE='/.svn/' ;;
esac
```

Another prerequisite for the analysis is identifying the source code files to analyze. Files associated with specific programming languages can be readily identified by their extension. For instance, C files end in .c; C++ files typically end in .cpp, .C, .cc, or .cxx; while Java files end in .java. Therefore, the following command

```
find . −type f −name \*.java
```

will output all the Java source code files residing in the current directory tree.

On the other hand, if we wish to process all source code files (e.g., to count the source code size in terms of lines) we must exclude binary files, such as those containing images, sound, and compiled third-party libraries. This can be done by running the Unix *file* command on each project file. By convention the output of *file* will contain the word text only for text files (in our case source code and documentation).

Putting all the above together, here is a pipeline that measures the lines in a repository snapshot checked out in the current directory.

```
# Print names of files
find . −type f |

# Remove from list version control data files
fgrep −−invert−match "$EXCLUDE" |

# Print each file's type
file −−files−from − |

# Print only the names of text files
sed −−quiet 's/: .*text.*//p' |

# Terminate records with \0, instead of new line
tr \\n \\0 |

# Catenate the contents of all files together
xargs −−null cat |

# Count the number of lines
wc −−lines
```

7.5.5 COMBINING FILES WITH METADATA

The version control system can also be used to help us analyze a project's files. An invaluable feature is the annotation (also known as "blame") command offered by many version control systems. This will display a source code file, listing with each line the last commit associated with it, the committer, and the corresponding date.

```
d62bd540 (linus1            1991-11-11  1) /*
d62bd540 (linus1            1991-11-11  2)  *  linux/kernel/sys.c
d62bd540 (linus1            1991-11-11  3)  *
cf1bbb91 (linus1            1992-08-01  4)  *  Copyright (C) 1991 Linus Torvalds
d62bd540 (linus1            1991-11-11  5)  */
d62bd540 (linus1            1991-11-11  6)
9984de1a (Paul Gortmaker    2011-05-23  7) #include <linux/export.h>
23d9e975 (linus1            1998-08-27  8) #include <linux/mm.h>
cf1bbb91 (linus1            1992-08-01  9) #include <linux/utsname.h>
8a219a69 (linus1            1993-09-19 10) #include <linux/mman.h>
d61281d1 (linus1            1997-03-10 11) #include <linux/reboot.h>
e674e1c0 (linus1            1997-08-11 12) #include <linux/prctl.h>
ac3a7bac (linus1            2000-01-04 13) #include <linux/highuid.h>
9a47365b (Dave Jones        2002-02-08 14) #include <linux/fs.h>
74da1ff7 (Paul Gortmaker    2011-05-26 15) #include <linux/kmod.h>
cdd6c482 (Ingo Molnar       2009-09-21 16) #include <linux/perf_event.h>
3e88c553 (Daniel Walker     2007-05-10 17) #include <linux/resource.h>
dc009d92 (Eric W. Biederman 2005-06-25 18) #include <linux/kernel.h>
e1f514af (Ingo Molnar       2002-09-30 19) #include <linux/workqueue.h>
c59ede7b (Randy.Dunlap      2006-01-11 20) #include <linux/capability.h>
```

Given such a list we can easily cut specific columns with the Unix *cut* command, and analyze version control metadata at the level of source code lines rather than complete files. For example, the following command will list the top contributors in the file cgroup.c of the Linux kernel at its current state.

```
# Annotated listing of the file
git blame kernel/cgroup.c |

# Cut the author name
cut --characters=11-29 |

# Order by author name
sort |

# Count consecutive author name occurrences
uniq --count |

# Order occurrences by their number
sort --reverse --numeric |

# Show top contributors
head
```

This is the command's output.

```
2425 Tejun Heo
1501 Paul Menage
 496 Li Zefan
 387 Ben Blum
 136 Cliff Wickman
```

```
106 Aristeu Rozanski
 60 Daniel Lezcano
 52 Mandeep Singh Baines
 42 Balbir Singh
 29 Al Viro
```

Similarly, we could find how many lines of the file stem from each year.

```
# Annotated listing of the file
git blame kernel/cgroup.c |

# Cut the commit's year
cut --characters=30-33 |

# Order by year
sort |

# Order occurrences by their number
uniq --count
```

This is the output we get by the preceding command.

```
1061 2007
 398 2008
 551 2009
 238 2010
 306 2011
 599 2012
2243 2013
  37 2014
```

7.5.6 ASSEMBLING REPOSITORIES

Projects with a long history provide an interesting source data. However, the data are seldom stored neatly in a single repository. More often than not we find snapshots from the beginning of a project's lifetime, then one or more frozen dumps of version control systems that are no longer used, and, finally, the live version control system. Fortunately, *Git* and other modern version control systems offer mechanisms to assemble a project's history retroactively, by piecing together various parts.

With *Git*'s *graft* feature, multiple *Git* repositories can be pieced together into a whole. This is, for instance, the method Yoann Padioleau used to create a *Git* repository of Linux's history, covering the period 1992–2010.[11] The last repository in the series is the currently active Linux repository. Therefore, with a single `git pull` command, the archive can be easily brought up to date. The annotated Linux file in Section 7.5.5 stems from a repository assembled in this way. A similar repository[12] covers 44 years of Unix development history [60].

If the repositories are not in *Git* format, then, given *Git*'s flexibility, the most expedient way to combine them into *Git* format is to use the methods we saw in this section for analyzing modern repositories.

---

[11] https://archive.org/details/git-history-of-linux.
[12] https://github.com/dspinellis/unix-history-repo.

Snapshots of a project can be imported into a *Git* repository with the correct date and committer (which must be derived from external sources, such as timestamps), using a Unix shell function like the following. This expects as its first argument the directory where the snapshot's files are located, and as its second argument an ISO-8601 basic date format (YYYYMMDD) date associated with the snapshot. When run within a directory where a *Git* repository has been checked out, it will add the files to the repository with a commit dated as specified. The code utilizes the `iso_b_to_epoch` function we saw in Section 7.5.3. To specify the code's author the `git commit --author` flag can be added to the code.

```
snapshot_add()
{
  rm --recursive --force *
  cp --recursive $1 .
  git add *
  GIT_AUTHOR_DATE="$(iso_b_to_epoch $2) +0000" \
  GIT_COMMITTER_DATE="$(iso_b_to_epoch $2) +0000" \
  git commit --all --message="Snapshot from $1"
  git tag --annotate "snap-$2" -m "Add tag for snapshot $2"
}
```

Importing into *Git* data stored in other repositories is relatively easy, thanks to existing libraries and tools that can be used for this purpose. Of particular interest is the (badly misnamed) *cvs2svn* program,[13] which can convert RCS [61] and CVS repositories into *Git* ones. In addition, the Perl VCS-SCCS library[14] contains an example program that can convert legacy SCCS [62] repository data into *Git* format.

Finally, if a program that can perform the conversion cannot be found, a small script can be written to print revision data in *Git*'s *fast import* format. This data can then be fed into the `git fast-import` command, to import it into *Git*. The data format is a textual stream, consisting of commands, such as `blob`, `commit`, `tag`, and `done`, which are complemented by associated data. According to the command's documentation and the personal experience of this chapter's author, an import program can be written in a scripting language within a day.

7.6 DATA VISUALIZATION

Given the volume and complexity of the data derived from the analysis methods we examined, it is easier to automate the process of diagram creation, rather than using spreadsheets or GUI-based graphics editors to draw them. The text-based tools we will see in this section do not beat the speed of firing up a drawing editor to jot down a few lines or a spreadsheet to create a chart from a list of numbers. However, investing time to learn them allows us to be orders-of-magnitude more efficient in repeatedly diagramming big data sets, performing tasks no one would dream of attempting in the GUI world.

7.6.1 GRAPHS

Perhaps the most impressive tool of those we will examine is *dot*. Part of the Graphviz suite [20], originally developed by AT&T, it lets us describe hierarchical relations between elements using a simple declarative language. For instance, with the following input *dot* will generate the diagram shown in Figure 7.3.

---

[13]http://cvs2svn.tigris.org/cvs2svn.html.
[14]http://search.cpan.org/dist/VCS-SCCS/.

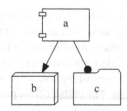

FIGURE 7.3

A simple diagram made with *dot*.

```
digraph {
  a [shape="component"];
  b [shape="box3d"];
  c [shape="folder"];
  a -> b;
  a -> c [arrowhead="dot"];
}
```

Dot offers a wide choice of node shapes, arrows, and options for controlling the graph's layout. It can handle graphs with thousands of nodes. This study's author has used it to display class hierarchies, database schemas, directory trees, package dependency diagrams, mechanical gear connections, and even genealogical trees. Its input language is simple (mostly graph edges and nodes), and it is trivial to generate a diagram from a script of just a few lines.

For example, the following Perl script will create a diagram of a directory tree. When run on the Linux source code tree, it will generate the Figure 7.4 [31]. This shows a relatively shallow and balanced tree organization, which could be a mark of an organization that maintains equilibrium between the changes brought by organic growth and the order achieved through regular refactorings. An architect reviewer might also question the few deep and narrow tree branches appearing in the diagram.

```perl
open(IN, "find $ARGV[0] -type d -print|");

while (<IN>) {
  chop;
  @paths = split(/\//, $_);
  undef $opath;
  undef $path;
  for $p (@paths) {
    $path .= "/$p";
    $name = $path;
```

FIGURE 7.4

The Linux directory tree.

```perl
  # Make name a legal node label
  $name =~ s/[^a-zA-Z0-9]/_/g;
  $node{$name} = $p;
  $edge{"$opath->$name;"} = 1 if ($opath);
  $opath = $name;
  }
}

print 'digraph G {
  nodesep=0.00001;
  node [height=.001,width=0.000001,shape=box,fontname="",fontsize=8];
  edge [arrowhead=none,arrowtail=none];
';

for $i (sort keys %node) {
  print "\t$i [label=\"\"];\n";
}
for $i (sort keys %edge) {
  print "\t$i\n";
}
print "}\n";
```

It is also easy to create diagrams from the version control system's metadata. The following Unix shell script will create a diagram of relationships between Linux authors and committers. The result of processing the first 3000 lines of the Linux kernel *Git* log can be seen in Figure 7.5.

```sh
(
  # Specify left-to right ordering
  echo 'digraph { rankdir=LR;'

  # Obtain git log
  git log --pretty=fuller |

  # Limit to first 3000 lines
  head -3000 |

  # Remove email
  sed 's/<.*//' |

  # Print author-committer pairs
  awk '
    # Store author and committer
    /^Author:/ { $1 = ""; a = $0}
    /^Commit:/{ $1 = ""; c = $0}
    /^CommitDate:/{
      if (a && c && a != c)
        print "\"" a "\" -> \"" c "\";"
    }' |

  # Eliminate duplicates
  sort -u
  # Close brace
  echo '}'
)
```

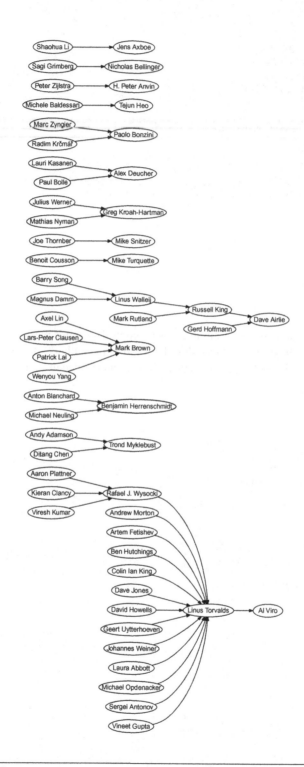

FIGURE 7.5

Relationships between Linux authors and committers.

Three cousins of *dot*, also parts of GraphViz, are *neato*, for drawing undirected graphs, and *twopi* and *circo*, for drawing radial and circular layout graphs. All use an input language similar to dot's. They are less useful for visualizing software systems, but in some cases they come in handy. For instance, this author has used *neato* has to draw the relationships between software quality attributes, links between Wikipedia nodes, and collaboration patterns between software developers.

7.6.2 DECLARATIVE DIAGRAMS

A slightly less declarative, but no less versatile, family of tools are those that target text-based typesetting systems: TikZ [63], which is based on TEX [64], and *pic* [65], which is based on *troff* [66]. The *pic* program was originally developed at AT&T's Bell Labs as part of the Unix document preparation tools [67], but these days it is more likely to appear in its GNU *groff* reincarnation. *Pic*'s language gives us commands such as `box`, `circle`, `line`, and `arrow`. Unlike the GraphViz tools, *pic* will not lay out the diagram for us, but it makes up for its lack of intelligence by letting us create macros and supporting loops and conditionals. This lets us define our own complex shapes (for our project's specialized notation) and then invoke them with a simple command. In effect, we are creating our own domain-specific drawing language. As an example, the following *pic* code, in conjunction with macros defined as part of the *UMLGraph* system [30], will result in Figure 7.6.

```
.PS
  copy "sequence.pic";

  # Define the objects
  pobject(E,"External Messages");
  object(T,"t:thread");
```

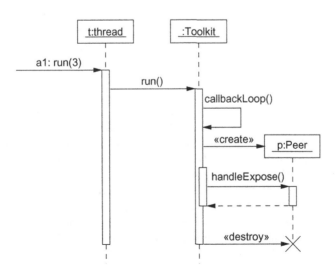

FIGURE 7.6

A diagram made with *pic*.

```
object(O,":Toolkit");
pobject(P);

step();

# Message sequences
message(E,T,"a1: run(3)");
active(T);
message(T,O,"run()");
active(O);
message(O,O,"callbackLoop()");
cmessage(O,P,"p:Peer"," ");
active(O);
message(O,P,"handleExpose()");
active(P);
rmessage(P,O,"");
inactive(P);
inactive(O);
dmessage(O,P);
inactive(T);
inactive(O);

step();

complete(T);
complete(O);
.PE
```

7.6.3 CHARTS

When dealing with numbers, two useful systems for generating charts are *gnuplot*[15] [68] and the *R Project* [69]. *Gnuplot* is a command-line driven graphing utility, whereas R is a vastly larger and more general system for performing statistical analysis, which also happens to have a very powerful plotting library.

Gnuplot can plot data and functions in a wide variety of 2D and 3D styles, using lines, points, boxes, contours, vector fields, surfaces, and error bars. We specify what our chart will look like with commands like `plot with points` and `set xlabel`. To plot varying data (e.g., to track the number of new and corrected bugs in a project), we typically create a canned sequence of commands that will read the data from an external file our code generates.

As an example of using *gnuplot* to draw a chart from software-generated data, consider the task of plotting a program's stack depth [37, p. 270]. The stack depth at the point of each function's entry point can be obtained by compiling the program's code with profiling enabled (by passing the -pg flag to GCC), and using the following custom profiling code to write the stack depth at the point of each call into the file pointed by the file descriptor fd.

---

[15]http://www.gnuplot.info/.

```
_MCOUNT_DECL(frompc, selfpc) /* _mcount; may be static, inline, etc */
   u_long frompc, selfpc;
{
   struct gmonparam *p;
   void *stack = &frompc;

   p = &_gmonparam;
   if (p->state != GMON_PROF_ON)
      return;
   p->state = GMON_PROF_BUSY;
   frompc -= p->lowpc;
   if (frompc > p->textsize)
      goto done;
   write(fd, &stack, sizeof(stack));
done:
   p->state = GMON_PROF_ON;
   return;
overflow:
   p->state = GMON_PROF_ERROR;
   return;
}

MCOUNT
```

Then, a small script, such as the following one written in Perl, can read the file and create the corresponding *gnuplot* file, which will then create a chart similar to the one seen in Figure 7.7. The information gathered from such a figure can be used to judge the size and variation of the program's stack size and therefore allow the tuning of stack allocation in memory-restricted embedded systems.

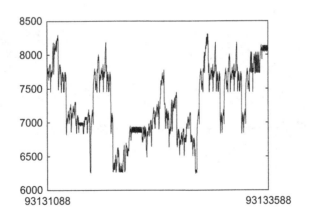

FIGURE 7.7

Stack depth measurements plotted using *gnuplot*.

```
print OUT qq{
set ytics 500
set format x "%.0f"
set terminal postscript eps enhanced "Helvetica" 30
set output 'stack.eps'
plot [] [] "-" using 1:2 notitle with lines
};
for (my $i = 0; $i < $nwords; $i++) {
  read(IN, $b, 4);
  my ($x) = unpack('L', $b);
  $x = $stack_top - $x;
  print OUT "$i $x\n";
}
print OUT "e\n";
```

More sophisticated diagrams can be plotted with R and the *ggplot2* library [70].

7.6.4 MAPS

The last domain we will covere involves geographical data. Consider data like the location of a project's contributors, or the places where a particular software is used. To place the corresponding numbers on the map, one option is the Generic Mapping Tools (GMT) [21].[16] We use these by plumbing together 33 tools that manipulate data and plot coastlines, grids, histograms, lines, and text using a wide range of map substrates and projections. Although these tools are not as easy to use as the others we have covered, they create high-quality output and offer extreme flexibility in a demanding domain.

As an example, consider the map depicting the contributions of FreeBSD developers around the world (Figure 7.8), showing that development is mainly concentrated in Europe, North America, and Japan.

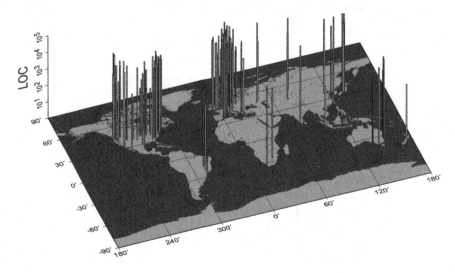

FIGURE 7.8

Contributions by FreeBSD developers around the world.

[16]http://gmt.soest.hawaii.edu/.

The map was generated using the following script, which ends with two GMT commands. Since this is the last script of this work, it brings together many of the techniques we have examined, integrating process and product data with their visualization.

```
# 1. List developer locations
# Remove comments, etc. from the FreeBSD contributor location file
sed '/^#/d;/^$/d;s/,/"/;s/,/"/;s/^#//;s/[   ]*//g' \
  /usr/ports/astro/xearth/files/freebsd.committers.markers |

# Print latitude, longitude, developer-id
awk 'BEGIN{FS="\x22"} {print $1, $2, $4}' |

# Split developers living in the same city
perl -na -e 'for $d (split(",", $F[2])) { print "$d $F[0] $F[1]\n"}'|

# Remove empty lines
sed '/^ /d' |

# Sort (for joining)
sort >dev-loc

# 2. Calculate lines per developer
# Find files in the FreeBSD checked-out repository
find . -type f |

# Remove version control files
grep --invert-match CVS |

# Create a log
xargs cvs -d /home/ncvs log -SN 2>/dev/null |

# Total lines each developer has contributed
awk '
  /^date/{lines[$5 " " hour] += $9}
  END {
    for (i in lines)
      print i, lines[i]}
  ' |
# Remove ;
sed 's/;//g' |

# Sort (for joining)
sort >dev-lines


# 3. Plot the map
# Join developer lines with their locations
join dev-lines dev-loc |

# Round location positions to integer degrees
sed 's/\.[0-9]*//g' |

# Total lines for each location
awk '
```

```
  {lines[$4 " " $2] += $2}
  END {
    for (i in lines)
      print i, lines[i]
  }' |

# Draw the map
{
  # Draw the coastlines
  pscoast -R-180/180/-90/90 -JX8i/5id -Dc -G0 -E200/40 \
    -K W0.25p/255/255/255 -G0/255/0 -S0/0/255 -Di -P
  # Plot the data
  psxyz -P -R-180/180/-90/90/1/100000 -JX -JZ2.5i1 \
    -So0.02ib1 -G140 -W0.5p -O -E200/40 -B60g60/30g30/a1p:LOC:WSneZ
} >map.eps
```

Another alternative involves generating KML, the Google Earth XML-based file format, which we can then readily display through Google Earth and Maps. The limited display options we get are offset by the ease of creating KML files and the resulting display's interactivity.

If none of the tools we have seen fits our purpose, we can dive into lower-level graphics languages such as PostScript and SVG (Scalable Vector Graphics). This approach has been used to annotate program code [33] and to illustrate memory fragmentation [37, p. 251]. Finally, we can always use *ImageMagick*[17] to automate an image's low-level manipulation.

The tools described in this section offer a bewildering variety of output formats. Nevertheless, the choice is easy. If we are striving for professional-looking output, we must create vector-based formats such as PostScript, PDF, and SVG; we should choose the format our software best supports. The resulting diagrams will use nice-looking fonts and appear crisp, no matter how much we magnify them. On the other hand, bitmap formats, such as PNG, can be easier to display in a presentation, memo, or web page. Often the best way to get a professional-looking bitmap image is to first generate it in vector form and then rasterize it through Ghostscript or a PDF viewer. Finally, if we want to polish a diagram for a one-off job, a clever route is to generate SVG and manipulate it using the *Inkscape*[18] vector-graphics editor.

7.7 CONCLUDING REMARKS

The software product and process analysis methods we have examined in this work offer a number of advantages.

> **Flexibility and Extensibility** The scripts we have seen can be easily modified and adapted to suit a variety of needs. New tools can be easily added to our collection. These can be existing tools, or tools developed to suit our own unique needs.

---

[17]http://www.imagemagick.org/.
[18]http://www.inkscape.org/.

Scalability The underlying tools have few if any inherent limits. Arbitrary amounts of data can flow through pipelines, allowing the processing of gigantic amounts of data. In our group we have used these approaches to process many hundreds of gigabytes of data.

Efficiency The workhorses of many pipelines, *git*, *sort*, and *grep*, have been engineered to be as efficient as possible. Other tools, such as *join*, *uniq*, and *comm*, are designed to run in linear time. When the tools run together in pipelines, the load is automatically divided among multiple processor cores.

Some may counter that the lack of a graphical user interface for using these analysis methods results in a steep learning curve, which hinders their use. This, however, can be mitigated in two ways. First, the use of each command can be easily learned by referring to its online manual page available through the *man* command, or by invoking the command with the `--help` argument. In addition, the creation of analysis scripts can be simplified by configuring, learning, and utilizing the shell's command-line editing and completion mechanisms.

Once the tools and techniques we examined are mastered, it is hard to find an alternative where one can be similarly productive.

REFERENCES

[1] Hemmati H, Nadi S, Baysal O, Kononenko O, Wang W, Holmes R, et al. The MSR cookbook: Mining a decade of research. In: Proceedings of the 10th working conference on Mining Software Repositories, MSR '13. Piscataway, NJ, USA: IEEE Press; 2013. p. 343–52.

[2] Johnson P, Kou H, Paulding M, Zhang Q, Kagawa A, Yamashita T. Improving software development management through software project telemetry. IEEE Softw 2005;22(4):76–85.

[3] Cubranic D, Murphy G, Singer J, Booth K. Hipikat: a project memory for software development. IEEE Trans Softw Eng 2005;31(6):446–65.

[4] Bevan J, Whitehead Jr EJ, Kim S, Godfrey M. Facilitating software evolution research with Kenyon. In: Proceedings of the 10th European software engineering conference held jointly with 13th ACM SIGSOFT international symposium on foundations of software engineering, ESEC/FSE-13. New York, NY, USA: ACM; 2005. p. 177–86.

[5] Gall H, Fluri B, Pinzger M. Change analysis with Evolizer and ChangeDistiller. IEEE Softw 2009;26(1): 26–33.

[6] Linstead E, Bajracharya S, Ngo T, Rigor P, Lopes C, Baldi P. Sourcerer: mining and searching internet-scale software repositories. Data Min Knowl Discov 2009;18:300–36. doi:10.1007/s10618-008-0118-x.

[7] Ossher J, Bajracharya S, Linstead E, Baldi P, Lopes C. SourcererDB: an aggregated repository of statically analyzed and cross- linked open source Java projects. In: Proceedings of the international workshop on mining software repositories. Vancouver, Canada: IEEE Computer Society; 2009. p. 183–6.

[8] Sarma A, Maccherone L, Wagstrom P, Herbsleb J. Tesseract interactive visual exploration of socio-technical relationships in software development. In: Proceedings of the 31st international conference on software engineering, ICSE '09. Washington, DC, USA: IEEE Computer Society; 2009. p. 23–33.

[9] Nierstrasz O, Ducasse S, Gîrba T. The story of moose: an agile reengineering environment. In: Proceedings of the 10th European software engineering conference held jointly with 13th ACM SIGSOFT international symposium on foundations of software engineering, ESEC/FSE-13. New York, NY, USA: ACM; 2005. p. 1–10.

[10] D'Ambros M, Lanza M. Distributed and collaborative software evolution analysis with Churrasco. Sci Comput Program 2010;75(4):276–87.

[11] Gousios G, Spinellis D. A platform for software engineering research. In: Godfrey MW, Whitehead J, editors, Proceedings of the 6th working conference on Mining Software Repositories, MSR '09. Piscataway, NJ, USA: IEEE Press; 2009. p. 31–40. http://www.dmst.aueb.gr/dds/pubs/conf/2009-MSR-Alitheia/html/GS09b.html.

[12] Gousios G, Spinellis D. Conducting quantitative software engineering studies with Alitheia Core. Empir Softw Eng 2014;19(4):885–925.

[13] Spinellis D. The Unix tools are your friends. In: Henney K, editor, 97 things every programmer should know. Sebastopol, CA: O'Reilly; 2010. p. 176–7. http://programmer.97things.oreilly.com/wiki/index.php/The_Unix_Tools_Are_Your_Friends.

[14] Spinellis D. Working with Unix tools. IEEE Softw 2005;22(6):9–11.

[15] Howison J, Conklin M, Crowston K. Flossmole: a collaborative repository for floss research data and analyses. Int J Inform Technol Web Eng 2006;1(3):17–26.

[16] Herraiz I, Izquierdo-Cortazar D, Rivas-Hernandez F, González-Barahona J, Robles G, Dueñas Dominguez S, et al. Flossmetrics: free/libre/open source software metrics. In: CSMR '09: 13th European conference on software maintenance and reengineering; 2009. p. 281–4.

[17] Gousios G. The GHTorrent dataset and tool suite. In: Proceedings of the 10th working conference on mining software repositories, MSR '13. Piscataway, NJ, USA: IEEE Press; 2013. p. 233–6.

[18] Mulazzani F, Rossi B, Russo B, Steff M. Building knowledge in open source software research in six years of conferences. In: Hissam S, Russo B, de Mendonça Neto M, Kon F, editors, Proceedings of the 7th international conference on open source systems. Salvador, Brazil: IFIP, Springer; 2011. p. 123–41.

[19] Friedl JE. Mastering regular expressions: powerful techniques for Perl and other tools. 3rd ed. Sebastopol, CA: O'Reilly Media; 2006.

[20] Gansner ER, North SC. An open graph visualization system and its applications to software engineering. Softw Pract Exp 2000;30(11):1203–33.

[21] Wessel P, Smith WHF. Free software helps map and display data. EOS Trans Am Geophys Union 1991;72:441, 445–6.

[22] R Core Team. R: a language and environment for statistical computing; 2012.

[23] Kechagia M, Spinellis D. Undocumented and unchecked: exceptions that spell trouble. In: Proceedings of the 11th working conference on mining software repositories, MSR '14. New York, NY, USA: ACM; 2014. p. 312–5.

[24] Spinellis D. Outwit: Unix tool-based programming meets the Windows world. In: Small C, editor, USENIX 2000 technical conference proceedings. Berkeley, CA: USENIX Association; 2000. p. 149–58.

[25] Lesk ME. Lex—a lexical analyzer generator. Computer science technical report 39. Murray Hill, NJ: Bell Laboratories; 1975.

[26] Aho AV, Lam MS, Sethi R, Ullman JD. Compilers: principles, techniques, and tools. Boston: Pearson/Addison Wesley; 2007.

[27] Lattner C, Adve V. LLVM: a compilation framework for lifelong program analysis and transformation. In: International symposium on code generation and optimization, CGO 2004. Piscataway, NJ, USA: IEEE Press; 2004. p. 75–86.

[28] Spinellis D. CScout: a refactoring browser for C. Sci Comput Program 2010;75(4):216–31.

[29] Kamiya T, Kusumoto S, Inoue K. CCfinder: a multilinguistic token-based code clone detection system for large scale source code. IEEE Trans Softw Eng 2002;28(7):654–70.

[30] Spinellis D. On the declarative specification of models. IEEE Softw 2003;20(2):94–6.

[31] Spinellis D. A tale of four kernels. In: Schäfer W, Dwyer MB, Gruhn V, editors, Proceedings of the 30th international conference on software engineering, ICSE '08. New York: Association for Computing Machinery; 2008. p. 381–90.

[32] Mitropoulos D, Karakoidas V, Louridas P, Gousios G, Spinellis D. The bug catalog of the maven ecosystem. In: Proceedings of the 2014 international working conference on mining software repositories, MSR '14, New York, NY, USA: ACM; 2014. p. 372–5.

[33] Spinellis D. Code reading: the open source perspective. Boston, MA: Addison-Wesley; 2003.

[34] Liu K, Tan HBK, Chen X. Binary code analysis. Computer 2013;46(8):60–8.

[35] Hovemeyer D, Pugh W. Finding bugs is easy. ACM SIGPLAN Not 2004;39(12):92–106. OOPSLA 2004 Onward! Track.

[36] Spinellis D, Louridas P. A framework for the static verification of API calls. J Syst Softw 2007;80(7): 1156–68.

[37] Spinellis D. Code quality: the open source perspective. MA, Boston: Addison-Wesley; 2006.

[38] Chidamber SR, Kemerer CF. A metrics suite for object oriented design. IEEE Trans Softw Eng 1994;20(6):476–93.

[39] Spinellis D. Tool writing: a forgotten art? IEEE Softw 2005;22(4):9–11.

[40] Rosenberg LH, Stapko R, Gallo A. Applying object-oriented metrics. In: Sixth international symposium on software metrics—measurement for object-oriented software projects workshop; 1999, Presentation available online. http://www.software.org/metrics99/rosenberg.ppt.

[41] Lippert M, Roock S. Refactoring in large software projects. Chichester, England/Hoboken, NJ: John Wiley & Sons; 2006.

[42] Spinellis D. Version control systems. IEEE Softw 2005;22(5):108–9.

[43] Spinellis D. Git. IEEE Softw 2012;29(3):100–1.

[44] Loeliger J, McCullough M. Version control with Git: powerful tools and techniques for collaborative software development. Sebastopol CA: O'Reilly Media, Inc.; 2012. ISBN 978-1449316389.

[45] Pilato CM, Collins-Sussman B, Fitzpatrick BW. Version control with Subversion. Sebastopol, CA: O'Reilly Media, Inc.; 2009. ISBN 978-0-596-51033-6.

[46] Grune D. Concurrent versions system, a method for independent cooperation. 1986. Report IR-114 Vrije University, Amsterdam, NL.

[47] Gala-Pérez S, Robles G, González-Barahona JM, Herraiz I. Intensive metrics for the study of the evolution of open source projects: case studies from apache software foundation projects In: Proceedings of the 10th working conference on mining software repositories, MSR '13. Piscataway, NJ, USA: IEEE Press; 2013. p. 159–68.

[48] Thomas SW, Adams B, Hassan AE, Blostein D. Modeling the evolution of topics in source code histories. In: Proceedings of the 8th working conference on mining software repositories, MSR '11. New York, NY, USA: ACM; 2011. p. 173–82, doi:10.1145/1985441.1985467.

[49] Capiluppi A, Serebrenik A, Youssef A. Developing an h-index for OSS developers. In: Proceedings of the 9th IEEE working conference on mining software repositories (MSR); 2012. p. 251–4.

[50] Steff M, Russo B. Co-evolution of logical couplings and commits for defect estimation. In: Proceedings of the 9th IEEE working conference on mining software repositories (MSR); 2012. p. 213–6.

[51] Eyolfson J, Tan L, Lam P. Do time of day and developer experience affect commit bugginess? In: Proceedings of the 8th working conference on mining software repositories, MSR '11. New York, NY, USA: ACM; 2011. p. 153–62, doi:10.1145/1985441.1985464.

[52] Bird C, Nagappan N. Who? where? what? Examining distributed development in two large open source projects. In: Proceedings of the 9th IEEE working conference on mining software repositories (MSR); 2012. p. 237–46.

[53] Giaglis GM, Spinellis D. Division of effort, productivity, quality, and relationships in FLOSS virtual teams: evidence from the FreeBSD project. J Universal Comput Sci 2012;18(19):2625–45.

[54] Kagdi H, Collard ML, Maletic JI. A survey and taxonomy of approaches for mining software repositories in the context of software evolution. J Softw Maint Evol Res Pract 2007;19(2):77–131.

[55] Mockus A. Amassing and indexing a large sample of version control systems: towards the census of public source code history. In: Proceedings of the 2009 6th IEEE international working conference on mining software repositories, MSR '09. Washington, DC, USA: IEEE Computer Society; 2009. p. 11–20.

[56] O'Sullivan B. Making sense of revision-control systems. Commun ACM 2009;52(9):56–62.

[57] Gyerik J. Bazaar version control. Birmingham, UK: Packt Publishing Ltd; 2013. ISBN 978-1849513562.

[58] O'Sullivan B. Mercurial: the definitive guide. Sebastopol, CA: O'Reilly Media, Inc.; 2009. ISBN 978-0596800673.

[59] Gousios G, Spinellis D. GHTorrent: Github's data from a firehose. In: Lanza M, Penta MD, Xie T, editors, Proceedings of the 9th IEEE working conference on mining software repositories (MSR). Piscataway, NJ, USA: IEEE Press; 2012. p. 12–21.

[60] Spinellis D. A repository with 44 years of Unix evolution. In Proceedings of the 12th Working Conference on Mining Software Repositories, MSR '15, IEEE; 2015. p. 13–16.

[61] Tichy WF. Design, implementation, and evaluation of a revision control system. In: Proceedings of the 6th international conference on software engineering, ICSE '82. Piscataway, NJ, USA: IEEE Press; 1982. p. 58–67.

[62] Rochkind MJ. The source code control system. IEEE Trans Softw Eng 1975;SE-1:255–65.

[63] Tantau T. Graph drawing in TikZ. In: Proceedings of the 20th international conference on graph drawing, GD'12. Berlin/Heidelberg: Springer-Verlag; 2013. p. 517–28.

[64] Knuth DE. TeX: the program. Reading, MA: Addison-Wesley; 1986.

[65] Bentley JL. Little languages. Commun ACM 1986;29(8):711–21.

[66] Kernighan B, Lesk M, Ossanna JJ. UNIX time-sharing system: document preparation. Bell Syst Tech J 1978;56(6):2115–35.

[67] Kernighan BW. The UNIX system document preparation tools: a retrospective. AT&T Tech J 1989;68(4): 5–20.

[68] Janert PK. Gnuplot in action: understanding data with graphs. Shelter Island, NY: Manning Publications; 2009.

[69] R: a language and environment for statistical computing. R foundation for statistical computing. 2nd ed. 2010.

[70] Wickham H. ggplot2: elegant graphics for data analysis. Berlin: Springer-Verlag; 2009.

DATA/PROBLEM FOCUSSED

ANALYZING SECURITY DATA

Andrew Meneely*

*Department of Software Engineering, Rochester Institute of Technology, Rochester, NY, USA**

CHAPTER OUTLINE

8.1 VULNERABILITY

Software engineers today are faced with a tough set of expectations. They are asked to develop their software on time, on budget, and with no bugs. The "no bugs" category, often called software quality, is a grab-bag of various types of mistakes that a developer can make. Bug reports might have statements like "the app crashes when I hit this button," or "the installation script fails on this operating system." Preventing, finding, and fixing bugs are an enormous portion of the software development lifecycle that manifests itself in activities like software testing, inspections, and design.

But bugs also have a darker, more sinister cousin: the *vulnerability*. Rather than the system failing to do what it's supposed to do, the system is abused in a cleverly malicious way. Instead of registering an email address in a web application, an attacker may inject operating system commands that leads to root access on the server. Or a common segmentation fault becomes a denial of service attack when it can be reproduced over and over again.

Informally, a vulnerability is a software fault that has security consequences. Our formal definition of a vulnerability is as follows (adapted from [1]), which is based on a standard definition of fault found in Definition 1.

Definition 1. A vulnerability is an instance of a fault that violates an implicit or explicit security policy.

Faults are the actual mistake a developer made in source code that results in a failure. The "security policy" of a system is an implicit or explicit understanding of how the system adheres to three properties: **confidentiality**, **integrity**, and **availability**. For example, if a healthcare system exposed patient records to the public, then the intended confidentiality of the system was violated. In some cases, a software development team may define a specific security policy as a part of their requirements document. In most cases, however, software development teams have a simple "I'll know it when I see it" policy regarding security.

Though vulnerabilities are considered to be a subset of faults, they are a different breed of faults altogether. A typical bug might be considered as some behavior where the system falls short, whereas a vulnerability is one where the system exhibits behavior beyond the specification. For example, if a user is allowed to type executable Javascript in a web application, then they can compromise other users who view that data, which also known as a cross-site scripting (XSS) vulnerability. Or, as another example, if an attacker is able to hijack another user's session, then they have provided themselves with another means of authentication that goes beyond the system's specification.

To visualize the difference between vulnerabilities and typical bugs conceptually, consider Figure 8.1. The perfectly-rounded circle is the system "as it is should be." The squiggly circle is what

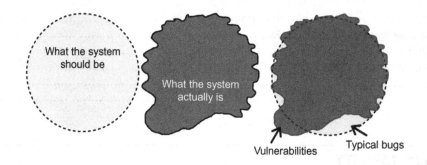

FIGURE 8.1

Conceptual difference between typical bugs and vulnerabilities.

the system actually is. In any practical setting the system will not match up perfectly to expectations, leading to two areas of mistakes: places where the system falls short of its expected functionality (typical bugs) and places where the system does *more* than what was specified. Vulnerabilities are in the areas where too much, or unintended, functionality is allowed.

We note that "as it should be" is not necessarily the system's specifications. What the system ought to be is often a combination of explicit statements and implicit assumptions. In fact, vulnerabilities often exist where the specifications themselves can be insecure.

Thus, with security, just getting a system working is not enough. The system must also not do what it is not supposed to. This conceptual difference between vulnerabilities and typical bugs not only alters the way developers approach software quality, it also introduces some "gotchas" regarding data analysis.

8.1.1 EXPLOITS

Vulnerabilities only become dangerous when they are actually taken advantage of with malicious intent. Exploits are the manifestation of that malicious intent. A single vulnerability can have many, potentially infinite exploits for it. In this chapter, our definition of an exploit is:

Definition 2. An exploit is a piece of software, a chunk of data, or a sequence of commands that takes advantage of a vulnerability in an effort to cause unintended or unanticipated behavior.

Exploits can come in many different forms. They can be a simple string that an attacker manually enters into a web application, or they can be sophisticated malware. One assumption that can be made about exploits is that a lack of exploits implies a lower risk. Just because no one has taken the time to write an exploit does not mean that a damaging one will not be written.

Exploit avoidance is a much different practice for software engineers than vulnerability prevention. Examples of exploit avoidance include intrusion detection systems and anti-virus systems that provide a layer of defense that can detect specific exploits. These systems, while important for users, cannot be relied upon fully.

8.2 SECURITY DATA "GOTCHAS"

Security data, especially vulnerability data, have many concepts that translate nicely from the software quality realm. Vulnerabilities can be tracked in the same way as bugs, e.g., using modern issue tracking systems. Vulnerabilities manifest themselves as design flaws or coding mistakes in the system, much like bugs. However, the malicious nature of their use and the conceptual difference of preventing unintended functionality means that any analysis of vulnerabilities are subject to a variety of caveats.

8.2.1 GOTCHA #1. HAVING VULNERABILITIES IS NORMAL

A common outsider's assumption is that admitting a large software product has vulnerabilities is a liability. After all, damage to a company brand is at stake, so why make a big deal about a few wrong lines of code.

However, companies have matured beyond this approach to practicing *responsible disclosure*, i.e., disclosing the details about a vulnerability after it is has been fixed. Responsible disclosure has led to a variety of benefits, such as the current cultural shift to the assumption that having vulnerabilities is normal. In fact, the practice of responsible disclosure has been a significant driver in modern vulnerability research as developers can learn from each other's mistakes.

8.2.1.1 Analytical consequences of Gotcha #1
- Having no vulnerabilities reported does not mean no vulnerabilities exist.
- Having no vulnerabilities reported could mean the team is not focusing on finding, fixing, and preventing vulnerabilities

8.2.2 GOTCHA #2. "MORE VULNERABILITIES" DOES NOT ALWAYS MEAN "LESS SECURE"

In the age of responsible disclosure, we have found that vulnerabilities are actually quite common. In 2013 alone the Chromium (the basis of Google Chrome) project and the Linux kernel self-reported over 150 vulnerabilities each. More broadly, the US National Vulnerability Database (NVD) has increased in size dramatically over the past several years. If one were to strictly adhere to the assumptions of metrics such as "defect density," one might assume that this influx of vulnerabilities means that software is becoming less secure, except that projects are simply keeping better records.

However, vulnerabilities are a unique defect due to several factors:

- Record-keeping practices have improved with the evolution of distributed version control systems, code review systems, and collaboration tools that maintain artifact traceability.
- Software projects are improving their responsible disclosure practices, leading to an increase in interest from the security enthusiast community.
- Due to the severe nature of vulnerabilities, prominent companies such as Google and Microsoft offer bounties in the thousands of US dollars for information leading to a vulnerability. Google currently pays out those bounties on a nearly monthly basis.
- Discovery of a single vulnerability often leads to the discovery of other, similar vulnerabilities since developers are learning security principles as they fix vulnerabilities.
- The availability and quality of comprehensive vulnerability taxonomies, such as the Common Weakness Enumeration have improved.
- Improved security awareness among developers has led to developers retroactively labeling traditional defects as vulnerabilities.

8.2.2.1 Analytical consequences of Gotcha #2
The main consequence is that, at face value, you cannot assume that an increase in vulnerability discovery implies decaying security. This consequence applies at both the micro and macro levels. Software development projects both mature and decay at the same time, so an increase or decrease in vulnerabilities overall is more often the result of external circumstances than intrinsic quality.

For individual source code files, the "vulnerability density" may not be as robust as its "defects density" counterpart. Since developers often discover vulnerabilities in batches based on their knowledge of prior vulnerabilities, the chances that a vulnerability is discovered is skewed toward particular vulnerability types.

To mitigate this density problem, many academic studies regarding vulnerabilities opt for a *binary labeling* of "vulnerable" and "neutral" files, as opposed to trying to predict the total number of vulnerabilities for a file. A vulnerable file is defined as a file that has been fixed by at least one vulnerability, and a neutral file is defined as a file that has had no known vulnerabilities fixed. This labeling alters the analysis to be more typically binary classification than regression techniques.

8.2.3 GOTCHA #3. DESIGN-LEVEL FLAWS ARE NOT USUALLY TRACKED

Vulnerabilities come in all sizes. A small, code-level mistake such as a format string vulnerability can be easily remedied at the line level, for example. Lacking the ability to provide audit logs to mitigate repudiation threats, however, is a much bigger problem. Historically, most vulnerabilities reported in databases such as the NVD tend to be code-level vulnerabilities. Design flaws, security-related or not, are rarely tracked in any consistent way.

8.2.3.1 Analytical consequences of Gotcha #3

While design vulnerabilities are common they are often not tracked. Thus, most of the academic research surrounding vulnerability data focuses primarily on coding mistakes. With a lack of empirical results on security-related design flaws, research that provides security at the design level may not have any empirical support to validate against. Empirical studies into secure design are far behind studies in coding-level mistakes.

8.2.4 GOTCHA #4. SECURITY IS NEGATIVELY DEFINED

The security of a software system is typically defined over three properties: Confidentiality, Integrity, and Availability. Confidentiality is the ability of a system to keep sensitive information from leaking out. Integrity is the ability of the system to prevent unauthorized tampering of data or functionality. Availability is the ability of the system to be continually accessible to the user.

Each of those properties, however, are defined according to what people should *not* be able to do. An attacker should *not* be able to steal passwords. An attacker should *not* be able execute arbitrary code.

From a requirements engineering point of view, security is considered to be a constraint on the entire system that does not trace to any one feature. Instead, security applies to all features. However, security is not alone in being negatively-defined. Other negatively-defined non-functional requirements include safety and resilience as they are properties the system must demonstrate in extreme circumstances.

Furthermore, security is an *emergent property* of software. An emergent property is one that builds upon many properties of the system, and can be brought down by a single flaw. Consider pitching a tent in the rain. The "staying dry" property is not a single feature of the tent, it's a combination of many different factors: the tent must be leak-free, deployed properly, the flap closed, and not be placed in a lake. Security must be achieved through a wide variety of means and can be compromised by one problem.

For all negatively-defined properties, developers cannot simply execute a checklist to maintain those properties. Improving security does not mean "do A, B, and C"; instead, it means "nowhere should A, B, C or anything like them be allowed."

8.2.4.1 Analytical consequences of Gotcha #4

Thus, many security practices today involve creating a potentially infinite list of past mistakes to avoid repeating. Avoiding past mistakes may improve the security of a system, but the overall security of a system cannot be fully defined in a single metric due to the above properties. Any methodology or metric provided for the assessment of security must account for more specific aspects of security. For example, metrics such as "the system was able to filter 96% of all exploit strings" must have the caveat that the list may be incomplete, and we don't know how many more exploits strings may pass if we keep writing. Thus, any assessment method of security must account for the fact that security is an emergent, negatively-defined, non-functional requirement of software.

8.3 MEASURING VULNERABILITY SEVERITY

Like their defect counterparts, not all vulnerabilities are the same. A vulnerability that exposes already-public information should be considered a lower severity than one that allows arbitrary code execution on a server, for example. To quantify differences, several vulnerability scoring systems have emerged in recent years. In 2005, a group of security experts collaborated on the Common Vulnerability Scoring System (CVSS), which today has been adopted by NIST and the National Vulnerability Database.

8.3.1 CVSS OVERVIEW

The CVSSv2 breaks down its metrics in to into three groups: Base Metrics, Temporal Metrics, and Environmental Metrics. Base Metrics are intended to represent the unchanging characteristics of a vulnerability regardless of time or environment. Temporal Metrics are intended to represent characteristics that may evolve over time. Environmental Metrics are intended to provide context for a vulnerability in its given environment. All of the answers to the metrics are given an ordinal label. The vector of answers for a vulnerability may look something like this: "(AV:N/AC:M/Au:N/C:P/I:P/A:P)"

The CVSSv2 Base Metrics include Access Vector, Access Complexity, Authentication, and three Impact Metrics. Access Vector denotes that the vulnerability is potentially exploitable over a network (choices: Local, Adjacent Network, Network). Access Complexity (choices: high, medium, low) denotes the expected level of expertise required to construct an exploit for this vulnerability. Authentication denotes how many layers of authentication were required to exploit the vulnerability. Finally, the three Impact Metrics are Confidentiality Impact, Integrity Impact, and Availability Impact, each with choices of "none," "partial," or "complete."

The CVSSv2 Temporal Metrics include measures of Exploitability, Remediation Level, and Report Confidence. Exploitability denotes whether or not an exploit is currently the wild. Remediation Level denotes what the vendor has done to fix, mitigate, or work around the vulnerability. Report Confidence denotes when information is currently still being gathered and investigation is developing. In all three cases, the intended understanding is to provide information as it is available so that the message can get out to users, system administrators, and other stakeholders as it becomes available.

The CVSSv2 Environmental Metrics are based on Collateral Damage Potential, Target Distribution, and the three Requirement Metrics of Confidentiality, Integrity, and Availability. Collateral Damage is about what other systems may be affected by the vulnerability. Target Distribution denotes whether a vulnerability only affects one release, or many releases of a given product. The Requirement Metrics are for Confidentiality, Integrity, and Availability and provide a way to denote the vulnerability's severity in the context of a larger product. Each of the three Requirements Metrics have choices of "low," "medium," or "high."

The CVSSv2 also provides a weighting scheme to combine all of the Base Metrics into a single number from 0 to 10, and to provide Temporal and Environment subscores.

8.3.2 EXAMPLE CVSS APPLICATION

To demonstrate the application of the CVSS, consider the following vulnerability entry number CVE-2011-3607:

> Integer overflow in the ap_pregsub function in server/util.c in the Apache HTTP Server 2.0.x through 2.0.64 and 2.2.x through 2.2.21, when the mod_setenvif module is enabled, allows local users to gain privileges via a .htaccess file with a crafted SetEnvIf directive, in conjunction with a crafted HTTP request header, leading to a heap-based buffer overflow.

The reported CVSSv2 base vector for this vulnerability was: (AV:L/AC:M/Au:N /C:P/I:P/A:P). The access vector was considered local since the integer overflow in this situation was through a utility function and not directly over the network. An attacker would have to have access to the server locally via an untrusted configuration file to exploit this. The access complexity was considered Medium, which according to the CVSSv2 guidelines indicates that the conditions would need to be somewhat specialized, such as a non-default configuration with mod_setenvif module enabled. Since local access would need to be through an .htacess file, authentication to HTTP Server would not be needed to access this vulnerability. The Confidentiality Impact was partial, since memory corruption vulnerabilities such as integer overflow can leak some information on how memory is laid out. The Integrity Impact is also Partial since remote code execution is technically feasible with heap-based buffer overflows, although since Apache HTTP Server employs distrustful decomposition the permissions of the exploited code would be limited. Finally, the Availability is also Partial since any memory corruption vulnerability can result in a segmentation fault on the server process, killing the process.

This example demonstrates the many different dimensions a vulnerability can be measured on. If we used the weighting scheme of the CVSSv2, then the measurement would be computed as 6.8 out of 10.

8.3.3 CRITICISMS OF THE CVSS

Given its widespread adoption into databases such as the NVD, researchers [2–5] have raised some concerns. Common criticisms of the CVSS include:

- High CVSS scores have not historically aligned with the availability of exploits [5].
- Subjectivity of the levels. However, the CVSSv2 specification does provide many historical examples on which to base one's decision [4].
- Reporters of vulnerabilities are not always those most familiar with the vulnerabilities.

Another concern we raise here of the CVSS scoring system is the practice of using numerical weights. The weighted average of the CVSSv2 does not appear to cite rigorous research, thus making the weighting number arbitrary. Furthermore, vulnerability severity is a multi-dimensional concept, so distilling that complexity into a single number does not yield useful results. Thus, our recommendation for the CVSS is to use the vector labeling to compare two vulnerabilities in a pair-wise fashion. This makes analysis of CVSS data more complex, but closer to the original meaning of vulnerability severity.

8.4 METHOD OF COLLECTING AND ANALYZING VULNERABILITY DATA

Vulnerability data can provide us with a rich history of some of the nastiest, most insidious bugs we've missed. A post-release vulnerability to a large open source product represents a list of potential mistakes the team made along the way. Mining this vulnerability data can provide some valuable insights into how the bugs were missed, found, and then fixed.

In this section, we will be demonstrating how to aggregate and process vulnerability data for useful empirical analysis. We will be using the Apache HTTP server as an example.

8.4.1 STEP 1. TRACE REPORTED VULNERABILITIES BACK TO FIXES

To analyze vulnerabilities in aggregate, we need to know the precise version control changes that fixed the vulnerability. With this fix, we will be able to see where vulnerabilities tend to reside, what source code issues were involved, and can then gather various metrics that tend to correlate with vulnerabilities.

While many software projects follow responsible disclosure practices and report their vulnerabilities, the data is not always consistent. In the case of vulnerability data, the situation is often urgent, handled outside of the usual defect tracking process, and kept a secret for a time until the fix is adequately disseminated. Thus, vulnerability data often requires extra manual treatment. Fortunately, vulnerabilities are also not so numerous that we can actually handle them individually.

In the case of the Apache HTTP Server, they provide a listing of vulnerabilities they have fixed. In each case, they have an entry in the NVD with a CVE identifier. In some cases, the HTTPD community has provided us with a link to the original fix in the source code. In other cases, we will need to do our own digging. Thus, tracing vulnerabilities back to their original fix in the version control system is often a manual process.

For a given vulnerability, many different pieces of information can be gathered as a part of this investigation:

- The NVD database stores confirmations from the vendors of the vulnerability. Often, these links do not tie directly into the fix commit, but can provide valuable information for the investigation.
- The version control logs, such as Git and Subversion, offer many ways of searching their archives. For example, searching the commit messages will sometimes reveal the CVE number or similar language. Limit the search in the Git and Subversion logs to the dates near where the CVE entry was created.
- Projects often maintain their own STATUS file or CHANGELOG file that records each major change. Use tools like Git Blame to examine what commit introduced a given change in the changelog, which sometimes leads to the fix commit.

- If the vulnerability description mentions a particular module or source code file, examine the history of that file around the dates the vulnerability was reported.
- Examine the logs from open source distributors such as Red Hat or Ubuntu. These companies have to maintain their own copies of commonly used open source systems and often keep their own patches to backport to their own versions. Their package management system will often have these patches as a part of source builds.
- If credit was given to an external person for finding this vulnerability, consider searching for that person's online presence in a blog or other article to gather more technical details.

Ultimately, the outcome of this step is to provide the fix commit(s) for each vulnerability. With each fix commit, you will need to check if that commit was an upstream commit, or a backport. Understanding what versions are affected may impact your analysis later.

For example, the above vulnerability CVE-2011-3607 in the CVSS section mentioned the specific file that was affected by this vulnerability. Furthermore, the history of that file around when the vulnerability was fixed by the team shows a CHANGELOG entry that was modified in response to this vulnerability. Thus, the fix was easily found in the version control system.

8.4.2 STEP 2. AGGREGATE SOURCE CONTROL LOGS

Once we have all of our vulnerabilities tied to fixes in the version control system, we can begin to reconstruct the timeline of the software project using version control. Systems such as Git and Subversion provide rich history that allow us to understand who committed what changes and when. By aggregating the version control logs into a relational database, we can query the data for our metrics in later steps.

Using commands such as "git log –pretty" or "svn log –xml" allows us output information from the version control systems into text files. The output formats for version control systems are configurable, so we can make our outputs easily parsed by scripts. Using a scripting language like Ruby or Python, we can develop scripts that step through the version control logs and insert data into the database.

A typical schema for version control logs might involve three tables: Commits, CommitFilepaths, and Filepaths. The commits table will have the commit date, commit message, and author. From our prior step we also add a field called "VulnFix" to indicate that the commit was fixing a vulnerability. The Filepaths will be the table that stores the files and their paths and the CommitFilepaths table links the two tables together. For example, if one commit changed "util.c" and "log.c" and another commit changed just "util.c," we would have two row in the Commits table, three rows in the CommitFilepaths table, and two rows in the Filepaths table.

If we are only looking at a limited period of time, at this point we must also take into account the fact that sometimes source code has no commits for a long time. A file might be untouched for months or years at a time. If so, be sure to have Filepath data that has no commits.

With that data and schema in place, we can now examine the history of a given file and determine if that file was later patched for a vulnerability. For example, a file patched for a vulnerability on January 20, 2011 would have had that vulnerability for some period prior to it and the team missed it. Thus, we can collect our metrics prior to January 20, 2011 and see if they correlate with the vulnerable files.

Regarding when a vulnerability was *introduced* rather than fixed, see the work by Meneely et al. [9] in Section 8.5.2.

8.4.3 STEP 3A. DETERMINE VULNERABILITY COVERAGE

Once we know what files were affected by vulnerabilities, we can now see what parts of the system were affected by them. Here are some relevant questions, keeping in mind our Gotchas from earlier in this chapter.

- What percentage of files were affected by at least one vulnerability? This number typically lies between 1% and 5% [6].
- What percentage of the subsystems was affected by vulnerabilities?
- What percentage of our developers have ever worked on a file with at least one vulnerability?
- Were there any files that had "bursts" of vulnerabilities fixed? What happened there?
- Were there any files that had been steadily, consistently fixed over time for a vulnerability? Why?

We note here that we are collecting coverage data, not necessarily vulnerability count data to keep in step with Gotcha #1 and Gotcha #2. Also, in the case of Apache HTTP Server, we cannot say that these are necessarily design flaws as those tend not to be tracked by project, as in Gotcha #3. We also recognize that files without vulnerabilities are not necessarily "invulnerable," so we typically refer to them as "neutral" according to Gotcha #4.

Examining vulnerability coverage can provide an enormous benefit to understanding the security posture of a system. Entire sub-communities of developers can be very active in fixing vulnerabilities and end up learning from their mistakes, often leading to "bursts." Or, some subsystems have a constant security concern (such as HTTPD's "protocol.c" that parses untrusted network packet traffic), leading to more of a "steady trickle" effect.

Coverage data can also provide empirical insight into the system's **assets**. An asset is an element of a running software system that has security consequences. A password table, for example, is an asset. The underlying file system for a web server is another asset. As more and more vulnerabilities are discovered, fixed, and aggregated, we can begin to see where the assets of the system tend to reside, and what elements of the architecture need restructuring.

8.4.4 STEP 3C. CLASSIFY ACCORDING TO ENGINEERING MISTAKE

Another consideration for using vulnerability fix data from Step 1 can be in classifying them by software engineering mistake. Developers are capable of making a wide variety of mistakes, and understanding the types of mistakes that you and your team tend to make can provide benefit. If you are collecting vulnerability data for your project, consider the following questions:

- Was this vulnerability the result of missing functionality or wrong functionality?
  - Ignore refactoring in the fix
  - Missing functionality involves adding a new method, new feature, or security-related check
  - Wrong functionality means the low-level design was there, but implemented incorrectly
- How large was the source code fix for this vulnerability?
  - Consider examining the Churn of the fix (number of lines added plus number of lines deleted in the patch)
  - Large changes are difficult to inspect

- Was this vulnerability the result of poor input validation?
  - If fixing the vulnerability involved reducing the input space in any way, then the answer is "yes"
  - Input validation should be the first, but not only line of defense against vulnerabilities
- Was this vulnerability the result of lack of sanitization?
  - If fixing the vulnerability involved altering the input to be safer (e.g., escaping characters), then the answer is "yes"
  - Sanitization is another layer of defense in addition to input validation
- Was this vulnerability domain-specific?
  - A domain-specific vulnerability is one that would not make any sense outside of the context of the current project. For example, a secretary having access to employee salaries in the HR system is a vulnerability entirely driven by the domain, not the technology. Examples of domain-independent vulnerabilities include buffer overflows, SQL injection, and cross-site scripting.
  - Domain expertise may be needed beyond hiring penetration testers
- Was this vulnerability the result of incorrect configuration?
  - If the fix involved altering a configuration file, such as upgrading a dependency or changing a parameter, then the answer is "yes"
  - Configuration files should be inspected alongside source code files
- Was this vulnerability the result of incorrect exception handling?
  - If the context of the fix was exception handling and the system did not react to an alternate subflow properly, then the answer is "yes"
  - Exception handling is difficult to reproduce for testing, but often involves integrity and availability concerns
- Were any of these vulnerabilities entries in the CWE?
  - Common Weakness Enumeration is a taxonomy of security-related mistakes
  - Common vulnerabilities may mean some education of developers is needed

The above questions are based on our experience analyzing vulnerability fixes in large open source systems and can provide a basis for discussion. Finding large occurrences of vulnerabilities in some of the above questions can help find some of the weak spots in your process.

8.5 WHAT SECURITY DATA HAS TOLD US THUS FAR

Analysis of security data has led to a variety of fascinating conclusions. The general methods outlined in this chapter have led to some interesting recent studies. We cover two lines of research here [6–9], but several other interesting empirical security studies have been conducted. For example:

- Neuhaus et al. [10] predicted vulnerable components in Mozilla based on import statements; Nguyen and Tran [11] did a similar study based on dependency graphs
- Manadhata and Wing [12], Manadhata et al. [13] and Howard et al. [14] provided measurements of the "attack surface" of a software system, which examines the "shape" of a system based on the avenues of attack (i.e., inputs and outputs)

- Scarfone and Mell [4] and Fruhwirth and Mannisto [2] provided an analysis on the robustness of the CVSS v2, examining flaws in the scoring process
- Bozorgi et al. [5] provided a security exploit classifier to predict whether a given vulnerability will be exploited
- DaCosta et al. [15] analyzed the security vulnerability likelihood of OpenSSH based on its call graph
- Cavusoglu et al. [16] analyzed the efficiency of vulnerability disclosure mechanisms
- Beres et al. [17] used prediction techniques and simulation to assess security processes

8.5.1 VULNERABILITIES HAVE SOCIO-TECHNICAL ELEMENTS

With each new developer to a software development team comes a greater challenge to manage the communication, coordination, and knowledge transfer amongst teammates. Lack of team cohesion, miscommunications, and misguided effort can lead to all kinds of problems, including security vulnerabilities. In this research, the authors focus on examining the statistical relationships between development team structure and security vulnerabilities. The statistical relationships demonstrated in this research provide us with (a) predictive models for finding security vulnerabilities in software prior to its release; and (b) insight into how effective software development teams are organized.

In several studies [6–8], Meneely et al. applied social network analysis techniques to open source software products and discovered a consistent statistical association between metrics measuring developer activity and post-release security vulnerabilities. In three case studies of Linux, PHP, and Wireshark, the authors analyzed four metrics related to Linus' Law and unfocused contributions. An empirical analysis of the data demonstrates the following observations:

(a) source code files changed by multiple, otherwise-separated **clusters** of developers are more likely to be vulnerable than changed by a single cluster;
(b) files are likely to be vulnerable when changed by many developers who have made many changes to other files (i.e., **unfocused contributions**); and
(c) a Bayesian network predictive model can be used on one project by training it on other projects, possibly indicating the existence of a **general predictive model**.

For the clustering analysis (a), we used the metric Edge Betweenness when computed over a developer network. A developer network is a graph where developers are nodes that are connected to each other when they make commits to the same source code file in the same release cycle. Developers have been known to cluster [18, 19] in open source projects to form sub-communities within a larger project. Edge Betweenness is one metric from social network analysis that can be used to identify connections between larger clusters. Edge Betweenness is based on the proportion of shortest paths that include a given edge (e.g., highways have a higher betweenness than residential streets because they connect traffic from neighborhood "clusters"). In that analysis, "highway" files with high betweenness were more likely to have vulnerabilities.

For the unfocused contributions result (b), we used the node betweenness metric on a contribution network. We formed a bipartite graph where developers and files are nodes, and developers are connected to files when a developer committed to a file. Files with a high betweenness in a contribution network, then, are ones where developers were working on many other files at the time. When a file was worked on by many developers, the contribution it had was "unfocused" (note: the developers themselves were not necessarily unfocused, but the aggregate contribution was unfocused because the developers were working on many other files). Files with unfocused contributions also had a higher likelihood of having a vulnerability.

Overall, while the results are statistically significant, the individual correlations indicate that developer activity metrics do not account for all vulnerable files. From a prediction standpoint, models are likely to perform best in the presence of metrics that capture other aspects of software products and processes. However, practitioners can use these observations about developer activity to prioritize security fortification efforts or to consider organizational changes among developers.

8.5.2 VULNERABILITIES HAVE LONG, COMPLEX HISTORIES

Even in open source projects, vulnerable source code can remain unnoticed for years. In a recent study, we traced 68 vulnerabilities in the Apache HTTP server back to the version control commits that contributed the vulnerable code originally [9]. Meneely et al. manually found 124 Vulnerability-Contributing Commits (VCCs), spanning 17 years. In this exploratory study, they analyzed these VCCs quantitatively and qualitatively with the over-arching question: "What could developers have looked for to identify security concerns in this commit?"

The methodology, which was adapted from related work [20, 21], can be summarized as follows:

1. Identify the fix commit(s) of the vulnerability;
2. From the fix, write an ad hoc detection script to identify the coding mistake for the given vulnerability automatically;
3. Use "git bisect" to binary search the commit history for the VCC; and
4. Inspect the potential VCC, revising the detection script and rerunning bisect as needed.

Specifically, the authors examined the size of the commit via code Churn Metrics, the amount developers overwrite each others' code via interactive Churn Metrics, exposure time between VCC and fix, and dissemination of the VCC to the development community via release notes and voting mechanisms. Results from the exploratory study of Apache HTTPD [9] show that:

- **VCCs are big commits**: VCCs average 608.5 lines of churn (vs. 42.2 non-VCCs), or 55% VCC relative churn (vs. 23.1% for non-VCCs).
- **VCCs are exposed for a long time.** The median for Days from VCC to Fix was 853 days; Median for Commits between VCC and Fix was 48 commits, indicating significant missed opportunities to find the vulnerability. Figure 8.2 shows this timeline.
- **Few VCCs are the original baseline import.** 13.5% of VCCs were original source code imports.
- **Few VCCs were "known offender" files.** 26.6% of VCCs were to files that had already been fixed for a prior vulnerability, covering only 20% of the total vulnerabilities.

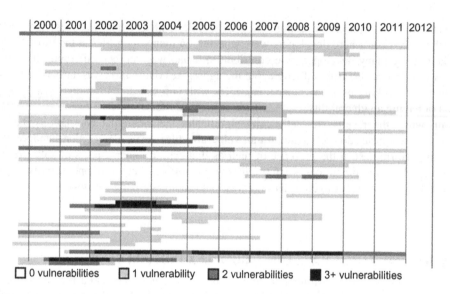

FIGURE 8.2

Timeline for source code files in HTTPD with vulnerabilities.

8.6 SUMMARY

Just as security is a difficult challenge for developers to face in their development, so it also poses a challenge to development data analysts. Security is not a concept that is easily quantified holistically, rather, security is an overarching concern with many facets to be measured. Security data is very useful, but has limitations such as a lack of design flaw tracking, or security being negatively defined. History has shown us that actionable metrics can be extracted from project histories that are correlated with vulnerabilities, but with vulnerabilities being small, rare, and severe, they are difficult to predict. In the age of responsible disclosure we have an enormous outpouring of vulnerability histories to learn from, yet we must also responsibly analyze those histories, knowing our limitations, to better understand how security can be engineered to remain secure.

REFERENCES

[1] Krsual IV. Software vulnerability analysis. PhD Dissertation; 1998.

[2] Fruhwirth C, Mannisto T. Improving CVSS-based vulnerability prioritization and response with context information. In: Proceedings of the 3rd international symposium on empirical software engineering and measurement, Washington, DC, USA; 2009. p. 535–44.

[3] Houmb SH, Franqueira VNL, Engum EA. Quantifying security risk level from CVSS estimates of frequency and impact. J Syst Softw 2010;83(9):1622–34.

[4] Scarfone K, Mell P. An analysis of CVSS version 2 vulnerability scoring. In: Proceedings of the 3rd international symposium on empirical software engineering and measurement, Washington, DC, USA; 2009. p. 516–25.

[5] Bozorgi M, Saul LK, Savage S, Voelker GM. Beyond heuristics: learning to classify vulnerabilities and predict exploits. In: Proceedings of the 16th ACM SIGKDD international conference on knowledge discovery and data mining, New York, NY, USA; 2010. p. 105–14.

[6] Shin Y, Meneely A, Williams L, Osborne JA. Evaluating complexity, code churn, and developer activity metrics as indicators of software vulnerabilities. IEEE Trans Softw Eng 2011;37(6):772–87.

[7] Meneely A, Williams L. Strengthening the empirical analysis of the relationship between Linus' Law and software security. In: Empirical software engineering and measurement, Bolzano-Bozen, Italy; 2010. p. 1–10.

[8] Meneely A, Williams L. Secure open source collaboration: an empirical study of Linus' Law. In: International conference on computer and communications security (CCS), Chicago, Illinois, USA; 2009. p. 453–62.

[9] Meneely A, Srinivasan H, Musa A, Tejeda AR, Mokary M, Spates B. When a patch goes bad: exploring the properties of vulnerability-contributing commits. In: Proceedings of the 2013 ACM-IEEE international symposium on empirical software engineering and measurement; 2013. p. 65–74.

[10] Neuhaus S, Zimmermann T, Holler C, Zeller A. Predicting vulnerable software components. In: Computer and communications security, New York, NY, USA; 2007. p. 529–40.

[11] Nguyen VH, Tran LMS. Predicting vulnerable software components with dependency graphs. In: Proceedings of the 6th international workshop on security measurements and metrics; 2010. p. 3:1–3:8.

[12] Manadhata PK, Wing JM. An attack surface metric. IEEE Trans Softw Eng 2011; 37(3):371–86.

[13] Manadhata P, Wing J, Flynn M, McQueen M. Measuring the attack surfaces of two FTP daemons. In: Proceedings of the 2nd ACM workshop on quality of protection, New York, NY, USA; 2006. p. 3–10.

[14] Howard M, Pincus J, Wing JM. Measuring relative attack surfaces. In: Lee DT, Shieh SP, Tygar JD, editors. Computer security in the 21st century, New York: Springer US; 2005.

[15] DaCosta D, Dahn C, Mancoridis S, Prevelakis V. Characterizing the 'security vulnerability likelihood' of software functions. In: Proceedings of the international conference on software maintenance, ICSM 2003; 2003. p. 266–74.

[16] Cavusoglu H, Cavusoglu H, Raghunathan S. Efficiency of vulnerability disclosure mechanisms to disseminate vulnerability knowledge. IEEE Trans Softw Eng 2007; 33(3):171–85.

[17] Beres Y, Mont MC, Griffin J, Shiu S. Using security metrics coupled with predictive modeling and simulation to assess security processes. In: Proceedings of the 3rd international symposium on empirical software engineering and measurement; 2009. p. 564–73.

[18] Bird C, Pattison D, D'Souza R, Filkov V, Devanbu P. Latent social structure in open source projects. In: Proceedings of the 16th ACM SIGSOFT international symposium on foundations of software engineering (FSE), Atlanta, Georgia; 2008. p. 24–35.

[19] Bird C, Gourley A, Devanbu P, Gertz M, Swaminathan A. Mining email social networks in postgres. In: International workshop on mining software repositories, Shanghai, China; 2006. p. 185–6.

[20] Kim S, Zimmermann T, Pan K, Whitehead EJ. Automatic identification of bug-introducing changes. In: 21st IEEE/ACM international conference on automated software engineering, ASE '06; 2006. p. 81–90.

[21] Williams C, Spacco J. Szz revisited: verifying when changes induce fixes. In: Proceedings of the 2008 workshop on defects in large software systems, New York, NY, USA; 2008. p. 32–6.

A MIXED METHODS APPROACH TO MINING CODE REVIEW DATA: EXAMPLES AND A STUDY OF MULTICOMMIT REVIEWS AND PULL REQUESTS

Peter C. Rigby[*], **Alberto Bacchelli**[†], **Georgios Gousios**[‡], **Murtuza Mukadam**[*]

Department of Computer Science and Software Engineering, Concordia University, Montreal, QC, Canada[*]
Department of Software and Computer Technology, Delft University of Technology, Delft, The Netherlands[†]
Institute for Computing and Information Sciences, Radboud University Nijmegen, Nijmegen, The Netherlands[‡]

CHAPTER OUTLINE

9.1 INTRODUCTION

Fagan's study [1] of software inspections (i.e., formal code review) in 1976 was one of the first attempts to provide an empirical basis for a software engineering process. He showed that inspection, in which an independent evaluator examines software artifacts for problems, effectively found defects early in the development cycle and reduced costs. He concluded that the increased upfront investment in inspection led to fewer costly customer-reported defects.

The techniques for conducting reviews have evolved along with the software industry, and have progressively moved from Fagan's rigid and formal inspection process to an incremental and more lightweight modern code review process. We have studied modern code review in a number of settings: Apache, Linux, KDE [2–5], Microsoft [6, 7], Android [8], and GitHub [9]. Since code review is an inherently complex social activity, we have used both quantitative and qualitative methods to understand the underlying parameters (or measures) of the process [7] as well as the rich interactions and motivations for doing code review [6]. The goal of this chapter is to introduce the reader to code review data and to demonstrate how a mixed quantitative and qualitative approach can be used to triangulate empirical software engineering findings.

This chapter is structured as follows. In Section 9.2, we compare qualitative and quantitative methods and describe how and when they can be combined. In Section 9.3, we describe the available code review data sources and provide a metamodel of the fields one can extract. In Section 9.4, we conduct an illustrative quantitative investigation to study how multiple related commits (e.g., commits on a branch) are reviewed. This study replicates many of the measures that have been used in the past, such as number of reviewers and the time to perform a review. In Section 9.5, we describe how to collect and sample nonnumerical data—for example, with interviews and from review e-mails—and extract themes from the data. Data is analyzed using a research method based on *grounded theory* [10]. In Section 9.6, we triangulate our findings on multicommit reviews by quantitatively examining review discussions on multiple commits. We also suggest how one might continue this study by using card sorting or interviews. Section 9.7 concludes the chapter by summarizing our findings and the techniques we use.

9.2 MOTIVATION FOR A MIXED METHODS APPROACH

While it is useful to develop new processes, practices, and tools, researchers suggest that these should not be "invented" by a single theorizing individual, but should be derived from empirical findings that can lead to empirically supported theories and testable hypotheses. Grounded, empirical findings are necessary to advance software development as an engineering discipline. With empirical work, one tries not to tell developers how they should be working, but instead tries to understand, for example, how the most effective developers work, describing the essential attributes of their work practices. This knowledge can inform practitioners and researchers and influence the design of tools.

There are two complementary methods for conducting empirical work [11]: quantitative and qualitative. *Quantitative* analysis involves measuring the case. For example, we can measure how many people make a comment during a review meeting. Since there is little or no interpretation involved in extracting these measurements, quantitative findings are objective. One of the common risks when extracting measures is construct validity. Do the measures assess a real phenomenon or is there a systematic bias that reduces the meaningfulness of the measurements?

In contrast, *qualitative* findings allow the researcher to extract complex rich patterns of interactions. For example, knowing the number of people at a review meeting does not give information about *how* they interacted. Using a qualitative approach, one must code data to find the qualitative themes, such as how reviewers ask questions. While qualitative approaches such as grounded theory ensure that each theme is tied back to a particular piece of data, potential for researcher bias is present.

Triangulation involves combining one or more research methods and data sources. The goal is to limit the weaknesses and biases present in each research method and dataset by using complementary methods and datasets. For example, one can measure attributes of archival review discussion and then interview developers involved in the reviews to check the validity of these measurements.

Replication involves conducting the same study using the same method for new cases. Yin [12] identified two types of case study replications: literal and contrasting. The purpose of a literal replication is to ensure that similar projects produce similar results. For example, do two similar projects, such as Apache and Subversion, yield similar findings? Contrasting replications should produce contrasting results, but for reasons *predicted* by one's understanding of the differences between projects. For example, one might compare how reviewers select contributions for review on the Linux project with Microsoft Office. We would expect to see differences between these two projects based on their drastically different organizational structures.

In subsequent sections, we will use quantitative methods to measure aspects of six case study replications, and we triangulate our findings by using qualitative coding of archival review discussion to understand how developers group commits for review.

9.3 REVIEW PROCESS AND DATA

To give the reader a sense of the different types of code review, we summarize how review is done traditionally, on open-source software (OSS) projects, at Microsoft, on Google-led OSS projects, and on GitHub. Subsequently, we provide a table of the different attributes of code review that we can measure in each environment.

9.3.1 SOFTWARE INSPECTION

Software inspections are the most formal type of review. They are conducted after a software artifact meets predefined exit criteria (e.g., a particular requirement is implemented). The process, originally defined by Fagan [1], involves some variations of the following steps: planning, overview, preparation, inspection, reworking, and follow-up. In the first three steps, the author creates an inspection package (i.e., determines what is to be inspected), roles are assigned (e.g., moderator), meetings are scheduled, and the inspectors examine the inspection package. The inspection is conducted, and defects are recorded, but not fixed. In the final steps, the author fixes the defects, and the mediator ensures that the fixes are appropriate. Although there are many variations on formal inspections, "their similarities outweigh their differences" [13].

9.3.2 OSS CODE REVIEW

Asynchronous, electronic code review is a natural way for OSS developers, who meet in person only occasionally and to discuss higher-level concerns [14], to ensure that the community agrees on what constitutes a good code contribution. Most large, successful OSS projects see code review as one of their most important quality assurance practices [5, 15, 16]. In OSS projects, a review begins with a developer creating a patch. A patch is a development artifact, usually code, that the developer feels will add value to the project. Although the level of formality of the review processes differs among OSS projects, the general steps are consistent across most projects: (1) the author submits a contribution by e-mailing it to the developer mailing list or posting it to the bug/review tracking system, (2) one or more people review the contribution, (3) the contribution is modified until it reaches the standards of the community, and (4) the revised contribution is committed to the code base. Many contributions are ignored or rejected and never make it into the code base [17].

9.3.3 CODE REVIEW AT MICROSOFT

Microsoft developed an internal tool, CodeFlow, to aid in the review process. In CodeFlow a review occurs when a developer has completed a change, but prior to checking it into the version control system. A developer will create a review by indicating which changed files should be included, providing a description of the change (similar to a commit message), and specifying who should be included in the review. Those included receive e-mail notifications and then open the review tool, which displays the changes to the files and allows the reviewers to annotate the changes with their own comments and questions. The author can respond to the comments within the review, and can also submit a new set of changes that addresses issues that the reviewers have brought up. Once a reviewer is satisfied with the changes, he or she can "sign off" on the review in CodeFlow. For more details on the code review process at Microsoft, we refer the reader to an empirical study [6] in which we investigated the purposes of code review (e.g., finding defects and sharing knowledge) along with the actual outcomes (e.g., creating awareness and gaining code understanding) at Microsoft.

9.3.4 GOOGLE-BASED GERRIT CODE REVIEW

When the Android project was released as OSS, the Google engineers working on Android wanted to continue using the internal Mondrian code review tool and process used at Google [18]. Gerrit is an OSS, Git-specific implementation of the code review tool used internally at Google, created by Google Engineers [19]. Gerrit centralizes Git, acting as a barrier between a developer's private repository and the shared centralized repository. Developers make local changes in their private Git repositories, and then submit these changes for review. Reviewers make comments via the Gerrit Web interface. For a change to be merged into the centralized source tree, it must be approved and verified by another developer. The review process has the following stages:

1. *Verified.* Before a review begins, someone must verify that the change merges with the current master branch and does not break the build. In many cases, this step is done automatically.
2. *Approved.* While anyone can comment on the change, someone with appropriate privileges and expertise must approve the change.
3. *Submitted/merged.* Once the change has been approved, it is merged into Google's master branch so that other developers can get the latest version of the system.

9.3.5 GitHub PULL REQUESTS

Pull requests is the mechanism that GitHub offers for doing code reviews on incoming source code changes.[1] A GitHub pull request contains a branch (local or in another repository) from which a core team member should pull commits. GitHub automatically discovers the commits to be merged, and presents them in the pull request. By default, pull requests are submitted to the base ("upstream" in Git parlance) repository for review. There are two types of review comments:

1. *Discussion.* Comments on the overall contents of the pull request. Interested parties engage in technical discussion regarding the suitability of the pull request as a whole.
2. *Code review.* Comments on specific sections of the code. The reviewer makes notes on the commit diff, usually of a technical nature, to pinpoint potential improvements.

Any GitHub user can participate in both types of review. As a result of the review, pull requests can be updated with new commits, or the pull request can be rejected—as redundant, uninteresting, or duplicate. The exact reason a pull request is rejected is not recorded, but it can be inferred from the pull request discussion. If an update is required as a result of a code review, the contributor creates new commits in the forked repository and, after the changes have been pushed to the branch to be merged, GitHub will automatically update the commit list in the pull request. The code review can then be repeated on the refreshed commits.

When the inspection process ends and the pull request is deemed satisfactory, it can be merged by a core team member. The versatility of Git enables pull requests to be merged in various ways, with various levels of preservation of the original source code metadata (e.g., authorship information and commit dates).

Code reviews in pull requests are in many cases implicit and therefore not observable. For example, many pull requests receive no code comments and no discussion, while they are still merged. Unless it is project policy to accept any pull request without reviewing it, it is usually safe to assume that a developer reviewed the pull request before merging it.

9.3.6 DATA MEASURES AND ATTRIBUTES

A code review is effective if the proposed changes are eventually accepted or bugs are prevented, and it is efficient if the time this takes is as short as possible. To study patch acceptance and rejection and

---

[1]GitHub pull requests: https://help.github.com/articles/using-pull-requests. Accessed July 2014.

Table 9.1 Metamodel for Code Review Analysis

Feature	Description
Code review features	
num_commits	Number of commits in the proposed change
src_churn	Number of lines changed (added and deleted) by the proposed change
test_churn	Number of test lines changed in the proposed change
files_changed	Number of files touched by the proposed change
num_comments	Discussion and code review comments
num_participants	Number of participants in the code review discussion
Project features	
sloc	Executable lines of code when the proposed change was created
team_size	Number of active core team members during the last 3 months prior to the proposed change creation
perc_ext_contribs	The ratio of commits from external members over core team members in the last n months
commits_files_touched	Number of total commits on files touched by the proposed change n months before the proposed change creation time
test_lines_per_kloc	A proxy for the project's test coverage
Developer	
prev_changes	Number of changes submitted by a specific developer, prior to the examined proposed change
requester_succ_rate	Percentage of the developer's changes that have been integrated up to the creation of the examined proposed change
reputation	Quantification of the developer's reputation in the project's community (e.g., followers on GitHub)

the speed of the code review process, a framework for extracting meta-information about code reviews is required. Code reviewing processes are common in both OSS [5, 9] and commercial software [6, 7] development environments. Researchers have identified and studied code review in contexts such as patch submission and acceptance [17, 20–22] and bug triaging [23, 24]. Our metamodel of code review features is presented in Table 9.1. To develop this metamodel we included the features used in existing work on code review. This metamodel is not exhaustive, but it forms a basis that other researchers can extend. Our metamodel features can be split in three broad categories:

1. *Proposed change features.* These characteristics attempt to quantify the impact of the proposed change on the affected code base. When external code contributions are examined, the size of the patch affects both acceptance and the acceptance time [21]. Various metrics have been used by researchers to determine the size of a patch: code churn [20, 25], changed files [20], and number of commits. In the particular case of GitHub pull requests, developers reported that the presence of tests in a pull request increases their confidence to merge it Pham et al. [26]. The number of participants has been shown to influence the amount of time taken to conduct a code review [7].

2. *Project features.* These features quantify the receptiveness of a project to an incoming code change. If the project's process is open to external contributions, then we expect to see an

increased ratio of external contributors over team members. The project's size may be a detrimental factor to the speed of processing a proposed change, as its impact may be more difficult to assess. Also, incoming changes tend to cluster over time (the "yesterday's weather" change pattern [27]), so it is natural to assume that proposed changes affecting a part of the system that is under active development will be more likely to merge. Testing plays a role in the speed of processing; according to [26], projects struggling with a constant flux of contributors use testing, manual or preferably automated, as a safety net to handle contributions from unknown developers.

3. *Developer.* Developer-based features attempt to quantify the influence that the person who created the proposed change has on the decision to merge it and the time to process it. In particular, the developer who created the patch has been shown to influence the patch acceptance decision [28] (recent work on different systems interestingly reported opposite results [29]). To abstract the results across projects with different developers, researchers devised features that quantify the developer's track record [30]—namely, the number of previous proposed changes and their acceptance rate; the former has been identified as a strong indicator of proposed change quality [26]. Finally, Bird et al. [31], presented evidence that social reputation has an impact on whether a patch will be merged; consequently, features that quantify the developer's social reputation (e.g., follower's in GitHub's case) can be used to track this.

9.4 QUANTITATIVE REPLICATION STUDY: CODE REVIEW ON BRANCHES

Many studies have quantified the attributes of code review that we discussed in Table 9.1 (e.g., [2, 22, 32]). All review studies to date have ignored the number of commits (i.e., changes or patches) that are under discussion during review. Multicommit reviews usually involve a feature that is broken into multiple changes (i.e., a branch) or a review that requires additional corrective changes submitted to the original patch (i.e., revisions). In this section, we perform a replication study using some of the attributes described in the previous section to understand how multiple related commits affect the code review process. In Section 9.6, we triangulate our results by qualitatively examining how and why multiple commits are reviewed. We answer the following research questions:

1. How many commits are part of each review?
2. How many files and lines of code are changed per review?
3. How long does it take to perform a review?
4. How many reviewers make comments during a review?

We answer these questions in the context of Android and Chromium OS, which use Gerrit for review; the Linux Kernel, which performs email-based review; and the Rails, Katello, and WildFly projects, which use GitHub pull requests for review. These projects were selected because they are all successful, medium-sized to large, and represent different software domains.

Table 9.2 shows the dataset and the time period we examined in years. We use the data extracted from these projects and perform comparisons that help us draw conclusions.

More details on the review process used by each project are provided in the discussion in Section 9.3. We present our results as boxplots, which show the distribution quartiles, or, when the range is large enough, a distribution density plot [33]. In both plots, the median is represented by a bold line.

Table 9.2 The Time Period we Examined		
Project	**Period**	**Years**
Linux Kernel	2005-2008	3.5
Android	2008-2013	4.0
Chrome	2011-2013	2.1
Rails	2008-2011	3.2
Katello	2008-2011	3.2
WildFly	2008-2011	3.2

9.4.1 RESEARCH QUESTION 1—COMMITS PER REVIEW

How many commits are part of each review?

Table 9.3 shows the size of the dataset and proportion of reviews that involve more than one commit. Chrome has the largest percentage of multicommit reviews, at 63%, and Rails has the smallest, at 29%. Single-commit reviews dominate in most projects. In Figure 9.1 we consider only multicommit reviews, and find that Linux, WildFly, and Katello have a median of three commits. Android, Chrome, and Rails have a median of two commits.

9.4.2 RESEARCH QUESTION 2—SIZE OF COMMITS

How many files and lines of code are changed per review?

Figure 9.2 shows that WildFly makes the largest changes, with single changes having a median of 40 lines churned, while Katello makes the smallest changes (median eight lines). WildFly also makes the largest multicommit changes, with a median of 420 lines churned, and Rails makes the smallest, with a median of 43.

In terms of lines churned, multicommit reviews are 10, 5, 5, 5, 11, and 14 times larger than single-commit reviews for Linux, Android, Chrome, Rails, WildFly, and Katello, respectively. In comparison with Figure 9.1, we see that multicommit reviews have one to two more commits than single-commit reviews. Normalizing for the number of commits, we see that individual commits in multicommit reviews contain more lines churned than those in single-commit reviews. We conjecture that multicommit changes implement new features or involve complex changes.

Table 9.3 Number of Reviews in our Dataset and Number of Commits per Review			
Project	**All**	**Single Commit (%)**	**Multicommit (%)**
Linux Kernel	20,200	70	30
Android	16,400	66	34
Chrome	38,700	37	63
Rails	7300	71	29
Katello	2600	62	38
WildFly	5000	60	40

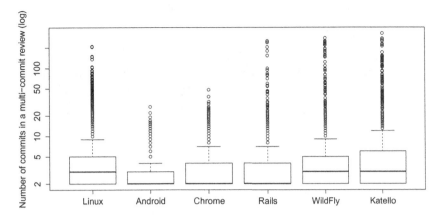

FIGURE 9.1

Number of patches.

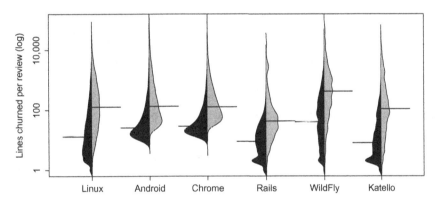

FIGURE 9.2

Number of lines churned: left, single-commit reviews; right, multicommit reviews.

9.4.3 **RESEARCH QUESTION 3—REVIEW INTERVAL**

How long does it take to perform a review?

The review interval is the calendar time since the commit was posted until the end of discussion of the change. The review interval is an important measure of review efficiency [34, 35]. The speed of feedback provided to the author depends on the length of the review interval. Researchers also found that the review interval is related to the overall timeliness of a project [36].

Current practice is to review small changes to the code before they are committed, and to do this review quickly. Reviews on OSS systems, at Microsoft, and on Google-led projects last for

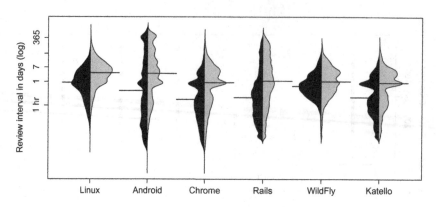

FIGURE 9.3

Review interval: left, single-commit reviews; right, multicommit reviews.

around 24 h [7]. This interval is very short compared with the months or weeks required for formal inspections [1, 35].

Figure 9.3 shows that the GitHub projects perform reviews at least as quickly as the Linux and Android projects. Single-commit reviews happen in a median of 2.3 h (Chrome) and 22 h (Linux). Multicommit reviews are finished in a median of 22 h (Chrome) and 3.3 days (Linux).

Multicommit reviews take 4, 10, 10, 9, 2, and 7 times longer than single-commit reviews for Linux, Android, Chrome, Rails, WildFly, and Katello, respectively.

9.4.4 RESEARCH QUESTION 4—REVIEWER PARTICIPATION

How many reviewers make comments during a review?

According to Sauer et al. [37], two reviewers tend to find an optimal number of defects. Despite different processes for reviewer selection (e.g., self-selection vs assignment to review), the number of reviewers per review is two in the median case across a large diverse set of projects [7]. With the exception of Rails, which has a median of three reviewers in multicommit reviews, reviews are conducted by two reviewers regardless of the number of commits (see Figure 9.4).

The number of comments made during a review varies with the number of commits. For Android, Chrome, and WildFly the number of comments increases from three to four, while for Rails and Katello the number increases from one to three. For Linux there is a much larger increase, from two to six comments.

9.4.5 CONCLUSION

In this section, we contrasted multicommit and single-commit reviews for the number of commits, churn, interval, and participation. We found that multicommit reviews increase the number of commits by one to two in the median case. The churn increases more dramatically, between 5 and 14 times the number of changed lines in the median case. The amount of time to perform a review varies quite substantially from 2.3 hours to 3.3 days in the median case. Multicommit reviews take 2-10

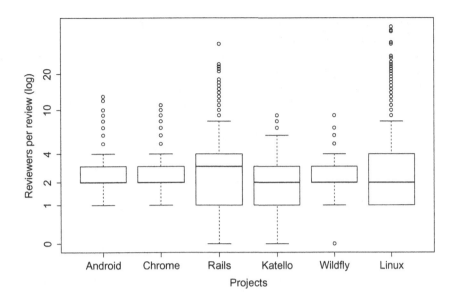

FIGURE 9.4

Number of reviewers in multicommit reviews.

times longer than single-commit reviews. The number of reviewers is largely unaffected by review: we see two reviewers per review, with the exception of Rails. The number of comments per review increases in multicommit reviews. We purposefully did not perform statistical comparisons among projects. Statistical comparisons are not useful because we have the entire population of reviews for each project and not a sample of reviews. Furthermore, given the large number of reviews we have for each project, even small differences that have no practical importance to software engineers would be highlighted by statistical tests.

No clear patterns emerged when we compared the multicommit and single-commit review styles across projects and across review infrastructures (e.g., Gerrit vs GitHub). Our main concern is that multicommit reviews will serve two quite different purposes. The first purpose would be to review branches that contain multiple related commits. The second purpose will be to review a single commit after it has been revised to incorporate reviewer feedback. In Section 9.5, we randomly sample multicommit reviews and perform a qualitative analysis to determine the purpose of each review. These qualitative findings will enhance the measurements made in this section by uncovering the underlying practices used in each project.

9.5 QUALITATIVE APPROACHES

Studies of formal software inspection [1, 34, 38] and code review [2, 7, 15, 22, 32, 39, 40] have largely been quantitative with the goal of showing that a new process or practice is effective, finds defects, and is efficient.

Unlike traditional inspection, which has a prescriptive process, modern code review has gradually emerged from industrial and open-source settings. Since the process is less well defined, it is important to conduct exploratory analyses that acknowledge the context and interactions that occur during code review. These studies are required to gain an in-depth *understanding* of code review, which is a complex phenomenon that encompasses nontrivial social aspects. Such understanding can be gained only by answering many *how* and *why* questions, for which numbers and statistics would give only a partial picture. For this reason, the studies were conducted using *qualitative methods*.

Qualitative methods involve the *"systematic gathering and interpretation of nonnumerical data"* [41]. Software engineering researchers collect the nonnumerical data by studying the people involved in a software project as they work, typically by conducting *field research* [42]. Field research consists of "a group of methods that can be used, individually or in combination, to understand different aspects of real world environments" [43]. Lethbridge et al. [43] surveyed how field research had been performed in software engineering, and accordingly proposed a taxonomy of data collection techniques by grouping them in three main sets: (1) direct, (2) indirect, and (3) independent. Direct data collection techniques (e.g., focus groups, interviews, questionnaires, or think-aloud sessions) require researchers to have direct involvement with the participant population; indirect techniques (e.g., instrumenting systems, or "fly on the wall") require the researcher to have only indirect access to the participants via direct access to their work environment; independent techniques (e.g., analysis of tool use logs or documentation analysis) require researchers to access only work artifacts, such as issue reports or source code.

In this section, we analyze two exploitative studies on code reviews. We dive into the details of the qualitative research methods used in two of those studies, to understand them in more detail and to show how qualitative research could be employed to shine a light on aspects of modern code review practices.

The first study manually examines archives of review data to understand how OSS developers interact and manage to effectively conduct reviews on large mailing lists [3]. The second study investigates the motivations driving developers and managers to do and require code review among product teams at Microsoft [6]. The two studies considered use both direct and independent data collection techniques. The data gathered is then manually analyzed according to different qualitative methods.

9.5.1 SAMPLING APPROACHES

Qualitative research requires such labor-intensive data analysis that not all the available data can be processed, and it is necessary to extract samples. This regards not only indirect data (e.g., documents), but also direct data and its collection (e.g., people to interview), so that the data can be subsequently analyzed.

In quantitative research, where computing power can be put to good use, one of the commonest approaches for sampling is random sampling: picking a high number of cases, randomly, to perform analyses on. Such an approach requires a relatively high number of cases so that they will be *statistically* significant. For example, if we are interested in estimating a proportion (e.g., number of developers who do code reviews) in a population of 1,000,000, we have to randomly sample 16,317 cases to achieve a confidence level of 99% with an error of 1% [44]. Although very computationally expensive, such a number is simple to reach with quantitative analyses.

Given the difficulty of manually coding data points in qualitative research, random sampling can lead to nonoptimal samples. In the following, we explain how sampling was conducted on the two qualitative studies considered, first in doing direct data collection, then in doing independent data collection.

9.5.1.1 Sampling direct data

As previously mentioned, one of the main goals of qualitative research is to see a phenomenon from the perspective of another person, normally involved with it. For this reason, one of the commonest ways to collect qualitative data is to use direct data collection by means of observations and interviews. Through observations and interviews, we can gather accurate and finely nuanced information, thus exposing participants' perspectives.

However, interviews favor depth over quantity. Interviewing and the consequent nonnumerical data analysis are time-consuming tasks, and not all the candidates are willing to participate in investigations and answer interview questions. In the two qualitative studies considered, the authors used different approaches to sample interview participants.

Rigby and Storey [3] selected interviewees among the developers of the Apache and Subversion projects. They ranked developers on the basis of the number of e-mail-based reviews they had performed, and they sent an interview request to each of the *top five* reviewers in each project. The researchers' purpose was to interview the most prolific reviewers, in order to learn from their extensive experience and daily practice, thus understanding the way in which experts dealt with submitted patches on OSS systems. Overall, the respondents that they interviewed were nine core developers, either with committer rights or maintainers of a module.

Bacchelli and Bird [6] selected interviewees among different Microsoft product teams (e.g., Excel and SQL Server). They sampled developers on the basis of the number of reviews they had done since the introduction of CodeFlow (see Section 9.3.3): They contacted 100 randomly selected candidates who signed off between 50 and 250 code reviews. In this case, they did not select the *top* reviewers, but selected a sample of those with an average mid-to-high activity. In fact, their purpose was to understand the motivation of developers who do code reviews. The respondents that they interviewed comprised 17 people: five developers, four senior developers, six testers, one senior tester, and one software architect. Their time in the company ranged from 18 months to almost 10 years, with a median of 5 years.

9.5.1.2 Sampling indirect data

Although, as shown in the rest of this chapter, indirect code review data can be used entirely when employing quantitative methods, this is not the case for qualitative analyses. In fact, if researchers are willing to qualitatively analyze review comments recorded in e-mails or in archives generated by code review tools, they have to sample this data to make it manageable.

In the studies considered, Rigby and Storey [3] analyzed e-mail reviews for six OSS projects, and Bacchelli and Bird [6] analyzed code review comments recorded by CodeFlow during code reviews done in different Microsoft product groups. In both cases, since no human participants were involved, the researchers could analyze hundreds of documents.

9.5.1.3 Data saturation

Although a large part of the qualitative analysis is conducted after the data gathering, qualitative researchers also analyze their data throughout their data collection. For this reason, in qualitative research it is possible rely on *data saturation* to verify whether the size of a sample could be large enough for the chosen research purpose [10]. Data saturation happens in both direct data collection and indirect data collection, and occurs when the researcher is no longer seeing, hearing, or reading new information from the samples.

In both studies the number of data points—for example, reviews and possible interviewees—was much larger than any group of researchers could reasonably analyze. During analysis, when no new patterns were emerging from the data, saturation had been reached, and the researchers stopped introducing new data points and started the next stage of analysis.

9.5.2 DATA COLLECTION

In the following, we describe how the researchers in the two studies collected data by interviewing and observing the study participants selected in the sampling phase. In both studies, the aim of this data collection phase was to gain an understanding of code reviewing practices by adopting the perspective of the study participants (this is often the main target of qualitative research [41]). Moreover, we also briefly explain how they collected indirect data about code reviews.

9.5.2.1 Observations and interviews at Microsoft

In the study conducted at Microsoft, each meeting with participants comprised two parts: an observation, and a following *semistructured* interview [45].

In the e-mails sent to candidate participants in the study, Bacchelli and Bird invited developers to notify them when they received the next review task, so that the researchers could go to the participant's office (this happened within 30 min from the notification) to observe how developers conducted the review. To minimize invasiveness and the Hawthorne effect [46], only one researcher went to the meeting and observed the review. To encourage the participants to narrate their work (thus collecting more nonnumerical data), the researcher asked the participants to consider him as a newcomer to the team. In this way, most developers thought aloud without the need for prompting.

With consent, assuring the participants of anonymity, the audio of the meeting was recorded. Recording is a practice on which not all the qualitative researcher methodologists agree [10]. In this study, researchers preferred to have recorded audio for two reasons: (1) having the data to analyze for the researcher who was not participating in the meetings; and (2) the researcher at the meeting could fully focus on the observation and interaction with participants during the interview. Since the researchers, as observers, have backgrounds in software development and practices at Microsoft, they could understand most of the work and where and how information was obtained without inquiry.

After the observations, the second part of the meeting took place—that is, the semistructured interview. This form of interview makes use of an *interview guide* that contains general groupings of topics and questions rather than a predetermined exact set and order of questions. Semistructured interviews are often used in an exploratory context to *"find out what is happening* [and] *to seek new insights"* [47].

The researchers devised the first version of the guideline by analyzing a previous internal Microsoft study on code review practices, and by referring to academic literature. Then, the guideline was iteratively refined after each interview, in particular when developers started providing answers very similar to the earlier ones, thus reaching saturation.

After the first five or six meetings, the observations reached the saturation point. For this reason, the researchers adjusted the meetings to have shorter observations, which they used only as a starting point for interacting with participants and as a hook to talk about topics in the interview guideline.

At the end of each interview, the audio was analyzed by the researchers, and then transcribed and broken up into smaller coherent units for subsequent analysis.

9.5.2.2 Indirect data collection: Review comments and e-mails
As we have seen in previous sections, code review tools archive a lot of valuable information for data analysis; similarly, mailing lists archive discussions about patches and their acceptance. Although part of the data is numerical, a great deal of information is nonnumerical data—for example, code review comments. This information is a good candidate for qualitative analysis, since it contains traces of opinions, interactions, and general behavior of developers involved in the code review process.

Bacchelli and Bird randomly selected 570 code review comments from CodeFlow data pertaining to more than 10 different product teams at Microsoft. They considered only comments within threads with at least two comments so that they were sure there was interaction between developers. Considering that they were interested in measuring the types of comments, this amount, from a quantitative perspective, would have a confidence level of 95% and an error of 8%.

Rigby and Storey randomly sampled 200 e-mail reviews for Apache, 80 for Subversion, 70 for FreeBSD, 50 for the Linux kernel, and 40 e-mail reviews and 20 Bugzilla reviews for KDE. In each project, the main themes from the previous project reoccurred, indicating that that saturation had been reached and that it was unnecessary to code an equivalent number of reviews for each project.

9.5.3 QUALITATIVE ANALYSIS OF MICROSOFT DATA
To qualitatively analyze the data gathered from observations, interviews, and recorded code review comments, Bacchelli and Bird used two techniques: a *card sort* and an *affinity diagram*.

9.5.3.1 Card sorting
To group codes that emerged from interviews and observations into categories, Bacchelli and Bird conducted a *card sort*. Card sorting is a sorting technique that is widely used in information architecture to create mental models and derive taxonomies from input data [48]. In their case, it helped to organize the codes into hierarchies to deduce a higher level of abstraction and identify common themes. A card sort involves three phases: (1) in the *preparation phase*, participants of the card sort are selected and the cards are created; (2) in the *execution phase*, cards are sorted into meaningful groups with a descriptive title; and (3) in the *analysis phase*, abstract hierarchies are formed to deduce general categories.

Bacchelli and Bird applied an *open card sort*: there were no predefined groups. Instead, the groups emerged and evolved during the sorting process. In contrast, a closed card sort has predefined groups and is typically applied when themes are known in advance, which was not the case for our study.

Bacchelli created all of the cards, from the 1047 coherent units generated from the interview data. Throughout the further analysis, other researchers (Bird and external people) were involved in developing categories and assigning cards to categories, so as to strengthen the validity of the result. Bacchelli played a special role of ensuring that the context of each question was appropriately considered in the categorization, and creating the initial categories. To ensure the integrity of the categories, Bacchelli sorted the cards several times. To reduce bias from Bacchelli sorting the cards to form initial themes, all researchers reviewed and agreed on the final set of categories.

The same method was applied to group code review comments into categories: Bacchelli and Bird printed one card for each comment (along with the entire discussion thread to give the context), and conducted a card sort, as performed for the interviews, to identify common themes.

9.5.3.2 Affinity diagramming

Bacchelli and Bird used an *affinity diagram* to organize the categories that emerged from the card sort. This technique allows large numbers of ideas to be sorted into groups for review and analysis [49]. It was used to generate an overview of the topics that emerged from the card sort, in order to connect the related concepts and derive the main themes. To generate the affinity diagram, Bacchelli and Bird followed five canonical steps: they (1) recorded the categories on Post-it notes, (2) spread them onto a wall, (3) sorted the categories on the basis of discussions, until all had been sorted and all participants had agreed, (4) named each group, and (5) captured and discussed the themes.

9.5.4 APPLYING GROUNDED THEORY TO ARCHIVAL DATA TO UNDERSTAND OSS REVIEW

The preceding example demonstrated how to analyze data collected from interviews and observation using a card sort and an affinity diagram. Qualitative analysis can also be applied to the analysis of archival data, such as records of code review (see Figure 9.5). To provide a second perspective on qualitative analysis, we describe the method used by Rigby and Storey [3] to code review discussion of six OSS projects. In the next section, we describe one of the themes that emerged from this analysis: patchsets. Patchsets are groups of related patches that implement a larger feature or fix and are reviewed together.

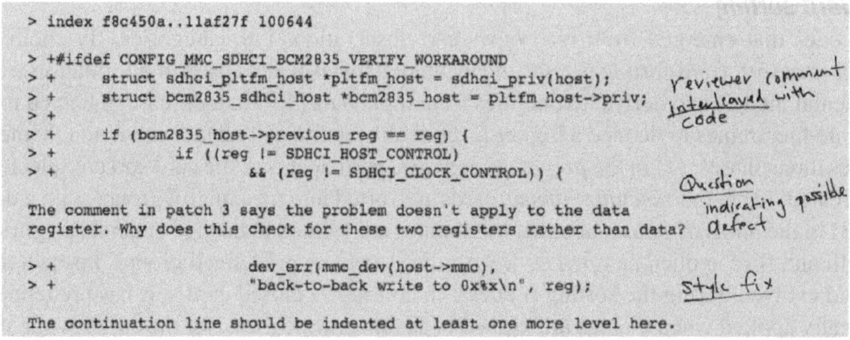

FIGURE 9.5

Example fragment of review with three codes written in the margins: a type of fix, a question that indicates a possible defect, and interleaved comments.

The analysis of the sample e-mail reviews followed Glaser's approach [10] to grounded theory, where manual analysis uncovers emergent abstract themes. These themes are developed from descriptive codes used by the researchers to note their observations. The general steps used in grounded theory are as follows: note taking, coding, memoing, sorting, and writing.[2] Below we present each of these steps in the context of the study of Rigby and Storey:

1. *Note taking.* Note taking involves creating summaries of the data without any interpretation of the events [10]. The comments in each review were analyzed chronologically. Since patches could often take up many screens with technical details, the researchers first summarized each review thread. The summary uncovered high-level occurrences, such as how reviewers interacted and responded.

2. *Coding.* Codes provide a way to group recurring events. The reviews were coded by printing and reading the summaries and writing the codes in the margin. The codes represented the techniques used to perform a review and the types and styles of interactions among stakeholders. The example shown in Figure 9.5 combines note taking and coding, with emergent codes being underlined.

3. *Memos.* Memoing is a critical aspect of grounded theory, and differentiates it from other qualitative approaches. The codes that were discovered on individual reviews were grouped together and abstracted into short memos that describe the emerging theme. Without this stage, researchers fail to abstract codes and present "stories" instead of a high-level description of the important aspects of a phenomenon.

4. *Sorting.* Usually there are too many codes and memos to be reported in a single paper. The researchers must identify the core memos and sort and group them into a set of related themes. These core themes become the grounded "theory." A theme was the way reviewers asked authors questions about their code.

5. *Writing.* Writing the paper is simply a matter of describing the evidence collected for each theme. Each core theme is written up by tracing the theme back to the abstract memos, codes, and finally the data points that lead to the theme. One common mistake is to include too many low-level details and quotations [10]. In the work of Rigby and Storey, the themes are represented throughout the paper as paragraph and section headings.

9.6 **TRIANGULATION**

Triangulation "involves the use of multiple and different methods, investigators, sources, and theories to obtain corroborating evidence" [50]. Since each method and dataset has different strengths and weakness that offset each other when they are combined, triangulation reduces the overall bias in a study. For example, survey and interview data suffer from the biases that participants self-report on events that have happened in the past. In contrast, archival data is a record of real communication and so does not suffer from self-reporting bias. However, since archival data was collected without a research agenda, it can often be missing information that a researcher needs to answer his or her questions. This missing information can be supplemented with interview questions.

---

[2]A simple practical explanation of grounded theory is given at http://www.aral.com.au/resources/grounded.html. Accessed March 2014.

In this section, we first describe how Bacchelli and Bird [6] triangulate their findings using follow-up surveys. We then triangulate our quantitative findings from Section 9.4 on multicommit reviews by first describing a qualitative study of branch reviews on Linux. We then manually code multicommit reviews as either branches or revisions in the Gerrit and GitHub projects that we examined in Section 9.4. We conclude this section with a qualitative and quantitative examination of why GitHub reviews are rejected.

9.6.1 USING SURVEYS TO TRIANGULATE QUALITATIVE FINDINGS

The investigation of Bacchelli and Bird about expectations, outcomes, and challenges of code review employed a mixed quantitative and qualitative approach, which collects data from different sources for triangulation. Figure 9.6 shows the overall research method employed, and how the different sources are used to draw conclusions and test theories: (1) analysis of the previous study, (2) meetings with developers (observations and interviews), (3) card sort of meeting data, (4) card sort of code review comments, (5) affinity diagramming, and (6) survey of managers and programmers.

The path including points 1-5 is described in Section 9.5, because it involves collection and analysis of nonnumerical data; here we focus on the use of surveys for additional triangulation. In Figure 9.6 we can see that the method already includes two different sources of data: direct data collection based on observations and interviews, and indirect data collection based on the analysis of comments in code review archives. Although these two sources are complementary and can be used to learn distinct stories, to eventually uncover the truth behind a question, they both suffer from a limited number of data points. To overcome this issue, Bacchelli and Bird used surveys to validate—with a larger, statistically significant sample—the concepts that emerged from the analysis of the data gathered from other sources.

In practice, they created two surveys and sent them to a large number of participants and triangulated the conclusions of their qualitative analysis. The full surveys are available as a technical report [51]. For the design of the surveys, Bacchelli and Bird followed the guidelines of Kitchenham and Pfleeger [52] for personal opinion surveys. Although they could have sent the survey in principle to all the employees at Microsoft, they selected samples that were statistically significant, but at the same time would not inconveniently hit an unnecessarily large number of people. Both surveys were anonymous to increase response rates [53].

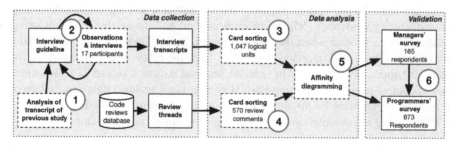

FIGURE 9.6

Triangulation-based method used by Bacchelli and Bird [6].

They sent the first survey to a cross section of managers. They considered managers for whom at least half of their team performed code reviews regularly (on average, one pr more per week) and sampled along two dimensions. The first dimension was whether or not the manager had participated in a code review himself or herself since the beginning of the year, and the second dimension was whether the manager managed a single team or multiple teams (a manager of managers). Thus, they had one sample of first-level managers who participated in a review, and another sample of second-level managers who participated in reviews, etc. The first survey was a short survey comprising six questions (all optional), which they sent to 600 managers who had at least 10 direct or indirect reporting developers who used CodeFlow. The central focus was the open question asking managers to enumerate the main motivations for doing code reviews in their team. They received 165 answers (28% response rate), which were analyzed before they devised the second survey.

The second survey comprised 18 questions, mostly closed questions with multiple choice answers, and was sent to 2000 randomly chosen developers who had signed off on average at least one code review per week since the beginning of the year. They used the time frame of January to June 2012 to minimize the amount of organizational churn during the time period and identify employees' activity in their current role and team. The survey received 873 answers (44% response rate). Both response rates were high, as other online surveys in software engineering have reported response rates ranging from 14% to 20% [54].

Although the surveys also included open questions, they were mostly based on closed ones, and thus could be used as a basis for statistical analyses. Thanks to the high number of respondents, Bacchelli and Bird could triangulate their qualitative findings with a larger set of data, thus increasing the validity of their results.

9.6.2 HOW MULTICOMMIT BRANCHES ARE REVIEWED IN LINUX

In Section 9.4, we quantitatively compared single-commit and multicommit reviews. We found that there was no clear pattern of review on the basis of the size of the project and the type of review tool (i.e., Gerrit, GitHub, or e-mail-based review). To enhance our findings and to understand the practices that underlie them, we qualitatively examine how multiple commits are handled on Linux. We find that multicommit reviews contain patches related to a single feature or fix. In the next section, we use closed coding to determine if the other projects group commits by features or if multicommit reviews are indicative of revisions of the original commit.

Instead of conducting reviews in Gerrit or as GitHub pull requests, the Linux kernel uses mailing lists. Each review is conducted as an e-mail thread. The first message in the thread will contain the patch, and subsequent responses will be reviews and discussions of review feedback (Rigby and Storey [3] provide more details on this point). According to code review polices of OSS projects, individual patches are required to be in their smallest, functionally independent, and complete form [2]. Interviews of OSS developers also indicated a preference for small patches, with some stating that they refuse to review large patches until they are split into their component parts. For Iwai, a core developer on the Linux project, "if it [a large patch] can't be split, then something is wrong [e.g., there are structural issues with the change]." However, by forcing developers to produce small patches, larger contributions are broken up and reviewed in many different threads. This division separates and reduces communication among experts, making it difficult to examine large contributions as a single unit. Testers and reviewers must manually combine these threads together. Interviewees complained about how difficult it is to combine a set of related patches to test a new feature.

Linux developers use patchsets, which allow developers to group related changes together, while still keeping each patch separate. A patchset is a single e-mail thread that contains multiple numbered and related contributions. The first e-mail contains a high-level description that ties the contributions together and explains their interrelationships. Each subsequent message contains the next patch that is necessary to complete the larger change. For example, message subjects in a patchset might look like this[3]:

- Patch 0/3: fixing and combining foobar with bar [no code modified].
- Patch 1/3: fix of foobar.
- Patch 2/3: integrate existing bar with foobar.
- Patch 3/3: update documentation on bar.

Patchsets are effectively a branch of small patch commits that implements a larger change. The version control system Git contains a feature to send a branch as a number patchset to a mailing list for code review [55].

Notice how each subcontribution is small, independent, and complete. Also, the contributions are listed in the order they should be committed to the system (e.g., the fix to foobar must be committed before combining it with bar). Reviewers can respond to the overall patch (i.e., $0/N$) or they can respond to any individual patch (i.e., $n/N, n > 0$). As reviewers respond, subthreads tackle subproblems. However, it remains simple for testers and less experienced reviewers to apply the patchset as a single unit for testing purposes. Patchsets represent a perfect example of creating a fine, but functional and efficient division between the whole and the parts of a larger problem.

9.6.3 CLOSED CODING: BRANCH OR REVISION ON GITHUB AND GERRIT

A multicommit review may be a related set of commits (a branch or patchset) or a revision of a commit. We conduct a preliminary analysis of 15 randomly sampled multicommit reviews from each project to understand what type of review is occurring. Of the 15 reviews coded for each of the GitHub-based projects, 73%, 86%, and 60% of them were branches for Rails, WildFly, and Katello, respectively. These projects conducted branch review in a manner similar to Linux, but without the formality of describing the changes at a high level. Each change had a one-line commit description that clearly indicated its connection to the next commit in the branch. For example, the commits in the following pull request implement two small parts of the same change[4]:

- Commit 1: "Modified CollectionAssociation to refer to the new class name."
- Commit 2: "Modified NamedScopeTest to use CollectionAssociation."

WildFly had the highest percentage of branch reviews, which may explain why it had the largest number of lines changed and the longest review interval of all the projects we examined (see Section 9.4).

---

[3] A Linux patchset: http://lkml.org/lkml/2008/5/27/278. Accessed in January 2014.
[4] Example of a pull request: https://github.com/rails/rails/pull/513/commits. Accessed in March 2014.

For GitHub, we also noted that some of the multicommit reviews were of massive merges instead of individual feature changes.[5] It would be interesting to examine "massive" merge reviews.

For Android and Chrome, we were surprised to find that none of the randomly selected reviews were of branches. Each multicommit review involved revisions of a single commit. While work is necessary to determine whether this is a defacto practice or enforced by policy, there is a preference at Google to commit onto a single branch [56]. Furthermore, the notion of "patchset" in the Gerrit review system usually applies to an updated version of a patch rather than a branch, as it does in Linux [19].

9.6.4 UNDERSTANDING WHY PULL REQUESTS ARE REJECTED

As a final example of mixed qualitative-quantitative research involving triangulation, we present new findings on why pull request reviews are rejected in GitHub projects. Previous work found relatively low rates of patch acceptance in large successful OSS projects. Bird et al. [17] found that the acceptance rate in three OSS projects was between 25% and 50%. In the six projects examined by Asundi and Jayant [16], they found that 28% to 46% of non-core developers had their patches ignored. Estimates of Bugzilla patch rejection rates for Firefox and Mozilla range from 61% [28] to 76% [15]. In contrast, while most proposed changes in GitHub pull requests are accepted [9], it is interesting to explore why some are not. Even though textual analysis tools (e.g., natural language processing and topic modeling) are evolving, it is still difficult for them to accurately capture and classify the rationale behind such complex actions as rejecting code under review. For this reason, a researcher needs to resort to qualitative methods.

In the context of GitHub code reviews, we manually coded 350 pull requests and classified the reasons for rejection. Three independent coders did the coding. Initially, 100 pull requests were used by the first coder to identify discrete reasons for closing pull requests (bootstrapping sample), while a different set of 100 pull requests was used by all three coders to validate the categories identified (cross-validation sample). After validation, the two datasets were merged, and a further 150 randomly selected pull requests were added to the bootstrapping sample to construct the finally analyzed dataset, for a total of 350 pull requests. The cross-validation of the categories on a different set of pull requests revealed that the categories identified are enough to classify all reasons for closing a pull request. The results are presented in Table 9.4.

The results show that there is no clearly outstanding reason for rejecting code under review. However, if we group together close reasons that have a timing dimension (obsolete, conflict, superseded), we see that 27% of unmerged pull requests are closed because of concurrent modifications of the code in project branches. Another 16% (superfluous, duplicate, deferred) are closed as a result of the contributor not having identified the direction of the project correctly and therefore submitting uninteresting changes. Ten percent of the contributions are rejected for reasons that have to do with project process and quality requirements (process, tests); this may be an indicator of processes not being communicated well enough or a rigorous code reviewing process. Finally, 13% of the contributions are rejected because the code review revealed an error in the implementation.

Only 13% of the contributions are rejected for technical issues, which are the primary reason for code reviewing, while 53% are rejected for reasons having to do with the distributed nature of modern

---

[5]Example of a massive pull request: https://github.com/Katello/katello/pull/1024.

Table 9.4 Reasons for Rejecting Code Under Review

Reason	Description	Percentage
obsolete	The pull request is no longer relevant, as the project has progressed	4
conflict	The feature is currently being implemented by other pull requests or in another branch	5
superseded	A new pull request solves the problem better	18
duplicate	The functionality was in the project prior to the submission of the pull request	2
superfluous	The pull request does not solve an existing problem or add a feature needed by the project	6
deferred	The proposed change is delayed for further investigation in the future	8
process	The pull request does not follow the correct project conventions for sending and handling pull requests	9
tests	Tests failed to run.	1
incorrect implementation	The implementation of the feature is incorrect, is missing, or does not follow project standards.	13
merged	The pull request was identified as merged by the human examiner	19
unknown	The pull request could not be classified owing to lacking information	15

code reviews or the way projects handle communication of project goals and practices. Moreover, for 15% of the pull requests, the human examiners could not identify the cause of not integrating them. The latter is indicative of the fact that even in-depth, manual analysis can yield less than optimal results.

9.7 CONCLUSION

We have used our previous work to illustrate how qualitative and quantitative methods can be combined to understand code review [3, 5, 6, 9]. We have summarized the types of code review and presented a metamodel of the different measures that can be extracted. We illustrated qualitative methods in Section 9.5 by describing how Rigby and Storey [3] used grounded theory to understand how OSS developers interact and manage to effectively conduct reviews on large mailing lists. We then contrasted this method with the card sorting and affinity diagramming used by Bacchelli and Bird [6] to investigate the motivations and requirements of interviewed managers and developers with regard to the code review tool and processes used at Microsoft.

To provide an illustration of a mixed methods study, we presented new findings that contrast multicommit reviews with single-commits reviews. In Section 9.4 we presented quantitative results. While no clear quantitative pattern emerges when we make comparisons across projects or types of review (i.e., Gerrit, GitHub, and e-mail-based review), we find that even though multicommit reviews take longer and involve more code than single-commit reviews, multicommit reviews have the same number of reviewers per review. We triangulated our quantitative findings by manually examining how multicommit reviews are conducted (see Sections 9.6.2 and 9.6.3). For Linux, we found that multicommit reviews involve patchsets, which are reviews of branches. For Android and Chrome, multicommit reviews are reviews of revisions of single commits. For the GitHub projects, Rails, WildFly, and Katello, there is a mix of branch reviews and revisions of commits during review. As a final contribution, we presented new qualitative and quantitative results on why reviews on GitHub pull requests are rejected (Section 9.6.4).

REFERENCES

[1] Fagan M. Design and code inspections to reduce errors in program development. IBM Syst J 1976;15(3):182–211.

[2] Rigby PC, German DM, Storey MA. Open source software peer review practices: a case study of the apache server. In: ICSE '08: Proceedings of the 30th international conference on software engineering. New York, NY, USA: ACM; 2008. p. 541–50. ISBN 978-1-60558-079-1. doi:10.1145/1368088.1368162.

[3] Rigby PC, Storey MA. Understanding broadcast based peer review on open source software projects. In: Proceeding of the 33rd international conference on software engineering, ICSE '11. New York, NY, USA: ACM; 2011. p. 541–50. ISBN 978-1-4503-0445-0.

[4] Rigby P, Cleary B, Painchaud F, Storey MA, German D. Contemporary peer review in action: lessons from open source development. IEEE Softw 2012;29(6):56–61. doi:10.1109/MS.2012.24.

[5] Rigby PC, German DM, Cowen L, Storey MA. Peer review on open source software projects: parameters, statistical models, and theory. ACM Trans Softw Eng Methodol 2014:34.

[6] Bacchelli A, Bird C. Expectations, outcomes, and challenges of modern code review. In: Proceedings of the international conference on software engineering. Washington, DC, USA: IEEE Computer Society; 2013.

[7] Rigby PC, Bird C. Convergent contemporary software peer review practices. In: Proceedings of the 9th joint meeting on foundations of software engineering, ESEC/FSE 2013. New York, NY, USA: ACM; 2013. p. 202–12. ISBN 978-1-4503-2237-9. doi:10.1145/2491411.2491444.

[8] Mukadam M, Bird C, Rigby PC. Gerrit software code review data from android. In: Proceedings of the 10th working conference on mining software repositories, MSR '13. Piscataway, NJ, USA: IEEE Press; 2013. p. 45–8. ISBN 978-1-4673-2936-1. URL: http://dl.acm.org/citation.cfm?id=2487085.2487095.

[9] Gousios G, Pinzger M, Deursen Av. An exploratory study of the pull-based software development model. In: Proceedings of the 36th international conference on software engineering, ICSE 2014. New York, NY, USA: ACM; 2014. p. 345–55. ISBN 978-1-4503-2756-5. doi:10.1145/2568225.2568260.

[10] Glaser B. Doing grounded theory: issues and discussions. Mill Valley, CA: Sociology Press; 1998.

[11] Creswell J. Research design: qualitative, quantitative, and mixed methods approaches. Thousand Oaks: Sage Publications, Inc.; 2009. ISBN 141296556X.

[12] Yin RK. Case study research: design and methods. In: Applied social research methods series, vol. 5. 3rd ed. Thousand Oaks: Sage Publications Inc.; 2003.

[13] Wiegers KE. Peer reviews in software: a practical guide. In: Addison-Wesley information technology series. Boston, MA: Addison-Wesley; 2001.

[14] Guzzi A, Bacchelli A, Lanza M, Pinzger M, van Deursen A. Communication in open source software development mailing lists. In: Proceedings of MSR 2013 (10th IEEE working conference on mining software repositories); 2013. p. 277–86.

[15] Nurolahzade M, Nasehi SM, Khandkar SH, Rawal S. The role of patch review in software evolution: an analysis of the Mozilla Firefox. In: International workshop on principles of software evolution; 2009. p. 9–18. ISBN 978-1-60558-678-6.

[16] Asundi J, Jayant R. Patch review processes in open source software development communities: a comparative case study. In: HICSS: proceedings of the 40th annual Hawaii international conference on system sciences; 2007. p. 10.

[17] Bird C, Gourley A, Devanbu P. Detecting patch submission and acceptance in OSS projects. In: MSR: proceedings of the fourth international workshop on mining software repositories. Washington, DC, USA: IEEE Computer Society; 2007. p. 4.

[18] Schwartz R. Interview with Shawn Pearce, Google Engineer, on FLOSS Weekly. http://www.youtube.com/watch?v=C3MvAQMhC_M.

[19] Gerrit. Web based code review and project management for Git based projects. http://code.google.com/p/gerrit/.

[20] Nagappan N, Ball T. Use of relative code churn measures to predict system defect density. In: Proceedings of the 27th international conference on software engineering, ICSE '05. New York, NY, USA: ACM; 2005. p. 284–92. ISBN 1-58113-963-2. doi:10.1145/1062455.1062514.

[21] Weißgerber P, Neu D, Diehl S. Small patches get in! In: MSR '08: proceedings of the 2008 international working conference on mining software repositories. New York, NY, USA: ACM; 2008. p. 67–76. ISBN 978-1-60558-024-1.

[22] Baysal O, Kononenko O, Holmes R, Godfrey M. The influence of non-technical factors on code review. In: Proceedings of the 20th working conference on reverse engineering (WCRE); 2013. p. 122–31.

[23] Anvik J, Hiew L, Murphy GC. Who should fix this bug? In: ICSE '06: proceedings of the 28th international conference on software engineering. New York, NY, USA: ACM; 2006. p. 361–70. ISBN 1-59593-375-1.

[24] Giger E, Pinzger M, Gall H. Predicting the fix time of bugs. In: Proceedings of the 2nd international workshop on recommendation systems for software engineering, RSSE '10. New York, NY, USA: ACM; 2010. p. 52–6. ISBN 978-1-60558-974-9. doi:10.1145/1808920.1808933.

[25] Ratzinger J, Pinzger M, Gall H. EQ-mine: predicting short-term defects for software evolution. In: Proceedings of the 10th international conference on fundamental approaches to software engineering, FASE'07. Berlin: Springer-Verlag; 2007. p. 12–26. ISBN 978-3-540-71288-6. URL: http://dl.acm.org/citation.cfm?id=1759394.1759399.

[26] Pham R, Singer L, Liskin O, Figueira Filho F, Schneider K. Creating a shared understanding of testing culture on a social coding site. In: Proceedings of the 2013 international conference on software engineering, ICSE '13. Piscataway, NJ, USA: IEEE Press; 2013. p. 112–21. ISBN 978-1-4673-3076-3. URL: http://dl.acm.org/citation.cfm?id=2486788.2486804.

[27] Girba T, Ducasse S, Lanza M. Yesterday's weather: guiding early reverse engineering efforts by summarizing the evolution of changes. In: Proceedings of the 20th IEEE international conference on software maintenance; 2004. p. 40–9. doi:10.1109/ICSM.2004.1357788.

[28] Jeong G, Kim S, Zimmermann T, Yi K. Improving code review by predicting reviewers and acceptance of patches. Technical Memorandum ROSAEC-2009-006, Research On Software Analysis for Error-free Computing Center, Seoul National University; 2009.

[29] Beller M, Bacchelli A, Zaidman A, Juergens E. Modern code reviews in open-source projects: which problems do they fix? In: Proceedings of MSR 2014 (11th working conference on mining software repositories); 2014. p. 202–11.

[30] Dabbish L, Stuart C, Tsay J, Herbsleb J. Social coding in Github: transparency and collaboration in an open software repository. In: Proceedings of the ACM 2012 conference on computer supported cooperative work, CSCW '12. New York, NY, USA: ACM; 2012. p. 1277–86. ISBN 978-1-4503-1086-4. doi:10.1145/2145204.2145396.

[31] Bird C, Gourley A, Devanbu P, Swaminathan A, Hsu G. Open borders? Immigration in open source projects. In: MSR '07: proceedings of the fourth international workshop on mining software repositories. Washington, DC, USA: IEEE Computer Society; 2007. p. 6. ISBN 0-7695-2950-X.

[32] Shihab E, Jiang Z, Hassan A. On the use of Internet Relay Chat (IRC) meetings by developers of the GNOME GTK+ project. In: MSR: proceedings of the 6th IEEE international working conference on mining software repositories. Washington, DC, USA: IEEE Computer Society; 2009. p. 107–10.

[33] Kampstra P. Beanplot: a boxplot alternative for visual comparison of distributions. J Stat Softw 2008;28(Code Snippets 1):1–9.

[34] Kollanus S, Koskinen J. Survey of software inspection research. Open Softw Eng J 2009;3:15–34.

[35] Porter A, Siy H, Mockus A, Votta L. Understanding the sources of variation in software inspections. ACM Trans Softw Eng Methodol 1998;7(1):41–79.

[36] Votta LG. Does every inspection need a meeting? SIGSOFT Softw Eng Notes 1993;18(5):107–14. doi:10.1145/167049.167070.

[37] Sauer C, Jeffery DR, Land L, Yetton P. The effectiveness of software development technical reviews: a behaviorally motivated program of research. IEEE Trans Softw Eng 2000;26(1):1–14. doi:10.1109/32.825763.

[38] Laitenberger O, DeBaud J. An encompassing life cycle centric survey of software inspection. J Syst Softw 2000;50(1):5–31.

[39] Cohen J. Best kept secrets of peer code review. Beverly, MA: Smart Bear Inc.; 2006. p. 63–88.

[40] Ratcliffe J. Moving software quality upstream: the positive impact of lightweight peer code review. In: Pacific NW software quality conference; 2009.

[41] Ko AJ. Understanding software engineering through qualitative methods. In: Oram A, Wilson G, editors. Making software. Cambridge, MA: O'Reilly; 2010. p. 55–63 [chapter 4].

[42] Burgess RG. In the field: an introduction to field research. 1st ed. London: Unwin Hyman; 1984.

[43] Lethbridge TC, Sim SE, Singer J. Studying software engineers: data collection techniques for software field studies. Empir Softw Eng 2005;10:311–41.

[44] Triola M. Elementary statistics. 10th ed. Boston, MA: Addison-Wesley; 2006. ISBN 0-321-33183-4.

[45] Taylor B, Lindlof T. Qualitative communication research methods. Thousand Oaks: Sage Publications, Inc.; 2010.

[46] Parsons HM. What happened at Hawthorne? new evidence suggests the Hawthorne effect resulted from operant reinforcement contingencies. Science 1974;183(4128):922–32.

[47] Weiss R. Learning from strangers: the art and method of qualitative interview studies. New York: Simon and Schuster; 1995.

[48] Spencer D. Card sorting: a definitive guide. http://boxesandarrows.com/card-sorting-a-definitive-guide/; 2004.

[49] Shade JE, Janis SJ. Improving performance through statistical thinking. New York: McGraw-Hill; 2000.

[50] Onwuegbuzie A, Leech N. Validity and qualitative research: an oxymoron? Qual Quant 2007;41(2):233–49.

[51] Bacchelli A, Bird C. Appendix to expectations, outcomes, and challenges of modern code review. http://research.microsoft.com/apps/pubs/?id=171426; 2012. Microsoft Research, Technical Report MSR-TR-2012-83 2012.

[52] Kitchenham B, Pfleeger S. Personal opinion surveys. In: Guide to advanced empirical software engineering; 2008. p. 63–92.

[53] Tyagi P. The effects of appeals, anonymity, and feedback on mail survey response patterns from salespeople. J Acad Market Sci 1989;17(3):235–41.

[54] Punter T, Ciolkowski M, Freimut B, John I. Conducting on-line surveys in software engineering. In: International symposium on empirical software engineering. Washington, DC, USA: IEEE Computer Society; 2003.

[55] Git. git-format-patch(1) manual page. https://www.kernel.org/pub/software/scm/git/docs/git-format-patch.html.

[56] Micco J. Tools for continuous integration at Google Scale. Google Tech Talk, Google Inc.; 2012.

MINING ANDROID APPS FOR ANOMALIES

10

Konstantin Kuznetsov*, Alessandra Gorla†, Ilaria Tavecchia‡, Florian Groß*, Andreas Zeller*

Software Engineering Chair, Saarland University, Saarbrücken, Germany* IMDEA Software Institute, Pozuelo de Alarcon, Madrid, Spain† SWIFT, La Hulpe, Bruxelles, Belgium‡

CHAPTER OUTLINE

10.1 INTRODUCTION

Detecting whether a mobile application behaves as expected is a prominent problem for users. Whenever they install a new app on their mobile device, they run the risk of it being "malware"— i.e., to act against their interests. Security researchers have largely focused on detecting malware in Android™ apps, but their techniques typically check new apps against a set of predefined known patterns of malicious behavior. This approach works well for detecting new malware that uses known patterns, but does not protect against new attack patterns. Moreover, in Android it is not easy to define what malicious behavior is and therefore to define its key features to detect malware. The problem is that any specification on what makes behavior beneficial or malicious *very much depends on the current context.*

Typical Android malware, for instance, sends text messages to premium numbers, or collects sensitive information from users, such as mobile number, current location, and contacts. However, this very same information, and the very same operations, frequently occur in benign applications as well. Sending text messages to premium numbers is for instance a legitimate paying method to unlock new app features; tracking the current location is what a navigation app has to do; and collecting the list of contacts and sending it to an external server is what most free messaging apps like WhatsApp do upon synchronization. The question thus is not whether the behavior of an app matches a specific malicious pattern or not; it is whether *an app behaves as one would expect.*

In our previous work we presented CHABADA, a technique to check *implemented* app behavior against *advertised* app behavior [1]. We analyzed the natural language descriptions of 22.500+ Android applications, and we checked whether the description matched the implemented behavior, represented as a set of application programming interfaces (APIs). The key of CHABADA is to associate descriptions and API usage to detect anomalies.

Our CHABADA approach includes the five steps illustrated in Figure 10.1:

1. CHABADA starts with a *collection* of 22,500+ supposedly "benign" Android applications downloaded from the Google Play Store.
2. Using Latent Dirichlet Allocation (LDA) on the app descriptions, CHABADA identifies the main *topics* ("theme," "map," "weather," "download") for each application.
3. CHABADA then *clusters* applications by related topics. For instance, if there were enough apps whose main description topics are "navigation" and "travel," they would form one cluster.
4. In each cluster, CHABADA identifies the APIs each app statically accesses. It only considers *sensitive* APIs, which are governed by a *user permission*. For instance, APIs related to Internet access are controlled by the "INTERNET" permission.
5. Using unsupervised learning, CHABADA identifies *outliers* within a cluster with respect to API usage. It produces a *ranked list of applications* for each cluster, where the top apps are most abnormal with respect to their API usage—indicating possible mismatches between description and implementation. Unknown applications would thus first be assigned to the cluster implied by their description and then be *classified* as being normal or abnormal.

By flagging anomalous API usage within each cluster, CHABADA is set up to detect any suspicious app within a set of similar apps and can therefore detect whether an app has any *mismatch between*

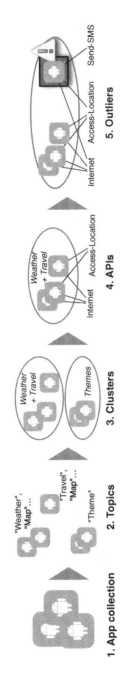

FIGURE 10.1

Detecting applications with anomalous behavior. Starting from a collection of "benign" apps (1), CHABADA identifies their description topics (2) to form clusters of related apps (3). For each cluster, CHABADA identifies the APIs used (4), and can then identify outliers that use APIs that are uncommon for that cluster (5).[1]

FEATURES:

– News: Real-time breaking news from the Jets, previews of upcoming matchups, post-game blogs

– Video: Video-on-demand clips of Jets' press conferences, coach and player interviews

– Photos: Gallery of game-time action

– Audio: Podcasts

– Stats: Real-time statistics and scores from the official NFL stats engine, head-to-head stats of the matchup, player stats, drive-by-drive stats, box score, out-of-town scores around the league

– Standings: Division and conference standings

– Fantasy: Keep track of your favorite fantasy players

– Depth chart: Shown by offense, defense and special teams

– Social media: Aggregated Twitter of all of your favorite Jets tweeps, check in to the stadium on game-day, one-click tweet of all media items, one-click Facebook posting of all media items

– Digital keepsake: Your game-time moment superimposed on the stadium jumbotron in the form of a unique digital keepsake

– Schedule: Schedule of upcoming games, and scores/stats of previous games from the season, ticket purchase for games

– Concessions: Interactive map of MetLife Stadium with searchable concessions-stands and amenities

– Problem-reporting: Reports of various problems and issues around the stadium

– Evolving home-screen: Pre-game, in-game, post-game, off-season countdown, draft-day

– In-stadium live video and replays: Limited beta test; connect to the MLSOpen Wi-Fi network at MetLife Stadium

Follow us @nyjets on Twitter for updates or visit www.newyorkjets.com. SUPPORT/QUESTIONS: Email support@yinzcam.com or send a tweet to @yinzcam The Official New York Jets app is created and maintained by YinzCam, Inc., on behalf of the New York Jets.

FIGURE 10.2

Official New York Jets app description.

advertised and implemented behavior. We show how this works in practice with a real app as an example. Figure 10.2 shows the description of the Official New York Jets team app,[2] available from the Google Play Store. Its description clearly puts it into the "sports" cluster.

In addition to expected common API calls, the version of the Official New York Jets app we analyzed can check whether GPS location is available, via the API method *Location-Manager.addGpsStatusListener()*, and can send text messages, via the API method *SmsManager.sendTextMessage()*, which are highly uncommon operations for this kind of application. These API method calls, together with similar others, make Official New York Jets an outlier within the "sports" cluster. By flagging such anomalies, CHABADA can detect false advertising, plain fraud, masquerading, and other questionable behavior. CHABADA can be used as a malware detector as well. By training it on a sample of benign apps, CHABADA can classify new apps as benign or malware, without any previous notion of malicious behavior.

---

[2]https://play.google.com/store/apps/details?id=com.yinzcam.nfl.jets.

This chapter extends our previous conference paper [1] by presenting several new techniques that lead to significant improvements:

1. We now *rank down irrelevant* APIs when looking for anomalies. Specifically, we give a lower weight to APIs that are common within a particular cluster (e.g., Internet access, which is frequently used in applications). By giving more importance to less common behavior, CHABADA can highlight outliers more easily.

2. We incorporate an *additional technique for anomaly detection.* The anomaly detection of CHABADA is now based on a distance-based algorithm, which allows clearly identifying the APIs that make an app anomalous.

3. To use CHABADA as a classifier of malicious applications, we now run anomaly detection as a preliminary step, and we exclude the anomalies from the training set. This allows to *remove noise* from the training set, and consequently to improve the abilities of the classifier. CHABADA can now predict 74% of malware as such (previously 56%), and suffers from only 11% of false positives (previously 15%).

4. We can now automatically select the *optimal parameters* for the classifier. This also contributes to the improvement of CHABADA as a malware classifier.

The remainder of this paper is organized as follows. We first describe how CHABADA clusters applications by description topics in Section 10.2. This book chapter does not improve our first paper [1] on this side, but we include a description of this step for the sake of completion. Section 10.3 describes how in each cluster we detect outliers with respect to their API usage. In particular, we describe the new algorithm that CHABADA uses, and we highlight the advantages of the new approach. Section 10.4 evaluates the improvements of CHABADA. After discussing the related work (Section 10.5), Section 10.6 closes with conclusions and future work.

10.2 CLUSTERING APPS BY DESCRIPTION

The intuition behind CHABADA is simple: applications that are similar, in terms of their descriptions, should also behave similarly. As a consequence, applications that behave differently from their similars should be further inspected, as they may have malicious behavior. For this, we must first establish what makes two descriptions "similar". We start with describing our Android apps collection, and how we collected it (Section 10.2.1). After initial processing (Section 10.2.2), CHABADA identifies *topics* of app descriptions (Section 10.2.3), and then *clusters* the apps based on common topics (Section 10.2.4 to Section 10.2.6).

10.2.1 COLLECTING APPLICATIONS

CHABADA is based on detecting anomalies from "normal," hopefully benign applications. As a base for such "normal" behavior, CHABADA relies on a large set of applications from the Google Play Store, the central resource for Android apps. Our automated crawler ran at regular intervals (i.e., every 2 weeks) during the Winter and Spring of 2013, and for each of the 30 categories in the Google Play

Store, downloaded the top 150 free [3] applications in each category. A single complete run of our script thus returned 4500 apps; as the top 150 apps shifted during our collection, we obtained a total of 32,136 apps across all categories.

In addition to the actual app (coming as an android application package (APK) file), we also collected the store *metadata*—such as name and description.

10.2.2 PREPROCESSING DESCRIPTIONS WITH NLP

Before subjecting app descriptions to topic analysis, CHABADA applies standard techniques of natural language processing (NLP) for filtering and stemming [2].

App descriptions in the Google Play Store frequently contain paragraphs in multiple languages—for instance, the main description is in English, while at the end of the description developers add a short sentence in different languages to briefly describe the application. To be able to cluster similar descriptions, CHABADA has to work on a single language, and because of its predominance we chose English. CHABADA relies on Google's *Compact Language Detector*[4] to detect the most likely language of the app description, and it removes non-English paragraphs.

After multi-language filtering, CHABADA removes *stop words* (common words such as "the," "is," "at," "which," "on," ...), and applies *stemming* on all descriptions employing the power of *Natural Language Toolkit*.[5] Stemming is a common NLP technique to identify the word's root, and it is essential to make words such as "playing," "player," and "play" all match to the single common root "plai". Stemming can improve the results of later NLP processes, since it reduces the number of words. CHABADA also removes non-text items such as numerals, HTML tags, links, and email addresses thanks to specific Python modules such as *HTMLParser*.[6]

As an example, consider the description of Official New York Jets in Figure 10.2; after the preprocessing phase, it appears as:

action aggreg amen android anytim anywher app around audio behalf beta blog box break can catch chart check clip coach com concess concessions-stand confer connect countdown creat defens depth devic digit divis draft-dai drive drive-by-dr email engin everi evolv experi facebook fantasi favorit featur follow form galleri game game-dai game-tim head-to-head home-screen ingam in-stadium inc interact interview issu item jet jumbotron keep keepsak leagu limit live maintain make map matchup media metlif mlsopen mobil moment network new newyorkjet nfl now nyjet off-season offens offici one-click out-of-town part photo player podcast post post-gam pre-gam press preview previou problem problem-report purchas question real-tim replai report schedul score searchabl season see send shown social special stadium stai stand stat statist superimpos support team test ticket touch track tweep tweet twitter uniqu upcom updat us variou video video-on-demand visit want watch wi-fi yinzcam york

---

[3]Section 10.4.4 discusses possible induced bias.
[4]http://code.google.com/p/chromium-compact-language-detector.
[5]http://www.nltk.org.
[6]https://docs.python.org/2/library/htmlparser.html.

We remove from our dataset those applications whose description has less than 10 words after the preprocessing we just described. We also eliminate all applications without any sensitive APIs (see Section 10.3 for details). This resulted in a final set of 22,521 apps, which form the basis for CHABADA.

10.2.3 IDENTIFYING TOPICS WITH LDA

To identify sets of topics for the apps under analysis, CHABADA resorts to *topic modeling* using *Latent Dirichlet Allocation* (LDA) [3].

LDA is an unsupervised, statistical algorithm that discovers latent semantic topics in a collection of text documents. LDA represents documents as random mixtures over multiple latent topics, where each "topic" is characterized by a distribution over a fixed vocabulary of words. Given a set of documents and the number of topics, LDA produces the probability distribution of each topic-document pair and of each word-topic pair, and consequently learns, for each topic, a set of words.

By analyzing a set of app descriptions on sports and social networking, for instance, LDA would group words such as "team," "soccer," "league," and "sport" into one topic, and "share," "facebook," "twitter," and "suggest" into another topic. Applications whose description is mainly about sports would thus be assigned to the first topic, since most of the words occurring in the description belong to the first group. Applications such as the Official New York Jets, however, would be assigned to both topics, as the words in the description appear in both groups.

CHABADA feeds the NLP pre-processing output (i.e., the English text without stop words and after stemming) into the *Mallet* framework [4]. CHABADA can be freely configured to choose the number of topics to be identified by LDA; by default it identifies 30, the number of categories covered by the apps in the Google Play Store. Furthermore, by default CHABADA is configured such that an app can belong to at most four topics. Limiting the number of topics an app can belong to makes the clustering more effective in our experience.

Table 10.1 shows the resulting list of topics for the 22,521 descriptions that we analyzed with CHABADA; the "assigned name" is the abstract concept we assigned to that topic. Our example application, Official New York Jets, is assigned to these four topics:

- Topic 24 ("sports") with a probability of 63.1%
- Topic 8 ("share") with a probability of 17.7%
- Topic 10 ("files and videos") with a probability of 10.4%
- Topic 6 ("game") with a probability of 6.7%

10.2.4 CLUSTERING APPS WITH *K-MEANS*

Topic modeling can assign application descriptions to topics with a certain probability. What we want, however, is to cluster applications with similar descriptions within the same group. It would appear reasonable to consider obtained topics as separate clusters, but unfortunately topic modeling does not provide a binary decision of whether a description belongs to a particular topic. Moreover, each description may be related to many topics, and even with equal probability, so it would not be clear how to choose a specific cluster for a given application description.

Table 10.1 Topics Mined from Android Apps

Id	Assigned Name	Most Representative Words (Stemmed)
0	"personalize"	galaxi, nexu, device, screen, effect, instal, customis
1	"game and cheat sheets"	game, video, page, cheat, link, tip, trick
2	"money"	slot, machine, money, poker, currenc, market, trade, stock, casino coin, finance
3	"tv"	tv, channel, countri, live, watch, germani, nation, bbc, newspap
4	"music"	music, song, radio, play, player, listen
5	"holidays" and religion	christmas, halloween, santa, year, holiday, islam, god
6	"navigation and travel"	map, inform, track, gps, navig, travel
7	"language"	language, word, english, learn, german, translat
8	"share"	email, ad, support, facebook, share, twitter, rate, suggest
9	"weather and stars"	weather, forecast, locate, temperatur, map, city, light
10	"files and video"	file, download, video, media, support, manage, share, view, search
11	"photo and social"	photo, friend, facebook, share, love, twitter, pictur, chat, messag, galleri, hot, send social
12	"cars"	car, race, speed, drive, vehicl, bike, track
13	"design and art"	life, peopl, natur, form, feel, learn, art, design, uniqu, effect, modern
14	"food and recipes"	recip, cake, chicken, cook, food
15	"personalize"	theme, launcher, download, install, icon, menu
16	"health"	weight, bodi, exercise, diet, workout, medic
17	"travel"	citi, guid, map, travel, flag, countri, attract
18	"kids and bodies"	kid, anim, color, girl, babi, pictur, fun, draw, design, learn
19	"ringtones and sound"	sound, rington, alarm, notif, music
20	"game"	game, plai, graphic, fun, jump, level, ball, 3d, score
21	"search and browse"	search, icon, delet, bookmark, link, homepag, shortcut, browser
22	"battle games"	story, game, monster, zombi, war, battle
23	"settings and utils"	screen, set, widget, phone, batteri
24	"sports"	team, football, leagu, player, sport, basketbal
25	"wallpapers"	wallpap, live, home, screen, background, menu
26	"connection"	device, connect, network, wifi, blootooth, internet, remot, server
27	"policies and ads"	live, ad, home, applovin, notif, data, polici, privacy, share, airpush, advertis
28	"popular media"	seri, video, film, album, movi, music, award, star, fan, show, gangnam, top, bieber
29	"puzzle and card games"	game, plai, level, puzzl, player, score, challeng, card

Table 10.2 Four Applications and Their Likelihoods of Belonging to Specific Topics

Application	$topic_1$	$topic_2$	$topic_3$	$topic_4$
app_1	0.60	0.40	–	–
app_2	–	–	0.70	0.30
app_3	0.50	0.30	–	0.20
app_4	–	–	0.40	0.60

As a consequence, CHABADA uses *K-means* [5], one of the most common clustering algorithms, to group applications with similar descriptions, and it does so by using topic probabilities as features. Given a set of elements and the number of clusters K to be identified, *K-means* selects one *centroid* for each cluster, and then associates each element of the dataset to the nearest centroid, thus identifying clusters. It should be noted that using words instead of topics would significantly increase the dimension of the feature space and would thus make *K-means* almost ineffective.

In this context, we use applications as the elements to be clustered, and we use the probabilities of belonging to topics as features. As an example, Table 10.2 shows four applications app_1 to app_4, with the corresponding probabilities of belonging to topics. If we applied *K-means* to partition the set of applications into two clusters, it would create one cluster with app_1 and app_3, and a second cluster with app_2 and app_4.

10.2.5 FINDING THE BEST NUMBER OF CLUSTERS

One of the challenges with *K-means* is to estimate the number of clusters that should be created. The algorithm needs to be given either some initial potential centroids, or the number K of clusters to identify. There are several approaches to identifying the best solution, among a set of possible clustering solutions. Therefore, CHABADA runs *K-means* several times, each time with a different K number, to obtain a set of clustering solutions it would then be able to evaluate. The range for K covers solutions among two extremes: having a small number of clusters (even just 2) with a large variety of apps; or having many clusters (potentially even one per app) and thus being very specific. CHABADA fixes *num_topics* $\times$ 4 as an upper bound, since according to the default settings an application can belong to up to four topics.

To identify the best solution, i.e., the best number of clusters, CHABADA uses the *elements silhouette*, as discussed in [6]. The silhouette of an element is the measure of how closely the element is matched to the other elements within its cluster, and how loosely it is matched to other elements of the neighboring clusters. When the value of the silhouette of an element is close to 1, the element is in the appropriate cluster. If the value is close to -1, instead, the element is in the wrong cluster. Thus, to identify the best solution, CHABADA computes the average of the elements' silhouette for each solution using K as the number of clusters, and selects the solution whose silhouette is closest to 1.

Table 10.3 Clusters of Applications

Id	Assigned Name	Size	Most Important Topics
1	"sharing"	1453	**share** (53%), settings and utils, navigation and travel
2	"puzzle and card games"	953	**puzzle and card games** (78%), share, game
3	"memory puzzles"	1069	**puzzle and card games** (40%), game (12%), share
4	"music"	714	**music** (58%), share, settings and utils
5	"music videos"	773	**popular media** (44%), **holidays and religion** (20%), share
6	"religious wallpapers"	367	**holidays and religion** (56%), design and art, wallpapers
7	"language"	602	**language** (67%), share, settings and utils
8	"cheat sheets"	785	**game and cheat sheets** (76%), share, popular media
9	"utils"	1300	**settings and utils** (62%), share, connection
10	"sports game"	1306	**game** (63%), battle games, puzzle and card games
11	"battle games"	953	**battle games** (60%), **game** (11%), design and art
12	"navigation and travel"	1273	**navigation and travel** (64%), share, travel
13	"money"	589	**money** (57%), puzzle and card games, settings and utils
14	"kids"	1001	**kids and bodies** (62%), share, puzzle and card games
15	"personalize"	304	**personalize** (71%), **wallpapers** (15%), settings and utils
16	"connection"	823	**connection** (63%), settings and utils, share
17	"health"	669	**health** (63%), design and art, share
18	"weather"	282	**weather and stars** (61%), **settings and utils** (11%), navigation and travel
19	"sports"	580	**sports** (62%), share, popular media
20	"files and videos"	679	**files and videos** (63%), share, settings and utils
21	"search and browse"	363	**search and browse** (64%), game, puzzle and card games
22	"advertisements"	380	**policies and ads** (97%)
23	"design and art"	978	**design and art** (48%), share, game
24	"car games"	449	**cars** (51%), game, puzzle and card games
25	"tv live"	500	**tv** (57%), share, navigation and travel
26	"adult photo"	828	**photo and social** (59%), share, settings and utils
27	"adult wallpapers"	543	**wallpapers** (51%), share, kids and bodies
28	"ad wallpapers"	180	**policies and ads** (46%), wallpapers, settings and utils
29	"ringtones and sound"	662	**ringtones and sound** (68%), share, settings and utils
30	"theme wallpapers"	593	**wallpapers** (90%), holidays and religion, share
31	"personalize"	402	**personalize** (86%), share, settings and utils
32	"settings and wallpapers"	251	**settings and utils** (37%), **wallpapers** (37%), personalize

"Size" is the number of applications in the respective cluster. "Most Important Topics" list the three most prevalent topics; most important (>10%) shown in bold. Topics less than 1% not listed.

10.2.6 RESULTING APP CLUSTERS

Table 10.3 shows the list of clusters that CHABADA identifies for the 22,521 apps we analyzed. Each of these 32 clusters contains apps whose descriptions contain similar topics, listed under "Most Important Topics". The percentages reported in the last column represent the weight of specific topics within each cluster.

The clusters we identified are quite different from the *categories* we would find in an app store such as the Google Play Store. Cluster 22 ("advertisements"), for instance, is filled with applications that do nothing but display ads in one way or another; these apps typically promise or provide some user benefit in return. Cluster 16 ("connection") represents all applications that deal with Bluetooth, Wi-Fi, etc.; there is no such category in the Google Play Store. The several "wallpaper" clusters, from adult themes to religion, simply represent the fact that several apps offer very little functionality.

The Official New York Jets app ended up in Cluster 19, together with other applications that are mostly about sports. Table 10.3 lists the clusters of apps related by their descriptions in which we now can search for outliers with respect to their behavior.

10.3 IDENTIFYING ANOMALIES BY APIs

After clustering apps based on similarity of their description topics, CHABADA searches for outliers regarding their actual behavior. Section 10.3.1 shows how CHABADA extracts API features from Android binaries. Section 10.3.2 describes how it filters the APIs to be used as features, and how it weighs APIs according to their importance. Section 10.3.3 describes how CHABADA detects API outliers, while Section 10.3.4 describes how CHABADA can be used as a classifier.

10.3.1 EXTRACTING API USAGE

As discussed in the introduction, CHABADA uses *static* API *usage* as a proxy for behavior. API use is straightforward: while Android bytecode can also be subject to advanced static analysis such as information flow analysis and standard obfuscation techniques that easily thwart any static analysis, API usage has to be explicitly declared; in Android binaries, as in most binaries on other platforms, static API usage is easy to extract. For each Android application, CHABADA extracts the (binary) APK file with *apktool*,[7] and with a *smali* parser extracts all API invocations.

10.3.2 SENSITIVE AND RARE APIs

Using *all* API calls would result in too much information to represent the behavior of an application. Therefore, we focus on a subset of APIs only, namely *sensitive* APIs that are governed by an Android *permission setting.* These APIs access sensitive information (such as the user's picture library, camera, or microphone) or perform sensitive tasks (altering system settings, sending messages, etc.). When installing an app, the user must explicitly *permit* usage of these APIs. For this purpose, each Android app includes a manifest file that lists the permissions the application needs to run. To obtain the set of sensitive APIs, we relied on the work of Felt et al., who identified and used the mapping between

---

[7]https://code.google.com/p/android-apktool.

permissions and Android methods [7]; CHABADA only considers a sensitive API to be used by the app if and only if it is declared in the binary and if its corresponding permission is requested in the manifest file. This allows eliminating API calls that are used within third party libraries, and not used by the application directly.

As an example for such sensitive APIs, consider Table 10.4. These are some of the APIs used by the Official New York Jets app that are governed by a specific permission; through these APIs, the app accesses the GPS status, accesses the WiFi status, sends text messages, and executes arbitrary shell commands. The score of each API method expresses its impact on the overall anomaly score of the app. The anomaly score will be introduced and explained in the next section. Table 10.4 reports the top APIs ordered by anomaly score.

As each permission governs several APIs, going for permissions alone would be too few features to learn from; going for sensitive APIs allows a much more fine-grained characterization of the application behavior. Section 10.4 provides empirical evidence that using APIs as features yields better results than using permissions.

Filtering the APIs by considering only the sensitive ones considerably limits the number of features. In [1] we show that it is possible to identify anomalous apps by using all sensitive APIs as features. However, we noticed that among the sensitive APIs there are some that are not as interesting as others. For instance, Internet access is governed by the "INTERNET" permission, and consequently any API requiring this permission should be considered as a sensitive one. However, most apps access the Internet, so accessing the Internet is not an important feature for an application, since it has no discriminating power. On the contrary, sending text messages (governed by the "SEND-SMS" permission) is not a common feature among Android apps, and should thus be considered more than others. The cluster context, however, must be taken into account, since wallpaper applications, for instance, do not often use Internet connection, and consequently this could be a discriminating feature.

Removing common features would be too aggressive. Instead, we employ feature ranking based on statistical analysis. We then use different weights either to emphasize or diminish a particular feature. Our strategy is similar to IDF (inverse document frequency) [8], which is a part of the TF-IDF measure, well known in information retrieval. It is intended to reflect how important a word is to a document in a collection of documents (typically referred to as corpus).

Table 10.4 Filtered APIs Used in *Official New York Jets* that Make this App an Outlier in its Cluster

com.yinzcam.nfl.jets	Anomaly Score 10,920.1
Feature importance:	
android.location.LocationManager.addGpsStatusListener()	2900.00
android.net.wifi.WifiManager.pingSupplicant()	2900.00
android.net.wifi.WifiManager.setWifiEnabled()	1452.51
android.telephony.SmsManager.sendTextMessage()	1162.01
java.lang.Runtime.exec()	970.02
Each application is associated to an anomaly score, which is explained in Section 10.3.	

Accordingly, we define *weights* with the following formula:

$$W_a = \log \frac{N}{\mathrm{df}_a}.$$

The weight W_a of an API a is obtained by dividing the total number of applications (N) in a cluster by the number of applications df_a calling the API a and then taking the logarithm of that quotient. Thus, the weight of a rare API is high, whereas the weight of a common API is likely to be low.

Section 10.4 provides empirical evaluation that using IDF helps CHABADA identify the important features for anomaly detection.

10.3.3 DISTANCE-BASED OUTLIER DETECTION

Now that we have all API features for all apps, the next step is to identify *outliers*—i.e., those applications whose API usage would be abnormal within their respective topic cluster. Since we have no notion about an underlying generating model for our data, it is reasonable to utilize a non-parametric approach to identify these outliers. Namely, we changed CHABADA such that it uses a distance-based technique [9], i.e., it uses the distance of an app to the other apps within the same cluster as a measure of anomaly. Distance-based approaches can identify outliers according to different definitions:

1. Outliers are those elements with fewer than k neighbors, where a neighbor is an element that is within a maximum specified distance [9].
2. Outliers are those elements whose distance to their respective k-th nearest neighbor is highest. This is what is usually referred as the k-Nearest Neighbors (k-NN) algorithm [10].
3. Outliers are those elements whose average distance to their respective k nearest neighbors is highest [11].

CHABADA uses *Orca*, an open source framework that implements distance-based outlier detection [12]. The distance function of Orca computes the Euclidean distance of two apps in the feature space (i.e., the APIs). The first definition of outliers requires specifying the maximum neighborhood, and does not provide ranking scores for the outliers. The second definition does not take into account the local density of samples. Thus, CHABADA identifies anomalies by considering the average distance of an element, i.e., an app in the cluster, to the k nearest neighbors. The idea is that if there are other samples that are close to the candidate in the feature space, then the sample is probably not an outlier. We use 5 as the value for k, since this number offers a good trade-off between two extremes: a small value for k would be too sensitive to noise, and would therefore miss many outliers; on the other hand, a high value for k would regard almost any app as an outlier.

CHABADA uses the average distance to the 5 closest neighbors as the "anomaly" score of each app in the cluster, and it ranks the apps according to this score. The higher the score, the more anomalous the behavior of an app is. Some apps may be flagged as anomalies because they use few APIs that are never (or seldomly) used in the cluster. Others may be considered anomalies because they use combinations of APIs that do not occur frequently. Table 10.4 shows the anomaly score for the *Official New York Jets* app, and shows the features with the highest values, i.e., the APIs that have the highest impact on the final anomaly score.

By virtue of this distance-based technique, CHABADA can assign an anomaly score to each app within each cluster. However, these anomalies are meant to be manually evaluated, and it is therefore critical to select a *cut-off* value. Apps whose anomaly score is above this cut-off value would be reported as anomalies, and the ones below this value would be considered normal. It is non-trivial to select a cut-off value, as it strongly depends on the data. An easy solution would be to report as outliers a certain fraction of the data, namely the apps with the highest score. An alternative common approach would be to use quartile statistics.

The potential outliers here would be those apps whose score exceeds the third quartile by more than 1.5 times the *interquartile range* (third quartile minus first quartile). This is one of the standard measures for identifying outliers in a dataset.

Within various clusters the anomaly scores differ widely in their their range, contrast, as well as in their meaning, and unfortunately this makes it difficult to interpret and compare the results. In many cases, an identical outlier score in two different clusters can denote substantially different degrees of outlierness, depending on different local data distributions. Simple normalization for k-NN does not result in good contrast between outliers and inlier scores, since it just scales data onto the range $[0, 1]$. A solution to this problem is to represent values as a *probability* of an application of being an outlier.

Following the approach proposed by Kriegel et al. [13] CHABADA transforms the anomaly scores into probabilities using *Gaussian Scaling*.

Without drawing any assumptions on the distribution of the data, we can suppose, according to the central limit theorem, that the computed anomaly scores have normal distribution. Given the sample mean μ and the sample standard deviation σ of the set of anomaly scores S, we can use its cumulative distribution function and the "Gaussian error function" *erf()* to turn the anomaly score into a probability value:

$$P(s) = \max\left\{0, erf\left(\frac{s - \mu}{\sqrt{2} \cdot \sigma}\right)\right\}.$$

All applications with non-zero probability are reported by CHABADA as outliers.

10.3.4 CHABADA AS A MALWARE DETECTOR

CHABADA can also be used to detect malware. For this task we use *One-Class Support Vector Machine learning* (OC-SVM) [14], which is an unsupervised machine learning technique to learn the features of *one class* of elements. The learned model can then be used to evaluate new apps, and the classifier can decide whether they are similar or different to the training set. Note that this is in contrast to the more common usage of support vector machines as classifiers, where each app additionally has to be *labeled* as belonging to a specific class—say, "benign" vs. "malicious"—during training.

OC-SVMs have been successfully applied in various contexts that span from document classification [15] to automatic detection of anomalous Windows registry access [16]. In our context, the interesting feature of OC-SVM is that one can provide only samples of one class (say, of regular benign applications), and the classifier will be able to identify samples belonging to the same class, tagging the others as malware. OC-SVMs, therefore, are mainly used in those cases in which there exist many samples of one class of elements (e.g., benign applications), and not many samples of other classes (e.g., malicious applications).

The OC-SVM algorithm first projects input data into a high dimensional feature space via an appropriate kernel function, and considers the origin as the only sample different from the training data.

It then identifies the maximal margin on the hyperplane that best separates the training data from the origin. The kernel mapping is necessary since usually data in the initial feature space are not separable via linear hyperplane division.

A training dataset containing anomalies would not result in a good model, since outliers could significantly influence the decision boundary of a OC-SVM. With the filtered APIs as features (as described in Section 10.3.2), CHABADA first identifies outliers, as described in Section 10.3.3, and then trains a OC-SVM within each cluster with the subset of the applications that were not tagged as outliers. Thus, the obtained model represents the APIs that are commonly used by the applications in that cluster. The resulting cluster-specific models are then used to classify new apps, which can be benign, and thus expected to have features that are similar to the trained model, or malicious, and thus expected to differ. Our OC-SVM uses a radial-bases-function (Gaussian) kernel, which is the most commonly used for OC-SVM. It has been shown that for this type of classification it performs better than other kernels (e.g., linear or polynomial) [17], which was confirmed by our experiments.

The Gaussian kernel size, which represents how tight the boundary should fit over the training data, has to be manually specified. It is essential to properly select this parameter, as it highly influences the performance of the classifier. Values that are too small will lead to overfitting, while a larger value of the kernel size will give a smoother decision surface and more regular decision boundary.

Selecting the kernel size of OC-SVM remains an open problem. In CHABADA we used the default kernel size value, as proposed by Schölkopf [18], which is equal to the inverse of the feature space dimension. Using the default kernel size, however, does not take into account the arrangement of data, and it is therefore not optimal. According to Caputo et al. [19], the optimal value of the inverse kernel size γ lies between the 0.1 and 0.9 quantile of the statistics involving distance from training samples to their center point. We thus now set γ to the mean of quantiles of this range, and this significantly improves the results, as we will show in the evaluation.

Section 10.4 shows how γ influences the classification ability of CHABADA.

10.4 EVALUATION

To evaluate the effectiveness of CHABADA, we investigated the following main research questions:

RQ1 *Can CHABADA effectively identify anomalies (i.e., mismatches between description and behavior) in Android applications?* For this purpose, we visualized how often anomalies occur in each cluster, and we manually analyzed the top anomalies (Section 10.4.1).

RQ2 *Are sensitive and rare APIs the appropriate features to detect anomalies?* We compare the results obtained with the sensitive and rare set of APIs, as described in Section 10.3.2, against different sets of features (Section 10.4.2).

RQ3 *Can CHABADA be used to identify malicious Android applications, and how does the improved technique compare to [1]?* For this purpose, we included in our test set of applications a set of known malware, and we ran OC-SVM as a classifier. We show how the improvements proposed in this paper lead to more accurate results (Section 10.4.3).

10.4.1 RQ1: ANOMALY DETECTION

To identify anomalies (i.e., mismatches between description and behavior) in Android applications, we ran CHABADA on all 32 clusters, as described in Section 10.3.

The best way to evaluate whether the outliers that CHABADA identifies are indeed anomalous applications is via manual evaluation. We did this in our conference paper [1], and we found similar results using the new outlier detection mechanism described in Section 10.3. Outliers fall into the following categories: (1) spyware applications, which mainly collect sensitive information about the user by means of third party advertisement libraries; (2) very unusual applications, i.e., applications that, although benign, behave differently from other similar applications; and (3) benign applications that were assigned to the wrong topic cluster, and thus behave differently from other applications in the cluster. The third category shows that we should improve the first step of the CHABADA approach (Section 10.2), but the other two categories show that the outliers reported by CHABADA indeed have suspicious behavior and should therefore be further analyzed. We give a few example applications that appeared as top outliers in the corresponding clusters. We list the cluster number, as reported in Table 10.3, the package identified of the application, the anomaly score, a brief description (which is a one line summary of the original one), the list of the top anomalous features, and a brief comment:

7th cluster (language): com.edicon.video.free Score: 29112.7
All-In-One multi language video player.

android.media.AudioManager.stopBluetoothSco()	3025.00
android.media.AudioManager.startBluetoothSco()	3025.00
android.media.AudioManager.setBluetoothScoOn(boolean)	3025.00
android.media.AudioManager.isWiredHeadsetOn()	3025.00
android.media.AudioManager.isBluetoothA2dpOn()	3025.00
android.bluetooth.BluetoothAdapter.getState()	3025.00
android.bluetooth.BluetoothAdapter.enable()	3025.00

The app has been associated with the "language" cluster because the description emphasizes the multi-language support. The main reason why this app was tagged as an outlier is because of the heavy bluetooth support, which is highly uncommon both for video and for language applications. The bluetooth connection is likely required to support external headsets.

10th cluster (sports game): com.mobage.ww.a987.PocketPlanes.Android Score: 21765.2
Flight simulator.

android.provider.Contacts.People.createPersonInMyContactsGroup(ContentResolver, ContentValues)	6595.00
android.provider.ContactsContract.RawContacts.getContactLookupUri (android.content.ContentResolver,android.net.Uri)	6595.00
android.provider.ContactsContract.Contacts.getLookupUri (android.content.ContentResolver, android.net.Uri)	6595.00
android.app.NotificationManager.notify(java.lang.String, int, android.app.Notification)	661.00
android.app.ActivityManager.getRunningTasks(int)	249.17
android.hardware.Camera.open()	191.33
android.location.LocationManager.getProvider(java.lang.String)	149.50

This application shows suspicious behavior. It can access the list of existing contacts, and it can add a new one. Moreover, it can look at what tasks are currently running, and it can access the photo camera.

22nd cluster (advertisements): com.em.lwp.strippergirl Score: 3799.35
Erotic wallpaper.

android.provider.Browser.getAllBookmarks(android.content.ContentResolver)	1900.00
android.location.LocationManager.getLastKnownLocation(java.lang.String)	952.51
android.location.LocationManager.isProviderEnabled(java.lang.String)	275.79
android.location.LocationManager.requestLocationUpdates(java.lang.String)	241.97
android.location.LocationManager.getBestProvider(android.location.Criteria, boolean)	241.97
android.net.wifi.WifiManager.isWifiEnabled()	65.23
android.net.wifi.WifiManager.getConnectionInfo()	65.23

This application is clearly spyware, since it can access sensitive information of the user, such as the browser bookmarks and the location. This app has been removed from the play store.

In addition to a qualitative analysis of the results, we tried to estimate the ability of CHABADA to detect anomalies by plotting the anomaly scores of the outliers of each cluster. Intuitively, a good result would be to have few outliers with high anomaly scores within each cluster. A worse result, instead, would be to have lots of outliers whose anomaly score is not too high. In the second case, in fact, it would mean that there is no clear border between the outliers and the normal applications. Figure 10.3 shows such a plot. We report the anomaly scores (on the y axis) of all the apps grouped per cluster (on the x axis) scaled such that all clusters have the same width, in order to ease the comparison. The cluster ids correspond to the ones listed in Table 10.3).

As expected, the results vary depending on the cluster. There are clusters in which the outliers are clear anomalies, e.g., Cluster 5 or 29, and others for which there are lots of outliers with high anomaly

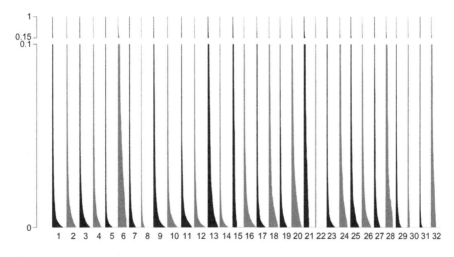

FIGURE 10.3

Apps grouped per cluster (*x* axis) according to their normalized anomaly score (*y* axis).

scores, e.g., Cluster 6 and 20. When clusters have too many outliers, they lack a proper model of "normal" behavior, and as a consequence our technique might be less effective in such clusters.

10.4.2 RQ2: FEATURE SELECTION

Section 10.3.2 describes how we select the list of features to detect anomalous applications within a cluster. In [1] we considered the sensitive API usage as binary features (i.e., 1 if the app used the API at least once; 0 otherwise), while we now use IDF to weigh APIs. To evaluate whether the feature selection is reasonable, we ran the anomaly detection process on each cluster with three different sets of features:

1. We considered binary values for sensitive API usage. These are the features used in our conference paper [1]. We refer to this setting as *api-binary*.
2. We weighed sensitive API according to IDF. This is, in our opinion, the optimal set. We refer to this setting as *api-idf*.
3. We used permissions instead of APIs, and we weighed permissions with IDF. With this, we wanted to evaluate whether using permissions could be considered a valid alternative to using APIs. We refer to this setting as *permission-idf*.

Comparing different settings is non-trivial, as it would require an extensive manual inspection. We instead visually compare the distance-based plots of several clusters. Figure 10.4 shows the plots of Cluster 29, which is one of the clusters for which we have better results. From left to right, the plots show the three different settings described above: *api-binary, api-idf, and permission-idf*.

We used multi-dimensional scaling, which is a statistical technique used to visualize dissimilarity of multi-dimensional data. This allowed us to plot data in two dimensions, and at the same time preserve the original distances in the multi-dimensional space as accurately as possible [20].

As we can see, by using permissions or APIs with IDF it is possible to differentiate the anomalies better, since the distance between the outliers and the rest of the cluster is emphasized. However, between the two options it is better to use APIs instead of permissions. In the next section we provide more evidence that using IDF can lead to better results.

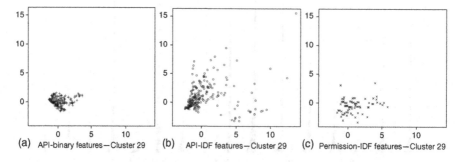

(a) API-binary features—Cluster 29 (b) API-IDF features—Cluster 29 (c) Permission-IDF features—Cluster 29

FIGURE 10.4

Plots of the distances among apps in Cluster 29. From left to right, these plots show the distance between apps when using *api-binary* features, as in [1], *api-idf*, as described in Section 10.3.2, and *permission-idf*.

10.4.3 **RQ3: MALWARE DETECTION**

Let us now turn to RQ3: *Can CHABADA be used to identify malicious Android applications? And do the improvements proposed in this paper lead to better results than the ones presented in [1]?* For this purpose, we used the dataset of Zhou et al. [21] that contains more than 1200 known malicious apps for Android. This is the same dataset we used in the original CHABADA paper [1]. In their raw form, these apps lack metadata such as title or description. Since many of these apps are repackaged versions of original apps, we were able to collect the appropriate description from the Google Play Store. We used the title of the application and the package identifier to search for the right match in the store. For 72 cases we could find exactly the same package identifier, and for 116 applications we found applications whose package identifiers were very similar. We manually checked that the match was correct. As with our original set of "benign" apps (Section 10.2.1), we only kept those applications with an English description in the set, reducing it to 172 apps.

As a malware detector, we used the OC-SVM classifier, as described in Section 10.3.4. Within each cluster, we trained the model using only the applications that were not tagged as outliers by the distance-based algorithm. Following K-fold validation, we partitioned the entire set of non-outlier benign applications in 10 subsets, and we used 9 subsets for training the model and 1 for testing. We then included the malicious applications in the test set, and we ran this 10 times, each time considering a different subset for testing. What we thus simulated is a situation in which the *malware attack is entirely novel*, and CHABADA must correctly identify the malware as such without knowing previous malware patterns. The number of malicious applications are *not* equally distributed across clusters, as malicious applications are assigned to clusters depending on their descriptions. In our evaluation setting, with our dataset, the number of malicious applications per cluster spans from 0 to 39.

To evaluate the performance of a classifier we use the standard approach of the Receiver Operating Characteristic (ROC) [22]. A ROC curve depicts the relative trade-offs between benefits (true positives) and costs (false positives). Figure 10.5 shows the results of our experiments in the form of this ROC curve, which plots the true positives rate against the false positives rate considering different thresholds.

Figure 10.5 shows the ROC curves of the worst and best clusters (Cluster 16 and 7, respectively), and the average performance on all clusters. To obtain these numbers, we computed the average over 10 different runs. We also report the Area Under the ROC curve (AUC) [22] metric, which can expose the predictive accuracy obtained by the classifier. When the AUC is equal to 1.0, the classification was perfect, while an area of 0.5 represents a worthless test. CHABADA as a classifier has a very good performance, as the AUC is 0.87 for the considered dataset, and thus we can claim that it is effective at detecting malware, reporting only limited false positives.

In our first paper, CHABADA used the set of sensitive Android APIs as binary features. Moreover, we did not filter anomalous applications when training the model for classification, and we used the default (and therefore not optimal) values for the kernel size and marginal error for OC-SVM. Section 10.3 described all the improvements we implemented in the new release of CHABADA. To evaluate the effectiveness of our technique as a malware detector, we evaluate how such improvements impact the final result.

Table 10.5 shows the detailed results of the evaluation considering different parameters. The first column (*Filter*) lists whether malware detection ran on filtered data. The + sign means that we ran the anomaly detection first, and we removed the outliers from the training set. The − sign means that we considered all the applications, as we did in [1]. The second column lists whether the γ parameter of

Table 10.5 Evaluation of the Malware Detection Ability of CHABADA with Different Settings

Filter	γ	ν	True Positive Rate (Malware Recognized as such)		True Negative Rate (Benignware Recognized as such)		Geometric Accuracy	
			IDF	Binary	IDF	Binary	IDF	Binary
-	Default	0.15	0.610	0.564	0.845	0.841	0.718	0.689
-	Optimal	0.05	0.592	0.484	0.889	0.915	0.726	0.666
-	Optimal	0.1	0.609	0.539	0.870	0.869	0.728	0.684
+	Default	0.02	0.633	0.535	0.962	0.96	0.780	0.716
+	Default	0.1	0.726	0.637	0.890	0.885	0.804	0.750
+	Optimal	0.02	0.737	0.695	0.890	0.902	0.810	0.791
+	Optimal	0.05	0.738	0.752	0.884	0.887	0.808	0.791
+	Optimal	0.1	0.752	0.738	0.850	0.856	0.799	0.795
+	Optimal	0.15	0.810	0.771	0.814	0.813	0.812	0.792

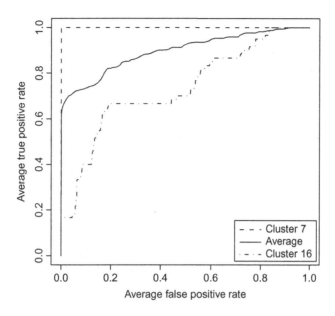

FIGURE 10.5

ROC curves, representing the fraction of true positives out of the total actual positives vs. the fraction of false positives out of the total actual negatives. We report the average performance of the classifier across all clusters, for which the Area Under Curve (AUC) is equal to 0.87. We also plot the performance for the worst (Cluster 16) and best clusters (Cluster 7).

OC-SVM was automatically selected to have optimal results, or whether the default value was selected, as in [1]. γ is related to the kernel size, as explained in Section 10.3.3. The third column lists the value assigned to the v parameter, which can be specified in OC-SVM. The parameter v is an upper bound on the fraction of margin errors in training data and a lower bound of the fraction of support vectors relative to the total number of training examples. Assigning a small value to v will produce less false positives and likely more false negatives, while assigning greater values to v would have the opposite effects. In [1] we used the default value. The last six columns report the results obtained with the corresponding settings using APIs as binary features (as in [1]) or weighing them using IDF (as explained in Section 10.3.2). We report the True Positive Rate (TPR) (i.e., the fraction of malicious Android apps that were recognized as such), the True Negative Rate (TNR) (i.e., the fraction of benign Android apps that were recognized as such), and the geometric accuracy. We report the geometric accuracy because we have highly unbalanced datasets (malicious vs. benign applications) and therefore common accuracy metrics would have distorting effects [23]. The geometric accuracy can be computed with the following formula:

$$g = \sqrt{TPR \times TNR}.$$

Just as we did for the plot in Figure 10.5, we report the average values of 10 runs. The first highlighted row reports the results and the setting used in the original CHABADA paper. This, in essence, represents the baseline for our malware detector. This row also reports how only applying IDF to the used features would have changed the results. As highlighted in bold, without any of the improvements we described in this paper we could detect 56.4% of malware and 84.1% of benignware.

The other two highlighted rows in Table 10.5 show the results of the using the improvements described in this paper. In essence, we propose two possible settings, which both achieve an **accuracy of over 79%** (instead of 69% as in [1]). Using a small ν value would report a limited number of false positives (**11%**), and at the same time would detect a high number of malicious apps (**73.7%**). Using a bigger ν value, instead, would increase the number of detected malicious apps up to **81%**, but at the cost of reporting more false positives (**19%**).

> *With the improvements proposed in this paper,* CHABADA *correctly recognizes 73.7% of malware as such, only 11% of false positives.*

The results in Table 10.5 clearly highlight the following facts:

- Training the OC-SVM model without the identified outliers clearly improves the classifier results. This is obvious, as removing outliers helps create a model that better represents the core features of the cluster.
- Tuning the γ value, which relates to the kernel size of the OC-SVM model, can also lead to significantly better results.
- Assigning weights to APIs with IDF produces consistently better results than using APIs as binary features.

Thus, the three main improvements we propose in this paper (filtering outliers, optimal selection of the OC-SVM kernel size, and using IDF to assign weights to APIs) can produce results that are significantly better than the ones we presented in [1].

Choosing parameter ν is a matter of taste, as it depends on whether it is more important to have as little false positives as possible (and consequently choose a smaller value for ν) or to have as little false negatives as possible (and consequently choose a higher value for ν). In this context it is probably better to detect as many malicious applications as possible, and consequently a higher value of ν should be chosen (last highlighted row in Table 10.5). However, if it is desirable to lower the number of false positives, a lower value of ν can be selected and still have comparable effectiveness (second highlighted row in Table 10.5). This trade-off can be tuned using the ROC curve of Figure 10.5.

10.4.4 LIMITATIONS AND THREATS TO VALIDITY

We inherit most of the limitations of the original CHABADA paper, and we include a new one that comes with the filtering phase. The most important threats and limitations are listed below.

Grey area in classification. Filtering outliers when building the model to classify new applications leads to significant improvements in malware detection. The consequence of this gain, however, is that the outlier apps that are filtered out in first place cannot be classified. More precisely, these apps are reported in a "grey area," i.e., they are suspicious since they are not part of the majority of the apps in the same cluster, but CHABADA does not report them as clearly malicious.

External validity. CHABADA relies on establishing a relationship between description topics and program features from existing, assumed mostly benign, applications. We cannot claim that these relationships can be applied in other app ecosystems, or be transferable to these. We have documented our steps to allow easy replication of our approach.

Free apps only. Our sample of 22,521 apps is based on free applications only; i.e., applications that need to generate income through ads, purchases, or donations. Not considering paid applications makes our dataset biased. However, the bias would shift "normality" more toward apps supported by ads and other income methods, which are closer to the undesired behavior of malware. Our results thus are conservative and would be improved through a greater fraction of paid applications, which can be expected to be benign.

App and malware bias. Our sample also only reflects the top 150 downloads from each category in the Google Play Store. This sample is biased toward frequently used applications and toward lesser used categories; likewise, our selection of malware (Section 10.4) may or may not be representative of current threats. Not knowing which actual apps are being used, and how, by Android users, these samples may be biased. Again, we allow for easy reproduction of our approach.

Native code and obfuscation. We limit our analyses to the Dalvik bytecode. We do not analyze native code. Hence, an application might rely on native code or use obfuscation to perform covert behavior, but such features may again characterize outliers. Further, neither of these would change the set of APIs that must be called.

Static analysis. As we rely on static API usage, we suffer from limitations that are typical for static analysis. In particular, we may miss behavior induced through *reflection,* i.e., code generated at runtime. Although there exist techniques to statically analyze Java code using reflection, such techniques are not directly applicable with Android apps [24]; in the long run, dynamic analysis paired with test generation may be a better option.

Static API declarations. Since we extract API calls statically, we may consider API calls that are never executed by the app. Checking statically whether an API is reached is an instance of the (undecidable) halting problem. As a workaround, we decided to consider an API only if the corresponding permission is also declared in the manifest.

Sensitive APIs. Our detection of sensitive APIs (Section 10.3.2) relies on the mapping by Felt et al. [7], which now, two years later, may be partially outdated. Incorrect or missing entries in the mapping would make CHABADA miss or misclassify relevant behavior of the app.

10.5 **RELATED WORK**

While this work may be the first to generally check app descriptions against app behavior, it builds on a history of previous work combining natural language processing and software development.

10.5.1 **MINING APP DESCRIPTIONS**

Most related to our work is the AsDroid prototype, which can detect malicious behavior by identifying mismatches between the program behavior and the user interface [25]. CHABADA and AsDroid share the same final intent, but AsDroid checks the text in GUI components, while we use the program description. Since AsDroid focuses on few permissions and works only if the GUI elements contain textual keywords. CHABADA, on the other hand, uses the application description, which is always available, and works with any permission or API call.

Also very related to our work is the WHYPER framework of Pandita et al. [26]. Just like our approach, WHYPER attempts to automate the risk assessment of Android apps and applies natural language processing to app descriptions. The aim of WHYPER is to tell whether the need for *sensitive permissions* (such as access to contacts or calendar) is given in the application description. In contrast to CHABADA, which fully automatically learns which topics are associated with which APIs (and by extension, which permissions), WHYPER requires manual annotation of sentences describing the need for permissions. Further, CHABADA goes beyond permissions in two ways: first, it focuses on APIs, which provide a more detailed view, and it also aims for general mismatches between expectations and implementations.

The very idea of app store mining was introduced in 2012 when Harman et al. mined the Blackberry app store [27]. They focused on app meta-data to find correlation patterns in consumer rating and rank of app downloads, but did not download or analyze the apps themselves.

Our characterization of "normal" behavior comes from mining related applications; in general, we assume that what most applications in a well-maintained store do is also what most users would expect them to. In contrast, recent work by Lin et al. [28] suggests *crowdsourcing* to infer what users expect from specific privacy settings; just like we found, Lin et al. also highlight that privacy expectations vary between app categories. Such information from users can well complement what we infer from app descriptions.

10.5.2 BEHAVIOR/DESCRIPTION MISMATCHES

Our approach is also related to techniques that apply natural language processing to infer specifications from comments and documentation. Lin Tan et al. [29] extract implicit program rules from the program Corpora and use these rules to automatically detect inconsistencies between comments and source code, indicating either bugs or bad comments. Rules apply to ordering and nesting of calls and resource access ("f_a must not be called from f_b").

Høst and Østvold [30] learn from Corpora which verbs and phrases would normally be associated with specific method calls and use these to identify misnamed methods.

Pandita et al. [31] identify sentences that describe code contracts from more than 2500 sentences of API documents; these contracts can be checked either through tests or static analysis.

All these approaches compare program code against formal program documentation, whose semi-formal nature makes it easier to extract requirements. In contrast, CHABADA works on end-user documentation, which is decoupled from the program structure.

10.5.3 DETECTING MALICIOUS APPS

There is a large body of industrial products and research prototypes that focus on identifying known malicious behavior. Most influential on our work was the paper by Zhou and Jiang [21], who use the permissions requested by applications as a filter to identify potentially malicious applications; the actual detection uses static analysis to compare sequences of API calls against those of *known* malware. In contrast to all these approaches, CHABADA identifies outliers even without knowing what makes malicious behavior.

The TAINTDROID system [32] tracks dynamic information flow within Android apps and thus can detect usages of sensitive information. Using such dynamic flow information would yield far more precise behavior insights than static API usage; similarly, profilers such as ProfileDroid [33] would provide better information. However, both TAINTDROID and ProfileDroid require a representative set of executions. Integrating such techniques in CHABADA, combined with automated test generation [34–37], would allow learning normal and abnormal patterns of information flow, which is part of our future work (Section 10.6).

10.6 CONCLUSION AND FUTURE WORK

By clustering apps according to description topics and identifying outliers by API usage within each cluster, our CHABADA approach effectively identifies applications whose behavior would be unexpected given their description. In [1] we identified several examples of false and misleading advertising; and as a side effect, obtained a novel effective detector for yet unknown malware. This chapter presented several improvements on the original technique and thus introduces a more powerful malware detector.

In the future we plan to provide better techniques to cluster applications according to their descriptions. This should improve the ability of CHABADA to identify relevant abnormal behaviors. Furthermore, we plan to integrate dynamic information in the approach, thus overcoming the known limitations of static analysis.

The dataset we used for our evaluation, as well as a list of more detailed results, are available on the CHABADA website: http://www.st.cs.uni-saarland.de/appmining/chabada/.

ACKNOWLEDGMENTS

This work was funded by the European Research Council (ERC) Advanced Grant "SPECMATE—Specification Mining and Testing."

REFERENCES

[1] Gorla A, Tavecchia I, Gross F, Zeller A. Checking app behavior against app descriptions. In: ACM/IEEE international conference on software engineering (ICSE); 2014. p. 1025–35. doi:10.1145/2568225.2568276.

[2] Manning C, Raghavan P, Schütze H. Introduction to information retrieval. UK: Cambridge University Press; 2008.

[3] Blei DM, Ng AY, Jordan MI. Latent Dirichlet allocation. J Mach Learn Res 2014;3:993–1022.

[4] McCallum AK. Mallet: a machine learning for language toolkit. 2002. URL: http://mallet.cs.umass.edu.

[5] MacQueen JB. Some methods for classification and analysis of multivariate observations. In: Cam LML, Neyman J, editors, Berkeley symposium on mathematical statistics and probability, vol. 1. University of California Press; 1967. p. 281–97.

[6] Rousseeuw P. Silhouettes: a graphical aid to the interpretation and validation of cluster analysis. J Comput Appl Math 1987;20(1):53–65. doi:10.1016/0377-0427(87)90125-7.

[7] Felt AP, Chin E, Hanna S, Song D, Wagner D. Android permissions demystified. In: ACM conference on computer and communications security (CCS). New York, NY, USA: ACM; 2011. p. 627–38. doi:10.1145/2046707.2046779.

[8] Salton G, McGill M. Introduction to modern information retrieval. New York: McGraw-Hill Book Company; 1983.

[9] Knorr EM, Ng RT. Algorithms for mining distance-based outliers in large datasets. In: Proceedings of the 24rd international conference on very large data bases (VLDB). San Francisco, CA: Morgan Kaufmann Publishers Inc.; 1998. p. 392–403.

[10] Ramaswamy S, Rastogi R, Shim K. Efficient algorithms for mining outliers from large data sets. In: Proceedings of the 2000 ACM SIGMOD international conference on management of data (SIGMOD). New York, NY, USA: ACM; 2000. p. 427–38. doi:10.1145/342009.335437.

[11] Angiulli F, Pizzuti C. Fast outlier detection in high dimensional spaces. In: Proceedings of the 6th European conference on principles of data mining and knowledge discovery (PKDD). Berlin: Springer-Verlag; 2002. p. 15–26.

[12] Bay SD, Schwabacher M. Mining distance-based outliers in near linear time with randomization and a simple pruning rule. In: 9th ACM SIGKDD international conference on knowledge discovery and data mining (KDD). New York, NY, USA: ACM; 2003. p. 29–38. doi:10.1145/956750.956758.

[13] Hans-Peter Kriegel ES, Kröger P, Zimek A. Interpreting and unifying outlier scores. In: 11th SIAM international conference on data mining (SDM), SIAM; 2011. p. 13–24. doi:10.1137/1.9781611972818.

[14] Schölkopf B, Platt JC, Shawe-Taylor JC, Smola AJ, Williamson RC. Estimating the support of a high-dimensional distribution. Neural Comput 2001;13(7):1443–71. doi:10.1162/089976601750264965.

[15] Manevitz LM, Yousef M. One-class SVMs for document classification. J Mach Learn Res 2002;2:139–54.

[16] Heller KA, Svore KM, Keromytis AD, Stolfo SJ. One class support vector machines for detecting anomalous windows registry accesses. In: ICDM workshop on data mining for computer security (DMSEC); 2003.

[17] Tax D, Juszczak P. Kernel whitening for one-class classification. In: Lee SW, Verri A, editors, Pattern recognition with support vector machines. Lecture notes in computer science, vol. 2388. Berlin/Heidelberg: Springer; 2002. p. 40–52. doi:10.1007/3-540-45665-1-4.

[18] Schölkopf B, Smola AJ. Learning with kernels: support vector machines, regularization, optimization, and beyond. Cambridge, MA, USA: MIT Press; 2001.

[19] Caputo B, Sim K, Furesjo F, Smola A. Appearance-based object recognition using svms: which kernel should I use? In: NIPS workshop on Statistical methods for computational experiments in visual processing and computer vision; 2002.

[20] Cox T, Cox M. Multidimensional scaling. Boca Raton: Chapman and Hall; 2001.

[21] Zhou Y, Jiang X. Dissecting Android malware: characterization and evolution. In: IEEE symposium on security and privacy (SP). Washington, DC, USA: IEEE Computer Society; 2012. p. 95–109. doi:10.1109/SP.2012.16.

[22] Fawcett T. Introduction to roc analysis. Pattern Recogn Lett 2006;27(8):861–74. doi:10.1016/j.patrec.2005.10.010.

[23] Kubat M, Matwin S. Addressing the curse of imbalanced training sets: one-sided selection. In: Proceedings of the fourteenth international conference on machine learning. San Francisco, CA: Morgan Kaufmann; 1997. p. 179–86.

[24] Bodden E, Sewe A, Sinschek J, Oueslati H, Mezini M. Taming reflection: aiding static analysis in the presence of reflection and custom class loaders. In: ACM/IEEE international conference on software engineering (ICSE). New York, NY, USA: ACM; 2011. p. 241–50. doi:10.1145/1985793.1985827.

[25] Huang J, Zhang X, Tan L, Wang P, Liang B. Asdroid: detecting stelthy behaviors in android applications by user interface and program behavior contradiction. In: ACM/IEEE international conference on software engineering (ICSE); 2014. p. 1036–46. doi:10.1145/2568225.2568301.

[26] Pandita R, Xiao X, Yang W, Enck W, Xie T. WHYPER towards automating risk assessment of mobile applications. In: USENIX Security Symposium; 2013. p. 527–42.

[27] Harman M, Jia Y, Zhang Y. App store mining and analysis: MSR for app stores. In: IEEE working conference on mining software repositories (MSR); 2012. p. 108–11. doi:10.1109/MSR.2012.6224306.

[28] Lin J, Amini S, Hong JI, Sadeh N, Lindqvist J, Zhang J. Expectation and purpose: understanding users' mental models of mobile app privacy through crowdsourcing. In: ACM conference on ubiquitous computing (UbiComp). New York, NY, USA: ACM; 2012. p. 501–10. doi:10.1145/2370216.2370290.

[29] Tan L, Yuan D, Krishna G, Zhou Y. /* iComment: Bugs or bad comments? */. In: ACM SIGOPS symposium on operating systems principles (SOSP); 2007. p. 145–58.

[30] Høst EW, Østvold BM. Debugging method names. In: European conference on object-oriented programming (ECOOP). Berlin: Springer; 2009. p. 294–317.

[31] Pandita R, Xiao X, Zhong H, Xie T, Oney S, Paradkar A. Inferring method specifications from natural language API descriptions. In: ACM/IEEE international conference on software engineering (ICSE); 2012.

[32] Enck W, Gilbert P, Chun BG, Cox LP, Jung J, McDaniel P, et al. TaintDroid: an information-flow tracking system for realtime privacy monitoring on smartphones. In: USENIX conference on operating systems design and implementation (OSDI), USENIX Association; 2010. p. 1–6.

[33] Wei X, Gomez L, Neamtiu I, Faloutsos M. ProfileDroid: multi-layer profiling of Android applications. In: ACM annual international conference on mobile computing and networking (MobiCom). New York, NY, USA: ACM; 2012. p. 137–48. doi:10.1145/2348543.2348563.

[34] Hu C, Neamtiu I. Automating GUI testing for Android applications. In: International workshop on automation of software test (AST). New York, NY, USA: ACM; 2011. p. 77–83. doi:10.1145/1982595.1982612.

[35] Yang W, Prasad MR, Xie T. A grey-box approach for automated GUI-model generation of mobile applications. In: International conference on fundamental approaches to software engineering (FASE). Berlin, Heidelberg: Springer-Verlag; 2013. p. 250–65. doi:10.1007/978-3-642-37057-1_19.

[36] Machiry A, Tahiliani R, Naik M. Dynodroid: an input generation system for Android apps. In: European software engineering conference held jointly with ACM SIGSOFT international symposium on foundations of software engineering (ESEC/FSE). New York, NY, USA: ACM; 2013. p. 224–34. doi:10.1145/2491411.2491450.

[37] Amalfitano D, Fasolino AR, Tramontana P, Carmine SD, Memon AM. Using GUI ripping for automated testing of Android applications. In: IEEE/ACM international conference on automated software engineering (ASE). New York, NY, USA: ACM; 2012. p. 258–61. doi:10.1145/2351676.2351717.

CHANGE COUPLING BETWEEN SOFTWARE ARTIFACTS: LEARNING FROM PAST CHANGES

Gustavo Ansaldi Oliva*, Marco Aurélio Gerosa*

*Software Engineering & Collaborative Systems Research Group (LAPESSC),
University of São Paulo (USP), São Paulo, Brazil**

CHAPTER OUTLINE

11.1 INTRODUCTION

Version control systems store and manage the history and current state of source code and documentation. As early as 1997, Ball and colleagues wrote a paper entitled *"If your version control system could talk…"* [1], in which they observed that these repositories store a great deal of contextual information about software changes. Over the years, researchers have leveraged such information to understand how software systems evolve over time, enabling predictions about their properties.

While mining these repositories, researchers observed an interesting pattern: certain artifacts are frequently committed together. These artifacts are connected to each other from an evolutionary point of view, in the sense that their histories intertwine. We call this connection *change coupling*. We also say that an artifact A is *change coupled* to B if A often co-changes with B. Other names employed in the literature include logical dependencies/coupling, evolutionary dependencies/coupling, and historical dependencies.

Change coupling can be calculated at different abstraction levels. In this chapter, we will focus on file-level change coupling. Analyzing change couplings at this level has two key benefits [2]: first and foremost, it can reveal hidden relationships that are not present in the code itself or in the documentation. For instance, a certain class A might be change coupled to another class B without structurally depending on it. Second, it relies on historical file co-change information only, which can be easily extracted from commit logs. Therefore, it does not require parsing code, making it more lightweight than structural analysis. It is also programming language agnostic, making it flexible and a good candidate to be used in studies that involve many subject systems written in different languages.

Most importantly, recent research has shown that detecting and analyzing change couplings supports a series of software development tasks. Suppose you are a software developer and just made a change to a certain part of a system. What else do you have to change? Based on the idea that artifacts that changed together in the past are bound to change together in the future, researchers leveraged change couplings to help answer this question [3]. Another traditional application regards discovering design flaws [2]. For instance, detecting and visualizing change couplings might reveal artifacts or modules that are being frequently affected by changes made to other parts of the system (encapsulation problem).

This chapter intends to provide researchers and practitioners with an overview of change coupling and its main applications. In Section 11.2, we introduce the concept of change coupling and highlight its key benefits. This will help you familiarize yourself with the topic and understand why it has been adopted so frequently in software engineering empirical studies. In Section 11.3, we present the main change coupling identification approaches, along with their key characteristics. We also link to tools and present code snippets that show how you can extract these couplings from the systems you develop, maintain, or analyze. In Section 11.4, we discuss the current key challenges of accurately identifying change coupling from version control systems. Besides highlighting fertile research areas that call for further exploration, we also provide some practical advice to help you identify change couplings more accurately. We conclude this section by discussing the trade-offs of identifying change coupling from monitored IDEs. In Section 11.5, we present the main applications researchers have discovered by detecting and analyzing change couplings from version control systems. This will provide you with a big picture of how researchers have leveraged these couplings to understand software systems, their evolution, and the developers around it. Finally, in Section 11.6, we draw our conclusions on the topic.

11.2 CHANGE COUPLING

According to Lanza et al. [8], "change coupling is the implicit and evolutionary dependency of two software artifacts that have been observed to frequently change together during the evolution of a software system." This term was introduced in late 2005 by Fluri et al. [4] and Fluri and Gall [5]. It gained more popularity with a book edited by Mens and Demeyer in 2008 called *Software Evolution* [6, 7]. Other studies then started employing it [8, 9]. As mentioned in the introduction, alternative terms found in the literature include logical dependency/coupling [10, 11], evolutionary dependencies/coupling [3, 12], and historical dependencies [13].

In the following, we go deeper into the concept of change coupling. In Section 11.2.1, we discuss the rationale behind change coupling by introducing one of the main forces that makes artifacts co-change. In Section 11.2.2, we highlight some key practical benefits of using change coupling.

11.2.1 WHY DO ARTIFACTS CO-CHANGE?

The ideas underlying the concept of co-changes and change coupling date back to the beginning of the 1990s when Page-Jones introduced the concept of "connascence" [14]. The term connascence is derived from Latin and means "having been born together." The Free Dictionary defines connascence as: (a) the common birth of two or more at the same time, (b) that which is born or produced with another, and (c) the act of growing together. Page-Jones borrowed the term and adapted it to the software engineering context: "connascence exists when two software elements must be changed together in some circumstance in order to preserve software correctness" [15].

Connascence assumes several forms and can be either explicit or implicit. To illustrate this point, consider the following code excerpt[1] written in Java and assume that its first line represents a *software element A* and that its second line represents a *software element B*:

```
String s;                //Element A (single source code line)
s = ''some string'';     //Element B (single source code line)
```

There are (at least) two examples of connascence involving elements A and B. If A is changed to `int s`; then B will have to be changed too. This is called *type connascence*. Instead, if A is changed to `String str`; then B will need to be changed to `str = ''some string''`. This is called *name connascence*. These two forms of connascence are called *explicit*. A popular manifestation of explicit connascence comes in the form of structural dependencies (e.g., methods calls). In turn, as we mentioned before, connascence can also be implicit, such as when a certain class needs to provide some functionality described in a design document.

---

[1] This example is adapted from Page-Jones' book [15].

In general, connascence involving two elements A and B occurs because of two distinct situations:

(a) A depends on B, B depends on A, or both: a classic scenario is when A changes because A structurally depends on B and B is changed, i.e., the change propagates from B to A via a structural dependency (e.g., a method from A calls a method from B). However, this dependency relationship can be less obvious, as in the case where A changes because it structurally depends on B and B structurally depends on C (transitive dependencies). Another less obvious scenario is when A changes because it semantically depends on B.

(b) Both A and B depend on something else: this occurs when A and B have pieces of code with similar functionality (e.g., use the same algorithm) and changing B requires changing A to preserve software correctness. As in the previous case, this can be less obvious. For instance, it can be that A belongs to the presentation layer, B belongs to the infrastructure layer, and both have to change to accommodate a new change (e.g., new requirement) and preserve correctness. In this case, A and B depend on the requirement.

Therefore, artifacts often co-change because of connascence relationships. This is what makes artifacts "logically" connected. Most importantly, the theoretical foundation provided by connascence is a key element that justifies the relevance and usefulness of change couplings.

11.2.2 BENEFITS OF USING CHANGE COUPLING

The use of change coupling in software engineering empirical studies is becoming more frequent every day. There are many reasons that justify this choice. In the following, we highlight some practical key benefits of detecting and analyzing change coupling.

Reveals historical relationships

Change couplings reveal hidden relationships undetectable by structural analysis. This means you may discover a change coupling involving two classes that are not structurally connected. Moreover, you may find change couplings involving artifacts of different kinds. For instance, you may find change couplings from domain classes to configuration files (e.g., XML files or Java .properties files), presentation files (e.g., HTML or JSP files), or build files (e.g., Maven's pom.xml file or Ant's build.xml file). These couplings are just undetectable by static analysis. Just to give a practical example, McIntosh and colleagues used change coupling to evaluate how tight the coupling is between build artifacts and production or test files [16]. Their goal was to study build maintenance effort and answer questions like "are production code changes often accompanied by a build change?"

Lightweight and language-agnostic

Change coupling detection from version control systems (file-level change coupling) is often lightweight, as it relies on co-change information inferred from change-sets. It is also programming-language-agnostic, as it does not involve parsing source code. This makes it a good choice for empirical studies involving several systems written in different languages. Approaches for detecting change couplings are presented in Section 11.3. We note, however, that accurately identifying change couplings is still a challenging task due to noisy data and certain commit practices. These problems are discussed in Section 11.4.

Might be more suitable than structural coupling

Certain empirical studies admit the use of both structural coupling and change coupling. Researchers have shown that using change coupling leads to better results for some specific applications. For instance, Hassan and Holt [17, 18] showed that change couplings were far more effective than structural couplings for predicting change propagation (more details in Section 11.5.1.1). In addition, Cataldo and Herbsleb [19] showed that change couplings were more effective than structural couplings for recovering coordination requirements among developers (more details in Section 11.5.4). An important aspect, however, is that change coupling requires historical data. If you are just starting a project and no historical data is available, then using structural analysis might be the only way out. In fact, a promising research area concerns conceiving hybrid approaches that combine structural analysis with historical data to cope with the dynamics of software development [20].

Relationship with software quality

Researchers have found evidence that change couplings detected from version control systems provide clues about software quality. D'Ambros et al. [8] mined historical data from three open source projects and showed that change couplings correlate with defects extracted from a bug repository. Cataldo et al. [21] reported that the effect of change coupling on fault proneness was complementary and significantly more relevant than the impact of structural coupling in two software projects from different companies. In another study, Cataldo and Nambiar [22] investigated the impact of geographic distribution and technical coupling on the quality of 189 global software development projects. By technical coupling, they mean overall measures of the extent to which artifacts of the system are connected. Their results indicated that the number of change couplings among architectural components were the most significant factor explaining the number of reported defects. Other factors they took into consideration include the number of structural coupling, process maturity, and the number of geographical sites. In Sections 11.5.2 and 11.5.3, we describe visualization techniques and metrics to help manage change couplings and uncover design flaws.

Broad applicability

Besides its relation with software quality, analyzing change couplings is useful for a series of key applications, which include change prediction and change impact analysis (Section 11.5.1), discovery of design flaws and opportunities for refactoring (Section 11.5.2), evaluation of software architecture (Section 11.5.3), and detection of coordination requirements among developers (Section 11.5.4).

11.3 CHANGE COUPLING IDENTIFICATION APPROACHES

Identifying and quantifying change couplings inherently depends on how the artifacts' change history is recovered. Due to practical constraints, change couplings are often detected by parsing and analyzing the logs of version control systems (e.g., CVS, SVN, Git, and Mercurial). In this case, the change history of an artifact (file) is determined based on the commits in which such artifact appears. In most cases, researchers assume that if two artifacts are included in the same commit, then these artifacts co-changed. The more two artifacts are committed together, the more change coupled they become. In older version control systems that do not support atomic commits, such as CVS, some preprocessing is often needed to reconstruct change transactions [23].

In this section, we show how change couplings can be both discovered and quantified from the logs of version control systems. In the following, we present three approaches: raw counting (Section 11.3.1), association rules (Section 11.3.2), and time-series analysis (Section 11.3.3). Given the broad adoption of the first two, we provide code snippets and instructions to help you run them in your projects. All code is available on GitHub at https://github.com/golivax/asd2014.

11.3.1 RAW COUNTING

Several studies identify change couplings using a raw counting approach. In this approach, change-sets are mined from the logs of the version control system and co-change information is stored in a suitable data structure or in a database. A commonly used data structure is an *artifact × artifact* symmetric matrix in which each cell $[i,j]$, with $i \neq j$, stores the number of times that artifact i and artifact j changed together (i.e., appeared in the same commit) over the analyzed period. In turn, cell $[i,i]$ stores the number of times artifact i changed in this same period. We call this a co-change matrix (Figure 11.1).

Once the co-change matrix is built, change couplings can be inferred using the following two strategies:

(a) Non-directed relationship. Every non-zero cell $[i,j]$ out of the main diagonal implies the existence of a change coupling involving artifacts i and j. In this approach, change coupling is regarded as a non-directed relationship, i.e., it is not possible to know if artifact i is coupled to artifact j, if artifact j is coupled to artifact i, or both. In the example from Figure 11.1, the cell $[2, 1] = 3$ implies the existence of a change coupling involving A and B whose strength is 3. That is, coupling strength simply corresponds to the number of times the involved artifacts changed

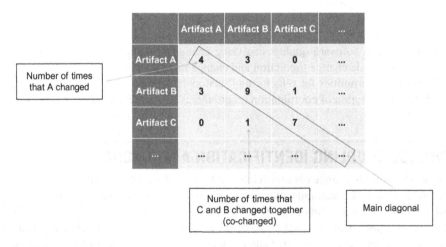

FIGURE 11.1

Hypothetical co-change matrix.

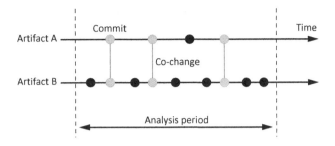

FIGURE 11.2

Scenario for change coupling analysis.

together. The rationale is that pairs of artifacts that co-change more often have a stronger evolutionary connection than those pairs that co-change less often. In the data mining field, this measure is known as *support*.

(b) Directed relationship. This approach is analogous to the previous one with regards to the identification of change couplings. However, this approach assumes that the strength of these couplings can be different. The strength of a change coupling from A to B is determined by the ratio of co-changes (support) and the number of times the artifact B changed. In the example from Figure 11.1, the strength of the change coupling from A to B would be cell[1, 2]/cell[2, 2] = 3/9 = 0.33. In turn, the strength of the change coupling from B to A would be cell[1, 2]/cell[1, 1] = 3/4 = 0.75. Therefore, this approach assumes that the last coupling is much stronger than the first one, since commits that include A often include B as well (Figure 11.2). In the data mining field, this measure is known as *confidence*.

Some of the studies that have employed this identification method include those of Gall et al. [24], Zimmermann et al. [25], and Oliva and Gerosa [26].

Determining relevant couplings

When identifying change couplings via *raw counting with non-directed relationship*, relevant couplings are often filtered by choosing a *support* threshold that is suitable for the study at hands. One approach is to iteratively test different values and qualitatively analyze the output. An alternative approach is to perform a statistical analysis of the distribution of support, such as a quartile analysis (Figure 11.3).

In the scope of a quartile analysis, one approach is to consider that sufficiently relevant couplings have a support value above the third quartile. The third quartile ($Q3$) is the middle value between the median and the highest value of the data, splitting off the highest 25% of data from the lowest 75%. Another approach consists of taking the upper whisker (a.k.a. upper fence) as the threshold. The upper whisker is determined using the following formula: $Q3 + [1, 5^* (IQR)] = Q3 + [1, 5^* (Q3 - Q1)]$. In a quartile analysis, values above the upper whisker are frequently considered as outliers. Therefore, this latter approach is more restrictive than the former, in the sense that only unusually highly evident couplings are selected. An even more restrictive approach would only take extreme outliers, which are those above the threshold given by the following formula: $Q3 + 3^* (IQR)$.

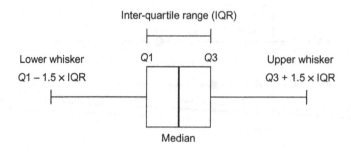

FIGURE 11.3

Schematics of a boxplot.[2]

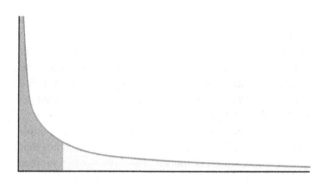

FIGURE 11.4

Power law distribution.[3]

Although the quartile analysis is simple and straightforward, we note that it might not be suitable for some studies, since the support distribution tends to follow a power law (Figure 11.4). This distribution is very right-skewed (long tail to the right) and traditional statistics based on variance and standard deviation often provide biased results. A more cautious approach would be thus to skip the green (left-hand side) part of Figure 11.4, which corresponds to 80% of the data, and stick to the yellow (right-hand side) part, which represents the frequently co-changed artifacts. In any case, researchers should always validate and analyze the output produced by each filtering strategy.

When identifying couplings via *raw counting with non-symmetric strength*, relevant couplings are determined based on paired values of support and confidence. In this mindset, support has been interpreted as a measure of how evident a certain change coupling is, in the sense that couplings

---

[2] Adapted from http://commons.wikimedia.org/wiki/File:Boxplot_vs_PDF.svg (CC Attribution-Share Alike 2.5 Generic).
[3] http://commons.wikimedia.org/wiki/File:Long_tail.svg Picture by Hay Kranen/PD.

supported by many co-changes are more evident than couplings supported by few co-changes [25]. In turn, confidence has been interpreted as a measure of the strength of the coupling. According to Zimmermann and colleagues, confidence actually answers the following question: of all changes to an artifact, how often (as a percentage) was some other specific artifact affected? Therefore, *relevant couplings* have sufficiently high values of support and confidence, i.e., they are simultaneously evident and strong.

A threshold for support is often the first parameter to be determined. As shown before, this can be calculated using different approaches. After having determined the couplings that are sufficiently evident, a confidence threshold is applied to filter those that are also sufficiently strong. The most conservative approach is to iteratively try different values of confidence, analyze the output, and pick the threshold that provides the best results for the study at hand [25]. To that end Zimmermann and colleagues implemented visualization techniques (*pixelmaps* and *3D bar charts*) to help spot coupling with high values of support and confidence (although high ends up being a little bit subjective in this case).

An alternative approach consists of performing a statistical analysis of the confidence distribution (such as a quartile analysis). Another idea is to establish three adjacent intervals for the confidence values [26] as follows:

- Confidence [0.00, 0.33]: low coupling
- Confidence [0.33, 0.66]: regular coupling
- Confidence [0.66, 1.00]: strong coupling

Tools

In this section, we show how to extract change couplings using the raw counting approach. In fact, we focus on how to parse a list of change-sets from either SVN or Git, since this is the most difficult part of the process. In the sections that follow, we show UML diagrams and Java code snippets. A complete implementation is available in GitHub.[4] We emphasize that such an implementation is just a starting point from you can develop more sophisticated or tailored solutions.

(1) Change-Set class

We use a very simple `ChangeSet` class to store the change-set of each commit (Figure 11.5). This class has an attribute called `commitID`, which stores the id of the commit. The other attribute is a set called `changedArtifacts`, which we will use to store the name of the artifacts changed in the associated commit. The class has two constructors: one to handle numeric commit ids (SVN) and another to handle alphanumeric commit ids (Git).

(2) Extracting change-sets from SVN

In order to extract change-sets from the SVN repository, we rely on the SVNKit[5] framework. SVNKit is a Java implementation of SVN, offering an API to work with both local and remote repositories. We use this framework to parse SVN commit logs and extract the change-sets. The class

---

[4]https://github.com/golivax/asd2014.
[5]http://svnkit.com/.

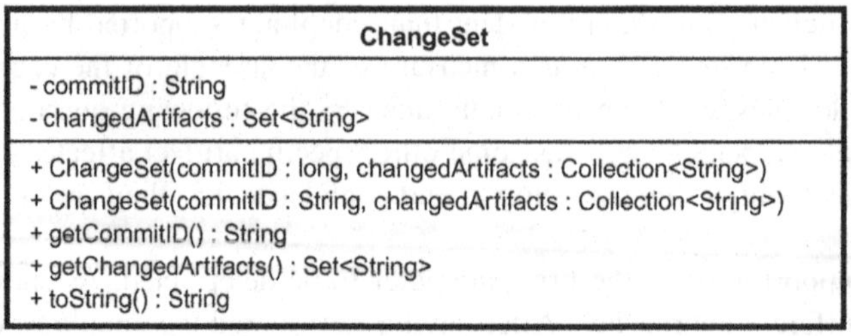

ChangeSet
- commitID : String - changedArtifacts : Set<String>
+ ChangeSet(commitID : long, changedArtifacts : Collection<String>) + ChangeSet(commitID : String, changedArtifacts : Collection<String>) + getCommitID() : String + getChangedArtifacts() : Set<String> + toString() : String

FIGURE 11.5

ChangeSet *class* (/src/main/java/br/usp/ime/lapessc/entity/ChangeSet.java).

/src/main/java/br/usp/ime/lapessc/svnkit/SVNKitExample.java in our GitHub is a complete example that shows how to extract change-sets from SVN.

In the code excerpt that follows, we show how to initialize the repository. It requires the URL of the repository and credentials access (username and password). Most repositories from open source software systems enable read permission with the username "anonymous" with password "anonymous."

```
DAVRepositoryFactory.setup();
try {
    SVNRepository repository = SVNRepositoryFactory.create(
            SVNURL.parseURIEncoded(url));
    ISVNAuthenticationManager authManager =
            SVNWCUtil.createDefaultAuthenticationManager(username, password);
    repository.setAuthenticationManager(authManager);
}catch(SVNException e){
    // Deal with the exception
}
```

After initializing the repository, we are ready to interact with it. The method `log (targetPaths, entries, startRev,endRev,changedPath,strictNode)` from the `SVNRepository` class performs a SVN log operation from `startRev` to `endRev`. The specific meaning of each parameter in this method call is summarized as follows. We refer readers to the SVNKit's documentation[6] for further details about this method.

- `targetPaths`—paths that mean only those revisions at which they were changed

---

[6]http://svnkit.com/javadoc/index.html.

- entries—if not null then this collection will receive log entries
- startRevision—a revision to start from
- endRevision—a revision to end at
- changedPath—if true then revision information will also include all changed paths per revision
- strictNode—if true then copy history (if any) is not to be traversed

This log method outputs a collection of SVNLogEntry, which are the objects that represent commit logs. In the following, we show an example of how to extract the commit id (revision number) and the change-set from each SVNLogEntry instance.

```
Set<ChangeSet> changeSets = new LinkedHashSet<ChangeSet>();
for(SVNLogEntry logEntry : logEntries){
    Map<String,SVNLogEntryPath> changedPathsMap = logEntry.
    getChangedPaths();
    if (!changedPathsMap.isEmpty()) {
        long revision = logEntry.getRevision();
        Set<String> changedPaths = logEntry.getChangedPaths().keySet();
        ChangeSet changeSet = new ChangeSet(revision, changedPaths);
        changeSets.add(changeSet);
    }
}
```

The main() method shown below triggers the mining with five important parameters: repository URL (url), user name (name), password (password), start revision number (startRev), and end revision number (endRev). In this example, we extract the change-sets from an open-source project called Moenia,[7] which is hosted by SourceForge and contains only 123 revisions.

```
public static void main(String[] args) {
        String url = "https://github.com/golivax/JDX.git";
        String cloneDir = "c:/tmp/jdx";
        String startCommit = "ca44b718d43623554e6b890f2895cc80a2a0988f";
        String endCommit = "9379963ac0ded26db6c859f1cc001f4a2f26bed1";
```

---

[7]http://sourceforge.net/projects/moenia/.

```
        JGitExample jGitExample = new JGitExample();
        Set<ChangeSet> changeSets =
            jGitExample.mineChangeSets(url,cloneDir,startCommit,
                endCommit);
        for(ChangeSet changeSet : changeSets){
            System.out.println(changeSet);
        }
    }
```

(3) Extracting change-sets from Git

In order to extract change-sets from Git repositories, we suggest using the JGit[8] framework. JGit is a Java implementation of Git, offering a fluent API to manipulate Git repositories. We use this framework to parse Git commit logs and extract the change-sets. Given the distributed nature of Git, as well as its particular notion of branching, extracting change-sets is a little bit more complicated. A complete example showing how to mine change-sets from Git repositories is available on GitHub.[9]

The first thing we need to do is to clone the Git repository (or open an already cloned repository). The code excerpt below shows how to accomplish this programmatically using the JGit API. In this example, the repository in the URL is cloned to `cloneDir`.

```
//Cloning the repo
Git git = Git.cloneRepository().setURI(url).
    setDirectory(new File(cloneDir)).call();
//To open an existing repo
//this.git = Git.open(new File(cloneDir));
```

After that, we need to decide from which branch we will extract the commits in the range [`startCommitID`, `endCommitID`]. A popular strategy to extract the "main branch" is follow the first parent of every commit. Hence, what we do is start at the `endCommitID` and keep on following the first parent of every commit until the first parent of the `startCommitID` is reached. This is equivalent to the following git command: git log `startCommitID`∧∧ `..endCommitID` –first-parent. The meaning of the –first-parent parameter is as follows (extracted from the Git manual):

–first-parent: Follow only the first-parent commit upon seeing a merge commit. This option can give a better overview when viewing the evolution of a particular topic branch, because

---

[8]http://eclipse.org/jgit.
[9]https://github.com/golivax/asd2014/src/main/java/br/usp/ime/lapessc/jgit.

merges into a topic branch tend to be only about adjusting to updated upstream from time to time, and this option allows you to ignore the individual commits brought in to your history by such a merge.

The method `List<RevCommit> getCommitsInRange(String startCommitID, String endCommitID)` in the `JGitExample` class implements this mining strategy, recovering the following commits:

```
endCommit,firstParent(endCommit),..., startCommit, firstParent(startCommit)
```

Git always determines change-sets by comparing two commits. However, if the chosen start commit happens to be the first commit in the repository, then it has no parent. We treat this special case by determining the artifacts that were *added* in the first commit. The following code excerpt shows how we implemented this algorithm using JGit. Note, however, that we omitted the details of recovering the actual change-sets, as the code is a bit lengthy.

```java
private Set<ChangeSet> extractChangeSets(List<RevCommit> commits) throws
        MissingObjectException, IncorrectObjectTypeException,
        CorruptObjectException, IOException {

    Set<ChangeSet> changeSets = new LinkedHashSet<ChangeSet>();

    for(int i = 0; i < commits.size() - 1; i++){
        RevCommit commit = commits.get(i);
        RevCommit parentCommit = commits.get(i+1);
        ChangeSet changeSet = getChangeSet(commit, parentCommit);
        changeSets.add(changeSet);
    }


    //If startCommit is the first commit in repo, then we
    //need to do something different to get the changeset
    RevCommit startCommit = commits.get(commits.size()-1);
    if(startCommit.getParentCount() == 0){
        ChangeSet changeSet = getChangeSetForFirstCommit(startCommit);
        changeSets.add(changeSet);
    }
```

```
            return changeSets;
        }
```

The `main()` method shown below triggers the `mineChangeSets()` method with four important parameters: remote repository URL (`url`), path to local repository (`cloneDir`), start commit id (`startCommit`), and end commit id (`endCommit`). In this example, we extract the change-set from an open-source project called JDX,[10] hosted on GitHub.

```
public static void main(String[] args) {
    String url = "https://github.com/golivax/JDX.git";
    String cloneDir = "c:/tmp/jdx";
    String startCommit = "ca44b718d43623554e6b890f2895cc80a2a0988f";
    String endCommit = "9379963ac0ded26db6c859f1cc001f4a2f26bed1";

    JGitExample jGitExample = new JGitExample();
    Set<ChangeSet> changeSets =
            jGitExample.mineChangeSets(url,cloneDir,startCommit, endCommit);
    for(ChangeSet changeSet : changeSets){
        System.out.println(changeSet);
    }
}
```

11.3.2 ASSOCIATION RULES

In this section, we present the concepts of *frequent itemsets* and *association rules*, which were introduced in the domain of data mining. To this end, we heavily rely on the reference book from Rajaraman, Leskovec, and Ullman entitled *Mining of Massive Datasets* [27] to introduce some fundamental definitions. Interested readers may want to refer to Chapter 4 of that book for more detailed information. As supplementary material, we also recommend the second chapter of the book from Liu entitled *Web Data Mining: Exploring Hyperlinks, Contents, and Usage Data* [28].

In the field of data mining, a model often referred to as *market-basket* is used to describe a common form of many-to-many relationship between two kinds of objects: *items* and *baskets* (or transactions). Each basket comprises a set of items, also known as an *itemset*. The number of items in a basket is usually assumed to be small, much smaller than the total number of different items available. In turn, the number of baskets is usually assumed to be very large, meaning that it would be not possible to store them all in main memory. A set of items (itemset) that appears in many baskets is said to be

---

[10]https://github.com/golivax/JDX/.

frequent. If I is an itemset, then the *support* for I, written as *support(I)*, indicates the number of baskets for which I is a subset.

Itemsets are often used to build useful if-then rules called *association rules*. An association rule is an implication of the form $I \Rightarrow J$, which states that when I occurs, J is likely to occur. In this context, I and J are two disjoint sets of items (itemsets). I is called the antecedent (left-hand-side or LHS) and J is called the consequent (right-hand-side or RHS). For instance, the rule $\{x, y\} \Rightarrow \{z\}$ found in the sales data of a supermarket would indicate that if a customer buys products x and y together, this same customer is also likely to buy z. If one is looking for association rules $I \Rightarrow J$ that apply to a reasonable fraction of the baskets, then the support for $I \cup J$ must be reasonably high. This value is called the *support of the rule* and is written as $support(I \Rightarrow J) = support(I \cup J)$. It simply corresponds to the number of baskets that contain both I and J. The strength of the rule, in turn, is given by a measure called *confidence*. It defines the fraction of baskets containing I where J also appears. Formally:

$$confidence(I \Rightarrow J) = \frac{support(I \Rightarrow J)}{support(I)} = \frac{support(I \cup J)}{support(I)}$$

As we showed in Section 11.3.1, *support* and *confidence* can be calculated for pairs of items using an exhaustive approach, which consists of determining (i) the number of times each item has changed, as well as (ii) the number of times two artifacts have changed together. The main difference here lies in the application of an algorithm to discover frequent itemsets (from which useful rules are then generated). Most frequent itemset mining algorithms, such as the often used *Apriori* [29], require an itemset support threshold as input. Hence, non-frequent (irrelevant) items are preemptively removed. Furthermore, *Apriori* is more flexible, in the sense that it can discover association rules involving an arbitrary number of items in both the LHS and the RHS.

Researchers have often formalized change couplings as association rules: the version control system (database) stores all commit logs, and each commit log (basket) contains a set of modified files (itemset). A change coupling from a versioned artifact x_2 (client) to another versioned artifact x_1 (supplier) can be written as an association rule $X_1 \Rightarrow X_2$, whose antecedent and consequent are both singletons that contain x_1 and x_2, respectively.

Some of the studies that have employed the association rules identification method include those of Bavota et al. [30], Zimmermann et al. [3, 31], Wang et al. [32], and Ying et al. [33]. The first applies the *Apriori* algorithm. The second and third studies perform adaptations to the original *Apriori* algorithm to speed up the calculation of rules, which often involve constraining antecedents and/or consequents based on some study-specific criteria. The last study uses a different (and more efficient) algorithm called FP-Growth [34], which avoids the step of generating candidate itemsets and testing them against the entire database.

Determining relevant couplings

When formalizing change couplings as association rules, researchers often determine their relevance based on thresholds for support and confidence (input to rule mining algorithms). However, as we showed in Section 11.3.1, determining thresholds from which rules become sufficiently relevant is complicated and depends on the characteristics of the project at hand. For instance, Zimmermann et al. [25] considered relevant those change couplings with support greater than 1 and confidence greater than 0.5. In turn, Bavota et al. [30] considered relevant those couplings that included elements that co-changed in at least 2% of the commits (support/number of commits) and whose confidence scored at least 0.8. According to Zimmermann et al. [3], in practice support against a combination of the average transaction size or the average number of changes per item should be normalized. However, as they pointed out themselves, choosing the right normalization is still research on its own.

Although support and confidence are the most common thresholds to capture relevant change couplings, other approaches do exist. One alternative is to use the *conviction* measure [35]. Given two elements A and B, conviction is $P(A)P(\sim B)/P(A \text{ and } \sim B)$. The implication $A \rightarrow B$ is tautologically equivalent to ($\sim A$ or B), which is in turn equivalent to $\sim(A \text{ and } \sim B)$. The idea is then to measure how far (A and $\sim B$) deviates from independence and invert the ratio to take care of the outside negation. According to Brin et al. [35], "conviction is truly a measure of implication, because it is directional, it is maximal for perfect implications, and it properly takes into account both $P(A)$ and $P(B)$" (as opposed to confidence, which ignores $P(B)$).

Tools

Implementations of the *Apriori*, as well as other frequent pattern mining algorithms, are available in Weka,[11] SPMF,[12] and R[13] (*arules* package[14]). These are all open-source projects licensed under GPL (GNU General Public License). In the following, we show how to extract change couplings using R and the arules package. As in Section 11.3.1, the subject system for this example will be Moenia.

(1) Load the library

The first step is to install and load the arules package into your R session. To load the package, run the following command:

```
library(arules)
```

(2) Read transactions from CSV file

The second step is to read change transactions (change-sets) from a CSV file:

```
trans = read.transactions("moenia.csv", format = "basket", sep = ",")
```

The `read.transactions()` function has three basic parameters. The first points to the CSV file, which is read from the working directory by default. You can execute the `getwd()` function in R to discover the current working directory. The second parameter indicates the format of this CSV. In the

---

[11]http://www.cs.waikato.ac.nz/ml/weka/.
[12]http://www.philippe-fournier-viger.com/spmf/.
[13]http://www.r-project.org/.
[14]http://cran.r-project.org/web/packages/arules/index.html.

basket format, each line in the transaction data file represents a transaction where the items (item labels) are separated by the characters specified bysep (third parameter). More information about this function can be found in the arules package manual.[15]

A CSV in basket format can be built out of a collection of ChangeSet instances very easily. In the following code snippet, we show one possible solution that captures files with the .java extension:

```java
public String toCSV(Set<ChangeSet> changeSets){
    String csv = new String();
    for(ChangeSet changeSet : changeSets){
        String cs = new String();
        for(String artifact : changeSet.getChangedArtifacts()){
            if(artifact.endsWith(".java")){
                cs+=artifact + ",";
            }
        }
        //StringUtils is a class from the Apache Commons Lang library
        cs = StringUtils.removeEnd(cs, ",");
        if(!cs.isEmpty()){
            csv+=cs + "\n";
        }
    }
    return csv;
}
```

(3) Compute rules using Apriori

In the third step, we run the *Apriori* algorithm to compute the association rules. This is done via the apriori() function. The function parameters we will use are as follows:

- transactions: the set of input transactions
- support: a numeric value for the minimal support of an item set (default: 0.1)
- confidence: a numeric value for the minimal confidence of rules (default: 0.8)
- minlen: an integer value for the minimal number of items per item set (default: 1)
- maxlen: an integer value for the maximal number of items per item set (default: 10)

The transactions will be the ones obtained in the following step. The support parameter is defined in relative terms. That is, if we want to find rules whose elements have changed together at least four

---

[15] http://cran.r-project.org/web/packages/arules/arules.pdf.

times, then the parameter should be 4/number of change-sets (i.e., number of lines in the CSV file). Confidence is defined just like we did in this section. Supposing we want to calculate rules with a single antecedent and a single consequent, then minlen and maxlen should be both 2.

If the data set is not too large, we can first obtain all possible rules and then start tweaking the parameters to obtain better rules. To obtain all rules, we use the following trick: set support equal to .Machine$double.eps. This reserved keyword outputs the smallest positive floating-point number the machine can produce. If we had set support equal to zero, then the apriori() function would generate artificial rules (rules with support equal to zero). The complete command is shown below.

```
rules <- apriori(trans, parameter = list(
    support = .Machine$double.eps,
    confidence = 0, minlen = 2, maxlen = 2))
```

(4) Inspect rules, analyze output, and fine-tune parameters

In this last step, we inspect rules, analyze the output, and fine-tune the parameters to obtain both evident and strong change couplings. The following command helps to investigate the rules produced in the prior step:

```
> summary(rules)
set of 10874 rules


rule length distribution (lhs + rhs):sizes
    2
10874

   Min. 1st Qu.  Median   Mean 3rd Qu.    Max.
      2      2       2      2      2       2

summary of quality measures:
    support            confidence            lift
 Min.   :0.01111   Min.   :0.02941   Min.   : 0.8823
 1st Qu.:0.01111   1st Qu.:0.25000   1st Qu.: 5.0000
 Median :0.01111   Median :0.33333   Median : 7.5000
 Mean   :0.01834   Mean   :0.45962   Mean   :12.0304
 3rd Qu.:0.02222   3rd Qu.:0.61538   3rd Qu.:15.0000
 Max.   :0.14444   Max.   :1.00000   Max.   :90.0000
```

Given the distribution of support, we use the extreme outliers approach shown in Section 11.3.1 to restrict the set of produced rules: $Q3 + 3^* \text{ IQR} = 0.02222 + 1.5^*(0.02222 - 0.01111) = 0.038885$. We also take a confidence value of 0.66. Now, we recalculate the rules as follows:

```
rules <- apriori(trans, parameter = list(
    support = 0.038885, confidence = 0.66, minlen = 2, maxlen = 2))
```

Analyzing the produced rules via the summary() command shows that we now have 304 rules. Of course, we could tweak the parameters again to obtain a smaller set of rules. To inspect all rules, we just type the following command:

```
inspect(rules)
```

Here, we should not forget that a certain rule $A_1 \Rightarrow A_2$ indicates that A_2 is impacted by changes to A_1, i.e., A_2 is the client and A_1 is the supplier. Finally, to export those rules to a CSV file, we can use the following command:

```
write(rules, file = "data.csv", sep = ",", col.names = NA)
```

11.3.3 TIME-SERIES ANALYSIS

Time-series representation has been successfully employed in different domains (e.g., image/speech processing and stock-market forecasting) to detect commonly occurring similar phenomena that evolve over time [36]. In fact, since the early days of mining software repositories, time-series analysis and associated metrics have been identified as a key research area in the understanding of how software structures change over time [1]. Time series analysis has emerged as a promising approach to cope with some of the problems found in earlier detection algorithms. According to Canfora et al. [37], "although association rules worked well in many cases, they fail to capture logical coupling relations between artifacts modified in subsequent change-sets."

11.3.3.1 Dynamic time warping

Dynamic time warping (DTW) is a technique introduced by Kruskal and Liberman [38] to find an optimal alignment between two given (time-dependent) sequences under certain restrictions (Figure 11.6). The algorithm warps sequences in a non-linear fashion so that they meet each other. In other words, DTW can distort (warp) the time axis, compressing it in some intervals and expanding it in others [39]. Originally, DTW was used to compare different speech patterns in automatic speech recognition systems [40, 41]. A traditional application consists of determining whether two wave forms represent the same spoken phrase under different pronunciation speed, accent, and pitch [39]. DTW was

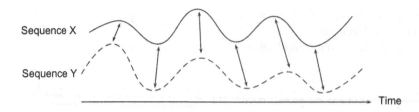

FIGURE 11.6

Time alignment of two time-dependent sequences. Arrows indicate aligned points.[16]

then successfully applied to a number of different domains, including medicine [42], robotics [43], and handwriting recognition [44]. More information about the DTW algorithm can be found in Chapter 4 of the book by Müller [45] entitled "Information Retrieval for Music and Motion."

In the case of change couplings, the set of time instants in which a versioned artifact changes is modeled as a time-series sequence. These sequences are then compared in a pair-wise fashion to determine how well they align. If such sequences align sufficiently well, then it is possible to state that there is a change coupling between the associated artifacts. Some of the studies that employed this identification method include those of Antoniol et al. [39] and Bouktif et al. [46].

Determining relevant couplings

Antoniol et al. [39] compute the DTW distance for every pair of time series in order to detect co-changing files in CSV. Instead of comparing the whole time series, they do it incrementally using windows that include a certain amount of data points (changes). They also do it backwards, i.e., time series starting from the most recent change. File histories with a distance below a certain threshold are considered indistinguishable and belonging to the same history group. In their paper, they experimented from 60 s up to 1200 s in the Mozilla project and showed that threshold values indeed change the number and size of groups (of co-changed files). This threshold can be used to fine-tune sensitivity, since its optimal value is project-dependent. In their paper, they report the results they obtained with threshold values of 270, 600, and 1200 s (4.5, 10, and 20 min, respectively). In a follow-up paper, Bouktif et al. [46] analyzed the change history of a small project called PADL stored in CVS. The authors showed that threshold values between 43,200 s (12 h) and 86,400 s (24 h) were a good compromise between precision and recall. They ended up using the threshold of 86,400 s in their case study, resulting in a minimum average (weighted) precision of 84.8% and recall of 71.8%. To calculate precision and recall, they performed a k-fold cross-validation, by dividing change histories in training and test sets. More details can be obtained in their papers.

Tools

The R statistical tool features a package called dtw[17] that implements the DTW algorithm. Using this package and running the algorithm with the default settings is straightforward, as shown in

---

[16]Extracted as is from Müller [45]—p. 70. Content licensed by Springer. Copyright cleared.
[17]http://dtw.r-forge.r-project.org/.

the package's guide.[18] The FastDTW[19] is a library written in Java that implements a variation of the original DTW algorithm called FastDTW [47]. This variation provides optimal or near-optimal alignments with an $O(N)$ time and memory complexity, in contrast to the $O(N^2)$ requirement of the standard DTW algorithm.

11.3.3.2 Granger causality test

Granger causality is a statistical hypothesis test for determining whether a time-series sequence is useful in forecasting another [48]. In other words, the algorithm tests for predictive causality. Formally, a time series X is said to Granger-cause Y if it can be shown, usually through a series of t-tests and F-tests on lagged values of X (and with lagged values of Y also included), that those X values provide statistically significant information about future values of Y. The basic idea is that the cause cannot come after the effect. Hence, if a variable x affects a variable y, then the former should help improving the predictions of the latter [37].

Ceccarelli et al. [49] used the bivariate Granger causality test to address the issue of detecting change couplings between artifacts that are modified in subsequent change-sets. They model the time series of a versioned artifact f_k as follows. Let $f_k(t)$, $t = 1, \ldots, t$ be the change time series of the versioned artifact f_k defined as:

$$f_k(t) = \begin{cases} 1, & f_k \in \Delta_t, \\ 0, & f_k \notin \Delta_t, \end{cases}$$

i.e., $f_k(t)$ is one if the file f_k was changed in snapshot Δ_t, zero otherwise. The authors found that the number of relevant recommendations provided by the Granger causality test is complementary to those inferred by association rules. In a follow-up study by the same authors [37], they used a slightly more sophisticated model, in which they replaced the binary variable $f_k(t)$ with a continuous variable that accounted for the number of changes that each file underwent during the test period. Their evaluation of four open source systems showed that while association rules provided more precise results, the Granger causality test achieved better results for recall and F-measure. Again, they highlighted that the set of true couplings provided by the two techniques is mostly disjoint.

Determining relevant couplings

The null hypothesis (H_0: file f_1 does not Granger-cause f_2) is rejected based on the calculation of a score S that takes into account the sum of squared residuals. If such score is higher than the 5% critical value for an $F(p,T-2p-1)$ distribution, then the hypothesis is rejected [37]. The set of relevant couplings comprise the top N in the list of versioned artifacts pairs ranked by S in decreasing order. The optimal value for N seems to be project-dependent.

---

[18] http://cran.r-project.org/web/packages/dtw/vignettes/dtw.pdf.
[19] http://code.google.com/p/fastdtw/.

Tools

The Granger causality test is available in R via the package MSBVAR.[20] The granger.test section of the reference manual[21] shows how to execute the statistical test. It also describes the input parameters, as well as the kind of output given by the function.

11.4 CHALLENGES IN CHANGE COUPLING IDENTIFICATION

Despite the importance of change couplings, accurately detecting them is far from trivial. In Section 11.4.1, we discuss how certain commit practices impair change coupling identification. In Section 11.4.2, we give some guidelines to help avoid noise and improve the accuracy of change coupling detection. Finally, in Section 11.4.3, we discuss the trade-offs of an alternative approach that involves detecting change couplings from monitored IDEs.

11.4.1 IMPACT OF COMMIT PRACTICES

Despite the flexibility and relevance of change couplings, accurately identifying them from the logs of version control system is far from trivial. When operationalizing change couplings this way, their detection become subject to different developers' commit practices. For instance, while a certain developer might commit very frequently, another developer might work for a long period in the code and commit all changes at once. This latter scenario favors the appearance of *overloaded commits*, i.e., commits with tangled changes [25, 50]. In turn, overloaded commits generate artificial change couplings, which link artifacts that belong to different changes. An example would be a commit in which a certain developer implements a new feature in a set of files, as well as fixes an unrelated bug in other files. In such case, change couplings will link artifacts related to the new feature with artifacts related to the bug fix. Another problematic situation refers to developers who produce *incomplete commits*. By incomplete commits, we mean those in which a developer forgets to perform a certain action or deliberately splits a single well-defined change into several consecutive commits. For instance, it might be that a developer changes certain domain classes but forgets to update an associated XML configuration file. This scenario leads to missing change couplings, because the developer will perform the forgotten actions in a separate commit. Finally, some commits might be the result of merging two branches from the repository. Such commits often involve a large number of artifacts and therefore originate several artificial change couplings. Detecting and coping with these problems is research on its own.

Researchers have recently tried to characterize developers' commit behavior. Ma et al. [51] conducted an empirical investigation on commit intervals in four open source projects from the Apache Software Foundation. In particular, they tried to fit lifecycle- and release-level commit intervals into well-known statistical distributions. They found that their datasets often presented a power-law distribution, i.e., most of the intervals between two consecutive commits in the repository were very short and only a few were distinctively high. Lin et al. [52] discovered that the number of commits per

---

[20] http://cran.r-project.org/web/packages/MSBVAR.
[21] http://cran.r-project.org/web/packages/MSBVAR/MSBVAR.pdf.

class (from creation of the class until its deletion) and the number of commits per time unit (e.g., one day, one week, one month) roughly follow a power-law distribution as well. These two studies provide empirical evidence that commits vary in size and frequency.

To make things even more complicated, commit practices are in turn influenced by a series of factors, including the project's development process, the way tasks are defined in Issue Tracking Systems or backlogs, and the specific version control system being used. For instance, recent studies have shown that the interaction protocol of version control systems influences commit frequency and the number of files in the change-sets. Brindescu et al. [53] conducted a large-scale empirical study (358k commits, 132 repositories, 5890 developers) and showed that commits made in distributed repositories were 32% smaller (fewer files) than in centralized repositories, and that developers split commits more often in distributed repositories.

All these studies leave us with several challenges. Should all commits be treated the same? What if the software development process does not enforce commit policies and developers end up having very different commit behaviors? How do we detect periods where commits have similar properties (size and frequency), so that the choice of thresholds for spotting relevant change coupling are meaningful and appropriate? What do we do when a project moves from a centralized version control system (e.g., SVN) to a distributed one (e.g., Git)? These are all challenges that call for further investigation. In the next section, we offer some hints to help detect change couplings in practice.

11.4.2 PRACTICAL ADVICE FOR CHANGE COUPLING DETECTION

In the following, we offer practical advice on how to collect and preprocess the input (commits) in order to extract file-based change couplings more accurately. We highlight that such recommendations are independent of the specific identification method chosen (Section 11.3), as they deal with the input only. These recommendations derive both from the aforementioned studies and from our own experience in the topic (lessons learned).

(1) Selecting subject projects

(a) Choose projects that use the same version control system. As we saw at the end of Section 11.4.1, the repository technology (e.g., centralized vs. distributed) influences commit frequency, as well as the average number of artifacts per change set. In order to reduce bias in empirical studies, we recommend selecting subject projects that use the same version control system product (e.g., SVN or Git). As a desirable consequence, this will also make the study's technological infrastructure lighter.

(b) Choose projects that link commits to tasks. Several open source projects, like Apache Lucene and Apache Hadoop, link commits to the tasks in the issue tracker (e.g., by explicitly mentioning the task id in the commit's comments). This adds contextual information to the commit and is beneficial for a series of purposes. For instance, having the task link enables you to calculate change couplings for specific types of software changes, such as bug fixes or new features. Most importantly, knowing the type of task also helps to conceive preprocessing mechanisms that improve the accuracy of change couplings (see advice item 4).

(c) Avoid projects that often move and migrate data. Most change coupling mining tools track files based on their paths. Although the tools are often able to track files that get renamed over time, they might face difficulties when tracking files that are moved to different paths. Cases in which files are deleted and then readded to a different path are especially complicated to deal with. Therefore, prefer projects where the "trunk" folder (or the folder you are mining) does not move over time. In addition, prefer projects that do not migrate data from other repositories. For example, an SVN repository that synchronizes with a CVS repository. The reason is that these migrations might alter the way developers originally made the commits, possibly leading to new commits that either group unrelated tasks or split cohesive changes.

(d) **Open source projects are at your disposal.** Thanks to the open source movement, several version control systems are freely available (in the sense that anyone can "read" them). Several research studies include projects from the Apache Software Foundation, a non-profit organization that has developed nearly a hundred distinguishing software projects that cover a wide range of technologies and domains. Examples of Apache projects include Apache HTTP Server, Apache Geronimo, Cassandra, Lucene, Maven, Ant, Struts, and JMeter. All Apache projects are hosted under a single SVN repository at https://svn.apache.org, which currently stores more than 1.6 million commits. A Git mirror with all projects is also available at http://git.apache.org/. Other hubs such as SourceForge and GitHub also contain a plethora of open source projects.

(2) Manipulating the repositories

(a) **Work locally.** To avoid dealing with network instability and other problems, we recommend mirroring (replicating) the repository locally when possible. The following sample script shows how to mirror the SVN repository of the Apache JMeter project to a local path in the filesystem:

```
1) Use the svnadmin utility to create a new (empty) repository
in the local file system.
   $ svnadmin create /mirrors/jmeter
After running the command, a non-empty directory called ''jmeter''
is created. The results should look similar to the following:
total 54K
drwxrwxr-x+ 1 user None 0   Dec 02 17:01 .
drwxrwxrwt+ 1 user None 0   Dec 02 17:01 ..
drwxrwxr-x+ 1 user None 0   Dec 02 17:01 conf
drwxrwxr-x+ 1 user None 0   Dec 02 17:01 db
-r--r--r-- 1 user None 2   Dec 02 17:01 format
drwxrwxr-x+ 1 user None 0   Dec 02 17:01 hooks
drwxrwxr-x+ 1 user None 0   Dec 02 17:01 locks
-rw-rw-r-- 1 user None 246 Dec 02 17:01 README.txt


2) Create an empty file "jmeter/hooks/pre-revprop-change" with the
''execute permission'' set. If in Windows, add a .bat extension to the
file. For more details, please read the template file
"/jmeter/hooks/pre-revprop-change.tmpl"
   $ touch /mirrors/jmeter/hooks/pre-revprop-change
```

```
$ chmod 777 /mirrors/jmeter/hooks/pre-revprop-change


3) Initialize the mirror repository using the "svnsync init" command.
This ties your local repository to the remote one
   $ svnsync init --username anonymous
   file:///mirrors/jmeter https://svn.apache.org/jmeter


4) Use the "svnsync sync" command to populate the mirror repository:
   $ svnsync sync filo:///mirrors/jmeter
```

The sample script above should work for most scenarios, but you can tailor it for your own requirements. Detailed instructions for mirroring a SVN repository are included in the free book "Version Control with Subversion."[22] Since mirroring and interacting with the repository might induce a lot of I/O, we also suggest using a solid-state drive (SSD) when possible.

(3) Determining the analysis scope

If the project has a stable release cycle, then identifying change couplings from each release can be a good approach. If not, then it is often better to analyze commit chunks (sequence of contiguous commits). The number of commits per chunk depends on the particular study and on the total number of commits the project has.

(4) Preprocessing commits to avoid noise and improve accuracy

Zimmermann and Weißgerber [23] emphasized that cleaning data is an important part of improving change coupling detection. In their work, they tackle two issues: large commits (i.e., commits with many files) and merge commits. They consider large commits as noise because the files they comprise often refer to infrastructure changes. In other words, these commits are not the consequence of relevant connascence relations (check Section 11.2.1). The authors advise filtering out commits of a size greater than a certain N, where N is a threshold defined on a per project basis.

The authors also regard *merge commits* (Figure 11.7) as noise. There are two main reasons. First, merge commits often contain unrelated changes. For instance, let us assume that commit 20 addresses a certain issue and commit 22 addresses a different one. In this case, commit 24 would contain unrelated changes, since A and C originally changed for different reasons. Second, merge commits rank changes on branches higher. For instance, A and B appear in both commit 20 and commit 24 (same thing happens to C).

Zimmermann and Weißgerber [23] note that depending on the purpose of the analysis, these merge commits should be ignored or at least receive some special treatment. Fluri and Gall [5] argue that commits including code styling and minor adjustments are also not significantly relevant in the context of change coupling identification.

---

[22]http://svnbook.red-bean.com/en/1.7/svn.reposadmin.maint.html#svn.reposadmin.maint.replication.

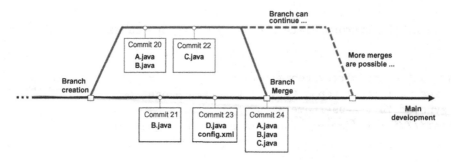

FIGURE 11.7

Influence of merges in change coupling identification.

In fact, the solution to these problems boils down to being able to classify or understand the kinds of changes implemented in each commit. Simply ignoring large commits might make you miss large refactorings or relevant changes. Our experience has shown that choosing projects that link commits to tasks in the issue track is often a better solution, since it helps to discover the purpose of each commit a lit bit better (see advice item 1b). Other strategies based on keyword matching against the commits' comments might also work reasonably well for certain applications (e.g., searching for "bug fix" or "refactoring"). This information can also be used to detect and bypass commits that link to two different tasks, thus mitigating the problem of overloaded commits. You may also leverage it to group commits that tackle the same tasks, thus mitigating the problem of incomplete commits. We note that Herzig and Zeller [50] performed a detailed manual classification of tasks found in the issue tracker of five open source systems: HTTPClient, Jackrabbit, Lucene, Rhino, and Tomcat 5. These data can be used to conceive preprocessing mechanisms that filter out unwanted commits, such as the ones that involve infrastructure changes, branch merging, and code styling.

11.4.3 ALTERNATIVE APPROACHES

The identification of change couplings from version control systems has one intrinsic shortcoming-*development information loss.* This problem was put in the spotlight by Robbes and colleagues [54, 55]. According to the author, versioned artifacts might undergo several changes in the period delimited by code checkout and commit. By analyzing such development session, one might conclude that although artifacts A, B, C, and D were modified, change couplings exist only between A and B, as well as between C and D. Moreover, it might be the case that A and B have a stronger change coupling when compared to the coupling level of C and D. However, the logs of version control systems will only store the set of modified files, the associated change operation (add, remove, replace, etc.), and the lines that changed. According to Robbes and colleagues [54, 55], this implies that "a large amount of data is needed before the measure can be accurate." They conclude that change coupling identification from periods of very active development (as opposed to projects in *maintenance mode*) may suffer even more from this issue.

Other researchers have an even stronger position. Negara et al. [56] consider that, although convenient, research based on version control systems is often incomplete and imprecise. They also note that many interesting research questions that involve code changes and other development activities (e.g., automated refactorings) require evolution data that is not captured by version control systems at all.

All these problems can be reduced to the fact that version control systems only store coarse-grained information. The alternative solution proposed by both Negara et al. and Robbes et al. relies on instrumenting developers' IDE. Quoting [56]:

> Code evolution research studies how the code is changed. So, it is natural to make changes be first-class citizens and leverage the capabilities of an Integrated Development Environment (IDE) to capture code changes online rather than trying to infer them post-mortem from the snapshots stored in VCSs (version control systems).

Negara et al. [56] developed an Eclipse plug-in called CodingTracker that unobtrusively collects fine-grained data about the code evolution of Java programs. This tool records every code edit performed by a developer, as well as other development actions, such as invocations of automated refactorings, tests and application runs, interaction with the version control system, etc. According to Negara and colleagues, the collected data is so precise that it enables them to reproduce the state of the underlying code at any point in time. To represent the raw code edits collected by CodingTracker uniformly and consistently, they implemented an algorithm that infers changes as Abstract Syntax Tree (AST) node operations. The solution from Robbes et al. [54, 55] is similar. They developed a tool called SpyWare that is notified by the Smalltalk compiler in the Squeak IDE whenever the AST of the underlying program changes. The solution from Negara and colleagues seems to be more complete and flexible, in the sense that their tool captures additional information (i.e., evolution data that does represent changes to code) and does not expect the underlying code to be compilable or even fully parsable.

What we see here is actually a trade-off. These studies show strong evidence that fine-grained information obtained from IDE monitoring is more accurate. However, they also have disadvantages. First, both approaches are targeted to specific IDEs: SpyWare interacts with Squeak IDE and CodingTracker is an Eclipse plug-in. Consequently, it can be that their software needs to be adjusted when new IDE versions are released (as often occurs with Eclipse plug-ins, for instance). Second, both approaches are targeted to specific programming languages: SpyWare records only Smalltalk code changes and CodingTracker records only Java code changes. What if the subject project is written in C#? What if the subject project is written mainly in Java, but also has a lot of XML files and other resources (which is common)? Third, although their tools seem unintrusive, they can only capture information from instrumented IDEs. In other words, all software development that occurred before the release of their tool is inevitably left behind. In particular, such period encompasses the core development of a huge amount of free/libre open source software (FLOSS) projects. In addition, given the highly collaborative and distributed nature of FLOSS development, instrumenting the IDEs of all developers becomes much more complicated (maybe even unfeasible in most cases). Therefore, while monitoring the IDE provides much more accurate data, it is also much more restrictive. In turn, research that mines version control systems only requires the existence of the log files (change-sets). Depending on the objective of the study, relying solely on these logs is perfectly adequate, as acknowledged by both Negara et al. [56] and Robbes et al. [54, 55] themselves.

11.5 CHANGE COUPLING APPLICATIONS

Now that we have presented different change coupling identification approaches and some pieces of practical advice, we will switch the focus to what we can do with the mined couplings. In the following sections, we present some key applications for change coupling, which include change prediction and change impact analysis (Section 11.5.1), discovery of design flaws and opportunities for refactoring (Section 11.5.2), architecture evaluation (Section 11.5.3), and identification of coordination requirements (Section 11.5.4).

11.5.1 CHANGE PREDICTION AND CHANGE IMPACT ANALYSIS

Change impact analysis (or simply *impact analysis*) concerns "identifying the potential consequences of a change, or estimating what needs to be modified to accomplish a change" [57]. Preventing side effects and estimating ripple effects have been two commons uses of impact analysis [58]. In a more general sense, developers use change impact analysis information for planning changes, deciding changes, accommodating certain types of changes, and tracing the effects of changes [57]. For more information, the interested reader might refer to the seminal book *Software Change Impact Analysis* by Arnold [57].

Change impact analysis probably constitutes the main application of change couplings. The rationale behind it is that *entities that have changed together in the past are likely to change together in the future* [10]. Zimmermann et al. [3, 31] developed an Eclipse plug-in that captures change couplings from the CVS version control system. Inspired by the way large e-commerce websites (e.g., Amazon[23] and eBay[24]) suggest related products to their visitors, their tool informs about related software changes: "programmers that changed these functions also changed..." More specifically, right after a certain developer changes a piece of code, the tool suggests locations where, in similar transactions in the past, other changes were made. These recommended locations can be very specific, like a class attribute or a class method. The tool captures change couplings using association rules, which are mined "on-demand" using a modified version of the *Apriori algorithm* [29]. After obtaining the rules and calculating their respective values of *support* and *confidence*, the tool displays them to the end-user (sorted by confidence).

The main benefits of the tool are: (a) suggesting and predicting likely changes, (b) showing coupling between items that would not be detectable via static analysis, and (c) preventing errors resulting from incomplete changes [3, 31]. These benefits are especially helpful for newcomers joining a software project, since they are less acquainted with the software architecture and with the semantics of certain classes. The results from the evaluation conducted by Zimmermann and colleagues showed that their tool was helpful in suggesting further changes and in warning about missing changes. However, they

---

[23]http://www.amazon.com.
[24]http://www.ebay.com.

highlight that the more there is to learn from history, the more and better suggestions that can be made. More details about this work can be found in their papers [3, 31] and at: http://thomas-zimmermann. com/publications/details/zimmermann-tse-2005/.

11.5.1.1 *Other research results*

Almost in parallel with Zimmermann and colleagues, a different group of researchers investigated the very same problem [33]. However, instead of generating association rules with the *Apriori* algorithm, they employed the more efficient FP-Growth algorithm [34] to find frequent itemsets, which avoids the step of generating candidate itemsets and testing them against the entire database. Ying and colleagues recommended the set of files to be changed by taking the union of frequent itemsets (change patterns) that includes the file being currently modified by the developer.

Hassan and Holt [17] conceived four different change propagation heuristics. The first heuristic (DEV) returns all program-level entities previously changed by the same developer who is performing the current change. The second one (HIS) returns all entities previously changed together with the entity being modified. The third heuristic (CUD) returns all entities structurally related to the entity being modified. The last heuristic (FIL) returns all entities defined in the same file as the entity being modified. The authors evaluated the performance of these heuristics in five open source systems: NetBSD, FreeBSD, OpenBSD, Postgres, and GCC. The heuristic based on change couplings (HIS) had the best recall (0.87) and the second best precision (0.06). Their results cast doubts on the effectiveness of using structural dependencies alone for predicting change propagation. Four years later, Malik and Hassan [20] worked on an adaptive change propagation recommender that relies on both structural and historical information to provide better suggestions.

Kagdi et al. [59] presented an approach for change impact analysis based on the combination of conceptual coupling analysis and change couplings analysis. Information retrieval techniques are used to derive conceptual couplings from the source code of a specific version of the subject system (e.g., a release). As usual, the authors identify change couplings by mining association rules from the logs of version control systems. The authors conducted an empirical study with historical data from four open source projects, Apache httpd, ArgoUML, iBatis, and KOffice. The results showed that the combination of the two techniques provide statistically significant improvement in accuracy when compared to the use of either technique individually. More specifically, the authors obtained improvements of up to 20% over the use of conceptual coupling technique alone in KOffice and up to 45% over the technique of change couplings in iBatis.

11.5.2 DISCOVERY OF DESIGN FLAWS AND OPPORTUNITIES FOR REFACTORING

Change couplings reveal how the evolution of versioned artifacts intertwine. In particular, artifacts that are highly change coupled to many other artifacts are intrinsically problematic, since this implies that these artifacts are frequently affected by changes made to other parts of the system. High change coupling among modules generally points to design flaws or even to architectural decay.

In order to help developers understand how change coupled artifacts are, D'Ambros and colleagues introduced a change coupling visualization tool called Evolution Radar [2, 10, 60, 61, 77]. The Evolution Radar is interactive and integrates information about change coupling at the file level and at the module level (group of files) in a scalable way. Furthermore, it enables developers to study and inspect change couplings in an interactive way by guiding them to the files responsible for strong change couplings (outliers). More specifically, the Evolution Radar helps to answer the following questions: (a) What are the components (e.g., modules) with the strongest (change) coupling? (b) Which low level entities (e.g., files) are responsible for these couplings?

Figure 11.8 shows the schematics of the Evolution Radar. The module chosen by the developer is visualized as a highlighted circle placed in the center of the radar. All other modules of the system are represented as sectors. The sector's size is proportional to the number of files it contains. Sectors are ordered according to their sizes, with the smallest one at 0 radian and the remaining ones arranged clockwise. Within each sector, files are represented as colored circles. Arbitrary metrics can be mapped to the color and size of file circles. Each circle is positioned according to polar coordinates, where the radius d and the angle θ are computed according to the following rules:

- Radius d (distance to the center): it is inversely proportional to the level of change coupling between the file (f) and the module (M). The more coupled they are, the closer they are to each other. In their study, Lanza and colleagues measured change coupling according to the following formula:

$$LC(M,f) = \max_{f_i \in M} LC(f_i, f), \quad \text{where}$$

$$LC(f_i, f_j) = \text{number of that } f_i \text{ and } f_j \text{ changed together}$$

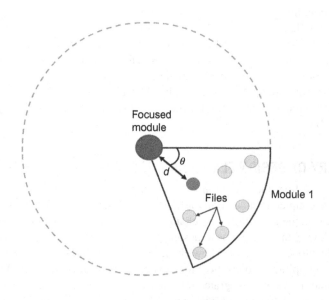

FIGURE 11.8

Schematics of Evolution Radar.

- Angle θ: the files in each module are ordered alphabetically considering their paths and uniformly distributed along the sector.

The main features of Evolution Radar are as follows [2]:

(a) Moving through time: When creating the radar, the end-user can divide the lifetime of the system into time intervals. For each of them a different radar is created (and change coupling is computed with respect to the given time interval). The radius coordinate has the same scale in all the radars, so that end-users can compare radars and analyze the evolution of coupling over time.

(b) Tracking: When a file is selected for tracking in a visualization related to a particular time interval, it is highlighted in all the radars (with respect to all the other time intervals) in which the file exists. This feature allows the end-user to keep track of files over time.

(c) Spawning: This feature enables end-users to discover how intensively files inside the module in focus are change coupled to other files of the system, thus providing a more detailed view of coupling.

In the following, we present an evaluation of the ArgoUML project done by D'Ambros and colleagues using the Evolution Radar [10]. Figure 11.9 depicts some of the radars they built for this evaluation. These radars focus on showing the change couplings between the Explorer module (the focused module in the center) and all other artifacts (all other circles) of the system for three consecutive analysis periods. A color temperature mapping is used: plain blue represents the lowest coupling and plain red represents the highest coupling.[25] The size of file circles is proportional to the total number of lines modified in all commits during the considered time interval.

The first radar (a) highlights a class named ModelFacade that underwent several modifications during the analysis period and that was highly coupled to the Explorer module. The authors further investigated the ModelFacade and discovered that it was a God class [62] with thousands of lines of code and around 450 methods (all static). The second radar (b) does not include the ModelFacade, i.e., a certain developer deleted it in the associated analysis period.

Using the tracking feature, the authors discovered that the NSUMLModelFacade class was the most coupled class in the second and third radars. In fact, its coupling with the Explorer module increased over time (its circle was getting closer to the central circle). A closer look revealed that the NSUMLModelFacade was also a God class with 317 public methods. The authors also discovered that more than 75% of its code was duplicated from the deleted ModelFacade class. Therefore, it appears the developers just relocated the problem instead of doing a proper refactoring. This example highlights how change couplings help detect design flaws and shows how artifacts (co)evolve over time. A more detailed evaluation of the ArgoUML project can be found in their journal article [10].

11.5.2.1 *Other research results*

Vanya et al. [63, 64] investigated whether interactive visualizations of co-changed software artifacts could be used beyond the mere identification of unwanted change couplings. More specifically, they investigated whether these techniques could help architects reason about and resolve these couplings. To evaluate their proposal, the authors conducted a case study in which they invited the architect and developers of a large medical system at Philips Healthcare to use iVIS to investigate unwanted change couplings in the system. The authors (i) selected the unwanted couplings the architect and developers

---

[25]Check the original paper for colored pictures [10].

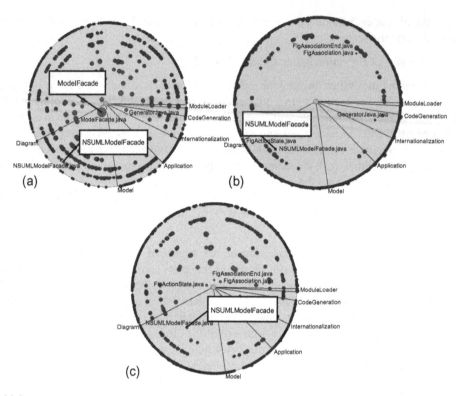

FIGURE 11.9

Evolution Radars for the ArgoUML.[26] (a) From June to December 2004; (b) From January to June 2005; (c) From June to December 2005.

decided to analyze, (ii) defined and implemented the interactions to be tested, and (iii) organized working sessions with the architect and developers to analyze the unwanted couplings. Solutions to unwanted couplings could be found in 7 out of the 10 working sessions conducted.

Beyer and Hassan [65, 66] introduced a visualization technique called *evolution storyboards*, which builds on a previous study by Beyer et al. [67] that clusters artifacts based on their change couplings. Just as directors and cinematographers use storyboards to study movie scenes and uncover potential problems before they occur, evolution storyboards were conceived to replay and study the history of software systems based on change coupling graphs. This is essentially an alternative to the Evolution Radar.

Ratzinger et al. [68] used change couplings to detect *bad smells*, which are somewhat subjective perceptions of design shortcomings. They developed a visualization tool called Evolens [68] that produces change coupling graphs, where large ellipses denote packages, smaller ellipses denote classes,

---

[26]Adapted from D'Ambros and Lanza [10, p. 6-7]. Content licensed by IEEE. Copyright cleared.

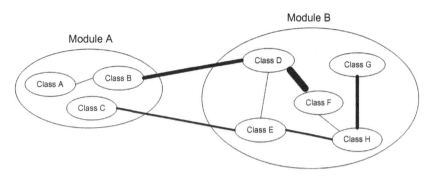

FIGURE 11.10

Schematic of the Evolens visualization.

and edges denote change couplings (Figure 11.10). The thickness of the edges is directly proportional to the number of co-changes involving the associated classes. The authors hypothesize that their tool assists developers in finding and fixing design flaws via refactoring. The authors introduced two *change smells*, i.e., *man-in-the-middle* and *data container*. Man-in-the-middle refers to a central class that is change coupled to many others scattered over several modules of the system. In turn, the data container smell involves two classes: one that holds the data and another that interacts with other classes of the system that require the data from the first class. The authors analyzed the history of a large industrial system for 15 months and found occurrences on both smells.

11.5.3 ARCHITECTURE EVALUATION

Zimmermann et al. [25] investigated the extent to which change history can be used to improve the assessment of software architectures. To this end, they detected change couplings between program-level entities (i.e., attributes and methods) and assessed the modularity of several open source projects, including GCC, DDD, Python, Apache, and OpenSSL. Such an assessment was driven by an analysis of the values produced by two metrics. One metric was the Evolutionary Density Index (EDI), which relates the number of actual change couplings to that of possible change couplings. The lower the EDI, the better the modularity. The other metric was the Evolutionary Coupling Index (ECI), which relates the actual number of external change couplings (i.e., couplings between entities defined in different files) to the actual number of internal change couplings. As in the previous case, the lower the ECI, the better the modularity. From their results, they concluded that a change history can either justify the organization and principles of the system architecture or show where reality diverges from policy (e.g., architectural rules).

Recently, Silva et al. [69] used change couplings to assess the modularity of software systems. The rationale comes from the principle that modules should confine implementation decisions that are likely to change together [70]. This is also known as the Common Closure Principle [71]. Silva and colleagues created co-change graphs, with edges representing the number of common changes between artifacts. They applied a clustering algorithm to extract co-change clusters from the graph and then compared such clusters against the hierarchical (package) structure of the system. Their evaluation included three open source systems: Geronimo, Lucene, and JDT Core. The authors performed this comparison using distribution maps [72], which is a visualization technique they leveraged to depict how clustered classes are distributed over the system packages. During the evaluation of the systems, they were able to see several of the distribution patterns introduced by Ducasse et al. [72]. For instance, some co-change clusters fit the *Octopus pattern*, since they were well encapsulated in one package (the "body") but also spread across others (the "tentacles").

11.5.4 COORDINATION REQUIREMENTS AND SOCIO-TECHNICAL CONGRUENCE

Organizations often cope with complex tasks by first dividing them into smaller interdependent work units and then assigning these units to teams. In this context, coordination among teams arises as a response to such interdependent work units [73]. Cataldo and colleagues conceived an approach to elicit coordination requirements [19, 74, 75]. More specifically, their approach tackles the following problem: *given a particular set of dependencies among tasks, identify which set of individuals should coordinate their activities.*

The approach from Cataldo et al. relies on two sets of relationships (Figure 11.11). The first set is called *Task Assignments* (T_A) and defines which individuals are working on which tasks. This set is represented by a matrix where each cell $[i, j]$ indicates that the developer i was assigned to the task j. In the context of software development, this set might be built upon the set of files modified by each developer on a modification request or throughout the development of a software release. The second set of relationships is called *Task Dependencies* (T_D) and defines the interdependencies between tasks. This set is also represented by a matrix where each cell $[i, j]$ (or $[j, i]$) indicates whether tasks i and j are interdependent. In the context of software development, this set might be built according to either structural coupling or change couplings. Cataldo and colleagues tested the two alternatives and concluded that change couplings provided better results [74]. In the particular case of change coupling, off-diagonal cells of T_D indicate the number of times the two files were changed together. In turn, the main diagonal indicates the total number of times the source code files were changed.

Once T_A and T_D matrices are built, coordination requirements are ready to be determined. Multiplying T_A by T_D results in a "people by task" matrix that represents the extent to which a particular

Task assignments	Task dependencies as co-changes	Task assignments transposed	Coordination requirements
(T_A)	(T_D)	$(T_A)^T$	(C_R)

$$
\begin{bmatrix} 0 & 1 & 0 & 1 & 1 & 0 \\ 0 & 0 & 1 & 0 & 0 & 0 \\ 1 & 1 & 0 & 0 & 1 & 0 \\ 1 & 1 & 0 & 1 & 1 & 0 \end{bmatrix}
\times
\begin{bmatrix} 25 & 5 & 0 & 1 & 2 & 8 \\ 5 & 32 & 3 & 5 & 0 & 7 \\ 0 & 3 & 9 & 1 & 0 & 0 \\ 1 & 5 & 1 & 20 & 3 & 5 \\ 2 & 0 & 0 & 3 & 10 & 1 \\ 8 & 7 & 0 & 5 & 1 & 27 \end{bmatrix}
\times
\begin{bmatrix} 0 & 0 & 1 & 1 \\ 1 & 0 & 1 & 1 \\ 0 & 1 & 0 & 0 \\ 1 & 0 & 0 & 1 \\ 1 & 0 & 1 & 1 \\ 0 & 0 & 0 & 0 \end{bmatrix}
=
\begin{bmatrix} - & 4 & 58 & 86 \\ 4 & - & 3 & 4 \\ 58 & 3 & - & 90 \\ 86 & 4 & 90 & - \end{bmatrix}
$$

FIGURE 11.11

Illustrative example of coordination requirements calculation.

worker should be aware of tasks that are interdependent to those that he or she is responsible for [74]. Multiplying the $T_A \times T_D$ product by the transpose of T_A results in a people by people matrix where a cell $[i, j]$ represents the extent to which person i works on tasks that share dependencies with the tasks worked on by person j [74]. In other words, this last matrix represents the Coordination Requirements (C_R), or the extent to which each pair of people needs to coordinate their work (values in the main diagonal should be ignored). When calculating T_D using co-changes, the resulting C_R matrix is symmetric (Figure 11.11).

11.6 CONCLUSION

In this chapter, we provided an overview of change coupling to researchers and practitioners. Our goals were to explain the concept (Section 11.2), present the main identification approaches (Section 11.3), discuss current challenges in coupling identification and offer some practical advice (Section 11.4), and present the main application areas (Section 11.5). To us, there is no doubt that detecting and analyzing change couplings is becoming an increasingly useful tool in software engineering empirical studies. Several studies have been published at top conferences, such as those on mining software repositories [12, 23], software engineering [2, 76], software evolution [25], and reverse engineering [10]. The work of Zimmermann et al. [31] on change prediction (Section 11.5.1) won the most influential paper award at the 26th International Conference on Software Engineering (ICSE 2014), the world's most important conference in software engineering. Having said that, we sincerely hope this chapter has given you the fundamentals to detect and analyze change couplings in practice. The authors of this chapter will be glad to answer questions and discuss researches revolving around the topic.

REFERENCES

[1] Ball T, Adam JMK, Harvey AP, Siy P. If your version control system could talk... In: ICSE workshop on process modeling and empirical studies of software engineering; 1997.

[2] D'Ambros M, Lanza M, Lungu M. Visualizing co-change information with the evolution radar. IEEE Trans Softw Eng 2009;35(5):720–35. doi:10.1109/TSE.2009.17.

[3] Zimmermann T, Weissgerber P, Diehl S, Zeller A. Mining version histories to guide software changes. IEEE Trans Softw Eng 2005;31(6):429–45. doi:10.1109/TSE.2005.72.

[4] Fluri B, Gall HC, Pinzger M. Fine-grained analysis of change couplings. In: Proceedings of the fifth IEEE international workshop on source code analysis and manipulation; 2005. p. 66–74. doi:10.1109/SCAM.2005.14.

[5] Fluri B, Gall HC. Classifying change types for qualifying change couplings. In: Proceedings of the 14th IEEE international conference on program comprehension, ICPC 2006; 2006. p. 35–45. doi:10.1109/ICPC.2006. 16.

[6] D'Ambros M, Gall H, Lanza M, Pinzger M. Analysing software repositories to understand software evolution. In: Mens T, Demeyer S, editors. Software evolution. Berlin: Springer; 2008. p. 37–67. Retrieved from doi:10.1007/978-3-540-76440-3.

[7] Mens T, Demeyer S. Software evolution. 1st ed. Berlin: Springer Publishing Company, Inc.; 2008.

[8] D'Ambros M, Lanza M, Robbes R. On the relationship between change coupling and software defects. Los Alamitos, CA, USA: IEEE Computer Society; 2009. p. 135–44. doi:10.1109/WCRE.2009.19.

[9] Zhou Y, Wursch M, Giger E, Gall H, Lu J. A Bayesian network based approach for change coupling prediction. In: Proceedings of the 15th working conference on reverse engineering, WCRE'08; 2008. p. 27–36. doi:10.1109/WCRE.2008.39.

[10] D'Ambros M, Lanza M. Reverse engineering with logical coupling. In: 13th working conference on reverse engineering, WCRE '06; 2006. p. 189–198. doi:10.1109/WCRE.2006.51.

[11] Gall H, Hajek K, Jazayeri M. Detection of logical coupling based on product release history. In: Proceedings of the international conference on software maintenance, ICSM '98. Washington, DC, USA: IEEE Computer Society; 1998. p. 190. Retrieved from http://dl.acm.org/citation.cfm?id=850947.853338.

[12] Alali A, Bartman B, Newman CD, Maletic JI. A preliminary investigation of using age and distance measures in the detection of evolutionary couplings. In: Proceedings of the 10th working conference on mining software repositories, MSR '13. San Francisco, CA, USA: IEEE Press; 2013. p. 169–72. Retrieved from http://dl.acm.org/citation.cfm?id=2487085.2487120.

[13] Hassan AE. The road ahead for mining software repositories. Front Softw Maint 2008; 2008:48–57. doi:10.1109/FOSM.2008.4659248.

[14] Page-Jones M. Comparing techniques by means of encapsulation and connascence. Commun ACM 1992;35(9):147–51. doi:10.1145/130994.131004.

[15] Page-Jones M. Fundamentals of object-oriented design in UML. 1st ed. Reading, MA: Addison-Wesley; 1999.

[16] McIntosh S, Adams B, Nguyen THD, Kamei Y, Hassan AE. An empirical study of build maintenance effort. In: Proceedings of the 33rd international conference on software engineering, ICSE '11. Waikiki, Honolulu, HI, USA: ACM; 2011. p. 141–50. doi:10.1145/1985793.1985813.

[17] Hassan AE, Holt RC. Predicting change propagation in software systems. In: Proceedings of the 20th IEEE international conference on software maintenance, ICSM '04. Washington, DC, USA: IEEE Computer Society; 2004. p. 284–93. Retrieved from http://dl.acm.org/citation.cfm?id=1018431.1021436.

[18] Hassan AE, Holt RC. Replaying development history to assess the effectiveness of change propagation tools. Empir Softw Eng 2006;11(3):335–67. doi:10.1007/s10664-006-9006-4.

[19] Cataldo M, Herbsleb JD. Coordination breakdowns and their impact on development productivity and software failures. IEEE Trans Softw Eng 2013;39(3):343–60. doi:10.1109/TSE.2012.32.

[20] Malik H, Hassan AE. Supporting software evolution using adaptive change propagation heuristics. In: Proceedings of the IEEE international conference on software maintenance, ICSM, 2008; 2008. p. 177–86. doi:10.1109/ICSM.2008.4658066.

[21] Cataldo M, Mockus A, Roberts JA, Herbsleb JD. Software dependencies, work dependencies, and their impact on failures. IEEE Trans Softw Eng 2009;35(6):864–78. doi:10.1109/TSE.2009.42.

[22] Cataldo M, Nambiar S. The impact of geographic distribution and the nature of technical coupling on the quality of global software development projects. J Softw Maint Evol Res Pract 2010. doi:10.1002/smr.477.

[23] Zimmermann T, Weißgerber P. Preprocessing CVS data for fine-grained analysis. In: Proceedings 1st international workshop on mining software repositories (MSR 2004). Los Alamitos, CA: IEEE Computer Society Press; 2004. p. 2–6.

[24] Gall H, Jazayeri M, Krajewski J. CVS release history data for detecting logical couplings. In: Proceedings of the 6th international workshop on principles of software evolution. Washington, DC, USA: IEEE Computer Society; 2003. p. 13. Retrieved from http://dl.acm.org/citation.cfm?id=942803.943741.

[25] Zimmermann T, Diehl S, Zeller A. How history justifies system architecture (or not). In: Proceedings of the sixth international workshop on principles of software evolution; 2003. p. 73–83. doi:10.1109/IWPSE.2003.1231213.

[26] Oliva GA, Gerosa MA. On the interplay between structural and logical dependencies in open-source software. In: Proceedings of the 25th Brazilian symposium on software engineering, SBES'11. Washington, DC, USA: IEEE Computer Society; 2011. p. 144–53. doi:10.1109/SBES.2011.39.

[27] Rajaraman A, Ullman JD, Leskovec J. Mining of massive datasets. 2nd ed. 2013.

[28] Liu B. Web data mining: exploring hyperlinks, contents and usage data. 2nd ed. Berlin: Springer Publishing Company, Inc.; 2011.

[29] Agrawal R, Srikant R. Fast algorithms for mining association rules in large databases. In: Proceedings of the 20th international conference on very large data bases, VLDB '94. San Francisco, CA, USA: Morgan Kaufmann Publishers Inc.; 1994. p. 487–99. Retrieved from http://dl.acm.org/citation.cfm?id= 645920.672836.

[30] Bavota G, Dit B, Oliveto R, Di Penta M, Poshyvanyk D, De Lucia A. An empirical study on the developers' perception of software coupling. In: Proceedings of the 2013 international conference on software engineering, ICSE '13. San Francisco, CA, USA: IEEE Press; 2013. p. 692–701. Retrieved from http://dl. acm.org/citation.cfm?id=2486788.2486879.

[31] Zimmermann T, Weissgerber P, Diehl S, Zeller A. Mining version histories to guide software changes. In: Proceedings of the 26th international conference on software engineering, ICSE'04. Washington, DC, USA: IEEE Computer Society; 2004. p. 563–72. Retrieved from http://dl.acm.org/citation.cfm?id=998675.999460.

[32] Wang X, Wang H, Liu C. Predicting co-changed software entities in the context of software evolution. In: Proceedings of the international conference on information engineering and computer science, ICIECS; 2009. p. 1–5. doi:10.1109/ICIECS.2009.5364521.

[33] Ying ATT, Murphy GC, Ng R, Chu-Carroll MC. Predicting source code changes by mining change history. IEEE Trans Softw Eng 2004;30(9):574–86. doi:10.1109/TSE.2004.52.

[34] Han J, Pei J, Yin Y. Mining frequent patterns without candidate generation. In: Proceedings of the 2000 ACM SIGMOD international conference on management of data, SIGMOD'00. Dallas, TX, USA: ACM; 2000. p. 1–12. doi:10.1145/342009.335372.

[35] Brin S, Motwani R, Ullman JD, Tsur S. Dynamic itemset counting and implication rules for market basket data. In: Proceedings of the 1997 ACM SIGMOD international conference on management of data, SIGMOD '97. Tucson, AZ, USA: ACM; 1997. p. 255–64. doi:10.1145/253260.253325.

[36] Kagdi H, Collard ML, Maletic JI. A survey and taxonomy of approaches for mining software repositories in the context of software evolution. J Softw Maint Evol 2007;19(2):77–131. doi:10.1002/smr.344.

[37] Canfora G, Ceccarelli M, Cerulo L, Di Penta M. Using multivariate time series and association rules to detect logical change coupling: an empirical study. In: Proceedings of the IEEE international conference on software maintenance (ICSM); 2010. p. 1–10. doi:10.1109/ICSM.2010.5609732.

[38] Kruskal JB, Liberman M. The symmetric time-warping problem: from continuous to discrete. In: Sankoff D, Kruskal JB, editors. Time warps, string edits, and macromolecules—the theory and practice of sequence comparison. Palo Alto, CA: CSLI Publications; 1999.

[39] Antoniol G, Rollo VF, Venturi G. Detecting groups of co-changing files in CVS repositories. In: Proceedings of the eighth international workshop on principles of software evolution; 2005. p. 23–32. doi:10.1109/ IWPSE.2005.11.

[40] Rabiner L, Rosenberg AE, Levinson SE. Considerations in dynamic time warping algorithms for discrete word recognition. IEEE Trans Acoust Speech Signal Process 1978;26(6):575–82. doi:10.1109/TASSP.1978. 1163164.

[41] Rabiner L, Juang BH. Fundamentals of speech recognition. Upper Saddle River, NJ, USA: Prentice-Hall, Inc.; 1993.

[42] Caiani EG, Porta A, Baselli G, Turiel M, Muzzupappa S, Pieruzzi F, et al. Warped-average template technique to track on a cycle-by-cycle basis the cardiac filling phases on left ventricular volume. Comput Cardiol 1998;1998:73–6. doi:10.1109/CIC.1998.731723.

[43] Oates T, Schmill MD, Cohen PR. A method for clustering the experiences of a mobile robot that accords with human judgments. In: Proceedings of the seventeenth national conference on artificial intelligence

and twelfth conference on innovative applications of artificial intelligence. Austin, TX: AAAI Press; 2000. p. 846–51. URL: http://dl.acm.org/citation.cfm?id=647288.721117.

[44] Rath TM, Manmatha R. Word image matching using dynamic time warping. In: Proceedings of the IEEE computer society conference on computer vision and pattern recognition, vol. 2; 2003. p. II-521–II-527. doi:10.1109/CVPR.2003.1211511.

[45] Müller M. Dynamic time warping. In: Information retrieval for music and motion. Berlin/Heidelberg: Springer; 2007. p. 69–84. doi:10.1007/978-3-540-74048-3{_}4.

[46] Bouktif S, Gueheneuc YG, Antoniol G. Extracting change-patterns from CVS repositories. In: Proceedings of the 13th working conference on reverse engineering, WCRE '06. Washington, DC, USA: IEEE Computer Society; 2006. p. 221–30. doi:10.1109/WCRE.2006.27.

[47] Salvador S, Chan P. Toward accurate dynamic time warping in linear time and space. Intell Data Anal 2007;11(5):561–80. URL: http://dl.acm.org/citation.cfm?id=1367985.1367993.

[48] Granger CWJ. Investigating causal relations by econometric models and cross-spectral methods. Econometrica 1969;37(3):424–38. doi:10.2307/1912791.

[49] Ceccarelli M, Cerulo L, Canfora G, Di Penta M. An eclectic approach for change impact analysis. In: Proceedings of the 32Nd ACM/IEEE international conference on software engineering, ICSE '10, vol. 2. Cape Town, South Africa: ACM; 2010. p. 163–6. doi:10.1145/1810295.1810320.

[50] Herzig K, Zeller A. The impact of tangled code changes. In: Proceedings of the 10th working conference on mining software repositories, MSR '13. San Francisco, CA, USA: IEEE Press; 2013. p. 121–30. Retrieved from http://dl.acm.org/citation.cfm?id=2487085.2487113.

[51] Ma Y, Wu Y, Xu Y. Dynamics of open-source software developer's commit behavior: an empirical investigation of subversion; 2013. CoRR, abs/1309.0897.

[52] Lin S, Ma Y, Chen J. Empirical evidence on developer's commit activity for open-source software projects. In: Proceedings of the 25th international conference on software engineering and knowledge engineering, SEKE'13, Boston, USA; 2013. p. 455–60. Retrieved from http://dl.acm.org/citation.cfm?id=257734.257788.

[53] Brindescu C, Codoban M, Shmarkatiuk S, Dig D. How do centralized and distributed version control systems impact software changes? (No. 1957/44927). EECS School at Oregon State University; 2014.

[54] Robbes R, Pollet D, Lanza M. Logical coupling based on fine-grained change information. In: Proceedings of the 15th working conference on reverse engineering, WCRE'08. Washington, DC, USA: IEEE Computer Society; 2008. p. 42–6. doi:10.1109/WCRE.2008.47.

[55] Robbes R. Of change and software. University of Lugano; 2008.

[56] Negara S, Vakilian M, Chen N, Johnson RE, Dig D. Is it dangerous to use version control histories to study source code evolution? In: Proceedings of the 26th European conference on object-oriented programming, ECOOP'12. Beijing, China: Springer-Verlag; 2012. p. 79–103. doi:10.1007/978-3-642-31057-7{_}5.

[57] Arnold RS. Software change impact analysis. Los Alamitos, CA, USA: IEEE Computer Society Press; 1996.

[58] Kagdi H, Maletic JI. Software-change prediction: estimated+actual. In: Proceedings of the second international IEEE workshop on software evolvability, SE'06; 2006. p. 38–43. doi:10.1109/SOFTWARE-EVOLVABILITY.2006.14.

[59] Kagdi H, Gethers M, Poshyvanyk D, Collard ML. Blending conceptual and evolutionary couplings to support change impact analysis in source code. In: Proceedings of the 17th working conference on reverse engineering (WCRE); 2010. p. 119–28. doi:10.1109/WCRE.2010.21.

[60] D'Ambros M, Lanza M, Lungu M. The evolution radar: visualizing integrated logical coupling information. In: Proceedings of the 2006 international workshop on mining software repositories, MSR '06. Shanghai, China: ACM; 2006. p. 26–32. doi:10.1145/1137983.1137992.

[61] D'Ambros M, Lanza M. Distributed and collaborative software evolution analysis with churrasco. Sci Comput Program 2010;75(4):276–87. doi:10.1016/j.scico.2009.07.005.

[62] Fowler M. Refactoring: improving the design of existing code. Boston, MA: Addison-Wesley; 1999. Object Technology Series.

[63] Vanya A, Premraj R, Vliet H. Interactive exploration of co-evolving software entities. In: Proceedings of the 14th European conference on software maintenance and reengineering, CSMR'10. Washington, DC, USA: IEEE Computer Society; 2010. p. 260–3. doi:10.1109/CSMR.2010.50.

[64] Vanya A, Premraj R, Vliet H. Resolving unwanted couplings through interactive exploration of co-evolving software entities—an experience report. Inf Softw Technol 2012; 54(4):347–59. doi:10.1016/j.infsof.2011. 11.003.

[65] Beyer D, Hassan AE. Animated visualization of software history using evolution storyboards. In: Proceedings of the 13th working conference on reverse engineering, WCRE '06. Washington, DC, USA: IEEE Computer Society; 2006; pp. 199–210. doi:10.1109/WCRE.2006.14.

[66] Beyer D, Hassan AE. Evolution storyboards: visualization of software structure dynamics. In: Proceedings of the 14th IEEE international conference on program comprehension, ICPC '06. Washington, DC, USA: IEEE Computer Society; 2006; pp. 248–51. doi:10.1109/ICPC.2006.21.

[67] Beyer D, Noack A. Clustering software artifacts based on frequent common changes. In: Proceedings of the 13th international workshop on program comprehension. Washington, DC, USA: IEEE Computer Society; 2005. p. 259–68. doi:10.1109/WPC.2005.12.

[68] Ratzinger J, Fischer M, Gall H. Improving evolvability through refactoring. In: Proceedings of the 2005 international workshop on mining software repositories, MSR'05. St. Louis, MO: ACM; 2005. p. 1–5. doi: 10.1145/1082983.1083155.

[69] Silva L, Valente MT, Maia M. Assessing modularity using co-change clusters. In: Proceedings of the 13th international conference on modularity; 2014. p. 1–12.

[70] Parnas DL. On the criteria to be used in decomposing systems into modules. Commun ACM 1972; 15(12):1053–8. doi:10.1145/361598.361623.

[71] Martin RC, Martin M. Agile principles, patterns, and practices in C#. 1st ed. Upper Saddle River, NJ: Prentice Hall; 2006.

[72] Ducasse S, Girba T, Kuhn A. Distribution map. In: Proceedings of the 22nd IEEE international conference on software maintenance, ICSM '06. Washington, DC, USA: IEEE Computer Society; 2006. p. 203–12. doi:10.1109/ICSM.2006.22.

[73] March JG, Simon HA. Organizations. 2nd ed. New York: Wiley-Blackwell; 1993.

[74] Cataldo M, Herbsleb JD, Carley KM. Socio-technical congruence: a framework for assessing the impact of technical and work dependencies on software development productivity. In: Proceedings of the second ACM-IEEE international symposium on empirical software engineering and measurement, ESEM '08. Kaiserslautern, Germany: ACM; 2008. p. 2–11. doi:10.1145/1414004.1414008.

[75] Cataldo M, Wagstrom P, Herbsleb JD, Carley KM. Identification of coordination requirements: implications for the design of collaboration and awareness tools. In: Hinds PJ, Martin D, editors, Proceedings of the 2006 ACM conference on computer supported cooperative work, CSCW 2006, Banff, Alberta, Canada, November 4-8. New York, NY, USA: ACM; 2006. p. 353–62. doi:10.1145/1180875.1180929.

[76] Kouroshfar E. Studying the effect of co-change dispersion on software quality. In: Proceedings of the 2013 international conference on software engineering, ICSE'13. San Francisco, CA, USA: IEEE Press; 2013. p. 1450–2. Retrieved from. http://dl.acm.org/citation.cfm?id=2486788.2487034.

[77] D'Ambros M, Lanza M. A flexible framework to support collaborative software evolution analysis. In: Proceedings of the 12th European conference on software maintenance and reengineering, CSMR '08. Washington, DC, USA: IEEE Computer Society; 2008. p. 3–12. doi:10.1109/CSMR.2008.4493295.

STORIES FROM THE TRENCHES

APPLYING SOFTWARE DATA ANALYSIS IN INDUSTRY CONTEXTS: WHEN RESEARCH MEETS REALITY

12

Madeline Diep[*], **Linda Esker***, **Davide Falessi***, **Lucas Layman***, **Michele Shaw***, **Forrest Shull**[†]

*Fraunhofer Center for Experimental Software Engineering, College Park, MD, USA**

Software Solutions Division, Software Engineering Institute, Arlington, VA, USA[†]

CHAPTER OUTLINE

12.1 INTRODUCTION

Software data analytics programs are founded upon the measurement of software products, processes, and organizations. Measurement is the "act or process of assigning a number or category to an entity to describe an attribute of that entity" [1]. Measurement allows us to build models or representations of what we observe so we can reason about relationships in context [2]. Measurement plays an important role in a number of analytical applications, from forecasting the cost of multi-billion dollar government defense systems to identifying faulty components from runtime execution logs. Measurement is crucial for process improvement, cost and effort estimation, defect prediction, release planning, and resource allocation.

As software data analytics matures as a discipline, the basic challenges remain of quantifying the resources, processes, and artifacts involved in software development. Practical software measurement, which serves as the basis of software data analysis, is challenging to execute. A well-intentioned developer who says, "We should measure the effort we spend on this project," has just exposed her/himself to a variety of challenges. Management must be convinced that measurement and analytics activities will be worth the cost. Instrumentation must be put in place to collect raw data. Raw measurement data must be cleaned for analysis. Developers may not like their work effort being scrutinized. The initial measurements collected may not provide the whole story of effort spent. There will be disputes, negotiations, and consequences regarding the results.

Our goal in this chapter is **to provide best practices and lessons learned for effective software data analysis in the software industry**, drawn from Fraunhofer's 15 years of measurement and data analysis experience in the software industry.[1] We provide practical advice both for researchers who need to know the real-world constraints of measurement in industry, and for practitioners interested in setting up a measurement program. In Section 12.2, we provide a brief background of our Fraunhofer team and our credentials in software measurement, together with a number of sources for the curious reader interested in implementing their own measurement program.

In Section 12.3, we discuss challenges and lessons learned around six key topics that must be considered when implementing a measurement program in industry. We present these issues in rough chronological order in which they occur during the lifecycle of implementing an applied software measurement and analytics program. This lifecycle roughly corresponds to a traditional software development lifecycle: gathering stakeholder requirements, formalizing measures, implementing data collection and analysis, and communicating results. The six topics are:

1. **Stakeholders, requirements, and planning: the groundwork for a successful measurement program**—Obtaining stakeholder buy-in, goal setting, and planning are the critical beginnings of an effective measurement program.
2. **Gathering measurements—how, when, and who**—Addressing the technical and organizational challenges of gathering measurement data, which extend beyond simply gaining access to data.
3. **All data, no information**—Facing the challenges of missing data, low quality data, or incorrectly formatted data.
4. **The pivotal role of subject-matter expertise**—Using qualitative input to understand the data and to interpret the results for practical software data analytics.
5. **Responding to changing needs**—Responding to changing goals, changing directions from consumers, and technical and budgetary challenges that occur during the lifetime of a project.
6. **Effective ways to communicate analysis results to the consumers**—Presenting the results to decision-makers and packaging the findings as reusable knowledge.

As we discuss these topics, we provide concrete examples of the challenges encountered and techniques used to overcome those challenges from past experiences in implementing measurement programs in industry. Each topic is punctuated with several short challenges and recommendations for the reader.

---

[1] One of the authors, Forrest Shull, established the Software Measurement division at Fraunhofer CESE; he moved to SEI while this chapter was being written.

Finally, in Section 12.4, we summarize the takeaways from our chapter and highlight several open issues in applied software measurement and analysis.

12.2 BACKGROUND

The background of this chapter consists of four main aspects: our experience in software measurement; terminology; our empirical method; and our high-level approach to measurement. Each of these aspects is described in a specific section in the remainder of this section.

12.2.1 FRAUNHOFER'S EXPERIENCE IN SOFTWARE MEASUREMENT

For 15 years, our team at the Fraunhofer Center for Experimental Software Engineering has performed software data analysis for government and commercial customers to provide actionable conclusions for key decision-makers. These analyses have covered all stages of product and service development, from proposal definition and requirements analysis to implementation, test, and operations. Fraunhofer has implemented measurement for projects of many types, from small web development projects in startup companies to safety-critical, systems-of-systems in government agencies. In small commercial projects, we have applied quantitative software data analyses to help organizations improve their process maturity level. In safety-critical, high-maturity contexts, we assisted government civil servants by using software data analytics to evaluate the progress of contractors and to quantify risk. Fraunhofer scientists and engineers have authored 40–50 publications on applied and theoretical software measurement; delivered software measurement keynotes; edited two measurement books [3, 4]; received multiple awards from the NASA on measurement-based research and program support; and assisted a commercial client in achieving CMMI®[2] Level 5 maturity [5].

Throughout this chapter, we draw on our practical experiences applying software measurement to government and industry projects. Table 12.1 summarizes 11 major projects from which we draw many of the measurement challenges and lessons learned in this chapter. Each project is described via six main characteristics: domain of the project, type of project, size of the team, lines of code, the specific phases covered by the measurement program, and the duration of the project.

12.2.2 TERMINOLOGY

Although there are other standards for measurement terminology [6], throughout this chapter we will use the following terminology, which we have adapted from the *IEEE Standard for a Software Quality Metrics Methodology* (IEEE Std 1061-1998) [1]:

- Metric—A function whose inputs are software data and whose output is a single numerical value that can be interpreted as the degree to which that software possesses a given attribute. Examples of metrics include Lines of Code (LOC), defects/LOC, and person-hours.
- To measure—(a) a way to ascertain or appraise value by comparing it with a norm; (b) to apply a metric.

---

[2]*CMMI® is registered in the U.S. Patent and Trademark Office by Carnegie Mellon University.*

Table 12.1 Excerpt of Project Characteristics

Project Domain	Project Type	Team Size	Lines of Code	Lifecycle Phases Covered by Metrics	Measurement Duration
Aerospace	Maintenance	Very large (100+)	1M+	Implementation	3+ years
Control	Greenfield	Very large (100+)	1M+	Implementation	3+ years
Aerospace	Greenfield	Very large (100+)	1M+	Design	<1 year
Aerospace	Both	Very large (100+)	1M+	Test, Operations	3+ years
Military health	Maintenance	Very large (100+)	1M+	DoD 5000—all aspects	1-3 years
Web applications	Both	large (30-100)	100K-500K	All	3+ years
Telecommunications	Maintenance	large (30-100)	1M+	Implementation	1-3 years
Software development	Maintenance	Very large (100+)	1M+	Implementation	1-3 years
Oil company	Maintenance	large (30-100)	100K-500K	Operations	1-3 years
FFRDC	Maintenance	N/A	N/A	Initiation	<1 year
Aerospace	Both	Small-very large	100K-500K	All	3+ years

- Measurement—(a) the act or process of assigning a number or category to an entity to describe an attribute of that entity. A figure, extent, or amount obtained by measuring, e.g., we use SonarQube^{TM}(i.e., the act) to determine LOC on our projects.
- Metric value—a metric output or an element that is from the range of a metric, e.g., the metric value for LOC is 520.

12.2.3 EMPIRICAL METHODS

Ad hoc and opportunistic "measurement for the sake of measurement" rarely yields useful results. Data that are collected for convenience suffer from data quality issues and rarely correlate with an organization's overall quality improvement goals. As a result, the effort required to transform data into useful information is likely to be substantial. Further, collected data that does not relate to an improvement goal is often viewed as wasted effort. Undirected measurement is hurtful in the long term; not only are resources from gathering and analyzing data wasted without yielding apparent benefit, but measurement programs in general will be viewed as a waste of resources.

In response to this phenomenon, many approaches and paradigms have been proposed to make measurement programs more systematic and formal. Fraunhofer has initiated and leveraged several such approaches to support applied software measurement with industry and government partners. Our approaches are goal-directed, where the focus is placed on identifying goals or objectives, using the goals and objectives to systematically derive information needs, and collecting the necessary data to provide the information. Fraunhofer has extensive experience applying several measurement-based approaches and methods, including:

1. The Goal Question Metric (GQM) approach [7] provides mechanisms for defining measurements goals, refining goals into specifications for data collection, and analyzing and interpreting the

collected data with respect to the formulated goals. Originally formulated for use at NASA's Software Engineering Laboratory [8], the GQM approach has been applied in many domains, including aeronautics, telecommunications, the oil industry, defense, and medical.

2. GQM+Strategies™(GQM+S) [9] is an extension to the GQM approach that supports alignment between goal definitions, strategy development, and measurement implementation existing in the various hierarchies of the organization. This extension enables integration of measurement across the organization. With GQM+Strategies, organizations make explicit how strategies implemented at the lower level in the organization support the highest level business goals of the organization, and how measurement collected at the lower level is used to track achievement of the business goals. For example, a top-level business goal of a commercial software company could be to "increase customer satisfaction," where it is supported by "perform effective code reviews" strategy at its technical division.

3. Quality Improvement Paradigm (QIP) [10] is a six-phase process for continuous organizational improvement that draws from the knowledge and experience gained executing individual projects. QIP consists of two cycles: (1) the organization-level cycle consists of phases for characterizing the organization, setting improvement goals, choosing processes to be implemented on projects, analyzing results, and packaging the experience for future organizational use; (2) the project-level cycle consists of phases for executing the selected process, analyzing results at the project scope, and providing feedback of the process.

4. Experience Factory (EF) [11] is a conceptual infrastructure supporting QIP for synthesizing, packaging, and storing work products and experiences provided by the projects as "reusable experience," and supplying the experience to (future) projects on-demand.

12.2.4 APPLYING SOFTWARE MEASUREMENT IN PRACTICE—THE GENERAL APPROACH

In this section, we briefly discuss Fraunhofer's general approach to implementing a measurement program with an industry or government partner. The steps of this process reflect, as we will discuss in Section 12.3, that many of the challenges facing an industry measurement program are not matters of processing or analyzing data, but rather in working with people and organizations.

As exemplified in the QIP, our general approach for measurement is comprised of three phases performed iteratively: (1) requirements gathering; (2) metrics planning and formalization; and (3) metric program execution consisting of implementation, interpretation, communication, and response (Figure 12.1).

In the *requirements gathering* phase, we identify the relevant stakeholders and elicit their business needs. Through the elicitation process, the available assets (e.g., existing data, process, and insight) as well as constraints and limitations (e.g., data availability and access, personnel engaged in measurement, etc.) are discovered. We also obtain the stakeholders' commitments by defining their roles and responsibilities in the measurement program.

In the *planning and formalization* phase, we articulate the business needs as measurement goals—specifying the purpose, object, focus, and context of the measurement. We also outline how the measures shall be analyzed and interpreted against the goal using GQM. We use the measurement goals, constraints, and limitations to define a measurement plan with specific metrics to gather, and the process (who, when, where, etc.) for gathering them. The formalization of the measurement plan

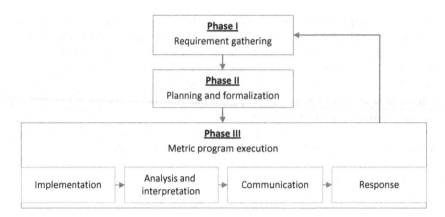

FIGURE 12.1

General applied software measurement approach.

includes the standardization of the vocabulary adopted in the measurement program. This alleviates the problem when dealing with a heterogeneous set of stakeholders.

The *execution* phase consists of four main activities: (1) implementation; (2) analysis and interpretation; (3) communication; and (4) response. In *implementation*, the measurement plan is executed and data is collected. During the data gathering, unanticipated changes and/or roadblocks may occur and need to be addressed. Next, the gathered data is *analyzed and interpreted* with respect to the business goals using the help of Subject Matter Experts (SMEs). Results are then *communicated* to the relevant stakeholders in an easy-to-understand format. Finally, we gather the organization's *responses* to the measurement program findings to define organizational improvement activities as well evaluations and improvements to the measurement program. New business needs may be identified, and the measurement process may be repeated.

In the remainder of this chapter, our discussion of challenges and lessons learned follows this progression from measurement requirement gathering, to formalization, to the many phases of implementation.

12.3 SIX KEY ISSUES WHEN IMPLEMENTING A MEASUREMENT PROGRAM IN INDUSTRY

12.3.1 STAKEHOLDERS, REQUIREMENTS, AND PLANNING: THE GROUNDWORK FOR A SUCCESSFUL MEASUREMENT PROGRAM

Whether you are applying software analyses in commercial or government settings, large or small organizations, the measurement process begins with requirements gathering, to understand the data analyses that the consumers, or end-users desire. As with any requirements-gathering process, there will be roadblocks along the way. This section highlights specific examples of challenges in three primary areas: *stakeholder relationships*, *goal setting*, and *measurement program planning*.

The first step in a successful measurement program is having a sponsor, i.e., a senior-level representative in the organization, who funds the activities as well as recognizes the value of the measurement program and communicates its importance to the organization at large. The sponsor may also act as the champion where the champion leads the measurement program initiative, assigns and motivates personnel resources, and ensures the measurement plan is managed and tracked to achieve the stated goals. In some cases, potential sponsors or champions may need to be convinced of the value of a measurement program. When doing so, one should focus on the general benefits of measurement to any organization:

- Understanding the business—Data collected from a measurement program can be used to build organizational baseline models to gain knowledge about the organization.
- Managing projects—Project management is supported by measurement, whether planning and estimating, tracking actual progress and cost versus estimates, or validating process/product models.
- Better prediction—Creation of process/product models through data collection improves the predictability of activity and decision-making within the organization.
- Guiding improvement—Measures and reports help to increase understanding by allowing users to analyze and assess the performance of processes and products and generate ideas for improvement.

The existence of both a sponsor and champion becomes critical to overcoming numerous challenges of implementing a measurement program, such as gaining buy-in from customer and supplier stakeholders, prioritizing measurement goals, obtaining data from project teams or subcontractors, attaining participation from subject matter experts, effectively communicating results to stakeholders, and more. As in software development project teams, paying attention to how well measurement program roles work together is extremely important [12].

FROM THE TRENCHES

Implementation of measurement programs is a multifaceted undertaking, particularly initiatives that are broad and affect many different groups of the organization. These programs are complex, organizational change efforts that require effective work, political, and/or cultural systems to achieve success. In a process improvement/measurement program in a commercial organization, both the sponsor and the champion were clearly identified in the program plan; however, two challenges occurred that ultimately resulted in the program ending without success. The champion was not positioned in the organization to influence change in all affected parts of the organization. In addition, there was a struggle between the sponsor and champion to keep program goals aligned, concrete, and explicit. On several occasions non-explicit or continually-changing goals confounded the activities of the program, thereby eliminating focused efforts and measurement success. This result highlighted the importance of the sponsor and champion working closely together including having the sponsor assist the champion to align the organization's differing factions and sub-interests to assure an environment where change is a priority and can take place.

Measurement stakeholders who will provide data, and subject matter experts who will interpret measurements must also be identified early so that they understand the importance of their contributions to the measurement effort. For example, in large acquisition projects, suppliers provide important measurement data to the acquirers so that overall program status can be monitored. In these situations, gaining buy-in from the supplier stakeholders who provide the data is essential. If possible, encourage the sponsor to build data collection requirements into the project requirements.

Stakeholder time is valuable, and measurement is often viewed as an overhead activity. Stakeholder commitment can be easier to obtain if the sponsor communicates the importance of the measurement program and incentivizes participation. When engaging stakeholders, explain the benefits the data and analyses will bring to the project and organization, rather than using metrics as a means to evaluate individuals. Maintaining the goodwill of your stakeholders throughout a measurement program is essential.

> "Setting goals is the first step in turning the invisible into the visible."
>
> *– Tony Robbins*

Aligning overarching business goals with individual team or organizational unit objectives is critical to a successful measurement program. For example, at a small business client of Fraunhofer's, the measurement sponsor wanted to increase product quality. The company's marketing group measured product quality using a customer satisfaction survey, whereas the software group measured software quality by post-release defects. Goals were set using different metrics within each division; however, both sets of metrics and division goals contributed to the overall goal of improving product quality. Aligning business goals with individual team or group goals can be difficult when eliciting measurement requirements with stakeholders. To make this problem easier, we apply the GQM+Strategies approach, which explicitly defines and aligns business goals and group strategies for achieving these goals into an integrated measurement program.

The measurement program must also be tailored to the needs of individual consumers (e.g., safety engineers, managers, technical staff, etc.). For example, managers on different levels have different needs. Project managers need to monitor and control their projects. Program managers need ways to manage a portfolio of projects, and higher-level managers need ways to manage the business based on even higher-level indicators. You cannot plan on a standard set of analyses that will be applicable to all stakeholders.

Consumers of the data analyses may find it difficult to express their desired goals or objectives for measurement and analyses especially when objectives are presented in abstract form, for example, quality objectives such as maintainability and portability. It may be helpful to define what *cannot* or *should not* happen, which can then be translated into measurable goals. When eliciting goals, be specific, "speak" in consumers' language, and, if possible, draw from data already available to ground the measurement objectives in relatable terms. In general, consumers will find it easier to respond to concrete ideas and feedback. We recommend developing a straw man of the measurement requirements using available documentation, including business goals, process documentation, organization website, and information collected at prior meetings, to make the limited time available with stakeholders as productive as possible.

When setting measurement goals, we recommend focusing on mature processes that have been institutionalized across the organization. Focusing on institutionalized processes has several benefits: (1) raw data to measure is more likely to exist; (2) the organization may already have baseline performance measures established; (3) the metrics can be applied to a broader set of projects within the organization; and (4) the measurements can be compared across projects for useful insights. However, while measurement with institutionalized processes is ideal, less mature organizations may not have this luxury. In these situations, measurement goals formulated around product quality may be the best starting point, since usually data on product or service quality are readily available and improved product or service quality goal(s) are valued by most organizations even when business goals are not well defined or explicitly communicated.

Goal development should ultimately result in a measurement plan. The measurement plan becomes the vehicle to capture measurement-related decisions, stakeholders involvement, measurement analysis needs, and measurement activities and risks. A measurement plan must have well specified individual metrics, and well-defined procedures for data collection, extraction, modification, aggregation, analysis, and reporting. Furthermore, the plan is a basis for allocating the resources needed for the measurement program. As mentioned earlier, measurement is often viewed as an overheard or assurance activity, rather than a contributor to product development. Thus, defining the resource needs from the organization is essential for project planning and to ensure that stakeholders participate in measurement activities. The measurement plan should include regular meetings with stakeholders to ensure that the measurement results are not just a deliverable to be filed away—an invisible measurement program is no better than a non-existent one [11].

In this section, we have discussed some of the key issues when initiating a measurement program in industry. Determining consumers' needs for measurement analyses is one of the first steps in applying software analytics in industry contexts. Doing so requires attention to stakeholder relationships, goal-setting, and measurement planning. The list below summarizes some of the key lessons learned from our experiences in laying the groundwork for a successful measurement program:

- Establish strong relationships with your sponsors and champion to leverage their support.
- Obtain and maintain buy-in from key stakeholders, including suppliers of data.
- Align consumer needs with the business goals and objectives of the organization.
- Understand measurement goals, questions, and metrics for each stakeholder.
- Tailor planned measurement analyses based on consumer needs.
- Explicitly capture the measurement goals, resources needed, and stakeholder involvement in a measurement plan.

12.3.2 GATHERING MEASUREMENTS—HOW, WHEN, AND WHO

> "Data! Data! Data!" he cried impatiently. "I can't make bricks without clay."
> – *Sir Arthur Conan Doyle, The Adventure of the Copper Beeches*

Once the goals of the organization are understood, the next challenge is to get the information for the analyses. Gathering data and other information for analysis can be expensive and time-consuming [13]. The needs of stakeholders often compete for priority when deciding which data to gather, how to collect it, how and where the data should be stored, who is responsible for the collection and integrity of the data, and how the information should be aggregated and reported [14]. Key considerations are automation and tools, establishing access to data, and designing the data storage that supports data collection as well as analysis needs.

A strong automated metrics infrastructure makes analysis easier. Automating the measurement process enables rapid feedback and improvement, and also reduces collection costs.

For even greater efficiency, an organization should leverage data collected by existing tools used by a project whether for project management, engineering, software development, or testing activities. These data are generated as a result of the natural process of work and often minimal effort is needed to collect the data. For example, a project manager can integrate automatic metrics collection using the project's build management tools. These tools provide many important metrics on the code size, churn (lines added, deleted, and modified), complexity, etc. Thus data collection can be a matter of copying comma separated values (CSV) files from a server. Projects can also use an effort estimation tool that stores data in a database as a valuable source of data to which researchers can connect and extract data with no burden on the project team members. By leveraging the output of existing tools and databases, we are able to accomplish more with our analyses in a shorter amount of time.

As beneficial as they are, data collection tools are not a "silver bullet" and can also be a hindrance. For example, on a large government project, the prime contractor decided to use a well-known commercial off-the-shelf (COTS) tool for data collection of work completed. The tool made it easy for teams to enter their data and to keep the data private to the specific teams. For basic analyses and predefined roll-ups or aggregations, it also worked well. However the tool's ad hoc analysis and reporting capabilities were very limited. When situations changed and the project or government needed to perform other analyses, extracting the data from the tool's proprietary data stores or reformatting the data within the tool was difficult or impossible. As a result, on subsequent projects, we have recommended that the project makes the government's/client's ability to extract and analyze data independently a priority.

For many projects, one tool or process cannot perform all the data collection and analyses needed. Furthermore, large programs often engage subcontractors or multiple project teams who each have their own processes and tools. To ensure that the data is useful, it is important that the same type of data is collected and the data have the same semantics. Thus, data must often be imported, processed, and transformed from many disparate files and tools, and merged before it is suitable for analysis. This collation process may be manual, semi-automatic, or automatic; but, in any case, it often requires significant effort to implement. The cost of collating such data is often overlooked, but a strong up-front measurement plan can help avoid this pain point.

Access to data must also be considered when planning the research and analyses. Access to some data may be impossible for both technical and organizational reasons, and these reasons are always difficult to overcome. An individual or organization may hide data or not allow access to it because it can make them look bad; the organization may not consider the data worth their time to collect; or stakeholders may simply distrust the researchers or the benefits of the analyses. On one project, we could not perform all of the analysis needed because we could not obtain the raw data, even though it existed somewhere electronically. The organization cited security concerns and it required extra time and upper management intervention to resolve the stalemate. Therefore, as much as possible, be sure to plan for access to data and tools as the project is being initiated to avoid delays or the inability to perform the work later. These issues are not easy to overcome, and it will require attacking the problem from viewpoints that include technical access and also political/social/ethical concerns (e.g., establishing trust among researchers and stakeholders and formalizing non-disclosure agreements).

Data analytics on large government projects also pose some unique situations and large-project-specific challenges. As explained in the following example from the trenches, the decisions made on how measurement data is stored can derail even the best intentions for a good measurement program.

FROM THE TRENCHES

On large government projects, measurement and analysis programs are often required by contract. Having the measurement program required rather than desired by the organization, can focus the project more on meeting the letter of the data collection and analyses requirements than on making the processes useful and efficient. On one large government contract, the prime contractor was required to keep a variety of data in an electronic data store. Unfortunately, the requirement did not specify what format or what analyses needed to be performed on this data. As a result, the contractor stored all the data and analyses as .pdf files. These .pdf files contained text documents, PowerPoint slides, and various other products developed and used by the project. It was impossible for researchers or the government to subsequently use the stored data for any further analysis without manually re-entering all the tables and numbers from the text reports. Obviously, this metrics repository was not useful and served no purpose. We now recommend that all projects we work with require project data to be stored in an electronic format that can facilitate and allow data aggregation and further electronic analysis.

In summary, lessons learned related to gathering measurements include:

- Automate data collection and transformation wherever possible:
  - Leverage existing data from other tools used by a project while keeping the goals in mind.
  - Be prepared to merge data from many sources, if necessary.
- Accessing data can be a difficult obstacle to overcome; it is important to plan ahead for data access.
- Make sure the data collected and stored is usable efficiently/electronically for analyses.

12.3.3 ALL DATA, NO INFORMATION—WHEN THE DATA IS NOT WHAT YOU NEED OR EXPECT

"The goal is to turn data into information, and information into insight."

– Cathy Fiorina

Once the data is accessible, the next step is to apply the metrics and gather measurements. When dealing with any form of raw data, there will always be issues of missing, incomplete, or incorrect data. However, these are just some of the issues that have to be addressed.

Often, when people think of software measurement, they think of code metrics. Yet, much of industry is focused on process improvement, and thus needs to quantify and understand their current processes and not just the process results (e.g., the resulting piece of software). When an organization's goals include process improvement, measuring the process is inevitable. Processes, unlike products, are much harder to define. For instance, while we have numerous methods for measuring the size of a software product, what is an equivalent metric for the size or scale of a process? To make something measurable implies that the object of measurement has some semi-rigorous definition to enforce measurement consistency. Thus, measuring a process can be a catalyst for defining the process. For example, on several of our projects, the client was interested in assessing the quality of their hazard analysis process. However, when we looked at the process artifacts (hazard reports), there were missing data, out-of-date information, a number of different formats, and inconsistent terminology. On another large defense project, there were no hazard reports to be measured even though, in management's eyes, they existed. Thus, trying to measure the process artifacts revealed a number of *process risks*, which could then be communicated to project management. Visibility into these risks was then the catalyst for process improvement initiatives. Ultimately, the measurement program provided the added benefit of helping to define the hazard analysis process and its expectations in the organization.

While "code" is the most recognizable process artifact, requirements documents, design diagrams, operating manuals, task descriptions, and other process artifacts are strong candidates for measurement. In our experience, industry partners are as interested in quantifying the quality of these artifacts as they are in code, particularly in projects with a long development period. Unfortunately, these artifacts do not lend themselves to insightful measurement. Process artifacts, such as requirements and designs, rarely follow a rigorous structured language, thus making the application of a scale (beyond a simple word count) a manual task. Those that do follow rigorous structures, such as formal models or standardized design languages (e.g., UML) lend themselves to counting-based analysis. However, artifacts, such as requirements and designs, are often evaluated according to their semantic content, thus making automated measurement a near impossibility. Thus, when an organization's goals involve improving non-coding activities, one must plan to spend significant effort understanding and applying metrics to non-code process artifacts. Further, additional effort should be allocated with the organization's subject matter experts to understand the artifacts and validate the proposed metrics. Partial automated analysis of non-code artifacts, such as requirements, defects, and anomalies is currently possible via the application of natural language processing techniques [15–17]. However, these techniques usually need a significant amount of effort to be institutionalized in the organization process and properly configured to the specific application context.

Even if we are measuring established concepts and sufficient planning for the measurement has been done, problems in data quality still occur. Problems such as missing data, incomplete data, data reported inconsistently, or incorrect data are prevalent and to be expected in any measurement program [18]. Such problems occur because of variations in the way the processes were performed—both in the process for gathering/reporting the data and/or the process that produced the artifacts being measured, creating variations in the process artifacts. Another reason could simply be that the activity of resolving missing data is expensive or impossible. In any case, problems with the quality of the data will likely cause bias in the resulting analyses or render it completely useless. Regardless of how sensitive or sophisticated the data analysis techniques are, the results they produce will not be useful if the underlying data is incorrect.

The general problem of the low quality of data in empirical software engineering has already been well documented [19, 20]. One such example is the problem with bug-fix datasets that has been studied in some detail [21–26]. We recall our own experience related to this problem in one of our projects. Our customer employs several Verification and Validation (V&V) techniques, e.g., peer review, user acceptance testing, and automated unit testing, and would like to assess their effectiveness against the different types of defects. Our customer's goal is to improve software quality by using the V&V technique that provides the most effective detection, given the type of defects they are expecting. To achieve this, they created and maintained a defect classification schema, which is used in their defect-fix reporting mechanism. However, they found that the defect classification schema was often used incorrectly by the personnel creating the reports, resulting in defects types being reported incorrectly.

As a consequence, errors exist in the defect report repository used in their data analysis, leading to the selection of inappropriate V&V techniques [27].

In our experience, we have found the following practices useful in reducing data quality issues:

1. Managers should communicate the importance of good data quality to the team and, when possible, put in place mechanisms for enabling convenient input of data. Managers should also ensure sufficient resources are allocated to enable the team to generate data as complete and as accurate as requested.
2. Data analysts should always validate the received data (e.g., check that data has valid or reasonable values, check underlying data if result analysis deviates from expectation), and provide the data submitter with constructive feedback when problems with the data are found and also provide suggestions for improving data collection (e.g., automate collection mechanisms, employ robust processes that place constraints on how values are entered—such as choosing from drop-down lists instead of free text, etc.)
3. Organizations should aim to institutionalize processes (i.e., processes that are well-documented, trained, repeatable, and consistently implemented) because such processes reduce variability in the artifacts produced.

Note, however, that even with the best intentions, eliminating data problems may still be infeasible, usually due to the significant cost associated with collecting, reviewing, or transforming it. When analyzing data with quality issues, it is important to understand how the analysis results may be impacted by them. Often, knowing which issues exist and their possible impact on the analysis can be taken into account during the interpretation of the analysis results. The caveats and limitations due to data irregularities should be clearly communicated along with the analysis results. Data analysts also need to be realistic in their expectations of the data and creative in their analyses to gain as much value from the data available.

FROM THE TRENCHES

On a large acquisition project, our customer (i.e., the acquirer) was interested in tracking software development progress. The lead development contractor was expected to provide sufficient data so that the plan and actual progress could be compared for deviations. However, for one particular activity, the contractor found that the week-by-week plan data was too difficult to generate; and when generated, the resulting plan was highly volatile, causing the analysis to be ineffective for informing the customer of progress issues. Instead of using the inaccurate weekly data, we decided to analyze the actual progress relative to what was needed (planned) to be accomplished in order to complete the activity on schedule. This data was readily available and relatively stable. We then derived the needed progress rate and assessed whether the planned rate was reasonable given past performance and industry standards. While this analysis did not provide insight about deviations on a weekly basis, it was still able to inform our customer when progress was starting to lag behind an expected schedule and the activity's timely completion was threatened. This measurement program has been perceived as critical to the project to the point that it is being explored for adoption throughout the acquiring organization.

In summary, lessons learned related to data quality include:

- Measuring process artifacts generally requires a well-defined process, but applying measures to an ill-defined process can still reveal useful insights to the organization.
- Extra time and customer resources should be planned when measuring non-code artifacts.
- Engage sponsors and champions to communicate the importance of data quality to the team.

- Validate all data prior to analysis.
- Data quality issues are inevitable, but being aware of their existence and their impact are key for obtaining analysis results that are useful in spite of the presence of problems.

12.3.4 THE PIVOTAL ROLE OF SUBJECT MATTER EXPERTISE

Subject Matter Expert—Person with bona fide expert knowledge about what it takes to do a particular job.

– U.S. Office of Personnel Management

Now that data are available, it is time for analysis and extracting the insights we hope can be used to improve our project. Regardless of the type of data, the analyst must first understand the context of the data so that it can be measured accurately. Furthermore, the measurements and analysis results will need an interpretation to be useful for project management—metrics are insightful, but rarely, if ever, tell the whole story on their own. Subject matter experts (SMEs) are key to overcoming the challenges in this area, which include *understanding the data* and *interpreting the analysis results.*

First, consider the scenario where one must *understand the data* so that it can be measured accurately. For example, on a government aerospace program, we wanted to measure *hazard reports,* which are PDF documents written in natural language that capture the output of safety analysis. Many terms used in the reports referred to software systems, but some familiarity with spaceflight systems was required to understand this. Understanding the language and domain was challenging, and we went through several iterations of measurement and review to ensure that our counts were accurate.

Consider a second scenario where the raw data have been collected and the measurements are ready for analysis. The challenge now is to *interpret the results of the analysis.* Analysis results may be interpreted in different ways depending on the assumptions and context that the analysts have regarding the data and/or the project. On one project, we calculated the effort estimation error for all of the features in the new release of the system [28] using data automatically extracted from a database. The analysis showed that a small subset of features had a high relative estimation error. However, we knew little about the technical aspects of the features or their implementation history, and could offer no insights for the project manager.

In both scenarios, SMEs from the development groups were essential to overcoming these challenges in a timely fashion. On the government aerospace project, we created a dictionary of common terms in the hazard reports, and asked software safety SMEs whether or not those subsystems contained software. The SMEs told us how to divide the system conceptually according to the development groups, thereby improving the utility of our results to project management. Such valuable insight can be difficult to obtain. Project SMEs are often most concerned with completing their project tasks, not contributing to a metrics initiative that they likely view as an overhead. The people most suitable to answer questions may be those with the least amount of time to spare. Once again, it is essential to have management support and "boots on the ground" who can identify and free the resources to assist in the measurement effort.

FROM THE TRENCHES

For a government aerospace program, one metric was a count of the number of hazards, causes, and controls (all contained within the hazard report) that involved software behavior. The simplest approach was to search for software-related terms, but the hazard reports contained a significant amount of technical jargon about spaceflight hardware design. For example, the same system handling spacecraft flight may be referred to as Avionics, Guidance, GNC, or Guidance Navigation and Control. This makes interpreting these terms as a single concept across artifacts challenging. Further, the relations between terms may be lost, e.g., a reference to the "flight computer" may include GNC and CD&H, but this implied relationship may not be explicit in the artifact. All of these issues arose when trying to accurately determine whether a hazard involved software components.

Many of the spacecraft engineers come from a hardware background, and thus did not appreciate the extent of software's involvement in safety-critical aspects of the design. For three major systems on the Program, 45-60% of the hazards were caused or prevented by software, which surprised many stakeholders. By having an accurate picture of the system decomposition, and their responsible parties, our measurements convinced systems engineers to allocate additional costly, yet essential, software assurance effort to certain areas of the system.

Sometimes, there is inconsistency between experts' opinions and quantitative results and it is important to investigate the reasons for disagreement. One of the main reasons for this inconsistency is that the underlying data (upon which results are computed) is unreliable or incorrectly filtered. For example, consider a scenario where one project has a high number of bugs and another has a low number of bugs. If the quality of the project is evaluated by the number of bugs, one may conclude that the project with the lower number of bugs is the higher quality project. The subject matter experts are puzzled because, in their opinion, the project with the lower number of bugs is actually the lower quality project, simply based on their own project insights. Further investigation reveals that the low-bug-count project was not following the bug reporting process and that some bugs have not been recorded. Thus, the project is actually of a lower quality than suggested by the analysis.

Subject matter expertise and familiarity with the development context are necessary to help identify such biases in the data.

On a commercial project, we presented some analysis results in a meeting with project managers and development leads. The features with high relative error estimates caused concern, but the development leads were able to provide justifiable reasons for the effort estimation errors, such as working with a new technology, developers taking medical leave, and other reasons not captured in the metrics. Understanding the development contributors to a measurement result is necessary for taking corrective action. In addition, for a small client pursuing high-maturity processes we established measurement-focused meetings at regular intervals to get the right people in the room. These meetings focused on assisting the project teams with goal definition, evaluating project performance given established goals and organizational models, using prediction models for decision-making, and adjusting project-specific processes to achieve goals, if needed.

In summary, lessons learned related to the role of subjects matter expertise include:

- Finding time with SMEs to validate metrics and interpret data is difficult. Data analysis is an overhead activity.
- The project must engage SMEs early to ensure that the metrics and measurements are meaningful for the project.

- SMEs should be available to answer specific questions about the project and domain.
- SMEs are necessary for interpreting data and taking corrective action.
- Raw data requires time and resources to understand, particularly in an unfamiliar domain.
- Measurements do not tell the whole story, and results can be meaningless or contentious without the qualitative insight of SMEs.

12.3.5 RESPONDING TO CHANGING NEEDS

> To improve is to change; to be perfect is to change often.
>
> *– Winston Churchill*

It never fails: just when you have successfully defined effective measures and established analysis processes, something changes and there are new management and stakeholder priorities; specific events to be analyzed or highlighted; and needs for new collection or aggregation methods that differ from what was planned. Most of the time, these changes cannot be predicted and are needed immediately. In these situations a project is left trying to adapt to change as best it can.

Edmunds and Morris noted succinctly that "A theme stressed in the literature is the paradoxical situation that, although there is an abundance of information available, it is often difficult to obtain useful, relevant information when it is needed" [29]. A challenge facing any measurement program is when the sponsoring organization, despite all of your planning and rigorous metric definitions, asks questions for which there is no direct data captured. This has happened routinely on many projects and it has required that the analysis teams become creative. Project managers/stakeholders urgently need the measurement program and analysts to provide a way to respond to the new situation. Politically, it is not an option to respond that there is just no information to assist the managers/stakeholders.

On one large government program, the project was cancelled but there were many functions that were almost complete. These pieces of software could be transferred over to another program, but the burning question was whether the software was mature enough to keep or whether it should just be thrown away when the project was terminated. The answer was needed very quickly and there wasn't time or budget to collect new data. So, answering the program's questions required analyzing what would give the program any insight into what a good decision would be. For example, the appropriateness of reusing the software could be characterized by the goodness of the software design, software complexity, quality (execution errors as well as code analysis), amount of code actually implemented, a qualitative technical assessment of the code, etc. Fortunately, the project had a mature measurement program and it already had collected some data for these attributes. We created a matrix with the attributes and the resulting analysis of the data to provide the customer with a valuable assessment of the current state and quality of the software, even though the software was still incomplete and not totally tested.

One common challenge for a software development project is the reorganization of its deliveries and software builds. Technical or logistic dependencies of software and its functions, changes in priorities, or schedule changes cause the contents and even the structure of major builds to change (possibly multiple times) during the project's life cycle. Transforming and re-aggregating the data to keep it in alignment with current reporting needs is an arduous task and it is very tempting to not change the project's data, but to work around it. However, most of the changes in the data can be performed via scripting and it is crucial to do if analysis of the data is to remain a value-added activity for the project. If the data and resulting analyses are no longer aligned with the current project goals and priorities, the analyses can no longer assist management or other stakeholders in their decision processes.

In addition to keeping data current with change, when there are tools to support the analysis of data, it is important that the tools be able to facilitate change. Tools need to provide the ability for the team to easily implement different what-if analyses. On a major government program, we provided the in-house cost estimate for the program. It was a very large program and even preparing the request for proposals required a few years' time. Over these years technology, politics, logistics and many aspects of the program changed. We had developed a tool to generate the cost estimate and structured it modularly so that the tool and the estimate were able to provide what-if-analyses and to adapt as more information was known, or as changes to the program were identified. To provide the maximum value added, not only must the data be able to adapt to changes, but tool development for analytics needs to be agile as well.

In summary, lessons learned related to the ability in responding to changing needs include:

- Use your investment in data collection and analyses creatively—do not expect to have a measurement directly collected for a purpose. Many measures can support more than one purpose.
- Keep the data aligned with program changes.
- Look for supporting tools that are agile and easily adaptable to change and for "what-if" exercises.

12.3.6 EFFECTIVE WAYS TO COMMUNICATE ANALYSIS RESULTS TO THE CONSUMERS

> "You can have brilliant ideas, but if you can't get them across, your ideas won't get you anywhere."
> *– Lee Iacocca*

Presenting the analysis results in the "right" way is important, as it affects how results are taken in and understood by the consumers. However, it is not trivial and it is an iterative process to arrive at the correct communication channels (e.g., written report versus oral presentation) and mechanisms.

As the literature recommends [29], today's professionals need value-added information that is filtered by software or subject matter experts. Reporting too much information at the wrong levels and without an indication of why the analysis results are meaningful to a manager/stakeholder will guarantee that the data and analyses are ignored. The challenge is to be able to summarize metrics across the program at a high level, while at the same time providing insights into the specific problem.

Ultimately, the outcome of the analysis must become an enabler for the consumers to make decisions with respect to the business needs that were identified early on. Therefore, the results, as communicated to the consumers, should be meaningful so as to aid the consumers in acting upon it. As the results of the analysis drive decision-making, effective communication also means providing the information in a timely manner. You want to present the analysis results while the stakeholders are still able to make decisions about it.

However, measurement programs tend to end up with large amounts of data, all of which are analyzed and dissected in various ways. It is tempting to unload all the data and their analysis onto the customers so as to show the value of the measurement program. The opposite typically holds: your customers will drown in the sea of information and will lose interest when they have to sift through the information just to find the subset of information that interests them. More problematically, with large amounts of information, especially when presented in incoherent ways, important issues may not be noticed and the appropriate actions not taken, all of which diminishes the value of the measurement program.

When communicating the analysis results, it is important to be aware to whom you are presenting the data and to tailor the analysis results accordingly. Different stakeholders care about different information, and at different levels of abstraction. For example, a manager tends to want to see a broader, "30,000-foot view" perspective, while technical personnel care about specific data at a much finer granularity. Therefore, different levels of data abstraction are needed to avoid overwhelming the consumers with the analysis, while providing the capability to drill down to detail when the need arises. However, it is possible that when abstracting data, important issues can become hidden, providing a false illusion that everything is fine. Recall the outcome of the *requirement gathering* phase, especially the elicitation discussion with the stakeholders, to identify the concerns of each stakeholder.

The point of a measurement program is to learn from the data through analysis and synthesis of the data in its context. Therefore, it is not sufficient just to present the results of data, but it is also necessary to present the data in context for comparison, to facilitate the interpretation of the data. Consider what other information is needed in order for the stakeholders to be able to take an action or make a decision.

FROM THE TRENCHES

On one of our large customer projects, an important business need was to understand how the development activity (e.g., requirements definition, code development, software testing) is progressing. The project manager is interested in knowing if delay in the completion of the activity may be anticipated, and, if so, how much of a delay it will be. The manager utilizes this information to make decisions regarding re-planning. When communicating the analysis of measurement results that track the development activity progress, it is important to include how the progress compares against the plan. However, while a comparison of actuals to plan provides a reasonable snapshot of the state of the progress, it is not sufficient to determine the progress toward the future and of potential delay. To do so, the manager also needs to know the trend of progress. This information can be used to infer past performance rate of progress, to compare it with the needed rate of progress, and to assess whether the past progress rate demonstrates the ability to meet the needed rate. Furthermore, if we communicate additional context of information in the form of industry benchmark value for progress rate, the manager can be even more confident in the determination of development delay risk. These presentations of development activity have become essential parts of weekly progress reporting to program and organizational management, and are used to assist in resource allocation and re-planning each month.

Visualization is integral for supporting communication of results. Visualization can quickly identify metric trends and raise issues. More than 80% of people exhibit a strong preference for visual learning [30]. Effective communication entails selecting the appropriate visualization methods. Bar charts and pie charts show proportions more easily than text numbers. Line charts show trends over time. Diagrams show relationships or process flow. Scatter plots can show groups and data trends. The human brain was built for pattern matching, and our visual cortex is the primary mechanism for doing this compared with our language processing centers, which interpret numbers and text [31]. When employing visualization, however, our advice is to keep visualization simple, as complicated visualization can distract from the message conveyed. If you find yourself expending much effort in explaining your visualization, it usually indicates that your visualization is too complex. Note that there are occasions where your stakeholders will have to look at the results on their own. In such cases, it is important to pay attention to correct and easily understood labeling as well as to be aware of color associations (e.g., red is usually associated as something that is in need of attention).

A sign of a successful measurement and analysis program is when measures and analyses are being used continuously and regularly by the decision-maker. While you have the eyes and ears of the decision-makers, be careful not to let the communicated results become repetitive, as the message becomes muted over time. This means that one should periodically revisit the communication channel and mechanisms used to ensure that they are still effective in conveying the message. At the same time, one should continuously explore the different ways to analyze data. The information needs to evolve over time as projects are at different phases or as new knowledge is being formed. Therefore, what analysis you do in the early phase of the project may be different from at the middle or at the end of the project.

In summary, lessons learned related to effectively communicating analysis results include:

- Provide value-added interpretations of all data and analyses.
- Tailor results to the appropriate levels of abstraction for individual consumers.
- Offer sufficient information to allow interpretation of the analysis result in a context that enables decision-making.
- Use visualization, and use the right one.
- Reflect and iterate on the responses to your communication so that you can improve how to communicate with consumers.

12.4 **CONCLUSIONS**

Drawing from examples from our 15 years of performing software analytics work, in this chapter we have discussed the process that has allowed us to deliver value across many different customers and types of organizations. Ultimately, software data analytics is about helping stakeholders to make decisions, and we have seen in our own work how powerful measurement-based decision-making can be. A grassroots analytics program to track and project development progress on a communications system project has been elevated to the highest levels of agency management as a best practice for managing software development on large acquisition programs. A data analytics program we implemented at a web application development company has driven process improvement to help that organization mature from CMMI Level 1 to CMMI Level 5, and is still used today for effort estimation and defect prediction. Data collected from years of software inspections helped form the basis for NASA's agency-wide Software Formal Inspections Standard [32]. The benefits of software data analytics will vary from organization to organization and project to project, hence any successful data analytics program must begin by understanding the needs and goals of the stakeholders involved.

Historically, the process of creating a successful data analysis program has been a largely manual one, for reasons that include:

- The necessity of finding champions and engaging with multiple stakeholders, and of conveying results in the language of those stakeholders.
- The necessity of scrubbing and quality-checking data sources, which requires human judgment and experience.

- The necessity of ensuring that conclusions are well-grounded and make sense for the domain.
- The frequent need to recalibrate all of the above in light of ever-changing organizational priorities.

A suite of proven methods (GQM [7, 9], QIP [10], EF [11]) have served us well. However, as in all other areas of software engineering, the fast pace of change in the field and the ever-increasing demand for software in all domains means that our technologies also need to continually improve to maintain their impact and relevance. Thus our recent research focus has been on topics that can augment our existing measurement framework with new capabilities and faster results. Moving forward, our research vision encompasses:

- Methods for aligning business goals and technical measures, including GQM+Strategies [9], to facilitate our ability to define appropriate metrics and report actionable results.
- Data mining approaches [15, 33] that can quickly find new and subtle relationships in our datasets from real customers, in order to increase the speed with which we can answer customer queries and to enable more fine-grained recommendations for projects.
- Automated and semi-automated tools [34] for extracting metrics from software artifacts into an analyzable form, in order to increase the speed and breadth with which data can be collected for analysis.
- Visualization approaches [35] that can aid in interactive exploration of relationships in the data as well as give our customers the ability to perform what-if analyses.

As promising as the results of the research by ourselves and others in these areas have been, we are well aware that none of these technologies are silver bullets. That is, they stand little chance of enabling effective, data-driven decision-making and other improvements in software development organizations, if they are not embedded into an intentional and end-to-end process, such as the one we have described here. While technology and the speed of analysis seem to constantly accelerate, the underlying fundamentals of human and organizational behavior do not.

Going forward, we must always guard against algorithmically correct and quick-performance algorithms that fail to take into account the messy reality of data, i.e., those that fail to account for data quality problems, that misinterpret biases in data collection (e.g., assuming that projects with few defects are high quality rather than possibly delinquent reporters), and that fail to sanity-check results against domain understanding. As automation and other research breakthroughs enable ever-larger volumes of data to be processed ever-more rapidly, such problems become more likely and have potentially wider repercussions.

REFERENCES

[1] IEEE. IEEE standard for a software quality metrics methodology. IEEE Std 1061-1998. p. i; 1998.
[2] Chrissis M, Konrad M, Shrum S. CMMI for development: guidelines for process integration and product improvement. In: SEI series in software engineering; 2011. p. 688.
[3] Basili V, Trendowicz A, Kowalczyk M, Heidrich J, Seaman C, Münch J, et al. Aligning organizations through measurement—the GQM+Strategies approach; 2014.
[4] Shull F, Singer J, Sjøberg DIK. Guide to advanced empirical software engineering. Secaucus, NJ, USA: Springer-Verlag New York, Inc.; 2007.

[5] Falessi D, Shaw M, Mullen K. A journey in achieving and maintaining CMMI maturity level 5 in a small organization. IEEE Softw 2014;31(5).

[6] Fenton NE, Pfleeger SL. Software metrics: a rigorous and practical approach, vol. 2. p. 38–42; 1997.

[7] Basili VR, Caldiera G, Rombach HD. The goal question metric approach. In: Encyclopedia of software engineering. New York: Wiley; 1994.

[8] Basili VR, Weiss DM. A methodology for collecting valid software engineering data. IEEE Trans Softw Eng 1984;SE-10.

[9] Basili VR, Lindvall M, Regardie M, Seaman C, Heidrich J, Munch J, et al. Linking software development and business strategy through measurement. Computer 2010;43:57–65.

[10] Basili VR, Caldiera G. Improve software quality by reusing knowledge and experience. Sloan Manage Rev 1995;37:55–64.

[11] Basili V, Caldiera G, Rombach HD. Experience factory. In: Encyclopedia of software engineering, vol. 1; 1994. p. 469–76.

[12] McConnell S. Software project survival guide. Redmond, WA: Microsoft Press; 1997.

[13] Campbell P, Clewell B. Building evaluation capacity: collecting and using data in cross-project evaluations. Washington, DC: The Urban Institute; 2008.

[14] Esker L, Zubrow D, Dangle K. Getting the most out of your measurement data: approaches for using software metrics. In: Systems software technology conference proceedings, vol. 18; 2006.

[15] Falessi D, Layman L. Automated classification of NASA anomalies using natural language processing techniques. In: IEEE international symposium on software reliability engineering workshops (ISSREW); 2013. p. 5–6.

[16] Falessi D, Cantone G, Canfora G. Empirical principles and an industrial case study in retrieving equivalent requirements via natural language processing techniques. IEEE Trans Softw Eng 2013;39(1):18–44.

[17] Runeson P, Alexandersson M, Nyholm O. Detection of duplicate defect reports using natural language processing. In: 29th international conference on software engineering (ICSE'07); 2007. p. 499–510.

[18] Wohlin C, Runeson P, Höst M, Ohlsson MC, Regnell B, Wesslén A. Experimentation in software engineering: an introduction; January 2000.

[19] Mockus A. Missing data in software engineering. In: Shull F, Singer J, Sjøberg DIK, editors. Guide to advanced empirical software engineering. London: Springer London; 2008.

[20] Liebchen GA, Shepperd M. Data sets and data quality in software engineering. In: Proceedings of the 4th international workshop on Predictor models in software engineering—PROMISE '08; 2008. p. 39.

[21] Antoniol G, Ayari K, Penta MD, Khomh F, Guéhéneuc YG. Is it a bug or an enhancement?. In: Proceedings of the 2008 conference of the center for advanced studies on collaborative research meeting of minds—CASCON '08; 2008. p. 304.

[22] Bachmann A, Bird C, Rahman F, Devanbu P, Bernstein A. The missing links. In: Proceedings of the eighteenth ACM SIGSOFT international symposium on foundations of software engineering—FSE '10; 2010. p. 97.

[23] Herzig K, Just S, Zeller A. It's not a bug, it's a feature: how misclassification impacts bug prediction. In: International conference on software engineering (ICSE '13); 2013. p. 392–401.

[24] Rahman F, Posnett D, Herraiz I, Devanbu P. Sample size vs. bias in defect prediction. In: Proceedings of the 9th joint meeting on foundations of software engineering—ESEC/FSE; 2013. p. 147.

[25] Nguyen THD, Adams B, Hassan AE. A case study of bias in bug-fix datasets. In: Proceedings of the 17th working conference on reverse engineering; 2010. p. 259–68.

[26] Kim S, Zhang H, Wu R, Gong L. Dealing with noise in defect prediction. In: Proceeding of the 33rd international conference on Software engineering—ICSE '11; 2011. p. 481.

[27] Falessi D, Kidwell B, Hayes JH, Shull F. On failure classification: the impact of 'getting it wrong'. In: Proceedings of the 36th international conference on software engineering (ICSE), novel ideas and interesting results track (NIER), June 2014, Hyderabad, India; 2013.

[28] Layman L, Nagappan N, Guckenheimer S, Beehler J, Begel A. Mining software effort data: preliminary analysis of visual studio team system data. In: Proceedings of the 2008 international working conference on Mining software repositories; 2008. p. 43–6.

[29] Edmunds A, Morris A. The problem of information overload in business organisations: a review of the literature. Int J Inform Manage 2000;20:17–28.

[30] Felder RM, Spurlin J. Applications, reliability and validity of the index of learning styles. Int J Eng Educ 2005;21:103–12.

[31] Bryant CD, Peck DL. 21st century sociology: a reference handbook; 2007. p. 738.

[32] NASA-STD-87399. Software formal inspections standard. NASA; 2013.

[33] Menzies T, Butcher A, Cok D, Marcus A, Layman L, Shull F, et al. Local versus global lessons for defect prediction and effort estimation. IEEE Trans Softw Eng 2013;39:822–34.

[34] Schumacher J, Zazworka N, Shull F, Seaman C, Shaw M. Building empirical support for automated code smell detection. In: Proceedings of the 2010 ACM-IEEE international symposium on empirical software engineering and measurement—ESEM '10; 2010. p. 1.

[35] Zazworka N, Basili VR, Shull F. Tool supported detection and judgment of nonconformance in process execution. In: Proceedings of the 3rd international symposium on empirical software engineering and measurement; 2009. p. 312–23.

USING DATA TO MAKE DECISIONS IN SOFTWARE ENGINEERING: PROVIDING A METHOD TO OUR MADNESS

13

Brendan Murphy*, **Jacek Czerwonka**[†], **Laurie Williams**[‡]

Microsoft Research Cambridge, Cambridge, UK * *Microsoft Corporation, Redmond, WA, USA*[†] *Department of Computer Science, North Carolina State University, Raleigh, NC, USA*[‡]

CHAPTER OUTLINE

13.1 **INTRODUCTION**

Each day, software development teams make decisions about their development process and the release-readiness of their product. The teams may be facing new challenges, such as the need to release more frequently, or the need to improve product quality. These teams may choose to use a different software process or different software practices to meet these challenges. Have other similar teams developing similar products achieved increased speed and quality by using these practices? Do results to-date suggest objectives will be met? Additionally, teams must decide if the software product is of high enough quality to release. Does the rate of test failures indicate the desired level of reliability has been achieved? And, are the teams actually following the process or actually incorporating the practices that were decided upon?

With the right data, important software engineering decisions can be made through evidence rather than through intuition or by following the latest process or technology trend. This era of "big data" provides a deluge of information. However, data only provides valuable information with carefully planned processing and analysis. Without a plan, the right data may not be collected, the wrong data may be analyzed, the research methods may not provide defensible or insightful results, or undesired comparisons, or inappropriate interpretations may be made.

The goal of this chapter is to aid software engineers and software engineering researchers by providing guidance for establishing a metrics-based decision support program in software engineering. This guidance has three components:

1. accentuating the need for establishing clear goals for the metrics-based program;
2. articulating important components of the metrics-based decision support program, including metrics to record project and product's context, constraints and development;
3. sharing pitfalls to avoid when collecting and interpreting metrics.

The five major components of an iterative and cyclical metrics-based decision support program are summarized in Figure 13.1. The cyclical process begins with the establishment of goals for the product and development for which the measurement program is being developed. Example software development goals include increased time to product deployment, improved quality, and increased

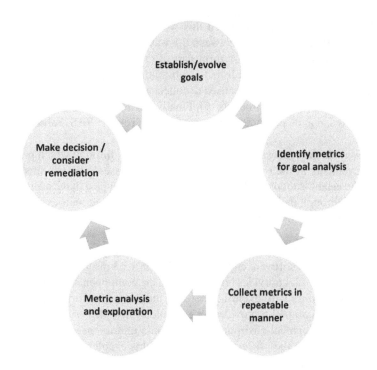

FIGURE 13.1

Metrics-based decision support program.

productivity. Next, the team determines which metrics need to be collected so that analysis can reveal whether the goals have been met or are predicted to be on target. The metrics are then collected. Procedures are documented so that the metrics collection can be repeated on the same product at a different time, or on other projects. The metrics data is then analyzed and explored. Based on the result of the metric analysis the team should determine if the development is on target and if it is not they need to determine if changes are required to the process or if the product goals need adjustment.

In software development, this data analysis and exploration is often called *software analytics* [1]. Through software analytics, insightful and actionable information is folded into the decision-making process. Once decisions are made, the goals of the measurement program can be evolved. The cycle is then repeated. The ultimate goal of such a program is to positively impact the behavior of the team and the success of the project. To illustrate this process, this chapter will provide an example of a Microsoft product group, who re-architected their development process based on data derived from benchmarking previous releases of their product.

We base our guidance on experiences and lessons learned when developing metrics-based decision support programs at Microsoft and when doing research with other companies. The first author previously worked at Digital Corporation monitoring customer systems to characterize hardware and software reliability [2], and initially continued this work in Microsoft [3, 4]. He then focused his research in understanding the relationship between the way software is developed and its post-release behavior. Both the first and second authors form part of the Empirical Software Engineering [ESE] team in Microsoft Research and have published a substantial body of work in this area. The second author manages CodeMine, a process that is used to collect and analyze the engineering processes used to develop the majority of Microsoft products [5]. Finally, the third author has conducted research on the use of agile process and agile practices at Microsoft, IBM, Telelec, SAS, Sabre Airlines [6–10], and other companies.

This chapter describes the process, as depicted in Figure 13.1, through which practitioners can use data to drive improvements in their software engineering processes. The key area that practitioners should focus on is the establishment of clear goals. Often, teams, at best, have aspirations of what they would like to achieve through their development process. Establishing metrics that can be repeatedly collected, and the careful analysis of the metrics can help teams understand if they have achieved their goals.

The rest of this chapter proceeds as follows: Section 13.2 provides information on a short history in the area of software metrics in software engineering. Section 13.3 discusses the need to provide clear goals for the project. Section 13.4 provides information on the components of a metrics-based program. Section 13.5 identifies the pitfalls to avoid in choosing metrics and information about interpretation challenges, respectively. Section 13.6 provides an example of how the Windows Server product team is re-architecting their development environment based on a metric-based decision support program. Section 13.7 shows how to use the processes described in this chapter to allow product teams to use data to drive their engineering process.

13.2 SHORT HISTORY OF SOFTWARE ENGINEERING METRICS

Software engineering differs from other engineering disciplines by its lack of a standardized set of metrics to manage projects. Other engineering disciplines have standardized processes and practices that have evolved over time. For instance, the railway industry standardized their total process for building and managing trains over the last 150 years [11].

Research into the relationship between metrics and software reliability can be traced back to the 1970s. John Musa took an empirical approach in his data collection works [12], whereas other researchers built reliability models based on the software structure [13]. The computer industry initially focused on hardware failures using reliability metrics, such as Mean Time Between Failures (MTBF) and Mean Time To Repair (MTTR) [14, 15]. In the 1980s, software was identified as increasingly impacting overall product reliability. Additionally, [16] identified that software reliability is also influenced by human factors.

In the late 1980s, a number of major computer manufacturers started providing real-time monitoring of their computer systems at the customer sites. This monitoring allowed the total behavior of the computers to be analyzed. Digital Equipment Corp identified that software was becoming the dominant factor impacting the overall system reliability, and its reliability could no longer be measured only in terms of system crash rates [2, 17]. Similarly, IBM analysts attempted to characterize software quality and productivity [18]. Barry Boehm built a model to analyze the economics of software development [19], while Fred Brooks highlighted the difficulty of bringing out-of-control software development projects back under control, based upon his experiences with the IBM System/360 [20]. Similarly Lehman and Belady [21] analyzed the impact of program evolution, from which Manny Lehman derived the "Lehman's laws of software evolution" [22], which assist in our understanding of how products evolve over time.

In the 1990s, in some areas, the perceived lack of standards was assumed to result in catastrophic failures as the new millennium approached. One solution was to apply formal development methods to control the software development process through the use of guidelines and standards, such as ISO 9000 Standard [23] or those promoted by the Software Engineering Institute [24]. During this same timeframe, Norman Fenton produced a comprehensive book on software metrics [25], and other authors focused on the analysis of software development methods [26].

At the same time, the 1990's saw the emergence of the Open Source community producing reliable software, such as Linux and Apache, without the use of these formal methods. The turn of the millennium (Y2K) came and went without catastrophic events. A backlash against the overemphasis of processes in software development resulted in a group of software engineering consultants publishing the *Manifesto for Agile Software Development* [27].

In this millennium, researchers in software engineering have performed numerous studies linking software metrics to post-release failures. For example, Li [28] examined factors that led to system and application unreliability. Mockus [29] discovered the effects of organizational volatility on software reliability, and Zimmermann [30] performed similar studies to identify the causes of security defects in released products. Cataldo [31] found that coordination breakdowns negatively impacted development productivity and software failures. Finally, Zimmermann [32] predicted defects using network analysis on dependency graphs. This sampling of studies found relationships between attributes of the development process and post-release failures for a specific set of products. However, researchers often have difficulty in replicating results on different product sets, suggesting the product and project context influence the metrics. Some practitioners have analyzed which metrics are applicable to specific coding practices, such as Lanza and Marinescu [33] providing assistance in developing object-oriented code.

This chapter incorporates a lot of the learning gained from all of this historical work to improve the effectiveness of managing software development through metrics; and provides a practical approach to this subject.

13.3 ESTABLISHING CLEAR GOALS

The development of any engineering project requires a clear set of goals to provide a focus for the engineers and a mechanism to ensure the development is on target. At times, the goals may change during the development period. Other engineering disciplines may have an established set of metrics that that can be used to determine if the overall product goals have been met. For instance, engineers building a bridge can decide on materials and the design of the bridge, but their usage must exist within defined bounds that are verified through a set of metrics and mathematical equations.

With a plethora of available data, the Goal-Question-Metric (GQM) [34] methodology can be used to guide the development of a metrics-based decision support program, as shown in Figure 13.1. GQM is focused, whereby only the data needed to determine if a goal has been met is processed and analyzed. The GQM approach forms the basis for any organization to measure its attainment of goals in a purposeful way. The first step is to build a *goal* statement. Then, a set of *questions* is developed that need to be answered to gain an understanding of whether the goal has been met. Finally, the *metrics* that need to be collected to answer the questions are enumerated. A set of data is associated with every question, such that the question can be answered in a quantitative way. In this way, the organization traces the goals to the needed data to define those goals operationally, and finally provides a framework for interpreting the data with respect to the stated goals. Other available data not required to answer the questions is ignored, even though it may intuitively look interesting.

The choice of any metric depends on the relevance of the metric to the attainment of product goals and also its accuracy. The accuracy of metrics, in turn, depends on how the data is collected, which often relies upon the tools and practices of the engineering teams. An effective way to establish the metrics and target values for those metrics is to benchmark an equivalent product, as discussed in Section 13.3.1. The benchmark provides a framework for collecting and interpreting metrics for the new product in the relevant context and provides a point of comparison [35]. Re-using metrics from previous projects will provide the analyst some confidence that the metrics accurately capture their development process. Once the metrics are defined, a project-specific criteria for metrics can be established, which more closely relate to the specific product goals.

This section describes the methods of obtaining benchmarking data and how that benchmarking data can then be used in interpreting the metrics. The section also describes the methods for quantifying the goals of the project.

13.3.1 BENCHMARKING

Many software products are either a new version of an existing system or derivatives of other products. The objective of the benchmarking process is to:

1. collect the metrics generated during the product development;
2. process the metrics to identify missing data and outliers;
3. ensure the metrics can be correctly interpreted.

Outside of major refactoring activities, which are typically evident, a new version of an existing product will rarely make a significant change to the core attributes of the product; especially as they relate to the product's architecture. Ideally, the products that are to be used as a benchmark should have developed using equivalent tools to the target product. If possible, metrics should be collected from more than one single product release. Product teams should not overly focus on the metrics from a problematic release. Rather, the objective should be to identify the normal value for a metric, because bad releases may only provide outlier values for a metric. Additionally, a team can consider the baseline being a product with a good reputation for quality and customer acceptance.

More generally, the same collection and analysis methods that were applied to previous versions of the product should be used for data collection and analysis of the release under study. Therefore, the methods for data collection and analysis should be clearly defined to enable replication. Additionally, the team interpreting the metrics should have knowledge of the data collection tools and their idiosyncrasies. The metrics collected from the prior release should be analyzed and an initial interpretation of the metrics should be produced. As part of this interpretation, the team should also focus on comparing metrics across the development cycle analyzing differences in trends to identify inaccuracies of the metrics or possible gaming of the system.

The creation of benchmarks for products that are significantly different from prior versions is more complex, and is dependent on the percentage of the new product that has been derived from the prior version. The smaller the percentage of derivation, the less applicable it is to use the prior development as a benchmark for the new product. But even in these circumstances, the benchmarking process can provide bounds for the metrics, whereby when metrics move outside of these bounds the product group should initiate investigations to identify if any potential issues exist.

The analysis of the metrics should be shared with the team that developed the product to clarify the discrepancies between the interpreted metrics and the product team's perception. During these discussions, the software engineers will often identify why the metrics may not be accurate. The team may reveal sources of noise in the data, gaming of the system, sources of inaccuracy, or outliers.

To illustrate the point of the relevance of choosing appropriate products to provide benchmarking data, we can consider how the Microsoft Bing team would choose a relevant benchmark. Bing is a service product that is continually deploying new features onto a single deployment target. Consequently, Bing does not support older versions, and it exposes its functionality through web servers. Alternatively, each release of Windows can be separated by years and it is deployed onto millions of computers whose failure profile is very different from Bing. So while the different product groups will share experiences, they would never attempt to benchmark their developments against each other.

Within a single product group, not all product releases may be used as benchmarks for other releases. For example, while the development tools and process are common for a Windows product and its Service Packs, neither would be a valid benchmark for the other. The focus of a main Windows release is to provide a new user experience, whereas for Service Packs the focus is on maintaining the current experience while correcting security or reliability issues. Therefore Windows 8.1 would use Windows 8 as a benchmark, whereas Windows 8.1 Service Pack 1 would use Windows 8 Service Pack 1 as a benchmark.

The phase of the product's development lifecycle should also be considered. For a product such as Windows, the development cycle is split into milestones that consist of periods of feature development and periods of stabilization. The expected product behavior should change between these milestones. In these circumstances, the development performance during Windows 8.1 feature development milestone would be compared against the equivalent feature development milestone in Windows 8.

13.3.2 PRODUCT GOALS

Once a clear relationship is established between the metrics and the development attributes of the previous release, the metric goals can be defined for the future products. The quantified metric targets are estimated based on the data calculated from benchmarks and the overall goals of the next release. Specifically, if the objective of the next release is to improve performance, then the goal could be a specified performance percentage increase over the previous release.

The goals should be realistic, which often takes considerable experience, judgment and restraint. For a complex product, improving all product attributes simultaneously is difficult. So, if the goal is to improve performance, then the goal for reliability may be to maintain the current level. The goals should also reflect any changes in development methodology.

A common mistake is to define goals at too detailed a level. For instance, if the goal is to improve productivity in terms of rate of code changes or feature added, defining that goal in terms of the increased productivity expected by individual engineers is discouraged. By breaking the goals down to the individual level, ownership of the goal from the teams is reduced, which removes the motivation of the team to innovate (e.g., assigning engineers to improve tools may be far more effective than asking them to code faster) and to work together as a team. The preferred way is to define and monitor the goal at the product level. If the product is not meeting the goals, then the causes of the issue should be investigated. The solution may be improved tools, sharing of best practices between teams or identifying that the goal itself is unachievable and needs to be reset.

13.4 REVIEW OF METRICS

This section provides the details of the metrics that are available to assist teams in the characterization of their software development process. Since the collection and analysis of metrics is a cost overhead for product teams, the objectives of the metrics must be to provide the developers with useful information that is not otherwise available to them. A small development team of five people may not need to collect daily metrics to know the amount of effort and bug fixes that occurred over the last few weeks. Their own experience would provide that knowledge. However, they may like to see trends over a period of time to monitor improvements. Conversely, a large product, such as Windows, benefits from detailed daily and weekly metrics, because no individual would have the knowledge of the amount and type of effort occurring in the entirety of its development. As the objective of the process is to use metrics to determine the status of a development, then the number and type of metrics that are required should be determined by the size and complexity of the product. Smaller teams and simpler products require fewer metrics to understand the product status.

The following should be considered in developing a metric framework for a product's development:

1. *The product's characteristics.* Is the product stand-alone, an application that is deployed on multiple platforms, or a service product? What is the objective of the next release of the product? For example, is the release focused on introducing new features or is the release intended to address customer feedback from prior release? If the objective is to add new features to a product, then the product goals can be complex, especially in regard to quality. The introduction of new features can change the product's user experience for the customers. Whereas, if the objective of a release is to improve reliability, reliability measures should be more precisely defined.

2. *The development process.* The chosen development process controls how the engineers behave, which has an obvious impact on interpretation of the metrics. One team may decide that features must be complete prior to integration into the master version of the product or component. For these teams, integrated features should be complete. Other teams may opt for continuous integration and will allow unfinished features to be submitted. For these teams, burst of changes until the product stabilizes is expected. Within Microsoft, and in most organizations, changes

being submitted into the master version of the product should not break that product in fundamental ways, often referred to as "not breaking the build". Often, teams opt for verification processes prior to checking into the trunk branch to prevent such build breakage. Quality metrics should reflect the verification processes available to the developers. If the developers are not able to perform a "system test" on a change, a higher failure rate for these changes would be predicted.

3. *The deployment and support characteristics.* Nowadays, product can be deployed via many different mediums. Some types of software are installed to be executed locally. Externally managed channels, such as app stores, may help with deploying such applications, or they can be deployed completely independently (such as via downloaded or shrink-wrapped packages). Other software can be shipped as a component of a larger product. In this case, the developer has much less control over the deployment and the usage scenario of the software. Deployment of the software can occur through a browser reaching a web service. In this case, software engineers have full control of their deployment and servicing of the product. Finally, some software might be deployed by multiple methods simultaneously.

All metrics collected and analyzed should be tied to a specified product goal, as discussed in Section 13.3. We grouped metrics into three classes, each with a different purpose. This grouping is an extension of the work of Williams et al. [20] when establishing the Extreme Programming Evaluation Framework. Product teams should aim at understanding all these aspects of the project and product characteristics to be able to make informed decisions regarding the way they develop software. These three classes are as follows:

1. *Contextual metrics.* Drawing conclusions from empirical studies of teams may be difficult because the results of any process largely depend upon the relevant context variables. One cannot assume *a priori* that a study's results generalize beyond the specific environment in which it was conducted [36]. Therefore, recording an experiment's context factors is essential for comparison purposes and for fully understanding the generality and utility of the conclusions and the similarities and differences between the case study and one's own environment. Factors such as team size, project size, criticality, and staff experience can help explain differences in the results of applying the practices. Product teams should look back at the project history as it creates a framework for assessing future performance. Organizational structure and relevant product expertise permeate the project and heavily influence the product and these also need to be understood.

2. *Constraint metrics.* While the goals of the product under development may be to release a set of new features, each release must meet a series of constraints. The majority of software products have to work under predefined constraints. For instance, applications distributed through an app store have to satisfy requirements of the particular store. Constraints can be related to past releases of products. For example, a new release may be required to maintain the same level of performance or reliability. Products may be required to ensure backward compatibility or security or privacy constraints. For instance, the new version of the product is required to improve the performance of data retrieval by 10%.

3. *Development metrics.* Assessing the state of development, verification, and deployment readiness and tracking these over time is an important part of managing a project. Is the development progressing according to plan? Is the progression rate higher or lower than in the past? How much time is spent in verification as opposed to design and implementation? These types of metrics can

be used to assess the achievement of a goal, such as the code should decrease in complexity by 20%.

This section discusses a set of metrics that individually can address some aspects of the above characteristics. Later parts of the document will discuss methods and challenges often occurring when interpreting these metrics. Table 13.1 provides an overview of the metrics discussed in this chapter, identifying the metric category, providing specific examples of the metrics, their goals.

13.4.1 CONTEXTUAL METRICS

The developments of software projects are varied in terms of scope, resources, and time commitments, and the resulting products have widely differing functionalities, intended audiences and lifecycles. An operating system that is deployed on servers will be, by necessity, differently scoped, produced and verified than a web service or a single-function application on a consumer-class device. The product and project context information explicitly describes some of the key attributes which later assist in identifying relevant products as benchmarks and in the interpretation of the metrics.

Among the most crucial context details are the project objectives, intended audience and the mode of deployment, project history and revision specifics, organizational structure and knowledge, and applied development methodology.

13.4.1.1 Product objective, audience, and delivery method

Understanding the project and the product context begins with business goals. These inform decisions around what value the product will provide, who the product is intended for, and how the functionality will be delivered and presented to the user. The differences between traditional software packages that need to be installed versus software exposing the functionality through a browser, are profound, and will require adjustments to the development methodology and the analyst's understanding of the data.

The output of this information will result in the adjustments of other metrics. For example, if a product moves from a traditional software package to a service, then that often results in increases in the frequency of releases.

13.4.1.2 Project scope, history, and revision specifics

Project size and scope can be measured in multiple ways, starting from counting source code artifacts, executables or higher-level functionality through a measure, such as function points. Unless the product is brand new, the product history is useful for putting metrics into context. History, moreover, provides the means of allowing for more precise analysis. The scope and timing of a release, put in context by the objectives and timing of the past releases, determine how relevant measurements are to understanding the project today. On the other hand, if past releases were focused on delivering new functionality and the current release is focused on improving reliability, historical comparisons might be less useful, although the past release will define the baseline for the minimum improvement in quality required for the current release.

In addition, previous releases at least partially determine the scope of the current release. The scope might take a form of addressing users' feedback from, or quality issues found in previous releases. Lastly, product history is invaluable in understanding persistent strong and weak points of the product; areas of concern across multiple releases in the product and in the development methods; and the levels

Table 13.1 Selected Product Metrics

Metric	Category	Example Metric	Goals	Challenges
Product objectives	Contextual	Product releases every month	Relate metrics to product goals	Each product may have unique characteristics
Product revision	Contextual	Service-based release	Assists in setting realistic development goals	Each release may have unique characteristics
Organizational structure	Contextual	% of experienced engineers	Ensure development teams have correct balance of experience	Sometimes this is not within the control of the product team
Development methodology	Contextual	Code velocity	Identify the most relevant product metrics	Product teams may use a variety of development processes
Quality	Constraint	MTBF	To improve the end-user experience	Some aspects of quality such as usage and visualization are difficult to measure
Performance	Constraint	Average response time on specific configurations	To understand the end-user performance	Performance is dependent upon a lot of environmental factors, such as network speed, outside product control
Compatibility	Constraint	Product is compatible with applications released since the previous version	Upgrading the software does not break compatibility	Difficult to emulate all the user's environments
Security and privacy	Constraint	Development complies with industry standards	Improve product security	Security threat landscape is constantly evolving making it less amenable to quantification
Legacy code	Constraint	Code age	Minimize technical debt	Can impact compatibility with older software
Code churn	Development	Files changed per week	Verify development activity match plan	Tracking only the code that forms the released product
Code velocity	Development	Time for feature completion	Increasing productivity	Difficult to interpret
Complexity	Development	McCabe's complexity	Minimize product complexity	Unclear what action to take based on McCabe's metrics
Dependency	Development	Count of direct dependencies on a module	Minimize product complexity	Tools do not calculate state dependencies
Quality	Development	Number of open defects	Improve product quality	Metrics are often gamed and not reflective of actual product quality

and concentrations points for accumulated technical debt. Technical debt is a metaphor for incomplete or inadequate artifacts in the software development lifecycle [37].

Data from prior releases can be used to determine the percentage change in the metric in a new release. For instance, if the goal is to improve the quality of the product, then the reliability goals can be set at a specified percentage improvement over a prior release. The previous product release may have focused on providing new functionality, and the current release is focused on addressing technical debt (e.g., a Service Pack release), then you would expect the current release would be more reliable than the previous release, without any changes to the development process.

13.4.1.3 Organizational structure and expertise

The organizational structure and the expertise of the team play a pivotal role in the success or failure of any project and the long-term viability of the product. Further, the architecture of the product is typically related to the organizational structure that created it; often referred to as Conway's law [38].

Understanding the organizational context starts from identifying the team's size, structure, defined and implied roles and responsibilities and, if possible, lines of communication. Distributed teams will work differently than co-located teams and will have different patterns of decision-making and knowledge sharing. Conflicts within teams may indicate goal- and role-definition problems, which often will translate into architectural, design, or quality issues later in the product lifecycle [39].

Finally, mapping out the longevity and churn of team members on the project is an indicator of retained organizational knowledge and expertise. Useful metrics in this space are the average level of experience per team. New people joining can bring new ideas and experiences to the teams but teams also benefit from retaining product expertise and experience. Another useful metric to track is the turnover of all the teams. Excessive turnover may indicate morale problems in the team.

13.4.1.4 Development methodology

The development methodology chosen by the team, and applied to developing the product, has an impact on the goals of the project, especially when changes to the methodology occur during or between product releases. Methodologies most often change in response to a project failure, inability to quickly respond to new requirements, quality issues with past releases, or frustration with the existing development workflow by the engineering team. If a team starts a project using deep branching hierarchy, then they may be focused on metrics, such as code velocity across branches. If the team then moves to a more agile approach during system verification, then code integration velocity may no longer be of prime interest to the team.

13.4.2 CONSTRAINT METRICS

During product development, the focus for engineers is the implementation of new features or the fixing or improvement of existing functionality. Changes to the software are verified through a number of different processes, such as code reviews, unit tests, static analysis, component verification, system verification, deployments, usability studies, or acceptance tests. The objective of the verification process is to ensure the change meets its goals by:

1. satisfying its functional requirements,
2. satisfying any constraints placed on the features by the system and the environment.

While functional requirements are product- and feature-specific and largely self-explanatory, constraint metrics focus on the system constraints. Typical constraints found in today's software relate to reliability, compatibility, security, standards and regulatory compliance, privacy, accessibility, UI guidelines, physical limitations, power consumption, and performance. Project goals should explicitly enumerate all the constraints the final product should meet, but often at least some of the constraints remain implicit. Users only perceive software meeting all its explicit and implicit constraints as high quality.

The constraints that a feature has to satisfy vary based on the product. A feature developed for a mobile application and for the kernel of an operating system would have to comply with completely different sets of constraints.

Lastly, all constraints can be expressed as absolute or relative. The former often have a form of a precise statement, creating a target for the engineers, for example, the start-up time of the software from a user initiating its launch to having the user interface ready to accept inputs should be less than 3 seconds. The latter is typically relative to the previous release or a competing product, such as to meet the value for the constraint in a prior release. For instance, a product's Service Pack may be required to be compatible with all the same applications as the original product.

13.4.2.1 Quality

The quality of the released product is dependent upon the ability of the product to match the needs of the customer. As such, quality is a difficult characteristic to measure. Often, product groups try to translate quality into the reliability attributes that are readily noticeable by end-users, which is translated into reliability constraints. In addition, reliability can also be characterized as the lack of availability of the product. Reliability targets and reliability trend monitoring are typically easy to establish, although care should be given to ensuring the target is appropriate for the scenario for which the product was designed. The traditional primary metric for measuring reliability is the mean time to failure (MTTF), which is still appropriate for most of the software written today. The secondary metric of mean time to recovery (MTTR) is often useful as a complement to the MTTF metric.

Depending on the nature of the product, increased MTTF may be traded off for decreased MTTR. For systems processing non-critical data where a failure will not corrupt any data, speed of recovery (MTTR) is more important to perceived quality than encountering a failure (MTTF). A system processing critical data would prioritize MTTF and the need to guarantee correctness of the data more than the MTTR.

13.4.2.2 Performance and scaleability

Performance or scalability constraints relate to resource consumption, both on the part of the software (e.g., ability to hold sufficient number of objects in its data structure) or the user (e.g., time spent waiting for an operation to complete). In certain product areas, such as communications, performance goals may be specified both in normal state and in a degraded state. In other software areas, performance and scalability is dependent on multiple factors, including those that the software cannot directly control, such as environment on which it runs. Performance and scalability metrics are typically expressed as distributions over a representative population of environments, for example, the response rate from the website for a user with a broadband connection should be between 1 and 2 seconds. The consequence of such representation is that the question of whether a product meets the constraints is subject to interpretation. At the very least, the boundary between meeting and not meeting a performance and scalability constraint is often soft. Performance metrics are often based around the performance of the software on representative equipment with representative user load, although some software, such as communications, often specify allowable performance degradation based on poor environments.

13.4.2.3 Compatibility

Compatibility relates to how the product interacts with its environment. The most prevalent case of having the ability to use data (and sometimes programs, for example, scripts) from its own previous versions is often referred to as providing backwards compatibility. Compatibility constraints come in a wide range depending on how interoperable the product needs to be with its environment and how big an installed-base it needs to support. In principle, the problem is confined to finding a representative set of configurations needing to maintain compatibility. In practice, fully establishing whether this constraint is met depends on how difficult it is to validate various combinations of the product interoperating with other software or its own previous versions. When such a representative validation set is established, the answer to how compatible the product is in relation to its requirements is straightforward.

The compatibility metrics often fall into two categories. One category is the type of equipment that can run the software and the other is the versions of the application that can interface with the software. Examples of equipment metrics are the software runs on computers running Windows 7 or above and have at least 1GB of memory. Examples of application compatibility are that the software must be compatible with browsers running at or above a specific version.

13.4.2.4 Security and privacy

Security of systems is another aspect of the product requirement set that becomes a constraint. Various ways of probing the security boundary of the system have been established over the years. Starting from performing a comprehensive analysis of threats, through analysis of entry points and paths through the software statically or through testing (including security focused fuzzing of inputs), to targeted penetration testing.

The security and privacy requirements of a software system must also comply within a legal system and laws governing the customer's location and, in case of companies, its line of business. The software has obligations for compliance with various policies, such as user data privacy, requirements around data storage and transmission, defined by the laws of the country (e.g., European Union (EU) data privacy laws).

Security metrics are often related to the process that product groups use to minimize the risk of security holes, rather than product goals. Examples of these metrics are whether the product groups follow the security development lifecycle (SDL). Privacy goals often relate to defining what types of data is classified as privacy related and how that data should be stored and accessed.

13.4.2.5 Legacy code

Legacy code is the amount of "old" code in a code base as compared with new code. Legacy metrics provide measurement in terms of age of the code or in terms of in which previous products did the code exist, depending on the definition of age. Engineers may use this to identify areas of accumulated technical debt, ripe for refactoring as old code is often not really well understood by current team members and a lack of expertise in such parts of the codebase may represent future risk.

Examples of legacy metrics are the percentage of the current code base that existed in prior releases of the product.

13.4.3 **DEVELOPMENT METRICS**

Development metrics capture the status of the product across its development cycle over time. These metrics are used by the development team to identify bottlenecks and problems with the development process. Different product development models will place different emphasis on different areas of its development. Therefore, the development metrics are organized into the categories below for different characteristics of the development process.

13.4.3.1 Code churn

The code churn occurring on a single file is defined as the lines added, modified, or deleted between two revisions of a file. These metrics are most often obtained through the use of textual diff'ing tools, which provide a convenient way for engineers to track and understand changes occurring at a level of a source line. Calculating churn is a lot easier when files are managed by a version control system (VCS), as the majority of VCSs have built-in diff tools.

For any type of software, a released product is comprised primarily of files that form the deployable artifacts; in addition, there can exist secondary software to perform the act of deployment or other process management functions. A project team may additionally store files that perform related tasks, such as testing or build process. These files need to be classified into their own category, as the churn of these files should be analyzed separately from the churn of the files that form the final deployed product. Monitoring the churn of these non-product related files and their correlations with testing efforts and product churn can be informative. If a correlation does not exist, the new features may not have been tested at the right level.

Numerous research has studied the relationship between code churn and reliability and through combining code churn with other progressive metrics. Nagappan [40] showed that characteristics of code churn can have a negative impact on overall system reliability.

The churn rate over the product lifecycle should correspond with the product lifecycle phase. For example, during feature development, the churn should consist of large changes while during stabilization, changes should be primarily smaller changes and bug fixes. Tracking churn provides a method to identify if the development process matches the plan. It is also invaluable to correlate where churn is occurring against where churn is planned to occur. A lot of churn happening in unplanned areas may be an indicator of problematic code, that is, code that continually requires patching. In these scenarios, the code should be investigated to identify if it requires to be refactored.

Code churn metrics are based on the number of changes that are occurring within specific time periods or within specific releases. The types of changes that are monitored are lines changed or files changed. For products with long development cycles the amount of churn is often tracked over time periods, such as a week. For short release cycles, such as services where a release could be weekly or monthly, the churn metric is the change occurring continuously within a release.

13.4.3.2 Code velocity

Code velocity is a term encompassing measures of efficiency of the development process, characterizing the time from the development of a new feature to its ultimate deployment to the end-user. In all product developments within Microsoft there is an intermediary stage, where the completed feature is merged into the master version of the product or component, this is traditionally managed within a trunk branch in the version control system. The applicability of the code velocity metrics assumes that the development process can be categorized into three phases:

1. feature development, this phase often includes unit testing;
2. system verification and the merging the feature into the trunk branch;
3. deployment of the feature to the end-user.

Based on these development phases the code velocity metrics can be deconstructed into the following:

1. *Implementation velocity*: The time between a team starting to write a feature and the feature being merged into the trunk branch. This does not include the time needed for clarification of requirements, designing a feature and performing design verification, as accurately measuring these time periods is difficult. This metric includes the time for the implementation and verification of the feature.
2. *Integration velocity*: The time from feature completion to the feature being integrated into the trunk branch. This metric is more relevant for teams that develop software within a branch structure and measures the time for the feature to move through intermediary branches, before being integrated into the trunk branch.
3. *Deployment velocity*: The time between a feature being integrated into the trunk branch to deploying that feature into a running service or into the shipped product.

To provide an example for these metrics we consider a feature being developed in its own feature branch and the master version of the product being managed in the trunk branch of a source tree. A team starts working on implementation at time $T1$; the feature is verified and ready for merging into the trunk branch at time $T2$. After going through an integration and verification process, the feature is merged into the trunk branch at time $T3$, and deployed to the end-user at time $T4$. The metrics characterizing the code movement are:

$$\text{Implementation velocity} = T2 - T1$$
$$\text{Integration velocity} = T3 - T2$$
$$\text{Deployment velocity} = T4 - T3$$

The appropriateness of the code velocity metrics is dependent upon the objective of the development process, for example, for a product such as Windows, the whole product is deployed yearly so measuring the deployment velocity for an individual feature is irrelevant, whereas for service products, features can be continuously deployed, and so the time for feature deployment is important.

If the code velocity of a development is slower than a team's goal (derived from past developments) a possible bottleneck may exist in the process or quality issues may be present necessitating additional verification and bug fixes that will slow the code flow into its trunk and subsequent deployment.

13.4.3.3 Complexity

The original complexity metric was defined by McCabe's and was defined as the number of branches in the flow of code at the level of a procedure. While this is accepted as a good metric for calculating the testability of a product, one complaint against this particular metric is that it does not handle loops very well.

Research results conflict relating to the importance of the complexity metrics, some indicating that the metric is correlated with failures [41] and others that do not find any such relationship. Additionally, measuring the total complexity of a product does not differentiate between legacy code and new code, and therefore is not an actionable metric.

A more relevant measure is the amount of change in complexity that is occurring over the project development. This metric is more actionable as it can be used to identify whether the increase in complexity matches planned changes to the product and helps detect mismatches between the intended design and implementation. This metric can also identify areas that are increasing in complexity or decreasing in their testability.

13.4.3.4 Dependencies

Dependency metrics are measures of architectural complexity. They typically count the number of artifacts that an artifact in question is dependent upon to perform its functionality. Artifacts can be binaries, components, modules, functions. In addition, dependencies can be measured in terms of direct dependencies (i.e., a binary calls a method or function of another binary) or indirect dependencies (a binary makes a call to another through an intermediary).

Engineers often analyze the dependency of the program at the start of the product development to identify areas of dependency complexity, which may require refactoring. Once the product development begins, it is important to track and characterize the changes in dependencies that occur over time. These changes should reflect the product plans. Areas of code that are increasing in complexity where no added functionality is planned may indicate issues.

Examples of dependency metrics are measures of the number of dependencies a component or binary is taking or has on them. Other useful measurements are identifying the total depth of dependencies in the program and the existence of cyclic dependencies.

13.4.3.5 Quality

Various in-process metrics, such as the number of defects found, tests executed and passed, achieved code coverage, or uptime under stress, are used as proxies for quality during development. Ultimately though, the level of quality of any software system is fully manifest in real world usage. Therefore, quality is most often equivalent to counting defects filed and/or fixed after release. Defects filed and fixed are the most common metrics collected by product groups but are among the most difficult metrics to correctly interpret. Issues with noise in defect data notwithstanding, some measures of overall quality collected from defect data are possible and often applied. These include:

1. the number of defects found during a period of time,
2. the number of defects resolved during a period of time,
3. the number of defects resolved through making a change to the product,
4. the number of defects that remain unsolved,
5. product availability under representative user load,
6. percentage of test executions succeeding.

Such metrics are often broken down by severity to give more weight to more urgent and important issues. These defect trends are quite often used as a proxy for determining the product's readiness to release.

A common practice is for engineers to use the product as it is being developed. This practice is often called "Eating your own dog food" or "dogfooding," for short. In these scenarios, it is possible to measure changes in end-user quality over the product lifecycle, such as system failure rates (e.g., MTTF), system availability (e.g., MTTR).

13.5 CHALLENGES WITH DATA ANALYSIS ON SOFTWARE PROJECTS

The greatest challenge for product groups is not collecting data for metrics but in their interpretation. For product groups to interpret the metrics to determine the current status of the product development, it is important to take into account how the data was collected to create the metric but also to understand and counteract common interpretation issues.

This section addresses both of these issues related to managing a project through metrics.

13.5.1 DATA COLLECTION

As described in Section 13.3, characterizing the software development process through metrics begins with goals, defining the specific questions that will be asked, and defining metrics appropriate for answering the questions. Once the objectives and definitions are established, typically the next step is the collection of data.

13.5.1.1 Collection methods

Data can be collected manually or automatically. Manual data collection takes a form of surveys, interviews, or manual inspections of artifacts. The process can be time-consuming but it is often the easiest to perform especially in the absence of any structured data collection available on the project. Automated data collection, on the other hand, typically consults some existing data source, such as a source version control system or a defect repository, and extracts the necessary information from there.

There is a trade-off between the two methods in terms of cost of the collection and quality of the data. Frequently, a combination of both methods is necessary for the collection to reach the desired level of precision and data volume. For example, the initial data extraction is often done automatically but then the result needs to be manually verified and noise removed. The noise at the level of the structure of data is quite easy to identify. This is the case, for example, with missing values or values not conforming to the prescribed schema. Much harder cases involve the data semantics where the knowledge of the product or the team's process is necessary for disambiguation and a successful resolution.

There are situations, however, in which automated data collection creates datasets of higher quality than those created by a manual process. This happens when the artifacts that the data is collected from are generated outside of the critical-path in the engineer workflow. A classic example of data of this kind are the various relationships between semantically-related artifacts, such a work item and a source code change or a code change and a code review performed on it. In many engineering workflows, explicitly saving such relationships in the repository is unnecessary for successful task completion and is often considered extra effort. Thus, work items, code reviews and code changes often form independent data silos. An engineer might be asked to make a connection between any two artifacts by a team policy but as the engineering system will work without them, the adherence to policy is based on managerial and peer pressure and often not universally applied. In such cases, being able to discover the relationships automatically from metadata surrounding the artifacts (code reviews and code submissions share many characteristics that can be retrieved from their metadata and correlated) often creates a more complete, higher quality dataset without requiring human input, making it less expensive.

13.5.1.2 Purpose of used data source

No matter if the collection is manual or automated; the particulars of the collection process can heavily influence the ability to draw conclusions from data. Therefore, it is important to have a full understanding not only of the data collection process but how the data was introduced into the system in the first place. Often, knowledge of details allows the analyst to work around data deficiencies. To that end it is important to know the objective of the process or tool that generates the metric.

The most accurate data often comes from tools designed to manage the workflow or process being measured. Such tools or processes are the primary source. Examples include source code version control systems when code churn is being analyzed.

The data accuracy is lower when the data is collected indirectly as it is, for example, when attempting to enumerate bug fixes in code from defect data (which is not the same as the data from source code). And when data needs to be interpreted, the accuracy depends on how well the interpretation aligns with the goal of the metric. For instance, metrics relating to the size of change can take the form of counting changed files or changed lines of code. In some circumstances a "changed file" would also include files newly added or deleted, the definition is dependent on the goal of the metric. In addition, defining a "changed line of code" is even more complex, as it depends on a chosen similarity measure and the format of files. For example, measuring changes in "lines" for XML files, is not very useful. In such cases, the interpretation tries to be as close as possible to the intuitive understanding of the concept of a "change size" by the engineers on a particular project. In the case of changed lines of code, this metric is best approximated by using the same tool the particular engineering team uses for viewing the code diffs. Here, the measurement is a side-effect of a tool.

Special care needs to be applied to any metric that concerns measuring people or teams. Especially if there are incentives attached to the metrics, the data will over time become unreliable as far as its initial objectives. A classic example is applying a "number of defects found" metric to judge the effectiveness of testing efforts. In such circumstances, it is not unusual to see multiple defects opened for each found symptom of one underlying problem where a single more comprehensive bug report would be more useful and would require less work filling out, triaging, and tracking. Counteracting the effects of gaming is hard because causes of the changes in metrics are often not easily distinguishable from naturally occurring events and requires in-depth knowledge of the project and the team. Normalization and using a set of metrics more resilient to gaming often helps. For example, instead of "defects opened", it might be worth applying "defects resolved through a code change" metric, since the latter is harder to game; performing a code change is typically more visible across the team than performing a defect record change. Since the problem of gaming might occur in any dataset involving events produced by incentivized people, recognition of its potential existence and applying countermeasures is therefore very important.

13.5.1.3 Process semantics

In many cases, specifics of the workflow are not explicit; but required for correct interpretation of data. Such workflow semantics can be understood in the context of and with deep knowledge of the process and the team working on a project. How important it is to understand the assumptions being made on the project is best illustrated with challenges faced when interpreting defect data.

Defect reports come from many sources: internal testing efforts, limited deployments, production deployments, telemetry collected directly from users, either automatically or through surveys and studies. The source of a defect report often determines the quality of the report and its fate. For example, crash data being reported automatically is precise as far as the symptom and, at least partially through the stack trace, the path software took to trigger the problem. Such defects often have a determinate root cause and a solution. On the other hand, when reporting issues found by usability studies, there is more subjectivity and consequently less precision in the defect report.

There is also a lot of subjectivity around categorization of defects. Assigning severity to a defect, even on teams with strong policies, is often unequal. A simple issue of deciding whether a task is tracking a bug fix or a more general work item can be difficult to deconstruct and varies even among teams working on the same product. Applying the concept of "bug triage" is frequently a way for a team to impose some measure of consistency of information gathered and resolution on the bug queue. Bug triage often removes noise from the defect data, for example, by requesting that all defects come into the queue with some minimum level of information provided, that work items tagged as defects are not in fact features (or vice versa), or that duplicates of the same issue are recognized and tagged properly. From the metrics point of view, defects which have gone through triage are typically carrying more data, are of higher quality and more readily amenable to analysis. In the absence of a team triage, the data clean up falls on the analyst who may be less knowledgeable about the team's policies and consequently less able to produce a high quality dataset.

Another class of problems with defect data stems from the fact that records for some of the defects do not exist (are omitted) so they may not reflect the reality of the product. Most commonly, omission of records happens when fixing a defect is less costly than the cost of tracking it in a formal system, or the visibility requirements at that stage of the project are not high. Code reviews, for example, depending on the level of formality attached to them, may result in defects being communicated to an engineer through a side channel, an informal conversation, or a comment attached to an e-mail. Customer-reported issues, on the other hand, are treated with more formality, in no small measure to ensure that there is a record of the interaction with the customer.

13.5.2 DATA INTERPRETATION

This section discusses some of the most common issues regarding interpreting metrics, and some methods to mitigate them.

13.5.2.1 Metrics as indicators

While metrics ideally should reflect the development process, they are often only indicators of the status of the project and not precise statements of fact about the project. Software development is a complex process and metrics provide windows into the development process but rarely a complete view. As such the metrics should assist in managing software development but they are not a substitute for management.

The people responsible for interpreting the metrics should continually validate their interpretation with the software engineers developing the product. Where divergence occurs between the interpretation and the engineer's perception, then the reasons for the divergences needs to be understood which may result in changes to how the metrics are interpreted.

13.5.2.2 Noisy data

There are two main classes of noisy data: missing data and unreliable data.

Missing data can occur due to tool issues or changes in practices. In these circumstances it is necessary to capture this data via different methods. Missing data should be investigated as it may be indicative of problems of either the development tools or the development process.

Unreliable data will always exist irrespective of the quality of the tools and the collection process. A common issue is the focus of development tools (which is not on metrics generation) so the metrics may not be totally accurate. For example, code diff'ing tools are inaccurate when the difference between files is large. Another common issue is default values in data fields; when data is entered manually it may not be clear if the person intended the field to be set to the value or they forgot to set the field to the correct value. A common issue is that a lot of defect reporting processes will have a default value for the defect priority and severity. These default values can bias any results. The greatest reason for noisy data, however, is data generated manually that is not strictly necessary for completion of primary tasks. Examples of auxiliary data often generated manually include: time spent on actions, ownership data, organization structure data. This data is often not kept up-to-date, or is liable to be gamed.

The models used for interpretation need to be able to handle missing data. If data is missing or becomes unreliable then it should be excluded from the model. But the model should be able to differentiate between a zero value for data and a null value, which represents missing data.

13.5.2.3 Gaming

Gaming of the system occurs when groups or individuals use the rules and procedures that are meant to protect or allow for understanding of a system, to manipulate the systems for a desired outcome. Gaming is more likely to occur when individuals or teams are being measured implicitly or explicitly by metrics. A common example of this is the effectiveness of test teams being measured in terms of the number of defects they find or code coverage achieved. This places pressure on the test team to find defects in a product irrespective of its quality or to add coverage in places that are not substantially at risk of failure only to achieve a desired number. If such gaming becomes prevalent, it invalidates the using of susceptible metrics as measures of quality.

Gaming can often be identified through correlations between metrics, so for instance, if the rate of defects opened is not correlated to the rate of defects fixed through code changes, this raises issues regarding the validity of using opened defects as a quality metric.

Where gaming has been identified then those metrics should not be used and other non-gamed metrics need to be identified. In the example above, where the rate of opened defects is not reflective of quality, then it can be replaced by the rate of code churn due to bug fixes.

13.5.2.4 Outliers

Metric outliers can skew statistics, such as averages, and so the temptation is to automatically ignore these values. Unfortunately, an outlier may either be due to noisy data or actual product issues. Monitoring and interpreting metrics from a single product makes it difficult to automatically interpret outliers. To understand the cause of outliers requires manual inspection of the data.

When applying the same set of metrics to multiple products it is possible to automatically differentiate between noisy data and truly problematic areas. Where the same set of outliers occurs across multiple products then it is more likely that the data is representative of normal product behavior and not corrupt data. Outliers should be discussed with the engineering team as some outliers indicating bad behavior may be normal development practice. For instance, the development team may decide to follow a different development methodology for a specific subtask of the development (as in certain cases of refactoring).

13.6 EXAMPLE OF CHANGING PRODUCT DEVELOPMENT THROUGH THE USE OF DATA

During the development of Windows Server 2012, the product team was frustrated by the length of time it was taking engineers to integrate completed features into the trunk branch.

The product team set two goals for themselves:

1. Increase the velocity of code integration from the feature branches into the trunk branch.
2. At least maintain but preferably improve product quality.

To achieve these goals the product team had to investigate what was the current code velocity for the product and what were the influencing factors. Windows Server is developed in a large branch tree, which shares the same trunk branch with Windows Client (Windows 8 and 8.1). The Windows Server development cycle is split into multiple milestones; some milestones are allocated for refactoring, some for feature development, and some for stabilization. The focus on code velocity is mainly during the feature development periods, so the investigation focused on that period.

To generate a benchmark for Windows Server 2012 R2, data analysts and engineers from the product team analyzed the metrics generated during the Windows Server 2012 development. Where the metrics were at odds with the perceptions of what the engineers believed occurred (e.g., a particular feature was problematic) the data analysts and the engineers met to understand these differences. The most common reasons for differences between the metrics and engineering perception was misinterpretation of a metric, the requirement for the metric to take into account other related measurements, or the engineering teams "forgetting" issues with the product development. The result of the exercise was to improve the accuracy of the metrics and also to increase the confidence of the engineering team with the metrics.

Analysis of the data identified that the branches with more engineers developing code on, had the fastest code velocity; and the more shallow the branch tree the faster the code velocity was. Analysis of factors influencing code velocity identified the necessity of treating implementation and integration velocity separately. For code quality, the main focus was on avoidance of code integration issues. Typical examples of such issues are: (i) merge conflicts where code simultaneously developed on two parallel branches does not cleanly merge into a branch dedicated to verification, resulting in failure of the merge; (ii) runtime issues discovered in testing. Analysis identified a correlation between the number of code conflicts and the integration velocity.

Based on the analysis, the decision was made to increase the number of teams who developed code simultaneously on the same branch and to decrease the depth of the branch tree. The resulting architectural changes are shown in Figure 13.2.

Reducing the depth of the branch tree was perceived as an increased quality risk, as certain branches where dedicated to verification purposes and now these branches were being removed. Additionally, the product group, recognizing that changing a complex process can have unforeseen side-effects, wanted to continuously monitor the impact of the changes in development architecture.

At the end of the first feature development milestone for Windows Server 2012 R2, a full analysis was performed comparing Windows Server 2012 R2 (the new branch model) behavior against that of Windows Server 2012 (old branch model serving as a benchmark). The product team was interested in comparison between old and new processes, not the absolute values achieved. The results of the analysis are displayed in Table 13.2, as interpretation of the metric value is dependent on the metric

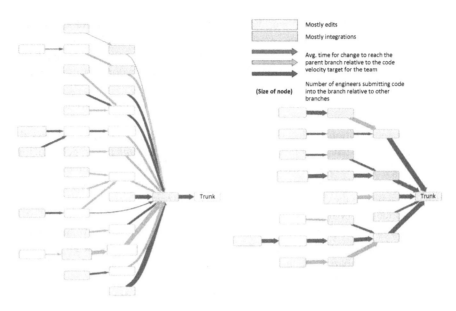

FIGURE 13.2

Branching structure used in Windows Server 2012 and 2012 R2, respectively.

Table 13.2 Comparable Metrics Between Product Developments

Category	Metric	Windows Server 2012	Windows Server 2012 R2	Status
Branch size	Number of Branches	1×	0.74×	Positive
	Engineers per Branch	1×	2.1×	Positive
	Teams Per Branch	1×	2.1×	Positive
Code velocity	Implementation Velocity	1×	0.88×	Positive
	Integration Velocity	1×	1.23×	Negative
Quality	Integration Conflicts	1×	0.56×	Positive
Volume of churn	Files	1×	1.28×	Positive
	Lines	1×	1.28×	Positive

itself, a status column is included to assist the readers. In the Status column, we indicate whether the change between releases was viewed as a positive or negative change.

Meetings were held with the product team to better understand these results. Specifically, questioned about changes to working practices, it was identified that while individual teams preferred to work separately in their own branches, they all felt that they benefited from working in branches with their related teams. The teams felt that the sharing of branches is the reason for the reduction in code conflicts. Previously, teams would develop their features separately and then merge the feature into a larger branch for verification. Often, during that verification stage, which could be days after the code was originally written, conflicts were identified. During Windows Server 2012 R2, as more teams worked simultaneously in the same branch conflicts were identified and corrected immediately. Further analysis confirmed that the teams were moving more towards a continuous integration style of development.

Ironically, the metric that showed the smallest overall improvement was the implementation velocity, additionally the integration velocity showed a decrease, which was the opposite of what was intended. The combination of these metrics identified that code was spending less time in the branch used to develop the feature but more time being processed through the branch structure. Further investigation highlighted that separate decisions had been made to increase the amount of system testing that the software had to undergo prior to being allowed to check into the trunk branch; this increase may have been a reaction to the decrease in the number of integration branches dedicated to testing.

Overall the amount of code generated by the development team during the milestone period increased by 28%, indicating a general improvement in productivity. This improvement of the Windows Server 2012 R2 development process was considered successful by the product team. Consequently and following that, the team embarked upon a second major round of changes to the branch architecture using the same metrics-based methodology.

The three main findings that readers should take from this example are:

1. *The importance for the product team to have clear measureable goals:* Through the considerable effort in analyzing Windows 8, the teams could both quantify goals and have confidence that the metric generation process would accurately characterize the development of Windows 8.1.
2. *Continuously meeting with the product team to interpret the metrics, during the product development:* These meetings quickly identified where changes in the development process resulted in incorrect interpretation of the metrics, due to missing data or changes in naming conventions, etc. This ensured that when the product teams needed the data to make decisions then the data was accurate and available.
3. *Changing a complex process will always have unpredicted side-effects:* The changes to the development process had a positive side-effect of improving the working practices of the engineering teams. But equally the changes could have resulted in negative impact on other aspects of the development process (e.g., an increase in the velocity measures could have resulted in a decrease in quality). Therefore, it is important to not only monitor those aspects of the development process that are planned to change, it is also important to monitor areas that are supposed to be unaffected by the change.

The next section takes the learnings gained from a number of similar studies within Microsoft and provides a generalized approach to develop a data-driven engineering process.

13.7 DRIVING SOFTWARE ENGINEERING PROCESSES WITH DATA

This section summarizes the overall approach a software engineering team should apply to use data to drive their engineering processes, based on the factors discussed previously in this chapter.

The minimum requirement to enable data to help drive the software engineering process is for companies or product teams to define goals for their software development process.

The act of setting development goals forces the product groups to define the metrics that will be used to monitor those goals. Through defining the goals the product teams will also define the relative importance of different aspects of the development process. While ideally, product groups will want all aspects of their process to improve, realistically, improving one development characteristic will often have, at least initially, a negative impact on another characteristic. For example, it is challenging to increase the speed of product release and maintain quality without sacrificing the number of features in the release without a period of adjustment.

Without goals, it is also difficult to interpret the collected metrics. If the product performance is monitored and the average response time increases, without understanding the intention of the product teams, it is difficult to determine if that change was good or bad. Under such conditions, discussions that are supposed to be about the actions to be taken from the metrics inevitably result in time spent trying to resolve the definition of the metrics. Discussions about the implicit goals of the product and the actions are deferred.

Since a standard set of metrics that product groups can use to monitor their development process does not exist, in Table 13.1 we provide a sample set of metrics that can help product teams in establishing their own scorecards. For all the metric categories, we provide examples of specific metrics, the goals for the metrics, and some of the challenges in interpreting those metrics.

Once the product group has determined the goals of the software engineering process and their metrics, they need to develop a process to collect and report on those metrics. The process of collecting metrics should be as automated as possible. The metrics and the data collection process can be verified through applying the process to prior releases of the same or similar products. The data analyst should characterize the behavior of the development of the prior product release and then verify their interpretation with the engineers who worked on the product. Through these discussions, the data analyst can improve their interpretation methods and also become aware of the accuracy and relevance of the chosen metrics. Ideally, this process should be applied to more than one development project, as that allows the data analysts to be better able to interpret whether statistical anomalies should be ignored or if they should be flagged as issues that need addressing.

Benchmarking the software engineering process based on the prior releases will allow the data analysts to translate the product goals into metric values. These metric values may vary over the total development cycle, for instance the code velocity during feature development periods should be longer than during stabilization periods.

This background work provides the information to allow the data analysts to track the performance of the product through comparing the collected metrics to the product goals. The focus of the data analysts during the development process should be to:

1. Continually validate the collected metrics through discussions with the engineering team and through correlate-related metrics to ensure their accuracy and lack of gaming.
2. Validate that the product development is still performing to plan based on the values of the collected metrics in relation to the product goals.
3. Examine the main drivers of any specific metric to identify opportunities to improve the metrics through optimizing the development process.

The process of creating product goals and translating those goals to validated metrics is expensive, but once a product group has a trusted set of metrics, and a set of metric-based goals, they can use those to drive product development and to optimize their development process.

REFERENCES

[1] Dongmei Z, Shi H, Yingnong D, Jian-Guang L, Haidong Z, Tao X. Software analytics in practice. IEEE Softw 2013;30(5):30–37. doi:10.1109/MS.2013.94.

[2] Murphy B, Gent T. Measuring system and software reliability using an automated data collection process. Qual Reliabil Eng Int 1995;11(5):341–53.

[3] Jalote P, Murphy B. Reliability growth in software products. In: IEEE international symposium on software reliability engineering; 2004.

[4] Murphy B. Automating software failure reporting. Queue 2004;November:42–48.

[5] Czerwonka J, Nagappan N, Schulte W, Murphy B. Codemine: Building a software analytic platform for collecting and analysing engineering process data at Microsoft. Microsoft Technical Report; 2013. MSR-TR-2013-7

[6] Williams L, Brown G, Nagappan N. Scrum + engineering practices: experiences of three Microsoft teams. In: International symposium on empirical software engineering and measurement; 2011. p. 463–71.

[7] Sanchez J, Williams L, Maximilien M. A longitudinal study of the test-driven development practice in industry. Washington, DC: Agile; 2007. p. 5–14.

[8] Ho CW, Johnson M, Williams L, Maximilien E. On agile performance requirements specification and testing. Minneapolis, DC: Agile; 2006. 6 p. ISBN 0-7695-2562-8/06. Electronic proceedings.

[9] Layman L, Williams L, Cunningham L. Motivations and measurements in an agile case study. J Syst Architect 2006;52(11):654–67.

[10] Williams L, Krebs W, Layman L, Antón A. Toward a framework for evaluating extreme programming. In: Empirical assessment in software engineering (EASE); 2004.

[11] Rolt LTC. Red for Danger. Stroud, UK: Sutton Publishing Limited; 1955.

[12] Musa J. A theory of software reliability and its applications. IEEE Trans Softw Eng 1975;1(3):312–30.

[13] Littlewood B. Software reliability model for modular program structure. IEE Trans Reliabil 1979;R-28(3):241–6.

[14] O'Connor P. Practical reliability engineering. Chichester, UK John Wiley & Sons; 1985. p. 133, 233–34.

[15] Siewiorek D, Swan R. The theory and practice of reliable system design. Bedford, MA: Digital Press; 1982.

[16] Gray J. Why do computers stop and what can be done about it. In: Proceedings of the 5th symposium on reliability in distributed software and database systems. Los Angeles, CA; 1986. p. 3–12.

[17] Moran P, Gaffney P, Melody J, Condon M, Hayden M. System availability monitoring. IEEE Trans Reliabil 1990;39(4):480–85.

[18] Jones C. Measuring programming quality and productivity. IBM Syst J 1978;17(1):39–63.

[19] Boehm B. Software engineering economics. Englewood Cliffs, NJ: Prentice-Hall; 1981.

[20] Brooks F. The mythical man month. Reading, MA: Addison-Wesley; 1986.

[21] Lehman M, Belady L. Program evolution—processes of software change. London: Academic Press; 1985.

[22] Lehman MM. Laws of software evolution revisited. In: Proceedings of European workshop on software process technology. LNCS, vol. 11491. Nancy: Springer Verlag; 1996. p. 108–24.

[23] ISO 9000 standard. URL: http://www.iso.org/iso/home/store/catalogue_tc/catalogue_detail.htm?csnumber=42180.

[24] Software Engineering Institute. URL: http://www.sei.cmu.edu/.

[25] Fenton N, Pfleeger S. Software metrics. Boston, MA: PWS Publishing Company; 1997.

[26] Jones C. Software assessments. Benchmarks and best practices. Reading, MA: Addison-Wesley; 2000.

[27] Beck K, et al. Manifesto for agile software development. Agile Alliance. 14 June 2001.

[28] Li P, Kivett R, Zhan Z, Jeon Se, Nagappan N, Murphy B, et al. Characterizing the differences between pre and post release versions of software. International conference on software engineering; 2011.

[29] Mockus A. Organizational volatility and its effect on software defect. In: ACM SIGSOFT international symposium on foundations of software engineering; 2010. p. 117–26.

[30] Zimmermann T, Nagappan N, Williams L. Searching for a needle in a haystack: predicting security vulnerabilities for Windows Vista, software testing, verification and validation (ICST); 2010.

[31] Cataldo M, Herbsleb J. Coordination breakdowns and their impact on development productivity and software failures. Trans Softw Eng 2013;39(3):343–60.

[32] Zimmerman T, Nagappan N, Predicting defects using network analysis on dependency graphs. In: International conference on software engineering. Leipzig, Germany; 2008.

[33] Ducasse S, Lanza M, Marinescu R. Object-oriented metrics in practice: using software metrics to characterize, evaluate, and improve the design of object-oriented systems. New York: Springer; 2010.

[34] Basili V, Caldiera G, Rombach D. The goal question metric paradigm. In: Encyclopaedia of software engineering, vol. 2. New York: John Wiley and Sons Inc.; 1994. p. 528–32.

[35] Sim S, Easterbrook S, Holt RC. Using benchmarking to advance research: a challenge to software engineering; In: International conference on software engineering. Portland; 2003.

[36] Basili V, Shull F, Lanubile F. Building knowledge through families of experiments. IEEE Trans Softw Eng 1999;25:4.

[37] Seaman C, Guo Y. Measuring and monitoring technical debt. Adv Comput 2011;82:25–46.

[38] Conway ME. How do committees invent? Datamation 1968;14(4):28–31.

[39] Nagappan N, Murphy B, Basili V. The influence of organizational structure on software quality: an empirical case study In: International conference on software engineering; 2008.

[40] Nagappan N, Ball T. Use of relative code churn measures to predict system defect density. In: International conference on software engineering; 2005.

[41] Nagappan N, Ball T, Zeller A. Mining metrics to predict component failure In: International conference on software engineering; 2006.

COMMUNITY DATA FOR OSS ADOPTION RISK MANAGEMENT

14

Xavier Franch*, Ron S. Kenett[†,‡], Angelo Susi[§], Nikolas Galanis*, Ruediger Glott[¶], Fabio Mancinelli[‖]

Department of Service and Information System Engineering, Universitat Politècnica de Catalunya, Barcelona, Spain* Department of Mathematics, "G. Peano", University of Turin, Turin, Italy[†] KPA Ltd., Raanana, Israel[‡] Fondazione Bruno Kessler, Trento, Italy[§] University of Maastricht, Maastricht, The Netherlands[¶] XWiki SAS, Paris, France[‖]

CHAPTER OUTLINE

14.1 INTRODUCTION

Open source software (OSS) has become a strategic asset for a number of reasons, such as its short time-to-market software service and product delivery, reduced development and maintenance costs, and its customization capabilities. Open source technologies are currently embedded in almost all commercial software—by 2016, up to 95% of mainstream IT organizations are expected to include OSS in their mission critical portfolios [1].

In spite of the increasing strategic importance of OSS technologies, IT organizations still face numerous difficulties and challenges when making the strategic move to the open source way of working (by adopting and/or developing OSS and integrating the company in the OSS ecosystems). The risks that IT organizations face when integrating OSS components into their solutions are not to be neglected and incorrect decisions may lead to expensive failures. Insufficient risk management has been reported as one of the five topmost mistakes to avoid when implementing OSS-based solutions [2]. In fact, according to the most popular OSS portal, SourceForge, most OSS projects have ended in failure: 58% do not move beyond the alpha developmental stage, 22% remain in the planning phase, 17% remain in the pre-alpha phase, and some become inactive. Similar results have been reported by the World Bank study which cites a failure rate of more than 50% for OSS projects [3]. Proper risk management and mitigation aims at reducing such failures and minimizing cost impacts. Therefore, the understanding and management of risks in OSS projects becomes necessary since they directly influence business, with strong effects on customer satisfaction, revenue, brand image, and time-to-market.

OSS-based solutions are not developed in isolation. Instead, they exist in the wider context of an organization or a community, in larger OSS-based software ecosystems, which include groups of projects that are developed and co-evolve within the same environment, but also further and beyond their context, including the organization itself, OSS communities, regulatory bodies, etc. All the elements in these wider and more strategic business ecosystems influence the risks to be managed.

Risk management involves collecting, aggregating, analyzing, and interpreting data from a risk perspective [4]. In the OSS case, several heterogeneous sources produce heterogeneous data that need to be aggregated:

- *OSS communities.* Observation of communities is a major source of data for risk management. The structure of the community is a first dimension to consider: How big is it? What is the distribution of roles (how many committers, ...)? But also, community dynamics has a strong influence on the risk of OSS adoption: How lively is the community? How often do releases occur? How happy do adopters appear to be? This data can be collected from resources like web pages, blogs, and mailing systems.
- *OSS projects.* The projects that deliver OSS components need to be considered when managing risks. Software engineering-related data repositories can be systematically reached and data therein gathered for analysis. Examples can be information about bugs during development and frequency of releases.
- *Expert opinions.* In addition to data that can be observed with the help of software artifacts, individuals can provide additional information. They can provide human-based judgment, that is,

expert assessment, to better understand the context of risk in a given organization. Also, they can eventually provide information that is missing in a particular context.

In this chapter, we present a methodology for risk management that considers these three types of sources as the "data fabric" that feeds a pipeline organized into three layers. The first layer is defining risk drivers by collecting and aggregating data; the second layer, is converting risk drivers into risk indicators; the third layer is assessing how risk indicators impact the business of the adopting organization. Throughout the chapter we refer to two cases, XWiki and Moodbile, representing different types of OSS components that can be considered individually and, eventually, in an integrated mode. The ultimate goal is that of promoting and supporting OSS adoption in institutions and IT organization. The work has been performed in the context of the European Project RISCOSS, whose objective is that of studying the risks in the adoption of open source software [5].

The rest of the chapter is organized as follows: Section 14.2 introduces the background as a short tutorial on the concepts and methods used in the work. Section 14.3 presents the proposed approach. Then detailed in Section 14.4 the basic OSS measures related to the quality of code, the statistical instruments to evaluate the community activeness and dynamics, and the risks and their impact on the business part of the organization are presented and illustrated via an example of use based on XWiki. Section 14.5 describes an integrated view of the approach through its application to the analysis of risks' impact and mitigation in the Moodbile case study. Section 14.6 presents relevant related works, while Section 14.7 concludes the chapter.

14.2 BACKGROUND

Here, we summarize the concepts and techniques we use throughout the chapter, mainly: risk management, OSS strategies and their effects on business goals, OSS communities and ecosystems, Bayesian networks, social network analysis, and the i^* goal-oriented methodology.

14.2.1 RISK AND OPEN SOURCE SOFTWARE BASIC CONCEPTS

14.2.1.1 Risk management

In order to effectively manage and control risk, management needs a clear and detailed picture of the risk and control environment in which they operate. Without this knowledge, appropriate actions cannot be taken to deal with rising problems. For this purpose, risks must be identified (this includes the risk sources, the risk events, and the risk consequences) and mitigated [4, 6].

Risk identification

All business areas within an organization include various activities and processes, which give several sources for risk. To manage and monitor risks efficiently in an organization, they need to be gathered and organized in an appropriate way, in a repository. This approach leads to a consolidated, organization-wide view of risk, indifferent of local interpretations and aggregation hierarchies, to monitor risk at a business unit level. This general repository needs to be completed with the local risks unique to each business unit with its particular responsibilities, which need to be identified and monitored.

Identification of risks specific to an enterprise is a critical step, since management cannot be expected to control risks they are unaware of. Risks can be identified, for example, by using event logs to extract risk events and risky situations; by eliciting expert opinions on what may go wrong in the enterprise; by simulating business processes and extracting a list of potential undesirable results; by systematically going through every existing business process and finding out problems; or by learning from experience of others, analyzing the risk events that materialized in similar businesses. Some of these methods produce only a list of risks, while others may produce accurate approximation of the frequency of the risk events actual occurrences. This frequency is used for calculating the expected potential damage that may become associated with a particular event and, consequently, for setting priorities of treating various contingencies.

Organizations ensure consistency in risk identification in two manners:

1. Risk identification is achieved via a centralized library of risks. This library covers generic risks that exist throughout the organization, and associates the risks with the organization's business activities. The library is typically created by using an industry list as an initial seed, and then continuously augmented.
2. Identification consistency is further aided by employing a classification model covering both risks and controls. Using this model, each risk in the risk library has an assigned risk classification that can be based on regulatory definitions, and each associated control also has a control classification.

The process of risk identification should be repeated at regular intervals as observed by Kenett and Raanan [4].

Key risk indicators, or KRIs, are metrics taken from the operations of a business unit, which are monitored closely in order to enable an immediate response by the risk managers to evolving risks. The number of risk indicators may be very large, thus making it very difficult to track, monitor and control. Therefore, a selected few risk indicators are chosen to serve as a warning mechanism for the Enterprise and are used as inputs to a risk management dashboard. These may be simple risk indicators, such as "number of bugs in the software project," or compound indicators made up of direct risk indicators for a given area of activity [4, 7, 8].

Risk mitigation

Risk mitigation is an action, consciously taken by management, also thanks to the indicators, to counteract, in advance, the effects on the business of risk events materializing. Possible risk mitigation strategies are: *Avoid the risk,* not taking the action that may generate it; *Accept the risk*, in the case the organization, while well aware of the risk, decides to go ahead and perform the operation that may end in the risk event occurring; *Transfer the risk*, for example, insuring the business against the occurrence of that risk event; and *Reduce the risk*, taking steps to lower either the probability of the risk event happening or the amount of the damage.

14.2.1.2 OSS business strategies

The business strategy describes the approach of a business to successfully compete with other businesses in a given market. The business strategy determines the goals of the enterprise and how resources and business partners are deployed in order to make the business model work and to achieve these goals. This includes cooperation and competition within the business ecosystem [9]. The key goal of a business strategy is to outperform competitors [10]. In the case of OSS-related business models, OSS may provide a means to create this competitive advantage, for instance through its potentially low cost, modifiability and availability.

There is a multitude of classifications of OSS business models and related business strategies [11–16]. In this work we refer to a generic typology of OSS business strategies determined by the purpose of OSS use, the way OSS is used, and the location within the company's business model and business ecosystem where OSS is deployed. In this context, for example, the *OSS integration* strategy requires sharing and co-creation of OSS with other actors, namely an OSS community. In this case, the company might use existing open source software or components that have been developed by the community, and "repay" in terms of bug reports, bug fixes, patches, or sponsoring events. In, *OSS acquisition* the adopter tries to benefit from existing OSS code and community support without paying back to the community.

Strictly connected to the strategies, an OSS business risk is any risk resulting from the direct or indirect involvement of OSS within the business model of a company that has the potential to significantly affect the company's business. Several categories of risks can be recognized that affect the business assets and goals of the organization. Among them, the *Strategic risks* are risks to the company's strategy and plan. Examples of these are demand shortfall, integration problems, pricing pressure; while the *Operational risks* are those related to the operations of the organization such as: cost overrun, poor capacity management, difficulty in OSS cost-benefit evaluation.

14.2.1.3 OSS communities and ecosystems

An OSS community consists of the people developing, using, improving, and making an OSS evolve. A community is engaged in many activities which are supported by an infrastructure providing services for carrying out these activities effectively. Usually a website is available to expose the OSS to the public describing the software and the services supporting the community. A space where people can discuss the OSS is also usually available. The specific system used can be different, but mailing lists or forum-like environments are mostly used. Usually, the community has several channels for discussing different topics, such as the OSS usage and OSS development and evolution. Code repositories play a crucial role in an OSS project and its community. In fact, community members use several tools in order to make their work more effective. Examples include: bug tracking systems for recording the defects of the OSS and for tracking their activity; continuous integration servers for spotting problems in the software as early as possible; Wiki for publishing and keeping up-to-date all the technical documentation about the OSS; code review systems for increasing the quality of the committed code. Communities rely on other OSS for building their own products. This fact positions a community in the same position of a generic adopter of OSS and makes the risks they are facing partially overlap the ones of industrial adopters.

No OSS community is an island: Several different players collaborate in the production and integration of OSS components, such as OSS communities, adopting IT organizations that commercialize OSS-based products and services. All these actors represent a complex ecosystem [17, 18] whose modeling is a prerequisite to the analysis of the gathered data. In fact, without a clear view of what the data is needed for, a meaningful analysis is not possible. In particular, it is crucial to identify the relationships between the entities in the ecosystem and to understand how these relationships are reflected in the internal structure of the organization in terms of strategies to be implemented and goals to be pursued through those strategies. Moreover, the OSS adopters may decide to follow different OSS strategies among those illustrated in Section 14.2.1.2.

Software ecosystems describe the commercial, legal (regulatory) and market context in which traditional software systems operate. According to Jansen et al., a software ecosystem is a set of actors functioning as a unit and interacting with a shared market for software and services, together with the relationships among them [17]. Ecosystems may be centered on a specific market (e.g., risk management tools), a particular technology (e.g., IPv6), a given platform (e.g., Eclipse), or a firm (e.g., Microsoft), as observed by Jansen et al. [19].

The participants of a software ecosystem may be diverse. The work by Boucharas et al. [20] identifies several actors, such as *Company of Interest* (CoI), which delivers the main software product in the business model, *supplier*, which is an actor that supplies one or more required products or services and *customer*, which is an actor that directly or indirectly acquires or makes use of the product delivered by the CoI.

These actors may eventually play different roles as identified by several researchers. For instance, the work of Iansiti and Levien [21] identifies the role of keystone (provider of a standard or platform technology) that provides a fundament for the ecosystem and niche player (requiring the standard or platform technology provided by the keystone player for creating business value). Hagel et al. [22] further classify niche players (who they call *followers*) into hedgers (who participate in two competing ecosystems to minimize risks), disciples (early adopters of a keystone technology) and influencers (who exert their influence on the keystone player).

In the scope of OSS ecosystems, participants can range from foundations, to commercial organizations, to independent developers [23]. Together, they compose the OSS community that develops the OSS itself.

14.2.2 MODELING AND ANALYSIS TECHNIQUES

14.2.2.1 Basic definitions and notation of social networks

A social network is typically described as a graph $G(N, L)$ consisting of a set of N nodes (or vertices) $N = \{n_1, n_2, ..., n_{|N|}\}$ and a set of L edges (or connections) $L = \{l_1, l_2, ..., l_{|L|}\}$, which denotes the links between nodes. An adjacency matrix Y, of dimension $|N| \times |N|$ can also be used to represent G, with $y_{ij} = 1$ if edge exists from node n_i to node n_j, 0 otherwise. Weighted networks are described using non-negative integer values for the entries in Y.

Reflexivity and symmetry in networks refers to the common behavior of many observed real-world networks; see [24]. A node n_i is reflexive if it is adjacent to itself, that is, if $y_{ii} = 1$. Ties within a network may be symmetric or reciprocal. For example, in many instances we expect ties of friendship to be returned, or mathematically, that between two nodes n_i and n_j, we have $y_{ij} = y_{ji}$. A third commonly observed phenomenon is that of transitivity. This may be loosely interpreted as "the friend of my friend is my friend." More formally, a graph displays transitivity if nodes n_i and n_j being connected and nodes n_j and n_k being connected implies that node n_i is likely to be connected to node n_k.

Graph theory provides tools to measure the connectivity structure of a network, such as the degree of separation between two nodes measured via the length of the shortest path between them that can be finite for all nodes in the network. The simplest way to quantify the connectivity of a node is to consider the number of nodes with which it is interacting. The degree of a node n_i in an undirected graph is the number of edges linked to the node. Highlighting actors of importance to the network is a common task of statistical network analysis. Centrality measures are ways of representing this importance in a quantifiable way. For example, the *Degree centrality* considers the number of nodes a node is connected to, with high numbers interpreted to be of higher importance, while *Betweenness* centrality measures the role of an actor in linking other nodes together in the network.

Many network visualization methods consist of laying out the nodes on the plot and adding the links as line segments (or arrows) connecting the nodes. These methods allow the analyst to have a view of the characteristics of connectivity of the network to identify, for example, areas of the network that are not, or loosely, connected.

14.2.2.2 Bayesian networks

Bayesian networks (BN) [25] implement a graphical model structure that is a directed acyclic graph (DAG) and can be used as a decision support engine. BNs enable an effective representation and computation of the joint probability distribution over a set of random variables. The structure of this type of DAG is defined by the set of nodes representing random variables labeled by the variables names and the set of edges representing directed links among the variables indicating that a value taken by variable x_j depends on the value taken by variable x_i. This property is used to reduce, sometimes significantly, the number of parameters that are required to characterize the joint probability distribution of the variables. This reduction provides an efficient way to compute the posterior probabilities given the evidence present in the data.

In learning the network structure, one can include white lists of forced causality links imposed by expert opinion and black lists of links that are not to be included in the network.

In order to fully specify a BN and thus fully represent the joint probability distribution it represents, it is necessary to specify for each node x the probability distribution for x conditional upon x's parents, which may take any form. Sometimes only constraints on a distribution are known. Often these conditional distributions include parameters which are unknown and must be estimated from data, for example using the maximum likelihood approach via the expectation-maximization (E-M) algorithm which alternates computing expected values of the unobserved variables conditional on observed data, with maximizing the complete likelihood assuming that previously computed expected values are correct.

14.2.2.3 The i* goal-oriented modeling language

$i*$ [26] is a goal-oriented modeling language that allows representing an organization in terms of the composing actors; their social relationships with other actors; their goals, that can be hard- and soft-goal depending on the existence of a clear cut criteria for their satisfaction or not; the tasks they perform; and the resources that are exploited to accomplish goals and perform the tasks. The language allows representing the relationships between the entities (see Figure 14.1). Actor dependencies model the relationships between two actors for the satisfaction of a goal, the execution of a task or the exchange, and use of a resource. Goals of an actor can be AND/OR decomposed into other goals and tasks, while contribution relationships allow representing the fact that the accomplishment of a given goal or the execution of a task can contribute in a positive or negative way to the accomplishment of other goals. The characteristic of the $i*$ language to allow representing the social relationships between actors in the domain makes it particularly suited to support the representation and modeling of OSS business and technical ecosystems, where several distributed and heterogeneous actors interact for the accomplishment of common and specific goals. The modeling part is complemented by the possibility to reason on the models in order to check several properties of the actors in the domain and of their relationships. For example, it is possible to check if some goals are obstructed by other goals or if there is an inadequate distribution of the responsibilities in goal achievement in the ecosystem exposing some actors of the ecosystem to possible risks. All these aspects will be considered in the rest of the chapter,

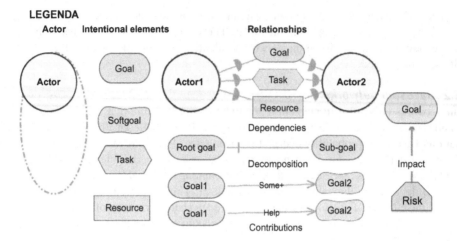

FIGURE 14.1

The *i** modeling language and risk modeling concepts.

to represent and reason on the risks the actors of a particular ecosystem are exposed to. Risks will be included in *i** models as new elements that impact on *i** entities, such as a goals and tasks.

14.3 AN APPROACH TO OSS RISK ADOPTION MANAGEMENT

Our approach to the problem of risk management in OSS is based on a three-layered strategy (see Figure 14.2). The layers cover the gathering of data from OSS communities, OSS projects, and experts (Layer I), a population of risk indicators variables (Layer II) that can be then analyzed in order to establish a top layer presenting the impact of risks on business goals (Layer III). Consequently, this approach provides an assessment of OSS risks at the strategic and business level of the organization.

In **Layer I** we deal with data collected from OSS communities, projects, and experts that determines the **risk drivers** resulting from raw data collected over time and aggregated over specific time windows. The data has a twofold nature. On the one side, it refers to the characteristics of the OSS components developed by the communities. This includes measures concerning the code, such as number of open bugs and number of file changes commits; the amount of activity in the information exchange, such as forum posts per day and mails per day; and measures concerning available information, such as the amount of documentation. On the other hand, other measures highlight the structure of the community in terms of its evolution, for example, changes in its roles and members and in the quality and quantity of relationships between them, mainly via social network analysis techniques [24]. These measures establish the "dynamic shape" of the community, recognizing for example, the presence of a core of active members and how this core changes in time, or a high interaction pattern between all the members of the community.

The data sources for these measures are community repositories, versioning systems, mail lists, bug trackers, and forums, among others. The corresponding measurement instruments are designed

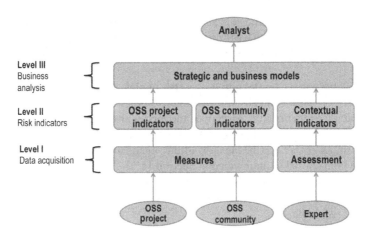

FIGURE 14.2

Three-layered approach to OSS adoption risk management.

to implement a continuous monitoring process to report data to the statistical and reasoning engines that are used in the other layers. Moreover, human intervention may be eventually needed in case data sources are unavailable for a particular component or community; values that concern subjective evaluation of some quality aspect, such as security or performance are missing; or values cannot be directly accessible or they are very costly to compute.

In **Layer II** the set of indicators of possible risks and models is defined that allow linking these risks to the possible objectives of the adopting organization. The indicators are variables extracted via the analysis of the data coming from Layer I. The different types of data gathered generate several categories of indicators:

(i) *Risk indicators* related to the particular OSS project can be grouped following some criteria, such as Reliability and Maintainability of the code.

(ii) *OSS Community Indicators*, that may be extracted from Community measures introduced in the next sections. This allows us to build indicators such as the *Community Activeness*, *Community Timeliness*, or *Community Cohesion*.

(iii) *Contextual indicators* that are more static and reflect the objective of the organization, such as its OSS business strategy, or the type of project in which the OSS component has to be introduced. These are sometimes also called "demographic indicators."

In our approach, statistical analysis [7, 27], Bayesian networks [4, 25], and social network analyses are exploited to determine values of risk. In fact, this three-layered approach is a particular realization of a seven-layered model introduced by Harel et al. [28] for analyzing usability of web services [29]. *Statistical analysis* of data from OSS communities allows us to determine trends and distributions of data, such as the number of bugs opened or fixed in a given number of days for a particular OSS component. In our case, this analysis was mainly implemented by functions and libraries from the R environment [27, 30]. *Bayesian networks* (BN) are used to link the community data gathered from the community data sources to the risk indicators and to the business risks using data generated by experts' assessment of various scenarios on the basis of their experience. *Community measures* that are derived via social network analysis techniques and tools used to understand the structure and evolution of the OSS community.

Risk indicators contribute to the definition of a risk model. This model allows the representation of the possible causes of risks, basically the risk indicators, and of their connection to the possible risk events for the adopter organization. Moreover, the model also allows representing the impact that the possible risk events have on the strategic and business goals of the organization as presented in in **Layer III**. Here, business goals describe the aims of the organization that adopts OSS. These goals are impacted by several kinds of risks summarized in Section 14.2.

In the following sections, we describe the different parts of the architecture logic focusing on data retrieval and analysis from different heterogeneous sources and on data aggregation into a comprehensive set of risk indicators.

14.4 OSS COMMUNITIES STRUCTURE AND BEHAVIOR ANALYSIS: THE XWiki CASE

This section describes methods used here for analyzing data characterizing the structure and behavior of the OSS communities. We aim at understanding *the roles in the OSS community* and the *relationships between its members* through, for example, the analysis of the mailing lists or forums, and *the capacity of an OSS community to solve issues*, such as bugs and new requests. We focus on dimensions, such as timeliness of an OSS community that can be measured by its capacity of following a roadmap or to release fixes and evolutions of the software in time, or reliability in terms, for example, of the number of bugs that are closed with respect to the total number of bugs. The methods are illustrated with data coming from the XWiki OSS community (http://www.xwiki.org), an Open Source platform for developing collaborative applications and managing knowledge using the Wiki metaphor. XWiki was originally written in 2003 and released at the beginning of 2004; since then, a growing community of users and contributors started to gather around it. The community is around 650,000 lines of code, around 95 contributors responsible for around 29,000 commits and with more than 200,000 messages, and 10,000 issues reported since the initial release of the XWiki OSS component in January 2004.

Specifically, the data we consider in our analysis consist of: user and developer mailing lists archives, IRC chat archives, code commits and code review comments, and information about bugs and releases.[1] The techniques we use for the analysis are the *Social Network Analysis*, the *Bayesian networks*, and other statistical techniques, such as the *run charts*, the *pareto charts*, the *analysis of frequencies* and the *association rules*. Moreover, we show how all the statistics and data are aggregated into the three layers approach introduced in Section 14.3.

---

[1] http://www.riscoss.eu/bin/download/Share/Public_Deliverables/D2-2IntermediateProposalforRiskManagement Techniquesv1-0.pdf.

14.4.1 OSS COMMUNITY SOCIAL NETWORK ANALYSIS

In order to apply the Social Network Analysis paradigm introduced in Section 14.2.2.1 we analyzed the data from XWiki community from 2008 to 2012 using data preprocessing of the IRC[2] chat archives so extracting the dynamics of the XWiki community over time to study the possible phenomena of isolation or forking in the community. Some of the challenges included a chat format change towards the end of 2010 and ambiguous names of a unique user (e.g., Vincent, VincentM, Vinny, Vinz). Eventually, names were fixed manually. Figure 14.3 represents the visual rendering of the dynamics, over time, of the community in terms of intensity and kind of relationships between the different groups of actors that are mainly contributors and managers of the community, and that can be captured by community metrics described before. In the graph is highlighted the increasing number of relationships between the groups of managers on the right and the contributors on the left during the years. The analysis has been performed using NodeXL,[3] a tool and a set of operations for analysis of networks in general and in particular of the social networks created when members interact for the sharing of goals and activities. The NodeXL-Network Overview, Discovery and Exploration add-in for Excel adds network analysis and visualization features to the spreadsheet. The core of NodeXL is an Excel workbook with six main worksheets for "Edges", "Vertices", and "Images" in addition to worksheets for "Clusters," mappings of nodes to clusters ("Cluster Vertices"), and a global overview of the network's metrics. NodeXL workflow typically moves from data import through steps such as import data, clean the data, calculate graph metrics, create clusters, create sub graph images, prepare edge lists, expand worksheet with graphing attributes, and show graph.

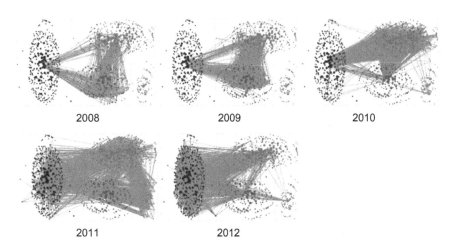

FIGURE 14.3

Network dynamics of the XWiki community, over time.

---

[2]http://dev.xwiki.org/xwiki/bin/view/IRC/WebHome.
[3]http://nodexl.codeplex.com/.

14.4.2 STATISTICAL ANALYTICS OF SOFTWARE QUALITY, OSS COMMUNITIES' BEHAVIOR AND OSS PROJECTS

In every software production organization, the activity of problem report tracking (such as bug reporting or project management issues) provides the capability to gain insights into both product quality and the ability of the organization to maintain the software. This data should be the basis for an analysis of the risks and their consequences on the business goals. Several possible measures and statistical analysis allow retrieval of these insights. This section introduces statistical methods applicable to the analysis of OSS communities and of their involvement in the OSS project they promote. We also illustrate how these measures are exploited in extracting a set of **Risk drivers** used to derive **Risk indicators**.

We give some examples of their application to the XWiki OSS community. In particular, two different forms of analysis were conducted. The first analysis focused on bug analysis and the ability of the XWiki core team to resolve these bugs across different priority levels, while the second focused on chat sessions between community members and the core team. Carrying out the analysis of the bugs provides an indication of the stability of the open source platform across various versions and the level of commitment to fixing those bugs, especially critical bugs. The chat session analysis provides an early warning signal of bugs that may potentially appear in the system. Both studies were based on readily accessible data from the XWiki OSS environment and can therefore be applied to other open source projects.

14.4.2.1 Run charts to illustrate bug resolution

Figure 14.4 shows the run-sequence chart also known as the run-sequence plot of XWiki bug resolution. The diagram represents the set of observed data in a time sequence. On the x-axis, the days of the year 2013, while on the y-axis, the number of bugs which appeared in each day, those that are not resolved, those fixed, those that are wrongly classified, and those that cannot be reproduced. It represents the ability of the XWiki core team and community to solve and fix open bugs[4] in a given period of time.

At the start of a new test phase, such as software integration testing, or acceptance testing, the number of problem reports opened usually increases fairly rapidly, creating a gap between the number of problems reported and closed. If the problems are straightforward, we expect the gap to quickly decrease. If not, this is an indication of a possibility serious condition or, alternatively, that the problems reported are of little operational consequence so that the resolution of them are being deferred to a later date. Enhancements to this chart apply to categories of problem severity, and an overlay the number of problems open by severity category [7]. The statistics calculated on the bug resolution data also allow populating the other statistical tools, such as the values of a subset of nodes in the Bayesian networks, allowing to characterize a situation in the OSS project that can influence the values of the other nodes in the network indicating risky situations. So, for example, the problem in bug fixing can influence the value of the risk of not timeliness of the community.

14.4.2.2 Pareto charts for analysis of issue types

The Pareto chart is a graphical display of the Pareto principle. When observing events, it is often a phenomenon that approximately 80% of events are due to 20% of the possible causes [27]. A classical application to software is the general fact that 80% of software failures can be attributed to 20% of

---

[4]The chart was derived from data XWiki data using R and specifically the applications ggplot2, reshape2.

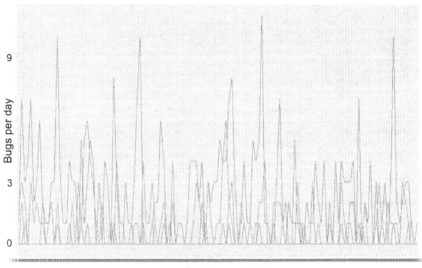

FIGURE 14.4

Run chart of XWiki bug statistics.

the code [4]. This observation was first made by Joseph M. Juran who, in the early 1950s, coined the term "Pareto Principle" which leads to the distinction between the "vital few" and the "useful many." The Pareto chart consists of bar graphs sorted in descending order of the relative frequency of errors by category. Pareto charts are used to choose the starting point for problem-solving, monitoring changes, or identifying the basic cause of a problem. An example of a Pareto chart of issues raised in the XWiki Jira[5] is presented in Figure 14.5.

The horizontal axis represents the attributes of interest for the analysis. The Pareto chart presents the findings from the highest to the lowest frequency for XWiki issues as indicated in the Jira. This type of analysis assists in indicating the few issues that cover the majority of cases and the connected line represents the cumulative percentage line for the attributes, issue types, so the added contribution of each issue can be evaluated. A total of 91% of the issue types are related to Bugs, Improvements and Tasks, where the highest issue as indicated within the Jira for XWiki is Bugs representing 57% of the total issue types. Also in this case the statistics related to the different issues can populate the Bayesian networks.

14.4.2.3 Analysis of the IRC chat archives
Here, we present the analysis of the chats by means of different statistical techniques in order to retrieve risk drivers. The chat session, in fact, can provide an early warning sign of issues related to the code

---

[5]http://jira.xwiki.org.

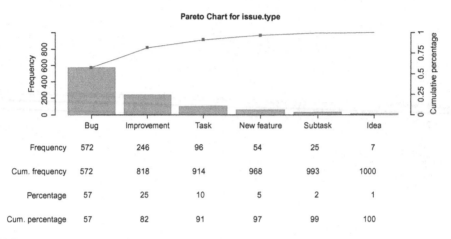

	Bug	Improvement	Task	New feature	Subtask	Idea
Frequency	572	246	96	54	25	7
Cum. frequency	572	818	914	968	993	1000
Percentage	57	25	10	5	2	1
Cum. percentage	57	82	91	97	99	100

FIGURE 14.5

Pareto chart of issues documents in XWiki Jira.

brought forward by users or contributors. The data used in the analysis are those related to the chats of XWiki.[6] The overall analysis consists of *Frequencies of Keywords across Chat Sessions* and the *Association rules*, which give two different perspectives to the analysis.

Frequencies of keywords across chat sessions: XWiki chat sessions were analyzed to locate keywords used in high frequency that could provide an indication of bugs or issues within the XWiki platform.[7] The frequency graph in Figure 14.6 highlights cells based on the frequency of the term within a specific chat session. The x-axis contains the chat sessions involved in the analysis and in the y-axis contains the terms used with the highest frequency levels across the eight chat sessions. The legend indicates the gray scale coding for the frequency levels of the terms used in the chat sessions. In addition to analyzing the frequency levels it is also important to spot certain keywords used in chat sessions including bugs or issue. Within the analysis of eight XWiki chat sessions the keyword "issue" is included during chat sessions XWikiArchive20130111, XWikiArchive20130116, and XWikiArchive20130117; the keyword "blocker" was used during chart session XWikiArchive20130110; and the term "XWikibot" is used in a relatively high frequency within the analyzed chat sessions.

Association rules: The association rule approach permits analysis of semantic data by identifying associations between various terms used within the chat sessions. The analysis was used to establish terms with high associations with the term "bug." The interesting associations that showed up within the analysis include "reported", "implementation," and "upgrade." For applications of association rules to risk management, see the work of Kenett and Raanan [4].

Figure 14.7 presents association rules for the term "bug" and "issue", ranked by the support measure of interest using the "arule" R application. Support is calculated as the ratio of the number of times the

---

[6]http://dev.xwiki.org/xwiki/bin/view/IRC/WebHome.
[7]To perform the analysis the *tm, Snowball, ggplot2, ggthemes, RWeka, reshape* applications of the R language have been used.

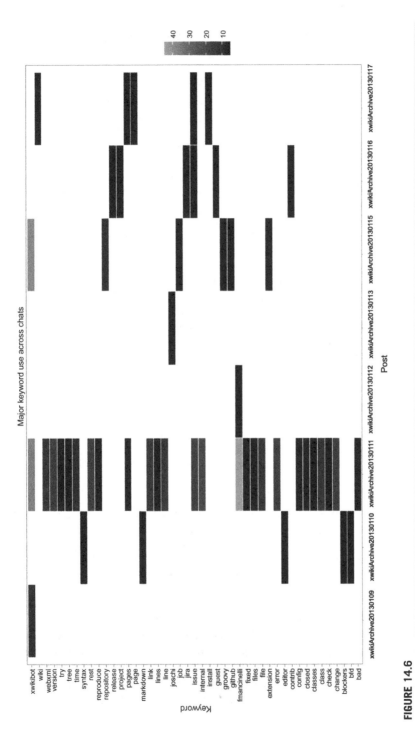

FIGURE 14.6

XWiki chat sessions to locate keywords used with high frequency.

Associated term	Association score	Associated term	Association score
yeah	0.97	depends	0.95
checking	0.93	wrong	0.94
display	0.93	ago	0.90
etc	0.93	broken	0.90
stuck	0.93	difference	0.90
weird	0.93	happens	0.90
reported	0.89	locally	0.90
idea	0.88	sorry	0.90
whats	0.87	unusable	0.90
busy	0.84	visible	0.90
care	0.84	level	0.89
charging	0.84	anyway	0.88
completely	0.84	checking	0.88
edit	0.84	cool	0.88
expert	0.84	email	0.88
fail	0.84	etc	0.88
fine	0.84	reproduce	0.88

FIGURE 14.7

Association with the term "bug" (left) and "issue" (right) from semantic analysis of XWiki chats.

association pair has been observed relative to the listed term. So, for example, 97% of the time "yeah" was used, the term "bug" was also used. This analysis can be associated with other analyses to better understand the behavior of the community and can contribute as an indicator of the possibility that the community is experiencing problems in its activity.

14.4.3 RISK INDICATORS ASSESSMENT VIA BAYESIAN NETWORKS

Here we aim at describing methods based on Bayesian networks (Pearl, 2000), introduced in Section 14.2.2.2, to involve OSS risk experts to give feedback about the impact of OSS community measures on the risk assessment in their own experience. The structure of the network is based on the OSS data analysis. On the other side, the Bayesian network feeds the qualitative goal-oriented model representing the organization, in order to reason about the impact of the structure and behavior of the communities on the risk suffered by OSS adopter organizations.

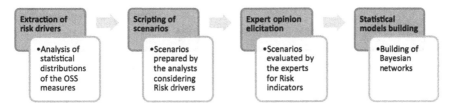

FIGURE 14.8

Process for Bayesian network specification.

Figure 14.8 illustrates a process for the specification and use of the BN paradigm to evaluate the link between the risk drivers and a possible risk indicator also thanks to the assessment of the experts.

Risk indicator values are determined in four steps. First, OSS data is analyzed in order to determine their relevant state values (distributions), for example, through the analysis of their distributions, using the measure introduced in Section 14.4.2 and their possible correlations with other variables. As a second step, an assessment is performed to evaluate the correlations between variables. For example, one of the variables affecting the Timeliness of an OSS community indicator is bug fix time. Bug fix time data has to be analyzed to determine low, medium, and high levels of fix time. Based on these limits an expert can assess the impact of a specific value on timeliness or a specific scenario. The output of the process is a BN that can be used to classify situations described via the basic indicators (both contextual indicators and risk drivers) and can give the status of a specific risk indicator.

Figure 14.9 shows a questionnaire about risk elements and scenarios. Experts are asked to review scenarios of risk drivers affecting Timeliness and provide a rating of Timeliness on a [1,5] scale. A rating of "5" represents low Timeliness (high risk) and a rating of "1" high Timeliness (low risk). Specifically, the workshops that we are currently conducting to elicit this information consist of about 50 scenarios with various combinations of community data and various scenarios of risk indicators. The scenarios were designed using random number generators to create a comprehensive coverage of risk situations. In the workshop instructions it is stated that scenarios that appear illogical should be skipped by the experts.

Figure 14.10 shows the resulting BN. The left part of the network contains the set of risk drivers and the distribution of probabilities for their values. For example, for the variable "bug fix time" four levels of probability are reported; the first one is referred to a bug fix time "below 14 days" and the probability is 23%, while the second is for a fix time between 14 and 44 days (probability 27%), the third between 44 and 74 (probability 25%), and the last one up to 74 days (probability 25%). The arrows connecting the variables describe the correlations between them. On the right side of the figure, the risk indicator "Timeliness" and its distribution is shown; its flat probability values (all 20%) let us deduce that Timeliness has low sensitivity to levels of bug fix times and commit frequency (for a deeper discussion on the use of BN, see also the work of Kenett coworkers [27, 31]).

14.4.4 OSS ECOSYSTEMS MODELING AND REASONING IN *i**

The representation of the ecosystem including OSS communities, OSS adopting organizations, other key actors, and the relationships between these actors, is performed through the *i** modeling language

Risk driver	State 1	State 2	State 3	State 4	State 5		Scenario 1	Scenario 2	Scenario N
Average bug fix time (days)	0	1	16	55	94		15	21	...
Bug fix time for critical & blocker level bugs	0	2	14	45	76		3	3	...
Commit frequency / week	0	21	44	90	113		15	23	...
Hour: When the commit was made	Mostly morning	Mid-day	Mostly night				Mostly morning	Mostly night	...
Weekday: When the commit was made	Mostly weekdays	Mixed pattern	Mostly week ends				Mostly weekdays	Mostly weekdays	...
Holiday: When the commit was made	Never	Sometimes	Always				Never	Sometimes	...
Timeliness	1	2	3	4	5		?	?	?

FIGURE 14.9

Questionnaire for expert assessment for the Risk driver "Timeliness."

presented by Yu [26] and Asnar et al. [32] (see Figure 14.1 for the description of the visual modeling language). In particular, the relationships between the actors of the ecosystem are represented as dependencies. Goals are represented using the Goal construct of i^* if they have a clear-cut criteria (e.g., *Bug fixed*) or the Softgoal otherwise (e.g., *Release delivered on time*). Goals are achieved through Tasks that may produce or consume Resources. Together with the concepts of AND/OR decomposition and positive or negative contributions to goals, i^* models allow representing, and reasoning about, business goals and business processes [33].

Figure 14.11 shows a model of a simple generic ecosystem reporting the two fundamental actors of an OSS ecosystem, the OSS Community, and the OSS Adopter, some of their internal goals and activities (such as *Release component* for the OSS Community and *Integrate OSS component* for the OSS Adopter), and the decompositions of these goals and activities into several lower level goals and activities. Moreover, the dependencies between the two actors are shown, such as the *Bugs to resolve* dependency between the OSS Adopter and the OSS Community (XWiki Project).

Referring to the OSS adoption strategies described in Section 14.2.1.2, this case is an implementation of an **OSS integration** strategy, in which the Adopter aims both at integrating the OSS component in its project, XWiki (see the activity "Integrate OSS component"), and to contribute to the OSS Community (see the activity "Contribute to OSS Community") for example repaying it via patches or new implementations of the OSS component. Together with the Organizational model we have then the risk model with the risk event (*Risk of missing documentation*) that "impacts" one of the activities of the OSS Adopter (in this case the development of a *Patch*). The risk event is identified via the measurement and statistical analysis of the behavior of the community and on the expert intervention that can rate the evidence of a risk indicator.

The reasoning on the i^* ecosystem model can be performed via label propagation algorithms, such as those described in Ref. [34] or logic-based techniques, such as those presented in Ref. [35]. The general process for the reasoning can be summarized in two main steps:

- The i^* ecosystem model is translated into a graph whose nodes are the different model entities, such as goals, tasks, and resources, while the relationships between these entities (mainly AND/OR decompositions and contribution relationships) are translated into graph arcs.

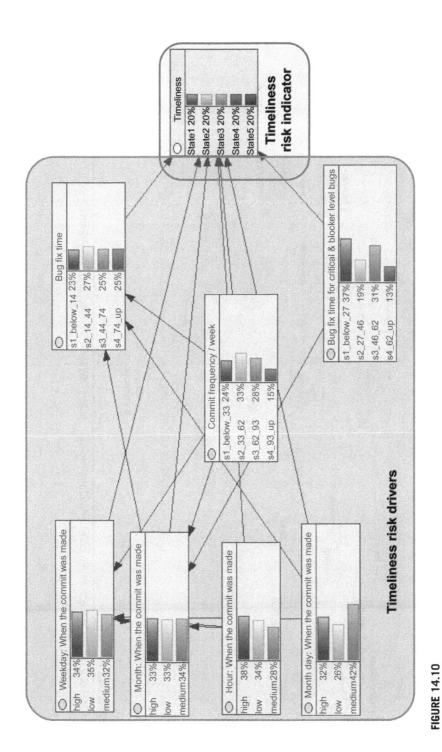

FIGURE 14.10

Bayesian Network resulting from Figure 14.9.

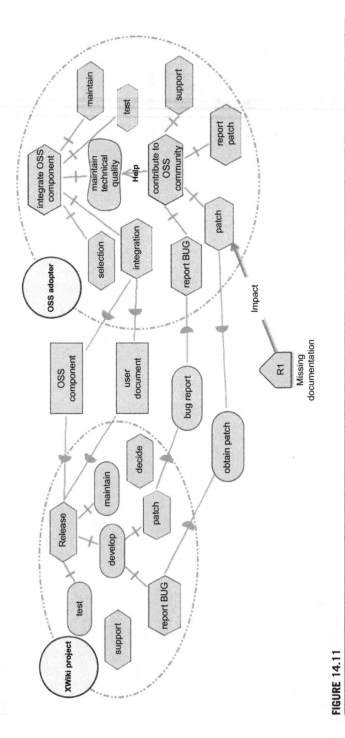

FIGURE 14.11

*i** model of a simple OSS ecosystem consisting of the two basic actors: XWiki OSS Project and OSS Adopter.

- The label propagation algorithm is applied to the graph in order to automatically retrieve the value of satisfaction of a set of given nodes (therefore of the corresponding entities in the model, such as the goals) starting from the evidence that the satisfaction of other nodes (goals) is, for example, compromised (or negated) by a risk.

Thus, starting from the knowledge about some known nodes of the graph, whose values come from the statistical and expert data and analysis illustrated in the previous sections, the propagation has the objective of inferring knowledge about unknown nodes. Following the model proposed by Giorgini et al. [36], two evidence values are associated to each node: a value for "*satisfaction*" evidence, and a value for "*denial*" evidence. For example, referring to the goal "Report Bug", a "*satisfaction*" evidence indicates that there is evidence that the bugs will be reported in the future; a "*denial*" evidence indicates that there is evidence for the possibility to not having the bug reported (e.g., because the documentation is poor or the adopting organization is not able to enter in the detail of the code). The node can have both values at the same time, indicating that there is some positive evidence but also some negative evidence about the node. This double value allows taking into account situations in which on a single organizational entity, for example, a goal, there are different possible evidences of risks impacting each one of them. Weighted arcs connect nodes with each other, and carry a positive or negative weight. Weighted propagation arcs always propagate a value from one node to the target node; the propagate value is a weighted function of the source nodes value. An example of propagation function is the simple multiplication $v * w$ of the value v, a real associated to the source node, and w, a real representing the weight associated to the relation (that can be AND, OR, and other contributions relationships). When more than one source nodes propagate a value to a target node, aggregation functions determine how the different propagations combine with each other. For example, a conjunction or disjunction function, that codifies an AND/OR decomposition of goals or tasks, propagates to the target node a value, which is a function of the values from multiple source nodes. So, in the case of a goal g AND decomposed into a set of subgoals $g_1, \ldots, g_n$, an example of propagation function can be the average of the values of the satisfaction (or denial) v_i of each goal g_i (that can be a Boolean value 1 for satisfied and 0 for not satisfied) times the weight of each link w_i so having a propagation function $sat(g)=sat(AND(g_1, \ldots, g_n))=avg(w_1 v_1, \ldots, w_n v_n)$ for the satisfaction values (and a similar one, $den(g)=den(AND(g_1, \ldots, g_n))$) for the denial value). The result of this analysis is a qualitative measure of the impact of a given risk scenario, described by the data coming from the XWiki OSS community and project analysis, on the goals of the adopting organization. For each node, a satisfaction and a denial value coexist to maintain the information about the evidence that a given goal can be satisfied or denied.

14.4.5 INTEGRATING THE ANALYSIS FOR A COMPREHENSIVE RISK ASSESSMENT

Here we show how to join the different types of analysis into the three layers defined in Section 14.3. In the next section, we describe the proposed method with a simple case study related to the evaluation of the risk in the adoption of OSS mobile learning technologies.

In Figure 14.12, the three layers are presented together with the corresponding main techniques. In Layer I the raw OSS measures (in these case via social network analysis and Pareto charts) are retrieved and the basic distributions of these data are computed. These statistical results, that make up the risk drivers, are exploited in Layer II that uses the BNs to produce the evidence of the existence of risk indicators, such as the "Community Timeliness" indicators based on the expert assessments that

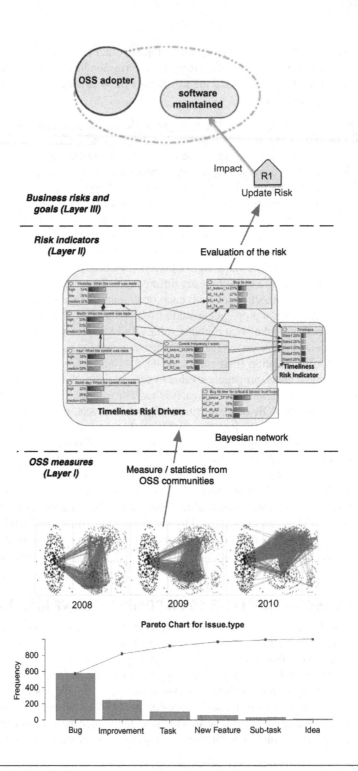

FIGURE 14.12

The elements characterizing the three layers.

expose to the component "Update Risk." Finally, in Layer III, the risks are connected to the goals of the XWiki adopting organization represented via the i^* diagrams as in the case of the goal "software maintained" impacted by the "Update Risk."

14.5 A RISK ASSESSMENT EXAMPLE: THE MOODBILE CASE

Here we describe the application of the proposed three-layered method to the case of risks identification and mitigation in the adoption of the OSS Moodbile project by an educational institution. Moodbile (http://www.moodbile.org/) is a project that aims to facilitate access and usage of the Moodle learning management system from internet-enabled mobile devices. To this end, the Moodbile's community ecosystem decided to develop a set of web services that allow external applications to access key Moodle functionalities thus exploiting the interest in mobile access and taking advantage of Moodle's open source nature. The Moodbile community exposes several types of data such as bug tracking and report milestones, the number of developers involved, communication data among the members of the community and finally the code history with all the various commits by the different developers. Moodbile consists of roughly 75,500 lines of code from about 70 contributors since 2010.[8]

The diagram in Figure 14.13 presents an i^* model of the organization of the Moodbile project, depicting the various actors involved and their relationships. The model shows how *Moodbile* is being managed as an open source applied research project. A second actor involved is the *Moodle project*, upon which Moodbile depends for their source code. Finally, a third actor is the Moodbile *Adopter* actor. Every adopter depends on the project for accessing the latest build for its platform, while the project depends on the adopter for reporting bugs and feature requests that help with the project development.

The Adopter can implement different kinds of adoption strategies related to Moodbile. Here, we refer to an adopter implementing an OSS services strategy or an OSS Integration strategy with a different technical involvement of the adopter for the community.

The relevant goals of Moodbile are also shown in Figure 14.13. The main goal is related to the management of the project that can be decomposed into several subgoals, such as to advertise the project, to manage the team of developers and the Moodbile system development, and to decide about the releases. All these goals can be further decomposed in a set of other subgoals. In particular, the Moodbile organization also disseminates the project using a dedicated project web, monitor the forums, participating in user discussions, post news, and forward feature requests and bug reports to the development team.

The diagram in Figure 14.13 also shows a subset of the business goals of an organization, typically a university or other teaching center, adopting Moodbile (the Moodbile Adopter actor). The organization aims at maximizing the value of the investment in the mobile e-learning platform ($g1$) in order to maintain its reputation. Several goals are directly connected to these high level goal, from the need of having a continuous availability and maintenance of the platform infrastructure ($g3$), to its reuse over the next years ($g4$), to the investment in distance learning reused ($g5$), to the continuous involvement of the students in the use of the e-learning services ($g6$). Moreover, the Adopter depends on Moodbile

---

[8]http://code.sushitos.org.

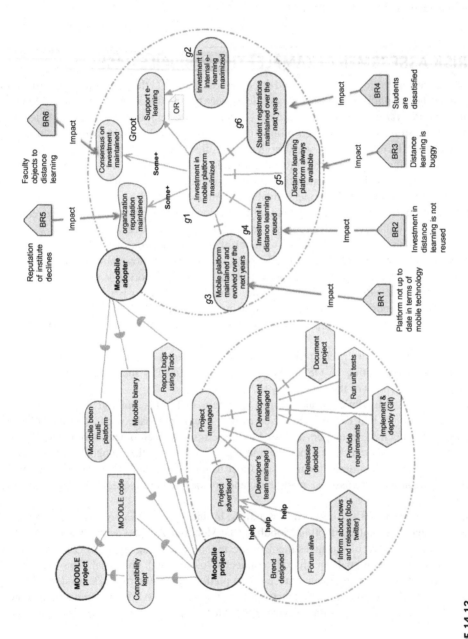

FIGURE 14.13

Moodbile *i** model.

to have a multi-platform version of Moodbile. The satisfaction of the business goals of the Adopter are subject to risks, shown as irregular pentagons and labeled BR1 to BR6 in Figure 14.13.

We apply our approach to the analysis of adoption risk that may impact the adopter organization. Going through the three layers permits us to evaluate the impact of a given scenario described by the OSS Moodbile project measures. These scenarios are determined by data being monitored by the risk management platform every 15 days. Combining the causality links derived from the BN analysis with updated data is providing a dynamic risk exposure dashboard to the adopting organization. The main objective of such adopting organizations is that of supporting e-learning represented by the goal *groot* = "Support e-learning" in Figure 14.13, that is then further OR decomposed in the two subgoals $g1$ = "investment in mobile platform maximized" and $g2$ = "investment in internal e-learning maximized."

In Layer I of the architecture, raw data is derived from the Moodbile community (and updated at pre-specified time stamps) and converted into risk drivers. In this layer we consider the following sources of data mainly related to bug reports:

- DS1: The bug tracker of the Moodbile project.[9] The community uses a web system to track development and report milestones, bugs, etc. The data retrieved from here are the different milestones, feature requests, the number of bugs, the time from a bug report to its solution, the number of developers involved and finally the code history with all the various commits by the different developers.
- DS2: The Moodbile entry in the ohloh.net open source directory.[10] The directory provides an analysis of the characteristics of the code like size, composition, commit history and general activity of the community.
- DS3: The Moodbile project's page in the Google source code repository.[11]

In Layer II, Moodbile risk drivers identified in the first Layer are converted into risk indicators. The Community Risk Indicators (RI) are derived from a social network analysis of the Moodbile developers ecosystem and from other statistics such as those related to bug fixing time. Examples of the Risk Indicators for Moodbile applications include:

- RI1. Timeliness: this is related to the data related to the OSS component and the behavior of the community with respect to activities such as the bug fixing.
- RI2. Activeness: this indicator is related to the activity of the members of the community extracted from chats and blogs data.
- RI3. Community timeliness (from network analysis).
- RI4. Community activeness (from network analysis).
- RI5. Community forking (from network analysis).

These risk indicators represent a range of characteristics of the OSS community that can impact the adopter organizations' business risks. Technical managers who are in charge of the operational systems typically identify them also via "Tactical workshops" using the methods introduced in the previous section.

---

[9] http://code.sushitos.org/moodbileserver.
[10] http://www.ohloh.net/p/moodbile.
[11] http://code.google.com/p/moodbile.

In Layer III, the Moodbile risk indicators are converted into business risks that impact the business goals of Moodbile adopters described via the i^* model as shown in Figure 14.13.

In this case, some operational and strategic risks, described in Section 14.2.1, become more detailed and contextual. These business risks have been defined via interviews to a number of possible Moodbile adopters mainly from academic institutions. The identified business risks represent the main concerns raised by the interviewed staff concerning a possible adoption of the Moodbile platform for use in their virtual campuses:

- BR1: Platform not up-to-date in terms of mobile technology.
- BR2: Investment in distance learning is not reused.
- BR3: Distance learning is buggy.
- BR4: Students are dissatisfied.
- BR5: Reputation of institute declines.
- BR6: Faculty objects to distance learning and is not taking part in the college distance learning program.

The mapping of risk indicator scenarios into business risks is achieved in the so-called "strategic workshops" which, similarly to the tactical workshops introduced above, present participants with scenarios (this time of risk indicators) to be mapped onto business risks.

After the analysis of the data and the workshops, we derive the BN linking risk indicators RI1-RI5 to business risks BR1-BR6. An example is presented in Figure 14.14. The figure compares the risk indicator values at low risk versus high risk. The values of the risk indicators range from very high (State 1) to very low (State 5). The business risks values range from low (State 1) to high (State 3) with State 0 representing non-relevant risks. We can see that at low risks, Timeliness is very low with 32% probability and activeness with 14%. With very high risks these numbers increase to 48% and 53%, respectively. This can be used, for example, to set a trigger for risk mitigation of 50% for low activeness and 45% for low timeliness. If these risk indicators cross these targets, the adopter is exposed to high risk and proactive actions are needed to address this condition.

The BN analysis allows for the evaluation of the initial risk exposure of the adopting university adopting Moodbile to identified business risks. As shown in Figure 14.13, the business risks are connected through impact relationships with some of the business goals of the adopter organization. This can be used to derive a view of the impact of the situation presented by the risk indicators and business risks on the organization actor.

In the OSS Moodbile adopter ecosystem model, the business risks BR1 to BR4 impact on four internal goals that are connected with AND decomposition with the higher level goal Investment in mobile platform maximized. For this goal there is no direct evaluation of the impact made via the risk indicators, which only evaluate some of the goals contributing to it. In this case, the evidence for possible risks to the contributing goals can be propagated following the relationships that connect the goals, thus providing an evaluation of the impact of the risk evidence to the satisfaction of internal goals of the organization. This is done automatically via the reasoning and label propagation techniques described in Section 14.4 applied to the i^* model. As envisaged in the method, the i^* model is translated into a graph whose nodes are the different model entities, such as goals, tasks, and resources, while the relationships between these entities (mainly AND/OR decompositions and contribution relationships) are translated into graph ar; then a label propagation algorithm is applied to the graph in order to retrieve the value of satisfaction of a set of given goals starting from the evidence

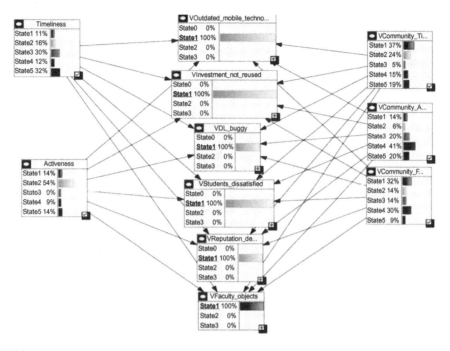

FIGURE 14.14

Linking risk indicators to business risks.

that the satisfaction of other goals is, for example, compromised (or negated) by a risk. In the example of the Moodbile Adopter in Figure 14.13 the goal $g1$="investment in mobile platform maximized" is AND decomposed in the four subgoals $g3$="mobile platform maintained and evolved over the next years", $g4$="investment in distance learning reused", $g5$="distance learning platform always available" and $g6$="student registrations maintained over the next years." So, all the four contributing subgoals should have an evidence to be satisfied in order to have the same evidence in the root goal.

Considering the case of low risk as in the BN in Figure 14.14 we have a situation in which all the Business risks have a very low probability. In this case, none of the Business Goals is impacted by the BR1–BR4 so none of the goals $g3,\ldots,g6$ have a "denial" value evidence while they have all "satisfied" evidences, so having weight v=1 for the satisfaction, as shown in Figure 14.15(a). These values of evidence are propagated through the four AND links (we assume each one of them having a weight w=0.25) and aggregated by the conjunction aggregation function (that makes the average of the four AND links), $sat(g1)=sat(AND(g3,\ldots,g6))=avg(\Sigma_{i=3..6}w_iv_i)=1$, $den(g1)=den(AND(g3,\ldots,g6))=0$ described in Section 14.4, to the higher-level goal $g1$="Investment in mobile platform maximized" that has the evidence of being satisfied and no evidence of being denied.

After a period of 15 days, the monitoring system starts a new risk assessment on the Moodbile community indicators. In this case, all the six business risks have a "state 3", so denoting a high probability. A "denial" value from all the four goals impacted by (BR1–BR4) is propagated through the links and the

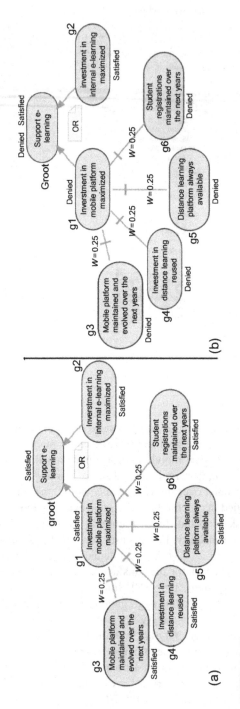

FIGURE 14.15

(a) a scenario in which all subgoals of goal *g1* of the Moodbile Adopter are "satisfied" and this value also propagates to top level goals;
(b) a scenario where some goals are "denied" causing a double value of "satisfied" and "denied" to be propagated on the root goal *groot*.

conjunction aggregation function sat($g1$)=sat(AND($g3,\ldots,g6$))=0, den($g1$)=den(AND($g3,\ldots,g6$))=1) to the higher-level goal $g1$="investment in mobile platform maximized" as shown in Figure 14.15(b).

Moreover, the "denial" value is propagated from the goal $g1$="investment in mobile platform maximized" to the two goals "organization reputation maintained" and "consensus on investment maintained" (through the "*some+*" relationships). In this case, the "denial" value coming from the propagation started in the internal goals is reinforced by the impact of the specific Business risks (BR5 and BR6) impacting these goals, increasing the evidence of a "denial" value for these two goals.

The result of this analysis is an evidence of the degree of risk and of the kind of impact on the business goals of the Moodbile Adopter and a means to explore mitigation activities. In particular, in this last case, a possible risk mitigation strategy for the University might be that of *avoiding the risk* via the exploration of possible alternative goals to be accomplished that are not denied by the Business risks. An example is the goal $g2$= "investment in internal e-learning maximized" that is part of the OR decomposition of the main University goal $groot$= "Support e-learning" (together with the goal $g1$ that is "denied") and that has a "satisfied" evidence, as reported in Figure 14.15(b).

14.6 RELATED WORK

This section discusses related work focused on the modeling, measure and analysis of OSS ecosystems and risks.

14.6.1 DATA ANALYSIS IN OSS COMMUNITIES

Several authors addressed the problem of studying the activities and decisions related to business and technical risks in OSS adoption processes in industrial environments. For instance, in the work of Ardagna et al. [37] the problem of software assurance in the adoption of open source products in telecommunication industry context is considered. The paper proposes a method to introduce assurance activities in the software development process when OSS components are exploited in order to ensure software technical quality and business objectives such as the reduction of Total Cost of Ownership (TCO). An extensive survey on the risks both at the technical and business level in industry has been reported by Li et al. [38]. Here several European IT organizations have been observed to understand which are the main risks and risks indicators related to OSS adoption that are perceived by technical and business managers.

The problem of evaluating the qualities and characteristics of OSS software via metrics and statistical analysis has been considered in several projects. In FLOSSMetrics[12] the objective was to construct, publish and analyze a large scale database with information and metrics from several thousands of software projects. In similar line, GHTorrent[13] project [39] aims at analyzing GIT repositories to mine interesting data to assess quality issues in the code. The objective of the QualiPSO[14] project designed a maturity model and supporting tools, similar to the CMMI [7], which is composed of a list of topics to be addressed by a project in order to be categorized in one of the three levels of maturity

---

[12]http://flossmetrics.org/.
[13]http://ghtorrent.org/.
[14]http://qualipso.org.

defined. Also, the QualOSS[15] project had the purpose of defining a method to assess the quality of OSS projects, more concretely, their qualities of robustness and evolvability. The quality model defined in QualOSS [30] is composed of three types of interrelated elements: quality characteristics, concrete attributes of a product or community, metrics, concrete aspects that can be measured, and indicators that define how to aggregate and evaluate the measurement values to obtain consolidated information. The SQO-OSS[16] project [40] aimed at producing a platform, namely Alitheia Core, serving as a basis of basis of an ecosystem of shared code quality analysis tools and research data to enable researchers to focus on their research questions at hand, rather than re-implementing analysis tools from scratch. Finally, OSSMETER[17] aims to develop a platform that will support decision makers in the process of discovering, comparing, assessing and monitoring the health, quality, impact and activity of open-source software. To achieve this, OSSMETER aims at computing trustworthy quality indicators by performing advanced analysis and integration of information from diverse OSS data sources.

The concept of Key Risk Indicators, or KRIs, are metrics used in the operations of a company or a particular business unit in order to enable an immediate response by the risk managers to evolving risks [7, 37]. The objective is to derive insights from links between risk events, indicators, and measurements representing the OSS development environment. Methodological and theoretical questions that need to be answered in order to derive risk related insights from measurable data are described in Refs. [4, 7, 8, 37, 41–44]. These include what indicators to use for monitoring risk events, how to operationalize an indicator into one or more specific risk mitigation actions and the validation of the predictive ability of risk related measurements.

14.6.2 RISK MODELING AND ANALYSIS VIA GOAL-ORIENTED TECHNIQUES

Several goal-oriented approaches focused on the identification of obstructing relationships between goals in order to model the risk for the goal not being achieved. We focus on two of the main approaches in literature. KAOS [45] is a framework for goal-oriented requirements modeling and analysis. The idea behind KAOS is that models of requirements, represented through the concept of goal, can be formally checked for interesting properties to derive a consistent requirements specification. Obstacle analysis in KAOS consists in analyzing the adverse conditions that may prevent a goal to be achieved. Possible obstacles are searched for every leaf goal and attached to the leaf goal through a negative contribution relation. The root obstacle (which basically is the negation of the leaf goal) if then AND- or OR-decomposed into more fine-grained obstacles. With the identification of the adverse conditions, it is possible to correct them by revising the model. A second approach by Asnar et al. [32] proposes a Goal–Risk framework based on i^* to capture, analyze, and assess risk at an early stage of the requirements engineering process, using goals models. A Goal–Risk model is a triplet $\{G, R, I\}$ where G is a set of goals, R a set of relations and I a set of a special type of relation called impact relations. The model is comprised of three layers. The *asset layer* is used to model the organizational assets. The *event layer* is used to model phenomena that could happen without having the possibility of controlling them. The *treatment layer* contains the countermeasures set up to mitigate the risks, by reducing their likelihood or attenuating their severity.

---

[15]http://www.qualoss.eu/.

[16]http://www.sqo-oss.org.

[17]http://www.ossmeter.eu.

14.7 CONCLUSIONS

This chapter presents a methodology for risk management in OSS adoption that considers data on the structure and behavior of OSS communities, the OSS project characteristics, and expert opinions as the basic sources of knowledge for risk assessment. Differently from other approaches in literature, an important aspect of the proposed methodology is that it aims at both the technological aspect of the OSS adoption as well as its business counterpart in a holistic view.

To implement this approach, we designed a scaffold organized into three layers that goes from the collection of data and the definition of risk drivers that aggregates them, to the conversion of risk drivers into risk indicators, up to the final assessment of the impact of risk on the business of the adopting organization. An important aspect of this approach is that the artifacts in each one of the layers give a view on some particular aspect of the risk identification process so progressively explaining the final risk assessment so that decision-makers can also understand partial results to have a holistic view of the assessment process.

The method also includes techniques for the continuous collection, deep analysis and correlation of the sources of knowledge. In fact, the area of OSS is characterized by the availability of very large sets of data rapidly evolving that can be exploited for the risk assessment, as we envisaged along the chapter. In parallel, it is important that the definition of methods for the expert assessment and feedback acquisition is continuously enriching the set of risk indicators and refining the evidences of correlations between raw data, risk predictors, and risks.

In the future, we envisage the definition and refining of other aspects of the methodology, such as the specification of new methods and algorithms for the risk awareness and mitigation strategies. Strictly connected to the previous point, the definition of assessment plans should allow support for different kinds of organizations, spanning from IT organizations to institutions, in the adoption of their own "OSS way" to software development. Finally, we will continuously enrich the data sources considering forums, mailing lists, such as those described in the work of Mamykina et al. [18] for community analysis and bug repositories for code quality analysis.

Our overall objective is to contribute to the safe and managed deployment of OSS by helping adopters design and implement effective risk management methodologies tailored to OSS adoption.

ACKNOWLEDGMENTS

This work is a result of the RISCOSS project, funded by the EC 7th Framework Programme FP7/2007-2013, agreement number 318249.

REFERENCES

[1] Driver M. Drivers and incentives for the wide adoption of open-source software. Gartner report; September 2012.

[2] Gartner Group. Five mistakes to avoid when implementing open-source software. Report; November 2011.

[3] Tom Lee S, Kim H, Gupta S. Measuring open source software success. Omega 2009;37(2):426–38.

[4] Kenett RS, Raanan Y. Operational risk management: a practical approach to intelligent data analysis. Chichester, UK: John Wiley & Sons; 2010.

[5] Franch X, Susi A, Annosi M, Ayala C, Glott R, Gross D, et al. Managing risk in open source software adoption. In: ICSOFT; 2013. p. 258–64.

[6] Soldal Lund M, Solhaug B, Stølen K. Model-driven risk analysis—the CORAS approach. Berlin: Springer 2011. 460 p.

[7] Kenett RS, Baker E. Process improvement and CMMI for systems and software: planning, implementation and management. Boca Raton, FL: Auerbach Pub, Taylor and Francis; 2010.

[8] Ligaarden O, Refsdal A, Stolen K. Validki: a method for designing key indicators to monitor the fulfillment of business objectives. In: Proc. BUSTECH 2011; 2011. p. 57–62.

[9] Moore J. Predators and prey: a new ecology of competition. Harv Bus Rev 1993;71(3):76–86.

[10] Porter M. What is strategy. Harv Bus Rev 1996;74(6):61–78.

[11] Bonaccorsi A, Giannangeli S, Rossi C. Entry strategies under competing standards: hybrid business models in the open source software industry. Manag Sci 2006;52(7):1085–98.

[12] Daffara C. Business models in floss-based companies; 2008. Available online at: http://ifipwg213.org/system/files/OSSEMP07-daffara.pdf.

[13] Gartner Group, Predicts 2009: the evolving open-source software model. Report; December 2008.

[14] Ghosh R. Study on the economic impact of open source software on innovation and the competitiveness of the information and communication technologies (ICT) sector in the EU; 2006. Available online at: http://ec.europa.eu/enterprise/sectors/ict/files/2006-11-20-flossimpact_en.pdf.

[15] Lakka S, Stamati T, Michalakelis C, Martakos D. The ontology of the oss business model: an exploratory study. Int J Open Source Softw Process 2011;3(1):39–59.

[16] Krishnamurthy S. An analysis of open source business models; 2003. URL: Availableonlineat:www.dbis.cs.uni-frankfurt.de/downloads/teaching/e-bmw/bazaar.pdf.

[17] Jansen S, Finkelstein A, Brinkkemper S. A sense of community: a research agenda for software ecosystems. In: 31st international conference on software engineering, new and emerging research track; 2009.

[18] Mamykina L, Manoim B, Mittal M, Hripcsak G, Hartmann B. Design lessons from the fastest q&a site in the west. In: CHI '11; 2011. p. 2857–66.

[19] Jansen S, Brinkkemper S, Finkelstein A. Business network management as a survival strategy: a tale of two software ecosystems. In: 1st international workshop on software ecosystems (IWSECO), CEUR; 2009. p. 505.

[20] Boucharas V, Jansen S, Brinkkemper S. Formalizing software ecosystem modeling. In: 1st international workshop on Open component ecosystems; 2009.

[21] Iansiti M, Levien R. The keystone advantage. What the new dynamics of business ecosystems mean for strategy, innovation, and sustainability. Boston, MA: Harvard Business School Press; 2004.

[22] Hagel I, Brown JS, Davison L. Shaping strategy in a world of constant disruption. Harvard Bus Rev 2008;86(10):80–89.

[23] Jansen S, Cusumano M. Defining software ecosystems: a survey of software platforms and business network governance. In: 4th international workshop on software ecosystems (IWSECO), CEUR; 2012. p. 879.

[24] Salter-Townshend M, White A, Gollini I, Murphy TB. Review of statistical network analysis: Models, algorithms, and software. Stat Anal Data Mining 2012;5(4):243–64.

[25] Pearl J. Causality models reasoning, and inference. Cambridge, UK: Cambridge University Press; 2000.

[26] Yu ESK. Modelling strategic relationships for process reengineering. Toronto, Ont.: University of Toronto; 1995.

[27] Kenett RS, Zacks S. Modern industrial statistics: with applications in R, MINITAB and JMP. 2nd ed. Chichester, UK: John Wiley and Sons; 2014.

[28] Harel A, Kenett R, Ruggeri F. Modeling web usability diagnostics on the basis of usage statistics. In: Statistical methods in ecommerce research. Chichester, UK: Wiley; 2009.

[29] Kenett RS, Harel A, Ruggeri F. Controlling the usability of web services. Int J Softw Eng Knowledge Eng 2009;19(5):627–51.

[30] Ciolkowski M, Soto M. Towards a comprehensive approach for assessing open source projects. Software process and product measurement; 2008.

[31] Kenett RS, Franch X, Susi A, Galanis N. Adoption of free libre open source software (FLOSS): a risk management perspective. In: COMPSAC; 2014. p. 171–80.

[32] Asnar Y, Giorgini P, Mylopoulos J. Goal-driven risk assessment in requirements engineering. Requir Eng 2011;16(2):101–16.

[33] Ayala CP, Franch X, López L, Morandini M, Susi A. Using i^* to represent oss ecosystems for risk assessment; In: 6th i^* workshop; 2013.

[34] Nilsson N. Problem-solving methods in artificial intelligence. New York, NY: McGraw-Hill; 1971.

[35] Leone N, Pfeifer G, Faber W, Eiter T, Gottlob G, Perri S, et al. The dlv system for knowledge representation and reasoning. ACM Trans Comput Log 2006;7(3):499–562.

[36] Giorgini P, Mylopoulos J, Nicchiarelli E, Sebastiani R. Formal reasoning techniques for goal models. J Data Semant 2003;1:1–20.

[37] Ardagna C, Banzi M, Damiani E, Frati F, El Ioini N. An assurance model for OSS adoption in next-generation telco environments. In: Proceedings of the 3rd IEEE international conference on digital ecosystems and technologies DEST '09; 2009. p. 619–24.

[38] Li J, Conradi R, Slyngstad O, Torchiano M, Morisio M, Bunse C. A state-of-the-practice survey of risk management in development with off-the-shelf software components. IEEE Trans Softw Eng 2008;34(2):271–86.

[39] Gousios G. The GHTorrent dataset and tool suite. In: MSR 2013; 2013. p. 233–6

[40] Gousios G, Spinellis D. Alitheia core: an extensible software quality monitoring platform. In: ICSE '09: proceedings of the 31st international conference on software engineering—formal research demonstrations Track: IEEE; 2009. p. 579–82.

[41] Aven T, Heide B. Reliability and validity of risk analysis. Reliabil Eng Syst Safety 2009;94(11):1862–68.

[42] El Emam K. A methodology for validating software product metrics. Technical report. National Research Council Canada, Institute for Information Technology; 2000.

[43] Fenton N, Neil M. A critique of software defect prediction models. IEEE Trans Softw Eng 1999;25(5):675–89.

[44] Wallace L, Keil M, Rai A. A understanding software project risk: a cluster analysis. Inf Manage 2004;42(1):115–25.

[45] van Lamsweerde A, Letier E. Handling obstacles in goal-oriented requirements engineering. IEEE Trans Softw Eng 2000;26(10):978–1005.

ASSESSING THE STATE OF SOFTWARE IN A LARGE ENTERPRISE: A 12-YEAR RETROSPECTIVE

15

Randy Hackbarth*, Audris Mockus*,†, John Palframan*, David Weiss‡

Software Technology Research, Avaya Labs, Santa Clara, CA, USA* The Department of Electrical Engineering and Computer Science, University of Tennessee, Knoxville, TN, USA† Computer Science Department, Iowa State University, Ames, IA, USA‡

CHAPTER OUTLINE

15.1 INTRODUCTION

How does a company evaluate and improve its software development capabilities? This chapter describes an annual software assessment process developed and used by Avaya. Avaya is a large telecommunications company that started as a spin-off from Lucent Technologies. It has evolved today to be a provider of open mobile collaborative platforms. Software has always been central to its success, and its software development and sustainment capabilities have evolved with the company. Its software assessment process has been in place for 12 years and continues to evolve.

Avaya's R&D organization, which numbers over 2000, is continually called upon to improve the quality of its software, to decrease its time-to-market, and to decrease the cost of development and maintenance of its software. Under these pressures it is critical to identify changes in development processes, environments, cultures, and tools that maximize improvement, that can be accomplished with existing resources, and that produce measurable results.

Avaya's assessment process was originated by and is carried out by the Avaya Resource Center for Software Technology (ARC), part of Avaya Research, a separate organization within Avaya R&D. A primary goal of the ARC is to improve the state of software in Avaya and to know it. "Knowing it" means that improvement should be subjectively evident and objectively quantifiable. Every year the ARC produces an annual report known as the State of Software in Avaya. The report describes software development trends throughout the company and contains prioritized recommendations for improvement. Priorities are assigned to the recommendations based on their expected impact and on the estimated capability of the software development organizations to implement them. Accordingly, part of the report is devoted to showing year over year changes in Avaya's development capabilities, with attention paid to the impact of previous recommendations. The report provides a feedback mechanism to help direct the evolution of Avaya's software development and sustainment capabilities so that the company may meet its goals. As the company's software capabilities have evolved, the report has evolved as well. The ARC is now at a point where it can look back and trace the evolution of the report, and assess its impact since its inception. Its methods may be a model for others to use.

In this chapter, we use examples taken from the annual reports to illustrate the methods used in and the lessons learned from them. We show why and how the scope of the report and the methods used evolved over time, how the report became a basis for software improvement in the company, what the impact of the report was and how we estimate that impact, both financially and subjectively. We also provide some suggestions for how others may initiate a corresponding effort. Section 15.2 describes the evolution of the approach used to create the report and Section 15.3 summarizes its impact. Section 15.4 provides more detail on the approach used, what aspects remained constant over time and what aspects changed. Section 15.5 describes our data sources, how we identified them, and how we validated the data and assured its accuracy. Section 15.6 gives examples of the different types of analyses performed over time, and how they evolved, focused primarily on software qualities, and Section 15.7 does the same with software practices within the company. Section 15.8 illustrates the types of recommendations provided in the report and how the recommendations are deployed. Section 15.9 provides examples of how we assess the impact of the report and its recommendations. Section 15.10 summarizes what the ARC has learned from producing the reports, how the report continues to evolve, how we expect it to evolve in the future, and the applicability to other organizations of the practices the ARC uses in crafting the report.

15.2 EVOLUTION OF THE PROCESS AND THE ASSESSMENT

Our primary project focus areas are derived from company goals, from the data available, and from what we think is feasible for the ARC to do. In 2002, most projects were single site projects, since Avaya had limited offshore and outsourced development at that time and our initial focus was, therefore, on assessment of individual projects. There follows a summary of our focus areas in 2002.

- *Project characteristics*: project descriptions, project goals, and number of releases approaching general availability (GA).
- *Technologies in use in Avaya projects:* the types of target and development platforms (e.g., VxWorks, LINUX), technologies (e.g., J2EE, .Net), protocols, development methodologies, and tools used across projects.
- *People skills*: a snapshot of the domain expertise, roles, and experience of the Avaya R&D community, and changes in these areas.
- *Software quality*: the quality goals of development projects, and customer perception of quality.
- *Project completion intervals (time it took to complete a project)*: an analysis of project intervals, including typical project intervals, and differences between forecast and actual intervals in Avaya projects.

As Avaya has evolved, the nature of project teams has changed. Many Avaya projects have become multi-site, moved offshore, and incorporate outsourced teams. As a result, the scope of the report has also evolved to assess the performance of teams of current nature (see Figure 15.1). This led us to analyze levels of experience, knowledge transfer techniques, multi-site project coordination, and communication mechanisms, among other distributed development factors.

Our initial assessment scope was primarily R&D development activities, including architecture, design, implementation, and functional and system test. These activities remain a focus of each report, but Avaya's business has changed, and the company has evolved from the goal of being a leader in

FIGURE 15.1

Evolution of product team scope in Avaya state of software assessments.

providing primarily voice-based enterprise-based telecommunications, to a goal of being the preferred provider of open mobile enterprise collaboration platforms.

Because of this business change, Avaya products are primarily software-based and need to interoperate effectively, which requires carefully coordinated cross-product planning, design, and testing. As a result, we have expanded the scope of the report in two ways. First is to include an assessment of full lifecycle activities (see Figure 15.2). Second is to include cross-project development activities (see Figure 15.3).

As shown in the figures, we now define the scope from both viewpoints, as follows:

Full lifecycle activities:

- front-end planning activities, such as requirements specification, requirements review and project estimation;
- full product development lifecycle, including product management and program management of functional teams (e.g., global market introduction, documentation, services, marketing, and sales);
- software services and support functions, such as time to resolve customer service requests and assessment of the completeness and ease of use of product information available to service staff.

Cross-project development activities:

- cross-project interoperability management, including interoperability specification, commitments, and testing;
- the creation, testing, and deployments of multi-product solutions;

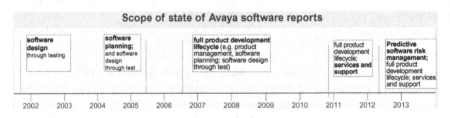

FIGURE 15.2

Evolution of the scope of state of Avaya software reports.

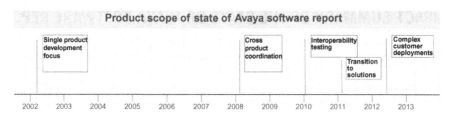

FIGURE 15.3

Evolution of the focus of state of Avaya software reports from single product to include cross-product interoperability management and development and deployment of solutions.

• the capability to predict and mitigate issues in complex customer environments.

The most recent step in the evolution of the reports is to include also an assessment of software risk management practices. For example, the focus of the 2013 report (excerpted from the report) is as follows (see Figure 15.2).

> Our emphasis in 2013 has been on software risk management practices focused on customer driven quality consistent with Avaya's mission to be the preferred provider of open mobile enterprise collaboration platforms.

Note that as the assessments evolve, some activities are transient because of evolution of goals, and some are long term, because they are associated with the company's long-term survival and success. We have taken our current focus, in partnership with Avaya leadership, in recognition of the transition of Avaya to a software-based company and the resulting importance to the business of effective software risk management practices.

Each report also analyzes a special topic of interest for the year. For example, in 2008 we analyzed the deployment of architecture guided iterative development in Avaya. We identify the focus area in cooperation with the company leadership, leading to greater interest in and relevance of the report. Each focus area analysis is based on a study of some set of input data. The data are carefully cleaned and validated throughout the process. Table 15.1 shows the annual focus areas of State of Avaya Software reports from 2009 through 2013. About 50% of each report is devoted to the focus area.

Table 15.1 Focus Areas of State of Avaya Software Reports (2009–2013)		
Year	**Focus**	**Requested by**
2009	Quality in Avaya	Avaya product quality VP
2010	Improving quality and operational efficiency	Avaya research leadership
2011	State of testing	Avaya CEO
2012	Critical software risk management approaches in Avaya	Avaya General Manager
2013	Software risk management: customer driven quality	Avaya CTO

15.3 IMPACT SUMMARY OF THE STATE OF AVAYA SOFTWARE REPORT

Because of changes in technology, market conditions, ownership, and other factors, over the past 12 years, as the company has evolved, Avaya has become a more software-focused company and the report has provided insight and guidance to R&D leaders and business leaders. New R&D leaders have typically provided feedback to Avaya Labs on the value of the report in providing a clear objective view of the strengths and areas for improvement in Avaya's software competencies.

The report is widely distributed to the entire R&D community, and the authors receive consistent feedback that it is read and appreciated by R&D staff.

> "It [the report] really helped me hit the ground running."
>
> —**new corporate quality leader**
>
> "The report has helped me focus on the right areas for quality improvement."
>
> —**new R&D leader**

We evaluate the impact of the assessments in the following ways:

- Usage and effectiveness of targeted areas, that is, once a set of related software practices, such as build management, has been targeted for improvement, we monitor how widely used and how effective it is in later years. As an example, automated build management was widely used but not very effective in 2002, but by 2008 it had become very widely used and very effective. (Section 15.9.1 discusses this example in more detail.)
- The extent of deployment of key software risk management practices, such as risky file management.
- Improvements in customers' view of Avaya quality as measured by the customer quality metric[1] [1].

Avaya leadership has had a strong focus on improving quality for the past three years, and our estimate of the financial benefit of the report and related quality-focused initiatives over this period of time is that operational costs per year have been reduced by at least $60M, which is many times more than the investment made to achieve the savings (Section 15.9).

15.4 ASSESSMENT APPROACH AND MECHANISMS

We do not attempt to characterize software development with a single number, such as with the CMMI approach [2]. Rather, we use the goal-question-metric approach [3–5]. We first establish the goals of software development in Avaya based on Avaya's business goals and on the goals established by the development organizations in order for the business goals to be achieved. As noted by Rifkin [6], different organizations adopt different product development styles depending on their approaches to their businesses. Companies that most highly prize innovation tend to have a different style than companies that most highly prize quality. We believe that it is a mistake to evaluate the different styles with the

---

[1]The customer quality metric is a measure of customers' view of a product's quality based on customer found product defects normalized by the number of installations of the product [1].

same set of measures. We use the goals to identify questions of interest and then define measures that we use to answer those questions. Section 15.6 includes some examples of questions and measures.

In addition, comparing our data and results with other enterprises is problematic because of the difficulty in assuring comparability among data. Validating our data internally is a difficult task, as we discuss in Section 15.5.1 and as the reader may infer from our discussions of the types of data that we analyze in our examples in Section 15.6. As an example, simply trying to determine how much code Avaya has in its code bases is complicated by a number of factors, including, but not limited to, the following:

1. What source code languages to consider. Avaya's products use C, C++, C#, Java, and many others, in very unequal parts.
2. Whether to include third party commercial or open source code or not, and how to identify it in code bases in either case.
3. How to identify duplicated code that occurs when a new configuration control system goes into use in a product and existing code is copied into it.

Comparing code size with other enterprises would require consistent answers to these questions from all enterprises involved in the comparison.

Furthermore, we do not have a way of validating and verifying non-Avaya enterprise data. Even assuming that we could be assured of comparability in the data, we would then have to take into consideration whether or not the enterprises had the same goals. For example, comparing product development time for a company whose goal is rapid time-to-market with a company whose goal is innovation or high quality may lead to misleading results and actions, particularly if one is not aware of the difference in goals. Put another way, we do not benchmark our software measures against other enterprises, either in an attempt to do better or to relax with the thought that we are better. Rather, we compare against our own goals and try to improve with respect to them.

In planning our approach, we have been particularly influenced by Walston and Felix's early work [7], by work on the Experience Factory by Basili and others [8], and by the foundational work on industrial software measurement by Grady and Caswell [9]. Like quality function design (QFD) [10], we analyze quantitative data as well as seek out and prioritize spoken and unspoken customer (Avaya R&D) needs, using a list of questions. The product we generate, in the form of the State of Software in Avaya report (SOSA), contains a series of recommendations with deliverable actions that we expect will improve Avaya's software development practices. Unlike QFD, we do this on a global scale, and quality is only one of the aspects we seek to optimize in R&D.

Since Avaya produces a number of different products for different markets and market segments, the business goals of the individual product development organizations differ, although all strive to meet certain common goals. As an example, in recent years improvement in customer satisfaction ratings has been a prominent goal. All divisions are striving to meet this goal. On the other hand, in certain markets, low cost and ease of installation and use are primary goals, whereas in others very high reliability is the dominant goal. Both common and individual goals color our assessments and the recommendations we make to different divisions. On presenting the report to a particular division we emphasize the results particular to that organization and make recommendations based on that emphasis. In doing so, we highlight their goals and present an analysis of their data, which is generally a subset of all the data we analyze for the year.

Data sources for the report include both quantitative and qualitative analysis of data. For example, in 2008 quantitative data came from sources such as distributions of defects found by customers, modifications made by software developers and described in modification reports (MRs), code in Avaya's software repositories, and demographic data. Qualitative data results from sources such as interviews with software developers, software managers, software product managers, and others,[2] from impressions and data gained from participating in architecture and other reviews, and from specialized assessments of particular issues, such as how well Avaya development organizations are applying iterative development techniques. The Introduction to the 2008 State of Software in Avaya Report describes the sources of information used in producing the report. It includes the following description (slightly edited to preserve confidentiality).

The State of Software in Avaya report series is published by the Avaya Resource Center for Software Technology (ARC) to provide periodic snapshots of Avaya's software production capability. Our goal is to give Avaya R&D organizations a picture of where they need to focus resources to make improvements to achieve operational excellence. Our intent is to give the reader insight into how well Avaya is using its software production capacity, including what resources are available for software development, how effective those resources are, where they are located, and whether they are sufficient.

The reports draw on learning from the services and analyses that the ARC provides to Avaya projects.[3] This year's report draws on the following sources:

- Our learning from our work with the divisions on a software improvement initiative based on last year's report
- Our 2008 assessment of iterative development deployment in Avaya R&D
- Our coordination of the 2007 Avaya Software Symposium and the 2008 Avaya Test Forum
- Our participation in a variety of software architecture reviews, and other services
- Our conduct of individual and small group input sessions with more than 120 members of the R&D community, and with program and product management from all divisions, distributed across Avaya's worldwide R&D locations. Our findings have been reviewed with and adapted based on feedback from these individuals
- Our quantitative analyses of data such as demographic data obtained from SAP and other sources, customer found defects, code in Avaya software repositories, project data, and MR data reported in the data warehouse and various configuration management systems used in Avaya.

Section 15.11 contains a list of example questions used in the interviews to which the report Introduction refers.

15.4.1 EVOLUTION OF THE APPROACH OVER TIME

The report initially gained credibility within R&D, but has now spread far outside R&D to the highest executives. This has affected how each year's theme is chosen and how follow-up is done.

---

[2] In 2008, we interviewed 120 people from R&D and Product Management specifically for the report.

[3] A project is undertaken to develop one or more releases of a product. In some cases, the development of a release is organized into multiple projects.

Twelve years ago the theme was chosen by Avaya Research, but for the last several years it has been chosen by corporate executives. The report evolves primarily based on the changing goals of the corporation.

Initially, we conducted follow-up sessions on the report with R&D management. Now we also meet with personnel from product management, quality, and services, as well as with Avaya business leaders. A version of the report is tailored for each organization based on data that focuses on that organization and recommendations that are the most relevant for it. For each recommendation we now suggest a role responsible for implementing the recommendation. Because of resource constraints in development we focus on the top few recommendations appropriate for an organization in order to increase the probability that action will be taken by that organization.

When Avaya was formed, there was a heavy emphasis on time-to-market. Since Avaya products can be used in mission critical situations corporate goals more recently place a heavier emphasis on product and solution quality [10]. There has also been increased emphasis on making R&D more efficient. This has affected what data are gathered and what analysis is performed.

The number of acquisitions has increased over time, bringing new issues, cultures, practices, market areas, and repositories. This has affected both the data gathered and the analyses performed.

Avaya products are increasingly interdependent, and the company is transitioning from a product management model to a "solution" development model. Along with this comes new data, such as interoperability matrices, that we use in our analysis.

The next two sections contrast what has changed with what has remained the same.

15.4.1.1 What has changed?

The mechanisms have evolved over time to accommodate the change in approach as well as the change in data available, as follows:

- More data sources are available, allowing more in-depth quantitative analysis (see Section 15.5 for details).
- The quality of the data collection practices has improved over time.
- Data are easier to access. Many of the software projects moved to Avaya Forge or started using central resources for issue tracking (see Section 15.5 for details on Avaya Forge).
- We regularly conduct interviews outside of R&D, including field services personnel, corporate quality personnel, managers in outsourced organizations doing Avaya product development, and Avaya executives. The number of interviews conducted has generally increased over time. Interview questions associated with the focus for a given year are specific to that year.
- Originally we conducted web-based surveys to get an overall view of R&D concerns and practices. Because we have built up significant relationships with the development community and because the response rate had become too low to be significant we discontinued surveys.
- We no longer track software development practice trends, so we do not gather data in this area. Instead we do an in-depth analysis of selected practices, such as testing or use of static analysis, and make recommendations focused on them.
- In our first year, we tried doing the report semi-annually. Because of the amount of work involved we quickly moved to an annual report. Since 2003, we have published the report for the preceding year during the first part of January.

15.4.1.2 What has remained the same?

We still rely on both quantitative and qualitative data. Many of the types of underlying data sources we use remain the same, even if the specifics have changed, for example, code repositories are accessed, though the technologies have changed. We still rely on partnerships with Avaya product teams, assessment of good software practice deployments in Avaya and industry, and data from internal software conferences.

We continue to do interviews to gather data as well as draw on engagements with projects and business units that occur throughout the year. Tailored questions for each interview are established in advance to give the interviewee time to think about the interview, though we emphasize that no preparation is required, given the busy schedules of the interviewees. In many cases the interview goes off in an unexpected direction, providing us more insight into development concerns. In this case, the concern may be factored into questions for subsequent interviews, and we typically add interviewees to our list to make sure the concern is properly understood. We document each interview for later analysis. As a result, we now maintain a large repository of interviews covering a 12-year period, which is very valuable when analyzing multi-year trends.

We review a draft of the report, including recommendations, with those from whom we obtained data. Such reviews are part of validating the report prior to completion and distribution.

We continue to meet with management after the report is published to get their view on recommendations and we track to see what recommendations get implemented.

15.5 DATA SOURCES

We access many types of data from a variety of sources, including the following:

- code repositories (lines of code, commit info, branching info, etc.);
- defect tracking systems (defects by stage, field escalations, service requests, etc.);
- demographics (distribution, experience, churn, distribution by roles, etc.);
- development data (code/document/design review information, metrics on code coverage, static analysis, performance, longevity, reliability, build metrics, etc.);
- document Repositories (requirements, designs, project plans, test plans, etc.);
- project WIKIs (processes and practices, project status);
- quality data (interoperability, in-process metrics, customer quality, customer satisfaction, quality improvement plans, etc.);
- use cases;
- sales information (distribution of products by release, product and solution configurations, upgrades);
- services information (escalations, customer found defects, trends, etc.).

There were several reasons for major changes in data sources as our assessment process evolved over time.

- First, the trend to an increasingly centralized (cloud-based) administration of software development support tools such as version control, problem tracking, and related systems continued to accelerate. A large fraction of projects moved to Avaya Forge and to a single instance of ClearQuest (an issue tracker). Avaya Forge is a corporate-source cloud-based tool similar to SourceForge that provides a suite of tools integrated by Atlassian, such as JIRA, Crucible, FindBugs, Subversion, Git, and Confluence. This trend has concentrated data from many of the hundreds of projects into a single location, making it simpler to access and use. In addition, this centralization has unified the identification of individuals. The typical projects analyzed in early state of software reports had their development support and issue tracking systems administered by individual projects and the same person often had multiple IDs associated with each system.

- Second, major new acquisitions brought in an entirely different set of systems and practices. To avoid fragmentation of developer support tools, the issue tracking systems for the projects in this acquisition were migrated to a single (ClearQuest or JIRA) platform.
- Third, projects continued to move to more advanced tools. In the early period, projects were moving from Sablime to ClearCase for version control. Later, Subversion became the standard tool with many projects moving from ClearCase to Subversion. Over the last few years another large migration to Git VCS has started. The employee directory system has changed to a new platform, but continued to provide similar types of data and continued to serve as a means to capture statistics for the entire enterprise.
One of the biggest changes in the use of advanced tools was a move to Siebel of the customer relationship management (CRM) system that was used to track and resolve customer issues.
- Fourth, as the business value of central data collection became more obvious, a data warehouse with information related to sales, field support, licensing, and other types of data was established. In addition, more aspects of software development were supported by tools providing additional data sources.

On the positive side, the collection of data became easier with the centralized tools, identifying individuals became simpler, and a wider set of tools, for example, Atlassian Crucible for inspection, JIRA, and others were introduced to provide additional opportunities to understand and improve software development. However, these migrations have substantially complicated historic analysis, because not all the past data were migrated, newer tools had different types of attributes, and the ways in which the tools were used changed substantially. Many of the no-longer-used tools were decommissioned, and the associated historic data were lost. This has validated our approach to store clones of the systems, such as Sablime, Subversion, Git, or ClearQuest, or to store snapshots for tools that do not keep track of state changes, for example, information from code coverage tools.

Because of the number and variety of Avaya products, the difficulty of accurately combining the data from the actively used and no longer used tools, and the transfer of reporting responsibilities to the business units, we no longer provide context data for the code size, the productivity of developers, and the quality for all Avaya projects. Instead, we have integrated a variety of measures and tools into a toolset for identifying and reducing risk in software projects. The measures we use allow answers to a number of specific practical questions, as described in Section 15.6.

Development still uses a variety of defect management tools (ClearQuest, JIRA, Rally) and Source Code Management (ClearCase, SVN, GIT, Sablime). With the increasing scope of the data warehouse there has been standardization of the semantics of the fields used by these tools. Also, as quality councils were established, the need for common reporting forced the standardization of semantics.

The rest of this section lists some of the new sources of data, some of the data sources that changed, and a few examples of the data and our analyses. Over time, many new sources of data became available, such as the following examples:

- Customer driven requirements and prioritization information are stored in a single repository covering all products.
- Coding data, such as static analysis repositories, code coverage data, automated test coverage, code inspection data, build frequency and breakage, interoperability, and technical debt are maintained for most Avaya products.
- Project management data as provided by Agile management systems like Rally or Green-hopper are available to gather data on project backlog trends, velocity, and quality.
- A comprehensive program management website was established that makes available planned and actual release data as well as other project-related data for each Avaya program.
- System test and developer test data such as test plans, test coverage, test pass and fail rates, and test efficiency are stored in a common repository for a large set of products.
- Open source data in the form of a repository of open source code described in Ref. [11] (that now includes over 200 million unique versions) and a Black Duck repository identifying open source use by projects have been created. As a result, we can filter out open source code from code growth trends.
- Product quality trends based on the "Customer Quality Metric" [1] are tracked and used to report on product field quality.
- Quality data are maintained, based on policies that Avaya developed for minor releases and patches, namely feature packs and service packs.
- Good software practices are tracked by Avaya's R&D quality council. This data is used to encourage improvement in software practices.
- Avaya now uses a Siebel customer relationships management tool that provides information on entitlements and service reports.
- SalesForce, which contains information about customers and their account managers, is used across the company.
- Billing, licensing, and download information is used to estimate the number of users of Avaya's software-based systems and the extent of usage. Downloads may be associated with licenses but also obtained from third parties, such as mobile application stores.

It is worth noting some of the difficulties encountered as projects migrated to new systems. For example, to determine which MRs are related to customer issues, distinct systems have to be linked: a CRM system Siebel, and an issue tracking system for development, such as JIRA or ClearQuest. Because CRM is used by a variety of the service personnel in almost all countries of the world, and MRs are tracked by different software development projects, it takes time to propagate uniform practices and definitions to this very large and diverse population. Active efforts from business units and quality organizations has, over time, led to more uniform and more accurate data entry and resulted in better quality data.[4]

Surprisingly, almost all data sources have changed over the considered period because of evolution of technology, because of the move to cloud-based systems, or other reasons listed above. Only one large project continues to use a custom set of tools built in the late 1980s. This toolset integrates many of the development process stages including inspections, testing, build, change control, and issue tracking.

---

[4]As usually happens, better quality data leads to more precise, more insightful, quicker analysis, which leads to better recommendations for improvements, which leads to faster improvement.

It is interesting to observe that only recently have the integrated suites, such as the one provided by Atlassian, started to approximate the functionality of the legacy tools mentioned earlier.

The main message from our experience of collecting data, however, is that over longer periods of time, it is reasonable to expect to see migrations to different development support tools. This suggests that one has to be ready to adapt to these long-term changes to stay relevant, and that studies done over the long term may require special techniques to adjust for the tool migration and the ways it affects collected data and analyses. For example, while some data were migrated in the projects we have been investigating, the decommissioned systems were not retained. Second, the data migrated from earlier systems were typically different from new data collected in the course of use of a new system. Third, the practices associated with using the new systems often are substantially different from practices previously employed. These three differences make it difficult to conduct historic analysis that crosses the migration boundary.

15.5.1 DATA ACCURACY

In addition to new data migration challenges noted previously, assuring and estimating the accuracy of our data is a major concern. We deal with large datasets that are distributed across a variety of repositories, and for which some of the data are entered manually, often by people far removed from the analysis of the data. For example, MR data are stored in different configuration control repositories and the descriptions of the changes in the MRs are entered by software developers or by support teams that may not be aware that their entries become part of a company-wide analysis. Human error or even just vagueness in such descriptions can be a major source of inaccuracy, as discussed and shown in Ref. [4]. The problem is compounded when performing analyses that include several different sources or types of data. We believe it is incumbent on us to estimate the error in the analyses that we do, and we continue to seek good methods for doing so. This is a research topic that the measurement community should address. In the following sections, where we present some examples of our analyses, we will provide error estimates where we can reasonably make them.

15.5.2 TYPES OF DATA ANALYZED

As previously noted, our quantitative data sources tend to focus on the process by which the requirements are obtained and tracked, the process by which software is developed, the demographics surrounding development, and the quality as seen by the developers and by the customers. Each area has a rich set of tools that can be used to quantify the history of events in the area and how they relate to, for example, customer-perceived quality downstream. Code commits and MRs are used to extract information about a variety of issues, including types of errors that occur and practices that are used. For example, by examining when an error is found we can usually determine the detection technique used, such as a code review or a system test. It is difficult to spot corporate-wide trends by looking at code measures since languages, platforms, and development tools vary across the company; we leave such analysis to the individual projects. However, as projects have deployed various static analysis tools, such as FindBugs and Coverity, and inspection tools such as Atlassian's Crucible, richer sources of data have become available.

15.6 **EXAMPLES OF ANALYSES**

The initial focus of our reports was analysis of demographic trends, domain expertise, code trends, software quality trends, productivity, predictability, transfer of work, and software practice trends. These trends continue to be important to Avaya, but the nature of our analyses has changed.

- We no longer perform annual analyses of some trends because Avaya product groups now track them on a regular basis as part of business operations. Two examples are regular tracking of the customer quality metric [1], which represents the probability that a customer will observe a failure within a certain interval after software release, and quarterly analyses of schedule performance, with a comparison of predicted schedule to actual schedule (Section 15.6.2). In both cases, mitigation steps are identified by the business operations team and taken as needed.
- As Avaya development has become a global endeavor, our demographic analyses have increased their focus on multi-project, multi-location, off shoring and outsourcing trends.
- We have discovered that it is even more important to help projects implement recommendations than to provide recommendations. In particular, we found that providing detailed recommendations with procedures and tools to help implement them was embraced the most readily and widely. Therefore we have started to provide integrated analyses of multiple data sources and tools and procedures to aid in the action steps for individual projects. For example, risky file management (Section 15.6.3) relates several sources of data, such as defect counts, file churn, author churn, and file size to identify the potentially most risky files in the code base. In addition to the risky file analysis, we provide procedures and tools to assist a product team in mitigating the riskiest files as described in Section 15.6.3

Our demographic analyses of the R&D community (Section 15.6.1) remain highly anticipated. For example, they help R&D and business leaders examine staffing, expertise, offshoring, outsourcing, and other R&D demographic trends. These trends are typically available for individual projects, but the report provides the trends at an organization and Avaya-wide basis and helps R&D and business leaders assess the capacity of their organization, its training needs, its ability to deliver products on time and with quality and similar factors.

Our analyses of other trends, such as domain expertise, code trends, software quality trends, transfer of work and productivity trends were performed independently in earlier reports [10]. In some cases, we compared two factors whose relationship we thought might be significant, such as product team productivity and lines of code in the product as shown in Figure 15.4. To measure developer productivity, we followed the approach introduced in Ref. [12]. We first select a subset of developers who together contributed 80% of the changes each year. We refer to them as the core group. The number of changes to the source code by this core group is then divided by the group's size to get the productivity measured by number of changes per developer per year. We consider only changes made to the source code files. Lines of code are calculated based on the contents of the project's code repository.

As previously noted, part of the validation process is showing the analysis results to people in a variety of roles in R&D and other organizations and noting their objections and confirmations. We then make a final pass through the data and analyses, making adjustments as necessary. The analyses that follow are each intended to answer some specific question(s), which are noted at the beginning of the section.

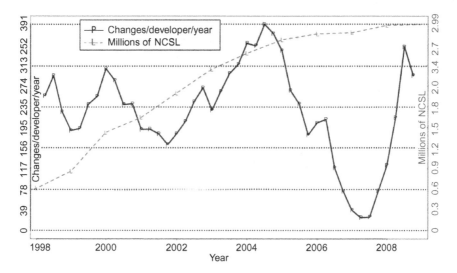

FIGURE 15.4

Productivity trend and lines of code trend for a sample product.

15.6.1 DEMOGRAPHIC ANALYSES

Questions: How is staff distributed across locations and divisions?
How much staff churn is there?

The reports look at the distribution of the current R&D population by location, titles, experience, division, company of origin, and by type of staff (employee, contractor, outsource, or offshore). Understanding the distribution and composition of the R&D organizations helps us to understand problems R&D is facing and to spot trends. For example, Figure 15.5 shows that many divisions in Avaya were spread across many locations, prompting us to study issues that projects have with distributed development. Figure 15.6 shows a major buildup in the use of contractors and in outsourcing, and so we are drawn to address issues such as knowledge transfer and how work is partitioned.

Both figures are based on an analysis of Avaya's corporate personnel directory, which includes information on the role and location of every employee. In addition, some data on outsourced teams is obtained by interviewing Avaya staff that is tasked with managing outsourced teams.

Analyzing the origins of the company's current employees provides insight into products, technologies, and markets with which they are familiar. This has impact on software development methodologies and on the locations of experts in various disciplines. A more detailed view (not shown here) reveals for each year hired how many employees remain and how many of the original set have left the company. This can be used to examine retention policies and morale issues.[5]

---

[5]This may only be possible because Avaya is a relatively new company and we can access records back to its origin in 2000.

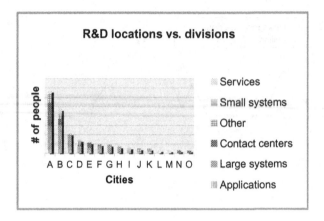

FIGURE 15.5

Distribution of divisions across locations.

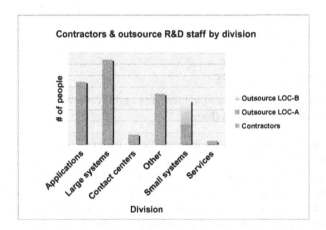

FIGURE 15.6

Outsourcing by division.

The demographic trends can be combined with other trends, such as code growth, to show where support may need to be rebalanced.

Another analysis displays staff churn trends, that is, the turnover rate at different locations, which allows us to estimate the rate of loss (or gain) of domain expertise. Because real-time telecommunications products are quite complex, it can take 6–12 months or more before a developer new to the product or company can be effective. In more complex projects we observed that it can take 3 years for a developer to become effective [13]. The churn trend can be used in analyzing productivity losses caused by staff loss or by training rates for new staff. Figure 15.7 shows long-term trends in Avaya product experience, and, along with more detailed charts, such as Figure 15.8, it is used to recommend what an appropriate balance of new to experienced staff should be based on historical data.

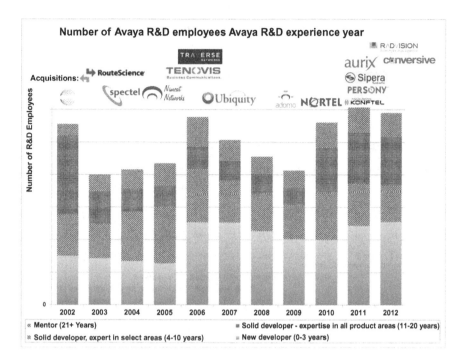

FIGURE 15.7

Long-term Avaya product experience trends.

The acquisitions demonstrate where infusion of developers new to Avaya occurs. Figure 15.8 shows a comparison of the geographic distribution for two specific points in time. Variations of this chart for individual organizations or functions highlight where the experience is out of balance and corrective action is needed. We do not have experience history from all acquired companies so the experience in the worst case could be understated by as much as 11%, but is more likely under 5%.

Our demographic analyses are based on our corporate personnel directory. We create a snapshot of the personnel directory every month and use this data to analyze trends.

In summary, the demographic analyses provide a background and context that assist us in understanding other significant trends in the company.

15.6.2 ANALYSIS OF PREDICTABILITY

Question: How well do Avaya projects predict their completion dates?

Avaya employs a business process with gated reviews for all projects to move projects forward and to synchronize such functions as development, training, documentation, services, installation, and customization. Depending on project characteristics, Avaya uses a variety of processes within the development phase, including iterative and traditional waterfall processes. Predictability of development

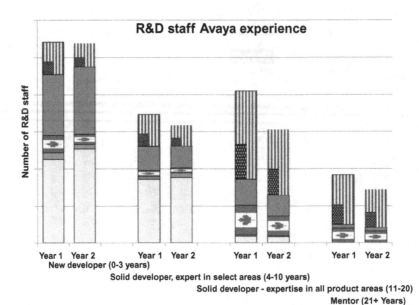

FIGURE 15.8

R&D product experience comparisons by location.

is important to make sure all functional areas allocate resources appropriately, including areas such as design, system test, interoperability test, documentation, globalization, localization, services for alpha trials, beta trials, general introduction, and support. Data are provided to and tracked by per-product Product Management Teams.

We are able to extract planned and actual dates from a number of sources and compare them for consistency. Figure 15.9 shows how well projects predict their completion dates at different gates in the development cycle. The y-axis shows how late or early a project completion estimate is relative to its actual completion. The horizontal line indicates on-time completion. The distribution of estimates at different gates in the development cycle is shown as shaded ovals. For example, at the OK-to-Plan gate, which marks the end of the feasibility phase, the shaded oval shows the distribution of estimates. The median estimate is indicated by a small black horizontal oval within the larger oval. One can see that very few projects fulfill their estimates. Furthermore, even when development has advanced to a later gate, there is only a small improvement.

Figure 15.9 was created by analyzing the predicted and actual project business gate dates for all Avaya projects over an 18-month period in 2004 and 2005. Schedule prediction is now closely tracked by Avaya's operations team and schedule performance has substantially improved

Figure 15.10 shows a relation between three factors and projects' ability to predict their schedule. For example, one factor is the degree of cross-project and cross-division cooperation required. We found that projects involving cooperation among divisions were worse at predicting completion dates than projects that were located within a single division but had development staff at several different sites, which were worse than projects that were located at a single site. Without quantitative data an

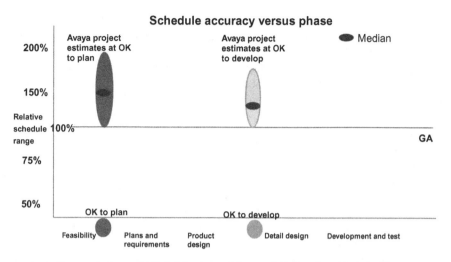

FIGURE 15.9

Schedule predictions.

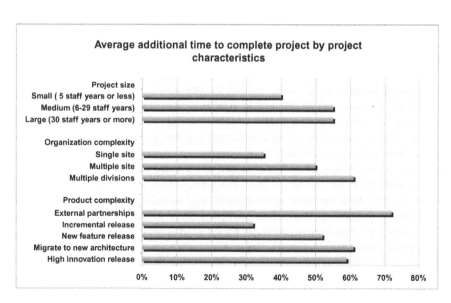

FIGURE 15.10

Some factors correlated with predictability (*circa* 2005).

experienced project manager might guess the same result, but would not know the magnitude of the difference. We also look at predictability by phase and predictability by variables, such as project complexity or size, number of sites, or development methodology. We track the predictability trend to ensure that practices are being put in place to improve predictability. At the time the charts in Figures 15.9 and 15.10 were generated we observed that Avaya was not good at prediction and that Avaya's ability did not improve as the development cycle progressed. Focusing attention on this issue through quantitative analysis led to the use of better prediction techniques and close tracking by Avaya's operations teams. Subsequent analysis showed improvements. This is a good example of an improvement resulting from (quantitatively) highlighting a problem.

Figure 15.10 shows factors that appear to be correlated with predictability. It was created by analyzing the predicted and actual project business gate dates for all Avaya projects over an 18-month period in 2004 and 2005. We identified project size and organizational complexity from project staffing profiles, and determined the product complexity from requirements and design documentation.

Our primary data sources for predictability analyses are the committed and actual dates that are tracked in Avaya's program management repository. These data are updated and tracked on a monthly basis and we estimate the data is about 95% accurate because it is carefully reviewed by Avaya's program managers.

15.6.3 RISKY FILE MANAGEMENT

We observed, based on empirical analysis, that 1% of project source code files contain changes for more than 60% of the customer reported defects in most Avaya products. The ability to identify these "1%" files helps prioritize risk mitigation activities.

Risky File Management (RFM) [14] helps to prioritize and determine the most appropriate risk mitigation actions. We have refined this approach while working with over 50 Avaya projects. Briefly, it involves annotating the source code at the file and module level with the historic information needed to identify risk, and proposes the most suitable actions to mitigate the particular types of risk. It is somewhat similar to approaches used to produce highly reliable software for critical situations, such as described in Ref. [15]. However, in contrast to work described in Ref. [15], the purpose of risky file management is to prioritize risk remediation by selecting risky areas and the remediation approaches that are likely to be most cost-effective. For example, to advocate static analysis techniques described in Ref. [15], we tried to find (but did not) instances of a defect flagged by static analysis techniques that caused a failure reported by a customer. In contrast, several projects reported a non-negligible fraction of fixes to static analysis warnings that introduced new defects. As a result, we prioritize fixes only for certain classes of static analysis defects and only for selected areas of the code.

The data we use comes from version control and MR tracking systems. Software projects use a version control system (VCS) to keep track of versions of the source code. Each revision of a source code file a developer makes is "committed" to the VCS. Information about the commit that can be retrieved includes author, date, affected file and its content, and a commit message that typically contains related Modification Request IDs. Examples of VCS include Subversion, ClearCase, Git, Mercurial, CVS, Bazaar, and SCCS. Developers create branches of a project source code to work on a particular release. VCS typically support creation of a branch so that changes made to one branch can be tracked separately from changes made to another branch. Most projects have at least two branches: a development branch with the latest features, and the release branch (for code that is in the product released to customers), which is unchanged except for important bug fixes. MR/Issue tracking systems are used to track the resolution of MRs (each commit is typically associated with an MR). The MR can be thought of as a software development task. The task may be to implement a new feature or to fix a defect. Among attributes associated with an MR is one that can be used to determine if the MR was customer-reported, so we can tell which defects were discovered by customers. Common issue tracking systems include Bugzilla, JIRA, ClearQuest, and Sablime.

The following lists the main steps of the RFM approach:

1. **Data collection and analysis**

   We gather data about each version of every file in a set of source code repositories for the majority of Avaya projects, and then prioritize the files and identify a candidate set of riskiest files (about 1% of all files) using a weighted algorithm based on the empirical results. While we create the risk profiles based on all files in all Avaya source code repositories, each project is presented with the most risky files that are in repositories related to that project. We obtain the following information for each revision of every file in each source code repository:

   1.1. Path name, which uniquely identifies the file in the repository. Pathnames will be different for each branch in some of the version control systems, for example, in SVN.

   1.2. Author, date, commit message, and content. We process the content of the file to obtain an Abstract syntax tree (AST), and size (in lines of code). We also process the commit message to identify MR identifiers, if present.

   1.3. To determine equivalence classes for a file, all versions of all files obtained in step 1.2 are examined as follows:

      1.3.1. If some version v1 of file f1 matches some version v2 of file f2 (matches means that they have identical content or that they have an identical abstract syntax tree (AST)) the files f1 and f2 are considered to be "related". Typically, the same file may be modified in multiple branches or even different repositories (when the same code is used in multiple projects).

      1.3.2. The "related" relationship is transitively closed, that is, if f1 is related to f2 and f2 is related to f3, then we declare that f1 is related to f3 even if f1 and f3 may not have a single version with the same content or AST.

      1.3.3. Open source software (OSS) files are identified by matching each version of each file for each equivalence class of the related files identified in step 1.3.2 to the large repository of open source code with more than 200M unique versions mentioned earlier. If a match is found, then the equivalence class is considered to be an OSS file.

   1.4. The corporate personnel directory is accessed to determine for each author obtained in step 1.2 if the author is an active employee. If the author is an active employee the employee's name, phone number and e-mail address are obtained. Any other information available in the corporate directory could also be obtained.

   1.5. We identify customer found defects (CFDs) and other MR attributes by matching MR identifiers obtained in step 1.2 to data in the MR tracking system.

   1.6. For each equivalence class of related files, aggregate the data over all related files to obtain the number of commits, number of authors, number of authors who left Avaya, and the number of CFDs.

1.7. Obtain an empirical relationship between properties of the file and CFDs using statistical models using all commits to the project's version control system for a period of time (typically a 3-year period) and fitting a logistic regression model with an observation representing an equivalence class of related files, with the response being whether or not any of the files in the equivalence class had a CFD, and the predictors including those described in step 1.6. For example, in several projects the most important predictors of future CFDs are the number of past changes, the number of SV MRs, and the number of authors who left Avaya.

The fitted model coefficients are then used to prioritize the list of candidate riskiest files.

2. **Presentation of the analysis results to relevant stakeholders.**

The approach provides a subject matter expert exploration view, an online dynamic table, and a downloadable spreadsheet. This is the critical and important part of the approach, as it provides information tailored to the decision-making needs of different stakeholders. Figure 15.11 shows an example of the subject matter expert exploratory view. The candidate-risky files and two most recent CFDs are identified in the first column. The second column contains the number of MRs requiring changes to the file or a related file and a hyperlink to a list and description of each MR. The third column contains the number of authors who have changed the file or a related file and a hyperlink to the list of authors. The third column also contains the number and percentage of authors who are no longer in the company. The fourth column contains the number of related files and a hyperlink to the list of related files

Results from different tables or different portions of the table can be tailored to the needs, interests, and skills of a particular stakeholder. The following are a few examples:

- A project manager sees the priority of the risk and an estimate of resources or time to remediate the risk.
- A subject matter expert sees more technical details of what the type of risk is, what underlying technical details led to the file or module being classified as risky, and so forth.
- A development manager sees who made changes to the file and can use that information to identify potential owners of the code or to identify reviewers for design or code reviews.

Table 15.2 shows key data needed by subject matter experts to reach the most appropriate risk remediation action.

Candidate Risky Files for EXAMPLE PROJECT — 1.0% of files (81 of 8017) contribute to 72% (188) of all CFDs (258)

CFDs by LATEST DATE (FILES by RISKIEST (Score for this project is: (# of CFDs*20) + (# of SV MRs*20) + (Ratio of # authors who have left AVAYA*10) + (# of MRs/10) + (# of file versions/100)))	MRS	AUTHORS	RELATED FILES
1) <PROJECT> /trunk/server/apps/usa/src/ <FILE1>.c : 81 versions			
wi01139190 **2014-11-22** *Empty drop-down box for VDN Override for ASAI Messages* wi01131999 **2014-10-17** *changed on CM 6.x directly is not populated in MSA after completing a Cache Update* 31 CFDs are 73% of the 42 MRs	42 MRs	5 Authors, 3 (60%) departed	51 Files
2) <PROJECT> /trunk/server/apps/usa/src/ <FILE2>.c : 40 versions			
wi00946394 **2014-10-11** *EC500 State field is missing in 96xx templates* wi00945438 **2014-10-07** *MSA application does not show the correct status of XMobile option if DECT is selected and saved.* 21 CFDs are 61% of the 34 MRs	34 MRs	2 Authors, 1 (50%) departed	78 Files

FIGURE 15.11

Extract of exploratory view provided by risky file management.

Table 15.2 Information Presented to Subject Matter Experts

Type of Data	Description of Data
List of CFDs	A link to the CFD, the date, and an abstract to aid the subject matter expert in understanding the defect to which the file contributed.
List of related files	The name of each related file, last commit date, first commit date, number of commit, and last author to make the commit. The list is sorted by the date of last commit.
List of file authors	The name, e-mail address, phone number, number of deltas made by the author, and total number of deltas made by the author to all related files. In addition the first and last date that the author made commits can be provided. The list is sorted by relative contribution (number of deltas) made by the author.
List of all MRs	A link to the MR, the date of the MR, an MR abstract, and an indication of whether the MR is a CFD is provided for each MR against the file. The list is sorted by most recent date.
Lines of Code	The size of the file in lines of code (LOC) is provided as well as the percentage of the current size of the file compared with its maximum size at any point in the past.[a]

[a]*The calculation comparing current size of a file with its maximum size is important, because if the percentage is significantly less than 100%, it is likely that the file has been refactored at some point.*

3. **Remediation actions.** A checklist of heuristics based on experience and empirical data to help the expert take the most appropriate action: for example, no action, control program, or reengineering. For each candidate or indicated risky file, the subject matter expert can analyze the file or module and any associated data. The system can provide an optional guideline, based on empirical data of previous actions taken to remediate risks.

   3.1. No action may be required, if, for example, development is complete for this file; the candidate file will not be used in the near future; the candidate file is changed with a risky file, but is not itself risky.

   3.2. The subject matter expert can recommend a control program involving additional review and testing of all changes to the file, or creating additional documentation to make clearer the design and implementation issues considered in producing the file. Such a control program mitigates risk from changes to the file. For example, if the file has many authors or other reasons warrant, the file owner can create a 1-page design guidance document that is available for anyone who changes the file. The same design guidance document may also apply to a set of files that all contribute to the same component or feature.

   3.3. Finally, the subject matter expert can recommend that the file be reengineered if development is active and the file is deemed to be fragile and difficult to change without introducing more risk.

Typically, the subject matter expert works with the development manager and project manager to schedule any recommended changes to the file. Figure 15.12 shows the distribution of actions taken in response to identification of risky files by an example project.

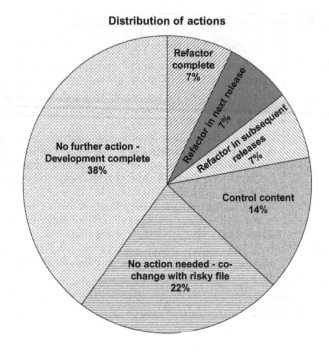

Distribution of actions

Refactor complete 7%

Refactor in next release 7%

Refactor in subsequent releases 7%

No further action - Development complete 38%

Control content 14%

No action needed - co-change with risky file 22%

FIGURE 15.12

Distribution of risky file actions for an example project.

15.7 SOFTWARE PRACTICES

Question: What software development practices are most often and most effectively used?

We originally assessed the extent of usage and the effectiveness of seven key software practice areas and individual practices that make up these areas (Section 15.7.1). These were based on the practices needed to meet stated Avaya goals, which changed over time, and our observation of industry practices. We have generated in-depth reports on the use of selected practices across most Avaya R&D projects, for example Metrics, Agile Practices, Estimation, Continuous Integration, Software Builds, Combinatorial Array Testing, Dynamic Analysis, and Risky File Management. These analyses and others have been used to share best practices across the R&D community.

Currently, the R&D quality council tracks four practices as representative of the larger set of development and test practices (Section 15.7.2). These, along with tracking of schedule adherence and product/solution quality, allow Avaya business leaders to gauge the health of a project's development processes without getting lost in the details.

Section 15.7.3 summarizes our assessment of an example practice area (Design Quality In) that focuses on 11 individual practices. Section 15.7.4 summarizes our assessment of static analysis, a key individual practice in Avaya R&D.

15.7.1 ORIGINAL SEVEN KEY SOFTWARE AREAS

The following seven practice areas were analyzed until 2011:

- Customer-focused development: Practices that emphasize customer input and feedback throughout the development lifecycle, for example, Root Cause Analysis, Customer Feedback, Front End Planning, Increase Customer Understanding, Empower Product Owner.
- Design quality in: Practices that provide a focus on quality early in the development lifecycle, for example, Adherence to Internal Technology Standards, Architecture, Baseline requirements, Build Management, Code Inspections, Collaborative Product Team, Cross Division Architecture reviews, Design Reviews, Interface Specifications, Management of third Party Deliverables, Refactoring, Reuse.
- Improve testing practices: Practices that improve the automation and comprehensiveness of developer and system tests, for example, Code Coverage, Memory Leak Detection, System Test Automation, Stress and Load Testing, Unit Test Automation, Test Focused Development.
- Software project management: Practices to support planning, monitoring and controlling an individual software project, for example, Cross-Division Cooperation, Knowledge Transfer, Measurement, Predictability, Product Management and R&D Learning, R&D Skills, Release Tracking.
- Multisite/offshore development: Practices that support the effective development of software across geographic boundaries, especially those involving offshore teams, for example, Cultural Training, Decouple Work, Ease of Communication, Empowered Teams, Knowledge Transfer, Multi-Site Development Environment, Trust.
- Architecture-guided iterative development: Practices drawn from agile and traditional methodologies that are organized into a family of iterative processes, where development is guided by a well-defined architecture, for example, Agile: Collaborative Product Team, Customer Feedback, Daily Stand-up, Document Just Enough, Ease of Communication, Empower Product Owner, Empowered Team Lead, Iteration Retrospective, Prioritized Feature List, Refactor, Test Automation, Test Focused Design, Time Boxed Iterations, Track Iteration; Traditional Architecture, Baseline Requirements, Build Management, Code Inspections, Manage third Party Deliverables, Track Releases.
- Cross-project cooperation and coordination: Practices that support cooperation and coordination across individual project boundaries. Such cooperation is required for platform-based development and solution-based development.

Our assessment for each practice was based on:

- Criteria for effective deployment of the practice based on accepted industry practices, such as those published in the International Conference on Software Engineering or IEEE Software, and Avaya good practices.
- The extent of usage based on input sessions and our partnerships with Avaya projects.
- Self-assessment of the effectiveness of the practices by a project and the reasons for that assessment.

Each practice was plotted on a grid showing effectiveness and extent of deployment (see Figure 15.13).

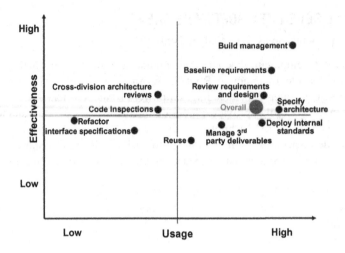

FIGURE 15.13

"Design quality in" practice assessment.

The areas and practices were kept relatively consistent until 2010 so that we could analyze trends and make recommendation based on those trends. In addition, several practices within the practice areas were selected as indicators of projects that focus on quality, as discussed in the next section.

15.7.2 FOUR PRACTICES TRACKED AS REPRESENTATIVE

Beginning in 2012, the following four practices are tracked by the Avaya quality council as necessary, but not sufficient, for achieving good quality while meeting schedules[6]:

- static analysis, using a commercial or open source tool;
- code review and inspections;
- automated regression testing, to prevent breakage and provide acceptance criteria for code being delivered to test or other projects;
- code coverage, to identify areas of the code that had not been adequately tested.

The report originally started tracking these as a group in 2011, contributing to the Avaya Quality Council's efforts to standardize and focus on a small set of representative good practices. Objective targets for these practices were established so that it was clear what actions were expected of projects. The scores of these four practices are averaged for each project to provide a development process measure that is easy to discuss with the quality council and with R&D leaders.

---

[6]We found that projects that do well on the assessment of these practices usually have embraced a host of other good development practices, and have established a culture of quality in the project.

A project's practices are assessed at each product development business gate, including prior to the start of development, when implementation is complete, for example, prior to beta testing, and prior to product launch. We have found these measures to be predictive of the quality of the end product [16].

15.7.3 EXAMPLE PRACTICE AREA—DESIGN QUALITY IN

The following 11 individual practices are representative individual practices associated with the "Design Quality In" practice area.

- Baseline requirements and place them under change control.
- Specify and update an architecture sufficient to guide development.
- Deploy internal technical standards.
- Create well-defined interface specifications [17, 18].
- Perform cross-division architecture reviews [19].
- Establish a component integration and reuse program.
- Review requirements, interface specifications, design artifacts, and test scripts.
- Perform inspections of new or changed code.
- Perform automated build management (at least daily) with automated sanity tests [12].
- Carefully manage third party deliverables and dependencies on other projects.
- Refactor a criteria-based selection of modules.

Each of these practices may be further partitioned into sub practices. For example, in Section 15.8.1.1, we identify six key sub practices of the automated build management practice.

We have defined criteria for effective deployment of each of these practices. For example, the criteria for effective deployment of "manage 3rd party deliverables" are the following.

- All third party deliverables are identified.
- Quality policies are in place and communicated to third party owners.
- Policies are in place on conditions for accepting updates.
- An acceptance test program is in place for each third party deliverable.
- A development team member is identified as "local owner" of each third party deliverable.
- Schedule and quality impact of third party deliverables is assessed.

An assessment of the individual practices for "Design Quality In" from several years ago is shown in Figure 15.13. The x-axis represents how widely the activity is deployed (Usage), and the y-axis represents how effectively the process has been deployed (Effectiveness) based on criteria for each practice. The evaluation of effectiveness and usage for a practice is a judgment based on our discussions with R&D project members and our analysis of quantitative data. In Figure 15.13, the judgments are represented by the positions of the black circles. For example, at the time of the assessment automated build management was widely deployed and Avaya R&D projects were highly effective in performing automated build management. On the other hand, there was limited usage of structured refactoring techniques [20] and where deployed the practice was judged to have medium effectiveness. The Overall circle, in blue (dark gray in print versions), represents our judgment of the usage and effectiveness of the total set of "Design Quality In" practices, which was medium to high usage and medium effectiveness.

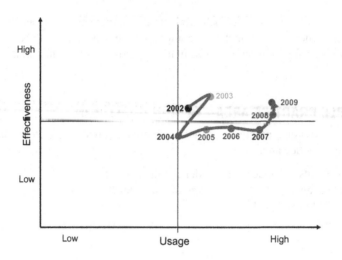

FIGURE 15.14

Multi-year trend for design quality in (2002–2008).

These charts provide guidance by identifying software practices to target for improvement. Avaya provides guidance on best practices to projects, but leaves the implementation of each specific practice to each project.

Figure 15.14 shows our overall assessment of design quality in from 2002 to 2008. This practice area shows initial improvement, then decline followed by slow improvement in usage and minimal improvement in effectiveness. Avaya has inherited a long tradition from Bell Labs of quality products and quality-focused development processes (see, e.g., [21]), and quality remains a strong emphasis for Avaya R&D leaders and staff.

15.7.4 EXAMPLE INDIVIDUAL PRACTICE—STATIC ANALYSIS

When a few products were not meeting quality goals many business units within Avaya made the use of static analysis mandatory. Projects had a choice of tools—either a centrally funded commercial tool or open source tools such as FindBugs for JAVA. Quality councils tracked how frequently static analysis was used and how aggressively projects fixed real violations. This proactive effort to remove defects complemented code inspections and automated testing.

We analyzed the strategies that projects were using to remove violations, tracked trends across projects that had used static analysis for multiple releases,[7] and summarized good project policies in addressing static analysis defects.

For example, depending on product quality, project stage, staff expertise and other characteristics, one or more of the following static analysis policies are typically used by Avaya development teams:

---

[7]Many business critical systems in Avaya have infrequent releases both because of the complexity and interaction of features, and because business customers cannot absorb frequent releases.

- no new or high impact violations allowed in any build,
- target critical violations (potentially high impact outliers),
- decrease or eradicate medium impact violations,
- cover fixed code by automated tests,
- fix when a file is being changed for other reasons, especially for legacy systems.

When fixing violations in legacy code where there was limited or no experience remaining with the file, projects took two approaches to minimize breakage:

1. If a file was being changed, and the developer had some familiarity with the file, the project took the opportunity to correct high and medium impacting violations.
2. A project addressed all violations of a particular type in legacy code all at once, regardless of whether a file was being changed for some other reason.

We found that a few types of violations accounted for the majority of violations. We also found that some violations had a more critical impact on the code than might be suggested by the vendor. We gave guidance on what type of violations to fix first. Figure 15.15 shows the distribution of the top violations across a sample of 32 Avaya projects. For these 32 projects, over 26% of all static analysis violations are "pass by value" or "uninitialized constructor" violations.

Similar charts are created for individual projects.

We track to determine if product teams are improving in their deployment of static analysis practices. Figure 15.16 shows an example for one Avaya R&D organization. The average static

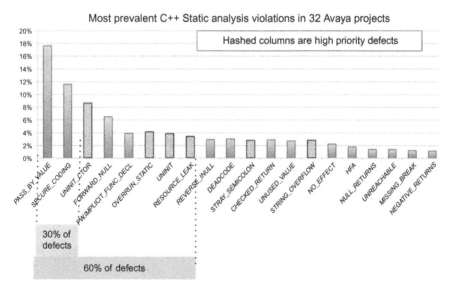

FIGURE 15.15

Distribution of static analysis violations.

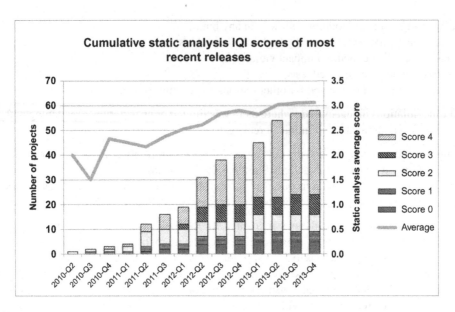

FIGURE 15.16

Trend in static analysis scores.

analysis score for the organization's product teams as determined by the R&D quality council increased year-over-year for most years leading up to 2013. In addition, the number of product teams with a static analysis score of 4[8] (the largest score possible) increased each year.

15.8 ASSESSMENT FOLLOW-UP: RECOMMENDATIONS AND IMPACT

We create a set of five to seven prioritized recommendations each year based on the assessment findings and identify a suggested owner for each recommendation. Suggested owners typically include the following roles:

- The project team leader if the recommendation is within the scope of an individual project.
- The R&D leader for an organization if the recommendation is within the scope of an individual R&D organization.
- The product management leader within a division if the recommendation requires the leadership of the product management team.
- The division general manager if the recommendation requires cooperation with a division across the entire functional areas of the business.
- Avaya's operations leader if the recommendation requires cross-division cooperation.

---

[8] A score of 4 means that the product team performs static analysis with every build, and the team addresses all serious defects; 2 means static analysis is run occasionally on new/changed code, there is no systematic approach to defect correction, but output is monitored and the most serious defects are corrected; 0 means no static analysis.

Table 15.3 Example Recommendations Summary Table (Excerpt)		
Recommendation	**Software Practice Area Addressed**	**Deployment Responsibility**
1. Recommendation One: Continue the software improvement program with a concentration on customer-focused development Monitor the impact of the program.	• Customer Focused Development	• Division Product Management leader
2. Recommendation Two: Improve build management practices as a lever to improve quality. Monitor the impact.	• Design Quality In	• Project team lead for each project
3. Recommendation Three: Improve the program for transfer … Monitor the impact.	• ….	• R&D Vice President for each division program

No individual role is assigned more than two or three areas of responsibility in any given year.

The report provides an abstraction of each recommendation in a summary table similar to Table 15.3, and a detailed description in the body of the report.

The first column of the summary table contains the recommendation abstract. The second column identifies the software practice addressed by the recommendation, and the third column identifies the suggested owner.

Two example recommendations are described in Section 15.8.1. Section 15.8.2 describes how the recommendations are deployed.

15.8.1 EXAMPLE RECOMMENDATIONS

Recommendations made between 2002 and 2013 cover a variety of topics, such as the following:

- front end planning;
- deployment of architecture-guided iterative and agile practices;
- software project management;
- multi-site and offshore development practices;
- domain expertise of the R&D staff.

The following sections describe two example recommendations. The automated build recommendation is an early recommendation (Section 15.8.1.1), initially made in 2003. The risky file management recommendation (Section 15.8.1.2) is more recent, initially made in 2012.

15.8.1.1 Automated build management recommendation

We classify automated build management as a practice in the "design quality in" practice area (see Section 15.7.3).

Avaya had several challenges in build management when the corporation was initially formed. While some Avaya projects had very sophisticated build management practices that supported distributed development and automated sanity testing,[9] the practices were not standard across the corporation. Build practices in many projects were inefficient, not fully automated and limited in their testing and reporting capabilities. In many projects, build management practices were more of a hindrance than a help to developers in rapidly integrating and testing their code.

Our recommendation was to improve build management practices as a lever to improve quality, including the following set of industry-proven good practices [22, 23].

- Good Practice 1   Treat load check-in as a quality gate
- Good Practice 2   Automatically track versions of all components of a load
- Good Practice 3   Establish a fully automated build and sanity test process
- Good Practice 4   Perform daily builds and sanity test
- Good Practice 5   Automatically link change tracking and version control
- Good Practice 6   Define and track load building metrics

We provided details on each practice in a separate report and identified example projects that could serve as mentors to other projects.

15.8.1.2 Risky file management: Target the riskiest files causing field defects for improvement

We identified risky file management as a key risk management technique to focus resources on the most critical files in a project's code repository (Section 15.6.3).

Our recommended action in the 2012 report was for product teams with field quality issues or a large customer base, to establish a standard practice of reviewing the project's riskiest files and determine an appropriate step, such as content control or refactor, to reduce the risk associated with changes to these files.

In 2013, Avaya Labs created a dashboard of candidate risky files for a large cross-section of Avaya products. The dashboard helps projects identify their riskiest files and is automatically updated weekly.

15.8.2 DEPLOYMENT OF RECOMMENDATIONS

Recommendations are deployed in partnership with business and R&D leaders. We conduct follow-up sessions with individual business leaders, R&D leaders, and product management leaders of each organization. The sessions are typically structured based on the following list of questions for each recommendation.

- Is the recommendation relevant to your organization/team?
- If relevant, is it already deployed in your organization/team?
- If relevant and not deployed, what are the barriers to deployment?
- What actions are you prepared to take?
- How can our team help in deployment?

---

[9]Sanity testing is the practice of running a few tests after a build to ensure that the product was built correctly and that basic functionality works.

Note that as a result of these sessions, a recommendation may not be deployed in a particular organization either because it is not relevant to that organization or the barriers for deployment are too large. In addition, the recommendation may be adapted to make it more deployable in a particular organization. When appropriate actions for an organization are identified for a recommendation, action plans are then defined, deployed and tracked. Results are incorporated into the next year's assessment report.

15.9 IMPACT OF THE ASSESSMENTS

As noted in Section 15.3, we evaluate the impact based on usage and effectiveness of the practices (see example in Section 15.9.1), on the extent and impact of deployment (Section 15.9.2), and on the improvements in the customers' view of quality as measured by the customer quality metric [1] (Section 15.9.3). Following are a few examples.

15.9.1 EXAMPLE: AUTOMATED BUILD MANAGEMENT

Our assessment in 2002 and 2003 was that Avaya projects had medium to high usage of automated build management practices with low to medium effectiveness[10] as shown in Figure 15.17. In 2003 and 2004, we made specific improvement recommendations as described in Section 15.8. These recommendations helped create a focus in Avaya R&D in 2004 and 2005 to improve build management practices. The good practices in build management described in Section 15.8.1.1 are now widely deployed and build

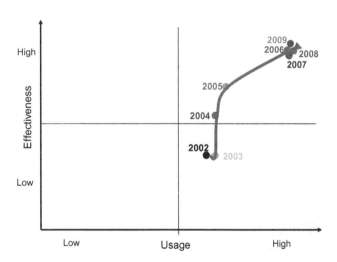

FIGURE 15.17

Multi-year trend of usage and effectiveness of automated build management practices (2002–2008).

---

[10]The scale for Usage and Effectiveness are defined in the same way as used in Section 15.7.

management is an effective, efficient practice for most Avaya projects (see Figure 15.17) for 2002 through 2008.

Automated build management continues to be a strength of Avaya product teams in 2014 with widespread and effective deployment. In fact, our assessment focus is no longer on automated build management, but on continuous build and integration practices.

15.9.2 EXAMPLE: DEPLOYMENT OF RISKY FILE MANAGEMENT

We provided briefings on risky file management to about 40% of the active projects in the first half of 2013 (i.e., the first several months after the 2012 State of Avaya Software report was published).

- 50% of those projects' products deployed risky file management as a part of their development process.
- 25% of the projects are considering deployment.
- 25% of the projects are not deploying, typically because the project is no longer doing significant new development—that is, they are now doing sustaining engineering.

We do not yet have post-release quality data for most of the projects that deployed risky file management, because they have not yet been deployed long enough to obtain reliable defect data. Two projects with sufficient defect data that used risky file management as part of their quality improvement program had significant improvements in quality.

- The customer quality metric (CQM) [1] for an Avaya contact center product improved by 30%.
- The CQM for an Avaya endpoints product improved by well over 50%.

15.9.3 IMPROVEMENT IN CUSTOMER QUALITY METRIC (CQM)

The operational cost of fixing a customer found defect includes the cost to diagnose the defect, to implement and test the fix to the defect, and to deploy the corrected fix.

We estimate the impact of the assessments based on the operational savings as a result of fewer customer found defects (CFDs).

The operational benefit for any product release is calculated as follows. First, we calculate or obtain the following data.

- Expected number of CFDs against the product release; the expected number is based on CQM (which is based on in-service time per customer) prior to improvement and the number of product release installations.
- Actual number of CFDs against the product release.
- Operational cost of fixing a CFD (cost provided by Avaya corporate quality team).

Then,

Operational benefit = Operational cost of fixing a CFD * (expected number of CFDs − Actual number of CFDs)

Table 15.4 shows the operational savings calculations for a sample of product releases over the past 3 years.

Table 15.4 Operational Savings Calculations for Product Releases of Four Avaya Products

Product Release	Operational Benefit
Product A Release 6.1	$328K
Product A Release 6.2	$406K
Product A Release 6.3	$27K
Product B Release 6.1	$450K
Product B Release 6.2	$773K
Product B Release 6.3	$932K
Product C Release 6.2	$5974K
Product D Release 6.0	$1686K
Product D Release 7.0	−$124K
Product D Release 8.0	$4073K
Product D Release 8.1	$3620K

The prior release of Product C (Release 6.1) did not deploy practices recommended in the reports and had numerous quality issues resulting in many millions of dollars in additional operational costs.

Using the approach described in this section, we estimate the annual operational savings based on the deployment of quality focused improvements for the past 3 years to be at least $60M per year based only on reduced cost of dealing with customer reported issues, and not including benefits resulting from increased customer satisfaction. The investment in the quality improvement effort was likely to be much lower. Approximately 20% of the effort of the ARC team goes into producing the report and obtaining relevant measures. The investments made by development, testing, and quality organizations are harder to quantify, but are highly likely not to have exceeded the savings.

15.10 **CONCLUSIONS**
15.10.1 **IMPACT OF THE ASSESSMENT PROCESS**

As noted in earlier sections, the process of assessing software development and sustainment in Avaya has had significant impact, on the way that software is developed, on the practices and processes targeted for improvement, on achieving company goals, and on the cost and value of software technology within the company.

The impact has been made possible by focusing on the goals of the company and on obtaining data that can be used to analyze how well software development within the company is contributing to meeting those goals, following the GQM approach to empirical studies. The idea has been to improve the way the company does software development and to know it.

The impact of the process is evident in several ways. The annual analysis, as described in the report The State of Software in Avaya, shows to all who are interested what improvements have occurred and what areas need improvement, often prompting allocation of resources to making improvements and monitoring those areas. It helps the company set goals and understand better whether or not it is achieving those goals. For example, improving software quality by reducing defects found by customers frees software developers' time to work on adding new features and capabilities to products rather than correcting bugs in those products. With appropriate focus on data collection, we are able to estimate how much the savings from improved quality is, providing more substance to the idea of knowing what the improvement is.

The assessment process can also be viewed as providing a competitive advantage to the company. It both allows the company to show customers the quality improvements and allows more rapid development of new features or customization to customers' needs. As a result, the company both retains existing customers and attracts new customers, instilling confidence in customers that the company has a systematic process in place to improve quality.

15.10.2 FACTORS CONTRIBUTING TO SUCCESS

The assessment process was started in 2002 and is a continuing process, producing the State of Software in Avaya report at the end of every year. Based on its longevity and continuing impact, we believe the assessment process has been a success. Factors contributing to that success include the following:

1. a well-defined measurement methodology, founded on the goal-question-metric approach [3, 4, 24];
2. the ability to identify organizational goals;
3. the availability of the necessary data and the willingness of the producers of the data to share it;
4. cooperation by people at all levels of technical and management positions, from software developers to the company's executives;
5. confidence by all involved that the conclusions drawn from analysis of the data, both quantitative and qualitative, are valid, with such confidence instilled by continuing discussion with development organizations, and retrospective views of the results;
6. acknowledgement from the software development organizations that the annual recommendations are useful and lead to (needed) improvements;
7. evidence that the assessment process is having a positive financial impact on the company, for example, that considerable time and effort is saved through improvements in quality of the type and by the means suggested in the state of software reports;
8. an incremental approach to implementing the assessment program, starting with relatively modest goals and an in-house focus, using a subset of the types of data that are currently analyzed, and proceeding over the years to a broader focus incorporating customer-focused data into the analysis.

In summary, the assessment process started with clear goals, a repeatable, systematic measurement process, gained the confidence of those who provided the data by providing them with useful analyses and recommendations, and then expanded the focus of the analysis and the breadth of the data analyzed. During the 12 years, so far, of the assessment process, the company has undergone significant changes in management and personnel, but the utility of the assessment process has remained clear to all, and it has continued to receive strong support from the software development organizations, from company executives, and from Avaya Research.

15.10.3 ORGANIZATIONAL ATTRIBUTES

The success of the process, of course, is also greatly owed to the skills and commitment of the ARC who, from the beginning, formed close relationships with the development organizations who both provided the data and were the subjects of the recommendations. The ARC was (and is) principally staffed by two or three people with considerable development experience and experience in working with development organizations to foster improvements. The ARC was established by a research director and was a part of a research department, and received direction from the director, and not from someone in the direct management line of the development organizations. Accordingly, it was perceived as being objective and non-competitive. It was also able to call on others in the research department for support in discussing and implementing different forms of data analysis. Furthermore, the ARC has remained a stable organization, with two of the same members that it had at its inception, and with continuing support from the same researchers.

15.10.4 SELLING THE ASSESSMENT PROCESS

As previously noted, there are a number of factors contributing to the success of the assessment process and the corresponding annual report. Perhaps most important to the success of the process was showing that the findings of the reports could have significant impact on the company by improving software development and related practices, and by making stakeholders out of a wide variety of people in roles throughout the company, ranging from typical software developers through the company CEO. Without continuing support from the stakeholders, the assessment process and report would have had no way to demonstrate value. Early in the process, we worked with small groups who had confidence in the ARC based on earlier dealings with its members. Based on the early results, as the process continued we broadened the stakeholder base, and always made sure we were focusing on issues of interest to stakeholders, often by showing them preliminary results and asking for their validation. As the process evolved, we could show the results of the recommendations from earlier analyses, thereby helping to validate the value of the process, and establishing a virtuous cycle. We think that such an approach helps assure success and would advise others who are interested in starting an assessment program to use a similar strategy.

15.10.5 NEXT STEPS

We will continue to prepare an annual state of software report for Avaya and expect to focus on the following areas in the coming years.

- Our demographic assessments focus on the R&D development and testing community and, because of the role of software across Avaya's business, we intend to include product management, services and support as well as other areas in future demographic assessments.
- As noted in Section 15.6, we have discovered that it is even more important to help projects implement recommendations than to provide them. As a result, we will continue to provide integrated analyses of multiple data sources and tools and procedures to aid in the action steps for individual projects. Risky file management (Section 15.6.3) is an example of this approach.
- As we utilize new data repositories (Section 15.5), we will improve our ability to estimate the accuracy of our data and analyses.

We are also interested in benchmarking with other companies who are performing similar analyses and with whom we could assure data comparability.

It is an open question as to how the various factors analyzed interact with each other, and is a subject of future research.

The techniques we use in producing the report could be applied in any organization that can define its goals, that is willing to collect the data needed to measure progress towards those goals, and that is willing to make an investment in improving its development practices. Although we typically think of such organizations as companies, or business units within companies, the techniques could be applied to any entity that develops software. For example, a worthwhile goal might be to produce a report on the state of software in the USA. Certainly, the challenges would be large, but the pay-offs in terms of knowing where one should invest to improve the way software is developed in the country would be large as well.

15.11 APPENDIX
15.11.1 EXAMPLE QUESTIONS USED FOR INPUT SESSIONS

As one source of input, we use individual and small group input sessions with R&D and product management. These sessions cover all divisions, major R&D sites, various levels of technical staff and management, and a variety of R&D roles, including architects, developers, project and program managers, testers, documentation, and support. Our findings are reviewed with them and adapted based on their feedback. Each session is based on two sets of questions and a set of software practices that we tailor based on the role of those in the input session. Common questions include:

- What are the three primary software-related areas that your project is doing particularly well?
- What are the three primary software-related issues facing your project?
- What is your assessment of the software quality for your project and why?
- What is your assessment of the productivity for your project and why?
- What is your assessment of the domain expertise of your staff? Why?
- What software development approach(es) are used in your project?
- If you could change one software related area in Avaya, what would you change?

The nature of these sessions and the questions that we ask has evolved over time. For early reports we had less data on trends and on a variety of factors, such as productivity, cost, and quality. Accordingly, we spent more time in individual discussion sessions. Currently, we are able to show session participants charts and graphs showing trends and, as necessary, data about their organizations, and use those to focus the session. As a result, sessions are more to the point and briefer.

ACKNOWLEDGMENTS

We thank the 300+ people who have contributed data, participated in interviews, validated results, and helped with the analysis of data for the State of Software in Avaya reports.

We especially thank David Bennett, Neil Harrison, Joe Maranzano, and John Payseur for their contributions to early assessments, Trung Dinh-Trong for his contributions to reports, especially in the areas of test automation and code coverage, Zhou Minghui for her work in Avaya on developer productivity, Evelyn Moritz for her analyses and feedback to the report as well as co-authorship of several reports, Pierre Osborne for his leadership in establishing and supporting Avaya's R&D data warehouse, and Jon Bentley for his careful and helpful reviews of the reports. Thanks to Lee Laskin, Dan Kovacs, Saied Seghatoleslami, and Patrick Peisker for their contributions around product quality processes and data. Thanks to Ravi Sethi, Brett Shockley, and Venky Krishnaswamy for their executive sponsorship and support of the ARC program and Christian Von Reventlow for his enthusiastic assistance in establishing deployment programs in partnership with business and R&D leaders. Thanks to Ashwin Kallingal Joshy for careful readings of earlier versions.

REFERENCES

[1] Mockus A, Weiss D. Interval quality: relating customer-perceived quality to process quality. In: 2008 international conference on software engineering. Leipzig, Germany: ACM Press; May 10-18 2008. p. 733–40.

[2] CMMI institute. URL: http://whatis.cmmiinstitute.com.

[3] Basili V, Weiss D. Evaluating software development by analysis of changes: some data from the software engineering laboratory; February 1985.

[4] Basili V, Weiss D. A methodology for collecting valid software engineering data. IEEE Trans. Softw Eng 1984;10:728–38.

[5] van Solingen R, Berghout E. the goal/qestion/metric method: a practical guide for quality improvement of software development. Cambridge, UK: McGraw-Hill Publishers; 1999.

[6] Rifkin S. Why software process innovations are not adopted. IEEE Software July/August 2001.

[7] Stokes D. Pasteur's quadrant. In: Basic science and technological innovation. Washington, DC: Brookings Institution Press; 1997.

[8] Basili V, Caldiera G, McGarry F, Pajeraki R, Page G, Waligora S. The software engineering laboratory—an operational software experience factory. In: International conference on software engineering; 1992. ISBN: 0-8791-504-6.

[9] Grady R, Caswell E. Software metrics. Englewood Cliffs, NJ: Prentice-Hall; 1987.

[10] Hackbarth R, Mockus A, Palframan J, Weiss D. Assessing the state of software in a large organization. J Empir Softw Eng 2010;15(3):219–49.

[11] Mockus A. Amassing and indexing a large sample of version control systems: Towards the census of public source code history. 6th IEEE Working Conference on Mining Software Repositories; May 16-17 2009.

[12] Mockus A, Fielding R, Herbsleb J. Two case studies of open source software development: Apache and mozilla. ACM Trans Softw Eng Methodol 2002;11(3):1–38.

[13] Zhou M, Mockus A. Developer fluency: Achieving true mastery in software projects. In: ACM Sigsoft/FSE. New Mexico: Santa Fe; November 7-11 2010. p. 137–46.

[14] Mockus A, Hackbarth R, Palframan J. Risky files: an approach to focus quality improvement efforts; June 3, 2013. CID 162981, ALR-2013-23, and Presented at foundations of software engineering conference/2013 August 18.

[15] Holzmann G. Mars code. Commun ACM 2014;57(2):64–73.

[16] Hackbarth R, Mockus A, Palframan J, Sethi R. Customer quality improvement of software systems. IEEE Softw 2015;PP(99). http://ieeexplore.ieee.org/xpls/abs_all.jsp?arnumber=7106410&tag=1

[17] Clements P, Britton K, Parnas D, Weiss D. Interface Specifications for the SCR (A-7E) extended computer module NRL report 4843. Washington, DC: Naval Research Laboratory; January 1983.

[18] Britton K, Parker R, Parnas D. A procedure for designing abstract interfaces for device interface modules. In: Proc 5th Int Conf Software Eng. San Diego, CA; 1981. p. 195–204.

[19] Maranzano J, Rozsypal S, Warnken G, Weiss D, Wirth P, Zimmerman A. Architecture reviews: practice and experience. IEEE Softw 2005;22(2):34–43.

[20] Fowler M. Refactoring: improving the design of existing code. Reading, MA: Addison-Wesley; 1999.

[21] Bell Labs Tech J, Special Issue Software. (April/June 2000), Available at URL: http://www3.interscience.wiley.com/journal/97518354/issue.

[22] Appleton B, Berczuk SP. <u>Software</u> configuration management patterns. Reading, MA: Addison-Wesley; 2003.

[23] McConnel S. Rapid development. Redmond, WA: Microsoft Press; 1996.

[24] Basili V, Caldiera G, Rombach HD. Goal question metric approach. In: Encyclopedia of Software Engineering. New York: John Wiley and Sons, Inc.; 1994. p. 528–32.

AUTHOR BIOGRAPHIES

Randy Hackbath

Randy coordinates a team dedicated to improving the state of the practice of software development in Avaya. Before joining Avaya, Randy worked for 20 years at Bell Labs with a focus on establishing, coordinating and contributing to business unit–research partnership projects. He has an MS in Computer Science and an MA in Mathematics, both from the University of Wisconsin-Madison. Randy is a member of IEEE and ACM. Contact him at randyh@avaya.com.

Audris Mockus

Audris Mockus received a B.S. in Applied Mathematics from Moscow Institute of Physics and Technology and a PhD in Statistics from Carnegie Mellon University. He teaches at the University of Tennessee and works part-time at Avaya Labs Research. Contact him at audris@utk.edu.

John Palframan

John is a research scientist with Avaya Labs. He works with Randy on improving software practices in Avaya. Before joining Avaya, John was a technical manager in Bell Labs responsible for developing communications software and software development tools. He has an M.Math and a B.Math (co-op) from the University of Waterloo. Contact him at palframan@avaya.com.

David Weiss

David M. Weiss received the B.S. degree in Mathematics in 1964 from Union College, an M.S. in Computer Science in 1974 and a PhD in Computer Science in 1981 from the University of Maryland. He is currently professor of software engineering at Iowa State University. Previously, he was the Director of the Software Technology Research Department at Avaya Laboratories, where he worked on the problem of how to improve the effectiveness of software development in general and of Avaya's software development processes in particular. To focus on the latter problem, he formed and led the Avaya Resource Center for Software Technology. Dr Weiss's principal research interests are in the area of software engineering, particularly in software development processes and methodologies, software design, software measurement, and globally-distributed software development. His best known work is the goal-question-metric approach to software measurement, his work on the modular structure of software systems, and his work in software product-line engineering.

LESSONS LEARNED FROM SOFTWARE ANALYTICS IN PRACTICE

Ayse Bener*, Ayse Tosun Misirli†, Bora Caglayan*, Ekrem Kocaguneli‡, Gul Calikli§

Mechanical and Industrial Engineering, Ryerson University, Toronto, ON, Canada* Faculty of Computer and Informatics, Istanbul Technical University, Istanbul, Turkey† Microsoft, Seattle, WA, USA‡ Department of Computing, Open University, Milton Keynes, UK§

CHAPTER OUTLINE

16.1 INTRODUCTION

Modern organizations operate in an environment shaped by the advances of information and communication technologies. The economic growth in highly populated countries such as China, India, and Brazil forces organizations from traditionally strong economies in Europe, North America, and

453

Japan to globally compete for resources as well as markets for their goods and services. This poses an unprecedented need for the organizations to be efficient and agile [1]. Meanwhile, today's ubiquitous communication and computing technologies generate vast amounts of data in many forms and many magnitudes greater than what was available even a decade ago. The ability of organizations of all sizes to gain actionable insights from such data sources, not only to optimize their use of limited resources [2], but also to help shape their future, is now the key to survival. Those who can beat their competitors in the effectiveness with which they handle their informational resources are the ones likely to go beyond survival and enjoy sustained competitiveness. Software development organizations also follow the same trend.

Most of the management decisions in software engineering are based on the perceptions of the people about the state of the software and their estimations about its future states. Some of these decisions concern resource allocation, team building, budget estimation, and release planning. As the complexity of software systems and the interactions between increasing numbers of developers have grown, the need for data-driven decision making has emerged to solve common problems in the domain, such as completing projects on time, within budget, and with minimum errors. Software projects are inherently difficult to control. Managers struggle to make many decisions under a lot of uncertainty. They would like to be confident in the product, the team, and the processes. There are also many blind spots that may cause severe problems at any point in the project development life cycle. These concerns have drawn much attention to software measurement, software quality, and software cost/effort estimation—namely, descriptive and predictive analytics.

Data science is vital for software development organizations because of a paradigm shift around many kinds of data in development teams. We essentially need to have intuition on data, and this is just not the statistics (statistical modeling, fitting, simulation) that we learned in school. Data science consists of analytics to use data to understand the past and present (descriptive analytics), to analyze past performance (predictive analytics), and to use optimization techniques (prescriptive analytics).

Software analytics is one of those unique fields that lies at the intersection of academia and practice. Software analytics research is empirically driven. Unlike traditional research methods, researchers study and learn from the data to build useful analytics. To produce insightful results for industrial practice, researchers need to use industrial data and build analytics.

Software analytics must follow a process that starts with problem identification—that is, framing the business problem and the analytics problem. Throughout this process, stakeholder agreement needs to be obtained through effective communication. The end goal for a software analytics project could be to address a genuine problem in the industry. Therefore, the outcome of the analytics project could be transferred and embedded into the decision making process of the organization. Sometimes, software analytics provides additional insights that stakeholders do not expect or imagine it can provide, and in such cases, the results could influence more than one phase in a software development process.

Data collection in software organizations is a complicated procedure. It requires identification and prioritization of data needs and available sources depending on the context. Qualitative and quantitative data collection methods are different depending on the problem. In some cases, data acquisition requires tool development first, followed by harmonizing, rescaling, cleaning, and sharing data within the organization. In discussing data collection, we will cover potential complications and data scaling issues.

The simplest way to obtain insight from data is through descriptive statistics. Even a simple analysis or visualization may reveal hidden facts in the data. Later, predictive models utilizing data mining techniques may be built to aid the decision making process in an organization. Selection of the suitable

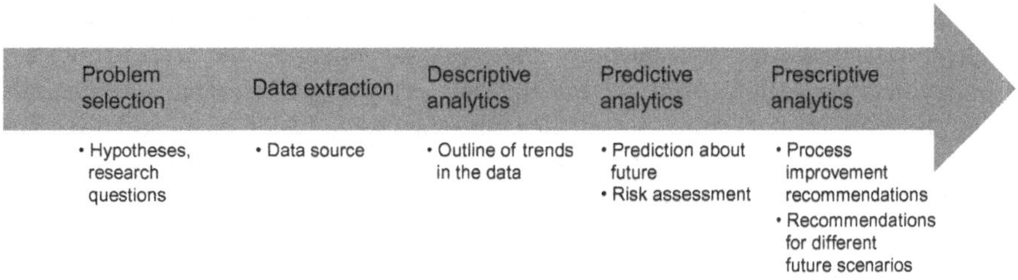

FIGURE 16.1

Our method in software analytics projects.

data mining techniques depending on the problem is critical when building the predictive model. Factors such as clarity of the problem, maturity of the data collection process in a company, and expected benefits from the predictive model may also affect model construction. In addition, insights gained from descriptive statistics may be used in the construction of predictive models. Finally, new predictive models could be evaluated, which requires the definition of certain performance measures, appropriate statistical tests, and effect size analysis.

In our software analytics projects, we have used a method adapted from a typical data mining process (problem definition, data gathering and preparation, model building and evaluation, knowledge deployment [3]) to define the main steps we performed. Figure 16.1 depicts the five main phases, the results of which could be used directly by practitioners, or could be linked to consecutive phases. The whole process does not necessarily end with a single cycle, but it is preferred to conduct several iterations in a software analytics project to make adjustments depending on the outcome of each phase.

In this chapter, we define each of these five phases in Figure 16.1 on the basis of our experience in state-of-the-art case studies concerning various software organizations. We provide example techniques, tools, and charts that we used to collect, analyze, and model data, as well as to optimize and deploy the proposed model in different industry settings in order to solve two main challenges: software defect prediction and effort estimation. In the following sections, we define the objectives of each phase in a software analytics project, share our experience on how to conduct each phase, and provide practical tips to address potential issues. All examples and lessons learned have come from our empirical studies rigorously conducted with industry partners. We do not provide the details of our past projects (e.g., the reasons behind our using a particular algorithm or a new metric, pseudocodes for model building, all performance measures, etc.) in this chapter because of space limitations. We suggest the reader refers to our articles listed at the end of this chapter for such information.

16.2 PROBLEM SELECTION

Problem selection in research differs depending on the nature of the research [4]. In the natural and social sciences, the researcher/scientist chooses a topic that he/she is simply curious about. In the natural sciences, the researcher aims to understand the natural phenomena to build the theoretical basis for prediction, and this becomes the basis for invention or engineering. In the social sciences, the researcher aims to understand human and societal phenomena to build the theoretical basis for prediction and intervention, and this becomes the basis for changing the world to create therapy, education, policy, motivation, etc. Both have a rigorous experimental basis. In the natural sciences, theories have to be testable, and testing is done in a physical world, which provides hard constraints on theories. In the social sciences, on the other hand, theories have to be testable, and testing is done in a behavioral world, which provides probabilistic constraints.

Empirical software engineering, compared with the natural sciences and social sciences, is still an immature field. It suffers from lack of understanding of empirical problems, issues, possibilities, and research designs. Software engineering is the study and practice of building software systems. It is an experimental field that uses various forms of experiments to test the theory (i.e., requirements) and its model (i.e., implementation). These experiments include independent and dependent variables, manipulations, data collection, and data analysis.

Software engineering is a very rich field where we have systems that execute programs and processes, people who design and use programs, and people who use and execute processes. This richness enables software engineering research and practice to cut across other disciplines, such as anthropology to understand families of systems, sociology to understand systems in context (i.e., relationships among systems as centralized, distributed, networked, etc.), social psychology to understand individual systems (i.e., component interaction), and personal psychology to understand individual system characteristics. People and processes can also be mapped to these disciplines—for example, anthropology to understand projects and disciplines, sociology to understand interactions among teams or projects, social psychology to understand interactions of people and technology, and personal psychology to understand traits and dispositions of developers and managers. These intersections enable researchers to observe and abstract specific parts of the world and create a theory. From that theory they can create a usable model to represent that theory. It then becomes an iterative process to adjust both the theory and the model as they evolve [5]. When the researcher is satisfied, he/she integrates the model into the world—that is, the existing environment with processes, systems, and technologies. Integrating the model into the world changes the current world, and this leads to adjustments and extensions to the original theory. This then leads to further changes in the model and the world.

A good question on which to conduct research is one that is testable with the materials at hand. A good question in empirical software engineering research is not only the one that the researcher pragmatically investigates, but it is also a relevant one that addresses a genuine issue in the daily life of software organizations. Every day, many decisions need to be made in software organizations, such as determining what users want/need, assessing architecture and design choices, evaluating functional characteristics or nonfunctional properties, evaluating and comparing technologies (i.e., supporting tools, product support, process support), determining what went wrong, and allocating resources effectively. Some of these challenges have also been addressed by process improvement (e.g., [6]) and data management models (e.g., [7]).

In many software development organizations, there is little evidence to inform decisions. Empirical studies are the key to show fundamental mechanisms of software tools, processes, and development techniques to software professionals, and to eliminate alternative explanations in decision making. An empirical study is a study that reconciles theory and reality. In order to conduct more valid empirical studies, researchers need to establish principles that are causal (correlated, testable theory), actionable, and general. They need to answer important questions rather than focusing on a nice solution and trying to map that solution to a problem that does not exist.

In the problem selection step, we need to ask the right or important questions. It is important to incorporate the domain expert/practitioner into this step. We may ask different types of questions: existence, description/classification, composition, relationships, and descriptive-comparative, causality, or causality-comparison interactions [8]. We need to make sure that the hypotheses are consistent with research questions, since these will be the basis of the statement of the problem. Failing to ask the right questions and inconsistencies in hypothesis formulation would also lead to methodological pitfalls such as hypothesis testing errors, issues of statistical power, issues in construction of dependent/independent variables, and reliability and validity issues [4].

Research, especially in software engineering, is all about balancing originality and relevance. Therefore, the researcher, before he/she starts the research, should always ask the following question "What is the relevance of this research outcome for the practice?" In a case study, we jointly identified the problem with the software development team during the project kickoff meeting [9]. The development team initially listed their business objectives (improve code quality, decrease defect rates, and measure the time to fix defects), while the researchers aligned the goals of our project (building code measurement and version control repository, and defect prediction model). To achieve these goals, the roles and responsibilities were defined for both sides (practitioners and researchers); the expectations and potential output of the analytics project were discussed and agreed. Furthermore, it was decided that any output produced during the project (e.g., metrics from data extraction, charts from descriptive analytics) would be assessed together before moving to the next step.

In some cases, the business need may be defined too generally or ambiguously, and therefore, the researchers should conduct further analysis to identify and frame the analytics problem. For instance, in a case study concerning a large software organization, the team leaders initially defined their problem as "measuring release readiness of a software product" [10]. The problem was too general for the researchers, since it may indicate building an analytics for (a) measuring the "readiness" of a software release in terms of the budget, schedule, or prerelease defect rates, or for (b) deciding which features could be deployed in the next release, or for (c) measuring the reliability of a software release in terms of residual (postrelease) defects. Through interviews with junior to senior developers and team leaders, the business need was redefined as "assessing the final reliability of a software product prior to release" in order to decide on the amount of resources that would be allocated for the maintenance (bug fixing) activities. We took this business need and transformed it into an analytics problem as follows: building a model that would estimate the residual (postrelease) defect density of the software product *at any time during a release*. At any given time during a release, the model could learn from the metrics that were available, and could predict the residual defects in the software product. To do that, we further decided on the input of the model as software metrics from requirements, design, development, and testing phases. The details of the model can be found in Ref. [10].

16.3 DATA COLLECTION

In our software analytics projects, we initially design the dataset required for a particular problem. Afterward, we extract the data on the basis of our initial data design through quantitative and qualitative techniques. In this section we describe these steps with guidelines for practitioners based on our past experience.

16.3.1 DATASETS

16.3.1.1 Datasets for predictive analytics

Most organizations want to predict the number of defects or identify defect-prone modules in software systems before they are deployed. Numerous statistical methods and artificial intelligence (AI) techniques have been employed in order to predict defects that a software system will reveal in operation or during testing.

One part of the approach in empirical software engineering research requires one to focus on the relevance of the outcome for the practice. Therefore, one of our main goals has so far been to find solutions to the problems of industry by improving the software development life cycle and hence software quality. We have used predictive analytics to catch defects for large companies and small- and medium-sized enterprises specialized in various domains, such as telecommunications, enterprise resource planning, banking systems, and embedded systems for white-good manufacturing. We collected data from industry and used these datasets in our research in addition to publicly available datasets from the Metrics Data Program repository for NASA datasets and the PROMISE data repository. Moreover, we donated all datasets we collected from industry to the PROMISE data repository, which consists of publicly available data for reusable empirical software engineering experiments [11].

The data employed in our studies consist of measurable attributes of software development, which are the objects of measurement (e.g., products, processes, and resources) according to the goal-question-metric approach [12]. Refining software metrics and their interactions using the goal-question-metric approach is a good practice to ensure data quality, and it has been employed by various researchers who propose metrics sets to quantify aspects related to the software development life cycle [13]. According to the information quality framework, some of the features of data collection and analysis that ensure high information quality are *data resolution*, *data structure*, *data integration*, *temporal relevance*, and *communication* [14]. While collecting data from industrial projects and using publicly available datasets, we focused on these features. *Data resolution* refers to the measurement scale and the aggregation level of data. Regarding *data resolution*, we decided on the data aggregation levels relative to the goal we would like to achieve. For instance, we collected metrics (e.g., static code and churn) at method-level granularity or aggregated data to file-level granularity in order to eliminate noise whenever necessary. *Data structure* relates to the type(s) of data (e.g., numerical, nonnumerical) and data characteristics such as corrupted and missing values because of the study design or data collection mechanism. We employed various techniques to handle the missing data problem [15]. *Data integration* refers to the need to integrate multiple data sources and/or data types. In terms of *data integration*, we used multiple data types (e.g., static code metrics, churn metrics, social interaction metrics, people-related metrics) to achieve better defect prediction performance. *Temporal relevance* is related to the temporal durations of the "data collection," "data analysis," and "study deployment" processes, and the gaps between these three processes. To address the *temporal relevance* of data, we kept the data collection and data analysis periods as short as possible in order to avoid uncontrollable transitions that might be disruptive. Moreover, we tried not to leave time gaps between the data collection and data analysis periods. To achieve information quality, we also improved our *communication* with software practitioners and other researchers. During the interpretation of the data, which we collected from industry projects, we conducted interviews with software engineers to gain more insight into the data. This helped us to perform more meaningful data analyses. We also shared our findings with software practitioners and discussed with them how these analysis results might help to improve their software development process.

In our previous industry collaborations, we mostly used static code metrics to build predictive analytics. The *static code metrics* consist of the McCabe, lines of code, Halstead, and Chidamber-Kemerer object-oriented (CK OO) metrics, as shown in Table 16.1.

McCabe metrics, which are one collection of static code metrics, provide a quantitative basis to estimate the code complexity on the basis of the decision structure of a program [16]. The idea behind McCabe metrics is that the more structural complexity a code gets, the more difficult it becomes to test and maintain the code, and hence the likelihood of defects increases. Descriptions of McCabe metrics and the relationship between them are given in Table 16.1.

Lines of code metrics are simple measures that can be extracted from the code. These include, but are not limited to, total lines of code, blank lines of code, lines of commented code, lines of code and comment, and lines of executable code metrics. A description of these metrics is given in Table 16.1.

Table 16.1 Static Code Metrics

Attribute	Description
McCabe metrics	
Cyclomatic complexity ($v(G)$)	Number of linearly independent paths
Cyclomatic density (vd(G))	The ratio of the file's cyclomatic complexity to its length
Decision density (dd(G))	Condition/decision
Essential complexity (ev(G))	The degree to which a file contains unstructured constructs
Essential density (ev(G))	$(ev(G) - 1)/(v(G) - 1)$
Maintenance severity	$ev(G)/v(G)$
Lines of code metrics	
Total lines of code	Total number of lines in source code
Blank lines of code	Total number of blank lines in source code
Lines of commented code	Total number of lines consisting of code comments
Lines of code and comment	Total number of source code lines that include both executable statements and comments
Lines of executable code	Total number of the actual code statements that are executable
Halstead metrics	
n1	Unique operands count
n2	Unique operators count
N1	Total operands count
N2	Total operators count
Level (L)	(2/n1)/(n2/N2)
Difficulty (D)	$1/L$
Length (N)	N1 + N2
Volume (V)	$N \times \log(n)$
Programming effort (E)	DV
Programming time (T)	$E/18$

Halstead metrics, which are also listed in Table 16.1, measure a program module's complexity directly from source code, with emphasis on computational complexity [17]. These metrics were developed as a means of determining complexity directly from the operators and operands in the module. The rationale behind Halstead metrics is that the harder the code is to read, the more defect-prone the modules are.

McCabe, lines of code, and Halstead metrics were developed with traditional methods in mind; hence they do not lend themselves to object-oriented notions such as classes, inheritance, encapsulation, and message passing. object-oriented metrics were developed by Chidamber and Kemerer (i.e., CK OO metrics) in order to measure unique aspects of the object-oriented approach [18]. CK OO metrics are listed in Table 16.2, together with their definitions.

Some researchers criticized the use of static code metrics to learn about defect predictors because of their limited content [19, 20]. However, static code metrics are easy to collect and interpret. In our early research, we used static code metrics to build defect prediction models for a local white goods manufacturing company [21] and for software companies specialized in enterprise resource planning software and banking systems [22]. For the best case, the defect prediction rate and the false positive (FP) rate were 82% and 33%, respectively, whereas for the worst case, they were 82% and 47%, respectively. These results are better than the results obtained for manual code reviews, which are currently used in industry. Moreover manual code inspections are quite labor intensive. Depending on the review methods, 8-20 lines of code can be inspected per minute per reviewer, and a review team mostly consists of four or six members [23].

To improve prediction performance, we proposed a "weighted naïve Bayes" technique, which consists in assigning relevant weights to static code attributes according to their importance, which improves defect prediction performance [24]. We employed eight different machine learning techniques mostly derived from attribute ranking techniques in order to estimate the weights for the static code

Table 16.2 Chidamber-Kemerer Object-Oriented (CK OO) Metrics	
Attribute	**Description**
Weighted methods per class	Sum of the complexity of the methods in a class
Depth of inheritance tree	The depth of the inheritance tree for a class is the maximum length from the node to the root of the tree of class inheritance
Number of children	Number of immediate subclasses subordinated in the class hierarchy
Coupling between object classes	Count of the number of other classes to which a class is coupled
Response for a class	The union of the set of methods called by each method in a class
Lack of cohesion in methods	The union of the set of instance variables used by each method in a class

attributes. The heuristics we used to assign relevant weights to the static code attributes consist of principal component analysis, information gain, the gain ratio, Kullback-Leibner divergence, the odds ratio, log probability, exponential probability, and cross entropy. Detailed information on these machine learning techniques can be found in Ref. [24]. Our proposed method yielded at least equivalent performance and in some cases better performance than the currently best defect predictor [25]. Furthermore, our proposed heuristics have linear-time computational complexities, whereas choosing the optimal subset of attributes requires an exhaustive search in the attribute space.

In another study, we reduced the probability of false alarms by supplementing static code metrics with a call-graph-based ranking (CGBR) framework [26, 27]. Call graphs can be used in tracing the software code module by module. Each node in a call graph represents a software module, and an edge (a, b) indicates that module a calls module b. Our CGBR framework is inspired by the PageRank algorithm of Page and Brin [28]. The PageRank algorithm, which is used by most search engines on the Web, computes the most relevant results of a search by ranking webpages. We have adopted this ranking method for software modules. We hypothesize that if a module is frequently used and the developers/testers are aware of that, they will be more careful in implementing/testing that module, whereas most of the defects in less used modules may not be detected, since such modules are not used frequently, and existing defects can be detected only with thorough testing. In one of our studies, where we also used the CGBR framework in order to increase the information content of prediction models, defect prediction performance improved for large and complex systems, while for small systems, prediction models without the CGBR framework achieved the same prediction performance [29].

During the research project we conducted for Turkey's largest GSM operator/telecommunications company, we built prediction models by employing 22 projects and 10 releases of one of the company's major software products [9]. When the research project started, defects were not matched with files in the issue management system. Developers could not allocate extra time to write all the defects they fixed during the testing phase because of their workload and other business priorities. In addition, matching those defects with the corresponding software files could not be handled automatically. Therefore, the prediction models could not be trained using company data. Instead, similar projects from cross-company data were selected by using nearest-neighbor sampling. Projects from the Metrics Data Program repository for NASA were selected as cross-company data. Following this study, the resulting defect prediction model was deployed into the company's software development process.

In another research project, we also used within-company data (i.e., data from same company but from different projects) in order to build defect predictors for embedded systems software for white goods [30] . During this research project, we mixed within-company data with cross-company data to train prediction models whenever within-company data data was limited. Complementing cross-company data with within-company data yielded better performance results.

There is still considerable room for improvement of prediction performance (i.e., obtaining lower false alarm rates and higher probability of detection). Researchers are actively looking for better code metrics which, potentially, will yield "better" predictors [13, 31, 32]. For this purpose, in one of our studies we used churn metrics as well as static code metrics and the CGBR framework in order to build defect predictors for different defect categories [33]. According to the results we obtained, churn metrics performed the best for predicting all types of defects. Code churn is a measure of the amount of code change taking place within a software unit over time. Churn often propagates across dependencies. If a component C_1, which has dependencies with component C_2, changes (churns) a lot between versions, we expect component C_2 to undergo a certain amount of churn in order to keep in

Table 16.3 Churn Metrics

Attribute	Description
Commits	Number of commits made for a file
Committers	Number of committers who committed a file
CommitsLast	Number of commits made for a file since the last release
CommittersLast	Number of developers who committed a file since the last release
rmlLast	Number of lines removed from a file since the last release
alLast	Number of lines added to a file since the last release
rml	Number of lines removed from a file
al	Number of lines added to a file
TopDevPercent	Percentage of top developers who committed a file

synch with component C_1. Together, a high degree of dependence plus churn can cause errors that will propagate through a system, reducing its reliability. A list of churn metrics is given in Table 16.3.

The above prediction models ignore the causal effects of programmers and designers on software defects. In other words, the datasets used to learn about such defect predictors consist of product-related (static code metrics) and *process*-related (churn) metrics, but not *people*-related metrics. On the other hand, people's thought processes have a significant impact on software quality as software is designed, implemented, and tested by people. In the literature, various people-related metrics have been used to build defect predictors, yet these are not directly related to people's thought processes or their cognitive aspects [13, 34–37].

In our research, we focused on a specific human cognitive aspect—namely, confirmation bias [38–41]. On the basis of founded theories in cognitive psychology, we defined a "confirmation bias metrics set." Confirmation bias metrics quantify software engineers' confirmatory behavior, which may result in overlooking defects, leading to an increase in software defect density [42] (i.e., the lower the confirmatory behavior of software engineers, the less likely it is to overlook defects in the software). We used confirmation bias metrics to learn about defect predictors [43]. The prediction performances of models that were learned from these metrics were comparable with those of the models that were learned from static code and churn metrics, respectively. Confirmatory behavior is a single human aspect, yet the results obtained were quite promising. Our findings support the fact that we should study human aspects further to improve the performance of defect prediction models.

In addition to individual metrics, metrics to quantify social interactions among software engineers (e.g., communication of developers on issue repositories by commenting on the same set of issues) serve as datasets having enhanced information content. In the literature, there are also other attempts where using social interaction networks to learn about defect predictors yielded promising performance results [31, 32, 44, 45]. In addition to these empirical studies, we also investigated social interaction among developers [46], and adapted various metrics from the complex network literature [47]. We also used social network metrics for defect prediction with two open source datasets—namely, development data from IBM Rational Team Concert and Drupal [46]. The results revealed that compared with other sets of metrics such as churn metrics, using social network metrics on these datasets either considerably decreases the high false alarm rates without compromising the detection rates or considerably increases the low prediction rates without compromising the low false alarm rates.

We have been building defect prediction models for large software development companies and small- to medium-sized enterprises specialized in domains such as enterprise resource planning, finance, online banking, telecommunications, and embedded systems. On the basis of our experience, we recommend the following road map to decide on the content of the dataset that will be collected to build defect prediction models:

1. **Start with static code metrics.** Although static code metrics (e.g., McCabe, lines of code, and Halstead metrics) have limited information content, they are easy to collect and use. They can be automatically and cheaply collected even for very large systems. Moreover, they give an idea about the quality of the code, and they can be used to decide which modules are worthy of manual inspection.

2. **Try to enhance defect predictors that are learned from static code metrics.** Try methods such as weighting static code attributes or employing the CGBR framework in order to improve the prediction performance of the models that are built using static code attributes.

3. **Do not give up on static code metrics even if you do not have defect data.** In some software development companies, defects may not be stored during the development activities. There might even not exist a process to match the defects with the files in order to keep track of the reasons for any change in the software system. It will not be a feasible solution to match defects manually because of the heavy workload of developers. One possible way might be to call emergency meetings with the software engineers and senior management in order to convince them to change their existing code development process. As a change in the development process, developers might be forced to check in the source code to the version management system with a unique ID for the test defect or requirement request. Referring to these unique IDs, one can identify which changes in the source code are intended to fix defects and which are for new requirement requests by referring to commit logs. Adaptation of the process change will take time; moreover, collection of adequate defect data will also take some time. While defect data is being collected, cross-company data can be used to build defect predictors. Within-company data that has been collected so far can be used in combination with cross-company data until enough local data has been collected. The methods mentioned in step 2 can be used with cross-company data and with cross-company and within-company data as well.

4. **Enhance defect prediction using churn metrics and/or social network metrics.** Churn metrics can be automatically collected from the logs of version management systems. Automated collection of social interaction metrics is also possible through mining issue management systems, version management systems, and developers' e-mails, which they send to each other to discuss software issues and new features. After static code, churn, and social interaction metrics have been extracted, defect prediction models can be built by employing all combinations of these three different types of metrics (i.e., static code metrics; churn metrics; social interaction metrics; static code and churn metrics; static code and social interaction metrics; churn and social interaction metrics; and static code, churn, and social interaction metrics). On the basis of the performance comparison results of these models, it can be decided which models will be used to identify defect-prone parts of the software.

5. **Include metrics related to individual human aspects.** It is much more challenging to employ individual human metrics to build defect prediction models. Formation of the metrics set and defining a method to collect metrics values requires interdisciplinary research, including fields

such as cognitive and behavioral psychology besides traditional software engineering. Moreover, one needs to face the challenges of qualitative empirical studies which are mentioned in detail in Section 16.3.2. Because of the challenges, we employed confirmation bias metrics to build prediction models at later stages during the field studies we conducted at software companies.

16.3.1.2 Datasets for effort estimation models

While building models for effort estimation, we used both datasets, which we prepared by collecting data from various local software companies in Turkey, as well as publicly available datasets such as the COCOMO database. Among the datasets we collected are SDR datasets [48–51]. We used the COCOMO II Data Collection Questionnaire in order to collect SDR datasets. SDR datasets consist of 24 projects, which were implemented in the first decade of this century. An exemplary dataset is shown in Table 16.4 in order to give an idea about the content and format of the datasets we used for software effort estimation. Each row in Table 16.4 corresponds to a different project. These projects are represented by the nominal attributes from the COCOMO II model along with their size in terms of lines of code and the actual effort expended to complete the projects. We also collected datasets from two large Turkish software companies, which are specialized in the telecommunication domain and the online banking domain, respectively [52, 53].

The publicly available datasets which we used in our research projects were obtained from the PROMISE data repository [11] and the International Software Benchmarking Standards Group, which is a nonprofit organization [54].

Project managers can benefit from the learning-based effort estimation models we have used when allocating resources among different software projects as well as among different phases of the software development life cycle. Moreover, the outputs of such effort estimation models can guide

	Table 16.4 An Example Dataset for Effort Estimation		
Project	**Nominal Attributes (as Defined in COCOMO II)**	**Lines of Code**	**Effort**
P1	1.00, 1.08, 1.30, 1.00, 1.00, 0.87, 1.00, 0.86, 1.00, 0.70, 1.21, 1.00, 0.91, 1.00, 1.08	70	278
P2	1.40, 1.08, 1.15, 1.30, 1.21, 1.00, 1.00, 0.71, 0.82 ,0.70, 1.00, 0.95, 0.91, 0.91, 1.08	227	1181
P3	1.00, 1.08, 1.15, 1.30, 1.06, 0.87, 1.07, 0.86, 1.00, 0.86, 1.10, 0.95, 0.91, 1.00, 1.08	177.9	1248
P4	1.15, 0.94, 1.15, 1.00, 1.00, 0.87, 0.87, 1.00, 1.00, 1.00, 1.00, 0.95, 0.91, 1.00, 1.08	115.8	480
P5	1.15, 0.94, 1.15, 1.00, 1.00, 0.87, 0.87, 1.00, 1.00, 1.00, 1.00, 0.95, 0.91, 1.00, 1.08	29.5	120
P6	1.15, 0.94, 1.15, 1.00, 1.00, 0.87, 0.87, 1.00, 1.00, 1.00, 1.00, 0.95, 0.91, 1.00, 1.08	19.7	60
P7	1.15, 0.94, 1.15, 1.00, 1.00, 0.87, 0.87, 1.00, 1.00, 1.00, 1.00, 0.95, 0.91, 1.00, 1.08	66.6	300
P8	1.15, 0.94, 1.15, 1.00, 1.00, 0.87, 0.87, 1.00, 1.00, 1.00, 1.00, 0.95, 0.91, 1.00, 1.08	5.5	18
P9	1.15, 0.94, 1.15, 1.00, 1.00, 0.87, 0.87, 1.00, 1.00, 1.00, 1.00, 0.95, 0.91, 1.00, 1.08	10.4	50
P10	1.15, 0.94, 1.15, 1.00, 1.00, 0.87, 0.87, 1.00, 1.00, 1.00, 1.00, 0.95, 0.91, 1.00, 1.08	14.	60
P11	1.00, 0.00, 1.15, 1.00, 1.00, 1.00, 1.00, 1.00, 1.00, 1.00, 1.00, 1.00, 1.00, 1.00, 1.00	16	114
P12	1.15, 0.00, 1.15, 1.00, 1.00, 1.00, 1.00, 1.00, 1.00, 1.00, 1.00, 1.00, 1.00, 1.00, 1.00	6.5	42
P13	1.00, 0.00, 1.15, 1.00, 1.00, 1.00, 1.00, 1.00, 1.00, 1.00, 1.00, 1.00, 1.00, 1.00, 1.00	13	60
P14	1.00, 0.00 ,1.15, 1.00, 1.00, 1.00, 1.00, 1.00, 1.00, 1.00, 1.00, 1.00, 1.00, 1.00, 1.00	8	42

project managers when they are deciding on whether a new software development project should be launched or not. Using our own datasets together with publicly available datasets helped us form cross-domain datasets (i.e., datasets from different application domains) in addition to within-domain datasets (i.e., datasets from a similar application domain). From our experience, we recommend practitioners build effort estimation models by using projects from different application domains rather than using projects from a similar application [55]. Analogy-based models, which are widely used for effort estimation, assume the availability of project data that are similar to the project data at hand, which can be difficult to obtain. In other words, there may be no similar projects in-house, and obtaining data from other companies may restricted because of confidentiality. Our proposed framework, which uses cross-domain data, suggests that it is not necessary to take care of particular characteristics of a project (i.e., its similarity with other projects) while constructing effort estimation models [55].

16.3.2 DATA EXTRACTION

The validity of the results obtained in software analytics projects is limited by the quality of the data extracted. For this reason, accurate data extraction is one of the most important phases in software analytics projects. In every research project, it is important to design the data extraction phase carefully.

The first step during data extraction is the choice of the right requirements for the data that will be extracted. If data requirements are changed after the data extraction phase, all the results of the study might be changed. Similarly, rescheduling extensions to surveys done with industry might be time-consuming.

Automation of the data extraction steps, when possible, reduces the extraction effort in the long term. On the other hand, tracking the history of the data extraction scripts helps in repeating older experiments when necessary. Over the years, we have employed several techniques for quantitative and qualitative data extraction for a given problem [56, 57]. In certain scenarios, we partly automated the qualitative techniques for efficiency. In this section, we describe these techniques and how we customized them for our problems.

16.3.2.1 Quantitative data extraction

Quantitative data can be either continuous data or discrete data. Quantitative data can be extracted from different software artifacts, including the source code and issue repositories. Similarly, quantitative techniques can be applied to postprocess the qualitative data extracted in surveys and questionnaires.

Source code repositories are arguably the primary data sources in software analytics projects. Source code repositories can be used to extract the state of a project at a given time snapshot or track the evolution of the software project over time. Evolution of the software in the source code repositories may be linear or may resemble a directed acyclic graph depending on the project method. For projects with multiple development branches, we have usually focused on the main development branch to keep the project history linear and for easier cross-project comparison [58].

For defect prediction, source code repositories may be mined to extract static code, churn, and collaboration metrics. Extraction of the static code metrics is dependent on the programming language. For extraction and storage of static code metrics and data storage, we have built tools to avoid rework over the years [57, 59]. In the case of effort estimation, software repositories may be mined to extract the attributes related to the size of the software.

Issue management software is used to track the issues related to software. It is the main repository of the quality assurance operations in a software project. We have used issue management software to map the defects to the underlying source code modules and to analyze the issue handling processes of organizations [60, 61].

Defect data may be used to label the defect-prone modules for defect prediction or to assess software quality in terms of defect density or defect count. The ideal method to map defects to issues is to associate source code changes with the issues. By mapping the issues to the source code directly, we can confidently label the defective source code modules. For some of our partners, this strategy has been used efficiently. In this case, text mining is necessary to map issues to changes in the source code as accurately as possible. In our studies, we have frequently used the change set (commit) messages to identify the defect-prone modules [56]. For projects in which even the commit messages are not available, manual inspection of the changes with a team member may be attempted as a last resort for defect matching.

These defect data extraction methods can be used with *within-company* defect data to train defect prediction models. In addition Turhan et al. [62] proposed certain methods to use *cross-company* data sources for cases where defect data is completely unavailable for individual software projects.

A few questions to be answered when choosing the time span for data extraction are as follows:

1. What is the specific software method employed by the organization for the given project? Practical implementation of a particular method is always different from its theoretical definition.
2. Which releases and which projects should be used in the analytics project? There may exist a difference among the data quality for different projects or releases. In addition, project characteristics such as size may change the outcome of experiments.
3. What is the estimated quality of the data? It is usually beneficial to check the quality of the data with the quality assurance teams. Identifying problematic parts in the data early may help researchers avoid rework.

Evaluation of qualitative results from surveys and questionnaires can also be done with quantitative methods. For extraction of metrics from qualitative data, digitizing the survey results to programmer-friendly formats (e.g., plain text, JSON, and XML) as early as possible would be useful.

Storage of metrics is a complicated task especially for datasets that may possibly be expanded in the future. These datasets may be used in future work with minimal effort if they are stored properly. The simplest method to store data is as a plain text file. For multidimensional data, we suggest storage of the data as a lightweight database such as an Sqlite database. Sqlite databases can be stored as a single file without the trouble of setting up a full database, and since it is a single file, the history of the database can be easily tracked. Every major language used frequently by software analysts, such as R, Python, and MATLAB, has native clients for Sqlite so it can be used. Sqlite can scale easily to store data with sizes of 1-10 GB in total [63].

Quality of the data, missing data, and data sparsity are three common problems we have encountered frequently. We had to modify our data extraction method for each of these problems. Over the years, we have used several techniques to reduce the noise in our data and to address these problems. For example, in a project we had trouble extracting cognitive bias metrics from all of the developers. We used a linear algebra approximation method named matrix factorization to complete the missing values in our case [42]. One of our partners had several problems in keeping the defect data for its projects because of the lack of maturity of its measurement process. In its case, we had to train our model with cross-company data sources. Finding the right training data for this particular project was a serious problem for us. For this goal, we evaluated sampling strategies to pick the right amount of data in our experiments [64].

16.3.2.2 Qualitative data extraction

Qualitative data is any form of feature set that cannot be expressed numerically [65]. Qualitative data can be extracted through questionnaires and surveys. We refer the reader to social science books for a through introduction to this area [65].

Some input for the software analytics models cannot be extracted directly from software repositories. We have extracted qualitative data for our models in many cases. For example, for modeling people we have used standardized tests to get cognitive biases of developers [38, 43]. In these tests, we interpreted the free text answers manually. We have also used questionnaires to assess process maturity in projects for reliability assessment models. We have used surveys to check the actual benefit of our analytics projects to software companies postmortem too [56]. In our surveys, we found that even for successful projects that within-organization adoption of the analytics model may change over time without some vocal advocates.

It is costly to change qualitative data extraction methods after the initiation of data extraction. Therefore, the design of the qualitative data extraction methods is more time-consuming than that of the quantitative data extraction methods.

16.3.2.3 Patterns in data extraction

Over the years, we have internally developed certain practices for extracting the relevant software data. Here is a short list of practices we recommend for software analysts on the basis of our experience:

1. Do not use proprietary data formats such as Microsoft Excel spreadsheets to store data since manual access to the data is time-consuming. Although these formats can be read through libraries, long-term availability of these formats is not certain. In addition, binary formats make tracking the difference between versions very hard.
2. Track the version of the extracted data and the scripts.
3. Store your parameters for data extraction for each run. It is possible to forget a set of parameters that provided a particular outcome. Keeping the parameters stored in addition to the analytics output would help to overcome this problem. For this goal, separating the parameters from the source code would be helpful.
4. Look for possible factors that may introduce noise into the data. Internal and external factors might include noise in the data. You can control internal factors easily by checking your data model and scripts. On the other hand, tracking the external factors is trickier. Certain parts of the projects might be missing.
5. Cross-check possible problems in the extracted data with a quality assurance team member as early as possible.
6. All of the data extraction and analysis tasks and code should be executable with a single script. Redoing some operations may be impractical in some cases, but if there is some problem with the data extraction method, the researcher saves a lot of time using this practice. Remembering all the custom parameters and script names on every reevaluation is time-consuming.

16.4 DESCRIPTIVE ANALYTICS

The simplest way to gain insight into data is through descriptive statistics. Even a simple correlation analysis or visualization of multiple metrics may reveal hidden facts about the development process, development team, or data collection process. For example, a graphical representation of commits extracted from a version control system would reveal the distribution of workload among developers—that is, what percentage of developers actively develop software on a daily basis [53], or it would highlight which components of a software system are frequently changed. On the other hand, a statistical test between metrics characterizing issues that were previously fixed and stored in an issue repository may identify the reasons for reopened bugs [60] or reveal the issue workload among software developers [61]. Depending on the questions that are investigated, we can collect various types of metrics from software repositories; but it is inappropriate to use any statistical technique or visualization approach without considering the data characteristics (e.g., types and scales of variables, distributions). In this section, we present a sample of statistical techniques and visualizations that were used in our previous work and explain how they were selected.

16.4.1 DATA VISUALIZATION

The easiest way to gain an understanding of the data collected from rich and complex software repositories is through visualization. Data visualization is a mature domain, with significant amounts of literature on charts, tables, and tools that can be used for visually displaying quantitative information [66]. In this section, we provide examples of the use of basic charts such as box plots, scatter diagrams, and line charts in our previous analytics projects to better understand the software data.

Box plots are helpful for visualization as they allow one to shape the distribution, central value (median), minimum and maximum values, and quartiles, and give clues about whether the data is skewed or contains noise—that is, outliers. Figure 16.2 illustrates a box plot used to visualize the distribution of a number of active issues owned by developers with different categories (defects found during functional testing, during system testing, and in the field) in a case study concerning a large software organization [61]. During this study, we used box plots to inform developers that the functional testing category dominates the issues owned by developers, and it has a slightly higher median than the system testing and field categories. Furthermore, outliers in each set (e.g., 48 functional testing issues are owned by a single developer) highlight potential noisy instances, or dominance of certain developers regarding issue ownership (Figure 16.3).

A scatter diagram is another visualization technique used to explore the relationship between two variables—that is, two metrics that you want to monitor. During an exploratory study on Eclipse releases [67], we used scatter diagrams to observe the trend between the number of edits of source files (first variable) and the number of days between edits (second variable) for three different file sets—that is, files with beta-release bugs, files with other types of bugs, and files with no bugs. Figure 16.4 shows the scatter diagrams for three file sets of an Eclipse release [67]. It is seen that that there is not a clear trend such as a positive monotonic relationship between the two variables. However, it is clear that files with beta-release bugs are concentrated in smaller regions, with very few edits done frequently (in small time periods). On the basis of these visualizations, we suggested that the developers should concentrate on those files that are not edited too frequently in order to catch beta-release bugs [67].

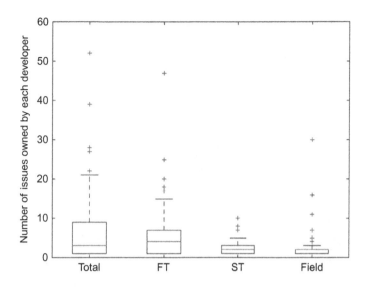

FIGURE 16.2

A box plot of issues owned by developers and their categories for a commercial software system. FT functional testing, ST system testing (from Ref. [61]).

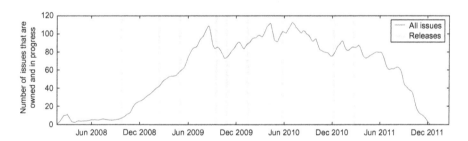

FIGURE 16.3

A line chart of activity in the issue repository of the Android system (from Ref. [61]).

Other types of charts are also useful for the purpose of visualizing software development, such as effort distribution of developers [53], issue ownership, or developer collaboration [61]. For example, we identified the collaboration network of developers and what factors affected the stability of the team working on a piece of large, globally developed and commercial software [68]. We used line charts to visualize the developer collaboration on the basis of the code that developers worked on together. In another study, we also used line charts to depict the number of issues owned and being fixed by developers on a monthly basis (see Figure 16.3). These charts are very easy to plot, and yet they are informative if they are monitored periodically—that is, every week/month or every sprint in agile practices, or per development team.

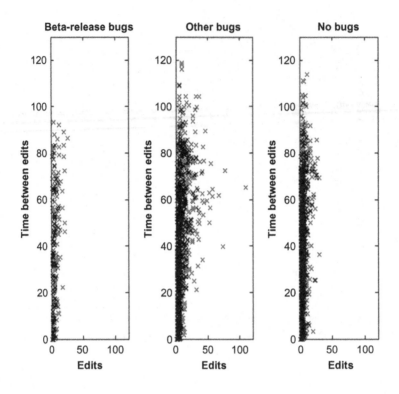

FIGURE 16.4

Three scatter diagrams for the number of edits and the time (in days) between edits for Eclipse source files containing beta-release bugs, other bugs, and no bugs (from Ref. [67]).

16.4.2 REPORTING VIA STATISTICS

Descriptive statistics such as minimum and maximum data points and mean, median, or variance of software metrics are computed prior to building analytics, since these statistics are informative about the distributional characteristics of metrics, central values, and variability. During an industry collaboration, it is a common practice to compute these descriptive statistics (e.g., [56, 61, 69]) or use visualizations at the beginning of a software analytics project, whereas other techniques such as statistical tests are more useful in the next steps to reveal existing relationships between software metrics or to identify differences in terms of distributions of two or more software metrics.

Below, we summarize a set of statistical analysis techniques that were reported in our previous projects conducted with our industry partners. Detailed descriptions of these techniques and their computations can be found in fundamental books on statistics (e.g., [70, 71]); here we explain the benefits of using these methods on software metrics to identify unique patterns.

Correlation analysis. This type of analysis identifies whether there are statistical relationships between variables, and in turn, it helps to decide on a set of independent variables that would be the input of a predictive analytics. Correlations can be computed among software metrics or between metrics and a dependent variable, such as the number of production defects, the defect category, the number of person-months (to indicate development effort), and issue reopening likelihood. Correlations between two variables can be measured using two popular approaches: Pearson's product-moment correlation coefficient and Spearman's rank correlation coefficient.

Pearson's correlation coefficient is a measure of the linear relationship between two variables, having a value between 1 (strong positive linear relation) and -1 (strong negative linear relation) [70]. The calculation of this coefficient is based on covariances of two variables, and there are different guidelines for interpreting the size of the coefficient depending on the problem being studied. For example, in empirical software engineering, a correlation coefficient above 75% may be interpreted as a strong relation between the variables, whereas in empirical studies in psychology, a quite small correlation coefficient of 37% may indicate a strong relation [72] .

In a case study concerning a large software organization operating in the telecommunications industry, we studied the linear relationship between confirmation bias metrics representing developers' thought processes and defect rates using Pearson's correlation coefficient and found that there is a medium (21%) to strong (53%) relationship between the variables [43]. On the basis of correlation analysis, we subsequently filtered the metrics that were significantly correlated and used the resulting metric set to build a predictive analytics that estimates the number of defects of a software system.

Spearman's rank correlation coefficient is a nonparametric measure of the statistical relationship between two variables [70]. Like Pearson's correlation coefficient, it takes values between 1 and -1, and is appropriate for both continuous and categorical variables. Differently, calculation of Spearman's correlation coefficient is based on the ranks that are computed from the raw values of the variables, and is independent of the distributional characteristics of the two variables. Thus, the correlation can indicate any monotonic relationship, in contrast to the linear relationship in Pearson correlation.

In a study that investigated the experience of software developers and testers, company size, and reasoning skills of software developers and testers in four to medium-sized to large software organizations [41], we computed Spearman's rank correlation coefficient to observe the relationship between the number of bugs reported by testers and production defects, and the relationship between developers' reasoning skills and defect-proneness of the code. Analyses showed that there is a significant (rank coefficient 0.82) positive relation between prerelease and production defects. We concluded that testers may report more bugs than the number that developers fix before each release, and hence, as more bugs are reported, the number of production defects increases.

In another case study concerning a large software development organization, we used Spearman correlation to analyze the relationship between metrics that characterize reopened issues (issues closed and opened again during an issue life cycle) [60]. We found a strong statistical relationship between the lines of code changed to fix a reopened issue and the dependencies of a reopened issue on other issues—that is, the higher the proximity of an issue to other issues, the more lines of code are affected during its fix.

In summary, although these results may sometimes look trivial, they are very influential for software teams, and development leads to observation of the hidden facts about the development process in an organization, and/or confirmation of assumptions that developers usually make in their daily decision making process. On the other hand, these types of correlation analyses show only whether there is a statistical relationship between two variables and the scale of that relationship. To further analyze what type of relationship (e.g., linear or nonlinear) exists between these two variables, scatter diagrams can be used or other statistical tests (e.g., hypotheses testing) may be applied. Below, we provide examples of some of these tests that were used in our previous work.

Goodness-of-fit tests. These tests can be used to compare a sample (distribution) against another distribution or another sample that is (assumed to be) generated from the same distribution. Similarly to correlation computation, there are several tests measuring the goodness of fit, and the appropriate one should be chosen depending on the number of instances in a sample, the number of datasets that will be compared, and the distributional characteristics of the sample. For example, in a comparative study between test-driven development and test-last programming, we used the Kolmogorov-Smirnov test to compare the code complexity and design metrics of a software system that is developed using test-driven development against a normal distribution [73]. The Kolmogorov-Smirnov test is a nonparametric test for checking the equality of two continuous probability distributions or for comparing two samples [71]. Our results [73] show that none of the metrics are normally distributed, and in turn, we applied analytics that are appropriate for samples generated from any type of distribution. In other studies, we applied the same goodness-of-fit test to compare development activities between experienced and novice team members of a software organization [40] or between developers and project managers [39].

In some of our studies, software metrics took categorical values, and hence other goodness-of-fit tests such as the chi-square test were more appropriate to compare the categorical metric values from two or more groups of samples. For example, during a case study concerning a software organization [42], the chi-square test was used to compare the distributions of confirmation bias metrics, which characterize developers' thought processes and reasoning skills, among developers, testers, and project managers. On the basis of the test results, we stated that reasoning skills are significantly different among the three development roles. Hence, we suggested using these metrics in deciding the assignment of roles and in forming a more balanced structure in the software organization.

Differences between populations. Though goodness-of-fit tests can be used to compare the differences between two or more populations—that is, samples—a better approach is to form a null hypothesis (H_0) and use statistical hypothesis tests to check if the null hypothesis is supported. For example, if we aim to check whether developers write more tests using test-driven development compared with test-last programming, we need to collect two samples that include the number of tests collected from a development activity using test-driven development and test-last programming. It is important that the samples are independently drawn from different populations. Later, we can form a null hypothesis as follows: *The difference between the number of tests written by developers using test-driven development and the test-last approach has a mean value of 0.*

A test (e.g., *t* test and the Mann-Whitney *U* test, also called the Wilcoxon rank-sum test) can reject the null hypothesis, meaning that the mean values are significantly different between two development practices, or it cannot reject the null hypothesis, meaning that the difference of means is not significant enough to make a statistical claim [71]. Hypothesis tests cannot actually prove or disprove anything, and hence they also calculate the power of the significance—for example, a *p* value of 0.05 tells us that there is a 95% chance of the means being significantly different. As this *p* value increases, it is more likely that the difference happens by chance.

We have often used hypothesis tests to compare two or more samples representing different software systems, development methods (e.g., Mann-Whitney *U* test [73]) and/or software teams (e.g., Mann-Whitney *U* test [41], and Kruskal-Wallis analysis of variance with more than two teams [43]).

Alternatively, these tests can be used to compare the performance of two predictive analytics in order to decide which one to choose—for example, *t* test [26, 49].

In summary, hypothesis testing techniques could be carefully selected by considering the information about sample distributions (e.g., *t* test for normally distributed samples, and nonparametric tests such as the Mann-Whitney *U* test for the others) during a descriptive analytics process. We also suggest that descriptive statistics, reporting via visualization or through statistical tests, could guide researchers or data analysts in software organizations in cases where there is rich, multivariate, and often noisy data.

16.5 PREDICTIVE ANALYTICS
16.5.1 A PREDICTIVE MODEL FOR ALL CONDITIONS

In this section, we present our experiences from multiple industry collaborative projects in terms of predictive analytics. Throughout this section we will review multiple algorithms, from simpler alternatives to more complex ones. However, our main intention is not to repeat the content of commonly used machine learning algorithms, since there are more than enough machine learning books [74–76]. We rather intend to share the lessons learned in the course of applying predictive analytics for more than a decade to industry-academia collaborative projects.

Often, we will see that knowing the learner (aka prediction algorithm) is only the part of the story, and the practitioner needs to be flexible and creative in terms of how he/she uses and alters the algorithm depending on the problem at hand. So, before going any further, just to set the right expectations, we briefly quote a conversation with an industry practitioner. Following the presentation of a predictive analytics model, a practitioner from a large software company asked the following question: "Would your predictive model work under all conditions?" ("Conditions" meaning different datasets and problem types.) The short answer to that questions is: "No." There is no predictive model that would yield high-performance measures under all the different conditions. Therefore, if you are looking for a silver-bullet predictive model, this section will disappoint you. On the other hand, we can talk about a certain approach to predictive models as well as some likely steps to be followed, which have been applied in real life to a number of industry projects by the authors of this chapter.

Terminology. A predictive model is a specific use of a learner that is often aided by preprocessing and postprocessing steps to improve predictive performance [30]. We will talk about improving the performance in Section 16.5.3. For the now, let us focus our attention on the learners, which are machine learning algorithms that learn the known instances and provide a prediction for an unknown instance. The known instances refer to instances for which we know the dependent variable information— for example, the defect information of software components. These instances are also referred as the "*training set*." The unknown instances are the ones for which we lack the dependent variable information—for example, the software components that have just been released, and hence that do not have defect information. These instances are referred to as the "*test set*." In the example of defective and nondefective software components, a predictive model is supposed to use the training set and learn the relationship between the metrics defining software components and the defects. Using the relationship learned, the predictive model is expected to provide accurate estimates for the test set—that is, the newly released components.

Go from simple to complex. One misleading approach to predictive modeling is to bluntly use whichever learner we come across. It may be possible to get a decent estimation accuracy with a randomly selected learner, but it is unlikely for such a random learner to be used by practitioners. For example, in a software effort estimation project for an international bank, every month we presented the results of the experiments to the management as well as the software developers [9, 52]. The focus of these presentations was never merely the performance, but how and why the algorithm presented could achieve the presented performance. In other words, merely using a complex algorithm, without a high-level explanation of how and why it applies to the prediction problem at hand, is unlikely to lead to adoption by product groups. Therefore, it is a good idea to start the investigation with an initial set of algorithms that are easy to apply and explain, such as linear regression [38], logistic regression [60, 77], and k-nearest neighbors (k-NN) [62, 78]. The application of such algorithms will also serve the purpose of providing a performance baseline, so that we can see how much added value the more complex additions will bring. These algorithms are relatively easier to understand, and in most of the industry projects in which the authors participated, they proved to have quite good performance [38, 60, 62, 77, 78]. On the other hand, simplicity just for the sake of choosing algorithms that nontechnical audiences can easily understand is also misleading. The simplicity of the algorithm for that purpose should have a minimal effect on the decision making process. If the best performing algorithm turns out to be some complex ensemble of relatively more difficult to understand learners, then so be it. But to make the case for deciding on a complex alternative, we should start simple and make sure that value is added with the complexity.

Linear regression is a predictive model that assumes a linear relationship between the dependent and independent variables [74]:

$$y = X\beta + \varepsilon. \tag{16.1}$$

The independent variables (defined by X) are multiplied by coefficients (β), and we want to set up the coefficients such that the error (ε) is minimized.

We have used linear regression in various industry settings for regression problems (the problems in which the dependent variable is a continuous value). The focus of a project in which we collaborated with a large telecommunications company was the effects of confirmation bias on the defect density (defect density measured in terms of the defect count, which is a continuous value, and hence a regression problem). We opted to use linear regression in this project as the confirmation bias metrics were observed to be linearly related to defect counts [38]. The observation of a linear relationship can be checked with the R^2 value (aka the coefficient of determination) as well as by plotting the metric value against the defect count. The R^2 value measures how much of the response variable variation (around its mean) is explained by a linear model. It can take values from 0 to 1, where 0 means none of the response variable variation is explained by the linear model, whereas 1 means all of the response variable variation is explained by the linear model. Therefore, values close to 1 mean a better model fit. In the confirmation bias project we defined the defect density for each developer group as the ratio of the total number of defective files created/updated by that group to the total number of files that group created/updated. So as to visualize the effect of confirmation bias on software defect density, we constructed a predictive model based on linear regression, with confirmation bias metrics as the predictor (independent) variables and defect density as the response variable. Our results showed that 42.4% of the variability in defect density could be explained by our linear regression model ($R^2 = 0.4243$)

Note that in the telecommunications company project, we used a linear regression model so as to predict a continuous value (defect count) [38]. However, not all the predictive problems that we face in real-life predictive analytics involve continuous variables. In the case of discrete dependent variables, we can make use of logistic regression [60, 77]. For example, assume that we know only whether a software module is defective or not (but not the exact defect count), then we can define the discrete classes of "*defective*" and "*nondefective*." Such a grouping would give us a two-class (aka binary) problem (instead of a continuous-variable prediction problem). In the case of two-class classification problems ($y_i = [0, 1]$), logistic regression is a frequently used prediction algorithm. The authors have employed logistic regression in various defect prediction projects [60]. The general logistic regression formula is as follows:

$$Pr(y_i = 1) = \text{logit}^{-1}(X_i \beta), \tag{16.2}$$

where $Pr(y_i = 1)$ denotes the probability of y_i belonging to class 1, X is the vector of independent variable values, and the β is the coefficient vector. One benefit of this predictive method is that—given the logistic regression provides high accuracy—one can use the corresponding coefficient values in order to see the importance of different input variables. An example application of this approach can be found in one of our projects [60], where we used logistic regression to analyze the possible factors behind issues being reopened in software development. For this purpose, we fit a logistic regression model to the collected issue data, but our main aim was to understand which issue factors are most important (through the use of coefficient values). Therefore, for the analysis of factors leading to reopened issues, logistic regression was an appropriate choice.

Another simple, yet quite successful learner for classification problems is naïve Bayes [33, 62, 78]. Particularly for software defect prediction studies, the authors have observed that naïve Bayes proved to be better than some more complicated rule-based learners (such as decision trees) [62]. As the name of the learner suggests, the naïve Bayes classifier is based on the Bayes theorem, which states that our next observation depends on how new evidence will affect old beliefs:

$$P(H|E) = \frac{P(H)}{P(E)} \prod_i P(E_i|H). \tag{16.3}$$

In Equation 16.3, given that we have old evidence E_i and a prior probability for a class H, it is possible to calculate its next (posterior) probability. For example, for a classifier trying to detect defective modules in a piece of software, class H would represent the class of defective modules. Then the posterior probability of an instance being defective ($P(H|E)$) is the product of the fraction of defective instances $P(H)/P(E)$ and the probability of each observation $P(E_i|H)$.

The success of this learner for defect prediction tasks also paved the way for us to use it in conjunction with other learners. For example, we have employed the k-NN learner as a cross-company filter for naïve Bayes [62]. Before going into how we made use of the k-NN learner as a filter, we briefly explain how it works: k-NN finds the labeled k instances most similar to the test instance. The distance is calculated via a distance function (e.g., Euclidean distance or Hamming distance).

k-NN can also be used for classification [78] and regression [79] problems. For a classification problem, usually the majority vote (i.e., the majority class of k-NN) is given as the predicted value. For a regression problem, the mean or median of the dependent variable value k-NN is given. Our use of k-NN as a filter in the defect prediction domain—that is, a classification problem [62]—questions whether organizations without data of their own (so-called within-company data) can use the data from other organizations (so-called cross-company data). In our initial experiments we use naïve Bayes as the predictive method and compare the performance when an organization uses within-company data versus cross-company data. The performance results show that the use of cross-company data yields a poor performance. This is understandable as the context of another organization may differ considerably. Then we use k-NN to filter instances from the cross-company data—for example, instead of using all the instances of cross-company data in a naïve Bayes classifier, we first find the closest cross-instances to the test instance (using k-NN). Filtering only the closest instances improves the performance of cross-company data such that it is very close to that of within-company data. The ability to use cross-company data has been quite important in a number of our projects, because our observation is that initially the within-company data will be quite limited at best. In other words, "*a practitioner will have to start the analysis with the data at hand.*" In such cases, the ability to use cross-company data has helped us provide initial predictions for the within-company test data [52].

Other relatively more complex learners are also frequently employed in software engineering research as predictive methods. Neural networks [49] and decision trees [50, 80] are examples of such learners that were used by the authors. We will not go deeply into the mechanics of these learners; however, we will provide the general idea and possible inherent biases because having an idea of how these algorithms work and their biases aids a practitioner in choosing the right learner for datasets of different characteristics.

Neural networks are known to be universal approximators [81]—that is, they can learn almost any function. Neural networks are defined to be a group of connected nodes, where the training instances are fed into the nodes that form the input layer (see Figure 16.5) and the information is transmitted to hidden layer nodes. During transmission, each connecting edge applies a weight to the number it receives from the previous node. Although there is one hidden layer in Figure 16.5, there may be multiple hidden layers to model more complex functions. Finally, the values are fed into the output layer, where a final estimate for each dependent variable is obtained. Note that instances can be fed into a neural network one by one—that is, the model can update itself one instance at a time as the training instances become

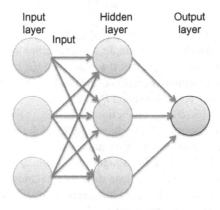

FIGURE 16.5

A sample neural network with a single hidden layer.

available. However, the problem with neural networks is that they are sensitive to small changes in the dataset [82]. Also, overtraining a neural network will have a negative impact for the future test instances that we want to predict. We addressed such issues related to neural networks by arranging the neural networks in the form of an ensemble [49]. Application of our neural network ensemble on software effort estimation data revealed that unlike the problems inherent in a single neural network, having an ensemble of neural networks provides stabler and improved accuracy values [49]. We will discuss ensembles of other learners further in the next section as a way to improve the predictive power of learners.

A capable and commonly used learner type is decision trees [50, 80]. Unlike neural networks that take instances one by one, decision trees require all the data to be available before they can start learning. Decision trees work by recursively splitting data into smaller and smaller subsets on the basis of the values of independent features [83]. At each split the instances that are more coherent with respect to the selected features are grouped together into a *node*. Figure 16.6 presents a hypothetical decision tree that uses two features, F1 and F2. The way this decision tree would work for a test instance is as follows: If F1 of this feature is smaller than or equal to x, then the decision tree will return the prediction of A. Otherwise, we will go down the node of F1 $> x$ and look at F2. If F2 $> y$ is true for our test instance, then we would predict B, otherwise we would predict C.

Particularly for datasets where instances form interrelated clusters, it is a good idea to try decision tree learners as their assumptions overlap with the structure of the data. Software effort estimation data is a good example of this case, where instances (projects) form local groups that are composed of similar projects. Therefore, we made use of decision trees in different industry projects focusing on estimating the effort of software projects [50, 52, 53]. One of our uses of decision tree learners on software effort data [50] includes the idea of grouping similar instances so as to convert the software effort estimation problem into a classification problem (recall that originally software effort estimation is a regression problem). By using decision trees, we form software effort intervals, where an interval is identified by the training projects falling in the final node of a decision tree. Then the test instance is

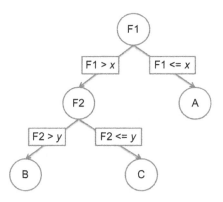

FIGURE 16.6

A sample decision tree that uses two features (F1 and F2).

fed into the decision tree and it finds its final node, where the estimate is provided as an interval instead of a single value.

Things to keep in mind:

1. *The learner is only part of the picture.* Until now we have reviewed some of the learners that we successfully applied on different real-life software engineering data. We have also seen how these learners can be altered for different tasks—for example, our use of k-NN as an instance-filtering method [62] or the use of decision trees to convert a regression problem into a classification problem [50]. However, the application of the learner on the data is only one part of the picture. There are possible pitfalls we identified over the course of different projects that a practitioner should be aware of when building a predictive model.

2. *Building a predictive model is iterative.* As you are applying different learners on the data, you should consider including the domain experts (or customers) of the data in the loop. In other words, we recommend discussing the initial results and your concerns with the domain experts. The initial benefit of having the customer in the loop is that you can get early feedback about the quality of the data. For certain instances that your learner yields a poor performance, you can get a clear explanation as to what the cause is. Another benefit will be to identify potential data issues early on. If there is a feature that looks suspicious, the domain experts may give you a clear answer as to whether the data is wrong. For example, in one of the industry projects, for some projects the bug count was surprisingly low, whereas the test cases for these projects were quite high. A domain expert who worked on this project may tell you whether this is indeed the case, or whether in this particular project bugs were not tracked consistently. Then you may decide not to include this unhealthy information in your model, as we did in that particular project.

3. *Automation is the key.* During any part of the project, you may need to rerun all your experiments. In an industry project, we learned halfway into the project that one of the assumptions we were told for a group of projects would be invalid for another group of projects developed within the preceding year. So we had to repeat all the analyses we had done up to this point for the projects developed within the preceding year. If we had not coded our experiments, it would have taken much time to repeat all the experiments. Therefore, it is beneficial to use machine learning toolkits such as WEKA [76], but it is also critically important to have your experiments coded for reruns of the experiments. Another reason why it is important to code your predictive models is customization. You may want to combine or alter different learners in a specific way, which may be unavailable through the user interface of a toolkit. Coding your experiments may provide you with the flexibility of customization.

16.5.2 PERFORMANCE EVALUATION

Depending on the problem being studied, performance evaluation of predictive analytics can be computed differently. Naturally, the output of a predictive analytics—that is, a prediction model—is compared against the data points in the test set, or against the actual data points after they have been retrieved and stored in data repositories of software organizations. The type of output variables can be categorical or continuous, which determines the set of performance evaluation measures. For instance, in a defect prediction problem, the output of a predictive analytics can take a categorical value (e.g., defect-proneness of a software code module, i.e., package, file, class, method, being defect-free (0), or being defect-prone/defective (1)) or it can take a continuous value ranging from zero to infinity (e.g., number of defect-prone code modules in a software product). For a model with a categorical output, a typical confusion matrix can be used for computing a set of performance measures. Table 16.5 presents a confusion matrix in which the rows represent the actual information about whether the software module is fixed or not because of a defect, whereas the columns represent the output of a predictive analytics.

All performance measures can be calculated on the basis of the four base measures presented in Table 16.5—namely, true positives (TPs), false negatives (FNs), false positives (FPs), and true negatives (TNs). For example, in the context of defect prediction, TPs are the actual number of defective modules that are correctly classified as defective by the model, FNs are the number of defective modules that are incorrectly marked as defect free, FPs are the number of defect-free modules that are incorrectly classified as defective, and TNs are the number of defect-free modules that are correctly marked as defect free by the model. A predictive analytics ideally aims to classify all defective and defect-free modules accurately—that is no FNs and no FPs. However, achieving the ideal case is very challenging in practice.

In our empirical studies, we have used six popular performance measures to assess the performance of a classifier: *accuracy*, *recall* (also called *TP rate* or *hit rate* or specifically in defect prediction, *probability of detection rate*), *FP rate* (also called *false alarms* in defect prediction), *precision*, *F measure*, and *balance*. The calculations of these six measures are shown below [30, 51, 77]:

$$ACC = (TP + TN)/(TP + TN + FN + FP), \qquad (16.4)$$

$$REC = TP/(TP + FN), \qquad (16.5)$$

$$PREC = TP/(TP + FP), \qquad (16.6)$$

$$FPR = FP/(FP + TP), \qquad (16.7)$$

$$F \text{ measure} = 2(PREC \times REC)/(PREC + REC), \qquad (16.8)$$

$$BAL = 1 - \sqrt{(1 - REC)^2 + (0 - FPR)^2}, \qquad (16.9)$$

where ACC is accuracy, REC is recall, PREC is precision, FPR is the FP rate, and BAL is balance. ACC, REC, PREC, *F* measure, and BAL should be as close to 1 as possible, while FPR should be close to 0. However, there is an inverse relationship between REC and PREC—that is, it is only possible to increase one (REC) at the cost of the other (low PREC). If these two are prioritized over all performance measures, it is useful to compute *F* measure, which depicts the harmonic mean between REC and PREC.

Furthermore, there is a positive relationship between REC and FPR—for example, an algorithm tends to increase REC at the cost of a high false alarm rate. BAL is a measure that incorporates the relationship between REC and FPR; it calculates the distance between an ideal case (REC = 1, FPR = 0) and the performance of a predictive analytics.

Achieving high REC and PREC while lowering FPR, and in turn, achieving high BAL and *F* measure, has been a real challenge for us when building predictive analytics in software organizations. A good balance between these measures needed to be targeted according to the business strategies in these organizations. For example, in software organizations operating in mission-critical domains (e.g., embedded systems), software teams aim to catch and fix as many defects as possible before deploying the production code. Thus, they prioritize achieving a high REC over a low FPR from a predictive

Table 16.5 A Typical Confusion Matrix Used for Performance Assessment of Prediction Models

		Predicted	
		True	False
Actual	True	TP	FN
	False	FP	TN

analytics. Conversely, in software organizations operating in competitive domains (e.g., telecommunications), reducing costs is the primary concern. Accordingly, they would like to reduce the additional costs caused by high FPR and achieve a balance between REC, PREC, and FPR.

We have preferred to use REC, FPR, and BAL in most of our work since reducing the cost of predictive analytics by lowering FPR has always been the focus of our industry partners. For example, in a case study concerning a software organization operating in the telecommunications domain, we deployed a software analytics for predicting code defects [9]. On the basis of user feedback, we calibrated the analytics to reduce FPR while getting as high REC as possible. The model that was later deployed in the company produced 87% recall and 26% false alarms [84]. In a study concerning a company operating in embedded systems, we built a predictive analytics for catching the majority of code defects at the cost of high false alarm rates [85]. We reported that an ensemble of classifiers was able to catch 82% recall and 35% false alarms. In other case studies, we have studied different techniques for lowering false alarm rates in defect prediction research (e.g., algorithm threshold optimization [29], increased information content of training data [24, 26, 30], and missing data imputation [15]).

For localizing the source of software faults, we built a predictive analytics that extracts unique patterns stored in previous fault messages of a software application and assigns a newly arrived fault message to where it belongs [51]. In the context of fault localization, both REC and PREC are equally important since misclassification of faults has equal costs for both classes. In other words, localizing a fault to component A even though it belongs to component B can be as costly as localizing a fault to component B though it belongs to component A. Therefore, the proposed model in Ref. [51] managed to achieve 99% REC and 98% PREC in the first application, whereas it achieved 76% REC and 71% PREC rates in the second application.

Another predictive analytics was built for a software organization to estimate software classes that need to be refactored on the basis of code complexity and dependency metrics [86]. The proposed model was able to predict 82% of classes that need refactoring (TP rate) using 13% inspection effort by developers.

If predictive analytics produces a continuous output (e.g., total number of defects, project effort in terms of person-months), evaluating its performance requires either a transformation of the output to categorical values or use of other performance measures that are more appropriate for a continuous model output. For example, we built a software effort estimation model that would dynamically predict the interval of a project's effort—that is, a categorical value that indicates which effort interval is the most suitable for a new project—rather than the number of person-months [80]. Since the output was categorical, performance measures that were used in defect prediction studies—that is, REC, PREC, FPR, and ACC—were used to assess the performance of the proposed effort estimation model.

A more convenient approach is to use other performance measures that are more suitable for evaluating the performance of a model that produces continuous output. Some of these measures that we have extensively used are the *magnitude of relative error* (MRE), the *mean MRE* (MMRE), and *predictions at level k* (PRED(k)). Calculation of each of these measures is shown below:

$$MRE_i = \frac{|x_i - \hat{x}_i|}{x_i},$$
(16.10)

$$MMRE = mean(all\ MRE_i),$$
(16.11)

$$PRED(k) = \frac{100}{N} \sum_{i=1}^{N} \begin{cases} 1 & \text{if } MRE_i \leq \frac{k}{100}, \\ 0 & \text{otherwise.} \end{cases}$$
(16.12)

Ideally, MRE and MMRE should be as low as 0, whereas PRED(k) should be close to 1. Instead of MMRE, the *median magnitude of relative error* (MdMRE) can abe used, since the mean of a sample is always sensitive to outliers in that sample compared with the *median*. In the context of software effort estimation, reducing MRE indicates that effort values are estimated with low error rates. As the error rate decreases, PRED increases. The value of k in the PRED calculation is usually selected as 25 or 30, meaning that the percentage of estimations whose error rates are lower than 25% or 30%. PRED might be a better assessment criterion for software practitioners, since it shows the variation of the prediction error—that is, what percentage of predictions achieve a level of error that was set by practitioners. Hence, it implicitly presents both the error rate (k) and the variation of this error among all predictions made by the analytics.

We have used MMRE and PRED(25) measures during our empirical studies in the context of software effort estimation, and we observed that there is not an optimal value for these measures that fits best for all software projects and teams. For example, in one study, one of our colleagues from our research laboratory built different predictive analytics to estimate the project effort in person-months [87]. Two datasets—that is, one public dataset and another dataset collected from different software organizations—were used to train the predictive analytics. The results show that the best model applied to the public dataset produced 29% MMRE, 19% MdMRE, and 73% PRED(30), whereas it produced 49% MMRE, 28% MdMRE, and 51% PRED(30) when applied to the commercial dataset.

In other studies, we have proposed relatively more complex analytics to estimate software projects' effort in the case of a limited amount of training data. For example, the intelligence in our predictive analytics proposed in Ref. [49] works as follows: it has an associative memory that estimates and corrects the error of a prediction on the basis of the algorithm's performances over past projects. The results obtained using this associative memory show that we could achieve 40% MMRE, 29% MdMRE, and 55% PRED(25), compared with a simple classifier that predicts 434% MMRE, 205% MdMRE, and 10% PRED(35) [49].

On the basis of the increase/decrease in performance measures, the best performing algorithm can be selected when building predictive analytics. A raw comparison between the values of a performance measure may sometimes be problematic—that is, the change in a measure might happen because of the sample used for training the algorithm and the improvements may not be statistically significant. So, even though an algorithm produces higher values in terms of a performance measure—say, 30% over 27%—statistical tests should be used to confirm that the change does not happen by chance.

Statistical tests, as explained in Section 16.4.2, can be used to identify patterns of software data as well as to compare the performance of predictive analytics that are built with different algorithms (e.g., the Mann-Whitney U test [73], and Nemenyi's multiple comparison test and the Friedman test [52]). Box plots are also useful visualization techniques to depict the differences between the performance measures of two or more predictive analytics [30, 62]. Other performance measures we used for predictive analytics that produce continuous output can be found in Ref. [38].

Finally, we calculated context-specific performance evaluations, such as cost-benefit analysis (in terms of the amount of decrease (in lines of code) in inspection effort for findings software defects [84, 85]) in empirical studies for software defect prediction. These types of analysis are also easy to understand and interpret for software practitioners as they represent the tangible benefits—that is, effort reduction—of using predictive analytics.

16.5.3 PRESCRIPTIVE ANALYTICS

Once you decide on an algorithm, it is possible to improve the performance via some simple methods such as the following:

- forming ensembles [49, 85, 88],
- applying normalization [50, 80],
- feature selection through methods such as information gain [62],
- instance selection via k-NN-based sampling.

Ensembles are one powerful way to combine multiple weak learners into a stronger learner [88]. The idea behind ensembles is that different learners have different biases (recall how neural networks and decision trees are different from one another); hence, they learn different parts of the data. When their predictions are combined, they may complement one another and provide a better prediction. For example, in one of our studies, we employed a high number of prediction methods and combined them in simple ways such as taking the mean and median of the predictions coming from single learners [88]. However, before combining single learners, we paid attention to choosing the successful ones, where we ranked the learners and combined only the ones that had a high performance. Such a selection of only the successful learners provided us with ensembles that are consistently more successful than all the single learners. In other words, in the formation of an ensemble, it is better not to include the single learners whose performance is already low when they are run alone.

Normalizing the values of features is "*a must*" to improve learner performance if some of the features have very high values compared with others. For example, a feature keeping the number of classes defined in a project will have much smaller values compared with another feature that keeps the number of lines of code in this project. If you are using a k-NN learner, the impact of lines of code will dominate over the impact of the number of classes in a Euclidean distance calculation. A very common method we use for a number of different datasets is min-max normalization [50, 80]:

$$\frac{x_i - \min(X)}{\max(X) - \min(X)},$$
(16.13)

where X represents the feature vector and x_i represents a single value in this vector. Although a very high number of features may be available to practitioners to be included in a data set, it is usually the case that some of these features are less important than the others. We have observed in different scenarios that it is in fact possible to improve the performance of a learner by selecting a subset of all the features [62, 88]. There are multiple ways to select features, such as information gain [62], stepwise regression [88], and linear discriminant analysis to name just a few.

Similarly to the idea of "not all features being helpful" for a prediction model, not all the instances are beneficial for a prediction problem too. There may be various reasons why certain instances should be filtered out of the data. For example, the instance may contain erroneous data, or the data stored concerning the instance may be correct, but it may be so different from all the rest of the instances that it turns out to be an outlier. In either case, we may want to filter out such instances from the dataset. We have discussed our use of k-NN-based instance filters prior to us of a naïve Bayes classifier [62], which is a good example of instance-based filtering. k-NN-based instance filters select only the training instances closest to the test instance, so the learner uses only filtered-out instances. Another algorithm that was inspired by the k-NN-based filters is filtering by variance [79], where we selected only the instances that form groups of low variance (of the dependent variable value).

The proposed methods of ensembles, feature and instance selection, and feature normalization are a subset of possible ways to improve the performance of a learner. However, their application should not be interpreted as a must. Depending on the problem and dataset at hand, a practitioner must experiment with his or her application separately or as combinations (e.g., feature and instance selection applied together). The combination that yields the best performance should be preferred.

In summary, predictive analytics requires a clear definition of business challenges from a statistical point of view: from understanding data through visualizations and statistical tests to defining the input-output of a predictive analytics; from the selection of an algorithm to performance assessment criteria, and finally, to improving the performance of the algorithm. On the basis our previous experience, we provide Table 16.6 to guide software data analysts toward building a software analytics framework. Note that Table 16.6 is by no means an exhaustive list of all the possible algorithms for predictive purposes. However, it covers the selected algorithms that were employed in the multiple industrial case studies that we have discussed so far.

16.6 **ROAD AHEAD**

In many real-world problems, there are lots of random factors affecting the outcomes of a decision making process. It is usually impossible to consider all these factors and their possible interactions. Under such uncertainty, AI methods are helpful tools for making generalizations of past experiences in order to produce solutions for the previously unseen instances of the problem. These past experiences are extracted from available data, which represents the characteristics of the problem. Many data mining applications deal with large amounts of data, and their challenge is to reduce this large search space. On the other hand, there exist domains with very limited amounts of available data. In this case, the challenge is making generalizations from limited amounts of data.

In this context, software engineering is a domain with many random factors and relatively limited data. Nevertheless, in the software domain, remarkably effective predictors for software products have been generated using data mining methods. The success of these models seems unlikely considering all the factors involved in software development. For example, organizations can work in different domains, have different process, and define/measure defects and other aspects of their products and processes in different ways. Furthermore, most organizations do not precisely define their processes,

Table 16.6 A Classification and Application of Some of the Statistical Methods for Building a Software Analytics Framework

| Type of Response Variable (Output) | Type of Learning | Predictive Analytics | | Prescriptive Analytics |
		Algorithms	Performance Measures	
Categorical (e.g., defect-proneness, issue reopening)	Classification	Logistic regression, naïve Bayes, k-NN, decision trees	Base measures from confusion matrix (TP, TN, FP, FN). Other derived measures: ACC, REC, PREC, false alarms, F measure, BAL	Normalization, feature and instance selection, ensembles
Continuous (e.g., number of defects, defect density, project effort in person-months)	Regression	Linear regression, k-NN, neural networks, decision trees	MRE, MdMRE, PRED(k), R^2	

products, measurements, etc. Nevertheless, it is true that very simple models suffice for generating approximately correct predictions for software development time and the location of software defects.

One candidate explanation for the strange predictability in software development is that despite all the seemingly random factors influencing software construction, the net result follows very tight statistical patterns. Building oracles to predict defects and/or effort via data mining is also an inductive generalization over past experience. All data miners hit a performance ceiling effect when they cannot find additional information that better relates software metrics to defect occurrence, or effort intervals. What we observe from our past results is that the research paradigm, which relied on relatively straightforward application of machine learning tools, has reached its limits.

To overcome these limits, researchers use combinations of metric features from different software artifacts, which we call information sources, in order to enrich the information content in the search space. However, these features from different sources come at a considerable collection cost, and are not available in all cases. Another way to avoid these limits is to use domain knowledge.

So far in our research we have combined the most basic type of these features—that is, source code measurements—with domain knowledge, and we propose novel ways of increasing the information content using these information sources. Using domain knowledge, we have shown that, for example, data miners for defect prediction can be easily constructed with limited or no data.

Research in AI, programming languages, and software engineering shares many common goals, such as high-level concepts, tools, and techniques: abstraction, modeling, etc. But there are also significant differences in the problem scope, the nature of the solution, and the intended audience. The AI community is interested in finding solutions to problems; the software engineering community tries to find efficient solutions, and as a result it needs to tackle simpler, more focused problems.

When we define intelligence, we have to be precise. What do we mean by intelligence? Which system is considered as intelligent? Those are the questions that are important to be able to create "smart" oracles. Building those systems becomes extremely important when we have large and distributed teams for software development. Users want an easy environment in which to switch between subsystems. For example, in the defect prediction domain, it is obvious that cooperative use of oracles with test benches is essential to support business decisions.

AI needs to be thought of as a large-scale engineering project. Researchers should build systems and design approaches that merge theory with empirical data, that merge science with large-scale engineering, and that merge methods with expert knowledge, business rules, and intuition.

In our previous work we saw that static code attributes have limited information content. Descriptions of software modules only in terms of static code attributes can overlook some important aspects of software, including the type of application domain, the skill level of the individual programmers involved in system development, contractor development practices, the variation in measurement practices, and the validation of the measurements and instruments used to collect the data. For this reason we have started augmenting and replacing static code measures with repository metrics such as past faults or changes to code or the number of developers who have worked on the code. In building oracles we have successfully modeled product attributes (static code metrics, repository metrics, etc.), and process attributes (organizational factors, experience of people, etc.). However, in software development projects people (developers, testers, analysts) are the most important pillar, but are very difficult to model. It is inevitable that we should move to a model that considers the product, process, and people.

We believe that in defect and effort estimation, more value will come from better understanding of developer characteristics, such as a grasp of how social networks are formed and how they affect the defect-proneness and/or effort allocation. Therefore, research in this area will include input from other disciplines, such as the social sciences, cognitive science, economics, and statistics.

REFERENCES

[1] Kenett RS. Implementing SCRUM using business process management and pattern analysis methodologies. Dyn Relationships Manage J 2013;2(2):29–48

[2] Powner DA. Software development: effective practices and federal challenges in applying agile methods. Technical report. US Office of Public Affairs, GAO-12-681; 2012.

[3] Shearer C. The CRISP-DM model: the new blueprint for data mining. J Data Warehousing 2000; 5:13–22.

[4] Creswell JW. The selection of a research design. In: Research design: qualitative, quantitative, and mixed methods approaches. Thousand Oaks: Sage; 2008. p. 3–21.

[5] Easterbrook S, Neves B. Empirical research methods for computer scientists; 2004. URL: http://www.cs.toronto.edu/sme/CSC2130/01-intro.pdf.

[6] Chrissis MB, Konrad M, Shrum S. CMMI for development: guidelines for process integration and product improvement. 3rd ed. Reading, MA: Addison Wesley; 2011.

[7] Why is measurements of data management maturity important. Technical report. CMMI Institute; 2014.

[8] Easterbrook S, Singer J, Storey MA, Damian D. Selecting empirical methods for software engineering research. Guide to advanced empirical software engineering. Berlin: Springer; 2008. p. 285–311.

[9] Tosun A, Bener AB, Turhan B, Menzies T. Practical considerations in deploying statistical methods for defect prediction: A case study within the Turkish telecommunications industry. Inform Software Technol 2010;52(11):1242–57.

[10] Misirli AT, Bener A. Bayesian networks for evidence-based decision-making in software engineering. IEEE Trans Softw Eng 2014; 40:533–54.

[11] Menzies T, Caglayan B, He Z, Kocaguneli E, Krall J, Peters F, Turhan B. The PROMISE repository of empirical software engineering data, 2012. URL: http://promisedata.googlecode.com.

[12] Basili VR. Software modeling and measurement: the goal/question/metric paradigm. Technical report. College Park, MD, USA; 1992.

[13] Nagappan N, Murphy B, Basili V. The influence of organizational structure on software quality: An empirical case study. In: 30th international conference on software engineering (ICSE 2008); 2008.

[14] Shmueli G, Kenett R. An information quality (InfoQ) framework for ex-ante and ex-post evaluation of empirical studies. In: 3rd international workshop on intelligent data analysis and management (IDAM); 2013.

[15] Calikli G, Bener A. An algorithmic approach to missing data problem in modeling human aspects in software development. In: Predictive models in software engineering conference (PROMISE); 2013.

[16] McCabe TJ. A complexity measure. IEEE Trans Software Eng 1976;SE-2.

[17] Halstead MH. Elements of software science, vol. 1. New York: Elsevier North-Holland; 1977.

[18] Chidamber SR, Kemerer CF. A metrics suite for object oriented design. IEEE Trans Software Eng 1994;20(6):476–93.

[19] Fenton NE, Neil M. A critique of software defect prediction models. IEEE Trans Software Eng 1999;25(3): 1–15.

[20] Fenton NE, Ohlsson N. Quantitative analysis of faults and failures in a complex software system. IEEE Trans Software Eng 2000;26(8):797–814.

[21] Oral AD, Bener A. Defect prediction for embedded software. In: 22nd international symposium on computer and information sciences (ISCIS 2007); 2007.

[22] Ceylan E, Kutlubay O, Bener A. Software defect identification using machine learning techniques. In: EURIMICRO SEAA 2006; 2006.

[23] Shull F, Basili V, Boehm B, Brown AW, Costa P, Lindvall M, Port D, Rus I, Tesoriero R, Zelkowitz M. What we have learnt about fighting defects. In: 8th international software metrics symposium; 2002.

[24] Turhan B, Bener A. Weighted static code attributes for software defect prediction. In: 20th international conference on software engineering and knowledge engineering; 2008.

[25] Menzies T, Greenwald J, Frank A. Data mining static code attributes to learn defect predictors. IEEE Trans Software Eng 2007;33(1):1–13.

[26] Turhan B, Kocak G, Bener A. Software defect prediction using call graph based ranking (CGBR) framework. In: 34th EUROMICRO software engineering and advanced applications (EUROMICRO-SEAA 2008); 2008.

[27] Kocak G, Turhan B, Bener A. Predicting defects in a large telecommunication system. In: ICSOFT; 2008. p. 284–8.

[28] Brin S, Page L. The anatomy of a large-scale hypertextual web search engine. In: Computer Networks and ISDN systems. Amsterdam: Elsevier Science Publishers; 1998. p. 107–17.

[29] Tosun A, Bener AB. Reducing false alarms in software defect prediction by decision threshold optimization. In: ESEM; 2009. p. 477–80.

[30] Turhan B, Misirli AT, Bener A. Empirical evaluation of the effects of mixed project data on learning defect predictors. Information and Software Technology 2013;55(6):1101–18.

[31] Pinzger M, Nagappan N, Murphy B. Can developer-module networks predict failures? In: 16th ACM SIGSOFT international symposium on foundations of software engineering, (FSE 2008); 2008.

[32] Meneely A, Williams L, Snipes W, Osborne J. Predicting failures with developer networks and social network analysis. In: 16th ACM SIGSOFT international symposium on foundations of software engineering (FSE2008); 2008.

[33] Misirli AT, Caglayan B, Miranskyy AV, Bener A, Ruffolo N. Different strokes for different folks: A case study on software metrics for different defect categories. In: Proceedings of the 2nd international workshop on emerging trends in software metrics; 2011. p. 45–51. ISBN 978-1-4503-0593-8.

[34] Graves TL, Karr AF, Marron JS, Siy H. Predicting fault incidence using software change history. IEEE Trans Software Eng 2000;26(7):653–61.

[35] Weyuker EJ, Ostrand TJ, Bell RM. Do too many cooks spoil the broth? using the number of developers to enhance defect prediction models. Empirical Software Eng 2008;13(5):539–59.

[36] Mockus A, Weiss DM. Predicting risk of software changes. Bell Labs Tech J 2000; 5.

[37] Weyuker EJ, Ostrand TJ, Bell RM. Using developer information as a factor for fault prediction. In: Proceedings of the third international workshop on predictor models in software engineering. IEEE Computer Society; 2007. p. 8.

[38] Calikli G, Bener AB. Preliminary analysis of the effects of confirmation bias on software defect density. In: ESEM; 2010.

[39] Calikli G, Bener A. Empirical analyses of the factors affecting confirmation bias and the effects of confirmation bias on software developer/tester performance. In: PROMISE; 2010.

[40] Calikli G, Bener A, Arslan B. An analysis of the effects of company culture, education and experience on confirmation bias levels of software developers and testers. In: ICSE; 2010.

[41] Calikli G, Arslan B, Bener A. Confirmation bias in software development and testing: An analysis of the effects of company size, experience and reasoning skills. In: 22nd annual psychology of programming interest group workshop; 2010.

[42] Calikli G, Bener A, Aytac T, Bozcan O. Towards a metric suite proposal to quantify confirmation biases of developers. In: ESEM; 2013.

[43] Calikli G, Bener A. Influence of confirmation biases of developers on software quality: an empirical study. Software Qual J 2013; 21:377–416.

[44] Bird C, Nagappan N, Gall H, Murphy B, Devanbu P. Putting it all together: Using socio-technical networks to predict failures. In: Proceedings of the 2009 20th international symposium on software reliability engineering. ISSRE '09, Washington, DC, USA: IEEE Computer Society; 2009. p. 109–19.

[45] Zimmermann T, Nagappan N. Predicting subsystem failures using dependency graph complexities. In: Proceedings of the 18th IEEE international symposium on software reliability. IEEE Computer Society; 2007. p. 227–36.

[46] Bicer S, Caglayan B, Bener A. Defect prediction using social network analysis on issue repositories. In: International conference on software systems and process (ICSSP 2011); 2011. p. 63–71.

[47] Easley D, Kleinberg J. Networks, crowds, and markets: reasoning about a highly connected world. Cambridge University Press; 2010.

[48] Kultur Y, Turhan B, Bener A. Enna: Software effort estimation using ensemble of neural networks with associative memory. In: 16th international symposium on foundations of software engineering (ACM SIGSOFT FSE 2008); 2008.

[49] Kultur Y, Turhan B, Bener AB. Ensemble of neural networks with associative memory (enna) for estimating software development costs. Knowl-Based Syst 2009;22(6):395–402.

[50] Bakir A, Turhan B, Bener AB. A comparative study for estimating software development effort intervals. Software Qual J 2011;19(3):537–52.

[51] Bakir A, Kocaguneli E, Tosun A, Bener A, Turhan B. Xiruxe: an intelligent fault tracking tool. In: International conference on artificial intelligence and pattern recognition; 2009.

[52] Kocaguneli E, Tosun A, Bener AB. AI-based models for software effort estimation. In: EUROMICRO-SEAA 2010. p. 323–6.

[53] Kocaguneli E, Misirli AT, Bener A, Caglayan B. Experience on developer participation and effort estimation. In: Euromicro SEAA conference; 2011.

[54] Lokan C, Wright T, Hill PR, Stringer M. Organizational benchmarking using ISBSG data repository. IEEE Software 2001;18(5):26–32.

[55] Bakir A, Turhan B, Bener AB. A new perspective on data homogeneity in software cost estimation: a study in the embedded systems domain. Software Qual J 2010;18(3):57–80.

[56] Misirli AT, Caglayan B, Bener A, Turhan B. A retrospective study of software analytics projects: in-depth interviews with practitioners. IEEE Softw 2013; 30(5):54–61.

[57] Caglayan B, Misirli AT, Calikli G, Bener A, Aytac T, Turhan B. Dione: an integrated measurement and defect prediction solution. In: Proceedings of the ACM SIGSOFT 20th international symposium on the foundations of software engineering. FSE '12, New York, NY, USA: ACM; 2012. p. 20:1–2.

[58] Caglayan B, Tosun A, Miranskyy AV, Bener AB, Ruffolo N. Usage of multiple prediction models based on defect categories. In: PROMISE; 2010. p. 8.

[59] Kocaguneli E, Tosun A, Bener AB, Turhan B, Caglayan B. Prest: an intelligent software metrics extraction, analysis and defect prediction tool. In: SEKE; 2009. p. 637–42.

[60] Caglayan B, Misirli AT, Miranskyy AV, Turhan B, Bener A. Factors characterizing reopened issues: a case study. In: PROMISE; 2012. p. 1–10.

[61] Caglayan B, Bener A. Issue ownership activity in two large software projects. In: 9th international workshop on software quality, collocated with FSE; 2012.

[62] Turhan B, Menzies T, Bener AB, Stefano JSD. On the relative value of cross-company and within-company data for defect prediction. Empirical Software Eng 2009;14(5):540–78.

[63] Owens M, Allen G. The definitive guide to SQLite, vol. 1. Springer; 2006.

[64] Turhan B, Kutlubay FO, Bener AB. Evaluation of feature extraction methods on software cost estimation. In: ESEM; 2007. p. 497.

[65] Yin RK. Case study research: design and methods, vol. 5. sage; 2009.

[66] Tufte E. The visual display of quantitative information. 2nd ed. Cheshire, CT: Graphics Press; 2001.

[67] Misirli AT, Murphy B, Zimmermann T, Bener A. An explanatory analysis on eclipse beta-release bugs through in-process metrics. In: 8th international workshop on software quality. ACM; 2011. p. 26–33.

[68] Caglayan B, Bener A, Miranskyy AV. Emergence of developer teams in the collaboration network. In: CHASE workshop colocated with ICSE; 2013.

[69] Kocak S, Miranskyy AV, Alptekin G, Bener A, Cialini E. The impact of improving software functionality on environmental sustainability. In: ICT for sustainability; 2013.

[70] Hocking RR. Methods and applications of lLinear models: Regression and the Analysis of Variance. Third edition ed.; Wiley Series in Probability and Statistics; 2013.

[71] Hollande M, Wolfe DA, Chicken E. Nonparametric statistical methods. 3rd ed. Wiley Series in Probability and Statistics; 2014.

[72] Cohen J. Statistical power analysis for the behavioral sciences. Hillsdale, NJ: Lawrence Erlbaum Associates Publishers; 1988.

[73] Turhan B, Bener A, Kuvaja P, Oivo M. A quantitative comparison of test-first and test-last code in an industrial project. In: 11th international conference on agile software development (XP); 2010.

[74] Alpaydin E. Introduction to machine learning. Cambridge MA: MIT Press; 2004.

[75] Bishop CM. Pattern recognition and machine learning, vol. 1. New York: Springer; 2006.

[76] Witten IH, Frank E. Data mining: practical machine learning tools and techniques. Morgan Kaufmann; 2005.

[77] Tosun A, Turhan B, Bener AB. Validation of network measures as indicators of defective modules in software systems. In: PROMISE; 2009. p. 5.

[78] Turhan B, Koçak G, Bener AB. Data mining source code for locating software bugs: A case study in telecommunication industry. Expert Syst Appl 2009;36(6):9986–90.

[79] Kocaguneli E, Menzies T, Bener A, Keung JW. Exploiting the essential assumptions of analogy-based effort estimation. IEEE Trans Softw Eng 2012;38(2):425–38.

[80] Bakir A, Turhan B, Bener AB. Software effort estimation as a classification problem. In: ICSOFT (SE/MUSE/GSDCA); 2008. p. 274–7.

[81] Hornik K, Stinchcombe M, White H. Multilayer feedforward networks are universal approximators. Neural Networks 1989;2(5):359–66.

[82] Geman S, Bienenstock E, Doursat R. Neural networks and the bias/variance dilemma. Neural Comput 1992;4(1):1–58.

[83] Breiman L, Friedman J, Stone CJ, Olshen RA. Classification and regression trees. CRC Press; 1984.

[84] Misirli AT, Bener AB, Kale R. AI-based software defect predictors: applications and benefits in a case study. AI Magazine 2011;32(2):57–68.

[85] Tosun A, Turhan B, Bener AB. Ensemble of software defect predictors: a case study. In: ESEM; 2008. p. 318–20.

[86] Kosker Y, Turhan B, Bener A. An expert system for determining candidate software classes for refactoring. Expert Syst Appl 2009;36(6):10000–3.

[87] Baskeles B, Turhan B, Bener A. Software effort estimation using machine learning methods. In: 22nd international symposium on computer and information sciences (ISCIS); 2007. p. 126–31.

[88] Kocaguneli E, Menzies T, Keung JW. On the value of ensemble effort estimation. IEEE Trans Softw Eng 2012;38(6):1403–16.

ADVANCED TOPICS

CODE COMMENT ANALYSIS FOR IMPROVING SOFTWARE QUALITY*

17

Lin Tan*

*Department of Electrical and Computer Engineering, University of Waterloo, Waterloo, ON, Canada**

CHAPTER OUTLINE

---

*This chapter contains figures, tables, and text copied from the author's PhD dissertation and the papers that the author of this chapter coauthored [1–4]. Sections 17.2.3, 17.4.3, 17.5, and 17.6 are new, and the other sections are augmented, reorganized, and improved.

17.1 INTRODUCTION

Code commenting is a standard practice in the software industry. Developers write comments to explain code, document specifications, communicate with other developers, annotate to-do tasks, etc. Software contains a large amount of comments. For example, for the six widely used open source projects written in different programming languages (C/C++ and Java) of different functionalities (operating systems (OS), servers, and desktop applications)—the Linux kernel, FreeBSD, OpenSolaris, MySQL, Firefox, and Eclipse—21.8-29.7% (0.3 million to 1.7 million lines) of their code bases are code comments [5].

Code comments contain a rich amount of information that can be leveraged to improve software maintainability [6] and software reliability [2–4]. Given the overwhelming amount of available code comments, text analytics including natural language processing (NLP) and machine learning techniques is in high demand to automatically analyze free-form and semistructured comments written in a natural language. In recent years, automated comment analysis has become an emerging topic [7]. Many recent studies showed that automated comment analysis can improve software reliability, programming productivity, software maintenance, and software quality in general [1–4, 8, 9]. For example, Tan et al. [2] leverage NLP techniques (e.g., part-of-speech (POS) tagging, chunking, and semantic role labeling) and machine learning techniques (e.g., decision tree classification) to automatically extract specifications from code comments, and check these specifications against source code to detect software defects (also known as bugs) and bad code comments. These techniques are capable of automatically detecting previously unknown defects in widely used large mature software projects.

17.1.1 BENEFITS OF STUDYING AND ANALYZING CODE COMMENTS

Studying and analyzing code comments can help in the following aspects:

17.1.1.1 Programming language

Comments can motivate the design of new programming language extensions or new programming languages. The comments in OpenSolaris shown below specify the field name to which a value is assigned—for example, assigning 15 to the `length` field. Specifying such information in comments is not only inconvenient but also error-prone when the `struct` definition changes. To address these limitations, the GNU Compiler Collection (GCC) *designator* extension was proposed to specify such field names in the code—for example, .length = 15. This example shows that some needs indicated by comments have *already* been addressed by programming language extensions. More programming language extensions could be designed by studying comments.

```
const struct st_drivetype st_drivetypes[] = {
    ...
    ''Unisys ...'', /* .name ... */
    15,             /* .length ... */
    ...
};
```

17.1.1.2 Annotation language
To broaden the impact of annotation languages, we would benefit from studying two questions regarding code comments. First, how often do programmers use comments instead of annotations for concerns that are already covered by existing annotation languages? If there are a significant number of such comments, it may be beneficial to convert comments into existing annotation languages for bug avoidance and automated bug detection. Second, what important concerns that are expressed in comments are not covered by existing annotation languages? The results can motivate new types of annotations.

17.1.1.3 Code editor features
Comments can be used by code editors to increase programmer productivity. For example, to make it easier to find relevant code, developers put cross-reference information in comments, such as /*
See comment in struct sock definition to understand why we need sk_prot_creator
*/.[1] It would be beneficial for a code editor to utilize such comments and display related code and comments in the same window to reduce code navigation time. Such a feature may greatly increase programmer productivity as it has been found that programmers spend on average 35% of their programming time on code navigation [10].

17.1.1.4 Specification mining and software bug detection
Analyzing comments can enable the extraction of specifications, also referred to as programming rules, which can be used (1) for detecting bugs and bad comments, and (2) as documentation to help developers avoid new bugs and better understand code, which improve software reliability and maintainability. For example, the comment in Figure 17.1 shows that the callers of reset_hardware() (functions that call reset_hardware()) must acquire a lock to protect shared data accesses in the function. Since the specification in the comment is not enforced, the code may violate the specification. Figure 17.1 illustrates such a violation from Linux kernel 2.6.11. No lock was held before calling the function reset_hardware() in the function in2000_bus_reset().

---

[1]The comment examples given in this chapter are extracted from real-world software such as the Linux kernel, FreeBSD, OpenSolaris, and Apache Commons Collections.

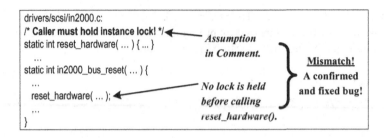

FIGURE 17.1

A Linux kernel bug automatically detected through comment analysis.

If we know that the developer intended to have function `reset_hardware()` called with the lock held, we could check if the code conforms to this specification. This checking process can uncover the bug. For example, we can analyze the comment sentence `/* Caller must hold instance lock! */` and the surrounding code to extract the specification "the lock `instance` must be acquired before entering the function `reset_hardware()`." Then a static or dynamic checker can examine the direct and indirect callers of the function `reset_hardware` to check if the specification is followed. It would discover that on a path in `in2000_bus_reset`, no lock is held before calling function `reset_hardware`, thus detecting this bug. This is a real bug in the Linux kernel that was automatically detected by the first comment analysis and bug detection tool iComment [2].

It is known that detecting software bugs is crucial yet challenging [2, 11]. Many bugs are mismatches between code and specifications. One fundamental challenge in detecting bugs is to know the specifications. Much work has been proposed to infer programming rules from source code [11–14] and execution traces [15, 16]. Many of the techniques assume that most of the code is correct for released mature software, and infer specifications from most of the code. For example, if many callers of the function `reset_hardware()` acquire a lock, a programming rule that all callers of this function must do the same can be inferred. The entire code base is then compared against the inferred programming rule. Such approaches are effective in detecting certain bugs; however, there are situations where they fail. If the code does not provide enough support for the rules, these approaches may fail. For example, `reset_hardware` is called with the lock held only once in Linux kernel 2.6.11. One will not be confident enough to conclude this is a rule. In addition, if `reset_hardware` is never called with the lock held, one cannot infer this rule from the source code. Moreover, some type of information is not available in the source code, such as the unit of a variable. Confusing different units—for example, megabytes with kilobytes—can cause bugs. Therefore, it would be beneficial to extract specifications from code comments, and use the specifications to detect new bugs. The specifications can also be used to help developers understand code and avoid bugs.

To analyze code comments, we need to have a deep understanding of existing comments. Therefore, studying code comments can help us understand what comments are available for us to analyze and what comments are useful for us to analyze. In addition, studying comments can help us listen to developers' needs, as developers often express their needs in comments when these needs are not supported or not fully supported by other types of development tools or mechanisms. Therefore, studying comments can help us understand how to build better tools to support software development [1].

17.1.2 CHALLENGES OF STUDYING AND ANALYZING CODE COMMENTS

It is extremely difficult to automatically analyze code comments [17]. As comments are written in a natural language, they are difficult to analyze and almost impossible to "understand" automatically, even with the most advanced NLP techniques [18], which focus on analyzing well-written news articles from the *Wall Street Journal* or other well-written corpora. Unlike news articles, comments are usually not well written, and many of them are not grammatically correct. In addition, many words in comments have different meanings from their general English meanings. For example, the words "buffer," "memory," and "lock" have program-domain-specific meanings that cannot be found in general dictionaries. In addition, many comments are also mixed with program identifiers (e.g., variable names and function names) that do not exist in any dictionary.

The usefulness of comments differs, and it is difficult to identify useful comments automatically. While some comments are useful for analysis as shown earlier, many are useless. For example, the comment in the code segment "i++; //increment i" is useless for developers' comprehension of the code segment, and is unlikely to help automated bug detection. It is difficult to automatically distinguish useful comments from useless comments.

17.1.3 CODE COMMENT ANALYSIS FOR SPECIFICATION MINING AND BUG DETECTION

Existing comment analysis techniques focus on analyzing comments for specification mining and bug detection [2–4, 8, 9], which is the main content of this chapter. This section uses examples to introduce automated comment analysis for specification mining and bug detection.

As discussed earlier, a large amount of comments that contain a rich amount of information exist in software. Certain information is available only in the code, as developers do not repeat all the information that is in the code in comments. On the other hand, comments contain information that cannot be extracted (easily) from source code—for example, changes that need to be made together (/* WARNING: If you change any of these defines, make sure to change the defines in the X server file (radeon_sarea.h) */), to-do tasks (/* FIXME: We should group addresses here. */), the unit of a variable, the reason why a particular algorithm is not chosen, and the author information for a file.

In addition, comments and code contain redundant information. For example, a comment in OpenSolaris states that the function taskq_ent_free() must be called with a lock held. In the code, the lock is indeed acquired before the function taskq_ent_free() is invoked from the function taskq_create_common(). The comment and the code segment contain redundant information. In this particular case, the redundancy is consistent. In some other cases, as shown in Figure 17.1, the comment and code are inconsistent, which is undesirable.

The redundant information about a program's semantic behavior creates a unique opportunity for checking for comment-code inconsistencies. When software evolves, it is common for comments and source code to be out-of-sync [19]. An inconsistency between the two indicates either the code does not follow the correct comment (*a bug*) or the code is correct but the comment is wrong (*a bad comment*):[2]

---

[2]To be complete, it is also possible that both the comment and the code are wrong and they are inconsistent with each other. In any case, something (the comment, the code, or both) is wrong, and therefore it is beneficial to detect comment-code inconsistencies.

(1) *Bugs—source code does not follow correct comments.* Such cases (see, e.g., Figure 17.1) may be caused because developers do not read the comments because of time constraints and lack of motivation to read comments. Another possible reason is that the assumption in a comment is used in many places throughout the source code and developers violate the assumption in some places—for example, in newly added code.

(2) *Bad comments that can later lead to bugs.* It is common for developers to change code without updating comments accordingly, as developers may not be motivated, may not have time, or simply forget to do so. In addition, as opposed to source code, which goes through software testing before release, comments are typically not tested for correctness. As a result, many comments are out of date and incorrect. Such comments are referred to as bad comments.

Figure 17.2 shows a bad comment in Mozilla that was automatically detected by iComment through automated comment analysis. The outdated comment, "the caller must hold cache lock when calling function ConvertToSID()," does not match with the code that releases the lock before calling ConvertToSID(). Mozilla developers confirmed that this mismatch is a bad comment.

Figure 17.3 presents two bad comments from a series of eight bad comments in Mozilla that has caused many new bugs. As pointed out by the developer in Mozilla's bug report #363114, whether PR_Write and PR_Recv are blocking depends on the blocking property of the sockets on which the two functions are applied. After reading the bad comments, many developers mistakenly conclude that the functions are always blocking and thus have written very wrong code. Bad comments impair software reliability and software development effectiveness; therefore, it is important to detect them and fix them promptly.

The rest of this chapter is organized as follows. Section 17.2 provides a tutorial on basic and advanced techniques for analyzing comments automatically or semiautomatically. Section 17.3 presents the characteristics and content of code comments. Section 17.4 describes the state-of-the-art comment analysis techniques. Section 17.5 summarizes the state-of-the-art techniques for studying and analyzing application programming interface (API) documentation. Section 17.6 concludes with future research directions and challenges.

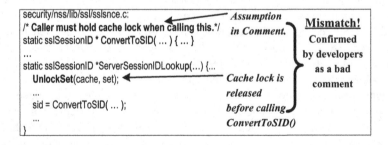

FIGURE 17.2

A Mozilla bad comment automatically detected through comment analysis. It has been confirmed by the Mozilla developers, who replied, "I should have removed that comment about needing to hold the lock when calling ConvertToSID."

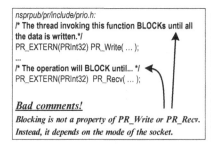

FIGURE 17.3

Two bad comments in Mozilla that have caused many new bugs.

17.2 TEXT ANALYTICS: TECHNIQUES, TOOLS, AND MEASURES

This section briefly describes common NLP and machine learning techniques, popular comment analysis software packages and tools, and standard metrics for measuring the accuracy of comment analysis.

17.2.1 NATURAL LANGUAGE PROCESSING

POS tagging, chunking and clause identification, and semantic role labeling are three mature NLP techniques [18]. Figure 17.4 shows an example of these three techniques on a Linux kernel comment. Section 17.4.2.1 describes how the three NLP techniques help iComment [2] parse comment sentences and build features for learning.

17.2.1.1 Part-of-speech tagging

POS tagging, also known as word tagging, identifies the POS (e.g., nouns and verbs) of each word within a sentence. The basic approach is to train a classification model from a manually labeled data set.

17.2.1.2 Chunking and clause identification

Chunking and clause identification is often referred to as phrase and clause parsing. Chunking is a technique to divide a sentence into syntactically correlated groups of words—for example, noun phrases and verb phrases. Clause identification recognizes clauses which are word sequences with a subject and a predicate. These two techniques form a coherent partial syntax of a sentence.

17.2.1.3 Semantic role labeling

Semantic role labeling identifies the semantic relationship among different phrases within a sentence by assigning to each phrase a semantic argument. Typically, semantic arguments include "agent," "patient," "instrument," and adjuncts such as "locative," "temporal," "manner," and "cause."

17.2.2 MACHINE LEARNING

A wide spectrum of machine learning techniques can be applied to analyze code comments. This section briefly introduces a few that are commonly used for code comment analysis and in software engineering

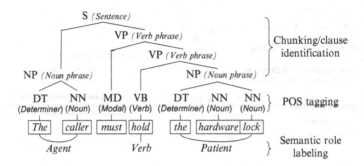

FIGURE 17.4

An example of POS tagging, chunking and clause identification, and semantic role labeling. The leaf nodes of this tree form a sentence.

research. Both supervised learning and unsupervised learning have been employed for code comment analysis. Supervised learning infers models from labeled training data, while unsupervised learning aims to find hidden structure in unlabeled data.

17.2.2.1 Supervised learning

Decision tree learning is a supervised machine learning technique for inducing a decision tree from training data. A *decision tree* (also referred to as a classification tree or a reduction tree) is a predictive model which is a mapping from observations about an item to conclusions about its target value. In the tree structures, leaves represent classifications (also referred to as labels), nonleaf nodes are features, and branches represent conjunctions of features that lead to the classifications [20].

Building a decision tree that is consistent with a given data set is easy. The challenge lies in building good decision trees, which typically means the smallest decision trees. A popular heuristic for building the smallest decision trees is ID3 by Quinlan, which is based on information gain. C4.5 is an improved version of ID3, which is implemented in the software package Weka [21]. Overfitting pruning can be used to prevent the tree from being overfitted just for the training set. This technique makes the tree general for unlabeled data and can tolerate some mistakenly labeled training data.

Other popular supervised learning techniques include support vector machines (SVM) [22], naive Bayes [23], and logistic regression [24]. Section 17.4.2.1 describes how iComment uses decision tree learning to build models to classify comments. iComment uses decision tree learning because it works well and its results are easy to interpret. It is straightforward to replace the decision tree learning with other learning techniques. From our experience, decision tree learning is a good supervised learning algorithm to start with for comment analysis and text analytics in general.

17.2.2.2 Clustering

Unsupervised clustering techniques include *k*-means clustering and mixture models. The former groups data into clusters on the basis of a distance metric. Mixture models use the distribution to cluster data.

For example, a generative probabilistic mixture model performs cross-collection clustering and within-collection clustering to help discover the main themes of documents [25]. Comments from different software may have common themes—for example, about concurrency issues. Within a common theme, comments in different software may have their own subthemes—for example, about interrupt-related concurrency issues in OS code. The cross-collection clustering approach [25] is appropriate for capturing such themes and subthemes. Section 17.3.2 presents a comment topic miner that uses mixture models to discover common topics in comments.

17.2.3 ANALYSIS TOOLS

Common comment analysis and text analytics tools include WordNet [26], Weka [21], Stanford Parser [27], OpenNLP [28], SPSS [29], and SAS Text Miner [30]. Lists of other available NLP, machine learning, and data mining tools can be found from [7, 31–34]. For example, iComment [2] uses a standard off-the-shelf decision tree learning algorithm called C4.5 [35], implemented in the software package Weka [21]. iComment also uses the Illinois Semantic Role labeler [36].

17.2.4 EVALUATION MEASURES

Many comment analysis techniques convert comments into specifications [2–4] by classifying comments into predefined categories first. To measure the accuracy of comment analysis, three standard metrics are *accuracy*, *F score*, and *kappa*. These metrics are widely used in text analytics, including the techniques described in Sections 17.4 and 17.5.

Accuracy measures the overall percentage of classification accuracy, which is defined as follows:

$$\text{Accuracy} = \frac{\text{total number of correctly classified comments}}{\text{total number of comments given for classification.}}$$

F score (also known as F1 score) is the harmonic mean of *precision* and *recall*. Precision is defined as $P = \frac{T_+}{T_+ + F_+}$, recall is defined as $R = \frac{T_+}{T_+ + F_-}$, and *F* score is defined as (F1 $= \frac{2PR}{P+R}$), where T_+, T_-, F_+, and F_- are true positives, true negatives, false positives, and false negatives, respectively.

Kappa (κ) is a statistical measure of interrater reliability. It measures the agreement between two raters, each of which classifies N items into C mutually exclusive categories. iComment uses it to measure the agreement between a rater produced by iComment and the oracle rater that labels all comments correctly. Kappa is defined as $\kappa = \frac{\text{pr}(a) - \text{pr}(e)}{1 - \text{pr}(e)}$, where $\text{pr}(a)$ is the percentage of correctly labeled comments, and $\text{pr}(e)$ is the percentage of correctly labeled comments resulting from pure chance.

17.3 STUDIES OF CODE COMMENTS

Many comment studies have been conducted since the 1980s [37]. While this section gives a brief introduction to these studies, it focuses on the recent work that studies the content and semantics of code comments to answer the following questions. What is in code comments? What are the common topics of comments? What comments are useful for bug finding, program comprehension, and other purposes?

Comment studies in the 1980s and 1990s examined the usefulness of comments for program comprehension [37] and ratio metrics between code and comments [38], under the assumption that software quality is better if code is more commented. A recent paper [39] studied the quality of comments qualitatively. Other work studied the evolution of comments in size and number during the software life cycle [19] and metrics about the coevolution of code and comments [40]. Marin [41] studied psychological factors that may push programmers to comment—for example, whether already commented code is an incentive for programmers to comment more on their own modifications to the code.

A few papers [1, 2, 17, 42] studied the content of code comments. Maalej and Robillard [43] designed a taxonomy for API documentation, and Monperrus et al. [44] focused on studying the directives of API documentation.

Next we discuss a few comment studies in detail, which should help us understand the common topics of comments, and help us identify comments that are useful for bug finding, program comprehension, etc.

17.3.1 CONTENT OF CODE COMMENTS

Padioleau et al. [1] designed a taxonomy for the content of code comments, and classified 2100 comments (one comment is defined as a block of comments) from six C and Java projects. The study designed categories for comments in seven dimensions based on four "W" questions. The first dimension is the "Content" of the comments based on the "What" is in a comment question, which is the focus of the study. The six categories for this dimension are "Type," "Interface," "Code Relationship," "PastFuture," "Meta," and "Explanation." They found that comments that belong to the first four categories (52.6%) can potentially be leveraged (e.g., by a bug detection tool, or by an integrated development environment (IDE)) to be useful for developers. Other findings include the following: (1) many comments describe code relationships, code evolutions, or the usage and meaning of integers and integer macros, (2) a significant number of comments could be expressed by existing annotation languages, and (3) many comments express synchronization-related concerns but are not well supported by annotation languages.

On the basis of the "Who" question, there are two dimensions: (1) the "Beneficiary" of the comments (who can benefit from a comment), and (2) the "Author" of the comments (who is the author of a comment). On the basis of the "Where" question, there are two dimensions: "Code entity" (where in a file is a comment located, e.g., the header or a function), and (2) "Subsystem" (in which subsystem is a comment, e.g., a file system). On the basis of the "When" question, the two dimensions are "Time" and "Evolution."

Ying et al. [17] and Storey et al. [42] studied the content and use of "TODO" comments, which are an important type of comment.

17.3.2 COMMON TOPICS OF CODE COMMENTS

Identifying common topics of code comments can help one understand comments and find useful comments to analyze. To find common topics of program comments, Tan et al. [2] used two miners, *common word miner* and *common cluster miner*. These two miners use NLP techniques, clustering techniques, and simple statistics to automatically discover common topics of program comments. Both miners first use POS tags to filter out words such as "we," "your," and "have" since they can prevent meaningful topic keywords from being found. To focus on specification-containing comments, the miners consider only comment sentences that contain imperative words such as "should," "must," "need," "ought to," "have to," "remember," "make sure," and "be sure" and their variants.

After the word-based filtering process, the common word miner uses simple word counting—that is, counting the number of comments in which a word appears, to find common nouns and verbs, which the user can use to determine common topics.

The common cluster miner is more sophisticated. Specifically, since many words are related and are about the same topic, the common cluster miner clusters related words together instead of using a simple word count. For example, words such as "lock," "acquire," and "release" are related and are all about the same topic. For this purpose, the common cluster miner uses mixture model clustering [45], which builds a generative probabilistic mixture model to perform clustering.

The results show that both lock and call rank high on the output of the common keyword miner and the common cluster miner on comments from four programs (the Linux kernel, Mozilla, Wine, and Apache). For example, "lock" is the highest ranked word in the kernel module of the Linux kernel and is ranked second in the memory management module of the Linux kernel. According to the common cluster miner, Mozilla and the kernel module of the Linux kernel contain up to 5 (out of 10) clusters having "lock" in their topic keywords.

Similarly, keywords related to function calls also appear in a significant portion of comments. "Call" is the highest ranked word in Mozilla and among the top 7 for all three Linux kernel modules. The common cluster miner shows that Mozilla and the kernel module of the Linux kernel have at least one "call" cluster.

In addition to locks and call relationships, many other topics are common and can potentially be analyzed for inconsistency detection. While some topics are general, such as memory allocation, locks and call relationships, programs have their specific common topics. For example, "interrupt" is a common topic of comments from the kernel module of the Linux kernel, whereas "error," "return," and "check" are common topics in Mozilla. In addition, a substantial percentage of comments in the kernel module contain the keyword "thread," "task," or "signal," whereas many comments in the memory management module contain the keyword "page," "cache," or "memory."

17.4 AUTOMATED CODE COMMENT ANALYSIS FOR SPECIFICATION MINING AND BUG DETECTION

This section presents the state-of-the-art techniques for automated comment analysis, which improves software quality by inferring specifications and detecting software bugs and bad comments. These state-of-the-art techniques analyze comments of various topics (locks, call relationships, interrupts, null pointers, and exceptions) in software written in different programming languages (Java and C/C++) by using different program analysis techniques (dynamic testing and static analysis) and different comment analysis techniques (POS tagging, chunking, semantic role labeling, heuristics, clustering, and decision tree learning). Specifically, this section describes the following three pieces of work in detail:

(1) iComment: Static code analysis combined with advanced analysis of C/C++ comments regarding locks and call relationships [2]. iComment is the first work that analyzes comments written in natural language to extract specifications automatically for bug detection.

(2) aComment: Static code analysis combined with analysis of C/C++ comments regarding interrupts and locks [3].

(3) @tComment: Dynamic testing combined with analysis of Javadoc comments regarding null pointers and exceptions [4].

The work mentioned above leverages different comment analysis techniques to fit the different characteristics and challenges of the types of comments. For example, @tComment uses simple keyword-based searches to extract null pointer and exception related Javadoc comments because these Javadoc comments are well formed. In contrast, keyword-based searches are inaccurate for iComment owing to the variability of lock- and call-related comments in C/C++ projects. Instead, iComment uses machine learning and NLP techniques to address the variability issue. However, the approach used in iComment is insufficient for analyzing interrupt-related comments owing to the small percentage of such comments. Therefore, aComment uses templates and heuristics with domain-specific knowledge to analyze interrupt-related comments. In the future, it may be feasible to leverage advanced learning techniques [46], such as resampling techniques, to increase the percentage of interrupt-related comments in the training set to learn more accurate models.

These techniques have extracted many programming rules from comments, and have used these programming rules to detect software bugs, including previously unknown bugs. While these techniques focus on leveraging the extracted rules to detect bugs, the rules can be used for many other purposes, such as helping developers understand code and avoid bugs.

To automatically extract rules from comments and use these rules to detect comment-code inconsistencies, we need to address three main challenges: (1) What should we extract from comments? (2) How should we extract the information? (3) How should we check for inconsistencies between comments and code? We will focus on the first two challenges since they are related to comment analysis, while the third challenge is related to program analysis.

17.4.1 WHAT SHOULD WE EXTRACT?

Addressing this challenge requires considering two factors. The first is what type of information is useful for us to extract from comments. The second consideration is what information can be checked against source code.

For the first factor, typically there are two types of comments, one explains code segments, and the other specifies important programming rules. For example, the Linux kernel comment "Find out where the IO space is" belongs to the first type, whereas the comment "Caller must hold bond lock for write" belongs to the second type.

It is less useful to check the first type of comments because they are usually consistent with the source code since they are together. Even in the case of inconsistencies, they are less likely to mislead programmers to introduce bugs later. The second type is more important—it specifies certain rules that programmers need to follow. For example, the second comment example given above requires all callers of the function to hold a lock before calling it. If such a comment is obsolete or incorrect, it can mislead programmers to introduce bugs. Therefore, the comment analysis that we discuss in this chapter

Table 17.1 Supported Rule Templates of iComment	
ID	**Rule template**
1	$\langle R \rangle$ must be claimed before entering $\langle F \rangle$
2	$\langle R \rangle$ must NOT be claimed before entering $\langle F \rangle$
3	$\langle R \rangle$ must be claimed in $\langle F \rangle$
4	$\langle R \rangle$ must NOT be claimed in $\langle F \rangle$
5	$\langle F_A \rangle$ must be called from $\langle F_B \rangle$
6	$\langle F_A \rangle$ must NOT be called from $\langle F_B \rangle$

R is a resource—for example, a lock, a buffer, or a file descriptor— that a system can claim and release. F can be one function or a group of functions.

focuses on the second type—*rule-containing comments*, comments that specify certain programming rules.

The second consideration in determining what to extract depends on what information can be checked against source code. Although both static and dynamic analysis for detecting software bugs have made impressive advances in recent years [11, 47], it is not that any arbitrary rule can be checked automatically. Therefore, we focus on extracting rules that can be checked against source code. Examples of such rules include "hold lock L before calling function A, " "acquire lock L in function A," "allocate memory for buffer B before entering function A," and "call function B before calling function A." We refer to each type as a *rule template*, and refer to the lock L, the function A, etc., as *rule parameters* for a rule template.

In addition to the two factors mentioned above, we consider what topics are common in comments, and what topics have not been well addressed by previous work. For example, previous work [11, 13] only checked general rules such as "must release the lock after acquiring a lock" but not software-specific rules such as "releasing lock L before entering function A."

On the basis of these factors, iComment supports six types of rules related to two important topics—locks and call relationships—as listed in Table 17.1.

aComment supports rules that annotate whether interrupts should be disabled or enabled on entry or exit of a function, which are shown in Table 17.2. The OS-specific interrupt context makes OS concurrency extremely complex and it has challenged the OS community for decades [48]. Analyzing interrupt-related comments can address some of the challenges [3].

The annotations of the rules are in the following format: `@IRQ(Precondition, Postcondition)`, where `Precondition` and `Postcondition` can have one of four values—that is, 0, 1, X, and P. The meanings of each of the four values are shown in Table 17.3. Value P indicates that a function—for example, `local_irq_restore`—restores the saved interrupt state. We use `(X, P)` to indicate functions that restore a saved interrupt state, and all other six annotations that contain a value P are not accepted. Therefore, although there are 16 possible annotations, only 10 of them are accepted by aComment, as shown in Table 17.2, and the other six should not appear in aComment.

@tComment infers from Javadoc comments null-related rules about method parameters. Java has standardized the writing of API specifications as Javadoc comments with tags such as `@param` to describe method parameters and `@throws` to describe what exceptions a method could throw.

Table 17.2 Valid Annotations Supported by aComment	
@IRQ **(Pre, Post)**	**Meaning**
@IRQ (0, 0)	Interrupts are disabled on entry and remain disabled on exit
@IRQ (0, 1)	Interrupts are disabled on entry but are enabled on exit
@IRQ (1, 0)	Interrupts are enabled on entry but are disabled on exit
@IRQ (1, 1)	Interrupts are enabled on entry and remain enabled on exit
@IRQ (X, X)	Either @IRQ (0, 0) or @IRQ (1, 1)
@IRQ (X, 0)	Don't care on entry and interrupts are disabled on exit
@IRQ (X, 1)	Don't care on entry and interrupts are enabled on exit
@IRQ (0, X)	Interrupts are disabled on entry and don't care on exit
@IRQ (1, X)	Interrupts are enabled on entry and don't care on exit
@IRQ (X, P)	Don't care on entry and interrupts are restored to the saved state on exit

"Pre" stands for "preconditions" and "Post" denotes "postconditions." The meanings of 0, 1, X, and P are shown in Table 17.3.

Table 17.3 The Meaning of the Four Annotation Values for aComment	
Value	**Meaning**
0	Interrupts are disabled
1	Interrupts are enabled
X	Don't care: interrupts are either disabled or enabled
P	Interrupts are restored to the saved interrupt state

API developers write Javadoc comments to describe their classes and methods. API users often read these comments to understand the code—for example, reading a Javadoc comment for a method instead of reading the body of the method.

For a parameter of a nonprimitive type, @tComment infers one of the four kinds of rules: *Null Normal, Null Any Exception, Null Specific Exception*, or *Null Unknown*, whose meanings are explained in Table 17.4.

Table 17.4 also shows four examples of comment tags and their corresponding inferred rules. For example, @tComment infers from the second tag, "@param collection the collection to add to, must not be null," that if the method parameter collection is null, then the method is expected to throw some exception, represented as *collection == null => exception*. Note that the tag could have another interpretation, describing a precondition such that passing null for the parameter collection allows the method to do anything, not necessarily throw an exception. @tComment uses the first interpretation because it focus on *library projects*, where the methods cannot trust their callers. This interpretation may differ for applications with more of a design-by-contract mentality where callers are more trusted.

Table 17.4 Supported Rule Templates of @tComment

Rules	Meaning	Comment Example	Notation
Null Normal	If the parameter is null, the method should execute normally, i.e., throw no exception.	`@param predicate the predicate` `to use, may be null`	predicate==null => normal
Null Any Exception	If the parameter is null, the method should throw *some* exception.	`@param collection the collection` `to add to, must not be null`	collection==null => exception
Null Specific Exception	If the parameter is null, the method should throw a *specific* type of exception.	`@throws IllegalArgumentException` `if the id is null`	id==null => IllegalArgu- mentException
Null Unknown	We do not know the expected behavior of the method when the parameter is null.	`@param array the array over` `which to iterate`	array==null => unknown

17.4.2 HOW SHOULD WE EXTRACT INFORMATION?

To extract rules from comments, we first identify comments that potentially contain rules, and then extract the relevant parameters to generate the concrete rules and annotations described in Section 17.4.1. iComment, aComment, and @tComment use different comment classification and rule generation techniques to best fit the need of the different types of rules and comments. This section explains these techniques in detail.

These techniques build models to identify comments that potentially contain rules. iComment builds models through supervised learning [18] automatically, while aComment and @tComment build models manually by leveraging prior experience and expertise. As explained in Section 17.2.2, supervised learning trains a model on a set of manually labeled documents from representative document collections. The model can then analyze *other* documents in the same collection or in other collections [18].

17.4.2.1 iComment's code comment analysis

Because it is virtually impossible to understand any arbitrary comment, iComment provides a general framework to analyze comments topic by topic (e.g., locks is a topic), and demonstrates its effectiveness by automatically analyzing comments of two topics (locks and call relationships) to detect bugs and bad comments in large software. Since using NLP techniques alone cannot solve the comment analysis problem, to address the fundamental challenges of comment analysis, iComment combines techniques from several areas, including NLP, machine learning, statistics, and program analysis techniques.

The rule extraction process is divided into two stages: (1) building rule generators, and (2) running rule generators to produce rules. The former builds the rule generation model, and the latter uses the model to classify comments and extract rules. For each topic, a separate rule generator is built.

Rule generators can be built *in-house* (a one-time cost) from a set of comments from representative software. After a user has obtained iComment's rule generators, he or she can use them to analyze comments of similar topics from his or her software without building rule generators. The rationale is that rule generators built from representative comments should work reasonably well for similar comments.

If a user desires higher analysis accuracy or wants to analyze an unsupported topic, he or she can use iComment's generator building components to train a rule generator specifically for his or her software on the selected topic.

Stage (1). *Building rule generators* consists of three steps: (1) comment extraction, which extracts all topic-related, rule-containing comments, called *TR-comments*, for a given topic keyword such as "lock" using NLP and statistics techniques; (2) comment sampling, which provides a set of randomly selected TR-comments for manual labeling; (3) rule training, which uses the manually labeled sample set to build the rule generator, which can then be used to analyze unlabeled comments from the same or different software.

To extract comments, iComment extracts all comments from a program and then breaks the comments into sentences. Next, it uses word splitters [49] to split each comment into words. Afterward, it uses POS tagging, chunking and clause identification, and semantic role labeling techniques [49–52] to tell whether each word in a sentence is a verb, a noun, etc., whether a clause is a main clause or a subclause, and what is the subject, the object, etc.

Feature selection is important for decision tree learning algorithms to achieve high accuracy. Features are used in a decision tree classifier to determine how to traverse the decision tree for a given input. The feature pool used in iComment's rule trainer can be divided into two categories. The first feature category is typical text classification features that are widely used in text classification studies [53]. The second feature category contains features that are unique to comment analysis but are general to different comment topics, different rule templates, and different software.

Some important features include the following: (1) *comment scope*—whether a comment is written outside a function (global scope) or written within the body of a function (local scope); (2) *conditional rule*—whether a comment contains any prepositions or conditional words (e.g., "if" and "whether"); (3) *modal word class*—whether a comment contains a word in a modal word class (e.g, "must," "should," "can," and "might"); and (4) *application scope*—whether a comment expresses a precondition, a postcondition, or an in-function-condition of a method.

iComment uses a standard off-the-shelf decision tree learning algorithm called C4.5 [35] implemented in the software package Weka [21]. The algorithm performs pruning to prevent the tree from being overfitted for the training set. Figure 17.5 shows the top of the decision tree model trained from a small set of manually labeled lock-related Linux kernel comments.

Stage (2). *Running rule generators to produce rules* is straightforward. Depending on the topic selected by the user, iComment uses the corresponding decision tree model to analyze all TR-comments from the target software by first mapping them to *rule templates*, and then uses semantic role labeling and program analysis to fill in the *rule parameters*. Finally, the rule generator produces all the rules whose confidence, produced by the decision tree model, is higher than certain a threshold.

iComment has inferred 1832 rules with high accuracy and has used the rules to detect 60 comment-code inconsistencies (33 new bugs and 27 bad comments) in the Linux kernel, Mozilla, Wine, and Apache. For rule extraction, iComment achieved a classification accuracy over 90% for all four projects. The F1 score is 0.89 or higher, except for Apache owing to its small size (0.67). Kappa is 0.85-1.

From the comment in Figure 17.1, iComment extracted the rule "*<The lock instance>* must be claimed before entering *<reset_hardware>*" (recall the rule templates in Table 17.1). As another

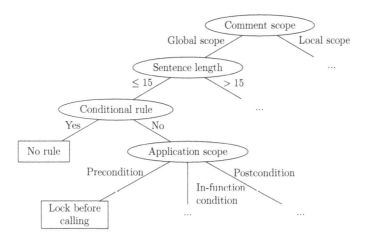

FIGURE 17.5

The top of the decision tree model built automatically by iComment from the Linux kernel's lock-related comments.

example, iComment extracted the rule "*<A lock>* must be claimed before entering *<ata_dev_select>*" from the Linux kernel comment "LOCKING: caller" right above the definition of the function ata_dev_select, and the rule "*<A lock>* must be claimed in *<pci_seq_start>*" from the Linux kernel comment "surely we need some locking for traversing the list" inside the function pci_seq_start.

17.4.2.2 aComment's code comment analysis

It is feasible to extract interrupt-related preconditions and postconditions from both source code and comments written in a natural language. This section uses examples to explain how aComment extracts postconditions and preconditions from comments and code. For *postconditions*, if one knows that local_irq_disable disables interrupts, one can infer that all functions that call local_irq_disable but not any interrupt-enabling function also disable interrupts.

aComment infers *preconditions* from both comments and code assertions. First, aComment infers preconditions from comments. For example, the comment in Figure 17.6a states that interrupts must be disabled before calling tick_init_highres. By combing keyword search and domain-specific knowledge, aComment converts this comment into the annotation /* @IRQ (0, X) */, where 0 indicates that interrupts must be disabled before calling the function, and X indicates that interrupts can be either disabled or enabled on exit of this function (Figure 17.6b). The postcondition, X, will be refined during the annotation propagation process.

Second, programmers often write code assertions such as BUG_ON(!irqs_disabled()) to print an error message if interrupts are not disabled, indicating that they assume that interrupts must already be disabled. The function run_posix_cpu_timers, for instance, starts with BUG_ON(!irqs_disabled()), indicating that this function must be called with interrupts disabled. Although such dynamic assertions can help detect bugs, they are limited because (1) they require bugs to manifest themselves in order for them to be detected, which is difficult for OS concurrency bugs, *linux/kernel/time/tick-oneshot.c:*

```
/* ... Called with interrupts disabled. */
int tick_init_highres(void) { ... }
```

(a) The original version

```
/* ... Called with interrupts disabled.  */
int /*@IRQ(0, X)*/ tick_init_highres(void) { ... }
```

(b) The annotated version

FIGURE 17.6

Converting a comment in the Linux kernel to an annotation.

and (2) these assertions incur high run-time overhead, and therefore are often disabled for production runs for better performance. aComment converts such assertions into annotations and checks these annotations statically. Such a static approach can complement dynamic assertions to detect more bugs with no run-time overhead. For example, the annotation /* @IRQ (0, X) */ was added to the function run_posix_cpu_timers, which enables aComment to detect a real bug in the Linux kernel.

aComment converts programmers' intentions inferred from the comments and code they write into formal annotations and uses these annotations to detect interrupt-related OS concurrency bugs. Two key techniques enable the generation of annotations for all functions in a code base for effective bug detection: *annotation extraction from both comments and code* and *annotation propagation*. Annotations inferred from comments and code complement each other. By combining them, aComment achieves better coverage and accuracy in annotation extraction, which help aComment detect more bugs more accurately. For effective bug detection, aComment also automatically propagates annotations from callee functions to caller functions when necessary [3].

In total, aComment generates 96,821 interrupt-related annotations from the Linux kernel, which are automatically propagated from a total of 245 *seed* annotations. These seed annotations are inferred directly from comments and code assertions with little manual effort (226 of which are from comments, and 24 of which are from code assertions). Only five of the seed annotations can be extracted from both comments and code assertions, meaning that the majority (221 from comments and 19 from code assertions) can be extracted from only one source. The result indicates that it is beneficial to infer annotations from both sources. aComment has used these annotations to detect nine real bugs (seven of which were previously unknown), which are more than one could have detected by using annotations extracted from code alone or using annotations extracted from comments alone.

17.4.2.3 @tComment's code comment analysis

Null-related and exception-related Javadoc comments are more structured, with fewer paraphrases and variants than the C/C++ comments analyzed by iComment and aComment. Therefore, @tComment uses three simple heuristics to extract null-related and exception-related constraints from the free-form Javadoc text. The authors of @tComment designed these heuristics on the basis of their experience and knowledge with Javadoc comments related to null pointers and exceptions. While the heuristics are not perfect, they are highly accurate in practice. First, if negation words, such as "not" and "never," are found *up to three words* before or after the word "null"—for example, "the collection to add to, must not be null" has "not" two words from "null"—@tComment infers the *Null Any Exception* rule. If no negation words are found up to three words from the word "null"—for example, the first tag in Table 17.4—@tComment infers the *Null Normal* rule.

Second, for @throws tags—for example, "@throws IllegalArgumentException if the id is null"—the Javadoc doclet parses the tag and outputs the specific exception (IllegalArgument Exception) and the free-form text ("if the id is null"). If the text contains the keyword "null," @tComment simply splits the text into words and searches for each word in the list of all method parameter names generated by the Javadoc doclet. If a valid parameter name is found—for example, id—@tComment infers the rule *id == null => IllegalArgumentException*.

Third, if the keyword "or" is in the @throws comment text—for example, "@throws NullPointerException if the collection or array is null," @tComment generates multiple rules—for example, *collection == null => NullPointerException* and *array == null => NullPointerException*. If both *Null Any Exception* and *Null Specific Exception* rules are inferred for the same method parameter, @tComment keeps only the *Null Specific Exception* rule.

@tComment assigns *Null Unknown* to a method parameter if no other rules are inferred for that method parameter by the heuristics described above. In total, 2713 @param and @throws tags contain "null" in seven evaluated projects. @tComment inferred 2479 *Null Normal, Null Any Exception*, and *Null Specific Exception* rules from these comments. It does not count *Null Unknown* rules, because one cannot test against the *Null Unknown* rules. Since the simple heuristics achieve a high accuracy of 97–100%, no advanced NLP techniques are necessary. @tComment detected 29 inconsistencies between Javadoc comments and method bodies. The authors of @tComment reported 16 of these inconsistencies to the developers, and five have already been confirmed and fixed by the developers, while the rest await confirmation by the developers.

17.4.3 ADDITIONAL READING

Collections of work related to comment analysis and software text analytics can be found from [7, 33].

Comments have been analyzed to improve program comprehension. For example, much work has been proposed to analyze comments and code identifiers (e.g., method names and class names) to extract synonyms and semantically related words [54–59]. On the other hand, researchers have proposed techniques to generate comments automatically [60–63].

17.5 STUDIES AND ANALYSIS OF API DOCUMENTATION

While this chapter has focused on studies and analyses of free-form and semistructured comments embedded in source code, we briefly discuss work that studies and analyzes API documents, some of which are generated from comments (e.g., Javadoc comments) that are embedded in source code.

17.5.1 STUDIES OF API DOCUMENTATION

Maalej and Robillard [43] examined 5574 Javadoc documentation units (a documentation unit is documentation that is associated with an API element, e.g., a class) and designed a taxonomy of API documentation. The knowledge types they defined are Functionality and Behavior, Concepts, Directives, Purpose and Rationale, Quality Attributes and Internal Aspects, Control-Flow, Structure, Patterns, Code Examples, Environment, References, and Noninformation.

Monperrus et al. [44] conducted an empirical study of the directives of API documentation. Since directives are the contracts (e.g., preconditions and postconditions) of API functions, they are particularly useful for automated bug finding and avoidance. Monperrus et al. [44] designed six categories to classify directives of API documentation (contracts of API methods), which are Method Call Directive, Subclassing Directive, State, Alternative, Synchronization, and Miscellaneous. The first three categories contain subcategories. The Method Call Directive is particularly relevant for extracting specifications for automated bug detection. The subcategories of the Method Call Directive are Not Null, Return Value, Method Visibility, Exception Raising, Null Allowed, String Format, Number Range, Method Parameter Type, Method Parameter, Correlation, Post-Call, and Miscellaneous. It is quite conceivable that these directives can be leveraged by a tool to automatically detect software defects.

17.5.2 ANALYSIS OF API DOCUMENTATION

Zhong et al. [8, 9] analyzed API documentation to generate resource-related specifications. The management of resources—for example, memory, locks, sockets, file descriptors, and files—is an important task for software. Typically, before using a resource, one needs to conduct preparatory tasks—for example, creating a file, connecting to a socket, and allocating memory. After finishing using a resource, one needs to perform cleaning up tasks—for example, closing the file, closing the socket, and freeing the memory. The work extracts state machines that represent how resources should be managed. Take the following API documentation describing "`javax.resource.cci.Connection`" [8] as an example:

"`createInteraction()`: '*Creates an interaction associated with this connection.*'

`getMetaData()`:'*Gets the information on the underlying EIS instance represented through an active connection.*'

`close()`: '*Initiates close of the connection handle at the application level.*'" [8].

The work infers a state machine that requires `createInteration()` to be called before `getMetaData()`, and `close()` to be called after `getMetaData()`. The approach leverages NLP techniques (e.g., named entity recognition and the hidden Markov model) to infer action-resource pairs for API methods, and cluster methods according to the resources that they manipulate. Then it uses the action words to map methods to the predefined state machine template to generate concrete state machines for the methods.

Zhong et al. manually tagged actions and resources for 687 methods, which were used to train the tool so that the tool could tag new unlabeled actions and resources. The proposed approach generated 3981 resource specifications from five Java projects, which enabled the detection of 383 violations of the specifications, 100 of which were suspected bugs, while the rest were false positives. Among the 100 suspected bugs, 35 have been confirmed as true bugs (30 known and five previously unknown), while the rest await confirmation from the developers. The $F1$ score of the specification extraction is 74.8–85.8%, the precision is 70.7–86.5%, and the recall is 74.0–86.2%.

Pandita et al. [64] analyzed API documentation to generate method-level contracts with 92% precision and 93% recall. The approach leverages a few manually designed shallow parsing semantic templates to identify a variety of sentence structures of similar meaning. POS tagging and chunking were used to parse API documentation sentences for matching with the templates. In addition, noun boosting was used to distinguish programming keywords (e.g., `true`, `null`) from English words.

17.6 FUTURE DIRECTIONS AND CHALLENGES

Automated code comment analysis is a relatively young topic. Existing techniques have analyzed a small fraction of code comments to demonstrate the big potential of comment analysis. There are great opportunities for new work from both academia and industry.

Analyzing new topics and new groups of comments

iComment, aComment, and @tComment analyzed comments of a few topics—locks, call relationships, interrupts, null pointers, and exceptions. Code comments of other topics can be analyzed automatically, some of which are shown in Section 17.3.2. For example, a common topic in C/C++ code is memory allocation/deallocation such as "allocating a certain buffer before calling some function." Other common topics include error returns and multithreading.

Most of the existing code comment analysis techniques analyze each comment sentence separately. Quite often, several comment sentences describe a coherent set of rules. It would be promising to analyze many comment sentences together or many blocks of comments together to extract more rules and more complex rules. @tComment analyzed blocks of Javadoc comments, and Zhong et al. [8] analyzed blocks of API documentation.

Automatically identifying useful comments for analysis

While a large number of comments are useful to analyze for purposes such as bug detection and improving code navigation, the rest do not contain useful information for analysis. It is an open question to automatically identify useful comments for analysis. Existing work [2–4] used keyword matching, clustering, supervised learning, heuristics, and manual inspection to identify useful comments. In the future, it would be interesting to apply data mining techniques (e.g., frequent itemset mining) and advanced NLP techniques (e.g., textual entailment) to automatically discover useful comments.

Automatically identifying useless comments for removal

One reason that developers ignore (some) comments is the mixed quality of comments: while some comments are useful, (e.g., code contracts), some are useless (e.g., the comment in `i++; //increment i by 1`). It would be beneficial to automatically identify useless comments, and remove them from code bases, so that it is easier for developers to find useful comments, and developers are then more likely to read comments for program comprehension, bug avoidance, etc.

Improving comment analysis accuracy, explaining classification results, designing comment languages, and more

It would be beneficial to further improve the comment analysis accuracy so that these comment analysis techniques are more likely to be adopted by industry. Results from machine learning techniques are often hard to interpret—for example, why a comment sentence is classified into a certain category. Better interpretation may help researchers and practitioners understand and adopt the results. In addition, we can design easy-to-learn and flexible comment languages that can be analyzed more easily, which can also encourage developers to write better comments.

In addition, it would be beneficial to automatically analyze other software documents written in a natural language [7, 33, 65, 66], such as manuals, bug reports, mailing lists, processor specifications, user interface text, mobile application descriptions, figures, and tables, to extract information for other purposes, including automatically tuning system performance, troubleshooting software configurations, and enhancing software security.

REFERENCES

[1] Padioleau Y, Tan L, Zhou Y. Listening to programmers—taxonomies and characteristics of comments in operating system code. In: Proceedings of the international conference on software engineering; 2009. p. 331–41.

[2] Tan L, Yuan D, Krishna G, Zhou Y. /* iComment: Bugs or bad comments? */. In: Proceedings of the symposium on operating systems principles; 2007. p. 145–58.

[3] Tan L, Zhou Y, Padioleau Y. aComment: mining annotations from comments and code to detect interrupt-related concurrency bugs. In: Proceedings of the international conference on software engineering; 2011. p. 11–20.

[4] Tan SH, Marinov D, Tan L, Leavens GT. @tComment: testing Javadoc comments to detect comment-code inconsistencies. In: Proceedings of the international conference on software testing, verification and validation; 2012. p. 260–9.

[5] Tan L. Leveraging code comments to improve software reliability. Ph.D. thesis, University of Illinois at Urbana-Champaign, 2009.

[6] Aggarwal K, Singh Y, Chhabra J. An integrated measure of software maintainability. In: Proceedings of the annual reliability and maintainability symposium; 2002. p. 235–41.

[7] Tan L, Xie T. Text analytics for software engineering. https://sites.google.com/site/text4se/home/biblio; 2014.

[8] Zhong H, Zhang L, Xie T, Mei H. Inferring resource specifications from natural language API documentation. In: Proceedings of the international conference on automated software engineering; 2009. p. 307–18.

[9] Zhong H, Zhang L, Xie T, Mei H. Inferring specifications for resources from natural language API documentation. Automat Software Eng J 2011;18(3-4):227–61.

[10] Ko AJ, Aung H, Myers BA. Eliciting design requirements for maintenance-oriented IDEs: A detailed study of corrective and perfective maintenance tasks. In: Proceedings of the international conference on software engineering; 2005. p. 126–35.

[11] Engler DR, Chen DY, Hallem S, Chou A, Chelf B. Bugs as deviant behavior: a general approach to inferring errors in systems code. In: Proceedings of the symposium on operating systems principles; 2001. p. 57–72.

[12] Kremenek T, Twohey P, Back G, Ng AY, Engler DR. From uncertainty to belief: inferring the specification within. In: Proceedings of the USENIX symposium on operating system design and implementation; 2006. p. 161–76.

[13] Li Z, Zhou Y. PR-Miner: automatically extracting implicit programming rules and detecting violations in large software code. In: Proceedings of the symposium on the foundations of software engineering; 2005. p. 306–15.

[14] Tan L, Zhang X, Ma X, Xiong W, Zhou Y. AutoISES: automatically inferring security specifications and detecting violations. In: Proceedings of the USENIX security symposium; 2008. p. 379–94.

[15] Ernst MD, Czeisler A, Griswold WG, Notkin D. Quickly detecting relevant program invariants. In: Proceedings of the international conference on software engineering; 2000. p. 449–58.

[16] Hangal S, Lam MS. Tracking down software bugs using automatic anomaly detection. In: Proceedings of the international conference on software engineering; 2002. p. 291–301.

[17] Ying ATT, Wright JL, Abrams S. Source code that talks: an exploration of eclipse task comments and their implication to repository mining. In: International workshop on mining software repositories; 2005. p. 1–5.

[18] Manning CD, Schütze H. Foundations of statistical natural language processing. Cambridge, MA: MIT Press; 2001.

[19] Jiang ZM, Hassan AE. Examining the evolution of code comments in PostgreSQL. In: International workshop on mining software repositories; 2006. p. 179–80. ISBN 1-59593-397-2.

[20] Mitchell T. Machine learning. McGraw Hill; 1997. ISBN 0070428077.

[21] Witten IH, Frank E. Data mining: practical machine learning tools and techniques. 2nd ed. Morgan Kaufmann; 2005.

[22] Chang CC, Lin CJ. LIBSVM: a library for support vector machines. ACM Trans Intell Syst Technol 2011;2:27:1-27. Software available at http://www.csie.ntu.edu.tw/cjlin/libsvm.

[23] John GH, Langley P. Estimating continuous distributions in Bayesian classifiers. In: Proceedings of the conference on uncertainty in artificial intelligence; 1995. p. 338–45.

[24] Landwehr N, Hall M, Frank E. Logistic model trees 2005;95(1-2):161–205.

[25] Zhai C, Velivelli A, Yu B. A cross-collection mixture model for comparative text mining. In: Proceedings of the international conference on knowledge discovery and data mining; 2004. p. 743–8.

[26] Miller GA. WordNet: a lexical database for English. In: Commun ACM 1995;38(11):39–41.

[27] Stanford NLP Group. The Stanford Parser: a statistical parser. http://nlp.stanford.edu/software/lex-parser.shtml; 2014.

[28] The Apache Software Foundation. Apache OpenNLP. https://opennlp.apache.org/; 2014.

[29] IBM. SPSS. http://www-01.ibm.com/software/analytics/spss/; 2014.

[30] SAS. SAS Text Miner. http://www.sas.com/en_us/software/analytics/text-miner.html; 2014.

[31] Borgelt C. Software for frequent pattern mining. http://www.borgelt.net/fpm.html; 2014.

[32] KDnuggets. Text analysis, text mining, and information retrieval software. http://www.kdnuggets.com/software/text.html; 2014.

[33] Software engineering community. Text analysis for software engineering wiki. http://textse.wikispaces.com/; 2014.

[34] Stanford NLP Group. Statistical natural language processing and corpus-based computational linguistics: An annotated list of resources. http://nlp.stanford.edu/links/statnlp.html; 2014.

[35] Quinlan RJ. C4.5: programs for machine learning. Morgan Kaufmann; 1993.

[36] Cognitive Computer Group of the University of Illinois, Urbana-Champaign. Illinois semantic role labeler. http://cogcomp.cs.illinois.edu/page/software_view/SRL; 2014.

[37] Woodfield SN, Dunsmore HE, Shen VY. The effect of modularization and comments on program comprehension. In: Proceedings of the international conference on software engineering; 1981. p. 215–23.

[38] Stamelos I, Angelis L, Oikonomou A, Bleris GL. Code quality analysis in open source software development. Informat Syst J 2002;12(1):43–60.

[39] Steidl D, Hummel B, Jürgens E. Quality analysis of source code comments. In: Proceedings of the international conference on program comprehension; 2013. p. 83–92.

[40] Fluri B, Wursch M, Gall HC. Do code and comments co-evolve? On the relation between source code and comment changes. In: Proceedings of the working conference on reverse engineering; 2007. p. 70–9.

[41] Marin DP. What motivates programmers to comment? Research report UCB/EECS-2005-18, University of California Berkeley; 2005.

[42] Storey MA, Ryall J, Bull RI, Myers D, Singer J. TODO or to bug: exploring how task annotations play a role in the work practices of software developers. In: Proceedings of the international conference on software engineering; 2008. p. 251–60.

[43] Maalej W, Robillard MP. Patterns of knowledge in API reference documentation. IEEE Trans Software Eng 2013;39(9):1264–82.

[44] Monperrus M, Eichberg M, Tekes E, Mezini M. What should developers be aware of? an empirical study on the directives of API documentation. Empiric Software Eng J 2012;17(6):703–37.

[45] Zhai C, Velivelli A, Yu B. A cross-collection mixture model for comparative text mining. In: Proceedings of the international conference on knowledge discovery and data mining; 2004. p. 743–8.

[46] He H, Garcia EA. Learning from imbalanced data. IEEE Trans Knowl Data Eng 2009;21(9):1263–84.

[47] Savage S, Burrows M, Nelson G, Sobalvarro P, Anderson T. Eraser: a dynamic data race detector for multithreaded programs. ACM Trans Comput Syst 1997;15(4).

[48] Dijkstra EW. The structure of the "THE"-multiprogramming system. In: Proceedings of the first ACM symposium on operating system principles; 1967. p. 10.1–6.

[49] Cognitive Computation Group of the University of Illinois, Urbana-Champaign. Illinois NLP tools. http://cogcomp.cs.illinois.edu/page/tools; 2014.

[50] Even-Zohar Y, Roth D. A sequential model for multi-class classification. In: Proceedings of the conference on empirical methods for natural language processing; 2001. p. 10–19.

[51] Punyakanok V, Roth D. The use of classifiers in sequential inference. In: Proceedings of the conference on advances in neural information processing systems; 2001. p. 995–1001.

[52] Punyakanok V, Roth D, Yih W. The necessity of syntactic parsing for semantic role labeling. In: Proceedings of the international joint conference on artificial intelligence; 2005. p. 1117–23.

[53] Teufel S, Moens M. Summarizing scientific articles—experiments with relevance and rhetorical status. Comput Linguist 2002; 28(4).

[54] Hill E. Integrating natural language and program structure information to improve software search and exploration. Ph.D. thesis, University of Delaware, 2010.

[55] Howard MJ, Gupta S, Pollock L, Vijay-Shanker K. Automatically mining software-based, semantically-similar words from comment-code mappings. In: Proceedings of the working conference on mining software repositories; 2013. p. 377–86.

[56] Shepherd D, Fry ZP, Hill E, Pollock L, Vijay-Shanker K. Using natural language program analysis to locate and understand action-oriented concerns. In: Proceedings of the 6th international conference on aspect-oriented software development; 2007. p. 212–24.

[57] Shepherd D, Pollock L, Vijay-Shanker K. Towards supporting on-demand virtual remodularization using program graphs. In: Proceedings of the international conference on aspect-oriented software development; 2006. p. 3–14.

[58] Yang J, Tan L. Inferring semantically related words from software context. In: Proceedings of the working conference on mining software repositories; 2012. p. 161–70.

[59] Yang J, Tan L. SWordNet: inferring semantically related words from software context. Empirical Software Eng J 2014;19(6):1856–86.

[60] Moreno L, Aponte J, Sridhara G, Marcus A, Pollock L, Vijay-Shanker K. Automatic generation of natural language summaries for Java classes. In: Proceedings of the international conference on program comprehension; 2013. p. 23–32.

[61] Sridhara G, Hill E, Muppaneni D, Pollock L, Vijay-Shanker K. Towards automatically generating summary comments for Java methods. In: Proceedings of the international conference on automated software engineering; 2010. p. 43–52.

[62] Sridhara G, Pollock L, Vijay-Shanker K. Automatically detecting and describing high level actions within methods. In: Proceedings of the international conference on software engineering; 2011. p. 101–10.

[63] Wong E, Yang J, Tan L. AutoComment: mining question and answer sites for automatic comment generation. In: Proceedings of the international conference on automated software engineering, new idea; 2013. p. 562–7.

[64] Pandita R, Xiao X, Zhong H, Xie T, Oney S, Paradkar A. Inferring method specifications from natural language API descriptions. In: International conference on software engineering; 2012. p. 815–25.

[65] Gorla A, Tavecchia I, Gross F, Zeller A. Checking app behavior against app descriptions. In: Proceedings of the international conference on software engineering; 2014. p. 1025–35.

[66] Huang J, Zhang X, Tan L, Wang P, Liang B. AsDroid: detecting stealthy behaviors in Android applications by user interface and program behavior contradiction. In: Proceedings of the international conference on software engineering; 2014. p. 1036–46.

MINING SOFTWARE LOGS FOR GOAL-DRIVEN ROOT CAUSE ANALYSIS

Hamzeh Zawawy*, Serge Mankovskii†, Kostas Kontogiannis‡, John Mylopoulos§

Department of Electrical & Computer Engineering, University of Waterloo, Waterloo, ON, Canada* CA Labs, San Francisco, CA, USA† Department of Electrical and Computer Engineering, National Technical University of Athens, Athens, Greece‡ Department of Information Engineering and Computer Science, University of Trento, Trento, Italy§

CHAPTER OUTLINE

18.1 INTRODUCTION

Software root cause analysis is the process by which system operators attempt to identify faults that have caused system application failures. By *failure* we mean any deviation of the system's observed behavior from the expected one, while by *fault* we refer to a software bug or system misconfiguration. For systems that comprise a large number of components that encompass complex interactions, the root cause analysis process may require a large volume of data to be logged, collected, and analyzed. It has been argued in the literature that the increase in the number of services/systems in a distributed environment can directly contribute to the increase of its overall complexity and the effort required to maintain it [1]. It has also been estimated that 40% of large organizations collect more than 1 TB of log data per month, and 11% of them collect more than 10 TB of log data monthly [2]. In this context, and in order to maintain the required service quality levels, IT systems must be constantly monitored and evaluated by analyzing complex logged data emanating from diverse components. However, the sheer volume of such logged data often makes manual log analysis impossible, and therefore there is a need to provide tools for automating this task to a large extent.

Nevertheless, there are challenges in automating log analysis for root cause identification. These challenges stem first from the complexity of interdependencies between system components, second from the often incomplete log data for explaining the root cause of a failure, and third from the lack of models that could be used to denote conditions and requirements under which a failure could be manifested. The problem becomes even more complex when the failures are caused not by internal faults, but rather by external actions initiated by third parties.

In this chapter, we present an approach to root cause analysis that is based on the use of requirements models (goal models) to capture cause-effect relationships, and a probabilistic reasoning approach to deal with partial or incomplete log data and observations. More specifically, first we use goal models to denote the conditions, constraints, actions, and tasks a system is expected carry out in order to fulfill its requirements. Similarly, we use antigoal models to denote the conditions, constraints, actions, and tasks that could be taken by an external agent to invalidate or threaten a system's functional or nonfunctional requirements. Second, we use latent semantic indexing (LSI) as an information retrieval technique in order to reduce the volume of the software logs that can be considered as observations for a given root cause analysis session so that the performance and tractability of the root cause analysis process can be increased. Third, we compile a knowledge base by transforming goal and antigoal models to a collection of weighted Markov logic diagnostic rules. In this context, when a failure is observed, the goal and antigoal models for which their root nodes correspond to the observed failure are analyzed in order to identify the tasks and actions that may explain the observed failure. The confidence for a root cause further increases when both a goal model and an antigoal model support this root cause hypothesis. Confidence levels are computed as part of the Markov logic reasoning process, combined with rule weights learned from past observations, thus providing a level of training in the reasoning process. The material presented in this chapter builds on previous work conducted by the authors [3, 4].

The chapter is organized as follows. Section 18.2 discusses related work in the areas of root cause analysis. Section 18.3, goal models, antigoal models, node annotations, and a running example are presented. Log reduction is discussed in Section 18.5, while reasoning using Markov logic is presented in Section 18.6. In Section 18.7, we describe in detail the framework and its application to detect failures caused by internal system faults. Section 18.8 describes the use of the root cause analysis framework for identifying the root causes of system failures stemming from external actions. In Section 18.9, we present and discuss the experimental results related to applying the framework to both internally and externally caused failures. Finally, Section 18.10 presents a summary and the conclusions of the chapter.

18.2 APPROACHES TO ROOT CAUSE ANALYSIS

In principle, root cause analysis approaches can be classified into three main categories: rule-based, probabilistic, and model-based approaches. Some approaches rely on natively generated low-level system traces [5, 6]. Others rely on log data obtained by instrumenting the source code [7], or by intercepting system calls [8]. In the following sections, we outline the main concepts behind each of these approaches.

18.2.1 RULE-BASED APPROACHES

This class of root cause analysis approaches uses rules to capture the domain knowledge of the monitored IT environment. Such rules are typically of the form *<If symptoms then diagnosis>*, where symptoms are mapped to root causes. This set of rules is built manually by interviewing system administrators, or automatically by using machine learning methods applied on past data. To find the root cause of an incident, the set of rules is evaluated for matching symptoms. When the conditions of a rule are satisfied, the rule is triggered and a conclusion for the root cause of the failure is derived.

In general, the drawback of the rule-based root cause analysis approaches is that it is hard to have a comprehensive set of rules that cover all the possible cases. Furthermore, the overhead work needed before these approaches can be used in practice is not trivial and requires there to be updating for new incidents. In our work we use goal models to represent cause-effect relationships at a higher level of abstraction, as well as probabilistic rules so that reasoning can be performed with partial or incomplete log data.

18.2.2 PROBABILISTIC APPROACHES

Traditional root cause analysis techniques assume that interdependencies between system components are fully known a priori and that log information about the monitored system's state is complete for all diagnostic purposes. Probabilistic approaches aim to model the cause and effect relationships between IT components using probabilities to represent the possible effect of one component on another. An example of using the probabilistic approach is the work of Steinder et al. [9]. They used Bayesian networks to represent dependencies between communication systems and diagnose failures while using dynamic, missing, or inaccurate information about the system structure and state.

Another example is the approach of Al-Mamory et al. [10], who used a history of alarms and resolutions in order to improve future root cause analysis. In particular, they used root cause analysis to reduce the large number of alarms by finding the root causes of false alarms. The approach uses data mining to group similar alarms into generalized alarms and then analyzes these generalized alarms and classifies them into true and false alarms.

18.2.3 MODEL-BASED APPROACHES

This class of root cause analysis techniques aims at compiling a model representing the normal behavior of the system, and detecting anomalies when the monitored behavior does not adhere to the model. Such models denoting the normal behavior of a system can take various forms. One form is to associate design decisions and components with functional and nonfunctional system properties. For example, these associations can be represented by goal models, antigoal models, or i*-diagrams. A system that uses model-driven engineering combined with run-time information for facilitating root cause analysis is presented in Ref. [11]. More specifically, models denoting system behavior and structure are used to annotate the source code at design time. At run time, logged data are compared with design-time models in order to infer possible root causes. Similarly, a model-based approach facilitating root cause analysis for business process compliance is presented in Ref. [12]. The system allows the specification of models denoting business processes, as well as constraints on/policies for these processes. A run-time monitoring infrastructure allows the collection of system events that are consequently analyzed against the constraints and the policies in the model repository. The analysis yields possible violations, as well as the causes of these violations. Linear temporal logic models were used in Ref. [13] to represent business process compliance constraints in complex service-oriented systems. Symptoms are associated with causes by utilizing current reality trees. An analysis engine allows the current reality trees to be traversed when a symptom is observed, evaluate whether a constraint is violated, and establish possible causes of this violation. Another example of model-based approaches is given in Ref. [7], and is based on the propositional satisfaction of system properties using SAT solvers. Given a propositional formula f, the propositional satisfiability (SAT) problem consists in finding values for the variables of the propositional formula that can make an overall propositional formula evaluate to true. The propositional formula is said to be true if such a truth assignment exists. In Ref. [7] effects (i.e., symptoms or requirement violations) are linked to causes using goal trees. Consequently, goal trees are transformed to propositional formulas. The objective of root cause analysis when a symptom is observed is to identify which combination of goal nodes (i.e., causes) could support or explain the observed violation. One way of solving this problem is by utilizing SAT solvers applied in the logic formula that stems from the goal tree.

18.3 ROOT CAUSE ANALYSIS FRAMEWORK OVERVIEW

As illustrated in Figure 18.1, the root cause analysis framework consists of three phases: *modeling*, *observation generation*, and *diagnostics*. The first phase is an off-line preparatory phase. In this phase, system administrators generate a set of models to represent the requirements of the monitored applications. For this, we use goal and antigoal models (discussed in Section 18.4) as a formalism of choice to represent the monitored applications. Goal models and antigoal models are transformed to collections of rules, forming a diagnostic rule base. Goal and antigoal model nodes are annotated with additional information that represents *precondition*, *postcondition*, and *occurrence* constraints for each of these nodes. The second phase of the framework starts when an alarm is raised indicating the monitored application has failed. In this phase (discussed in Section 18.5), the goal model that corresponds to the observed failed requirement is triggered and its node annotations are used to extract a reduced event set from the logged data. This event set is used, along with the goal and antigoal models, to build a fact base of observations. In the third phase of the framework (discussed in Section 18.6), a reasoning process that is based on Markov logic networks (MLNs) is applied to identify root causes from the diagnostic knowledge base. The overall behavior of the proposed framework is outlined in the sequence diagram depicted in Figure 18.2.

18.4 MODELING DIAGNOSTICS FOR ROOT CAUSE ANALYSIS
18.4.1 GOAL MODELS

Goal models are tree structures that can be used to represent and denote the conditions and the constraints under which functional and nonfunctional requirements of a system can be delivered. In these structures, internal nodes represent *goals*, while external nodes (i.e., leafs) represent *tasks*. Edges between nodes represent either AND or OR goal decompositions or *contributions*.

The AND decomposition of a goal G into other goals or tasks $C_1, C_2, \ldots, C_n$ implies that the satisfaction of each of G's children is necessary for the decomposed goal to be fulfilled. The OR decomposition of a goal G into other goals or tasks $C_1, C_2, \ldots, C_n$ implies that the satisfaction of one of these goals or tasks suffices for the satisfaction of the parent goal. In Figure 18.3, we show goals g_1 and g_3 as examples of AND and OR decompositions.

In addition to AND/OR decompositions, two goals may be connected by a *contribution* edge. A goal may potentially contribute to other goals in four ways—namely, $++S$, $--S$, $++D$ and $--D$. In this chapter, we adopt the semantics of Chopra et al. [14] for the interpretations of contributions:

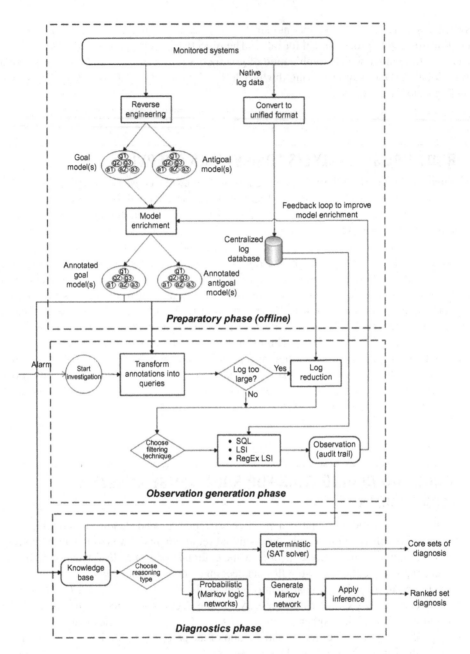

FIGURE 18.1

Root cause analysis framework.

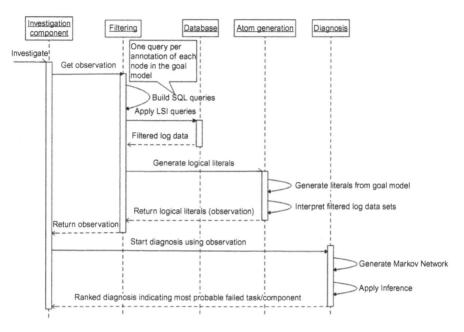

FIGURE 18.2

Sequence diagram for the inner workings of the diagnosis framework.

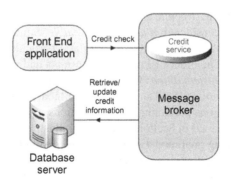

FIGURE 18.3

Loan application goal model and corresponding antigoal attacks.

$$++S/D : g_s \text{ satisfaction/denial implies } g_t$$
$$satisfaction/denial,$$
$$--S/D : g_s \text{ satisfaction/denial implies } g_t$$
$$denial/satisfaction. \tag{18.1}$$

18.4.2 ANTIGOAL MODELS

Similarly to goal models, antigoal models represent the goals and actions of an external agent with the intention to threaten or compromise specific system goals. Antigoal models are also denoted as AND/OR trees built through systematic refinement, until leaf nodes (i.e., tasks) are derived. More specifically, leaf nodes represent tasks (actions) an external agent can perform to fulfill an antigoal, and consequently through the satisfaction of this antigoal to deny a system goal. In this respect, root cause analysis can commence by considering root causes not only due to internal system faults but also due to external actions. Antigoal models were initially proposed by Lamsweerde et al. [15] to model security concerns during requirements elicitation.

An example of antigoal models is the trees with roots ag_1 and ag_2, depicted in Figure 18.3, where the *target* edges from antigoal ag_1 to tasks a_2 and a_3 as well as from antigoal ag_2 to tasks a_4 and a_6 model the negative impact an antigoal has on a system goal.

18.4.3 MODEL ANNOTATIONS

Since a generic goal model is only an abstract description of cause and effect relationships, it is not sufficient on its own to capture whether goals are satisfied on the basis of input from the collected log data. For this reason, we consider three annotations per goal or task node: *precondition*, *postcondition*, and *occurrence* annotations. *Precondition* annotations denote the structure and contents the log data must have at a particular (logical) time instant for the goal or task be considered for evaluation. *Occurrence* annotations denote the structure and contents the log data must have at a particular (logical) time instant for the goal to be considered *potentially satisfiable*. Similarly, *postcondition* annotations denote the structure and contents the log data must have at a particular (logical) time instant for the goal to be *tagged* as *satisfied*. The order of *logical time* instants and the logical relationship between *preconditions*, *occurrence* and *postconditions* for a given goal or task are presented in Equations 18.9-18.12 for goal models, and Equations 18.17 and 18.18 for antigoal models.

Goal and task node annotations pertaining to preconditions, occurrence, and postconditions take the form of expressions as discussed in Section 18.7.1.2 and illustrated in Equation 18.10. Figure 18.3 depicts an example of annotating goal model nodes with precondition, postcondition, and occurrence expressions. Once goal and antigoal models have been formulated and annotated, they are consequently transformed into collections of Markov logic rules in order to form a diagnostic knowledge base, as will be discussed in the following sections.

In addition to assisting in inferring whether a goal or action node is *satisfied*, annotations serve as a means for reducing, through information retrieval approaches, the volume of the logs to be considered for the satisfaction of any given node, increasing the overall root cause analysis processing performance.

Logs are filtered on a per goal node basis using the metadata annotation information in each node. Log reduction uses LSI and is discussed in more detail in Section 18.5. Other approaches to log reduction that are based on information theory were proposed in Ref. [16]. The reduced logs that are obtained from the running system are also transformed to collections of facts, forming a fact base of *observations*. The rule base stemming from the goal and antigoal models and the facts stemming from the observed log files form a complete knowledge base to be used for root cause analysis reasoning. Root cause analysis reasoning uses a probabilistic rule engine that is based on the Alchemy tool [17]. In the following sections we discuss in more detail log filtering, reasoning fundamentals using Markov logic, and the application of the framework used for root cause analysis for (a) failures that occur because of internal system errors and (b) failures that occur as a result of external actions.

18.4.4 LOAN APPLICATION SCENARIO

Throughout this chapter, as a running example to better illustrate the inner workings of the proposed root cause analysis technique, we use example goal and antigoal models pertaining to a loan application scenario as depicted in Figure 18.3. The scenario is built on a test environment that is composed of a set of COTS application components. As depicted in Figure 18.4, the experimentation environment includes a business process layer and a service-oriented infrastructure. In particular, this test environment includes four subsystems: the front-end application (SoapUI), a middleware message broker, a credit check service, and a database server.

We have built the *Apply_For_Loan* business service, specifying the process of an online user applying for a loan, having the loan application evaluated, and finally obtaining an accept/reject decision based on the information supplied. Technically, the business process is exposed as a Web service. The *Apply_For_Loan* service starts when it receives a SOAP request containing loan application information. It evaluates the loan request by checking the applicant's credit rating. If the applicant's credit rating is "good," his/her loan application is accepted and a positive reply is sent to the applicant. Otherwise, a loan rejection result is sent to the applicant. If an error occurs during processing, a SOAP fault is sent to the requesting application. The credit rating evaluation is performed via a separate Web service (*Credit_Rating*). After the credit evaluation terminates, the *Credit_Rating* service sends a SOAP reply to the calling application containing the credit rating and the ID of the applicant. If an error occurs during the credit evaluation, a SOAP error is sent to the requesting application. During the credit rating evaluation, the *Credit_Rating* application queries a database table and stores/retrieves the applicants' details.

18.4.4.1 Goal model for the motivating scenario

The loan application is represented by the goal model in Figure 18.3, which contains three goals (rectangles) and seven tasks (circles). The root goal g_1 (loan application) is AND-decomposed to goal g_2 (loan evaluation) and tasks a_1 (eeceive loan Web service request) and a_2 (send loan Web service reply), indicating that goal g_1 is satisfied if and only if goal g_2 and tasks a_1 and a_2 are satisfied. Similarly, g_2 is AND-decomposed to goal g_3 (extract credit rating) and tasks a_3 (receive credit check Web service request), a_4 (update loan table), and a_5 (send credit Web service reply), indicating that goal g_2 is satisfied if and only if goal g_3 and tasks a_3, a_4, and a_5 are satisfied. Furthermore, subgoal g_3 is OR-decomposed into tasks a_6 and a_7. This decomposition indicates that goal g_3 is satisfied if either

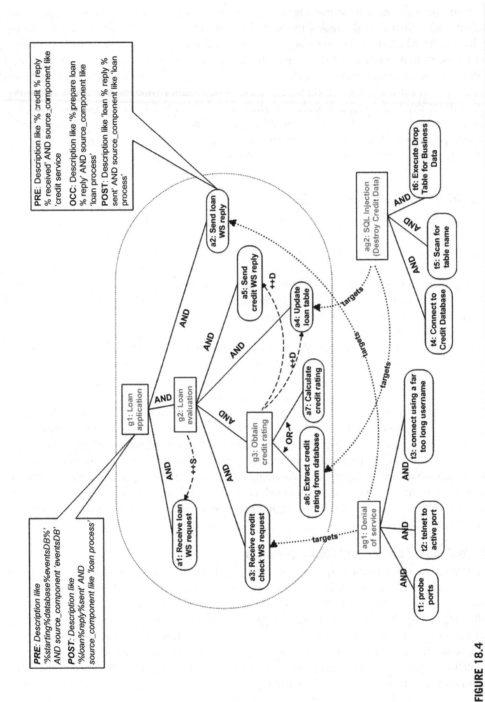

PRE: Description like '% credit % reply
% received' AND source_component like
'credit service'

OCC: Description like '% prepare loan
% reply' AND source_component like
'loan process'

POST: Description like 'loan % reply %
sent' AND source_component like 'loan
process'

PRE: Description like
'%starting%database%eventsDB%'
AND source_component 'eventsDB'

POST: Description like
'%loan%reply%sent' AND
source_component like 'loan process'

g1: Loan application

g2: Loan evaluation

g3: Obtain credit rating

a1: Receive loan WS request

a2: Send loan WS reply

a3: Receive credit check WS request

a4: Update loan table

a5: Send credit WS reply

a6: Extract credit rating from database

a7: Calculate credit rating

ag1: Denial of service

t1: probe ports

t2: telnet to active port

t3: connect using a far too long username

ag2: SQL Injection (Destroy Credit Data)

t4: Connect to Credit Database

t5: Scan for table name

t6: Execute Drop Table for Business Data

FIGURE 18.4

Layout of the test distributed environment.

Table 18.1 Loan Application Goal Model's Node/Precondition/Postcondition Identifiers

Node	Precondition	Postcondition
g1	InitialReq_Submit	Reply_Received
g2	ClientInfo_Valid	Decision_Done
a1	BusinessProc_Ready	BusProc_Start
a2	LoanRequest_Submit	LoanRequest_Avail
a3	Decision_Done	LoanReply_Ready
a4	SOAPMessage_Avail	SOAPMessage_Sent
a5	ClientInfo_Valid	Prepare_CreditRating_Request
a6	Prepare_CreditRating_Request	Receive_CreditRating_Rply
a7	Receive_CreditRating_Rply	Valid_CreditRating
a8	Valid_CreditRating	CreditRating_Available
a9	CreditRating_Available	Decision_Done

task a_6 or task a_7 is satisfied. Contribution links $(++D)$ from goal g_3 to tasks a_4 and a_5 indicate that if goal g_3 is denied, then tasks a_4 and a_5 should be denied as well. Contribution link $(++S)$ from goal g_2 to task a_1 indicates that if goal g_2 is satisfied, then so must be task a_1. Table 18.1 provides a complete list of the goals and tasks in the loan application goal model. We will discuss the role of antigoals ag_1 and ag_2 later in the chapter.

18.4.4.2 Logger systems in the test environment

The test environment includes four logging systems that emit log data. The logging systems we have used include the following:

1. Windows Event Viewer: This is a Windows component that acts as a Windows centralized log repository. Events emanating from applications running as Windows services (middleware and database server) can be accessed and viewed using the Windows Event Viewer.
2. SoapUI: This is an open source Web service testing tool for service- oriented architecture. SoapUI logs its events in a local log file.
3. Web Service logger: This corresponds to the Credit_Rating application, and generates events that are stored directly in the log database.

18.5 **LOG REDUCTION**

Log reduction pertains to a process that allows the selection of a subset of the available logs to be used for root cause analysis purposes. The motivation is that by reducing the size of the log files (i.e., the number of events to be considered), we can make root cause analysis more tractable and efficient with respect to its time performance. However, such a reduction has to keep entries important to the analysis, while discarding irrelevant ones, thus maintaining a high recall and high precision for the results obtained. The basic premise used here for log reduction is that each log entry represents a document, while terms and keywords obtained from the goal and antigoal model node annotations are treated as queries. The documents (i.e., log entries) that conform with the query form then the reduced set. Here, we discuss the background techniques which we use to reduce the size of the logged data to be considered for the satisfaction of each goal model node, and that thus make the whole process more tractable. More specifically, we consider LSI and probabilistic latent semantic indexing (PLSI) as two techniques used to discover relevant documents (i.e., log entries) given keywords in a query (i.e., keywords and terms obtained by annotations in goal model nodes related to the analysis). A detailed discussion on how annotations are used for log reduction is presented in Section 18.7.1.2.

18.5.1 LATENT SEMANTIC INDEXING

Some of the well-known document retrieval techniques include LSI [18], PLSI [19], latent Dirichlet allocation [20], and the correlated topic model [21]. In this context, semantic analysis of a corpus of documents consists in building structures that identify concepts from this corpus of documents without any prior semantic understanding of the documents.

LSI is an indexing and retrieval method to identify relationships among terms and concepts in a collection of unstructured text documents. LSI was introduced by Deerwester et al. [18]. It takes a vector space representation of documents based on term frequencies as a starting point and applies a dimension reduction operation on the corresponding term/document matrix using the singular value decomposition algorithm [22]. The fundamental idea is that documents and terms can be mapped to a reduced representation in the so-called latent semantic space. Similarities among documents and queries can be more efficiently estimated in this reduced space representation than in their original representation. This is because two documents which have terms that have been found to frequently co-occur in the collection of all documents will have a similar representation in the reduced space representation, even if these two specific documents have no terms in common. LSI is commonly used in areas such as Web retrieval, document indexing [23], and feature identification [24]. In this context, we consider each log entry as a document. The terms found in the goal and antigoal node annotation expressions become the search keywords. LSI is then used to identify those log entries that are mostly associated with a particular query denoting a system feature, a precondition, an occurrence, or a postcondition annotation of a goal or antigoal node.

18.5.2 PROBABILISTIC LATENT SEMANTIC INDEXING

PLSI is a variation of LSI [19] that considers the existence of three types of random variables (topic, word, and document). The three types of class variables are as follows:

(1) An unobserved class variable $z \in Z = \{z_1, z_1, ...z_K\}$ that represents a topic
(2) Word $w \in W = \{w_1, w_2, ...w_L\}$, where each word is the location of a term t from the vocabulary V in a document d
(3) Document $d \in D = \{d_1, d_2, ...d_M\}$ in a corpus M

PLSI aims to identify the documents d_i in a collection of documents $\{d_1, d_2, .., d_j\}$ that best relate to a word w (or words), presented as query—that is, to compute $P(d_i, w)$. The major difference of PLSI from LSI is that its model is based on three layers—namely, the documents layer, the latent topics layer, and the words (i.e., query) layer. Each document d_i is associated with one or more concepts c_k (i.e., a latent variable). Similarly, each word is also associated with a concept. The overall objective is to compute the conditional probabilities $P(c_k|d_i)$ and $P(w|c_k)$. By computing the inner product of $P(w|c_k)$ and $P(d_i|c_k)$ over latent variables c_k for each document d in the collection of documents separately, as the "similarity" score between the query w and a document d_i, we can then select the documents that produce the maximum score. Such documents are considered as the most relevant to the query.

18.6 REASONING TECHNIQUES

As discussed in Section 18.4, we use goal models to represent dependencies between system requirements and design decisions, components, and system properties. Each goal model is represented as a goal tree. The root of the tree represents a functional or a nonfunctional requirement for the given system. When a failure is observed (i.e., a failure to observe the delivery of a functional or nonfunctional requirement), the corresponding goal tree is analyzed. Goal models are transformed to first-order logic formulas so that a SAT solver or a reasoning engine can determine the assignment of truth values to the nodes of the tree in a way that explains the failure of the requirement that corresponds to the root node of the goal or antigoal tree. However, to evaluate the actual truth value of each node we would require that the node annotations are evaluated using observations (i.e., events) and information found in the system logs as presented in Sections 18.7.1.4, 18.7.1.6, and 18.8.1. In practical situations though, observations can be missing, erroneous, or considered as valid within a degree of likelihood or probability. For this reason, we resort to the use of a probabilistic reasoning engine to cope with uncertain, erroneous, or missing observations. In this section, we discuss such a probabilistic reasoning technique that we use, and that is based on the Markov logic theory [17].

18.6.1 MARKOV LOGIC NETWORKS

MLNs were recently proposed in the research literature as a framework that combines first-order logic and probabilistic reasoning. In this context, a knowledge base denoted by first-order logic formulas represents a set of hard constraints on the set of possible worlds (i.e., if a world violates one formula, it has zero probability of existing). Markov logic softens these constraints by making a word that violates a formula be less probable, but still possible. The more formulas it violates, the less probable it becomes. A detailed discussion on MLNs can be found in Ref. [25].

Markov network construction. In MLNs, each logic formula F_i is associated with a nonnegative real-valued weight w_i. Every grounding (instantiation) of F_i is given the same weight w_i. In this context, a Markov network is an undirected graph that is built by an exhaustive grounding of the predicates and formulas as follows:

- Each node corresponds to a ground atom x_k which is an instantiation of a predicate.
- If a subset of ground atoms $x_{\{i\}} = \{x_k\}$ are related to each other by a formula F_i with weight w_i, then a clique C_i over these variables is added to the network. C_i is associated with a weight w_i and a feature function f_i defined as follows:

$$f_i(x_{\{i\}}) = \begin{cases} 1 & F_i(x_{\{i\}}) = \text{true,} \\ 0 & \text{otherwise.} \end{cases} \tag{18.2}$$

Thus, first-order logic formulas serve as templates to construct the Markov network. In the context of a Markov network, each ground atom, X, represents a binary variable. The overall Markov network is then used to model the joint distribution of all ground atoms. The corresponding global energy function can be calculated as follows:

$$P(X = x) = \frac{1}{Z} \exp \left(\sum_i w_i f_i(x_{\{i\}}) \right), \tag{18.3}$$

where Z is the normalizing factor calculated as

$$Z = \sum_{x \in X} \exp \left(\sum_i w_i f_i(x_{\{i\}}) \right), \tag{18.4}$$

where i denotes the subset of ground atoms $x_{\{i\}} \in X$ that are related to each other by a formula F_i with weight w_i and feature function f_i.

Learning. Learning in an MLN consists of two steps: structure learning, or learning the logical clauses, and weight learning, or determining the weight of each logical clause. Structure learning is typically done by heuristically searching the space for models that have a statistical score measure that fits the training data [17]. As for weight learning, Singla et al. [26] extended the existing voted perceptron method and applies it to generate the MLN's parameters (weights for the logical clauses). This is done by optimizing the conditional likelihood of the query atoms given the evidence.

Inference, Assuming $\phi_i(x_{\{i\}})$ is the potential function defined over a clique C_i, then $\log(\phi_i(x_{\{i\}})) = w_i f_i(x_{\{i\}})$. We use the Markov network constructed to compute the marginal distribution of events. Given some observations, probabilistic inference can be performed. Exact inference is often intractable, and thus Markov chain Monte Carlo sampling techniques, such as Gibbs sampling, are used for approximate reasoning [25]. The probability for an atom X_i given its Markov blanket (neighbors) B_i is calculated as follows:

$$P(X_i = x_i / B_i = b_i) = \frac{A}{(B + C)}, \tag{18.5}$$

where

$$A = \exp \left(\sum_{f_j \in F_i} w_j f_j(X_i = x_i, B_i = b_i) \right), \tag{18.6}$$

$$B = \exp \left(\sum_{f_j \in F_i} w_j f_j(X_i = 0, B_i = b_i) \right), \tag{18.7}$$

$$C = \exp \left(\sum_{f_j \in F_i} w_j f_j(X_i = 1, B_i = b_i) \right). \tag{18.8}$$

F_i is the set of all cliques that contain X_i, and f_j is computed as in Equation 18.2.

The Markov network is used to compute the marginal distribution of events and perform inference. Because inference in Markov networks is #P-complete, approximate inference is proposed to be performed using the Markov chain Monte Carlo method and Gibbs sampling [27].

As already mentioned, the above expressions are used to compute the probability an atom X (i.e., an instantiated predicate in one of the logic formulas stemming from the goal models) belongs to a clique in the Markov network. Intuitively, this probability gives the likelihood this atom is satisfied in the "world" represented by the clique. As an example, consider the first-order logic formula $A \wedge B \rightarrow C$. If we have atoms A and B, then we can infer C exists. But if we consider that we have seen a "world" where B and C coexist on their own in 40% of cases without A, then even in the absence of observing A, we can still deduce C exists with a degree of likelihood if we observe B alone without A. In the sections below, we elaborate more on the use of probabilistic reasoning for root cause analysis for failures due to internal system errors or due to external maliciously induced actions.

18.7 ROOT CAUSE ANALYSIS FOR FAILURES INDUCED BY INTERNAL FAULTS

In this section, we present the elements of the probabilistic-based root cause analysis framework and we illustrate its use through the loan application example. The framework consists of three main components: system modeling, observation generation, and diagnosis. This framework takes as input, first, the set of annotated goal models that represent the monitored systems and, second, the log data stored in unified format in a centralized database. It generates as output a ranked list of diagnostics that represents the weighted possible root cause(s) of the failure.

18.7.1 KNOWLEDGE REPRESENTATION

In the following sections, we discuss in more detail the steps pertaining to modeling a diagnostic knowledge base from a collection of goal models.

18.7.1.1 Goal model compilation

The root cause analysis framework is built on the premise that the monitored system's requirements goal model is available to system analysts or can be reverse engineered from source code using techniques discussed in Ref. [28]. Tasks in a goal model represent simple components in the source code. These are treated as black boxes for the purposes of monitoring and diagnosis in order to enable us to model a software system at different levels of abstraction.

18.7.1.2 Goal model annotations

We extend the goal models representing the monitored systems by annotating the goal model nodes with additional information. In particular, tasks (leaf nodes) are associated with preconditions, occurrence, and postconditions, while goals (nonleaf nodes) are associated with preconditions and postconditions only. The annotations are expressed using string pattern expressions of the form [*not*]*column_name*[*not*]*like*"*match_string*", where *column_name* represents a field name in the log database and *match_string* can contain the following symbols:

- %: matches strings of zero or many characters;
- _ (underscore): matches one character;
- [...]: encloses sets or ranges, such as [abc] or [a − d].

An annotation example is the precondition for goal g_1 (in Figure 18.3) shown below:

> Pre(g_1): Description like '%starting%Database%eventsDB%' AND source_component like 'eventsDB'

This annotation example matches events containing keywords or attribute values indicating that they have been generated by the "*eventsDB*" database system, and have a description text or attribute values containing the keyword "*starting*," followed by a space, then followed by the keyword "*Database*," then a space, followed by the keyword "*eventsDB*." More annotation examples are shown in Figure 18.3.

18.7.1.3 Goal model predicates

We use first-order logic to represent semantic information on goal and antigoal models. More specifically, we represent the monitored systems/services' states and actions as first-order logic predicates. A predicate is *intentional* if its truth value can only be inferred (i.e., it cannot be directly observed). A predicate is *extensional* if its truth value can be observed directly. A predicate is *strictly extensional* if it can only be observed and not inferred for all its groundings [29]. We use the extensional predicates *ChildAND(parent_node,child_node)* and *ChildOR(parent_node,child_node)* to denote the AND/OR goal decomposition. For instance, *ChildAND(parent,child)* is true when *child* is an AND-child of *parent* (similarly for *ChildOR(parent,child)*). Examples of AND goal decomposition are goals g_1 and g_2 shown in Figure 18.3. An example of OR decomposition is goal g_3. We use the extensional predicates *Pre(node,timestep)*, *Occ(node,timestep)*, and *Post(node,timestep)* to represent preconditions, task occurrences, and task postconditions at a certain timestep. For our work, we assume a total ordering of events according to their logical or physical timestamps [30]. The predicate *Satisfied* is predominantly intentional except for the top goal for which satisfaction is observable (i.e., the observed system failure that triggers the root cause analysis process). If the overall service/transaction is successfully executed, then the top goal is considered to be satisfied, otherwise it is denied.

18.7.1.4 Goal model rules

The satisfaction of goals, antigoals, and tasks is expressed using the truth assignment of the *Satisfied(node, timestep)* predicate, which, in turn, are inferred as follows: A task *a* with a precondition *{Pre}* and a postcondition *{Post}* is satisfied at time $t + 1$ if and only if *{Pre}* is true at time $t − 1$ just before task *a* occurs at time t, and *{Post}* is true at time $t + 1$ as follows:

$$Pre(a, t − 1) \land Occ(a, t) \land Post(a, t + 1) \Rightarrow Satisfied(a, t + 1) \tag{18.9}$$

The satisfaction of the *Pre(task, timestep)* and *Post(task, timestep)* predicates is based on whether there are events or event patterns that match the *node* annotations tagged as *Pre*, *Occ*, or *Post*, for the given task *node*.

Annotation expressions are string patterns linked by logical operators of the form

$$< Precond > \mid < Postcond > \mid < Occur > (node):$$
$$[not]column\ name[not]like\ <\ match\ string > \qquad (18.10)$$

where *column name* represents a field name in the log database, and the search pattern string contains symbols such as % (percent), which matches strings of zero or more characters, and _ (underscore), which matches one character.

The following is an annotation example for the precondition of node a_2:

Precond(a_2): Description like 'Windows.%starting.up'
AND Source Component like alpha.com.ca'

The satisfaction of the *Occ*(*task*, *timestep*) predicate for leaf nodes is based on the same principles as the satisfaction of the *Pre*(*node*, *timestep*) and *Post*(*node*, *timestep*) predicates as presented above.

Unlike *tasks* (i.e., the leaf nodes), which occur at a specific moment of time, *goal* occurrences (i.e., internal nodes) may span an interval $[t_1, t_2]$ that is based on the satisfaction timesteps of the child goals/tasks. Thus, a goal g with precondition *{Pre}* and postcondition *{Post}* is satisfied at time t_3 if the goal precondition *{Pre}* expression is observed at t_1, the goal occurrence is observed at timestep t_2, and *{Post}* expression is observed at timestep t_3, where ($t_1 < t_2 < t_3$) (see Equations 18.11-18.13). The truth values of the predicate *Occ(goal, timestep)* (used in Equation 18.13) can be inferred only on the basis on the satisfaction of all its children in the case of AND-decomposed goals (Equation 18.11) or at least one of its children in the case of OR-decomposed goals (Equation 18.12).

$$\forall a_i, i \in \{1, 2, ...n\}, ChildAND(g, a_i) \wedge Satisfied(a_i, t_i) \wedge \Rightarrow Occ(g, max(t_1, t_2, ...t_n)) \qquad (18.11)$$

$$\exists a_i, i \in \{1, 2, ...n\}, ChildOR(g, a_i) \wedge Satisfied(a_i, t_i) \wedge \forall j \in \{1, ...n\}s.t.j \neq i \wedge$$
$$Satisfied(a_j, t_j) \wedge t_i > t_j \Rightarrow Occ(g, t_i) \qquad (18.12)$$

From the above, the rule for the satisfaction of an internal goal node is given as follows:

$$Pre(g, t_1) \wedge Occ(g, t_2) \wedge Post(g, t_3)) \Rightarrow Satisfied(g, t_3) \qquad (18.13)$$

Contribution links of the form $node_1 \xrightarrow{++S} node_2$ are represented in Equation 18.14 (similarly for $++D, --S,$ and $--D$):

$$Satisfied(node_1, t_1) \Rightarrow Satisfied(node_2, t_1) \qquad (18.14)$$

18.7.1.5 *Generation of ground atoms from filtered system logs*

There are two inputs to this process: first, the log data stored in a common database, and second, the goal model for the monitored system with *precondition*, *postcondition*, and *occurrence* patterns annotating each node of the model. The output is a totally timestep-ordered set of literals (ground atoms) of the form *literal*(*node,timestep*).

The framework uses pattern expressions that annotate the goal models and applies these annotations as queries to the log data in order to extract evidence for the occurrence of events associated with each goal model node. More specifically, once the logged data have been stored in a unified format, the pattern expressions that annotate the goal and antigoal model nodes (see Figure 18.3) can be used, first, to generate LSI queries that are applied to collect a subset of the logged data pertaining to the analysis and, second, as patterns to satisfy *Pre*, *Occ*, and *Post* predicates for a node. An example of a log data pattern matching expression for the precondition of goal g_1 in Figure 18.3 is shown below:

The truth assignment for the extensional predicates is performed on the basis of the pattern matched log data. We show below a sample subset of the ground atoms for the goal model in Figure 18.3:

> *pre(g_1,1), pre(a_1,1), occ(a_1,2), post(a_1,3), pre(g_2,3), !pre(a_3,3), ?occ(a_3,4), ..., ?post(g_1,15), !satisfied(g_1,15)*

The set of literals above represents the observation of one failed loan application session. However, for some of the goals/tasks, there may be no *Pre*, *Occ*, or *Post* supporting evidence, which can be interpreted as either they did not occur, or they were missed from the observation set. We model this uncertainty by adding a question mark (?) before the corresponding ground atoms. In cases where there is evidence that a goal/task did not occur, the corresponding ground atom is preceded by an exclamation mark (!). For example, in Figure 18.3 the observation of the system failure is represented by *!satisfied(g_1,15)*, which indicates top goal g_1 denial, at timestep 15. Note that in the above example, the precondition for task a_3 was denied and the occurrence of a_3 was not observed, leading to the denial of task a_3, which led to goal g_2 not occurring and thus being denied. In turn, the denial of goal g_2 supports goal g_1 not being satisfied.

The filtering of the predicate with timesteps of interest is performed in two steps. First, a list of literals is generated (see the example above) from the nodes annotations (preconditions, occurrences, and postconditions) by depth-first traversing the goal model tree. In the second step, literals are used to initiate searches in the logged data set looking for events containing such literals (and within a certain time interval). The following is an example of the generation of ground atoms. A log entry of the form

> (2010-02-05 17:46:44.24 Starting up database eventsDB ... DATABASE)

that matches the pattern of the precondition of goal g_1 represents evidence for the satisfaction of the precondition of g_1. For other logical literals that do not have supporting evidence in the log data that their preconditions, postconditions, or occurrence expressions are matched, a question mark is assigned to these literals. Such a case is illustrated in the *precondition* of of a_7 ($Occ(a_7, 5)$) in Table 18.2 for scenario 1.

The ground atom generation process is further illustrated through the examples in Figures 18.5 and in 18.6.

18.7.1.6 Uncertainty representation

The root cause analysis framework relies on log data as the evidence for the diagnostic process. The process of selecting log data (described in the previous step) can potentially lead to false negatives and false positives, which in turn lead to decreased confidence in the observation. We address uncertainty in observations using a combination of logical and probabilistic models:

Table 18.2 Four Scenarios for the Loan Application

Scenario	Observed (& missing) events	Satisfied ($a1,3$)	Satisfied ($a3,5$)	Satisfied ($a6,7$)	Satisfied ($a7,9$)	Satisfied ($a4,11$)	Satisfied ($a5,13$)	Satisfied ($a2,15$)
1. Successful execution	Pre(g_1,1), Pre(a_1,1), Occ(a_1,2), Post(a_1,3), Pre(g_2,3), Pre(a_3,3), Occ(a_3,4), Post(a_3,5), Pre(g_2,5), Pre(a_6,5), Occ(a_6,6), Post(a_6,7), ?Pre(a_7,5), ?Occ(a_7,6), ?Post(a_7,7), Post(g_3,7), Pre(a_4,7), Occ(a_4,8), Post(a_4,9), Pre(a_5,9), Occ(a_5,10), Post(a_5,11), Pre(a_2,11), Occ(a_2,12), Post(a_2,13), Post(g_1,13), Satisfied(g_1,13)	0.99	0.99	0.99	0.49	0.99	0.99	0.99
2. Failed to update loan database	Pre(g_1,1), Pre(a_1,1), Occ(a_1,2), Post(a_1,3), Pre(g_2,3), Pre(a_3,3), Occ(a_3,4), Post(a_3,5), Pre(g_3,5), Pre(a_6,5), Occ(a_6,6), Post(a_6,7), ?Pre(a_7,5), ?Occ(a_7,6), ?Post(a_7,7), Post(g_3,7), Pre(a_4,7), ?Occ(a_4,8), ?Post(a_4,9), ?Pre(a_5,9), ?Pre(a_5,9), ?Occ(a_5,10), ?Post(a_5,11), ?Pre(a_2,11), ?Occ(a_2,12), ?Post(a_2,13), ?Post(g_1,13), !Satisfied(g_1,13)	0.99	0.99	0.99	0.43	0.45	0.45	0.36
3. Credit database table not accessible	Pre(g_1,1), Pre(a_1,1), Occ(a_1,2), Post(a_1,3), Pre(g_2,3), Pre(a_3,3), Occ(a_3,4), Post(a_3,5), Pre(g_2,5), ?Pre(a_6,5), ?Occ(a_6,6), ?Post(a_6,7), ?Pre(a_7,5), ?Occ(a_7,6), ?Post(a_7,7), Post(g_3,7), Pre(a_4,7), Occ(a_4,8), Post(a_4,9), Pre(a_5,9), Occ(a_5,10), Post(a_5,11), Pre(a_2,11), Occ(a_2,12), Post(a_2,12), ?Post(g_1,13), !Satisfied(g_1,13)	0.99	0.99	0.33	0.32	0.45	0.43	0.38
4. Failed to validate loan application Web service request	?Pre(g_1,1), Pre(a_1,1), ?Occ(a_1,2), ?Post(a_1,3), Pre(g_2,3), ?Pre(a_3,3), ?Occ(a_3,4), ?Post(a_3,5), Pre(g_3,5), Pre(a_6,5), ?Occ(a_6,6), ?Post(a_6,7), Pre(a_7,5), ?Occ(a_7,6), ?Post(a_7,7), ?Post(g_3,7), Pre(a_4,7), ?Occ(a_4,8), ?Post(a_4,9), ?Pre(a_5,9), ?Occ(a_5,10), ?Post(a_5,11), ?Pre(a_2,11), ?Occ(a_2,12), ?Post(a_2,13), ?Post(g_1,13), !Satisfied(g_1,13)	0.48	0.48	0.35	0.36	0.47	0.48	0.46

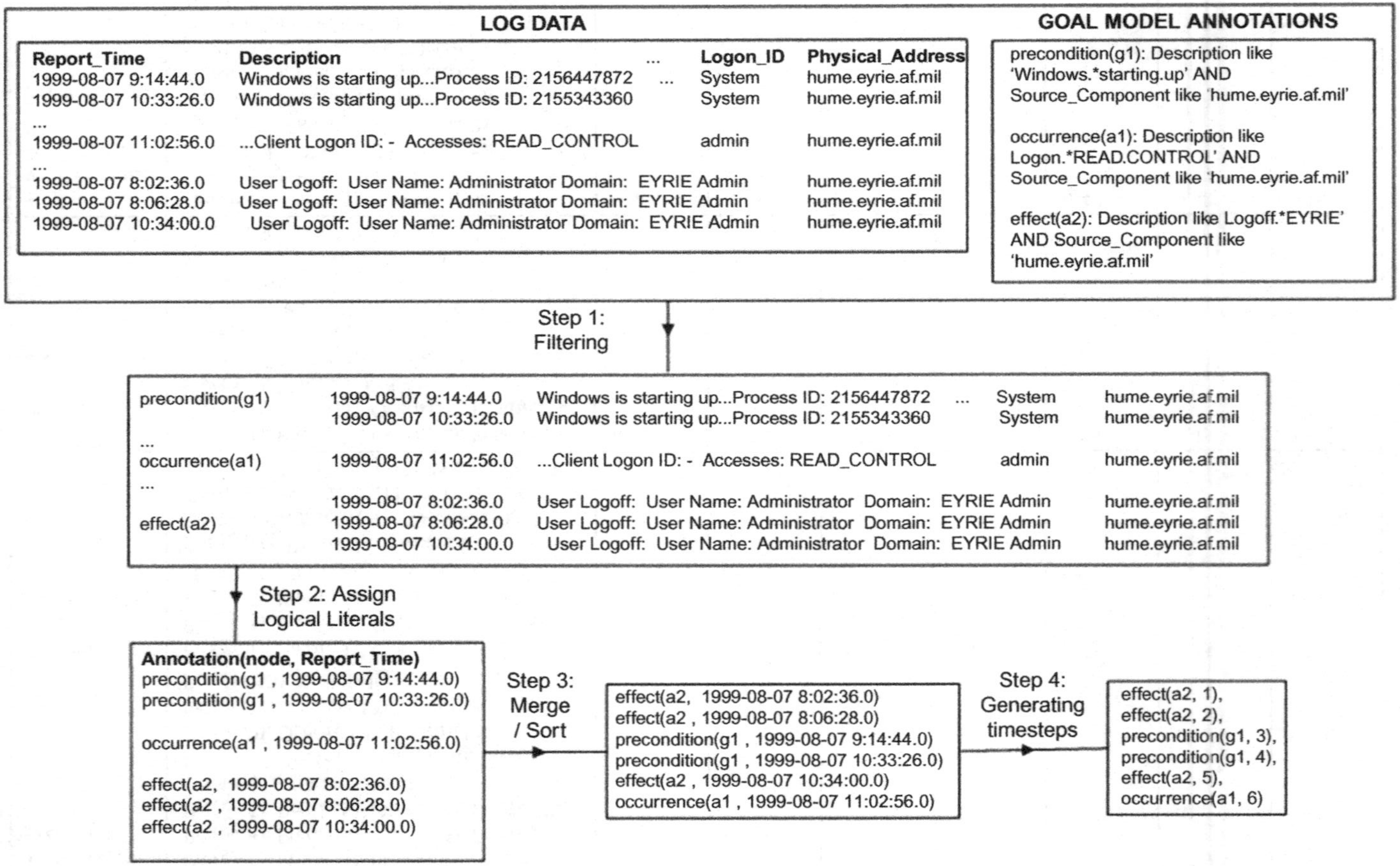

FIGURE 18.5

Transforming filtered log data subsets into ground atoms.

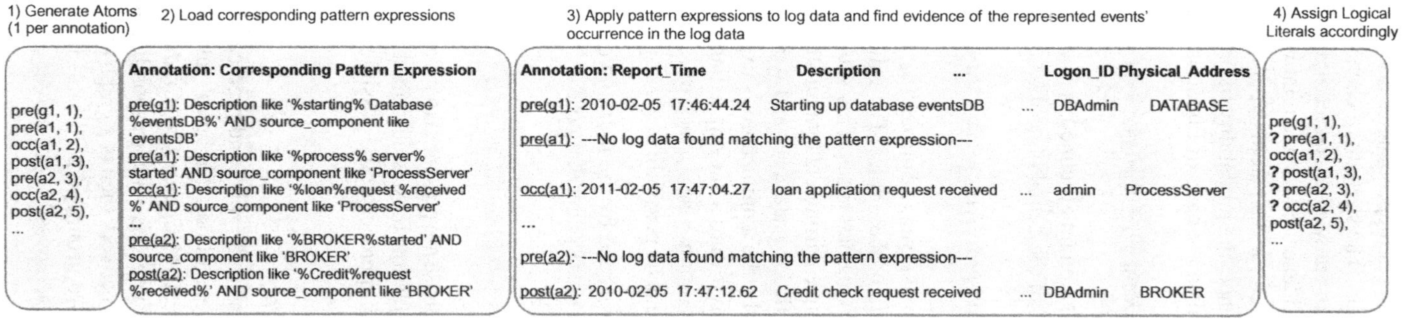

1) Generate Atoms
2) Load corresponding pattern expressions
(1 per annotation)

3) Apply pattern expressions to log data and find evidence of the represented events'
occurrence in the log data

4) Assign Logical
Literals accordingly

pre(g1, 1);
pre(a1, 1);
occ(a1, 2);
post(a1, 3);
pre(a2, 3);
occ(a2, 4);
post(a2, 5);
...

Annotation: Corresponding Pattern Expression
pre(g1): Description like '%starting% Database %eventsDB%' AND source_component like 'eventsDB'
pre(a1): Description like '%process% server% started' AND source_component like 'ProcessServer'
occ(a1): Description like '%loan%request %received %' AND source_component like 'ProcessServer'
...
pre(a2): Description like '%BROKER%started' AND source_component like 'BROKER'
post(a2): Description like '%Credit%request %received%' AND source_component like 'BROKER'

Annotation: Report_Time	Description	...	Logon_ID	Physical_Address
pre(g1): 2010-02-05 17:46:44.24	Starting up database eventsDB	...	DBAdmin	DATABASE
pre(a1): ---No log data found matching the pattern expression---				
occ(a1): 2011-02-05 17:47:04.27	loan application request received	...	admin	ProcessServer
...				
pre(a2): ---No log data found matching the pattern expression---				
post(a2): 2010-02-05 17:47:12.62	Credit check request received	...	DBAdmin	BROKER

pre(g1, 1),
? pre(a1, 1),
occ(a1, 2),
? post(a1, 3),
? pre(a2, 3),
? occ(a2, 4),
post(a2, 5),
...

FIGURE 18.6

Generating observation from log data.

- The domain knowledge representing the interdependencies between systems/services is modeled using weighted first-order logic formulas. The strength of each relationship is represented by a real-valued weight set, based on domain knowledge and learning from a training log data set. The weight of each rule represents our confidence in this rule relative to the other rules in the knowledge base. The probability inferred for each atom depends on the weight of the competing rules where this atom occurs. For instance, the probability of the satisfaction of task $a4$ in Figure 18.3 ($Satisfied(a4, timestep)$) is inferred on the basis of Equation 18.15 with weight $w1$:

$$w1: \quad Pre(a4, t-1) \wedge Occ(a4, t) \wedge Post(a4, t+1) \Rightarrow Satisfied(a4, t+1) \qquad (18.15)$$

On the other hand, the $(--S)$ contribution link (defined in Section 18.4) with weight $w2$: (Equation 18.16) quantifies the impact of the denial of goal $g3$ on task $a4$,

$$w2: \quad !Satisfied(g_3, t_1) \Rightarrow !Satisfied(a_4, t_1) \qquad (18.16)$$

Consequently, the probability assignment given to $Satisfied(a_4, timestep)$ is determined by the rules containing it, as well as the weight of these rules. The values of these weights are determined by system administrators and by observing past cases. This situation though implies that the structure of the system and its operating environment remain stable for a period of time, so that the system has the ability to train itself with adequate cases and stable rules. It should be noted that the accuracy of the weights is determined by the administrator's expertise and access to past cases.
- The lack of information or observations toward achieving a diagnosis is based on the application of an open world assumption to the observation, where a lack of evidence does not absolutely negate an event's occurrence but rather weakens its possibility.

Weights $w1$ and $w2$ can be initially assigned by the user and can be learned by the MLN as root cause analysis sessions are applied for various system diagnoses.

18.7.2 DIAGNOSIS

In this section the details of the diagnosis phase are presented in more detail. This phase aims to generate a Markov network based on goal model relationships as described in Section 18.7.1 and then uses the system events obtained to proceed with an inference of the possible root causes of the observed system failure.

18.7.2.1 Markov network construction

In this context, an MLN is constructed using the rules and predicates as discussed in Section 18.6.1. The grounding of the predicates comes from all possible literal values obtained from the log files. For example, in Figure 18.7 the ground predicate $t4$ $Connect\_to\_Credit\_Database(DB1)$, where DB1 is a specific database server, becomes true if there exists a corresponding logged event denoting that there is such a connection to DB1. The Markov network then is a graph of nodes and edges where nodes are grounded predicates and edges connect two grounded predicates if these coexist in a grounded logic formula. Weights w_i are associated with each possible grounding of a logic formula in the knowledge base [17].

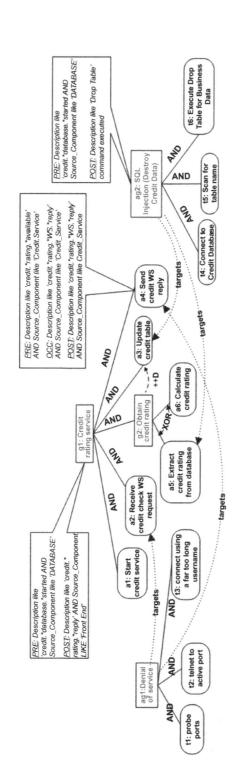

FIGURE 18.7

Goal and antigoal models for the credit history service.

18.7.2.2 Weight learning

Weight learning for the rules is performed semiautomatically, by first using discriminative learning based on a training set [17], and then with manually refining by a system expert. During automated weight learning, each formula is converted to its conjunctive normal form, and a weight is learned for each of its clauses. The learned weight can be further modified by the operator to reflect his or her confidence in the rules. For example, in Figure 18.3, a rule indicating that the denial of the top goal g_1 implies that at least one of its AND-decomposed children (a_1, g_2, and a_2) have been denied, should be given higher weight than a rule indicating that a_1 is satisfied on the basis of log data proving that $pre(a_1)$, $occ(a_1)$, and $post(a_1)$ are true. In this case, the operator has without any doubt witnessed the failure of the system, even if the logged data do not directly "support" it, and therefore can adjust the weights manually to reflect this scenario.

Report_Time	Description	Source_Address
2010-02-05 17:46:44.24	Starting database eventsDB	DATABASE

18.7.2.3 Inference

The inference process uses three elements. The first element is the collection of *observations* (i.e., facts extracted from the logged data) that correspond to ground atom *Pre*, *Occ*, and, *Post* predicates. As mentioned earlier, these predicates are generated and inserted in the fact base when the corresponding expression annotations match log data entries and the corresponding timestep ordering is respected (i.e., the timestep of a precondition is less than the timestep of an occurrence, and the latter is less than the timestep of a postcondition). See Section 18.7.1.5 for more details on the generation of ground atoms from logged data using the goal and task node annotations. The second element is the collection of rules that are generated by the goal models as presented in Section 18.7.1.4. The third element is the inference engine. For our work we use the Alchemy [17] probabilistic reasoning environment, which is based on MLNs. More specifically, using the MLN constructed as described in Section 18.7.2.1 and the Alchemy tool, we can infer the probability distribution for the ground atoms in the knowledge base, given the observations. Of particular interest are the ground atoms for the *Satisfied(node, timestep)* predicate, which represents the satisfaction or denial of tasks and goals in the goal model at a certain timestep. MLN inference generates weights for all the ground atoms of *Satisfied(task,timestep)* for all tasks and at every timestep. On the basis of the MLN rules listed in Section 18.4.4, the contribution of a child node's satisfaction to its parent goal's occurrence depends on the timestep of when that child node was satisfied. Using the MLN set of rules, we identify the timestep t for each task's *Satisfied(n,t)* ground atom that contributes to its parent goal at a specific timestep (t'). The same set of rules can be applied to infer the satisfaction of a child based on observing the parent's occurrence (remember that the occurrence of the top goal represents the overall service failure that has been observed and thus can be assigned a truth value). The *Satisfied* ground atoms of tasks with the identified timesteps are ordered on the basis of their timesteps. Finally, we inspect the weight of each ground atom in the secondary list (starting from the earliest timestep), and identify the tasks with grounds atoms that have a weight of less than 0.5 as the potential root cause of the top goal's failure. A set of diagnosis scenarios based on the goal model in Figure 18.3 are depicted in Table 18.2. For each scenario, a set of ground atoms representing this particular instance's observation is applied to the set of MLN rules representing the goal model in order to generate the probability distribution for the *Satisfied* predicate, which in turn is used to infer the root cause of the failure.

18.8 ROOT CAUSE ANALYSIS FOR FAILURES DUE TO EXTERNAL THREATS

In this section, we extend the root cause analysis framework discussed in the previous section, and develop a technique for identifying the root causes of system failures due to external interventions. There are two main differences between this framework and the previously described framework (root cause analysis for failures caused by *internal* errors). Here the first phase not only consists in modeling the conditions by which a system delivers its functionality using goal models, but also denotes the conditions by which system functionality can be compromised by actions that threaten system goals, by using antigoal models. Essentially, antigoal models aim to represent the different ways an external agent can threaten the system and cause a failure. As discussed earlier, logged data as well as goal and antigoal models are represented as rules and facts in a knowledge base. Consequently, the diagnosis phase involves identifying not only the tasks that possibly explain the observed failure, but also identifying antigoals induced by an external agent that may hurt system goals and explain the observed failure. Ground atom generation, rule construction, weight learning, and uncertainty representation follow the same principles and techniques as in the case of root cause analysis for failures due to internal errors, as presented in the previous section. Similarly to the case of root cause analysis for failures due to internal errors, antigoal model nodes are also extended by annotations in the form of pattern expressions. An example of such annotations is illustrated in Figure 18.7. More specifically, in Figure 18.7, antigoal *ag2* has *Pre*, *Post*, and *Occ* annotations, exactly as ordinary goal nodes have. Furthermore, it is shown that *ag2* targets action *a3* in the goal tree rooted at *g1*. These annotations pertain to string patterns and keywords that may appear in log entries and relate to the semantics of the corresponding goal or antigoal model node being annotated. The format of the log entries depends though on the logging infrastructure of each application.

In this section we focus on the definition of antigoals for root cause analysis for failures due to externally induced errors, and the inference strategy. The overall architecture of the framework of root cause analysis for failures due to externally induced errors is depicted in Figure 18.8.

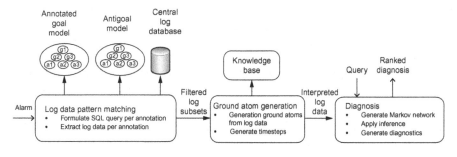

FIGURE 18.8

Logical architecture of the malicious behavior detection framework.

18.8.1 ANTIGOAL MODEL RULES

Here, the goal model rules are similar to the rules applied to detect internal errors and described in Section 18.7.1.4.

As is the case with goal models, antigoal models also consist of AND/OR decompositions; therefore antigoal model relationships with their child nodes are represented using the same first-order logic expressions as for goal models (Equations 18.11 and 18.12). The satisfaction of tasks (leaf nodes) in antigoal models follows the same rule as in Equation 18.9. The satisfaction of antigoals is expressed using the truth assignment of the *Satisfied(node)* predicates, which in turn is inferred as follows:

$$Pre(ag_1, t_1) \wedge Occ(ag_1, t_2) \wedge Post(ag_1, t_3) \Rightarrow$$
$$Satisfied(ag_1, t_3) \tag{18.17}$$

The satisfaction of an antigoal ag_i at timestep t_1 presents a negative impact on the satisfaction of a target task a_j at timestep $t_1 + 1$.

$$Satisfied(ag_i, t_1) \wedge Targets(ag_i, a_j) \Rightarrow$$
$$!Satisfied(a_j, t_1 + 1) \tag{18.18}$$

The outcome of this process is a set of ordered ground atoms that are used in the subsequent inference phase as the dynamic part of the system observation.

18.8.2 INFERENCE

The flowchart in Figure 18.10 represents the process of root cause analysis for failures due to externally induced errors. This process starts when an alarm is raised indicating a system failure, and terminates when a list of root causes of the observed failure is identified. For the diagnostic reasoning process to proceed, we consider that the annotated goal/antigoal models for the monitored systems and their corresponding Markov networks and logical predicates have been generated as described earlier in the chapter. The diagnostic reasoning process is composed of seven steps as discussed in detail below:

Step 1: The investigation starts when an alarm is raised or when the system administrator observes the failure of the monitored service, which is the denial of a goal g.

Step 2: On the basis of the knowledge base, which consists of all goal models and all observations (filtered log data and visual observation of the failure of the monitored service), the framework constructs a Markov network, which in turn is applied to generate a probability distribution for all the *Satisfied(node, timestep)* predicates for all nodes in the goal tree rooted at the denied goal g and the nodes of all other trees connected to it. This probability distribution is used to indicate the satisfaction or denial of tasks and goals at every timestep in the observation period. More specifically, if the probability of satisfaction of a task a_i at a timestep t is higher than a threshold value thrs, then we conclude that a_i is satisfied at t—that is, *Satisfied(a_i, t)*. Typically the timestep t starts at 0, and thrs is chosen to be 0.5.

An example of the outcome of this step is as follows based on Figure 18.9:

$$\begin{cases} Satisfied(a_1, 3) : 0.36 \\ Satisfied(a_3, 7) : 0.45 \end{cases}$$

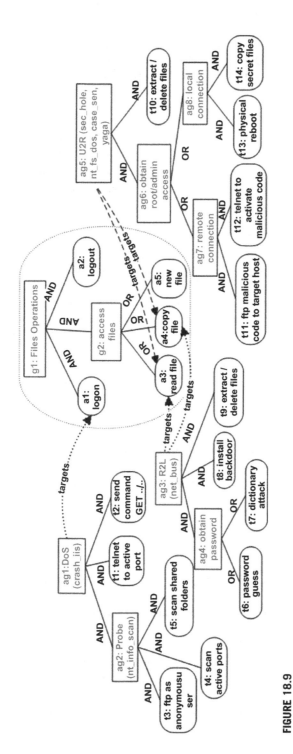

FIGURE 18.9

Antigoal attacks against g_1, the goal model for file services (center).

Step 3: The outcome of the previous step is a ranked list of denied tasks/goals, where the first task represents the node that is most likely to be the cause of the failure. In step 3, the framework iterates through the denied list of tasks identified in step 2, and loads the antigoal models targeting each of the denied tasks.

Step 4: For each antigoal model selected in step 3, we generate the observation literals from the log data by applying the ground atom generation process described in Section 18.7.1.5. Note that a task may have zero, one, or multiple antigoal models targeting it. The goal model in Figure 18.9 contains task a_2, which has no antigoal models targeting it, task a_1, which has one antigoal (ag_1) targeting it, and task a_3, which has two antigoals (ag_3 and ag_5) targeting it.

Step 5: This step is similar to step 2, but instead of evaluating a goal model, the framework evaluates the antigoal model identified in step 4 using the log-data-based observation and determines wether the top antigoal is satisfied. This is done by constructing a Markov network based on the antigoal model relationships (see Section 18.8.1) and inferring the probability distribution for the *Satisfied(antigoal, timestep)* predicate for the nodes in the antigoal model. In particular, we are interested in the probability assigned to *Satisfied(ag_j, t)* where t represents the timestep at which ag_j is expected to finish. Using the example in Figure 18.9, we see ag_1 takes 11 steps to complete execution, while ag_3 takes seven steps. In this case, we are interested in *Satisfied(ag_1, 11)* and *Satisfied(ag_2, 7)*.

Step 6: On the basis of the value of *Satisfied(ag_j, t)* identified in step 5, we distinguish the following two cases:

1. If *Satisfied(ag_j, t)* $\geq$ thrs (typically thrs $= 0.5$), this indicates that ag_j is likely to have occurred and caused a_i to be denied. In this case, we add this information (antigoal and its relationship with the denied task) to the knowledge base. This knowledge base enrichment is done at two levels: first, a new observation is added to indicate that antigoal ag_j has occurred, and second, a rule is added on the basis of the pattern in Equation 18.18.
2. If *Satisfied(ag_j, t)* $<$ thrs, this indicates that ag_j did not occur; thus we exclude it as a potential cause of failure for a_i.

Before going to next step, the framework checks whether the denied task a_i is targeted by any other antigoal models. If it is, it iterates through the list of other antigoals ag_j that are targeting a_i by going back to step 4. Once all antigoals targeting a denied task a_i have been evaluated, the framework checks whether there are more denied tasks, and if there are, it repeats step 2.

Step 7: On the basis of the new knowledge acquired from evaluating the antigoal models, the satisfaction of tasks based on the enriched knowledge base is reevaluated to produce a new ranking of the denied tasks. The fact that an attack is likely to have occurred targeting a specific task that has failed increases the chances that this task is actually denied because of the intrusion, leading to the overall system failure. This overall process helps improve the diagnosis, but also provides interpretation for the denial of tasks.

18.9 **EXPERIMENTAL EVALUATIONS**

To evaluate the proposed framework, we conducted the following set of case studies. The first set aims at examining the diagnostic effectiveness of the framework, using the experimental setup described in Section 18.4.4, by detecting root causes of observed failures due to internal errors. The second set focuses on detecting root causes of observed failures due to external actions. Finally, the third set aims to evaluate the scalability and measure the performance of the framework using larger data sets.

18.9.1 **DETECTING ROOT CAUSES DUE TO INTERNAL FAULTS**

The first case study consists of a set of scenarios conducted using the loan application service. These scenarios are conducted from the perspective of the system administrator, where a system failure is reported, and a root cause investigation is triggered.

The normal execution scenario for the system starts with the receipt of a loan application in the form of a Web service request. The loan applicant's information is extracted and used to build another request, which is sent to a credit evaluation Web service as illustrated in Figure 18.3.

The four scenarios in this study include one success and three failure scenarios (see Table 18.2). Scenario 1 represents a successful execution of the loan application process. Tthe denial of task a_7 does not represent a failure in the process execution, since goal g_3 is OR-decomposed into a_6 (*extract credit history for existing clients*) and a_7 (*calculate credit history for new clients*), and the successful execution of either a_6 or a_7 is enough for g_3's successful occurrence (see Figure 18.3). The probability values (weights) of the ground atoms range from 0 (denied) to 1 (satisfied). During each loan evaluation, and before the reply is sent to the requesting application, a copy of the decision is stored in a local table (a_4 (*update loan table*)). Scenario 2 represents a failure to update the loan table leading to failure of top goal g_1. Next, as described in Section 18.7.2.3, we identify a_4 as the root cause of the failure. Note that although a_7 was denied ahead of task a_4, it is not the root cause since it is an OR child of g_3, and its sibling task a_6 was satisfied. Similarly, for scenario 3, we identify task a_6 as the root cause of the failure. Scenario 4 represents the failure to validate Web service requests for the loan application. Almost no events are observed in this scenario. Using the diagnosis logic described in Section 18.7.2.3, we identify task a_1 (*receive loan application Web service request*) as the root cause of the observed failure.

18.9.2 **DETECTING ROOT CAUSES DUE TO EXTERNAL ACTIONS**

In this case study, we consider failures of the loan application scenario due to externally induced errors. As in the case of failures due to internal actions, we consider that the logs have the same format and the results are presented to the administrator in the same way—that is, in the form of lists of goal or antigoal nodes that correspond to problems that may be responsible (i.e., causes) for the observed failure. Each node is associated with a probability as this is computed by the reasoning engine as discussed in previous sections.

The experiment is conducted from the perspective of the system administrator, where a system failure is reported and an investigation is triggered. This case study scenario consists in running an attack while executing the credit history service (see the goal model of the credit service in Figure 18.7). The antigoal ag_1 is executed by probing the active ports on the targeted machine, and then the attacker attempts to log in but uses a very long username (16,000 characters), disrupting the service authentication process, and denying legitimate users from accessing the service. Traces of this attack can be obtained in the Windows Event Viewer.

The antigoal ag_2 models an SQL injection attack that aims at dropping the table containing the credit scores. One way to implement such an attack is to send two subsequent legitimate credit history Web service requests that contain embedded malicious SQL code within a data value. For example, to implement this malicious scenario, we embed an SQL command to scan and list all the tables in the data value of the field *ID* as follows:

$$< ID > 12345; selectfromSYSOBJECTSwhereTYPE =' U' orderbyNAME < /ID >$$

The system extracts the credential data value (e.g., ID) and uses it to query the database, thus inadvertently executing the malicious code. The scan is followed by a second Web Service request that contains a command to drop the Credit_History table:

$$< ID > 12345; DropTableCredit\_History < /ID >$$

Traces of the credit service sessions are found in the SQL Server audit log data and in the message broker (hosting the credit service). The first antigoal ag_1 represents the attacker's plan to deny access to the credit service by keeping busy the port used by that service. The second antigoal ag_2 aims at injecting an SQL statement that destroys the credit history data.

18.9.2.1 Experiment enactment

In this section, we outline a case where there is an observed failure, and we seek the possible causes. In this particular scenario there is a goal model and an antigoal model, and we illustrate how in the first phase of the process a collection of goal model nodes are identified as possible causes, but when in the second phase we consider also the antigoal model, where we identify the satisfaction of an antigoal that "targets" a goal node, the probability of the goal node failing (and thus becoming the leading cause) increases when we reevaluate it. The case is enacted with respect to the goal and antigoal models depicted in Figure 18.7.

We run a sequence of credit service requests and in parallel we perform an SQL injection attack. The log database table contained 1690 log entries generated from all systems in our test environment.

The first step in the diagnosis process (Figure 18.10) is to use the filtered log data to generate the observation (ground atoms) in the form of Boolean literals representing the truth values of the node annotations in the goal (or antigoal) model during the time interval where the log data is collected. The *Planfile1* model segment below represents the observation corresponding to one credit service execution session:

Planfile1: $Pre(g_1,1)$; $Pre(a_1,1)$; $Occ(a_1,2)$; $Post(a_1,3)$; $Pre(a_2,3)$; $Occ(a_2,4)$; $Post(a_2,5)$; $Post(g_2,5)$; $?Pre(a_5,5)$; $?Occ(a_5,6)$; $?Post(a_5,7)$; $Pre(a_6,5)$; $?Occ(a_6,6)$; $?Post(a_6,7)$; $?Post(g_2,7)$; $?Pre(a_3,7)$; $?Occ(a_3,8)$; $?Post(a_3,9)$; $?Pre(a_4,9)$; $?Occ(a_4,10)$; $?Post(a_4,11)$; $?Post(g_1,11)$, $!Satisfied(g_1,11)$

In the case where we do not find evidence for the occurrence of the events corresponding to execution of goals/antigoals/tasks (precondition, postcondition, etc.), we do not treat this as proof that these events did not occur, but we consider them as uncertain. We represent this uncertainty by adding a question mark before the corresponding ground atoms. In cases where there is evidence that an event did not occur, the corresponding ground atom is preceded by an exclamation mark.

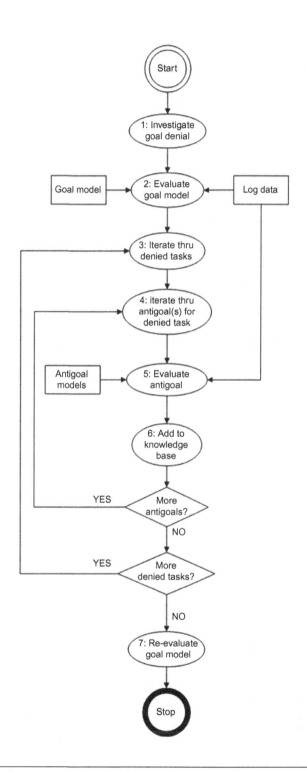

FIGURE 18.10

Malicious behavior detection process.

By applying inference based on the observation in *Planfile1* (step 2 in the flowchart in Figure 18.10), we obtain the following probabilities for the ground atoms using the Alchemy tool:

$$Satisfied(a_1, 3) : 0.99, \; Satisfied(a_2, 5) : 0.99,$$
$$Satisfied(a_5, 7) : 0.30, \; Satisfied(a_6, 7) : 0.32,$$
$$Satisfied(a_3, 9) : 0.34, \; Satisfied(a_4, 11) : 0.03.$$

Using step 2 in the diagnostics flowchart (Figure 18.10), we deduce that a_4, a_5, a_6, and a_3 are in that order, the possible root causes of the failure of the top goal g_1 (i.e., they have the lowest success probability, meaning they have high failure probability).

Using steps 3 and 4 in the diagnostics flowchart, we first generate the observation for antigoal ag_1 (*Planfile2*), and then apply inference based on the antigoal model ag_1 relationship and the generated observation.

Planfile2: $Pre(ag_1, 1)$, $?Pre(t_1, 1)$, $?Occ(t_1, 2)$, $?Post(t_1, 3)$, $?Pre(t_2, 3)$, $?Occ(t_2, 4)$, $?Post(t_2, 5)$, $?Pre(t_3, 5)$, $?Occ(t_3, 6)$, $?Post(t_3, 7)$, $?Post(ag_1, 7)$

In step 5, the outcome of the inference indicates that ag_1 is denied (satisfaction probability is 0.0001). We iterate through step 3, and the next denied task a_5 is targeted by antigoal ag_2. The observation generated for antigoal ag_2 is depicted in the *Planfile3* snippet below:

Planfile3: $Pre(ag_2, 1)$, $Pre(t_4, 1)$, $Occ(t_4, 2)$, $Post(t_4, 3)$, $Pre(t_5, 3)$, $Occ(t_5, 4)$, $Post(t_5, 5)$, $Pre(t_6, 5)$, $Occ(t_6, 6)$, $Post(t_6, 7)$, $Post(ag_2, 7)$

The outcome of the inference indicates that ag_2 is satisfied (satisfaction probability is 0.59). Using step 6, we add the result to the goal model knowledge base. In step 7, we reevaluate the goal-model-based knowledge base and generate a new diagnosis as follows:

$$Satisfied(a_1, 3) : 0.95, \; Satisfied(a_2, 5) : 0.98,$$
$$Satisfied(a_5, 7) : 0.23, \; Satisfied(a_6, 7) : 0.29,$$
$$Satisfied(a_3, 9) : 0.11, \; Satisfied(a_4, 11) : 0.26.$$

The new diagnosis now ranks a_3 as the most likely root cause of the failure of the top goal g_1 (i.e., it has the lowest success probability), whereas in the previous phase a_4 was the most likely one. Next, a_5, a_4, and a_6 are also possible root causes, but are now less likely. This new diagnosis is an improvement over the first one generated in step 2 since it accurately indicates a_3 as the most probable root cause. We know that this is correct since the SQL injection attack ag_2 targeted and dropped the credit table.

18.9.3 PERFORMANCE EVALUATION

The third experiment is an evaluation of the processing performance of the framework. We used a set of extended goal models representing the loan application goal model to evaluate the performance of the framework when larger goal models are used. The four extended goal models contained 10, 50, 80, and 100 nodes, respectively. This experiment was conducted using Ubuntu Linux running on an Intel Pentium 2 Duo 2.2 GHz machine. From the experiments conducted, we observed that the matching and ground atom generation performance depends linearly on the size of the corresponding goal model and

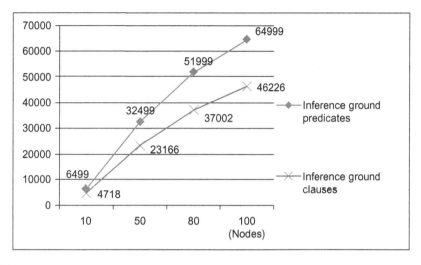

FIGURE 18.11

Impact of goal model size on ground atoms/clauses for inference. The time is given in seconds.

log data, and thus led us to believe that the process can easily scale for larger and more complex goal models. In particular, we are interested in measuring the impact of larger goal models on the learning and inference aspects of the framework.

Figure 18.11 illustrates that the number of ground atoms/clauses, which directly impacts the size of the resulting Markov model, is linearly proportional to the goal model size. Figure 18.12 illustrates that the running time for the off-line learning of the rule weights increases linearly with the size of

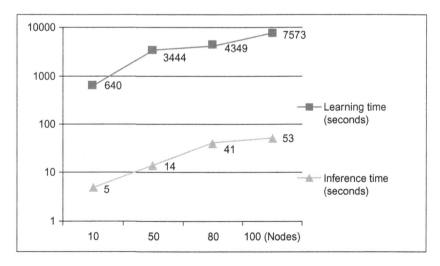

FIGURE 18.12

Impact of goal model size on learning/inference time. The time is given in seconds.

the goal model. The learning time ranged from slightly over 10 min for a goal model with 10 nodes, to over 2 h for a model with 100 nodes. The inference time ranged from 5 s for a goal model with 10 nodes to 53 s for a model with 100 nodes. As the initial results indicate, this approach can be considered for applications with sizeable logs, entailing the use of small to medium-sized diagnostic models (approximately 100 nodes).

18.10 CONCLUSIONS

In this chapter, we have presented a root cause analysis framework that allows the identification of possible root causes of software failures that stem either from internal faults or from the actions of external agents. The framework uses goal models to associate system behavior with specific goals and actions that need be achieved in order for the system to deliver its intended functionality or meet its quality requirements. Similarly, the framework uses antigoal models to denote the negative impact the actions of an external agent may have on specific system goals. In this context, goal and antigoal models represent cause and effect relations and provide the means for denoting diagnostic knowledge for the system being examined. Goal and antigoal model nodes are annotated with pattern expressions. The purpose of the annotation expressions is twofold: first, to be used as queries in an information retrieval process that is based on LSI to reduce the volume of the logs to be considered for the satisfaction or denial of each node; and second, to be used as patterns for inferring the satisfaction of each node by satisfying the corresponding *precondition*, *occurrence*, and *postcondition* predicates attached to each node. Furthermore, the framework allows a transformation process to be applied so that a rule base can be generated from the specified goal and antigoal models.

The transformation process also allows the generation of *observation facts* from the log data obtained. The rule base and the fact base form a complete, for a particular session, diagnostic knowledge base. Finally, the framework uses a probabilistic reasoning engine that is based on the concept of Markov logic and MLNs. In this context, the use of a probabilistic reasoning engine is important as it allows inference to commence even in the presence of incomplete or partial log data, and ranking the root causes obtained by their probability or likelihood values.

The proposed framework provides some interesting new points for root cause analysis systems. First, it introduces the concept of log reduction to increase performance and is tractable. Second, it argues for the use of semantically rich and expressive models for denoting diagnostic knowledge such as goal and antigoal models. Finally, it argues that in real-life scenarios root cause analysis should be able to commence even with partial, incomplete, or missing log data information.

New areas and future directions that can be considered include new techniques for log reduction, new techniques for hypothesis selection, and tractable techniques for goal satisfaction and root cause analysis determination. More specifically, techniques that are based on complex event processing, information theory, or PLSI could serve as a starting point for log reduction. SAT solvers, such as Max-SAT and Weighted Max-SAT solvers, can also be considered as a starting point for generating and ranking root cause hypotheses on the basis of severity, occurrence probability, or system domain properties. Finally, the investigation of advanced fuzzy reasoning, probabilistic reasoning, and processing distribution techniques such as map-reduce algorithms may shed new light on the tractable identification of root causes for large-scale systems.

REFERENCES

[1] Hirzalla M, Cleland-Huang J, Arsanjani A. Service-oriented computing — ICSOC 2008 workshops. Berlin: Springer-Verlag; 2009. p. 41–52. ISBN 978-3-642-01246-4. doi:10.1007/978-3-642-01247-1_5.

[2] Gray J. Designing for 20TB disk drives and enterprise storage. research.microsoft.com/Gray/talks/NSIC_HighEnd_Gray.ppt; 2000.

[3] Zawawy H, Kontogiannis K, Mylopoulos J, Mankovski S. Requirements-driven root cause analysis using Markov logic networks. In: CAiSE '12: 24th international conference on advanced information systems engineering; 2012. p. 350–65.

[4] Zawawy H. Requirement-based root cause analysis using log data. PhD thesis, University of Waterloo; 2012.

[5] Huang H, Jennings III R, Ruan Y, Sahoo R, Sahu S, Shaikh A. PDA: a tool for automated problem determination. In: LISA'07: proceedings of the 21st conference on large installation system administration conference. Berkeley, CA, USA: USENIX Association; 2007. p. 1–14. ISBN 978-1-59327-152-7.

[6] Chen M, Zheng AX, Lloyd J, Jordan MI, Brewe E. Failure diagnosis using decision trees. In: International conference on autonomic computing; 2004. p. 36–43.

[7] Wang Y, Mcilraith SA, Yu Y, Mylopoulos J. Monitoring and diagnosing software requirements. Automated Software Eng 2009;16(1):3–35. doi:10.1007/s10515-008-0042-8.

[8] Yuan C, Lao N, Wen JR, Li J, Zhang Z, Wang YM, Ma WY. Automated known problem diagnosis with event traces. In: EuroSys '06: proceedings of the 1st ACM SIGOPS/EuroSys European conference on computer systems 2006. New York, NY, USA: ACM; 2006. p. 375–88. ISBN 1-59593-322-0. doi:http://doi.acm.org.proxy.lib.uwaterloo.ca/10.1145/1217935.1217972.

[9] Steinder M, Sethi AS. Probabilistic fault diagnosis in communication systems through incremental hypothesis updating. Comput Netw 2004;45(4):537–62. doi:10.1016/j.comnet.2004.01.007.

[10] Al-Mamory SO, Zhang H. Intrusion detection alarms reduction using root cause analysis and clustering. Comput Commun 2009;32(2):419–30.

[11] Szvetits M, Zdun U. Enhancing root cause analysis with runtime models and interactive visualizations. http://st.inf.tu-dresden.de/MRT13/; 2013.

[12] Holmes T, Zdun U, Daniel F, Dustdar S. Monitoring and analyzing service-based internet systems through a model-aware service environment. In: CAiSE '10: 22nd international conference on advanced information systems engineering; 2010. p. 98–112.

[13] Elgammal A, Turetken O, van den Heuvel WJ, Papazoglou M. Root-cause analysis of design-time compliance violations on the basis of property patterns. In: ICSOC'10: 8th international conference on service oriented computing; 2010. p. 17–31.

[14] Chopra A, Dalpiaz F, Giorgini P, Mylopoulos J. Reasoning about agents and protocols via goals and commitments. In: Proceedings of the 9th international conference on autonomous agents and multiagent systems. AAMAS'10, Laxenburg, Austria, Austria: International Federation for Information Processing; 2010. p. 457–64. ISBN 978-0-9826571-1-9. URL: http://dl.acm.org/citation.cfm?id=2147671.2147737.

[15] Van Lamsweerde A, Darimont R, Massonet P. Goal-directed elaboration of requirements for a meeting scheduler: problems and lessons learnt. In: RE '95: Proceedings of the second IEEE international symposium on requirements engineering. Washington, DC, USA: IEEE Computer Society; 1995. p. 194. ISBN 0-8186-7017-7.

[16] Kalamatianos T, Kontogiannis K. Schema independent reduction of streaming log data. In: CAiSE '14: 26th international conference on advanced information systems engineering; 2014. p. 394–408.

[17] Kok S, Sumner M, Richardson M, Singla P, Poon H, Lowd D, Domingos P. The alchemy system for statistical relational AI. Technical report, Department of Computer Science and Engineering, University of Washington, Seattle, WA. http://alchemy.cs.washington.edu; 2007.

[18] Deerwester S, Dumais ST, Furnas G, K LT, Harshman R. Indexing by latent semantic analysis. J Amer Soc Informat Sci 1990; 41:391–407.

[19] Hofmann T. Probabilistic latent semantic indexing. In: SIGIR '99: proceedings of the 22nd annual international ACM SIGIR conference on research and development in information retrieval. New York, NY, USA: ACM; 1999. p. 50–7. ISBN 1-58113-096-1. doi:http://doi.acm.org/10.1145/312624.312649.

[20] Blei DM, Ng AY, Jordan MI. Latent Dirichlet allocation. J Mach Learn Res 2003;3:993–1022. URL: http://dl.acm.org/citation.cfm?id=944919.944937.

[21] Lee S, Baker J, Song J, Wetherbe JC. An empirical comparison of four text mining methods. In: HICSS '10: proceedings of the 2010 43rd Hawaii International Conference on System Sciences. Washington, DC, USA: IEEE Computer Society; 2010. p. 1–10. ISBN 978-0-7695-3869-3. doi:10.1109/HICSS.2010.48.

[22] Golub G, Reinsch C. Singular value decomposition and least squares solutions. Numer Math 1970;14(5):403-20, doi:10.1007/BF02163027.

[23] Wu L, Feng J, Luo Y. A personalized intelligent web retrieval system based on the knowledge-base concept and latent semantic indexing model. ACIS international conference on software engineering research, management and applications; 2009. p. 45–50. doi:10.1109/SERA.2009.40.

[24] Poshyvanyk D, Marcus A, Rajlich V, Gueheneuc YG, Antoniol G. Combining probabilistic ranking and latent semantic indexing for feature identification. In: ICPC '06: proceedings of the 14th IEEE international conference on program comprehension. Washington, DC, USA: IEEE Computer Society; 2006. p. 137–48. ISBN 0-7695-2601-2. doi:10.1109/ICPC.2006.17.

[25] Domingos P. Real-world learning with Markov logic networks. In: Boulicaut JF, Esposito F, Giannotti F, Pedreschi D, editors. Machine learning: ECML 2004. Lecture notes in computer science, vol. 3201. Berlin/Heidelberg: Springer; 2004. p. 17.

[26] Singla P, Domingos P. Discriminative training of Markov logic networks. In: Veloso MM, Kambhampati S, editors. AAAI. AAAI Press/The MIT Press; 2005. p. 868–73. ISBN 1-57735-236-X.

[27] Richardson M, Domingos P. Markov logic networks. Mach Learn 2006; 62:107–36.

[28] Yu Y, Lapouchnian A, Liaskos S, Mylopoulos J, Leite J. From goals to high-variability software design; 2008. p. 1–16. doi:10.1007/978-3-540-68123-6_1.

[29] Tran SD, Davis LS. Event modeling and recognition using Markov logic networks. In: European conference on computer vision; 2008. p. 610–23. doi:10.1007/978-3-540-88688-4_45.

[30] Dollimore J, Kindberg T, Coulouris G. Distributed systems: concepts and design. In: International Computer Science Series. 4th ed. Reading, MA: Addison Wesley; 2005. ISBN 0321263545.

ANALYTICAL PRODUCT RELEASE PLANNING

19

Maleknaz Nayebi*, Guenther Ruhe*

Software Engineering Decision Support Laboratory, University of Calgary, Calgary, AB, Canada*

CHAPTER OUTLINE

19.1 **INTRODUCTION AND MOTIVATION**

Release planning is a decision-centric problem with comprehensive information and knowledge needs. A release is a major (new or upgraded) version of an evolving product characterized by a collection of (new, corrected, or modified) features. Good release planning is a mandatory part of incremental and iterative software development. Release decisions address the questions about the functionality (What?), time (When?) and quality (How good?) of offering product releases. All types of release decisions are part of software product management, the discipline of governing a software product from its inception to the market until it is closed down [1].

Adaptive software development [2] as well as other domain of product development is increasingly affected by ongoing changes in business conditions. It also raises the need to adapt related decision-making processes. The formerly reactive mode of operation needs to be replaced by real-time or pro-active decisions based on highly up-to-date and comprehensive information. Big data analytics offers the principal pathway to make pro-active decisions. Information about changing customer and stakeholder product preferences and demands, knowledge about possible feature synergies in terms of added value or reduced effort estimation, as well as the possibility of performing pro-active product evaluation will increase the likelihood of developing the "right" product. A product manager can get additional information about product performance and mine industry trends and investigate on customer needs for achieving actionable insight.

The paradigm of Open Innovations is emphasizing on the range of opportunities available to get access to distributed knowledge and information. Open innovation integrates internal and external ideas and paths to market at the same level of importance [1] and merges distributed talent, knowledge and ideas into innovation processes [3]. Analytical Open Innovation (AOI) approach is designed in this context in order to make use of more knowledge containers for comprehensive decision-making and to address wickedness of the problem under study. We define AOI as being the integration of Open Innovation with (a portfolio of) analytical methods. AOI is positioned as a response to existing challenges of mining software repositories in software engineering. Some of the challenges are listed as follow:

- Mainly tame (well-defined) problems are considered. However, many software engineering planning and design problems incorporate some form of wickedness [4–6].

- Primarily, internal knowledge and repositories are used for the mining process. However, knowledge is available and retrievable from a broader range of information sources [4, 5].
- Often, a "closed world" and quantitative type of analysis is considered. However, problems need qualitative analysis as well as human expertise [7, 8].
- Mining software repositories (MSR) efforts, are mainly intended to support developers and, increasingly, project managers, but the role of a product manager has been largely ignored so far [6, 9, 10].

Current release planning methods are largely based on a "Closed Innovation", with information, knowledge, and stakeholders introduced (just) being largely static and pre-defined. Main deficits of current release planning techniques are related to their inability to handle the large amounts of data related to the ongoing change that is happening in the underlying development and business processes. In this chapter: (1) we propose the Analytical Open Innovation (AOI); (2) we discuss the application of AOI to the area of release planning decision support and will call this AOI@RP.

In this chapter, a taxonomy of (data-intensive) release planning problems is given in Section 19.2 Therein, special emphasis is on the content and impact of data analytics in all these problems. Information needs for software release planning are studied in Section 19.3. Data analytics techniques, as part of open innovation, are discussed in more detail in Section 19.4. The techniques are applied for an illustrative case study presented in Section 19.5. Finally, an outlook is presented on future research in Section 19.6.

19.2 TAXONOMY OF DATA-INTENSIVE RELEASE PLANNING PROBLEMS

There is a wide range of decision problems that altogether are subsumed under the term "Release planning". In what follows, seven classes of release planning problems are described.

19.2.1 WHAT-TO-RELEASE PLANNING

As part of any incremental and iterative software development, the question of which new features should be offered in upcoming releases is of key importance for product success. From an existing pool of features, the selection and schedule decisions are highly information intensive. To decide about the features, and assign them to one of the upcoming releases, one requires a good understanding of the features, their market value, their mutual dependencies and synergies, their effort to get them implemented and the market needs and trends to select the most appropriate feature for enhancing or updating the existing product. The main difficulty of the problem is that a large portion of the requested information is continuously changing.

19.2.2 THEME-BASED RELEASE PLANNING

The question of what constitutes a good release (content) is hard to answer. The formulation given in Section 19.4.2.1 assumes that the total value of a release is the sum of the value of the individual features, implemented and offered in this release. However, this is likely just an approximation of the truth. Some features are highly dependent and would have higher value when they are released along with a specific set of features.

A theme is meta-functionality of a product release, integrating a number of individual features under a joint umbrella. It can be thought of as an abstraction, that is, a group of features that are inter related to each other in a way that they depict a context and can be viewed as a single entity from a higher level [11, 12].

Theme-based release planning not only considers the value of individual features, but also utilizes synergy effects between semantically related features. Detection and formulation of dependencies are supported by performing cross consistency assessment (CCA), as discussed in Section 19.4.2.2. Pairwise consistency assessment between features shows the explicit dependencies and synergies, as well as hidden dependencies and synergies between features.

19.2.3 WHEN-TO-RELEASE PROBLEM

When-to-release decisions are trade-off decisions by their nature. The product manager needs to balance the possible gain (expressed by the value function) against the potential risks of delivering (too) early. This risk is essentially related to quality and customer acceptance. Although it is difficult to express formally, our assumption is that the risk is higher if the earlier the release date is chosen.

Various factors are relevant for deciding about when-to-release. The notion of *release readiness* incorporates a variety of factors related to requirements, coding and testing. Port et al. [13] illustrated the value of knowing RR in project success with aid of an explorative study at NASA's Jet Propulsion Laboratory (JPL). RR facilitates confident release decisions along with proactive addressing of problems related to releases. A list of frequently used release attributes and factors is given in Table 19.1

19.2.4 RELEASE PLANNING IN CONSIDERATION OF QUALITY

The traditional view of release planning favors delivery of pieces of functionality (called "features" or "requirements," depending on the granularity) in a best possible way. For a feature to become part of a product release, it needs to be implemented and thus, it consumes resources. The core question at this point is how to utilize the resources in the best possible way to provide the best combination of pieces of functionality. However, what is completely lacking in this view is the quality aspect of the resulting release product(s).

Table 19.1 List of Release Readiness Attributes and Related Metrics

Attributes (C_i)	RR Metrics (M_i)
Satisfaction of feature completion	Feature Completion Rate (FCR)
Satisfaction of features implemented	Features Implemented (FI)
Satisfaction of build/continuous integration trends	Build Success Rate (BSR)
Satisfaction of implementation effort	Code Churn Rate (addition and deletion per day) (CCR)
Satisfaction of defect finding	Defect Find Rate (DFR)
Satisfaction of defect fixing	Bug Fixing Rate (BFR)
Satisfaction of change completion	Change completion Rate (CR)
Satisfaction of pull request completion	Pull-request Completion Rate (PCR)

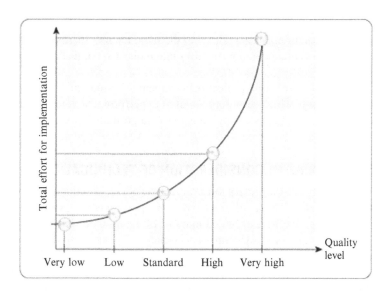

FIGURE 19.1

Total implementation effort of a feature in dependence of the target quality level.

Depending on the granularity of the planning, the specific effort attributed to higher target levels of quality can be feature-related and/or related to the whole product release (as a form of cross-cutting concern). The relation between quality and effort is demonstrated in Figure 19.1. With this formulation given, the problem is no longer just finding a plan to implement the most comprehensive and attractive set of features. Instead, the problem now becomes a trade-off analysis where the balance is between providing the most comprehensive and attractive functionality in dependence of varying levels of target quality. A prototype tool for supporting release planning of quality requirements and its initial industrial evaluation has been presented by Svensson et al. [14]. As part of the underlying planning method called "QUPER" [15], the tool helps to reach an alignment between practitioners, for example, product managers and developers, of what level of quality is actually needed [11].

19.2.5 OPERATIONAL RELEASE PLANNING

Once a strategic release plan is confirmed, the question becomes how to realize this plan. At this stage, planning gets more detailed, taking into account the existing pool of developers, their skills, as well as the order of tasks needed to implement the features. The problem; called *Operational Release Planning;* is to assign developers in the best possible way to the tasks constituting the features. It includes scheduling of tasks in consideration of possible technological constraints. Typically, the time horizon for operational planning is just before the upcoming release (or iteration).

For the staffing problem, each feature is considered as the result of performing a sequence of tasks. All objectives and constraints of the staffing problem(s) are formulated in terms of features and their related tasks. The solution method to the staffing problem considers the characteristics of the individual tasks and makes suggestions about the allocation of developers to the tasks and the order in which they should be performed. Among the tasks related to the same feature, there might be different types of dependencies. Another conceptual component looks into requested competences for performing the tasks [11].

Project scheduling as part of software project management was studied, for example, by Alba and Chicano [16]. In order to decide which resources are used to perform which tasks and when each task should be performed, the authors suggested applying genetic algorithms (GAs).

19.2.6 RELEASE PLANNING IN CONSIDERATION OF TECHNICAL DEBT

The metaphor of "technical debt" [17] refers to the actual versus ideal status of an evolving software system. Analogously to financial debt, different types of opportunistic development shortcuts and related temporary advantages (debt) are accepted in terms of the systems design, coding, testing, and documentation. In organizations, it is very common to strategically put off fixing a (non-critical) issue in order to implement new features as proposed by the release planning process.

It is a challenge for organizations to manage and track technical debt [18]. Accumulated debts, without appropriate refactoring, could threaten the maintainability of the products, and hinder future development due to unpredictable and poorly-designed architecture. Mining data can help in understanding the amount and potentially the root causes of the technical debt and what can be done about that principle (refactoring, redesign, etc.). Technical debt needs to be measured and tracked since the requirements gathering stage. Software design and requirements engineering need to identify the right, meaningful things to measure, such as the number of assumptions you make, the number of postponed functionality, the decision of technology platforms, etc. A wrong requirement is already a debt on future development, as the team will need to redesign or rebuild already made items to fit into requirements.

19.2.7 RELEASE PLANNING FOR MULTIPLE PRODUCTS

Instead of looking into the planning of just one product, often a suite of related products is considered. This increases not only the functionality, but also allows better customization, providing the customer with options to select the most appropriate products of the suite. As the development of a product suite typically follows the same paradigm of incremental and evolutionary development, the problem of release planning for one product is generalized that way to a problem with multiple products. At this point, the product can be either software or hardware related or a mixture of both.

The higher complexity of planning for a product suite instead of just a single product, results from the demand that the individual products of the suite should be offered synchronously. If this is not the case, a substantial part of the overall inherent value expected from offering a product suite is jeopardized, and/or the release of the suite needs to be delayed until the last part in the chain is finished.

Planning for release of product lines is another emerging topic. Schubanz et al. [19] proposed a conceptual model and corresponding tool support to plan and manage the systematic evolution of software-intensive systems. Their approach allows providing support for in time, continuous planning over long periods of time and many releases.

19.3 **INFORMATION NEEDS FOR SOFTWARE RELEASE PLANNING**

The paradigm of Open Innovation is aimed to enhance knowledge and information to qualify products decision-making. Information needs in software development and management was studied by Buse and Zimmermann [4]. In this chapter, we discuss expected information needs in the context of release planning. The evaluation is based on a combination of literature research and practical experience [20–25]. In order to utilize Open Innovation techniques in the context of release planning, the information needs are investigated in this section.

19.3.1 **FEATURES**

Wiegers [17] has defined a product feature as a set of logically related requirements that provide a capability to the user and enable the satisfaction of business objectives. For the actual description of features, different types of information need to be collected in a feature repository. As an example for a description scheme (Table 19.2), we present the structure suggested in adaptation of the scheme suggested by Regnell and Brinkkemper [26]. While all information is of strong relevance for release decisions, the information is hard to retrieve and to maintain. The situation worsens due to the degree of change inherent in the information.

Table 19.2 Feature Characterization Scheme (Based Upon [26])	
Attribute	**Value**
State	Candidate / approved / specified / discarded / planned / developed / verified / released
ID	Unique identity
Submitter	Who issued it?
Company	Submitter's company
Domain	Functional domain
Description	Short textual description
Contract	Link to sales contract enforcing requirement
Priorities	Prioritization for different criteria by different stakeholders on a 9-point scale
Motivation	Rational: Why it is important?
Line of business	Market segment for which feature is important
Specification	Link to use cases, textual specification
Dependencies	Precedence, coupling or other dependencies between features
Resource estimation	Estimated effort per defined resource type
Risk	Projected risks of implementation and market penetration
Schedule	Release for which it is planned for
Design	Link to design documents
Test	Link to test documents
Novelty	Novelty of the features when compared with competitors
Release version	Official release name

19.3.2 FEATURE VALUE

The question of what constitutes the value of a feature is difficult to answer. Value definition is context-specific and user-specific. The feature value is time-dependent, as the value might change under changing market or business conditions. Furthermore, the individual value of a feature is not additional to the overall release value. Offering certain features in conjunction, for example, related to themes (see Section 19.2.2), will provide synergies that are important to take into account [12].

A comprehensive value-map is suggested by Khurum et al. [27]. Utilizing knowledge from state-of-the-art in software engineering, business, management, and economics, and gathered through extensive literature reviews, as well as working with professionals in industry, the authors studied a broad range of value constructs and classified them as belonging to customer, internal business, financial, or innovation and in learning perspective. The authors also performed some industrial evaluation of the proposed taxonomy. They reported a fundamental impact within Ericsson, attributed to the creation and use of the software value map, indicated by the shift from cost-based discussions and reasoning, to value-based decision support.

19.3.3 FEATURE DEPENDENCIES

From analyzing industrial software product release planning projects in the domain of telecommunications, Carlshamre et al. [28] observed that features are often dependent on each other. For the projects and the domain analyzed, the percentage of features being dependent in one way or the other was as high as 80%.

There is a variety of dependencies which create different meanings of the term "dependency." We distinguish between dependencies in the following categories, based on Dahlstedt and Persson [1]:

- implementation space (two features are "close" in their implementation and should be treated together);
- feature effort space (two features are impacting each other in their implementation effort if provided in the same release);
- feature value space (two features are impacting each other in their value if provided in the same release);
- feature usage space (two features are only useful for the customer if provided in the same release).

Elicitation of dependencies is a form of knowledge elicitation and inherently difficult. Potentially, there are a large number of dependencies. Knowing at least the most critical ones will increase the chances of generating meaningful plans. Similarly, ignoring them will create plans lacking fulfillment of the required conditions between features [29].

19.3.4 STAKEHOLDERS

Stakeholders can play very different roles in the product planned for. They can be related to the design and/or development of the product, they can have a financial interest by the sale or purchase of the product; they can be responsible for the introduction and maintenance of the product; or they can have an interest in the use of the product. All of them are relevant, and their opinions are often contradictory. One of the challenges of product release planning is to determine a well-balanced product plan, which addresses the most relevant concerns.

Sharp et al. in Ref. [30] presented an approach of constructive guidance on how to actually find "the right set" of stakeholders. As a first (baseline) approach, four groups of stakeholders are summarized:

* users and customers,
* developers,
* legislators (such as professional bodies, trade unions, legal representatives, safety executives or quality assurance auditors),
* decision-makers (such as the CEO or shareholders).

Once the baseline stakeholders are established, the authors suggest a 5-step procedure to add further stakeholders to one of the four established groups. With regard to attaining access to stakeholder opinion, it can come from anywhere in the organization, or can be systemized and structured through personas.

19.3.5 STAKEHOLDER OPINIONS AND PRIORITIES

Stakeholder opinions and priorities are of key relevance to the plan and design of product releases. The process refers to the determination of priorities for the features under consideration for the next release(s). With the range of different segments, stakeholder opinions need to be clustered. Sample segmentation can be performed, based on criteria such as:

* demographic — gender, age, race, ethnicity;
* psychographic — personality, values, attitudes, interests, lifestyles;
* behavioral — product purchase patterns and usage, brand affinity;
* geographic — location-specific by city, state, region, or country.

The process of attracting stakeholder priorities is complex and reliable information is hard to get. However, without this information, product development becomes very risky. Gorschek et al. found that, too often critical stakeholders are overlooked and priorities are given in an ad hoc fashion [31].

More recently, discussion forums and user groups have been used to get access to stakeholder opinions [32]. This way, partial automation of information retrieval is possible. Social network analysis is another direction for improving the requirement prioritization process. Fitsilis et al. [33] applied meta-networks, where basic entities are combined for prioritizing requirements. They analyzed the required collaboration/knowledge within the requirements and analysis project team (including clients, managers, analysts, developers, etc.) in order to efficiently/effectively prioritize the requirements through the identification of a proper requirements prioritization technique.

19.3.6 RELEASE READINESS

Release readiness is a composite attribute intended to describe the degree of readiness to ship a product release. It comprises different aspects of the processes needed to implement a software product. Key dimensions of release readiness are:

* Implementation of functionality
* Testing
* Source code quality
* Documentation.

Monitoring all these dimensions with specific metrics is mandatory to further create predictive models for release readiness, or for analyzing the current status of it. An analytical method for evaluating release readiness is presented in Ref. [34].

19.3.7 MARKET TRENDS

In proactive software development, the analysis of customer needs is of great importance and in principle, the development processes are different from bespoke ones [35]. A target market or target audience is the market segment to which a particular product is marketed. It is often defined by age, gender, and/or socio-economic grouping. Market targeting is the process in which intended actual markets are defined, analyzed, and evaluated just before making the final decision to enter a market [36].

Information about current needs, competitors in these markets, and even more so about future trends, is of pivotal importance to decide on a future product release.

19.3.8 RESOURCE CONSUMPTIONS AND CONSTRAINTS

Development and testing of new features and their proper integration into the existing product consumes effort, time, and includes different types of human resources. Planning without investigating the resource constraints is risky, as the resulting plans are likely to fail. However, effort prediction is known to be very difficult and is impacted by many factors. Different methods are applicable for providing estimates [37]. Most of these methods incorporate some form of learning based on information available from former projects. In addition, often these methods are hybrid, in the sense that they combine formal techniques with the judgment and expertise of human domain experts. In all cases, no reliable estimates can be expected without proper and up-to-date information related to factors, such as product size, complexity, development processes, tools used, organization, productivity [17].

19.3.9 SYNTHESIS OF RESULTS

In this section, we gave an informal definition of seven classes of release planning problems, with special emphasis on their data and information needs. Using literature research and our practical experience [1, 20–25], we have applied information needs described in Section 19.3 and provided an evaluation of the needs for the different types of release planning problems. The results are summarized in Table 19.3.

19.4 THE PARADIGM OF ANALYTICAL OPEN INNOVATION

Open innovation integrates internal and external ideas and paths to market at the same level of importance [1], and merges talent, knowledge and ideas into innovation processes [3]. Analytical open innovation (AOI) is defined as the integration of open innovation with (a portfolio of) analytical methods. Its main goal is to make use of both internal and external knowledge for comprehensive decision-making and to address wickedness of the problem under study [38]. Data analytics is the use of advanced analytical techniques against very large diverse datasets that include different types, such as

Table 19.3 Information Needs for Different Types of Release Planning Problems								
	Information Needs							
Type of Release Planning Problem	**Features**	**Feature Dependencies**	**Feature Value**	**Stakeholder**	**Stakeholder Opinion and Priorities**	**Release Readiness**	**Market Trends**	**Resource Consumptions and Constraints**
What to release	×	×	×	×	×		×	×
Theme-based	×	×	×	×	×		×	×
When to release	×	×	×	×	×	×		×
Consideration of quality requirements	×		×	×	×	×	×	×
Operational release planning	×		×					×
Consideration of technical debt	×	×				×	×	
Multiple products	×	×	×	×	×	×		×

structured/unstructured and streaming/batch [39]. AOI subsumes all the methods, tools, and techniques to extract operational knowledge and insight from existing datasets.

AOI includes a great variety of methods and techniques, such as text and data mining, reasoning, and machine learning, clustering, optimization and simulation, as well as all forms of predictive models. For the approach described in this chapter, we discuss the effect of analytical techniques for leveraging release decisions in Section 19.4.1 We focus on the application and integration of two analytical techniques describes in Section 19.4.2. The methodology is then illustrated in Section 19.5.

19.4.1 THE AOI@RP PLATFORM

The AOI@RP platform is intended to support the application of AOI for different classes of release planning problems. Its main architecture is shown in Figure 19.2. The AOI@RP platform consists of three layers. Each of them is explained in more detail in the subsequent sections.

19.4.1.1 Open innovation system

This system is designed to satisfy the data needs presented in Section 19.3. Data gathering and generation is covered by following the open innovation approach and crowdsourcing is selected with the aim of direct-user involvement. The crowdsourcing platform provides the crowd for answering questions;

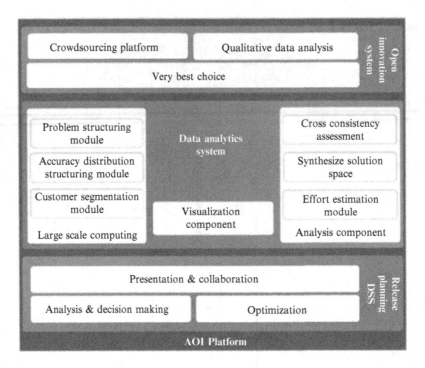

FIGURE 19.2

Proposed AOI platform.

facilitates controlling and verifying their works and task distribution. Here, *Amazon Mechanical Turk* [40] service as a micro-task market is employed. In addition, this platform in collaboration with Very Best Choice^{TM} maintains contact with the crowd. In order to manage collaboration between systems feedback management and representation alongside in-house collaboration with crowd, *Very Best Choice*^{TM} (VBC light) software is used. VBC light is a lightweight decision support system designed to facilitate priority decisions [41]. A text mining platform is used along with other platforms to enable automatic understanding of crowd's response in order to generate meaningful data.

19.4.1.2 Release planning DSS

This layer is presented as the release planning DSS in Figure 19.2. The different dimensions of release planning problems are presented in Section 19.2. *ReleasePlanner*^{TM} provides a proven [11, 21, 42] functionality to facilitate voting and prioritization as well as generating optimized plans although the *ReleasePlanner*^{TM} was designed to work in close innovation context; the underlying model of that platform needs to be adapted to the needs of handling more comprehensive data from different sources. The *Presentation & collaboration* component represents process outcomes to the organization and stakeholders. It is also responsible for initiating the work of other platforms. The *Optimization component* is responsible for computation of optimized and diversified alternative release plans based on specialized integer programming and the special structure of the problem. The *Analysis & decision component* defines alternative features and plans with their resource consumption and the degree of stakeholder excitement.

19.4.1.3 Data analytics system

This layer comprises of several analytical techniques leading to solving the problem of semi-wickedness of the release planning, by meaningfully analyzing the wide variety of gathered and generated data. Some of these techniques are described in Section 19.4.2. This platform is aligned with employed techniques and consists of modules, which are adapted with three technology pillars employed in a successful analytics platform [43]. Several silos of data are delivered as input to the data analytics platform. This data may have a variety of sources, such as former projects, expert's opinions, or similar projects. This layer interprets and structures the data. The large-scale computing module evaluates large sets of generated data and detects inconsistencies in the data. The analysis component provides the results of analysis on solution space.

19.4.2 ANALYTICAL TECHNIQUES

With the different types of data retrieved from the various sources of information, the follow-up question is how to analyze them and create new insight. While there is a broad range of existing techniques available, there are a few of them that have been successfully used in the context of release planning. In what follows, we describe two of these techniques. In addition, we present the analytical dimension of the technique called *morphological analysis* and describe its usage in the context of (release planning) problem structuring.

19.4.2.1 Identification of customer segments from applying clustering

A density-based clustering algorithm is used for identifying segments of customers having similar preference structures for product features [44]. We consider a set of L customers represented by $C = \{c(1), c(2), \ldots, c(L)\}$. A given set of M features represented by $F = \{feature(1), feature(2), \ldots, feature(M)\}$ is studied for their (complete) implementation in an evolving software system.

Definition 1. *Cluster configuration* is a partition of the set C into Q subsets. A cluster configuration is represented as $CC(i) = \{cc(i, 1), \ldots, cc(i, Q)\}$ where cc(i,j) is the *j*th cluster of customers in the *i*th cluster configuration such that $\bigcup_{j=1\ldots Q} cc(i,j) = C$ and $cc(i,j_1) \cap cc(i,j_2) = \emptyset$ for all pairs of j_1 and j_2.

Multiple cluster configurations can be generated by changing input parameters to the clustering algorithm. In Figure 19.8, the cluster configuration $CC(1)$ partitions the customers into two clusters $cc(1, 1)$ and $cc(1, 2)$.

Definition 2. For a given cluster configuration $CC(i)$, a *product variant* $p(i,j)$ is defined as the subset of the set of features F offered to the cluster of customers $cc(i,j)$ where $(1 \leq j \leq Q)$.

Using this, a company could offer one product variant per cluster of customers for all the cluster configurations.

Definition 3. *Product portfolio* is a set of product variants corresponding to a given cluster configuration. CC(i) corresponds to a product portfolio $PP(i) = \{p(i, 1), \ldots, p(i, Q)\}$ such that $\bigcup_{j=1\ldots Q} p(i,j) = F$ and $p(i,j_1) \cap p(i,j_2) \neq \emptyset$ for all pairs of j_1 and j_2.

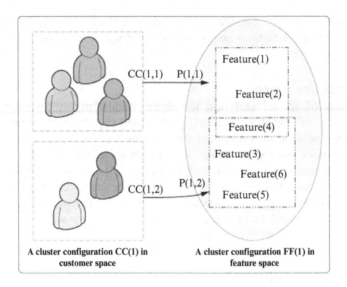

FIGURE 19.3

A cluster configuration and corresponding feature clusters.

For example, the product portfolio $PP(1)$ shown in Figure 19.3 contains two product variants corresponding to the two clusters in $CC(1)$. The product variants differ in their feature sets but have feature(4) in common.

We describe the assumptions for customer's clustering as follows:

1. The number of clusters is not pre-defined as clustering is preformed based on preferences.
2. The customers represent organizations with different market shares and seeing different level of value in each product.
3. Having similar preferences for features of the product defines the cohesiveness of the clusters. Each member of a cluster should be within the maximum distance (predefined) of at least one other member of the same cluster.
4. Clusters are non-overlapping, meaning that clusters should be at some distance from each other.

DBSCAN as a density-based spatial clustering algorithm for applications with noise [45] meets the first condition, since it does not require the number of clusters as an input parameter. It also meets the third condition listed above through the neighborhood distance parameter. The fourth condition is also fulfilled, since DBSCAN forms clusters with any arbitrary shape and they are separated by areas of low density (noise). However, DBSCAN treats all the customers as equally important. DBSCAN algorithm is used for identification of clusters of customers, since it meets most of the conditions listed above.

Once we plan for product release, each segment of customers becomes a data point in the dataset. Each data point is represented by a vector containing M values, where M1 is the number of features planned for the next release.

The major advantage of using DBSCAN is that clusters are formed only if there is sufficient level of cohesion among the data points in groups of customers representing unique market segments. Each market segment is mapped with a tentative product variant containing the features highly desired by customers.

19.4.2.2 Morphological analysis

Morphological analysis (MA) is a method for identifying, structuring and investigating the total set of possible relationships contained in a given multidimensional problem complex. MA allows small groups of subject specialists to define, link, and internally evaluate the parameters of complex problem spaces, creating a solution space and a flexible inference model [46, 47]. MA has been applied successfully in strategic planning and decision support in various domains, such as governance of technological development and modeling the Bioethics of drug redevelopment, which were reported more comprehensively by Ritchey [46].

MA provides an "if-then" laboratory within which drivers, and certain conditions, can be assumed and a range of associated solutions found, in order to test various inputs against possible outputs [48]. Generally, MA is intended to broaden the space of alternatives by systematic search for combinations of attributes and systematically narrow them down through the results. The result of MA is called *a morphological field*. Morphological fields describe the total problem complex. MA consists of the steps given below [48].

ANALYSIS PHASE

1. Extracts dimensions, parameters, or variables, which define the essential nature of the problem complex or scenario.
2. Defines a range of relevant, discrete values, or conditions, for each variable.

SYNTHESIZE PHASE

3. Assesses the internal consistency of all pairs of variable conditions.
4. Synthesizes an internally consistent outcome space.
5. Iterates the process, if necessary.

In what follows, we provide the key concept and notation from MA, which is needed to understand the remainder of this chapter.

Definition 4. A *morphological field* is a field of constructed dimensions or parameters, which is the basis for a morphological model. This will be shown by $F(n, l)$, as:

$F(n,l) \in FEATURES \mid$ *for all n, l where* $n \in \{f \mid F$ *is feature} refers to the functionality of the features, and* $l \in \{L \mid L$ *is level of functionality for M}* *indicates the level of functionality implemented.*

Definition 5. *Cross consistency assessment* (CCA) pertains to the process by which the parameter values $V(n, l) \in$ VALUE (or parameter conditions) in the morphological field are compared with each other. This process is intended to reduce the total problem space to a smaller (internally consistent) solution space.

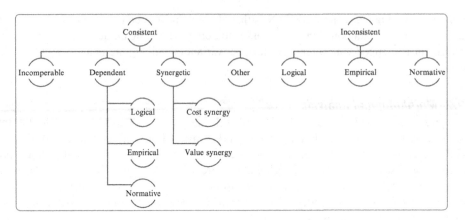

FIGURE 19.4

Hierarchy of relations detected in Morphological Analysis.

In order to dive deeper into the problem and examine internal relationships between field parameters [46], cross consistency assessment (CCA) analysis is performed. This analysis acts as "garbage detector" and takes contradictory value pairs out of the solution space. Several types of relation between elements are detected. The data is extracted in two different stages, first, by utilizing stakeholders' expertise, and second by using ideas coming from the "crowd." The result of CCA are the $V(n, l)$ values inside the (symmetric) CCA matrix. The different values (illustrated and classified in Figure 19.4) are defined as follows:

- *Logical relation* in the form of contradictions or dependency, based on the nature of involved concepts.
- *Empirical constraints* in the form of contradictions or dependency, which is not probable, based on experience.
- *Normative constraints* in the form of contradictions or dependency, which is accepted as a contextual norm.
- *Incomparable relation* indicates the type of relations that will not lead to any meaningful comparison, as there is a difference in nature of the elements.
- *Synergetic relation* indicates the cost or effort impact of implementing one feature on another feature.

CCA analysis is providing a way to examine a set of parameters representing one context (i.e., decision criteria), against another set, which represents another context (i.e., features) and is providing a tool for presenting one modeling context set as input and another set as output. There are different and conflicting criteria influencing release decisions [49]. At this step, by defining a solution set as an input, the probable output solutions on the other side are studied.

In the following, we summarize the usage of MA related to these sub-problems.

Table 19.4 Applications of MA for Release Planning			
No.	**Subproblem**	**MA Application**	**Extracted Data**
1	Planning criteria	Criteria modeling & assessment	Decision making criteria for selecting features
2	Features elicitation	Feature model & assessment	Influential features on choosing a product
3	Feature dependency and synergy elicitation	Cross consistency assessment	Dependencies and synergies between features
4	Prioritization of features	Feature-criteria relational model & assessment	Prioritization of features towards a set of consistent criteria
5	Plan evaluation	Object modeling & assessment	Objectives of plan evaluation

Definition of planning criteria

Providing and maintaining close relations with the market in order to first understand the needs and second, audit the response of the market to the offers by utilizing open innovation approach followed by MA (subproblems 2-4).

Definition of utility function

Defining utility function based on important criteria of decision-making in the context of project criteria and then assessing the utility of having a set of the extracted criteria (subproblem 1) supported by open innovation platform followed by MA (Table 19.4).

Elicitation and structuring of dependencies

Detection and formulation of dependencies are supported by performing CCA. Pairwise consistency assessment between features shows the explicit dependencies and synergies, as well as hidden dependencies and synergies between features.

Feature prioritization

Prioritization of features towards a given set of criteria.

Objectives of plan evaluation

Defining resource and quality as objectives of plan evaluation, helps in evaluating plans toward these considerations.

19.5 ANALYTICAL RELEASE PLANNING—A CASE STUDY

This section demonstrates the usage and customization of the AOI approach. While applicable for all the classes of release planning problems discussed in Section 19.2, in what follows, we describe the application of AOI for two of them in more detail. Before that, we present the context and the content of a case study.

19.5.1 OTT CASE STUDY—THE CONTEXT AND CONTENT

The case study is in the context of decisions for real over-the-top TV (OTT) features offered by a service provider. Over the top TV is referred to the media provided over the internet apart from operator infrastructure to distribute the content and putting the responsibility of media transportation on the ISP side [50, 51].

Company X has a new OTT product with various features, which were initially extracted from market expectations and by doing research on similar products in other markets. The stakeholders estimate the cost of implementing each feature. The company aims to extract sets of services for each quarter of the year, ensuring the best income and largest set of customers. To do so, they gather customer's willingness to pay for each feature from current customers (via customer management system (CMS) surveys) and potential customers (via crowdsourcing). The utility for the company is to achieve maximum income, while maintaining their market share. In order to perform crowdsourcing, the HIT submitted to Amazon Mechanical Turk was targeting 100 workers. Also, some context-specific validation was done on these 100 individuals, including metrics to indicate the truth worthiness of their answers (these metrics are defined by AMT and include ones such as expertise of worker, worker's score, number of rejected tasks . . .); 10 out of these 100 were not validated due to these issues (this is shown as a step in Figure 19.5).

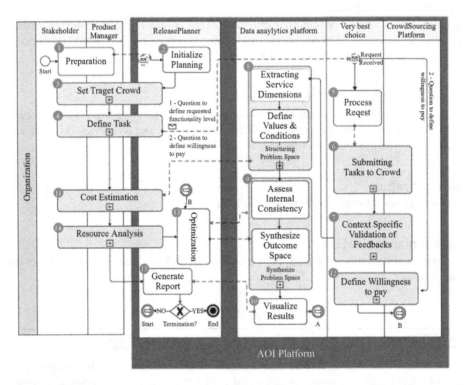

FIGURE 19.5

Process steps performed in the case study.

19.5.2 **FORMALIZATION OF THE PROBLEM**

The problem studied as part of the case study is a variant of the What-to-release problem, including advance feature dependencies as outlined in Section 19.2.1. In what follows, we give a more detailed formal description of the problem. For that, we consider a set of features called FEATURE. $F(n, l) \in$ FEATURE presents a specific feature in which n is the feature number and l is the functionality level. These features are planned over K release where $k = 1 \ldots n$, and each release has a release weight $\in \{1, \ldots, 9\}$.

A *release plan* is the assignment of features F(n,l) $\in$ FEATURES at functionality level l to one of the upcoming releases (or deciding to postpone the feature):

$$x(n, l) =: \begin{cases} k & \text{if } F(n,l) \text{ is offered at relase } k \\ 0 & \text{otherwise} \end{cases} \tag{19.1}$$

Each feature to be provided causes certain amount of (fixed) cost abbreviated by $F\_cost(n, l)$.

From the stakeholders' perspective each $F(n, l) \in$ FEATURE has a cost of implementation, the weighted average of stakeholders' prediction (and considering the person's importance) is used in the model:

$$F\_cost(n, l) = \frac{\sum_{s=1\ldots s} \text{Estimate}(n, l, s) \times \text{importance}(s)}{\sum_{s=1\ldots s} \text{importance}(s)} \tag{19.2}$$

Assuming capacities budget(k) for the different time periods k (e.g., quarters of a year), the budget constraint related to release k is formulated as:

$$\sum_{n,l:x(n,l)=k} F\_cost(n, l) \times x(n, l) \le \text{budget}(k) \tag{19.3}$$

Also, feature dependency constraints need to be considered for release decision-making. The detailed constraints are presented in Section 19.7. Next, we define the objectives of planning. For each F(n,l) $\in$ FEATURE we assume that we have information about the willingness to pay (defined as a monthly fee) from two groups of customers: (i) current customers of the company and (ii) potential new customers. The median of the data collected is used in order to make the data less affected by skewed and outlier data.

$$F\_WillingnessToPay(n, l) = median(WillingnessToPay(n, l)) \tag{19.4}$$

Problem: For a set of candidate features, FEATURE (which includes different types of features and their related functionality level), the problem is to:

(i) Find a subset of features named feat* $\subseteq$ FEATURES which is of maximum overall utility.
(ii) Assign all F(n,l) $\in$ feat* to a release where the feature will be offered.

The utility function is as follows:

$$Utility = \sum_{n,l:x(n,l)\neq0} Weight(x(n, l)) \times F\_WillingnessToPay(n, l) \times weight\_CustomerGroup(x(n, l)) \tag{19.5}$$
$$Utility \to Max!$$

19.5.3 **THE CASE STUDY PROCESS**

The detailed case study process is described in Figure 19.5. The process consists of 16 steps, utilizing the different parts of the AOI platform as described in Section 19.4.

Steps 1, 2, and 3 are initializing the project by defining the decision-making criteria, inviting stakeholders and defining the special crowd needs, respectively. In our case, the crowd was constituted from individuals living in North America. In order to extract features and desirable levels of functionality (Step 4), Task 1 and Task 2 were submitted to the crowd:

Task 1: What are the features you are looking for in an OTT service?
Task 2: Which level of quality (degree of functionalities) do you expect from OTT services?

Amazon Mechanical Turk [40] is used as a micro-task market to establish the collaboration with the crowd. In order to manage collaboration between systems Very Best Choice [41] is used as the lightweight decision support system. This system is designed to facilitate proper priority decision-making, based on comprehensive stakeholder involvement. In this case, two groups of stakeholders, namely technical and managerial experts, are involved. Tasks 1 and 2 were assigned to 90 participants. The extracted features and their rankings are shown in Figure 19.6.

Context specific validation and applying qualification type, such as "degree of experience based on acceptance rate of the worker at the Amazon Mechanical Turk" is applied in Step 7. The top 10 claimed features are used to describe the case study. The features and their related levels of functionality are defined as below:

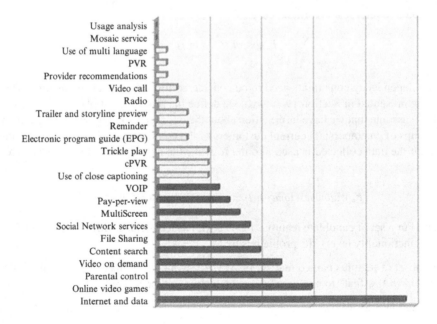

FIGURE 19.6

Features extracted from crowdsourcing and their ranking. The top 10 most attractive (dark) ones were selected for the case study.

$F(Online\ video\ game, l_1) |\ l_1 \in \{Paid,\ Free\}$

$F(VOIP, l_2) |\ l_2 \in \{Yes,\ No\}$

$F(Social\ network, l_3) |\ l_3 \in \{Rate,\ Comment,\ FB\ integration,\ twitter\ integration\}$

$F(Video\ on\ demand, l_4) |\ l_4 \in \{Yes,\ No\}$

$F(Parental\ control, l_5) |\ l_5 \in \{Basic,\ Advanced,\ Premium\}$

$F(Content\ search, l_6) |\ l_6 \in \{Basic,\ Advanced,\ Premium\}$

$F(File\ sharing, l_7) |\ l_7 \in \{Limited,\ Limited\ Chargeable,\ Unlimited\}$

$F(Pay-per-view, l_8) |\ l_8 \in \{Yes,\ No\}$

$F(Internet\ and\ data, l_9) |\ l_9 \in \{Limited,\ Limited\ Chargeable,\ Unlimited\}$

$F(Multiscreen, l_{10}) |\ l_{10} \in \{Basic,\ Advanced,\ Premium\}$

For ease of notation, we have used $F_1, F_2, \ldots, F_{10}$ (sequentially in the above list) for expressing all selected features including their different levels of functionality. Step 8 is designed to extract features and their related functionality levels. Extracting features and defining the content of a morphological box is an attempt to further structure the release planning problem space.

19.5.4 RELEASE PLANNING IN THE PRESENCE OF ADVANCED FEATURE DEPENDENCIES AND SYNERGIES

Step 9 in this case study process, is designed to detect service dependencies and inconsistencies, as well as extracting cost and value synergies. All these relations between features are taken as an input for the subsequent release optimization process. In addition to inconsistency analysis, cost and value synergy relationships between features' functionality levels offered in conjunction are taken as input for optimizing release plans. Some examples are presented below:

Example 1. x(parental control, Basic) NAND x(Online video games, Paid) means that x(parental control, Basic) $= 0\ ||\ x$(Online video games, Paid) $= 0$

Example 2. F(Multi-Screen, Premium) becomes 30% less expensive if offered no earlier than F(Multi-Screen, Basic)

Example 3. The sum value of $\{F$(Online Video Gaming, Premium), F(Parental Control, Premium)$\}$ is increased by 25% if these items are all offered in the same release.

The values extracted during the process of assessment are applied in Figure 19.7 and further analyzed to extract the inconsistencies. Without performing CCA, the proposed feature implementations would violate these constraints and thus creating customer and user concerns.

The estimation process is initiated for an agreed upon criterion (willingness to pay). Each feature and the different levels of functionality are evaluated on a 9-point scale ranging from "extremely low" to "extremely high" (corresponding to Step 12 in Figure 19.5).

In addition, customers are requested to articulate their willingness to pay for each functionality level of features. In Step 13 of the process, data from the two separate customer groups are gathered, and potential customers' ideas are investigated via crowdsourcing, while the data from current users are extracted from customer service surveys of the company. A task was submitted to the crowd in order to indicate their willingness to pay. For each functionality level, 50 participants completed the task via crowdsourcing, indicating the potential customer's willingness. Also the willingness to pay is investigated among the current customers via customer service surveys. Having all the data needed, in Step 15, ReleasePlanner is generating the alternative plans shown in Figure 19.8. Each column

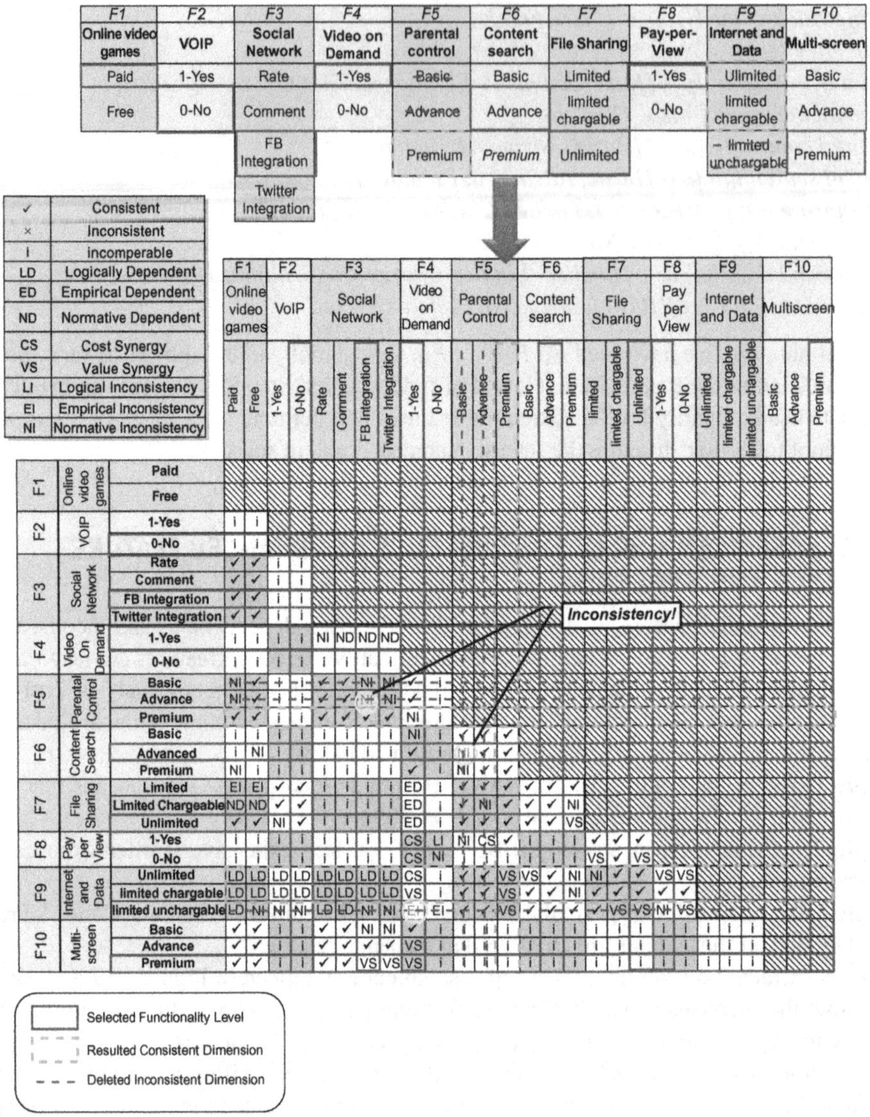

FIGURE 19.7

CCA analysis of top 10 features and their functionalities via Crowdsourcing.

represents a plan alternative, and each row corresponds to a feature. The table entries of Figure 19.8 describe that the respective feature is offered in Q1, Q2, Q3, and Q4 or that it is postponed (Q5).

Ignoring cost and value synergies ignores potential resource savings and additional value creation opportunities. Figure 19.9 shows the structural changes of release plans, while we consider synergies between features. As it is shown in Figure 19.9, considering synergies will affect the planning results.

ID	Feature	Alternative 1	Alternative 2	Alternative 3	Alternative 4	Alternative 5
1	Online video games_paid	Q2	Q2	Q2	Q2	Q2
2	Online video games_free	Q4	Q4	Q4	Q4	Q5
3	Social Network Access_Twitter Integration	Q2	Q2	Q2	Q2	Q2
4	Social Network Access_Rate	Q2	Q2	Q2	Q2	Q2
5	Social Network Access_Comment	Q1	Q1	Q1	Q1	Q3
6	Social Network Access_FB Integration	Q3	Q1	Q1	Q3	Q1
7	Parental Control Basic	Q5	Q5	Q5	Q5	Q5
8	Parental Control Advanced	Q5	Q5	Q5	Q5	Q5
9	Parental Control Premium	Q1	Q1	Q1	Q1	Q1
10	File Sharing_Limited	Q5	Q5	Q5	Q5	Q5
11	File Sharing_Limited chargable	Q5	Q5	Q5	Q5	Q5
12	File Sharing_Unlimited	Q5	Q5	Q5	Q5	Q5
13	Internet and Data_Unlimited	Q2	Q2	Q2	Q2	Q2
14	Internet and Data_Limited Chargable	Q5	Q5	Q5	Q5	Q4
15	Internet and Data_Limited Unchargable	Q5	Q5	Q5	Q5	Q5
16	VoIP_YES	Q1	Q1	Q1	Q1	Q1
17	VoIP_NO	Q1	Q1	Q1	Q1	Q1
18	Video on demand_YES	Q5	Q5	Q5	Q5	Q5
19	Video on demand_NO	Q1	Q1	Q1	Q1	Q1
20	Content search basic	Q4	Q4	Q3	Q4	Q4
21	Content search Advanced	Q3	Q3	Q4	Q4	Q3
22	Content search Premium	Q1	Q1	Q1	Q1	Q5
23	Pay-Per-View_NO	Q1	Q1	Q1	Q1	Q1
24	Pay-Per-View_YES	Q3	Q3	Q3	Q3	Q3
25	Multi-Screen Basic	Q1	Q3	Q3	Q3	Q3
26	Multi-Screen Advanced	Q3	Q1	Q1	Q1	Q3
27	Multi-Screen Premium	Q1	Q3	Q3	Q3	Q1

FIGURE 19.8

Optimized and diversified release plans in fulfilment of all types of dependencies and utilizing synergies.

Besides, they not only change the offered feature but they also affect the release value presented as the stakeholder's satisfaction; the value improvement is more than 10% in the discussed case.

19.5.5 REAL-TIME WHAT-TO-RELEASE PLANNING

Incrementally building and deploying products, relying on deep customer insight and real-time feedback is expected to create products with a higher customer hit rate and faster development. The process for achieving these goals needs to be based upon continuously up-to-date and most relevant information and deep and comprehensive data analytics to utilize business and market patterns, trends, and predictions. Short feedback cycles need to be performed, with the goal of evaluating the attractiveness of features and their combination. After each quarter of the year, with one set of features implemented, we created synthetic data for both customer groups to simulate real-time changes of customer value and priorities.

The individual and collective value of features is hard to predict. The value depends on a number of factors which themselves are dynamically changing (e.g., competition, market trends, user acceptance). As trend of planning is shown in Figure 19.10, the features' values are changed during time based on stakeholders' point of view. In Figure 19.10, the structural changes of features in release plans are

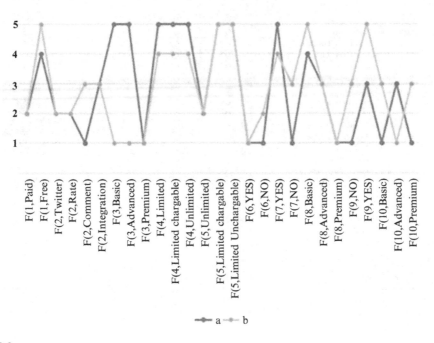

FIGURE 19.9

Comparison of the structure between optimized release plans (a) with and (b) without synergies. The placements of dotes on horizontal lines, are showing the release quarter for each feature (Q1-Q5).

shown in the right-most column. One circle shows that the feature was released in the first cycle and one line demonstrates that the release plan has not changed over time for a specific feature.

Figure 19.11 summarizes the changes caused by updated feature cost estimates and value predictions for the case that re-planning is conducted at the beginning of each quarter. Accommodating the most recent project information increases the validity and value creation capability of the generated release plans.

Re-planning adds significant value to the release plans and completely changes the structure of plans. The change of value during the four quarters of our planning is shown in Figure 19.12. In this figure, Plan 1 shows the values of all four releases at the initial point of planning. Plan 2 is calculated after implementing the first release plan and when the priorities and capacities were updated and re-planning conducted. The same process was applied for Plan 3 and Plan 4 at the end of implementing Q2 and Q3. This is mainly derived by the need to refine market needs to address uncertainty in the customers' needs and detecting the market trends.

19.5.6 RE-PLANNING BASED ON CROWD CLUSTERING

The cases studied in Sections 19.5.3-19.5.5 were presented by gathering the preferences of two different customer groups and utilizing the median of the preferences to eliminate the skewed and outlier data.

ID	Feature	Alternative 1-plan1	Alternative 1-After Q1 replan	Alternative 1-After Q2 replan	Alternative 1-After Q3 replan	Changes applied in replanning
1	Online video games_paid	2	3	5	4	
2	Online video games_free	4	4	4	5	
3	Social Network Access_Twitter Integration	2	3	5	4	
4	Social Network Access_Rate	2	3	5	4	
5	Social Network Access_Comment	1				
6	Social Network Access_FB Integration	3	2			
7	Parental Control Basic	5	5	3		
8	Parental Control Advanced	5	5	3		
9	Parental Control Premium	1				
10	File Sharing_Limited	5	5	5	5	
11	File Sharing_Limited chargable	5	5	5	5	
12	File Sharing_Unlimited	5	5	5	5	
13	Internet and Data_Unlimited	2	3	5	4	
14	Internet and Data_Limited Chargable	5	4	3		
15	Internet and Data_Limited unchargable	5	5	5	5	
16	VoIP_YES	1				
17	VoIP_NO	1				
18	Video on Demand_YES	5	5	5	5	
19	Video on Demand_NO	1				
20	Content search basic	4	2			
21	Content search Advanced	5	5	5	5	
22	Content search Premium	1				
23	Pay-Per-View_NO	1				
24	Pay-Per-View_YES	3	2			
25	Multi-Screen Basic	1				
26	Multi-Screen Advanced	3	4	3		
27	Multi-Screen Premium	1				

FIGURE 19.10

Initial plan (first column) and evolution of plans over the time considering re-evaluation of feature values. The structural changes of features within plans are summarized in the right-most column.

The intention of AOI is to gather and maintain the various types of relations and satisfy different groups of potential and current customers.

Based on the approach presented in Section 19.4.2.1, we cluster individuals inside the crowd with different neighborhood distance (Epsilon). By choosing epsilon as 10, the individuals inside the crowd are clustered into six categories. By choosing neighborhood distance as 11, clustering resulted in two categories. In order to investigate the effect of clustering on product planning, the impact of re-planning is shown by comparing the results of planning based on two versus six clusters (the clusters are shown in Figure 19.13).

The results of re-planning based on clusters are compared in Figures 19.14 and 19.15. In Figure 19.14, we used the six clusters defined in Figure 19.13, and we re-planned for releases. The results show significant differences in structure and value and a slightly better degree of optimization. In Figure 19.15, we re-planned for releases considering the two clusters we presented in Figure 19.13. For confidentiality reasons, the detailed data of current customers are not available and the clustering is done only base on the potential customer groups.

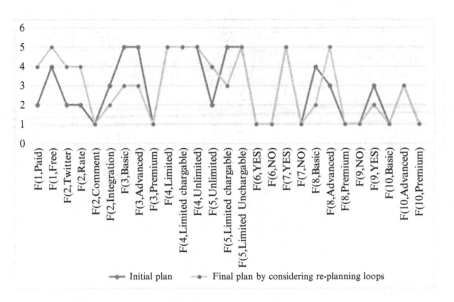

FIGURE 19.11

Comparison of the initial plan with implemented plan after considering three re-planning loops. The placements of dots on horizontal lines compare the release quarter for each feature being issued (initial plan versus plan after three revisions).

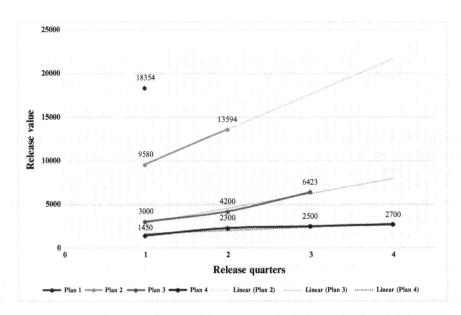

FIGURE 19.12

The increase of release value based on total number of stakeholder feature points by re-planning. The linear forecast of the value is shown for each level.

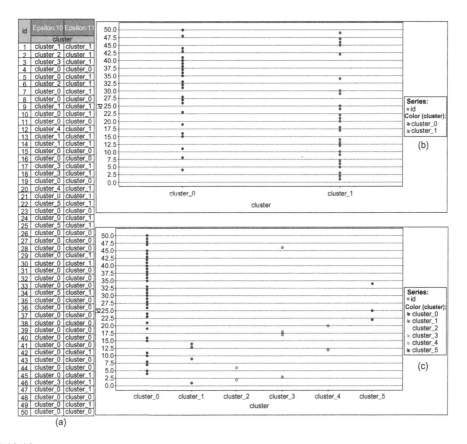

id	Epsilon:10 cluster	Epsilon:11 cluster
1	cluster_1	cluster_1
2	cluster_2	cluster_1
3	cluster_3	cluster_1
4	cluster_0	cluster_0
5	cluster_0	cluster_1
6	cluster_2	cluster_1
7	cluster_0	cluster_1
8	cluster_0	cluster_0
9	cluster_1	cluster_1
10	cluster_0	cluster_1
11	cluster_0	cluster_0
12	cluster_4	cluster_1
13	cluster_1	cluster_1
14	cluster_1	cluster_1
15	cluster_0	cluster_0
16	cluster_0	cluster_0
17	cluster_3	cluster_1
18	cluster_3	cluster_1
19	cluster_0	cluster_0
20	cluster_4	cluster_1
21	cluster_0	cluster_1
22	cluster_5	cluster_1
23	cluster_0	cluster_0
24	cluster_0	cluster_1
25	cluster_5	cluster_1
26	cluster_0	cluster_0
27	cluster_0	cluster_0
28	cluster_0	cluster_0
29	cluster_0	cluster_1
30	cluster_0	cluster_1
31	cluster_0	cluster_0
32	cluster_0	cluster_0
33	cluster_0	cluster_0
34	cluster_5	cluster_1
35	cluster_0	cluster_0
36	cluster_0	cluster_0
37	cluster_0	cluster_0
38	cluster_0	cluster_0
39	cluster_0	cluster_0
40	cluster_0	cluster_0
41	cluster_0	cluster_0
42	cluster_0	cluster_1
43	cluster_0	cluster_0
44	cluster_0	cluster_0
45	cluster_0	cluster_1
46	cluster_3	cluster_1
47	cluster_0	cluster_1
48	cluster_0	cluster_0
49	cluster_0	cluster_1
50	cluster_0	cluster_0

FIGURE 19.13

(a) Result of clustering of 50 individuals with two different epsilons. (b) Clustering results with $\varepsilon = 10$ (c) Clustering results with $\varepsilon = 11$.

19.5.7 CONCLUSIONS AND DISCUSSION OF RESULTS

The case study was done in the domain of a real industrial project for over the top TV (OTT) product and its related features. This case was mainly derived by the crowdsourcing technique and morphological analysis (see Section 19.4.2.2) among analytical metrics. During planning, the stakeholders are involved for defining the problem constraint with the focus on cost estimation while two groups of users (i) current users and (ii) potential users are involved in stating their willingness to pay for features in the crowdsourcing process. The purpose of the case study is primarily to serve as a proof-of-concept. The results are considered preliminary and no claims on external validity can be made.

As the non-trivial part of the release planning problem, the extraction and consideration of feature dependencies and synergies are highly desirable. This is supported in the AOI process when the effect of

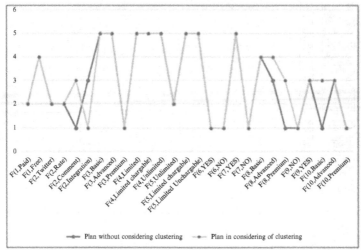

Structural comparison of first alternative of plans before and after clustering

Criteria for Planning	Explanation	Alternative 1	Alternative 2	Alternative 3	Alternative 4	Alternative 5
9-Willingness to pay • 0-Cost Estimate	Degree of optimality	100.0%	99.7%	99.3%	98.6%	98.3%
	(Stakeholder feature points)	(18354)	(18308)	(18220)	(18095)	(18045)

Value without considering clustering

Criteria for Planning	Explanation	Alternative 1	Alternative 2	Alternative 3	Alternative 4	Alternative 5
9-Willingness to pay • 0-Cost Estimate	Degree of optimality	100.0%	99.9%	99.6%	99.5%	99.7%
	(Stakeholder feature points)	(19085)	(19060)	(19013)	(18994)	(18840)

Value in consideration of clustering

FIGURE 19.14

Comparison of planning without clustering and by considering six clusters created from the crowd. The placements of bold points on horizontal lines show the release quarter for each feature. The degree of optimality for five alternative release plans are compared (below).

synergy and dependency detection were investigated and the results showed a significant improvement in both release value (in terms of stakeholder's feature points) and the structure of the release plan.

Based on the existing real-world data, additional synthetic data was used to perform re-planning before each release (quarter of the year). This re-planning process not only changed the structure of the plan but also demonstrated the likely improvement in terms of the release value of the release as shown in Figure 19.12.

The crowdsourced data has wide variety and needs precise analysis to consider the exceptional group of customers as well as majority trend toward product needs. The clustering approach introduced in Section 19.4.2.1 is applied to the crowdsourced data and the significant improvements in plan value were observed[1].

---

[1]The crowdsourced data used in this case study is available at: http://ucalgary.ca/mnayebi/files/mnayebi/dataset-book-chapter.pdf.

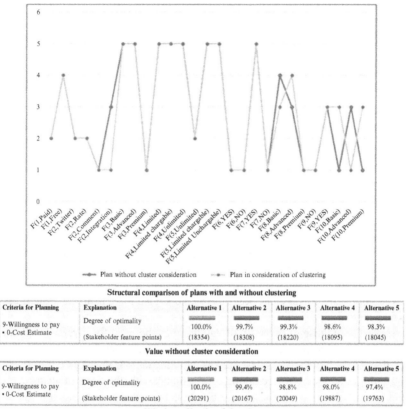

Structural comparison of plans with and without clustering

Criteria for Planning	Explanation	Alternative 1	Alternative 2	Alternative 3	Alternative 4	Alternative 5
9-Willingness to pay • 0-Cost Estimate	Degree of optimality	100.0%	99.7%	99.3%	98.6%	98.3%
	(Stakeholder feature points)	(18354)	(18308)	(18220)	(18095)	(18045)

Value without cluster consideration

Criteria for Planning	Explanation	Alternative 1	Alternative 2	Alternative 3	Alternative 4	Alternative 5
9-Willingness to pay • 0-Cost Estimate	Degree of optimality	100.0%	99.4%	98.8%	98.0%	97.4%
	(Stakeholder feature points)	(20291)	(20167)	(20049)	(19887)	(19763)

Value in consideration of clustering

FIGURE 19.15

Comparison of planning without clustering and considering two clusters.

The relation and synergy between features were extracted with stakeholder participation and crowdsourcing, although the process of information extraction was done manually and thus may have human errors, though text mining support would be further investigated.

19.6 SUMMARY AND FUTURE RESEARCH

Open innovation is seeking for significant value by looking beyond organizational boundaries and extending the scope of research and development limits to include outside institutions. The AOI approach is looking for variety of data containers to achieve the insightful and precise needs of the markets. The AOI domains of data gathering techniques are shown in Figure 19.16.

Crowdsourcing is taking advantage of web technologies and social media, with the ability to actively involve users and control the community to achieve organizational tasks. This can be conceptualized as a type of sourcing model, which is the intersection of outsourcing and sophisticated web technologies

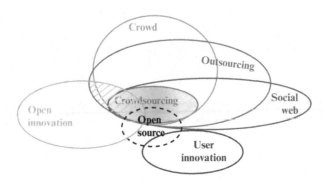

FIGURE 19.16

Open innovation related concepts—AOI use of open innovation is positioned with yellow (light gray in print versions) texture.

[52]. Crowdsourcing also seen as the "small scale outsourcing" [53]. Outsourcing is a mean of contracting internal business needs or functions to outside business providers [54] which are closely connected to an institution. Open source with the spirit of peer production does not have a clear boundary between problem 'solvers' and solution 'seekers' also there is no clear hierarchical structure of ownership and control [3].

Analytics under the premise of diversity of data implies the need for diversity and combination of analytical techniques. In this chapter, we have outlined an approach that is intended to support this process. Analytical Open Innovation is designed as an extendable framework combining the strengths of various individual methods and techniques. Combined with the idea of using a broader range of internal and external knowledge containers, the AOI framework is intended to overcome current limitations of (big) data analytics.

In this chapter, we have described the idea of AOI and have applied it to the problem of (analytical) product release planning. The concrete implementation called AOI@RP comprises analytical techniques used in the different stages of the release planning process. Although still in its infancy, the AOI@RP approach and its related techniques show promising results [29, 55]. From the illustrative case study, we demonstrated that the main contributions of the AOI@RP approach are towards:

- Structuring the problem: by detecting problem dimensions.
- Defining solution space: by detecting and maintaining probable ranges of solutions and relations.
- Prediction and estimation of planning attributes: by exploring the historical data for extracting features and predicting the value.
- From an enlarged and improved input for data and information of planning, we have a better chance to address the right problem. From applying advance optimization techniques, we are able to include all types of dependencies between features as well as cost and value synergies.

As outlined by Menzies [56], we are currently in the era of decision systems and leading into the discussion systems, which needs to satisfy four layers of social reasoning, namely: *do* (prediction and decision), *say* (summarization, plan and describe), *reflect* (trade-offs, envelopes, diagnosis, monitoring), *share* and *scale*. Our AOI platform not only supports the decision systems but is also aligned with these dimensions. Morphological analysis discussed in Section 19.4.2.2 provides a unique opportunity to maintain the relationships between well-defined dimensions of the problem and to reduce the threat of wickedness in the nature of planning problem, although the approach needs to be further investigated. In particular, we are planning and suggesting future research in the following four main directions:

(i) Mining inter-organizational repositories will provide context-specific data, which helps in solving planning aspects by analogy. Previous work on automating feature analysis from distributed repositories [57] opens new ways to utilize the available data on the internet. Mining open forums to gather software-related information would be a next step to be integrated into AOI@RP.

(ii) The new data analytics approach should be able to handle the dynamically changing data and to adjust the target of data analytics and find satisfactory solutions to the problem. Furthermore, in order to create real-time value while planning, AOI needs to swiftly process the dynamic data, which is changing over time. Swarm intelligence as a collective behavior of decentralized, self-organized systems [58], studies the collective behavior of systems composed of many individuals interacting locally with the environment and with each other. Swarms inherently use forms of decentralized control and self-organization to achieve their goals. Swarm intelligence has been widely applied to solve stationary and dynamical optimization problems specifically in presence of a wide range of uncertainties [59].

Generally, there are two kinds of approaches that apply swarm intelligence as data mining techniques [60]:

1. Techniques where individuals of a swarm move through a solution space and search for solution of the data mining task. This approach is applied to optimize the data mining techniques in order to perform effective search.
2. Swarms move data instances that are placed on a low-dimensional feature space in order to come to a suitable clustering or low-dimensional mapping solution of the data to organize the data.

As the next step, we will investigate the applicability of different swarm optimization algorithms, such as the particle swarm optimization [61], ant colony optimization (ACO) and brain storm optimization algorithm [62] on AOI approach to make the data analysis more efficient.

(iii) Smooth integration of the different components integrated under the AOI@RP platform label. This includes a higher degree of automation of the analysis steps to be done and the implementation of data exchange processes.

(iv) More comprehensive empirical analysis is needed for the implemented framework to demonstrate its usefulness. AOI@RP is planned to perform continued evaluation with the intention to further qualify the decision-making by performing scenario-playing and other forms of variation of project parameters. Also, the scalability of the whole approach needs to be investigated in terms of its effectiveness and efficiency.

19.7 APPENDIX: FEATURE DEPENDENCY CONSTRAINTS

Definition 6. The set CFD of coupling dependencies is presented by a set of coupled features based on the definition:

$$x(n_1, l_1) = x(n_2, l_2) \text{ for all pairs of coupled features } (F(n_1, l_1), F(n_2, l_2)) \in \text{CFD}$$

Definition 7. The set PFD of precedence dependencies is defined by:

$$x(n1, l1) \leq x(n2, l2) \text{ for all pairs of precedence features } (F(n1, l1),\ F(n2, l2)) \in \text{PFD}$$

Certain features and their related instances are not compatible with each other and do not make sense to be offered in conjunction. Detection of these incompatibilities is a complex problem itself, and we will later use MA/CCA analysis to find them.

Definition 8. NAND indicates that:

$$x(n_1, l_1) \, NAND \, x(n_2, l_2) \text{ if and only if features } (F(n_1, l_1), F(n_2, l_2)) \text{ cannot be offered both inconjunction}$$

Definition 9. The combination of different features is creating less cost than the individual feature values. We call them the set of *cost synergies FCS*:

$$\textit{If ItemSet} = \{F(n_1, l_1), \dots, F(n_y, l_y)\} \subseteq \textit{FCS then}: \textit{ Sum cost of ItemSet is decreased by}$$
$$\textit{Factor\% if none of these items is postponed.}$$

Similarly, from a value perspective, the combination of certain features will increase the attractiveness to the user which is called value synergy.

Definition 10. The set of *value synergies FVS* is defined as:

$$\textit{If ItemSet} = \{F(n_1, l_1), \dots, F(n_y, l_y)\} \subseteq \textit{FVS then}: \textit{ Sum value of ItemSet is increased by}$$
$$\textit{Factor\% if none of these items is postponed.}$$

ACKNOWLEDGMENTS

This research was partially supported by the Natural Sciences and Engineering Research Council of Canada, NSERC Discovery Grant 250343-12. We very much appreciate all the comments provided by reviewers, they helped us in presenting the content in a more understandable way. We also thank Kornelia Streb for her help in editing the chapter and for preparation of high quality figures. Finally, we would like to thank the book editors for their initiative, comments provided, and the overall support in publishing this book.

REFERENCES

[1] Ebert C, Brinkkemper S. Software product management-an industry evaluation. J Syst Softw 2014;95:10–18.
[2] Highsmith J. Adaptive software development: a collaborative approach to managing complex systems. Reading, MA: Addison-Wesley; 2013.

[3] Marjanovic F, Joanna C. Crowdsourcing based business models: in search of evidence for innovation 2.0. Sci Public Policy 2012;39:318–32.

[4] Buse R, Zimmermann T. Information needs for software development analytics. In: 2012 34th international conference on the software engineering (ICSE); 2012.

[5] Vasilescu B, Serebrenik A, Mens T. A historical dataset of software engineering conferences. In: Proceedings of the 10th international workshop on mining software repositories; 2013. p. 373–6.

[6] Johnson PM. Searching under the streetlight for useful software analytics. IEEE Softw 2013;30:57–63.

[7] Demeyer S, Murgia A, Wyckmans K, Lamkanfi A. Happy birthday! a trend analysis on past MSR papers. In: Proceedings of the 10th international workshop on mining software repositories. 2013. p. 353–62.

[8] Hassan A. Software analytics: going beyond developers. IEEE Softw 2013;30:53.

[9] Menzies T, Zimmermann T. Software analytics: so what? IEEE Softw 2013;30:31–7.

[10] Hemmati H, Nadi S, Baysal O, Kononenko O, Wang W, Holmes R, et al. The MSR cookbook mining a decade of research. In: MSR'13. San Fransisco, CA; 2013. p. 343–52.

[11] Ruhe G. Product release planning: methods, tools and applications. Boca Raton, FL CRC Press; 2010.

[12] Agarwal N, Karimpour R, Ruhe G. Theme-based product release planning: an analytical approach. In: The HICSS-47. Hawaii; 2014.

[13] Port D, Wilf J. The value of certifying software release readiness: an exploratory study of certification for a critical system at JPL. In: 2013 ACM/IEEE international symposium on empirical software engineering and measurement; 2013. p. 373–82.

[14] Svensson RB, Parker PL, Regnell B. A prototype tool for QUPER to support release planning of quality requirements. In: The 5th international workshop on software product management; 2011. p. 57–66.

[15] Regnell B, Svensson R, Olsson T. Supporting roadmapping of quality requirements. IEEE Softw 2008;25: 42–47.

[16] Alba E, Chicano JF. Software project management with gas. Inform Sci 2007;177:2380–401.

[17] Boehm B, Valerdi R. Impact of software resource estimation research on practice: a preliminary report on achievements, synergies, and challenges In: 2011 33rd international conference on software engineering (ICSE); 2011. p. 1057–65.

[18] Klinger T, Tarr P, Wagstrom P, Williams C. An enterprise perspective on technical debt. In: Proceedings of the 2nd workshop on managing technical debt; 2011. p. 35–38.

[19] Schubanz M, Pleuss A, Pradhan L, Botterweck G, Thurimella AK. Model-driven planning and monitoring of long-term software product line evolution. In: Proceedings of the 7th international workshop on variability modelling of software-intensive systems; 2013. p. 18.

[20] Zorn-Pauli G, Paech B, Beck T, Karey H, Ruhe G. Analyzing an industrial strategic release planning process—a case study at Roche diagnostics. In: bibinfobooktitleRequirements engineering: foundation for software quality. Berlin: Springer; 2013. p. 269–84.

[21] Heikkilae V, Jadallah A, Rautiainen K, bibinfoauthorRuhe G. Rigorous support for flexible planning of product releases—a stakeholder-centric approach and its initial evaluation. In: HICSS. Hawaii; 2010.

[22] Kapur P, Ngo-The A, Ruhe G, Smith A. Optimized staffing for product releases and its application at Chartwell technology. J Softw Mainten Evolut 2008;20:365–86.

[23] Bhawnani P, Ruhe G, Kudorfer F, Meyer L. Intelligent decision support for road mapping—a technology transfer case study with siemens corporate technology. In: Workshop on technology transfer in software engineering; 2006. p. 35–40.

[24] Momoh J, Ruhe G. Release planning process improvement—an industrial case study. Softw Process Improv Pract 2006;11:295–307.

[25] Lindgren M, Land R, M CN, Wall A. Towards a capability model for the software release planning process—based on a multiple industrial case study. Lecture notes in computer science (including subseries lecture notes in artificial intelligence and lecture notes in bioinformatics); 2008. p. 117–32.

[26] Regnell B, Brinkkemper S. Market-driven requirements engineering for software products. In: Aurum A, Wohlin C, editors. Engineering and Managing Software Requirements. Berlin: Springer; 2005. p. 287–308.

[27] Khurum M, Gorschek T, Wilson M. The software value map—an exhaustive collection of value aspects for the development of software intensive products. J Softw Evolut Process 2013;25:711–41.

[28] Carlshamre P. An industrial survey of requirements interdependencies in software product release planning. In: The 5th international symposium on requirements engineering (RE'01); 2001. p. 84–91.

[29] Naycbi M, Ruhe G. An open innovation approach in support of product release decisions. In: ICSE 2014—CHASE workshop. Hyderabad, India; 2014.

[30] Sharp H, Finkelstein A, Galal G. Stakeholder identification in the requirements engineering process. In: 10th international workshop on database and expert systems applications. Florence, Italy; 1999. p. 387–91.

[31] Gorschek T, Fricker S, Palm K, Kunsman S. A lightweight innovation process for software-intensive product development. IEEE softw 2010;27:37–45.

[32] Cleland-Huang J, Dumitru H, Duan C, Castro-Herrera C. Automated support for managing feature requests in open forums. Commun ACM 2009;52:68–74.

[33] Fitsilis P, Gerogiannis V, Anthopoulos L, Savvas I. Supporting the requirements prioritization process using social network analysis techniques. In: 2010 19th IEEE international workshop on enabling technologies: infrastructures for collaborative enterprises (WETICE); 2010. p. 110–15.

[34] Shahnewaz S, Guenther R. RELREA–An analytical approch for evaluating release readiness. In: Proceedings of the International Conference on Software Engineering and Knowledge Engineering; 2014. p. 437–42.

[35] Berander P, Andrews A. Requirements prioritization. Eng Manag Softw Requir 2005;69–94.

[36] International software product management association. Available: URL: http://ispma.org/glossary/.

[37] Shepperd M. Software project economics: a roadmap. In: Future of software engineering, 2007 (FOSE'07); 2007. p. 304–15.

[38] der Hoek AV, Hall R, Heimbigner D, Wolf A. Software release management. Proc. sixth European software engineering conference; 1997. p. 159–75.

[39] What is big data analytics? Available at http://www-01.ibm.com/software/data/infosphere/hadoop/what-is-big-data-analytics.html.

[40] MTurk; 2013. MTurk, URL: https://www.mturk.com/mturk/.

[41] Very Best Choice light, Expert Decisions Inc., URL: http://edi.lite.verybestchoice.com:3000/.

[42] URL: www.releaseplanner.com. March 2008. ReleasePlanner (1.7 ed.).

[43] Zhang D, Han S, Dang Y, Lou J, Zhang H, Xie T. Software analytics in practice. IEEE Softw 2012;30:30–37.

[44] Ullah MI, Ruhe G, Garousi V. Decision support for moving from a single product to a product portfolio in evolving software systems. J Syst Softw 2010;83:2496–512.

[45] Ester M, Kriegel HP, Sander J, Xu X. A density-based algorithm for discovering clusters in large spatial databases with noise. In: KDD; 1996. p. 226–31.

[46] Ritchey T. Wicked problems-social messes: decision support modelling with morphological analysis. vol. 17. Springer Science & Business Media; 2011.

[47] Ritchey T. Problem structuring using computer-aided morphological analysis. J Operat Res Soc 2006;57: 792–801.

[48] T Ritchey MS, Eriksson H. Using morphological analysis for evaluating preparedness for accidents involving hazardous materials. In: Proceedings of the 4th LACDE conference. Shanghai; 2002.

[49] Ngo-The A, Ruhe G. A systematic approach for solving the wicked problem of software release planning. Soft Comput 2008;12:95–108.

[50] Montpetit MJ, Klym N, Mirlacher T. The future of IPTV (connected, mobile, personal and social). Multimedia Tools Appl 2011;53:519–32.

[51] Boever JD, Grooff DD. Peer-to-peer content distribution and over-the-top tv: An analysis of value networks. In: Handbook of peer-to-peer networking. New York: Springer; 2010. p. 961–83.

[52] Saxton G, Oh O, Kishore R. Rules of crowdsourcing: Models, issues, and systems of control. Inf Syst Manag 2013;30:2–20.

[53] Gefen D, Carmel E. Is the world really flat? a look at offshoring at an online programming marketplace. MIS Quart 2008; 367–84.

[54] Kishore R, Rao H, Nam K, Rajagopalan S, Chaudhury A. A relationship perspective on it outsourcing. Commun ACM 2003;46:86–92.

[55] Nayebi M, Ruhe G. Analytical open innovation for value-optimized service portfolio planning. In: ICSOB conference. Paphos, Cyprus; 2014.

[56] Menzies T. Beyond data mining; towards idea engineering. In: Proceedings of the 9th international conference on predictive models in software engineering; 2013. p. 11.

[57] Dumitru H, Gibiec M, Hariri N, Cleland-Huang J, Mobasher B, Castro-Herrera C, et al. On-demand feature recommendations derived from mining public product descriptions. In: The 33rd international conference on software engineering, ICSE. Waikiki, Honolulu, HI; 2011.

[58] Martens D, Bart B, Tom F. Editorial survey: swarm intelligence for data mining. Machine Learning 2011;82.1:1–42.

[59] Dorigo M, Birattari M. Swarm intelligence. Scholarpedia 2007; 2:1462.

[60] Martens D, Baesens B, Fawcett T. Editorial survey: Swarm intelligence for data mining. Mach Learn 2011;82:1–42.

[61] Kazman R, Klein M, Barbacci M, Longstaff T, LH, Carriere J. The architecture tradeoff analysis method. In: International conference on engineering of complex computer systems (ICECCS 98). Monterey, CA; 1998. p. 68–78.

[62] Shi Y. Brain storm optimization algorithm. In: Advances in swarm intelligence. Berlin: Springer; 2011. p. 303–309.

DATA ANALYSIS AT SCALE (BIG DATA)

BOA: AN ENABLING LANGUAGE AND INFRASTRUCTURE FOR ULTRA-LARGE-SCALE MSR STUDIES

20

Robert Dyer*, Hoan Nguyen[†], Hridesh Rajan[‡], Tien Nguyen[†]

Department of Computer Science, Bowling Green State University, Bowling Green, OH, USA

Department of Electrical and Computer Engineering, Iowa State University, Ames, IA, USA[†]

Department of Computer Science, Iowa State University, Ames, IA, USA[‡]

CHAPTER OUTLINE

20.1 OBJECTIVES

Mining software repositories (MSR) on a large scale is important for more generalizable research results. Therefore, a number of recent studies in the MSR area have been conducted using corpus sizes that are much larger than the corpus size used by studies in the previous decade [1–15]. Such a large collection of software artifacts is openly available for analysis—for example, SourceForge has more than 350,000 projects, GitHub has more than 10 million projects, and Google Code has more than 250,000 projects. This is an enormous collection of software and information about software.

It is extremely difficult to capitalize on this vast amount of information to conduct MSR studies. Specifically, setting up ultra-large-scale MSR studies is challenging because they simultaneously require expertise in programmatically accessing version control systems, data storage and retrieval, data mining, and parallelization. These four requirements significantly increase the cost of scientific research in this area. Last but not least, building analysis infrastructure to process such ultra-large-scale data efficiently can be very difficult. We believe that for beginning practitioners or for practitioners with insufficient resources these obstacles can be a deal breaker.

This chapter describes Boa [16], an infrastructure that is designed to decrease the barrier to entry for ultra-large-scale MSR studies. Boa consists of a domain-specific language, its compiler, a dataset that contains almost 700,000 open source projects as of this writing, a back end based on MapReduce to effectively analyze this dataset, and a Web-based front end for writing MSR programs. While previous work has focused on Boa as a research result [16], this chapter serves as a reference guide for Boa and focuses on how researchers and software practitioners could start using this resource.

20.2 GETTING STARTED WITH BOA

Before attempting to solve real mining tasks with Boa, one must understand what is happening behind the scenes. In this section we describe Boa's architecture.

20.2.1 BOA'S ARCHITECTURE

Even though Boa provides a very large dataset with almost 700,000 projects in it and users write queries that look sequential, Boa's architecture efficiently executes those queries transparently to the user. Figure 20.1 gives an overview of Boa's architecture.

At the back end, Boa clones the data from the source code repository, such as SourceForge. It then translates the data into a custom format necessary for efficient querying. The translated data is then stored as a cache on Boa's cluster of servers. This forms the data infrastructure for Boa and abstracts many of the details of how to find, store, update, and query such a large volume of data.

Users interact with Boa via its Web interface. Users submit a query written in Boa's domain-specific query language to the website. The servers then compile that query and translate it into a Hadoop [17] MapReduce [18] program. This program is then deployed onto the cluster and executes in a highly parallel, distributed manner. All of this is transparent to the users. Once the query finishes executing, the output of the program is made available via the Web interface.

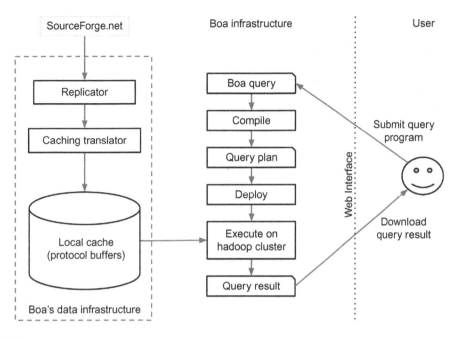

FIGURE 20.1

Overview of Boa's architecture. Data is downloaded, translated, and cached on Boa's servers. Users interact with a Web-based interface to submit queries, which are compiled into Hadoop distributed programs, run on a cluster, and the results are given via the Web interface.

```
1    count: output sum of int;
2    p: Project = input;

3    exists (i: int; input.programming_languages[i] == "Java")
4            count << 1;
```

FIGURE 20.2

A Boa program counting the number of Java projects.

As an example, Figure 20.2 shows a simple Boa program that counts the number of projects that use Java. First we declare an output variable named count (line 1). This output uses the aggregation function sum, which produces the arithmetic sum of each integer value emitted to it. The program takes as input a single project (line 2). It then looks at the metadata for that project, examining the declared programming languages (line 3) to see if at least one of those is Java. If there exists a value matching that condition, it outputs a value 1 (line 1) to indicate one project was found that uses Java.

Figure 20.3 shows the semantic model of how this program executes. Our input dataset consists of all projects on SourceForge. The Boa program is instantiated once for each of these projects, which

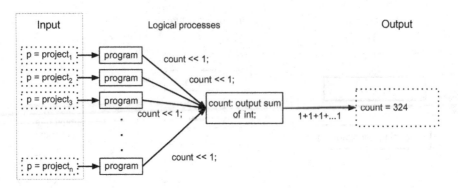

FIGURE 20.3

The semantic model of a Boa program. Inputs are single projects. Each input has its own process and analyzes one project. Outputs are also their own processes and receive data, aggregate the data, and generate the resulting output.

are given as input. If the dataset has 700,000 projects, then (logically) there are 700,000 instances of the program running on our cluster. Each instance of the program then analyzes a single project, in isolation. When an instance finds the project it is analyzing uses Java as a programming language, it sends the value 1 to the output variable.

Each output variable can be thought of as its own separate process. Sending values is similar to a message send between processes. After all the input processes finish, the output process has a list of values (in this case, a bunch of 1s). It then aggregates the data by summing the values and producing the final output. The final output is the name of the output variable and its result.

20.2.2 SUBMITTING A TASK

Boa queries are submitted via the Web interface [19] (see Figure 20.4). The interface provides standard integrated development environment features such as syntax highlighting and code completion. Additionally, there are many example queries across several domains provided which are easily accessible from a drop-down box above the query editor.

Once a user has written the query, the user selects the dataset to use as input. Boa provides snapshots of the input data, marked with the timestamp of when the snapshot was taken. Boa periodically produces these datasets (at least yearly, in the future perhaps even monthly). Once a dataset has been created, it will never change. This enables researchers to easily reproduce previous research results, by simply providing the same query and selecting the same input dataset.

When the query is submitted, Boa creates a job (see Figure 20.5). All jobs have a unique identifier and allow you to control them, such as stopping the job, resubmitting the job, and viewing the results of the job. The job page will show if compilation succeeded and any error messages. It will also show the status of executing the query. Once execution has finished, it provides information about how long execution took and links for viewing and downloading the output.

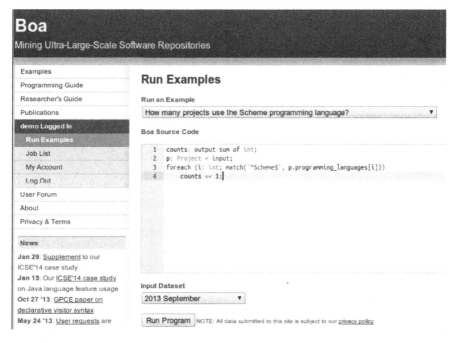

FIGURE 20.4

Submitting a mining task to Boa via the Web interface.

20.2.3 OBTAINING THE RESULTS

Once a job has finished without error, the output of the Boa program is available from the job's page. There are two options: users may view up to the first 64 kB of the output online (see Figure 20.6) or they may download the results as a text file.

20.3 BOA'S SYNTAX AND SEMANTICS

In this section we describe Boa's syntax and semantics. Boa's syntax is inspired by Sawzall [20], a procedural programming language designed by Google for processing large numbers of logs. Despite looking sequential, Boa programs are translated into MapReduce [18] programs, and thus run in a parallel, distributed manner. The language abstracts away many of the details of this framework. Most of a Boa program is actually the map phase, which takes a single project as input, processes it, and outputs the results. Users describe the output of a Boa program and select from a set of predefined aggregators, which acts like the reduce phase. In the remainder of this section we describe Boa's language features in more detail.

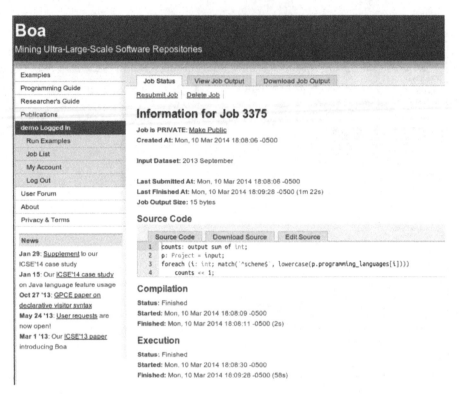

FIGURE 20.5

Viewing details of the submitted job. Users can view the output of the program online or download it as a text file.

Table 20.1 Basic Types Provided by Boa	
Type	**Description**
`bool`	Boolean values (true, false)
`string`	Array of Unicode characters
`int`	64-bit signed integer values
`float`	64-bit IEEE floating point values
`time`	Unix-like timestamp, unsigned integer representing number of microseconds since 00:00:00 UTC 1 January 1970

20.3.1 BASIC AND COMPOUND TYPES

Boa provides several built-in types. The first set of types are the basic types available in the language, and they are shown in Table 20.1. These include many standard types such as boolean values, strings, integers, and floats.

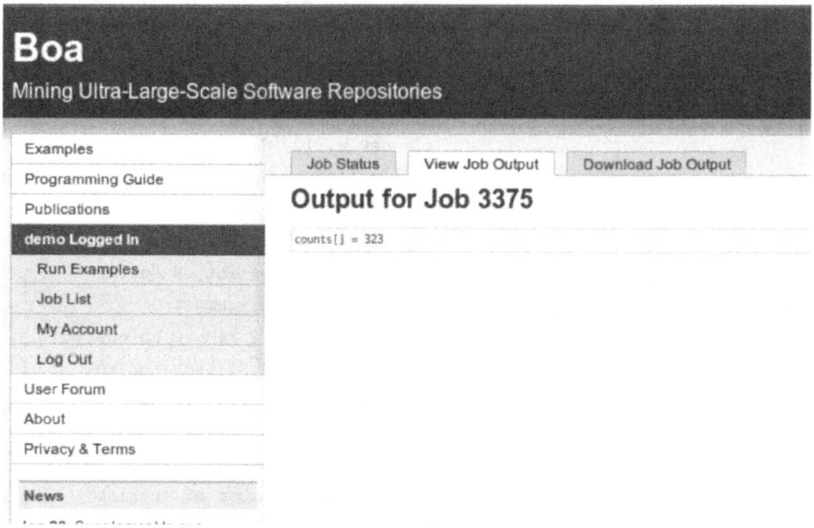

FIGURE 20.6

Viewing the job's output online.

Boa also provides a type called `time` to represent Unix-like timestamps. All date/time values are represented using this type. There are many built-in functions for working with time values, including obtaining specific date-related parts (such as day of the month, month, year, etc.), adding to the time by day, month, year, etc., and truncating to specific granularities.

Strings in Boa are arrays of Unicode characters. Strings can be indexed to retrieve single characters. Strings can be concatenated together using the plus (+) operator. There are also many built-in functions for working with strings to uppercase/lowercase them, get substrings, match them against regular expressions, etc.

Boa also provides several compound types, which are shown in Table 20.2. These types include arrays, maps, stacks, and sets, and are composed of elements of basic type.

Arrays can be initialized to a set of comma-delimited values surrounded by curly braces. They can also be initialized to a fixed size using the `new()` function, which initializes all entries to a given value. Individual elements in the array can be indexed for both reading and assigning values. Array indexing is 0-based. Arrays can also be concatenated together using the plus (+) operator. The size of the array can be retrieved (using the function `len(a)`).

Maps provide simple map functionality, based on hashing functions. Maps are initially created empty, and can also be cleared (using the `clear(m)` function). Assigning values can be accomplished with an assignment operator (=) with an index into the map on the left-hand side and the value on the right-hand side. Entries can also be removed from a map (using the `remove(m, k)` function). The keys in the map can be retrieved as an array (using the `keys(m)` function). Similarly, the values in the map can be retrieved as an array (using the `values(m)` function). The number of entries in the map can also be retrieved (`len(m)`).

Table 20.2 Compound Types Provided by Boa

Type	Example uses

array of basic_type	`a: array of int = 0, 2; # initialize`
	`a = new(a, 10, 0); # initialize`
	`a[0] = 1; # assignment`
	`a = a + a; # concatenation`
	`i = len(a); # size of array`

map[basic_type] of basic_type	`m: map[string] of int; # declare`
	`m["k"] = 0; # assignment`
	`remove(m, "k"); # remove an entry`
	`b = haskey(m, k); # test for key`
	`ks = keys(m); # array of keys`
	`vs = values(m); # array of values`
	`clear(m); # clear map`
	`i = len(m); # number of entries`

stack of basic_type	`st: stack of int; # declare`
	`push(st, 1); # push value`
	`i = pop(st); # pop stack`
	`clear(st); # clear stack`
	`i = len(st); # number of values`

set of basic_type	`s: set of int; # declare`
	`add(s, 1); # add value to set`
	`remove(s, 1); # remove value`
	`b = contains(s, 1); # test for value`
	`clear(s); # clear set`
	`i = len(s); # number of values`

Stacks of values can be maintained using a stack type. Stacks are initially empty. Values can be pushed onto the stack (`push(st, v)`) and popped off the stack (`pop(st)`). Stacks can also be cleared (`clear(st)`). The number of elements on the stack can also be retrieved (`len(st)`).

Finally, sets of unique values are created using a set type. Values can be added (`add(s, v)`) or removed from sets (`remove(s, v)`), and the set can be queried to check for their existence (`contains(s, v)`). Sets may also be cleared (`clear(s)`). The number of unique values in the set can also be retrieved (`len(s)`).

20.3.2 OUTPUT AGGREGATION

As previously mentioned, Boa provides a notion of output variables. Output variables declare an output aggregation function to use on the output. A list of available aggregation functions is given in Table 20.3.

Table 20.3 Output Aggregators Provided by Boa

Aggregator	Description
collection [indices] of T	A collection of data points. No aggregation is performed.
	Example: `output collection[string] of string`
set (param) [indices] of T	A set of the data, of type T. If *param* is specified, the set will contain at most the first *param* sorted elements.
	Example: `output set(5) of int # limit to first 5 elements`
	Example: `output set of int`
sum [indices] of T	An arithmetic sum of the data, of type T.
	Example: `output sum[string][time] of int`
mean [indices] of T	An arithmetic mean of the data, of type T.
	Example: `output mean of int`
bottom (param) [indices] of T	A statistical sampling that records the bottom *param* number of elements of type T.
bottom (param) [indices] of T weight T2	Similar, but groups items of type T and uses their combined *weight* for selecting elements.
	Example: `output bottom(10) of string weight int`
top (param) [indices] of T	A statistical sampling that records the top *param* number of elements of type T.
top (param) [indices] of T weight T2	Similar, but groups items of type T and uses their combined *weight* for selecting elements.
	Example: `output top(10) of string weight int`
minimum (param) [indices] of T weight T2	A precise sample of the *param* lowest *weight*ed elements, of type T. Unlike bottom, does not group items.
	Example: `output minimum(10) of string weight int`
maximum (param) [indices] of T weight T2	A precise sample of the *param* highest *weight*ed elements, of type T. Unlike top, does not group items.
	Example: `output maximum(10) of string weight int`

All aggregators can optionally take indices. Indices act as grouping operators. All output is sorted and grouped by the same index. Then the aggregation function is applied to each group. It is also possible to have multiple indices, in which case the grouping is performed from left to right.

The `collection` aggregator provides a way to simply collect some output without applying any aggregation to the values. Any value emitted to this aggregator will appear directly in the results.

The `set` aggregator is similar, but will output a value only once. Thus, if you emit the value "1" 50 times, it will appear only once in the output.

The `sum` aggregator takes values and computes their arithmetic sum. The param defines the maximum number of elements allowed in the set. If no param is given, the set can be of any size. The `mean` aggregator computes the statistical mean of the values.

The `top/bottom` aggregators produce at most param values in the output. The aggregators group all values together and for each value compute the total weight. Then the values are sorted on the basis of their weight and the aggregator outputs the top or bottom param values. If no weight values are given, a default weight of 1 is used.

So, for example, if the values and weights sent to the aggregator are

```
"foo" weight 2
"bar" weight 1
"baz" weight 2
"foo" weight 3
"bar" weight 4
"foo" weight 3
```

then the aggregator would see the following sorted list

```
"foo", 8
"bar", 5
"baz", 2
```

and would select the top/bottom param values from that list.

The `minimum/maximum` seem similar to top/bottom; however, these aggregators do not compute the total weight. Instead they consider every value individually and pick the top/bottom values on the basis of their individual weights. So while a value can appear only once in the output of top/bottom, with minimum/maximum it can appear more than once. Consider the previous list. For these aggregators they would see the following sorted list

```
"bar", 4
"foo", 3
"foo", 3
"foo", 2
"baz", 2
"bar", 1
```

and would select the first/last param elements from this list. So while `top(3)` would have `"foo"` appearing only once, `maximum(3)` would contain `"foo"` twice.

20.3.3 EXPRESSING LOOPS WITH QUANTIFIERS

A lot of the data in Boa is represented in arrays. Being able to easily loop over this data is important for many mining tasks. To ease dealing with looping over data, Boa provides three quantifier statements:

foreach, exists, and ifall. Quantifiers are simply a sugar, but are useful in many tasks. This sugared form makes programs much easier to write and comprehend.

All quantifiers expect a variable declaration (usually an integer type) with no initializer, a boolean condition, and a statement. The foreach quantifier executes the statement for each value of the quantifier variable where the condition holds. The quantifier variable is available and bound inside the statement. For example,

```
foreach (i: int; match('^java', lowercase(input.programming_languages[i])))
{ .. } # body, can access matching values of i
```

runs the body for each programming language the project declares whose name starts with the string 'java'.

The exists quantifier is different, in that it will execute the statement at most once if and only if there exists (at least) one value of the quantifier variable where the condition holds. If the statement executes, the quantifier variable will be bound to the first occurrence where the condition held. For example,

```
exists (i: int; match('^java', lowercase(input.programming_languages[i])))
{ .. } # body, runs at most one time
```

runs the body once if at least one programming language the project declares has a name starting with the string 'java'. In this case, the value of i will be bound to the first match.

Finally, the ifall quantifier also executes the statement at most once if and only if for all values of the quantifier variable the condition holds. In this case, the quantifier variable is not available inside the statement. For example,

```
ifall (i: int; !match('^java', lowercase(input.programming_languages[i])))
{ .. } # body, runs at most one time
```

runs the body once if there are no programming languages the project declares with a name starting with the string 'java'. In this case, the value of i is not available in the body.

20.3.4 USER-DEFINED FUNCTIONS

The Boa language allows users to write their own functions directly in the query program. This gives users the ability to customize the built-in functions or expand the framework by writing their own mining functions. This is critical for the usability of the framework since different users might have different needs, want different values for the parameters of an algorithm, or even would like an algorithm or algorithms which have not yet been provided by the framework.

The basic syntax for defining a function is as follows:

```
id := function([id : T]*) [: T] { body };
```

which gives the name id to the function, defines zero or more named arguments, has an optional return type, and defines the body of the function. Note that the syntax is actually a variable declaration with an initialization—this means the semicolon after the closing brace is required!

Since functions are just variables with a function type, they may be passed into other functions as an argument or even assigned to multiple variables, assuming the function types are identical. For example, we could write a function to find the maximum int value in an array of integers:

```
1    maxint := function(a: array of int, cmp: function(l: int, r: int) : int) : int
2    {
3            v := a[0];
4            for (i := 1; i < len(a); i++)
5                    if (cmp(v, a[i]) < 0)
6                            v = a[i];
7            return v;
8    };
```

which accepts an array and a comparator function. We could then call this function by passing in a custom comparator (in this case, it is an anonymous function):

```
    i := maxint(a, function(l: int, r: int) : int { return l - r; });
```

which performs the standard comparison between two integers.

20.4 MINING PROJECT AND REPOSITORY METADATA

The dataset provided by Boa contains metadata on projects and source code repositories. This section presents our domain-specific types for the metadata and some examples demonstrating how to use them to query the projects and code repositories.

20.4.1 TYPES FOR MINING SOFTWARE REPOSITORIES

The Boa language provides five domain-specific types for mining project and repository metadata. Table 20.4 shows these five types. Each type provides several attributes that can be thought of as read-only fields. The types form a tree, which is rooted at the `Project` type. This type serves as the input to a Boa program.

The `Project` type contains metadata about a project in the code corpus. Its attributes include the project's `name`, homepage `url`, a `description` of the project, information about its `maintainers` and `developers`, and a list of `code_repositories`. See Table 20.4 for all possible attributes. Depending on which repository the project came from, some of these attributes might be undefined.

The `Person` type represents a user on the repository. This includes project maintainers, developers, and committers. It contains their `username` in the repository, their `real_name`, and their `email` address.

The `CodeRepository` type provides metadata about a code repository of a project. It contains the `url` of the repository, the `kind` of version control system (e.g., Subversion (SVN), Git), and a list of all `revisions` which have been committed.

Each revision has the type `Revision`, which contains the unique revision `id`, the `log` message attached to the commit, the `commit_date`, information about the `author` of the commit as well as the actual `committer` (which are often the same person, and in SVN are *always* the same person), and the list of `files` changed in that revision.

All changed files are represented by the `ChangedFile` type, which contains the file's `name` (the relative path to the file in the repository), the file's `kind` (e.g., Java source file, C source file, binary file), and the kind of `change` performed on the file (e.g., added, deleted, or modified). The contents of source files that parse without error are available, while the contents of other files are not (for space reasons). In the future, Boa may contain file contents for other file types other than source code.

Type	Attributes
Table 20.4 Types Provided by Boa for Project and Repository Metadata	
Project	id: string
	name: string
	created_date: time
	code_repositories: array of CodeRepository
	audiences: array of string
	databases: array of string
	description: string
	developers: array of Person
	donations: bool
	homepage_url: string
	interfaces: array of string
	licenses: array of string
	maintainers: array of Person
	operating_systems: array of string
	programming_languages: array of string
	project_url: string
	topics: array of string
Person	username: string
	real_name: string
	email: string
CodeRepository	url: string
	kind: RepositoryKind
	revisions: array of Revision
Revision	id: int
	log: string
	committer: Person
	commit_date: time
	files: array of ChangedFile
ChangedFile	name: string
	kind: FileKind
	change: ChangeKind

20.4.2 EXAMPLE 1: MINING TOP 10 PROGRAMMING LANGUAGES

Some example questions which could be asked about programming languages are as follows: Which ones are the most popular? What has been the trend of using languages in the last few years? The answers would be useful for many people, from beginners who are choosing between dozens of

```
1        counts: output top(10) of string weight int;
2        foreach (i: int; input.programming_languages[i])
3                counts << input.programming_languages[i] weight 1;
```

FIGURE 20.7

A Boa program mining the top 10 most used programming languages.

programming languages to language designers who would like to improve their language(s). Figure 20.7 shows an example of a Boa program which could answer such a question.

This simple program contains only three lines of code. Similarly to the example in Figure 20.2, this program contains a declaration for the output (line 1). However, it uses a different aggregation function, top, to get the 10 languages which are used the most in our database. The output is a ranked list of 10 string elements based on their weights of type integer. The program runs on each input project (line 2). Note that this time we do not give a name to the input, and we just use it directly. For each programming language used in the project, it emits the language name and a weight of 1 to the output (lines 2-3). The aggregator collects those language names and increases their weights accordingly in the variable counts. The final outcome is a decreasingly ranked list of 10 language names having the highest weights.

From this simple starting Boa program, you could run the same program on different datasets for different years in the past to see the trend of language uses. You could also customize it to query a lot of different information about programming languages. For example, you could use different weight values for different criteria on usage popularity. You could use the amount of code written in a language to measure the popularity by replacing the weight value 1 by the number of lines of code written in that language. Or if you wish to study the relation between programming languages and the topic of the project, you could easily modify this program to compute the top k most popular pairs between topics and languages:

```
1        pairs: output top(10) of string weight int;
2        foreach (i: int; input.programming_languages[i])
3                foreach (j: int; input.topics[j])
4                        pairs << input.programming_languages[i] + ", " + input.
     topics[j] weight 1;
```

20.4.3 INTRINSIC FUNCTIONS

Besides the standard built-in functions as in Sawzall, Boa also provides several intrinsic functions for certain common tasks that involve processing the project and code repository metadata. This section will introduce two of those functions.

The first function is hasfiletype, which receives two arguments: a revision from some repository and a string containing a file extension. This function returns a boolean value which is true if the revision contains a changed file that has the given extension in its name and which is false otherwise. It uses pattern matching to check if there is a file name that ends with the given extension (line 2). This function could be useful for queries that are interested in the revisions which contain source code files

```
1      counts: output sum of int;

2      IsFixingRev := function(rev: Revision) : bool {
3              if (match('\bfix(s|es|ing|ed)?\b', rev.log)) return true;
4              if (match('\b(bug|issue)(s)\b', rev.log))    return true;
5              return false;
6      };

7      foreach (i: int; input.code_repositories[i])
8              foreach (j: int; IsFixingRev(input.code_repositories[i].revisions[j]))
9                      counts << 1;
```

FIGURE 20.8

A Boa program mining the bug-fixing revisions using a custom mining algorithm.

written in certain programming languages, such as C, C++, Java, and C#, or in an certain format, such as comma-separated values, XML, or text.

```
1      hasfiletype := function(rev: Revision, ext: string) : bool {
2              exists (i: int; match(format('\.%s$', ext), lowercase(rev.files[i].name)))
3                      return true;
4              return false;
5      };
```

The second intrinsic function is `isfixingrevision`, which also works on the metadata of the repository. This function receives a `Revision` or a string, which is the content of a commit log message, and determines if it is the log of a bug fixing revision or not. It figures that out by using pattern matching to check if the log message contains certain keywords indicating bug-fixing activities (lines 2-3). In this implementation, we consider the words `fix`, `error`, `bug`, and `issue`, and some of their variations as indicators of fixing bugs. Users who would like to use different sets of keywords or even different approaches could define custom functions in their query Boa code to achieve their goal, such as in the program shown in Figure 20.8 for the example in the next section.

```
1      isfixingrevision := function(rev: Revision) : bool {
2              if (match('\bfix(s|es|ing|ed)?\b', rev.log))    return true;
3              if (match('\b(error|bug|issue)(s)\b', rev.log)) return true;
4              return false;
5      };
```

20.4.4 EXAMPLE 2: MINING REVISIONS THAT FIX BUGS

Developers evolve software projects by committing changes to their repositories. Among them are the changes that fix bugs in the source code. Researchers have been studying those bug-fixing changes to improve the quality of software and software development. For example, one would like to characterize the buggy code (before the fix) and train a classifier to predict buggy code in future commits. Other work might learn from the bug fixes in the past to automatically derive patches for similar bugs in the

```
1      rates: output mean[string] of int;

2      foreach (i: int; input.code_repositories[i].kind == RepositoryKind.SVN)
3          foreach (j: int; input.code_repositories[i].revisions[j])
4              rates[input.id] << len(input.code_repositories[i].revisions[j].files);
```

FIGURE 20.9

A Boa program computing the churn rates for projects using SVN.

future. Others might model the trend of bug appearance in the previous development cycles to plan for the next cycles.

One core task of these works is identifying the bug-fixing revisions from the history. Figure 20.8 shows an example of a Boa program for doing this task. For an input project, the program accesses each repository (line 7) and checks each revision of that repository for if it could have fixed a bug or not by calling the function IsFixingRev to examine its commit log message (line 8). IsFixingRev is a user-defined function declared on lines 2-6. This function matches the given log message with certain patterns (lines 3-4). If there is a match, it considers the revision to be a bug-fixing revision. This program does not use the built-in function isfixingrevision, which has a similar purpose, because we wanted slightly different patterns for the matching.

20.4.5 EXAMPLE 3: COMPUTING PROJECT CHURN RATES

The final example of mining project and repository metadata is a query about the changed files in SVN repositories. It computes the churn rate, which we define as the average number of changed files per revision, in each project using SVN. The Boa program for this query is shown in Figure 20.9.

For each input project, the query accesses the SVN repository (if any) (line 2) and iterates all revisions (line 3). For each revision, the number of changed files is emitted to the output (line 4). The output is indexed by the project's id, meaning that the values will be grouped by each project. The output variable uses the mean aggregator and computes the mean of all values for each project, giving us our final answer.

20.5 MINING SOURCE CODE WITH VISITORS

Expressing source code mining tasks can be very challenging. Boa attempts to make this easier with custom syntax inspired by object-oriented visitor patterns.

20.5.1 TYPES FOR MINING SOURCE CODE

Previously we introduced the five types available for mining project and code repository metadata. In this section we introduce nine more types for mining source code data. These types are shown in Tables 20.5-20.7.

Table 20.5 Types Provided by Boa for Source Code Mining	
Type	**Attributes**
ASTRoot	imports: array of string
	namespaces: array of Namespace
Namespace	name: string
	declarations: array of Declaration
	modifiers: array of Modifier
Declaration	name: string
	parents: array of Type
	kind: TypeKind
	modifiers: array of Modifier
	generic_parameters: array of Type
	fields: array of Variable
	methods: array of Method
	nested_declarations: array of Declaration
Type	name: string
	kind: TypeKind
Modifier	kind: ModifierKind
	visibility: Visibility
	other: string
	annotation_name: string
	annotation_members: array of string
	annotation_values: array of Expression

For any ChangedFile representing a source file, the parsed representation of that source code is provided as a custom abstract syntax tree (AST). As of August 2015, only Java source code is supported, although support for more languages is planned. The root of a source file's AST is the type ASTRoot. This type contains information about any types or modules imported as well as any namespaces contained in the file. The ASTRoot of a file can be accessed by calling the intrinsic function getast(), described in detail later.

A Namespace is similar to a package in Java. Namespaces have a name and optional Modifiers, and contain declarations. A Declaration represents the declaration for types, and can be a class, interface, enum, annotation, etc. A Type represents a type symbol in the source file. The type's name is exactly as it appears in the source text at that location in the source, which means it may or may not be fully qualified.

Declarations have Method and Variable types (fields), which are shown in Table 20.6. These types are self-explanatory.

Finally, Boa provides Statement and Expression types as shown in Table 20.7. When we created these nine types, we had several goals in mind. First, we wanted to keep the total number of types as

Table 20.6 Method and Variable Types Provided by Boa for Source Code Mining

Type	Attributes
Method	name: string modifiers: array of Modifier arguments: array of Variable exception_types: array of Type return_type: Type generic_parameters: array of Type statements: array of Statement
Variable	name: string modifiers: array of Modifier variable_type: Type initializer: Expression

small as possible to make them easier for users to remember. Second, we wanted them to be flexible enough to support most object-oriented languages. Third, we wanted them to be extensible so we can add support for other languages over time.

Because of these goals, the `Statement` and `Expression` types are union types. This means that instead of having almost 50 different types, one for each kind of expression, we have a single unified type. The types have an attribute named `kind` to indicate what kind of statement or expression they are. Depending on the value of that attribute, other attributes will have values.

For example, a for statement in Java such as

```
for (int i = 0; i < 5; i++) { .. }
```

would be represented as follows:

```
Statement {
        kind = StatementKind.FOR,
        initializations = [ /* int i = 0 */ ],
        updates = [ /* i < 5 */ ],
        expression = /* i++ */,
        statements = ...
}
```

The variable_declaration, type_declaration, and condition attributes are undefined. A different language feature, such as Java's enhanced-for loop, could still use this same type. For example, consider the Java code

```
for (int i : coll) { .. }
```

which would be represented as follows:

```
Statement {
        kind = StatementKind.FOR,
        variable_declaration = /* int i */,
```

Table 20.7 Statement and Expression Types Provided by Boa for Source Code Mining

Type	Attributes
Statement	kind: StatementKind
	condition: Expression
	expression: Expression
	initializations: array of Expression
	statements: array of Statement
	type_declaration: Declaration
	updates: array of Expression
	variable_declaration: Variable
Expression	kind: ExpressionKind
	annotation: Modifier
	anon_declaration: Declaration
	expressions: array of Expression
	generic_parameters: array of Type
	is_postfix: bool
	literal: string
	method: string
	method_args: array of Expression
	new_type: Expression
	variable: string
	variable_decls: array of Variable

```
        expression = /* coll */,
        statements = ...
    }
```

The remaining attributes are undefined. A mining task can easily distinguish between the two statements by noticing if `variable_declaration` is defined.

20.5.2 INTRINSIC FUNCTIONS

Boa provides several domain-specific functions for dealing with source code. In this section we outline some of those.

The first function is `getast()`:

```
getast (file: ChangedFile) : ASTRoot
```

This takes a `ChangedFile` and returns the `ASTRoot` for that revision of that file. If a file has no AST, then the function returns an empty `ASTRoot`.

The `getsnapshot()` function

```
getsnapshot := function(cr: CodeRepository, t: time, filters: array of string) : array
    of ChangedFile {
```

```
2              snapshot: map[string] of ChangedFile;

3          visit(cr, visitor {
4                  before node: Revision -> if (node.commit_date > t) stop;
5                  before node: ChangedFile -> {
6                          filter := len(filters) > 0;

7                          exists (i: int; iskind(filters[i], node.kind))
8                                  filter = false;

9                          if (!filter) {
10                                 if (node.change == ChangeKind.DELETED)
11                                         remove(snapshot, node.name);
12                                 else
13                                         snapshot[node.name] = node;
14                         }
15                 }
16         });

17         return values(snapshot);
18     };
```

returns a view in time of the code repository. These views, called snapshots, are all the files that existed at that point in time. The function also accepts an array of strings, which are used to filter files of a specific kind. The filtering is done on the basis of matching the string to the start of each file's kind. For example, FileKind contains SOURCE_JAVA_ERROR (for Java source files that do not parse), SOURCE_JAVA_JLS2 (for Java 1.4), SOURCE_JAVA_JLS3 (for Java 5), etc. If you pass in "SOURCE_JAVA" it will retain all Java source files, even ones that do not parse. However if you pass in "SOURCE_JAVA_JLS" it will retain only Java source files that parsed without any errors. The last two arguments are optional and if not provided will default to the current time and include all files.

isliteral() is a useful function while mining source code that needs to know if an expression is a specific literal (e.g., null)

```
1      isliteral := function(e: Expression, s: string) : bool {
2              return e.kind == ExpressionKind.LITERAL && def(e.literal) && e.literal == s;
3      };
```

that tests an expression to see if it is of kind literal and if it is, if the literal string matches the one provided. This is a commonly occurring pattern so we provide it as a reusable function.

20.5.3 VISITOR SYNTAX

Boa also provides language features for easily mining source code. The syntax is inspired by object-oriented visitor patterns [21]. Since all data for a project is represented as a tree, visitors allow easy traversal of the structure of that tree and easily specifying actions while visiting nodes of specific types.

The general syntax for defining a visitor is

```
id := visitor {
        before n: T -> statement;
        after  n: T -> statement;
        ...
};
```

which declares a new visitor and gives it a name id. Visitors have one or more visit clauses, which can be either a before visit or an after visit. While traversing the tree, if a node has a type T, any matching before and after clauses will execute their statements. The before clause executes immediately on visiting the node and before visiting the node's children. The after clause executes after visiting the node's children. By default, visitors provide a depth-first traversal strategy. Visitors also automatically call getast() when visiting a ChangedFile, thus ensuring the source code nodes are visited.

To begin a visit, simply call the visit() function

```
visit(node, v);
```

and provide the starting node (which is typically just the input) and provide which visitor to use. Note that visitors can be anonymous as most of our examples will show.

There are three ways for a visit statement to match the type. The first form

```
before n: T -> statement;
```

matches exactly one type and (optionally) gives it a name. If a name is provided, then attributes in the type are accessible in the body. The second form

```
before T1, T2, .. -> statement;
```

is a list of types. This clause will execute when the node being visited is of any type listed. This allows easily sharing functionality in visitors. The last form

```
before _ -> statement;
```

is a wildcard. The wildcard acts as a default visit. When visiting a type, if there is no matching clause in the visitor and a wildcard is provided, the wildcard executes.

20.5.4 EXAMPLE 4: MINING AST COUNT

Now consider a simple example to illustrate how this syntax works. Consider a mining task to *find the number of AST nodes for every project in the corpus*. A solution to this task is shown in Figure 20.10.

First we declare our output, which we name AstCount (line 1). The output expects values of type integer. It contains an index of type string, so we can group the values by project, and will sum the values together.

```
1    AstCount: output sum[string] of int;

2    visit(input, visitor {
3            # by default, count all visited nodes
4            before _ -> AstCount[input.id] << 1;

5            # these nodes are not part of the AST, so do nothing when visiting
6            before Project, Person, CodeRepository, Revision, ChangedFile -> ;
7    });
```

FIGURE 20.10

Mining the number of AST nodes in each project.

Next we declare a visitor (lines 2-7). We start the visit at the input (line 2) and use the anonymous visitor we declared. This visitor contains two clauses.

The first clause (line 4) provides our default behavior. By default we want to count nodes as we visit them. So as we visit each node, we send a value of 1 to the output variable, giving the current project's id as the index.

The second clause (line 6) handles special cases. Since we are interested only in counting AST nodes, we list the non-AST node types and provide overriding behavior. In this case, we simply do nothing, as we wish to not count these node types.

This completes our mining task. The result of running this query will be a list of project ids and the total number of AST nodes for that project.

20.5.5 CUSTOM TRAVERSAL STRATEGIES

Visitors provide a default depth-first traversal strategy. This works well for many, but not all, source code mining tasks. For example, to collect all the fields of a class, a visitor would have to visit the `Variable` type; however, this type is also used for local variables. Thus, a custom traversal strategy is needed to ensure only the fields are visited. For such cases where the default traversal strategy will not work, Boa also provides syntax to easily allow you to specify your own traversals.

First, Boa has syntax for manually traversing a subtree rooted at any node:

```
visit(node);
```

which is similar to a normal visit call, but omits the second argument as the current visitor is implied. You may of course provide a different visitor as well as the second argument. This syntax allows you to manually visit any child nodes, in any order, as many times as you wish.

The second piece of syntax is the *stop statement*:

```
stop;
```

which says the current traversal should stop at that point. These statements act similarly to a return inside a function, so no code may appear after them. Stop statements are useful (and allowed) only for *before visits*, since an *after visit* has already traversed the children of that node.

A useful example of a custom traversal strategy is for traversing the current snapshot of the source code. This is useful for any mining task that does not need to analyze the history of the source and instead is interested only in the current state.

This pattern (shown in Figure 20.11) provides a before visit for all code repositories. Inside the body, we use the `getsnapshot()` intrinsic function to retrieve the latest snapshot of the code provided in the code repository (which we named n). Once we have the snapshot (which we store in a local variable named `snapshot`), we manually visit each of the `ChangedFiles` and then stop the default traversal.

20.5.6 EXAMPLE 5: MINING FOR ADDED NULL CHECKS

Now let us consider a more complex example. Consider a mining task that *finds how many null checks were added to source code*. A null check is an if statement containing either an equals or not-equals conditional check where one of the arguments is a null literal. A solution to this task is shown in Figure 20.12.

```
1    # only look at the latest snapshot
2    before n: CodeRepository -> {
3            snapshot := getsnapshot(n);
4            foreach (i: int; snapshot[i])
5                    visit(snapshot[i]);
6            stop;
7    }
```

FIGURE 20.11

Mining only the latest snapshot of the source code.

```
1    AddedNullChecks: output sum of int;

2    nullChecks := 0;

3    # find null check expressions, of the form:
4    #   null == expr *OR* expr == null *OR* null != expr *OR* expr != null
5    nullCheckVisitor := visitor {
6            before node: Expression ->
7                    if (node.kind == ExpressionKind.EQ || node.kind == ExpressionKind.NEQ)
8                            exists (i: int; isliteral(node.expressions[i], "null"))
9                                    nullChecks++;
10   };

11   counts: map[string] of int; # map of files to previous count for that file

12   visit(input, visitor {
13           before node: CodeRepository -> clear(counts);
14           before node: ChangedFile    -> nullChecks = 0;
15           after  node: ChangedFile    -> {
16                   # if there are more null checks, log it
17                   if (haskey(counts, node.name) && nullChecks > counts[node.name])
18                           AddedNullChecks << 1;

19                   counts[node.name] = nullChecks;
20           }
21           # look for IF statements where the boolean condition is a null check
22           before node: Statement ->
23                   if (node.kind == StatementKind.IF)
24                           visit(node.expression, nullCheckVisitor);
25   });
```

FIGURE 20.12

Mining source code to find how many null checks were added.

This solution needs one output variable, named `AddedNullChecks`, which will expect values of type integer and output their arithmetic sum. This will be the total count of all null checks added.

The first part of the solution is to write a visitor that looks for null checks (lines 2-10). This code creates a global variable `nullChecks` to keep track of how many null checks it found. The visitor (lines 5-10) looks for any expression that is an (in)equality conditional operator (`==` or `!=`) where either operand is a null literal. It makes use of the `isliteral()` function described previously.

The second part of the solution requires finding changed files, counting how many null checks are in the file ,and if the number of checks increased. A map is used (line 11) to track the last count for each file. The map is initialized at the start of each code repository (line 13) and is updated after each changed file has been visited (line 19). Since we update the map at the end of the visit clause, newly added files will not be in the map when we check for increased null checks (line 17).

The visitor looks for if statements (line 22) and on finding one, calls the null check visitor previously defined. Thus, we will look only for null checks that are in the condition of an if statement.

Finally, before visiting a changed file, we reset the null check counter (line 14). After visiting a changed file, we see if the number of null checks has increased (line 17), and if it has, we output this fact.

20.5.7 EXAMPLE 6: FINDING UNREACHABLE CODE

The final example we show is a standard static analysis technique to detect unreachable statements. Many compilers detect (and eliminate) unreachable code. Java's compiler actually considers many unreachable statements to be a compilation error. This task answers the question: *Are there existing files with unreachable statements?* A solution to this task is shown in Figure 20.13.

This example needs one output variable, named `DEAD`, which will expect string values and simply show all of them in the output. The idea is to first find unreachable statements, and then output a path for the method containing such statements. So there is no need for aggregation here, we simply collect all results as is.

Next we need a variable and code to store the name of the current file being analyzed (lines 2 and 7). We also need a variable to track the name of the current method (lines 3 and 9). These variables are used when we find unreachable statements and need to output that fact (line 14).

The analysis needs a variable to track if we consider the current statement to be alive (line 4), which we initialize to true on entering a method (line 11). Since methods can actually be nested inside each other, we also need a stack (line 5), which we update by pushing and popping the alive variable when we enter and leave a method (lines 10 and 15).

Finally, we are ready to find statements that stop the flow of execution and require our setting the alive variable to false (lines 19-23). These are things such as return statements, throw statements, and break and continue (for loops).

Since we do not want our analysis to produce false positives (at the cost of possibly missing some unreachable statements, aka false negatives), we need to consider special cases for a few things. First, break and continue may have labels and thus might not actually create dead code after them. For these we just assume if there is a label the following statements are still alive (line 20).

Second, if blocks and labeled blocks can create problems with the analysis, we avoid analyzing their bodies (line 24).

```
1        DEAD: output collection of string;

2        cur_file: string;
3        cur_method: string;

4        alive := true;
5        s: stack of bool;

6        visit(input, visitor {
7                before node: ChangedFile -> cur_file = string(node);
8                before node: Method -> {
9                        cur_method = node.name;
10                       push(s, alive);
11                       alive = true;
12               }
13               after node: Method -> {
14                       if (!alive) DEAD << format("%s - %s", cur_file, cur_method);
15                       alive = pop(s);
16               }
17               before node: Statement ->
18                       switch (node.kind) {
19                               case StatementKind.BREAK, StatementKind.CONTINUE:
20                                       if (def(node.expression)) break;
21                               case StatementKind.RETURN, StatementKind.THROW:
22                                       alive = false;
23                                       break;
24                               case StatementKind.IF, StatementKind.LABEL: stop;
25                               case StatementKind.FOR, StatementKind.DO, StatementKind.WHILE,
26                                               StatementKind.SWITCH, StatementKind.TRY:
27                                       foreach (i: int; node.statements[i]) {
28                                               push(s, alive);
29                                               visit(node.statements[i]);
30                                               alive = pop(s);
31                                       }
32                                       stop;
33                               default:
34                                       break;
35                       }
36       });
```

FIGURE 20.13

Finding unreachable code using static analysis.

Finally, for other statements with blocks we have to have special handling (lines 25-32). Since we do not know for certain these blocks will execute, in general we ignore the results of analyzing their bodies. However, we do want to visit the bodies in case there are nested methods inside them, which may themselves have unreachable statements.

20.6 GUIDELINES FOR REPLICABLE RESEARCH

One of the main principles of the scientific method is being able to confirm or replicate prior research results. However, exactly replicating previous research results is often difficult or impossible. There are many reasons why: the raw dataset is not clearly defined in the paper, the processed dataset is not available, the tools and infrastructure used are not available, the mining task itself is ambiguous in the paper, etc. One of the main goals of Boa is to solve this problem. In this section, we give researchers using Boa guidance so that their work may be replicable by others.

The first step in this process is handled by Boa's administrators. Boa provides timestamp-marked datasets for querying. These datasets, once published on the Boa website, will not change over time and will continue to be made available for researchers. This means other researchers will have access to the actual data used in your studies.

The second step is up to each individual researcher. For their research to be replicated, the program(s) used to query these fixed datasets must also be made available to other researchers. This can be accomplished in one of two ways:

(1) Researchers can publish the Boa program(s) and the dataset used for their research in a research publication. They can then make the results of the program(s) available on a website.
(2) Researchers can use the Boa website to publish the program(s), the dataset used, and the results of the program(s). They can then provide a link to this archive in their research publication(s).

The second method is preferred, as the public Boa archival page will contain all information, including the original source code, the execution date/time, the input dataset used, and the output of the program. In the rest of this section, we describe how to generate a Boa archival link for a job.

The first step is to view each Boa job used in the research project. Toward the top of the job page, there is text indicating if the job is PRIVATE or PUBLIC. To share the job, it must be marked PUBLIC. If it lists the job as PRIVATE, a link is provided to make it PUBLIC.

Now the job should be marked as a PUBLIC job. There is also a new link to view the public page. This is the URL for the archival page for this job. Click that link and verify the information matches what was used in your study.

The page you are now viewing is the public archival page for the job. This is the archival page for which you should provide a link in your research publication(s). This page contains all necessary information for replicating your research results, including the original source code, the input dataset used, and the original output of the program.

It is important to note that the necessary information for replicating this result (the program and the input dataset) can never be changed for this job! If you attempt to modify the job, Boa will create a new job and keep the original information intact. This helps avoid accidentally changing previously published results and ensures future researchers have the original information!

20.7 CONCLUSIONS

MSR on a large scale is important for more generalizable research results. Large collections of software artifacts are openly available (e.g., SourceForge has more than 350,000 projects, GitHub has more than 10 million projects, Google Code has more than 250,000 projects) but capitalizing on this data is extremely difficult. This chapter is a reference guide to using Boa, a language and infrastructure designed to decrease the barrier to entry for ultra-large-scale MSR studies.

Boa consists of a domain-specific language, its compiler, a dataset that contains almost 700,000 open source projects as of this writing, a back end based on MapReduce to effectively analyze this dataset, and a Web-based front end for writing MSR programs. The Boa language provides many useful features for easily looping over data, writing custom mining functions, and easily mining source code. Boa also aids reproducibility of research results by providing an archive of the data queried, the query itself, and the output of the query.

Currently Boa contains project metadata and source code data for Java source files. It also contains only data from SourceForge. Soon, Boa should support additional data such as issues/bug reports as well as additional sources of data such as GitHub. The goal of Boa is to provide the ability to easily query as many different data sources as possible, by simply using one infrastructure and query language. While this is an ambitious goal, we feel it is obtainable and look forward to the future of mining ultra-large-scale software repositories!

20.8 **PRACTICE PROBLEMS**

In this section we pose several software repository mining tasks. Your job is to write a query in Boa to solve the task. The tasks start easy and get substantially more difficult. Solutions to some of these tasks appear on Boa's website [19].

PROJECT AND REPOSITORY METADATA PROBLEMS

1. Write a Boa query to find in which year the most projects were created.
2. Write a Boa query to compute the average commit speed of each project.
3. Write a Boa query to find which developer has committed the most changes to each repository.
4. Write a Boa query to find, for each project, who commits changes to only a single file and who commits changes to the largest number of files.
5. Write a Boa query to find who has committed the most changes bug-fixing revisions for each project.
6. Write a Boa query to correlate the projects' topics and the programming language used.

SOURCE CODE PROBLEMS

7. Write a Boa query to compute the average number of methods per file in the latest snapshot of each project.
8. Write a Boa query to find, for each project, the top 100 methods that have the most AST nodes.
9. Write a Boa query to find top 10 most imported libraries.
10. Write a Boa query to find top five most used application programming interface methods.
11. Write a Boa query to compute the average number of changed methods/classes per revision for each project.

12. Write a Boa query to find the average number of changes to a class/file, or the average number of changes to a method.

13. Write a Boa query to find the distribution of the number of libraries over projects.

14. Write a Boa query to find the year that JUnit was added to projects the most.

15. Write a Boa query to find the adoption trend of using graphic libraries (AWT, Swing, and SWT) in Java projects.

16. Write a Boa query to find all sets of projects that use the same set of libraries.

17. Write a Boa query to compute how often classes/files are in a bug-fixing revision.

18. Write a Boa query to find which pairs of methods/classes/files are always co-changed in all bug-fixing revisions of a project.

19. Write a Boa query to find all methods that contain an uninitialized variable.

20. Write a Boa query to correlate the developers and the technical terms in the source code that they have touched. The terms are tokens extracted from the classes' name after tokenization.

REFERENCES

[1] Livshits B, Whaley J, Lam MS. Reflection analysis for Java. In: Proceedings of the third Asian conference on programming languages and systems, APLAS; 2005. p. 139–60.

[2] Baldi PF, Lopes CV, Linstead EJ, Bajracharya SK. A theory of aspects as latent topics. In: Proceedings of the 23rd ACM SIGPLAN conference on object-oriented programming systems languages and applications. OOPSLA, 2008. p. 543–62.

[3] Tempero E, Noble J, Melton H. How do Java programs use inheritance? An empirical study of inheritance in Java software. In: Proceedings of the 22nd European conference on object-oriented programming. ECOOP, 2008. p. 667–91.

[4] Linstead E, Bajracharya S, Ngo T, Rigor P, Lopes C, Baldi P. Sourcerer: mining and searching internet-scale software repositories. Data Mining Knowl Discov 2009; 18.

[5] Grechanik M, McMillan C, DeFerrari L, Comi M, Crespi S, Poshyvanyk D, Fu C, Xie Q, Ghezzi C. An empirical investigation into a large-scale Java open source code repository. In: International symposium on empirical software engineering and measurement, ESEM; 2010. p. 11:1–10.

[6] Gabel M, Su Z. A study of the uniqueness of source code. In: Proceedings of the 18th ACM SIGSOFT international symposium on foundations of software engineering. FSE '10, New York, NY, USA: ACM; 2010. p. 147–56. ISBN 978-1-60558-791-2. doi:10.1145/1882291.1882315.

[7] Parnin C, Bird C, Murphy-Hill ER. Java generics adoption: how new features are introduced, championed, or ignored. In: 8th IEEE international working conference on mining software repositories, MSR; 2011.

[8] Callaú O, Robbes R, Tanter E, Röthlisberger D. How developers use the dynamic features of programming languages: the case of Smalltalk. In: Proceedings of the 8th working conference on mining software repositories. MSR, 2011. p. 23–32.

[9] Richards G, Hammer C, Burg B, Vitek J. The eval that men do: A large-scale study of the use of eval in JavaScript applications. In: Proceedings of the 25th European conference on object-oriented programming, ECOOP; 2011. p. 52–78.

[10] Hindle A, Barr E, Su Z, Gabel M, Devanbu P. On the naturalness of software. In: 2012 34th international conference on software engineering (ICSE); 2012. p. 837–47. doi:10.1109/ICSE.2012.6227135.

[11] Dyer R, Nguyen HA, Rajan H, Nguyen TN. Boa: A language and infrastructure for analyzing ultra-large-scale software repositories. In: Proceedings of the 2013 international conference on software engineering. ICSE '13, Piscataway, NJ, USA: IEEE Press; 2013. p. 422–31. ISBN 978-1-4673-3076-3. URL: http://dl.acm.org/citation.cfm?id=2486788.2486844.

[12] Meyerovich L, Rabkin A. Empirical analysis of programming language adoption. In: 4th ACM SIGPLAN conference on systems, programming, languages and applications: software for humanity, SPLASH, 2013.

[13] Nguyen HA, Nguyen AT, Nguyen TT, Nguyen T, Rajan H. A study of repetitiveness of code changes in software evolution. In: 2013 IEEE/ACM 28th international conference on automated software engineering (ASE); 2013. p. 180–90. doi:10.1109/ASE.2013.6693078.

[14] Dyer R, Rajan H, Nguyen HA, Nguyen TN. Mining billions of ast nodes to study actual and potential usage of java language features. In: Proceedings of the 36th international conference on software engineering. ICSE 2014, New York, NY, USA: ACM; 2014. p. 779–90. ISBN 978-1-4503-2756-5. doi:10.1145/2568225.2568295.

[15] Negara S, Codoban M, Dig D, Johnson RE. Mining fine-grained code changes to detect unknown change patterns. In: Proceedings of the 36th international conference on software engineering. ICSE 2014, New York, NY, USA: ACM; 2014. p. 803–13. ISBN 978-1-4503-2756-5. doi:10.1145/2568225.2568317.

[16] Dyer R, Nguyen HA, Rajan H, Nguyen TN. Boa: a language and infrastructure for analyzing ultra-large-scale software repositories. In: Proceedings of the 35th international conference on software engineering, ICSE'13; 2013. p. 422–31.

[17] Apache Software Foundation. Hadoop: Open source implementation of MapReduce. http://hadoop.apache.org/.

[18] Dean J, Ghemawat S. MapReduce: simplified data processing on large clusters. In: Proceedings of the 6th symposium on operting systems design & implementation, OSDI'04, vol. 6; 2004.

[19] Rajan H, Nguyen TN, Dyer R, Nguyen HA. Boa website. http://boa.cs.iastate.edu/; 2014.

[20] Pike R, Dorward S, Griesemer R, Quinlan S. Interpreting the data: parallel analysis with Sawzall. Sci Program 2005;13(4):277–98.

[21] Gamma E, Helm R, Johnson R, Vlissides J. Design patterns: elements of reusable object-oriented software. Reading, MA: Addison-Wesley Professional; 1994.

SCALABLE PARALLELIZATION OF SPECIFICATION MINING USING DISTRIBUTED COMPUTING

21

Shaowei Wang*, David Lo*, Lingxiao Jiang*, Shahar Maoz[†], Aditya Budi[‡]

School of Information Systems, Singapore Management University, Singapore* School of Computer Science, Tel Aviv University, Tel Aviv, Israel[†] School of Information Systems, BINUS University, Jakarta, Indonesia[‡]

CHAPTER OUTLINE

Methods:

- Specification mining algorithms

  1. Frequent pattern-based specification miner
  2. Value-based invariant miner
  3. Finite-state machine specification miner
  4. Live sequence chart miner
  5. Temporal rule miner

- Distributed computing models

  1. Message-passing model
  2. MapReduce
  3. Hadoop

21.1 INTRODUCTION

Specification mining is a family of program analysis techniques that extract likely specifications from code or execution traces. "Specifications" refers to certain patterns or properties that should hold in a program. The specifications can take various forms, such as temporal rules about the order of certain method calls, and invariants that constrain method parameters and return values. The extracted specifications can provide much information about program properties which are not explicitly documented, and can be used to improve program documentation, comprehension, and verification tasks [1].

An important challenge for many specification mining algorithms relates to their scalability, since they need to take many potentially large program behavioral profiles as input to search for common patterns. A common way to collect behavioral profiles is to execute a subject program with many test cases. To exercise the many behaviors of a large program, many test cases would need to be run. Also, the resultant execution traces are likely to be huge. The size of a code base, the number of test cases, and the sizes of traces generated are all hurdles to the scalability of existing specification mining algorithms. For example, our evaluation on four existing specification mining algorithms—(1) CLIPPER [2], a recurring pattern mining algorithm, (2) Daikon [3], a value-based invariant mining algorithm,

(3) k-tails [4, 5], a finite-state machine inference algorithm, and (4) LM [6], a sequence diagram mining algorithm—shows that they fail to analyze the large traces ranging from 41 MB to 157 GB generated from seven DaCapo benchmark programs [7]. A fifth algorithm, Perracotta [8], a temporal rule mining algorithm, takes hours to analyze the traces before producing some specifications. To analyze many large traces from a large code base, existing specification mining algorithms need to be made much more scalable.

We observe that most specification mining algorithms are data intensive, on one hand, but computationally relatively repetitive, on the other hand, and many repetitive tasks in those algorithms can be executed concurrently. Even though tasks in different algorithms may require various levels of synchronization, the synchronization needed can be minimized with careful arrangements of the tasks to facilitate speedup when the algorithms are distributed onto multiple computers. This is the main insight that drives this chapter to address the scalability issue of many existing specification mining algorithms. Similar observations and ideas have been proposed to parallelize various algorithms in scientific computing, software engineering, data mining, and many other domains [9–13]. However, as far as we know, there is little prior study on parallelization of various kinds of specification mining algorithms.

To help address the challenge of making various existing specification mining algorithms more scalable,[1] we propose a general specification mining algorithm that can perform repetitive specification mining tasks across multiple computers based on a general distributed computing model. The general algorithm is designed in such a way that it abstracts away specific algorithmic details but captures the essences of many existing specification mining algorithms that mine specifications from program execution traces. We present this algorithm in the context of a message-passing-based distributed computing model, in particular MapReduce. An algorithm designer can transform a *sequential* specification mining algorithm into a *distributed* one by following the guided steps in our algorithm and instantiating it with concrete algorithm-specific details.

To evaluate our general algorithm, we instantiate it with five existing sequential specification mining algorithms on top of a popular distributed computing model—MapReduce [14]—and one of its open-source implementations—Hadoop [15]—and evaluate the scalability of the distributed versions of these algorithms. In particular, we show how we follow the guidance of our general algorithm, and use a common input-trace splitting scheme and several algorithm-specific techniques to divide and conquer five specification mining algorithms—(1) CLIPPER [2], (2) Daikon [3], (3) k-tails [4, 5], (4) LM [6], and (5) Perracotta [8]—and transform them into distributed ones. The five algorithms produce different kinds of specifications expressed in different target languages, such as frequent patterns, value invariants, finite-state machines, sequence diagrams, and temporal rules. We evaluate the distributed algorithms on seven Java programs from the DaCapo benchmark [7], whose traces range from 41 MB to 157 GB. The results are encouraging. Perracotta's distributed version implemented within MapReduce (Perracotta^{MR}) running on four machines (using up to eight CPU cores in total) can speed up the original version by 3-18 times. The other four original algorithms are unable to analyze the large traces, while their distributed versions (CLIPPER^{MR}, Daikon^{MR},

---

[1] It is not our goal to improve the accuracy of existing specification mining algorithms in inferring correct specifications. Rather, our goal is to improve their *scalability*. When evaluating the accuracy of the parallelized algorithms, we need only compare it against their sequential versions, instead of human developers' ground truth.

k-tails^{MR}, and LM^{MR}) can complete the analysis within hours, and gain more performance improvement when more machines are employed.

Our main finding is that many specification mining algorithms fit distributed computing models well as they are composed of many repetitive computational tasks dealing with data that may be split into partitions with limited overlapping. Our general algorithm also captures the essence of many specification mining algorithms well, and can be used to help transform sequential algorithms into distributed ones to gain much performance improvement and scalability improvement by implementing them within the MapReduce framework and executing them on clusters of computers. We believe our findings are applicable to many other specification mining algorithms, especially those that mine specifications expressed in one of the five target languages that we have investigated.

The contributions of this chapter are as follows:

1. Similarly to many prior studies on parallelization of other algorithms in various domains, we observe that many *specification mining* algorithms can be fit into a distributed programming model, and much performance gain and scalability gain can be achieved by parallelizing them within a distributed computing framework, such as MapReduce.
2. We present a general distributed specification mining algorithm that abstracts away particular algorithmic details and represents the essences of many existing specification mining algorithms.
3. We propose an input-trace splitting scheme and several algorithm-specific techniques to instantiate the general algorithm with five existing sequential specification mining algorithms to create five distributed algorithms.
4. We perform an empirical evaluation with seven Java programs from the DaCapo benchmark and show that the five distributed algorithms perform significantly faster than the original algorithms on many large traces.

This chapter is organized as follows. Section 21.2 provides a brief introduction to the five specification mining approaches and the distributed computing model we use in our work. Section 21.3 presents the main technical contribution of the chapter—that is, the general distributed specification mining algorithm and its instantiations with the five existing algorithms. Our implementation and empirical evaluation are described in Section 21.4. Section 21.5 discusses related work. Section 21.6 concludes the chapter with proposals for future work.

21.2 BACKGROUND

In this section, we first briefly introduce each of the five mining algorithms that we parallelize. Then, we introduce the distributed computing model used in this chapter—the message-passing model and MapReduce.

21.2.1 SPECIFICATION MINING ALGORITHMS

On the basis of the format of the specifications that a specification mining algorithm produces [1], many algorithms can be grouped into ones that produce (1) frequent patterns, (2) value-based invariants, (3) finite-state machines, (4) sequence diagrams, and (5) temporal rules. We briefly describe these families of algorithms in the following.

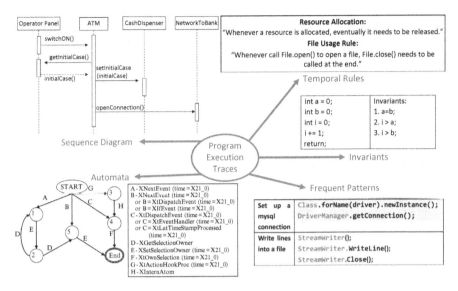

FIGURE 21.1

Sample outputs of specification mining algorithms.

We present in Figure 21.1 sample outputs of the five kinds of specification mining algorithms, which can be mined from various kinds of program execution traces.

21.2.1.1 Mining frequent patterns

Discovering patterns that appear many times in large input datasets is a well-known problem in data mining [16]. Many algorithms, such as frequent itemset mining, sequential pattern mining, and graph pattern mining, aim to capture frequent patterns. A number of algorithms specific to software engineering tasks have been proposed. For example, interaction pattern mining [17] analyzes traces of system-user interactions to discover frequently recurring activities and uses them as parts of functional requirements for reengineering. Iterative pattern mining (CLIPPER) [2] takes in a set of execution profiles containing methods invoked during the executions and then identifies methods that often need to be invoked together or in a particular order as usage specifications for the methods.

21.2.1.2 Mining value-based invariants

A value-based invariant captures the relation (e.g., x==y) among program variables that should be satisfied at a program point (e.g., when a method returns x). Daikon is the pioneer and most well-known system for extracting value-based invariants [3]. It has many invariant templates, such as Equality (e.g., x==y), IntGreaterThan (e.g., iVal1>=iVal2), and IntArraySorted (e.g., isSorted(iArray1)). On the basis of a set of input execution traces, Daikon matches the traces to the templates at various program points of interest (e.g., method entries and exits). Instances of the invariant templates satisfied by all (or most) of the input traces are outputted.

Value-based invariants generated by Daikon can be used independently, or can be used in conjunction with other kinds of specifications,—for example, to enrich finite-state machines [5] or sequence diagrams [18].

21.2.1.3 Mining finite-state machines

Many of these algorithms extend or make use of techniques from the grammar inference community [5, 19, 20]. One of these algorithms, k-tails [20], builds a prefix tree acceptor from a set of execution traces that capture input-output behaviors; the nodes of the prefix tree acceptor are then merged on the basis of some evaluation criteria—for example, the similarity of the subsequent k-paths, whose lengths are at most k—to form finite-state machines, which are then used as specifications of program behaviors.

21.2.1.4 Mining sequence diagrams

Sequence diagrams are a visual formalism to specify the ordering of events among components in a system. Different algorithms exist for mining various kinds of sequence diagrams, such as UML sequence diagrams [21], message sequence charts [22], message sequence graphs [4], and live sequence charts (LSCs) [6, 23, 24]. Such visual diagrams can help maintainers of a program to better understand how various components in the program interact with each other.

21.2.1.5 Mining temporal rules

Temporal rules can be expressed in various formats, such as association rules [8, 25],and temporal logics [26, 27] (e.g., "Whenever $x_1, \ldots, x_n$ occur, $y_1, \ldots, y_m$ also occur"). Such rules help to make it clearer which operations should or should not occur in certain orders so that maintainers of the program may make changes accordingly. Most temporal rule mining algorithms evaluate the validity of a rule on the basis of the likelihood that the x's are followed by the y's, and the number of times x is followed by y in the execution traces. They mainly differ in the semantics of the mined rules, the allowable values of n and m, and the metrics used to evaluate rule validity. For example, Perracotta extracts association rules of short length (n and m being 1) [8]; other algorithms extract temporal rules of longer lengths [27].

21.2.2 DISTRIBUTED COMPUTING

Similarly to what was observed in many prior studies on parallelization of other algorithms in various domains, we observe that many specification mining algorithms can be broken into computational tasks that are repetitively applied to various parts of input data, and thus fit well to a distributed computing model. This section summarizes the concepts we need.

21.2.2.1 Message-passing model

We focus on distributed algorithms in the message-passing model where multiple processes on multiple computing nodes have their own local memory and communicate with each other by message passing, although our general algorithm may be adapted to other distributed computing models as well.

The processes share information by *sending/receiving* (or *dispatching/collecting*) data to/from each other. The processes most likely run the same programs, and the whole system should work correctly regardless of the messaging relations among the processes or the structure of the network. A popular standard and message-passing system is the message passing interface (MPI) defined in [13]. Such models themselves do not impose particular restrictions on the mechanism for messaging, and thus

Table 21.1 The *Map* and *Reduce* Operations

Operation	Input	Output
map	(K_{ip}, V_{ip})	list(K_{int}, V_{int})
reduce	$(K_{int}, \text{list}(V_{int}))$	O_{part}

give programmers much flexibility in algorithm/system designs. However, this also means that programmers need to deal with actual sending/receiving of messages, failure recovery, managing running processes, etc.

21.2.2.2 MapReduce

MapReduce is a simplified distributed computing model for processing large data in a cluster of computers [14], reducing programmers' burden of dealing with actual sending/receiving of messages and various system issues so that programmers may focus more on the algorithmic issues. It can be implemented on top of a message-passing system, such as MPI [28]. In this chapter, we base our implementation on Hadoop [15], a free and open-source implementation of MapReduce.

The model splits the problem at hand into smaller subproblems as requested, distributes these subproblems among the computers in the cluster, and collects and combines the results that are passed back. Besides the splitting function, the key to using the MapReduce framework is to define two functions: (1) *map*, which takes one input key/value pair (K_{ip}, V_{ip}), and generates zero or more intermediate key/value pairs (list(K_{int}, V_{int})), and (2) *reduce*, which composes all intermediate values associated with the same key into a final output. The splitting function, customizable to split input data differently, partitions the whole input dataset into small pieces, and transforms each piece into a set of key/value pairs.

MapReduce works by automatically applying the *map* function on each of the key/value pairs from the splitting function to produce an intermediate set of key/value pairs. It then automatically groups all intermediate values associated with the same key together; the *reduce* function is then applied to each group, resulting in a partial output O_{part}; all partial outputs are concatenated to form the final output. The inputs and outputs of the *map* and *reduce* functions are illustrated in Table 21.1. The following sections use the same symbols to represent the inputs and outputs of the functions as well.

21.3 DISTRIBUTED SPECIFICATION MINING

We now present the main contribution of this chapter: a general distributed specification mining algorithm and redefinitions of five concrete algorithms in the MapReduce model.

21.3.1 PRINCIPLES

We first present our general principles and algorithm for parallelizing specification mining algorithms.

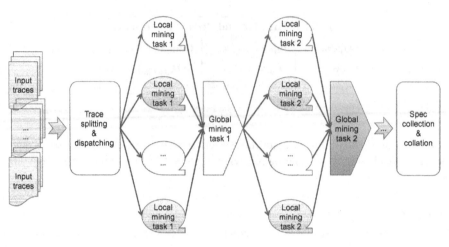

FIGURE 21.2

Overview of our distributed specification mining algorithm.

21.3.1.1 Abstracting specification mining algorithms

Even though many specification mining algorithms are not initially designed to be distributed, we can *divide and conquer* them by exploiting the parallelism in various parts of the algorithms on the basis of our observation that many computational tasks in the algorithms are repetitively applied to various parts of input data. Figure 21.2 illustrates the design idea of our general, distributed specification algorithm.

The key is to extract such tasks from existing algorithms that are repetitively applied to different parts of the input traces so that the input traces can be split and dispatched to and processed at different computing nodes. We note that many algorithms contain *local mining tasks* that can be done completely on a small part of the input data without the need of other parts. For some algorithms, however, there are still *global mining tasks* that need to operate on all data, and we need to ensure those tasks can run scalably. Fortunately, we note that the mining algorithms rely on various "statistics" that measure the likelihood of a candidate specification being valid. It is rarely necessary for the mining algorithms to really operate on all data at once in memory. Thus, we may also split the data (either the input traces or the intermediate results from other tasks) needed by the global mining tasks so that they operate on smaller data and become more parallelizable and scalable; or we can replace the global mining tasks with certain local ones plus certain specification compositions since many specifications are compositional. Multiple iterations of local and global mining tasks may be interweaved to find specifications mined by the normal sequential algorithms.

The general steps of our approach for parallelizing a given specification mining algorithm that takes a set of execution traces as input are as follows:

(1) Extract "local" operations in the algorithm that can be done in a separate trunk of the traces. The boundaries of trace trunks can be defined on the basis of the operations and can be algorithm specific.

(2) Extract "global" operations in the algorithm that may need to be done with all data and decide how the data needed by the global operations may be split and/or replace the global operations with local ones.

(3) Split the input traces into trunks accordingly, and dispatch them to different computing nodes for either local or global operations.

(4) Collect results from different computing nodes, and combine them to produce final specification outputs.

To produce efficient distributed versions of the sequential specification mining algorithms, one needs to ensure that the extracted local/global operations can be independent and executed concurrently with little or no synchronization. The steps described here are generic, although many details (what the local and global operations are, how to split data, how to dispatch/collect data, how to compose results, etc.) are algorithm specific, and are further explained in Section 21.3.2.

21.3.1.2 Distributed specification mining with MapReduce

MapReduce simplifies the general distributed computing model by providing automated mechanisms for setting up a "master" process that manages work allocated to "worker" processes, dispatching work to a worker, collecting results from a worker, recovering from failures, utilizing data locality, etc. We further describe our general specification mining steps in the context of MapReduce as follows:

(1) Define an appropriate *map* function that corresponds to a local mining task. Each instance of the *map* function runs in parallel with respect to other instances; it takes one trace trunk V_{ip} as input to produce a set of intermediate specification mining results (*intermediate key/value pairs*, list(K_{int}, V_{int}), in MapReduce's terminology). The *map* function must be designed in such a way that the operation on V_{ip} is independent of the operation on other trace trunks.

(2) Define an appropriate *reduce* function that corresponds to a global mining task or a composition operation that combines results (i.e., the intermediate key/value pairs, list(K_{int}, V_{int})) from local mining tasks. Many algorithms rarely need global mining tasks, and the composition operations may be as simple as concatenation or filtering or recursive applications of some local mining tasks (see the algorithm-specific steps in Section 21.3.2).

(3) Define an appropriate *record reader* that splits input traces into trunks suitable for the *map* function. For example, if the *map* function from a mining algorithm deals with invariants within a method, a trace may be split at method entry and exit points. Each trace trunk can be identified by a *trace identifier* K_{ip} and its content V_{ip}.

(4) Let the MapReduce framework automatically handle the actual trace splitting, dispatching, and result collection.

The general steps above provide guidance to make it easier to transform sequential specification mining algorithms into distributed ones, although the strategies and techniques used to identify the local/global tasks in various algorithms might be different from each other, and there can be multiple ways to define the local/global operations, split the data, etc., for a given algorithm.

In the following, we describe our concrete instantiations of the general algorithm on five specification mining algorithms: (1) CLIPPER [2], a recurring pattern mining algorithm, (2) Daikon [3], a value-based invariant mining algorithm, (3) k-tails [4, 5], a finite-state machine inference algorithm, (4) LM [6], a sequence diagram mining algorithm, and (5) Perracotta [8], a temporal rule mining algorithm. We believe our findings can be easily adapted to other specification mining algorithms, especially those that mine specifications in languages similar to one of the five algorithms.

21.3.2 ALGORITHM-SPECIFIC PARALLELIZATION

21.3.2.1 Iterative pattern mining with MapReduce

We illustrate how to instantiate our general algorithm with CLIPPER, an iterative pattern mining algorithm [2], to create the distributed version CLIPPER^{MR}.

CLIPPER, similarly to many frequent pattern/sequence mining algorithms, explores the search space of all possible patterns. It starts with small patterns and then *grows* these patterns to larger ones. *Pattern growth* is performed repeatedly; each iteration grows a pattern by one unit. The iterations follow the depth-first search procedure. During the traversal of the search space, every pattern that is *frequent* (i.e., appearing many times in the dataset) is outputted. There have been studies on parallelization of frequent sequence mining algorithms, such as [9]. Their work uses MapReduce too, but our data sources and the subject algorithms are specific to specification mining, which requires different parallelization strategies and techniques. The semantics of the sequential patterns mined by their approaches is also different from that of iterative patterns mined by CLIPPER. Their approach relies on the w-equivalency property, which may hold only for their sequential patterns.

A piece of pseudocode for CLIPPER, as well as many frequent pattern mining algorithms, is shown in Algorithm 1. Intuitively, checking if a pattern is frequent or not could potentially be a parallelizable

---

Algorithm 1 Generic algorithm of frequent patter mining.

1: **Procedure** MinePatterns:
2: Let SMALL = Small frequent patterns
3: **for all** s in SMALL **do**
4:     TraverseSSpace(s)
5: **end for**
6:
7: **Procedure** TraverseSSpace(Pattern s):
8: Output s
9: Let NEXT= GrowPattern(s)
10: **for all** n in NEXT **do**
11:     TraverseSSpace(n)
12: **end for**
13:
14: **Procedure** GrowPattern(Pattern s):
15: Let BIGGER = s++e , where e is a growth unit and ++ is a grow operation
16: **for all** s' in BIGGER **do**
17:     **if** s' is frequent **then**
18:         Output s'
19:     **end if**
20: **end for**

---

task. Unfortunately, it is not straightforward to break the pattern mining problem into *independent* tasks. On one hand, as we grow a pattern one unit at a time, if the pattern is not frequent, the longer pattern is not frequent either. In other words, some tasks can be omitted after the evaluation of other tasks and are thus dependent on other tasks. On the other hand, without the strategy of omitting longer patterns, the number of tasks grows exponentially with respect to the length of the traces.

Fortunately, we identify a common operation that is shared by these tasks—namely, *pattern growth* (i.e., the procedure `GrowPattern` in Algorithm 1). As pattern growth is performed many times, it is the critical operation that the mining algorithm spends many resources on. Thus, rather than trying to parallelize the whole pattern mining algorithm, we parallelize the pattern growth procedure.

The pattern growth procedure considers a pattern P and tries to extend it to patterns $P{+}{+}e$, where e is a growth unit and $+{+}$ is a growth operation (e.g., appending an event to an iterative pattern—from $\langle m_1 \rangle$ to $\langle m_1, m_2 \rangle$).

For an iterative pattern P and trace T, we store the indices pointing to the various instances of the pattern in T. When we try to grow the pattern P to each pattern $P' \in \{P{+}{+}e\}$, we can update these indices to point to instances of the pattern P'. From the instances of P', we could then know if P' is frequent and thus should be in the output. Thus, we break this operation of checking *all* $P' \in \{P{+}{+}e\}$ into parallelizable tasks, each of which is in the following format: check if *one* pattern P' is frequent.

We realize `GrowPattern(Pattern P)` by instantiating the *map* and *reduce* functions in our general algorithm as follows. The *map* function works in parallel on each trace and updates the indices pointing to instances of P to indices of instances of $P' \in \{P{+}{+}e\}$. It creates an intermediate key/value pair (K_{int}/V_{int}) where the key corresponds to a P' and the value corresponds to the indices pointing to instances of P' in the trace. MapReduce groups all indices corresponding to a P'. Each intermediate key K_{int} and all of its corresponding intermediate values form a task that is sent to the *reduce* function. The *reduce* function computes the support of a pattern P' and outputs it if the support is more than the minimum support threshold min_sup (i.e., if P' is frequent). We list the inputs (K_{ip}, V_{ip}), intermediate key/value pairs (K_{int}, V_{int}), and outputs (O_{part}) in column (a) in Figure 21.3 for CLIPPER^{MR}.

Given a large execution trace, the pattern growth operation can be performed in parallel. Each trace is processed in parallel by multiple instances of the *map* function. Also, the process to check if a pattern P' is frequent or not could be done in parallel by multiple instances of the *reduce* function.

Note that we only parallelize the `GrowPattern` operation, and thus each MapReduce procedure in our implementation performs only one unit of pattern growth operation (i.e., $P \rightarrow P{+}{+}e$). Since many software properties are short and may be specified with only a few operation units (e.g., rules used in Static Driver Verifier [29]), we restrict the size of the patterns mined to be at most three to limit the experimental costs.

Example 4. Given two traces trace$_1$ = $\langle a, b, c \rangle$ and trace$_2$ = $\langle a, b \rangle$, we want to mine patterns with support values above min_sup = 2 using CLIPPER^{MR}. In the first iteration, CLIPPER^{MR} mines patterns of length 1. We have two instances of the *map* function, map$_1$ and map$_2$, which take as input trace$_1$ and trace$_2$, respectively. Then map$_1$ creates the following intermediate key/value pairs: $\{K_{int} = \langle a \rangle, V_{int} = (\text{trace}_1, \{1\})\}$, $\{K_{int} = \langle b \rangle, V_{int} = (\text{trace}_1, \{2\})\}$, and $\{K_{int} = \langle c \rangle, V_{int} = (\text{trace}_1, \{3\})\}$. The *map* function map$_2$ produces $\{K_{int} = \langle a \rangle, V_{int} = (\text{trace}_2, \{1\})\}$, and $\{K_{int} = \langle b \rangle, V_{int} = (\text{trace}_2, \{2\})\}$. We have three instances of the *reduce* function—reduce$_1$, reduce$_2$, and reduce$_3$: reduce$_1$ takes pairs with the key $\langle a \rangle$ and checks whether the number of instances is larger than min_sup; similarly, reduce$_2$ and reduce$_3$ collect pairs with the keys $\langle b \rangle$ and $\langle c \rangle$, respectively. The *reduce* functions output patterns $\langle a \rangle$ and $\langle b \rangle$ because they satisfy the threshold min_sup. In the

	(a)	(b)	(c)
K_{ip}	Trace identifier	Trace identifier	Trace identifier
V_{ip}	(Trace content, Indices)	Trace content	Trace content

MAP

	(a)	(b)	(c)
K_{int}	Next pattern: $P' = P ++ e$	Method signature	Event Group: G_x
V_{int}	(Id , Indices) Id = Trace identifier Indices = Indices for P'	(Metadata, Entries, Exits)	Sub-trace with events in G_x

REDUCE

	(a)	(b)	(c)
O_{part}	P', if sup(P') ≥ min_sup Nothing, otherwise	Daikon invariants	Finite-state machine

FIGURE 21.3

MapReduce inputs (K_{ip}, V_{ip}), intermediate key/value pairs (K_{int}, V_{int}), and outputs (O_{part}) for GrowPattern(Pattern P) of CLIPPER (column (a)), Daikon (column (b)), and k-tails (column (c)).

next iteration, CLIPPER^{MR} mines patterns of length 2. The *map* functions generate the following intermediate key/value pairs: $\{K_{int} = \langle a, b \rangle, V_{int} = (\text{trace}_1, \{1\})\}$, $\{K_{int} = \langle a, c \rangle, V_{int} = (\text{trace}_1, \{1\})\}$, $\{K_{int} = \langle b, c \rangle, V_{int} = (\text{trace}_1, \{2\})\}$, and $\{K_{int} = \langle a, b \rangle, V_{int} = (\text{trace}_2, \{1\})\}$. The *reduce* functions group the instances on the basis of the key values, and find that pattern $\langle a, b \rangle$ satisfies the min_sup threshold. Finally, CLIPPER^{MR} returns the following frequent patterns: $\langle a \rangle$, $\langle b \rangle$, and $\langle a, b \rangle$.

21.3.2.2 Value-based invariant mining with MapReduce

We parallelize Daikon into a distributed version Daikon^{MR} by instantiating our general algorithm in MapReduce.

Similarly to Daikon, Daikon^{MR} takes as input a set of execution traces and outputs invariants for each method that hold for all execution traces. We parallelize Daikon by splitting the input traces: rather than feeding the whole set of traces to one instance of Daikon, we process the traces for each method separately, and in parallel the trace logs for each method are fed into one instance of Daikon. This allows us to instantiate our general algorithm for Daikon relatively easily without the need for synchronization because the traces of different methods are independent of one another for inferring method-level invariants.

In Daikon^{MR}, the *map* function processes a set of traces and outputs ⟨*method signature, (metadata, entries, and exits)*⟩ pairs. The latter part of each pair contains method metadata (e.g., the number of parameters a method has, the types of the parameters, etc.), and parts of the execution traces corresponding to the states of the various variables when entries and exits of the methods are executed. The *reduce* function runs an instance of Daikon on (*metadata, entries, and exits*) of the same method and the outputs ⟨*method signature, method invariants*⟩ pair. We illustrate the inputs, intermediate key/value pairs, and outputs for Daikon^{MR} in MapReduce's terminology in column (b) in Figure 21.3.

Many instances of Daikon are executed in parallel, each of which runs on a rather small input. Thus, each instance of Daikon requires much less memory and is able to quickly produce a subset of the results.

21.3.2.3 Finite-state machine mining with MapReduce

Many finite-state machine mining algorithms are variants of the k-tails algorithm [20]. The algorithms investigate a set of execution traces and produce a single finite-state machine. However, this finite-state machine may be too large and difficult to comprehend. Many studies propose methods to *split* the traces and learn a finite-state machine for each subtrace, whose ideas can be instantiated in MapReduce with our general algorithm, and we name it k-tails^{MR}.

Consider the mapping function EVENTS→GROUP, where EVENTS is the set of events (i.e., method calls) in the execution traces, and GROUP is a group identifier. Events in the same group are *related*. Many notions of relatedness may be defined (see [30]). In this chapter we consider one such notion: a group of events is composed of invocations of methods appearing in the same class.

The *map* function slices each trace into a set of subtraces on the basis of the group membership of each event. MapReduce collects the subtraces belonging to the same group. The *reduce* function produces one finite-state machine for a group of subtraces by invoking an instance of the k-tails algorithm. We illustrate the inputs, intermediate key/value pairs, and outputs for k-tails^{MR} in column (c) in Figure 21.3.

The slicing could be done in parallel for separate execution traces. In addition, the learning of multiple finite-state machines could be done in parallel.

21.3.2.4 Sequence diagram mining with MapReduce

We illustrate how to transform the LM algorithm [6], which mines LSCs [23, 24], into LM^{MR}.

An LSC contains two parts: a prechart and a main chart. The semantics of LSCs dictates that whenever the prechart is observed, eventually the main chart will also be observed. The goal of the mining task is to find all LSCs that appear frequently (i.e., the support of the LSC is more than min_sup), and for which the proportion of the prechart followed by the main chart in the execution traces is greater than a certain min_conf threshold. LSCs obeying these criteria are considered significant.

The LSC mining algorithm works in two steps:

(1) mine frequent charts,
(2) compose frequent charts into significant LSCs.

For the first step, we employ the same strategy as described in Section 21.3.2.1. For the second step, we consider the special case of min_conf = 100% (i.e., mining of LSCs that are always observed in the execution traces—the prechart is always eventually followed by the main chart).

In LSC mining, Lo and Maoz [31] define *positive witnesses* of a chart C, denoted by pos(C), as the number of trace segments that obey chart C. They also define *weak negative witnesses* of C, denoted by w_neg(C), as the number of trace segments that do not obey C because of the end of the trace being reached. The *support* of an LSC L = pre → main is simply the number of positive witnesses of pre++main. The *confidence* of an LSC L is given by

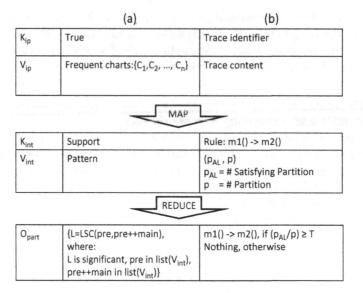

	(a)	(b)
K_{ip}	True	Trace identifier
V_{ip}	Frequent charts:$\{C_1, C_2, ..., C_n\}$	Trace content

MAP

	(a)	(b)
K_{int}	Support	Rule: m1() -> m2()
V_{int}	Pattern	(p_{AL}, p) p_{AL} = # Satisfying Partition p = # Partition

REDUCE

	(a)	(b)
O_{part}	{L=LSC(pre,pre++main), where: L is significant, pre in list(V_{int}), pre++main in list(V_{int})}	m1() -> m2(), if $(p_{AL}/p) \geq T$ Nothing, otherwise

FIGURE 21.4

MapReduce inputs (K_{ip}, V_{ip}), intermediate key/value pairs (K_{int}, V_{int}), and outputs (O_{part}) for LM (column (a)) and Perracotta (column (b)).

$$\text{conf}\,(L) = \frac{|\text{pos(pre ++main)}| + |\text{w\_neg(pre ++main)}|}{|\text{pos(pre)}|}.$$

We first note that LSCs with 100% confidence must be composed of a prechart and a main chart, where $|\text{pos(pre++main)}| + |\text{w\_neg(pre++main)}|$ equals $|\text{pos(pre)}|$. We could break up the task of constructing all significant LSCs into subtasks: find all significant LSCs of a particular support value.

We name the MapReduce version of LM as LM^{MR}. For LM^{MR}, we use the following *map* and *reduce* functions. The *map* function works on the set of patterns and simply groups pattern C where either $\text{pos}(C) + \text{w\_neg}(C)$ or $\text{pos}(C)$ has a particular value into a bucket. If a pattern C has different $\text{pos}(C) + \text{w\_neg}(C)$ and $\text{pos}(C)$ values, it is put into two buckets. The *reduce* function constructs significant LSCs by composing two patterns in each bucket. We list the inputs, intermediate key/value pairs, and outputs involved in column (a) in Figure 21.4.

The composition of charts to form LSCs is done in parallel for separate buckets. If the significant LSCs have many different support values, the speedup in the second stage of LSC mining due to the parallelization could be substantial.

Finally, LM^{MR} applies the MapReduce framework twice, sequentially in a pipeline. The first application computes the frequent charts using the solution presented in Section 21.3.2.1. The output of this application is used as an input for the second application described above. Composition of instances of MapReduce in a pipeline is also common (see, e.g., [32]).

21.3.2.5 Temporal rule mining with MapReduce

We illustrate how to reimplement basic Perracotta [8] by using our general algorithm and MapReduce. Perracotta proposes several extensions and variants to the main algorithm—for example, chaining. We consider only the basic Perracotta, which computes alternating properties. We call the resultant algorithm Perracotta^{MR}.

For n unique methods in the execution traces, Perracotta checks n^2 possible temporal specifications of the format "Whenever method m_1 is executed, eventually method m_2 is executed" (denoted as $m_1 \rightarrow m_2$) to see if the specification is strongly observed in the execution traces. A measure known as the *satisfaction rate* is defined on the basis of the proportion of partitions in the traces that satisfy $m_1^+ m_2^+$ (i.e., p) that also satisfy the temporal rule $m_1 \rightarrow m_2$ (i.e., p_{AL}). It is often the case that n is large, and Perracotta would require a lot of memory to process the traces together. We break up the original task into small subtasks by splitting each long trace into smaller subtraces of size k and process them independently—by default we set k to be 300,000 events for Perracotta^{MR}. As k is relatively large, by the principle of locality (i.e., related events appear close together; see [33]), there will be no or little loss in the mined specifications.

Following our general algorithm, we define the following *map* and *reduce* functions. The *map* function is applied to each execution subtrace independently. For each execution subtrace, the *map* function computes for each potential rule $m_i \rightarrow m_j$ two numbers: the number of partitions in the subtrace (i.e., p) and the number of partitions in the subtrace that satisfy the rule (i.e., p_{AL}). The method pair is the intermediate key, while the two numbers p and p_{AL} are the value in the intermediate key/value pair (K_{int} and V_{int}). MapReduce groups the counts for the same rule together. The *reduce* function simply sums up the p and p_{AL} for the separate execution subtraces and computes a *satisfaction rate* for the corresponding rule. Rules that satisfy a user-defined threshold of the satisfaction rate (i.e., S) are provided as output. By default, the satisfaction rate is 0.8. We list the inputs, intermediate key/value pairs, and outputs involved in column (b) in Figure 21.4.

Notice that the subtraces can now be processed in parallel using multiple runs of the *map* and *reduce* functions on potentially different machines. Also, the computation and checking of the satisfaction rate could be done in parallel. No synchronization is needed among different subtraces.

21.4 IMPLEMENTATION AND EMPIRICAL EVALUATION

We have implemented the algorithms described in the previous sections in Hadoop [15], one of the most popular MapReduce implementations. We describe our datasets, experimental settings, research questions, and experimental results in the following.

21.4.1 DATASET AND EXPERIMENTAL SETTINGS

We use seven programs—avrora, batik, fop, luindex, lusearch, xalan, and tomcat—from the DaCapo benchmark [7] as our subjects. We have also implemented a Java instrumentation tool to collect all methods that are executed (referred to as *trace databases* later) for the experiments with CLIPPER, k-tails, LM, and Perracotta; we use Chicory, a part of Daikon, to collect the traces for Daikon. The sizes of the Daikon traces for these seven programs range from 18 GB to 157 GB, while the sizes of the trace databases range from 41 MB to 533 MB. The experiments are run on four Acer M680G machines, each having an Intel Core i5 quad-core CPU, 4 GB of memory, and a 2 TB hard disk, on which the operating system Ubuntu version 12.04 is installed. One of the machines is used as the master; the three other machines are slaves. We also configure Hadoop (version 2.0.0-alpha) to use *up to* three cores for distributed map and reduce tasks on each slave machine to reduce the effects of potential resource contentions. We set the maximum memory of each map/reduce task to 1200 MB and leave the other settings at their default values (e.g., the Hadoop file system's replication factor). Before running the MapReduce versions of the specification mining algorithms, we also copy all traces from the usual ext4 file system under Ubuntu into the Hadoop file system as a one-time cost. To reduce experimental bias, we run each experiment with each version of the various specification mining algorithms two times and report the averages across the two runs.

21.4.2 RESEARCH QUESTIONS AND RESULTS

Our study aims to answer the following research questions:

(1) Could existing specification mining algorithms scale to process large execution traces?
(2) Could MapReduce be used to improve the scalability of existing specification mining algorithms?
(3) How much more scalable would our mining algorithms be if we increased the number of processing cores?

We discuss the answers to these research questions for each of the five specification mining algorithms.

21.4.2.1 Mining frequent patterns

To answer research question 1, we run the original version of CLIPPER on the traces. This version mines patterns recursively, and needs to load the complete trace database into memory. Thus, even for the smallest trace database with a size of 41 MB (from batik), original CLIPPER is unable to run.

To answer research question 2, we examine the performance of CLIPPER^{MR} with up to eight parallel map and reduce tasks. CLIPPER$^{MR(8)}$ (i.e., with eight parallel map and reduce tasks) outputs the invariants for all traces from the seven programs within 1493 min. This shows CLIPPER^{MR} improves the scalability of the original CLIPPER.

To answer research question 3, we compare the time cost for CLIPPER^{MR} as we increase the number of parallel tasks (see Figure 21.5). We find that the performance improves as we increase the number of parallel tasks. By increasing the number of parallel MapReduce tasks from one to four, we gain a speedup ranging from 1.4 to 3.2 times. By increasing the number of parallel MapReduce tasks from one to eight, we gain a speedup ranging from 1.7 to 4.6 times. The reason why CLIPPER^{MR} cannot speed up as much as parallelized versions of the other mining algorithms (see later) is that it needs to process a lot of I/O operations across different nodes in the Hadoop system.

21.4.2.2 Mining value-based invariants

To answer research question 1, we run the original Daikon on the traces. Since the traces from the seven programs are all larger than 18 GB, the original Daikon runs out of memory before outputting any invariant.

To answer research question 2, we examine the performance of the original Daikon and that of Daikon^{MR} with up to eight parallel map and reduce tasks. Daikon$^{MR(8)}$ outputs the invariants for *all*

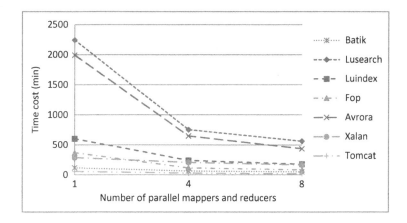

FIGURE 21.5

Performance improvements for CLIPPER.

traces from seven programs within 2374 min, and we are unable to infer the invariants of only less than 5% of the methods (since we terminate a Daikon instance if it takes more than 600 s to finish). Obviously, Daikon^{MR} improves the scalability of the original Daikon.

To answer research question 3, we compare the time cost for Daikon^{MR} as we increase the number of parallel tasks (see Figure 21.6). We find that the performance improves when we increase the number of parallel tasks. By increasing the number of parallel MapReduce tasks from one to four, we gain a speedup ranging from 2.7 to 3 times. By increasing the number of parallel MapReduce tasks from one to eight, we gain a speedup ranging from 4.2 to 5.4 times. We notice that the rate of speedup decreases as we increase the number of parallel tasks from four to eight. This is so as there are more resource contentions between the mappers and reducers as the number of parallel tasks is increased in our small four-machine cluster with limited memory.

21.4.2.3 Mining finite-state machines

To answer research questions 1 and 2, we compare the performance of the original k-tails with that of k-tails$^{MR(8)}$. The original k-tails ran out of memory before outputting any finite-state machines. On the other hand, k-tails$^{MR(8)}$ is able to output finite-state machines for *all* programs in 40 min. Similarly to what we did for Daikon^{MR}, we also employ a timeout, and terminate an instance of the k-tails construction process run in one reducer if it does not finish within 120 s. We find that we are unable to run k-tails to completion for only 5% of the classes. Obviously, k-tails^{MR} improves the scalability of the original k-tails.

To answer research question 3, we compare the time cost for k-tails^{MR} as we increase the number of parallel tasks (see Figure 21.7). We find that the performance improves as we increase the number of parallel tasks. By increasing the number of parallel MapReduce tasks from one to four, we gain a speedup ranging from 2 to 3.7 times. By increasing the number of parallel MapReduce tasks from one to eight, we gain a speedup ranging from 2.3 to 5.6 times.

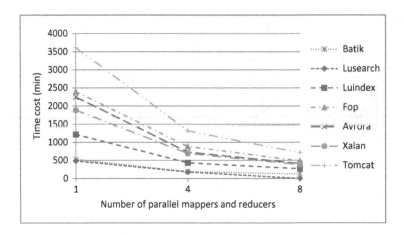

FIGURE 21.6

Performance improvements for Daikon.

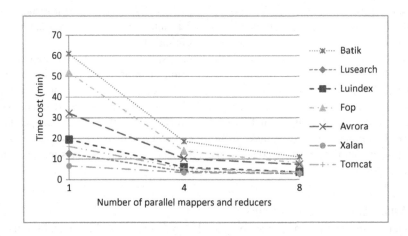

FIGURE 21.7

Performance improvements for k-tails.

21.4.2.4 Mining sequence diagrams

To answer research questions 1 and 2, we compare the performance of the original LM with that of $LM^{MR(8)}$. The original LM is unable to run because of memory problems, while LM^{MR} is able to get the sequence diagrams (since LM^{MR} is based on $CLIPPER^{MR}$). $LM^{MR(8)}$ can output the invariants for all traces from the seven programs within 1508 min. This shows LM^{MR} can improve the scalability of the original LM.

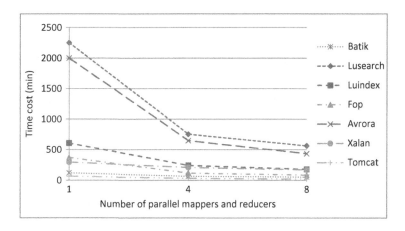

FIGURE 21.8

Performance improvements for LM.

To answer research question 3, we compare the time cost for LM^{MR} as we increase the number of parallel tasks (see Figure 21.8). We find that the performance improves as we increase the number of parallel tasks. By increasing the number of parallel MapReduce tasks from one to four, we gain a speedup ranging from 1.4 to 3 times. By increasing the number of parallel MapReduce tasks from one to eight, we gain a speedup ranging from 1.7 to 4.6 times. The performance improvement of LM^{MR} over LM is similar to that of CLIPPER^{MR} over CLIPPER. This is reasonable as the first of the two steps of LM^{MR} is based on CLIPPER^{MR} (see Section 21.3.2.4), and the second step for composing frequent charts into significant LSCs takes little time with respect to the time spent in the first step.

21.4.2.5 Mining temporal rules
To answer research question 1, we mine temporal rules with the original Perracotta, which was able to mine the temporal rules from all of the traces. Perracotta's memory cost is quadratic to the number of unique events in the traces. In our study, the unique events are the methods that are invoked when the program is run. The number of unique events is not so big, and is no more than 3000.

To answer research question 2, we compare the performance of the original Perracotta with that of Perracotta^{MR}, and we present the results in Figure 21.9. We see that Perracotta$^{MR(8)}$ achieves a speedup ranging from 3.5 to 18.2 times. Note that Perracotta$^{MR(8)}$ may achieve a speedup of more than eight times in comparison with Perracotta on average. This may be related to the fact that Perracotta is a memory-intensive algorithm (with space complexity $O(n^2)$ and time complexity $O(nL)$, where n is the number of unique events in the traces and L is the total length of all traces). Its sequential version needs to load all traces into memory sequentially, while the parallelized version may load many split smaller traces into memory simultaneously even when there is only one core available for map/reduce tasks. At the same time, the accuracy of Perracotta^{MR} is 100% with respect to Perracotta: when we compare the output of Perracotta^{MR} with that of Perracotta, there is no temporal rule that is missed.

To answer research question 3, we compare the time cost for Perracotta^{MR} as we increase the number of parallel tasks (see Figure 21.10). We find that the performance improves as we increase

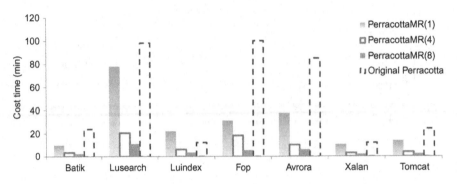

FIGURE 21.9

Original Perracotta versus parallelized Perracotta.

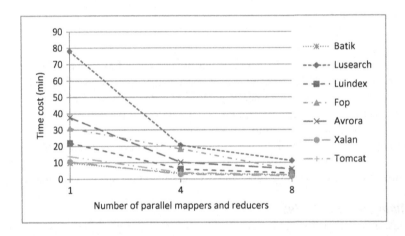

FIGURE 21.10

Performance improvements for Perracotta.

the number of parallel tasks. By increasing the number of parallel MapReduce tasks from one to four, we gain a speedup ranging from 1.6 to 3.8 times. By increasing the number of parallel MapReduce tasks from one to eight, we gain a speedup ranging from 4.1 to 7 times. Figure 21.10 also shows that the rate of speedup decreases as we increase the number of parallel tasks from four to eight. This is so as there are more resource contentions between the mappers and reducers as the number of parallel tasks is increased in our small four-machine cluster.

21.4.3 THREATS TO VALIDITY AND CURRENT LIMITATIONS

In this work, we have considered five families of specification mining algorithms: those mining frequent patterns, value-based invariants, finite-state machines, sequence diagrams, and temporal rules. For each family, we have considered one algorithm. There are other specification mining algorithms that we have not considered in this study—for example, those that analyze program code rather than execution traces [26, 34–37]. It is not clear if our approach can be easily extended to all other specification mining algorithms. In this study, we modified and adapted the algorithms to follow a divide-and-conquer strategy; it is not clear if all specification mining algorithms can be modified to follow this strategy. In the future, we would like to investigate even more algorithms and algorithm families and show how they can be modified to follow appropriate divide-and-conquer strategies to leverage the power of MapReduce.

We have evaluated our approach using seven programs from the DaCapo benchmark [7]. This benchmark has been used extensively in many previous studies (e.g., [38, 39]). Still, these programs might not be representative of all open-source and industrial software systems. We plan to reduce this threat to validity further by investigating more programs in addition to those in the DaCapo benchmark. Also, we have experimented with a cluster of four machines running eight cores. We plan to extend our experiment to even more machines and more cores. However, even with four machines, we have shown how the power of MapReduce could be tapped to scale various specification mining algorithms.

One limitation is imposed by the implementation of MapReduce that we use—that is, Hadoop. One of the most important issues for a distributed platform is locality, as network bandwidth is the bottleneck when processing a large amount of data. To solve this problem, Hadoop attempts to replicate the data across the nodes and to always locate the nearest replica of the data. However, a substantial proportion of the time may still be spent on data transmission, typically for algorithms which involve a heavy data transmission load. Our experiments used the default Hadoop file system replication factor 3 (i.e., each block of data is replicated to three machines) to minimize the transmission overheads during computation. The speedup factor of the parallelized versions of the specification mining algorithms may be affected if more machines are used or the replication factor is changed. We plan to perform a more comprehensive investigation of the effect of data transmission load, identify factors that may significantly affect the performance of distributed specification mining algorithms, and design improved algorithms that can reduce such overheads further.

21.5 RELATED WORK

We now discuss closely related studies on specification mining, uses of MapReduce in software engineering, and parallelizing data mining algorithms in general. By no means does this section cover all related work.

21.5.1 SPECIFICATION MINING AND ITS APPLICATIONS

Mined specifications can help developers to understand legacy systems [8], to detect potential bugs [26]. They can also be used as input for model checkers and for the purpose of program verification [40] or can be converted into test cases [41].

Some families of specification mining algorithms were described in Section 21.2. Here we describe other related recent work. Beschastnikh et al. [42] mined three kinds of temporal invariants from system logs and merged them into a state-based behavioral model. Wu et al. [43] proposed an approach that mines specifications from a variety of application programming interface (API) data, including information from API client programs, library source code, and comments. Lo and Maoz [44] used three concepts—equivalence classes among LSCs, isomorphic embeddings, and delta-discriminative similarity measures—to mine a succinct set of LSCs and improve the readability of mining results. Alrajeh et al. [45] presented a semiautomated approach that detects vacuously satisfiable scenarios by leveraging a model checker and generates new scenarios to avoid the vacuity using machine learning (inductive logic programming). Kumar et al. [4] presented a framework for mining message sequence graphs that can represent concurrent behaviors of a distributed system. Zhong et al. [46] inferred API specifications from documentations expressed in English. Lee at al. [47] implemented the tool jMiner to mine parametric specifications by using the concept of trace slicing. The proposed approach first slices independent interactions from program traces. The independent interactions are then fed into a variant of the k-tails algorithm to produce a probabilistic finite-state machine. The work of Wei et al. [48] builds on Daikon to infer contracts for Eiffel programs.

All five specification mining algorithms that we studied in this chapter (CLIPPER, Daikon, k-tails, LM, and Perracotta) analyze program execution traces. Other approaches to specification mining use program code as input (e.g., [26, 34–37]). A technique called *DySy* mines invariants, similar to those generated by Daikon, by performing symbolic execution to reduce the number of test cases needed to mine the invariants and improve the quality of the mined invariants [49]. There are also algorithms that mine specifications in forms different from the five families described in Section 21.2—for example, algebraic specifications [50] and separation logic invariants [51]. It would be interesting to examine how one can apply our general algorithm and MapReduce to the diverse mining algorithms mentioned above.

Some recent studies propose ways to better understand, extend, and compare existing specification mining algorithms. An approach called *InvariMint* allows users to construct a model inference algorithm by using a declarative specification [52]. Beschastnikh et al. [52] show that their approach could help users understand, extend, and compare algorithms that mine specifications in the form of finite-state machines. Different from their work, we propose an approach to adapt existing algorithms to the MapReduce framework and make them more scalable and efficient.

Comprehensive surveys of past studies on specification mining are available in a recent article [53] and in a book on specification mining [1].

21.5.2 MAPREDUCE IN SOFTWARE ENGINEERING

Shang et al. [12, 54] have presented experience reports on scaling tools for mining software repositories using MapReduce. They investigated several case studies to analyze the potential of the MapReduce platform to scale up tools for mining software repositories, including (1) J-REX, which mines a CVS repository for calculating changes of software metrics over the history of a software project, (2) CC-Finder, which is a token-based clone detection tool designed to extract code clones from systems developed in several programming languages, and (3) JACK, which is a log analyzer that uses data mining techniques to process system execution logs and automatically identify problems in load tests. Specification mining approaches are not covered in these studies. Recently, Dyer et al. [11] proposed a language and an infrastructure called Boa to ease the analysis of software repositories. Users can specify queries in a domain-specific language, and these queries can be processed by Boa's processing engine, which uses the MapReduce distributed computing model.

Different from these studies, we specifically focus on specification mining algorithms and investigate the potential of using MapReduce to make them more scalable.

21.5.3 PARALLEL DATA MINING ALGORITHMS

Kang et al. [55] used MapReduce to propagate beliefs on a sparse billion-node graph. Liu et al. [56] used MapReduce to parallelize an algorithm inferring document relevance for a Web search. Ene et al. [10] sped up general clustering algorithms by using MapReduce. Miliaraki et al. [9] recently proposed a parallelization of a frequent sequence mining algorithm that can run on MapReduce. Their approach relies on the w-equivalency property that holds only for sequential patterns, and the semantics of the sequential patterns mined by their approach is different from that of iterative patterns mined by CLIPPER (which is the closest algorithm considered in this chapter to the frequent sequence mining algorithm). Although our approach employs MapReduce too, our data sources and the subject algorithms are specific to specification mining, which requires different parallelization strategies and techniques.

21.6 CONCLUSION AND FUTURE WORK

In this chapter, we have addressed the challenge of making specification mining algorithms scalable. We have presented a general algorithm design that helps to transform sequential specification mining algorithms into distributed ones on the basis of the observation that many specification mining algorithms are data intensive but computationally repetitive. In particular, we have shown how five different kinds of algorithms—CLIPPER, Daikon, k-tails, LM, and Perracotta—can be parallelized by following our general algorithm and leveraging the popular distributed computing framework MapReduce. We have evaluated the distributed versions of these algorithms with seven programs from the DaCapo benchmark, and we found that the distributed versions can significantly improve the scalability of the original algorithms for every trace dataset of size ranging from 41 MB to 157 GB. The distributed Perracotta running on four machines (using up to eight CPU cores in total) speeds up the original version by 3-18 times. The original CLIPPER, Daikon, k-tails, and LM are unable to handle the large traces, while our distributed versions can finish in hours and much performance improvement can be gained by using more machines.

We consider the following for future work. First, our distributed algorithms are not necessarily optimal; we plan to investigate whether defining the *map* and *reduce* functions differently and/or splitting input data differently would improve the scalability of these algorithms. For example, Daikon has more than 100 invariant templates that are checked against traces when it looks for actual invariants. Checking each kind of template is independent from checking other kinds of templates, and thus could be parallelized as a *map* function as well. Second, our distributed algorithms are evaluated only with gigabyte traces in a four-machine cluster with many default settings; we would like to evaluate them with terabyte traces in a commercial cluster and see how the performance improves when the number of processors increases and various cluster system settings are used. Third, we consider the application of our general algorithm and MapReduce to additional kinds of specification mining algorithms not covered in this chapter—for example, algorithms leveraging other information besides traces (e.g., text, software repository). Fourth, some variants of the algorithms we have investigated may also deserve special attention—for example, the variants of LSC mining triggers and effects [31], or the combination of scenario-based and value-based invariants [18].

REFERENCES

[1] Lo D, Khoo SC, Han J, Liu C, editors. Mining software specifications: methodologies and applications. CRC Press Data Mining and Knowledge Discovery Series; 2011.

[2] Lo D, Khoo SC, Liu C. Efficient mining of iterative patterns for software specification discovery. In: KDD; 2007. p. 460–9.

[3] Ernst MD, Perkins JH, Guo PJ, McCamant S, Pacheco C, Tschantz MS, Xiao C. The Daikon system for dynamic detection of likely invariants. Sci Comput Program 2007;69(1-3):35–45.

[4] Kumar S, Khoo SC, Roychoudhury A, Lo D. Mining message sequence graphs. In: ICSE; 2011. p. 91–100.

[5] Lorenzoli D, Mariani L, Pezzè M. Automatic generation of software behavioral models. In: ICSE; 2008. p. 501–10.

[6] Lo D, Maoz S, Khoo SC. Mining modal scenario-based specifications from execution traces of reactive systems. In: ASE; 2007. p. 465–8.

[7] Blackburn SM, Garner R, Hoffmann C, Khan AM, McKinley KS, Bentzur R, Diwan A, Feinberg D, Frampton D, Guyer SZ, Hirzel M, Hosking AL, Jump M, Lee HB, Moss JEB, Phansalkar A, Stefanovic D, VanDrunen T, von Dincklage D, Wiedermann B. The DaCapo benchmarks: Java benchmarking development and analysis. In: OOPSLA; 2006. p. 169–90.

[8] Yang J, Evans D, Bhardwaj D, Bhat T, Das M. Perracotta: mining temporal API rules from imperfect traces. In: ICSE; 2006. p. 282–91.

[9] Miliaraki I, Berberich K, Gemulla R, Zoupanos S. Mind the gap: large-scale frequent sequence mining. In: SIGMOD conference; 2013. p. 797–808.

[10] Ene A, Im S, Moseley B. Fast clustering using MapReduce. In: KDD; 2011. p. 681–9.

[11] Dyer R, Nguyen HA, Rajan H, Nguyen TN. Boa: a language and infrastructure for analyzing ultra-large-scale software repositories. In: Proceedings of the 2013 international conference on software engineering, ICSE '13; 2013. p. 422–31. ISBN 978-1-4673-3076-3.

[12] Shang W, Adams B, Hassan AE. An experience report on scaling tools for mining software repositories using MapReduce. In: ASE; 2010. p. 275–84.

[13] Message Passing Interface Forum. MPI: a message-passing interface standard; 2012. URL: http://www.mpi-forum.org/docs/docs.html.

[14] Dean J, Ghemawat S. MapReduce: Simplified data processing on large clusters. In: OSDI; 2004. p. 107–13.

[15] Apache Software Foundation. Hadoop; 2013. URL: http://hadoop.apache.org/.

[16] Han J, Kamber M. Data mining: concepts and techniques. Morgan Kauffman; 2006.

[17] El-Ramly M, Stroulia E, Sorenson PG. From run-time behavior to usage scenarios: an interaction-pattern mining approach. In: KDD; 2002. p. 315–24.

[18] Lo D, Maoz S. Scenario-based and value-based specification mining: better together. In: ASE; 2010. p. 387–96.

[19] Ammons G, Bodík R, Larus JR. Mining specifications. In: POPL; 2002. p. 4–16.

[20] Biermann A, Feldman J. On the synthesis of finite-state machines from samples of their behavior. IEEE Trans Comput 1972;21:591–7.

[21] Briand LC, Labiche Y, Leduc J. Toward the reverse engineering of UML sequence diagrams for distributed Java software. IEEE Trans Software Eng 2006;32(9):642–63.

[22] de Sousa FC, Mendonça NC, Uchitel S, Kramer J. Detecting implied scenarios from execution traces. In: WCRE; 2007. p. 50–9.

[23] Damm W, Harel D. LSCs: breathing life into message sequence charts. Formal Meth Syst Design 2001; 45–80

[24] Harel D, Maoz S. Assert and negate revisited: modal semantics for UML sequence diagrams. Software Syst Model 2008;7(2):237–52.

[25] Livshits VB, Zimmermann T. Dynamine: finding common error patterns by mining software revision histories. In: ESEC/SIGSOFT FSE; 2005. p. 296–305.

[26] Wasylkowski A, Zeller A. Mining temporal specifications from object usage. Autom Softw Eng 2011;18 (3-4):263–92.

[27] Lo D, Khoo SC, Liu C. Mining temporal rules for software maintenance. J Software Maintenance 2008;20(4):227–47.

[28] Ho YF, Chen SW, Chen CY, Hsu YC, Liu P. A Mapreduce programming framework using message passing. In: International computer symposium (ICS); 2010. p. 883–8.

[29] Microsoft. Static driver verifier: DDI compliance rules. URL: http://msdn.microsoft.com/en-us/library/ff552840(v=vs.85).aspx.

[30] Pradel M, Gross TR. Automatic generation of object usage specifications from large method traces. In: ASE; 2009. p. 371–82.

[31] Lo D, Maoz S. Mining scenario-based triggers and effects. In: ASE; 2008. p. 109–18.

[32] Chambers C, Raniwala A, Perry F, Adams S, Henry RR, Bradshaw R, Weizenbaum N. FlumeJava: easy, efficient data-parallel pipelines. In: PLDI; 2010. p. 363–75.

[33] Gabel M, Su Z. Online inference and enforcement of temporal properties. In: ICSE; 2010. p. 15–24.

[34] Li Z, Zhou Y. PR-Miner: automatically extracting implicit programming rules and detecting violations in large software code. In: ESEC/SIGSOFT FSE; 2005. p. 306–15.

[35] Nguyen TT, Nguyen HA, Pham NH, Al-Kofahi JM, Nguyen TN. Graph-based mining of multiple object usage patterns. In: ESEC/SIGSOFT FSE; 2009. p. 383–92.

[36] Shoham S, Yahav E, Fink S, Pistoia M. Static specification mining using automata-based abstractions. In: ISSTA; 2007. p. 174–84.

[37] Weimer W, Necula GC. Mining temporal specifications for error detection. In: TACAS; 2005. p. 461–76.

[38] Bond MD, Coons KE, McKinley KS. Pacer: proportional detection of data races. In: PLDI; 2010. p. 255–68.

[39] Chen F, Rosu G. Mop: an efficient and generic runtime verification framework. In: OOPSLA; 2007. p. 569–88.

[40] Li W, Forin A, Seshia SA. Scalable specification mining for verification and diagnosis. In: DAC; 2010. p. 755–60.

[41] Dallmeier V, Knopp N, Mallon C, Hack S, Zeller A. Generating test cases for specification mining. In: ISSTA; 2010. p. 85–96.

[42] Beschastnikh I, Brun Y, Schneider S, Sloan M, Ernst MD. Leveraging existing instrumentation to automatically infer invariant-constrained models. In: SIGSOFT FSE; 2011. p. 267–77.

[43] Wu Q, Liang GT, Wang QX, Mei H. Mining effective temporal specifications from heterogeneous API data. J Comput Sci Technol 2011;26(6):1061–75.

[44] Lo D, Maoz S. Towards succinctness in mining scenario-based specifications. In: ICECCS; 2011. p. 231–40.

[45] Alrajeh D, Kramer J, Russo A, Uchitel S. Learning from vacuously satisfiable scenario-based specifications. In: FASE; 2012. p. 377–93.

[46] Zhong H, Zhang L, Xie T, Mei H. Inferring resource specifications from natural language API documentation. In: ASE; 2009. p. 307–18.

[47] Lee C, Chen F, Rosu G. Mining parametric specifications. In: ICSE; 2011. p. 591–600.

[48] Wei Y, Furia CA, Kazmin N, Meyer B. Inferring better contracts. In: ICSE; 2011. p. 191–200.

[49] Csallner C, Tillmann N, Smaragdakis Y. DySy: dynamic symbolic execution for invariant inference. In: ICSE; 2008. p. 281–90.

[50] Henkel J, Reichenbach C, Diwan A. Developing and debugging algebraic specifications for Java classes. ACM TOSEM 2008;17(3):14:1–37.

[51] Magill S, Nanevski A, Clarke E, Lee P. Inferring invariants in separation logic for imperative list-processing programs. In: SPACE; 2006.

[52] Beschastnikh I, Brun Y, Abrahamson J, Ernst MD, Krishnamurthy A. Unifying FSM-inference algorithms through declarative specification. In: ICSE; 2013. p. 252–61.

[53] Robillard MP, Bodden E, Kawrykow D, Mezini M, Ratchford T. Automated API property inference techniques. IEEE Trans Software Eng 2013; 39(5):613–37

[54] Shang W, Jiang ZM, Adams B, Hassan AE. MapReduce as a general framework to support research in mining software repositories (MSR). In: MSR; 2009. p. 21–30.

[55] Kang U, Chau DH, Faloutsos C. Mining large graphs: algorithms, inference, and discoveries. In: ICDE; 2011. p. 243–54.

[56] Liu C, Guo F, Faloutsos C. BBM: Bayesian browsing model from petabyte-scale data. In: KDD; 2009. p. 537–46.

Printed in the United States
By Bookmasters